Securing Web Services:
Practical Usage of Standards and Specifications

Dr. Panos Periorellis
Newcastle University, UK

Information Science REFERENCE
INFORMATION SCIENCE REFERENCE
Hershey · New York

Acquisitions Editor:	Kristin Klinger
Development Editor:	Kristin Roth
Senior Managing Editor:	Jennifer Neidig
Managing Editor:	Sara Reed
Copy Editor:	Lanette Ehrhardt
Typesetter:	Amanda Appicello
Cover Design:	Lisa Tosheff
Printed at:	Yurchak Printing Inc.

Published in the United States of America by
Information Science Reference (an imprint of IGI Global)
701 E. Chocolate Avenue, Suite 200
Hershey PA 17033
Tel: 717-533-8845
Fax: 717-533-8661
E-mail: cust@igi-global.com
Web site: http://www.igi-global.com/reference

and in the United Kingdom by
Information Science Reference (an imprint of IGI Global)
3 Henrietta Street
Covent Garden
London WC2E 8LU
Tel: 44 20 7240 0856
Fax: 44 20 7379 0609
Web site: http://www.eurospanonline.com

Library of Congress Cataloging-in-Publication Data

Securing Web services : practical usage of standards and specifications / Panos Periorellis, editor.

p. cm.

Summary: "This book collects a complete set of studies addressing the security and dependability challenges of Web services and the development of protocols to meet them. Encompassing a complete range of topics including specifications for message level security, transactions, and identity management, it enables libraries to provide researchers an authoritative guide to a most challenging technological topic"--Provided by publisher.

Includes bibliographical references and index.

ISBN 978-1-59904-639-6 (hardcover) -- ISBN 978-1-59904-641-9 (ebook)

1. Web services. 2. Computer security. 3. Internet--Security measures. I. Periorellis, Panos.

TK5105.88813S43 2007

005.8--dc22

2007023433

British Cataloguing in Publication Data
A Cataloguing in Publication record for this book is available from the British Library.

Table of Contents

Detailed Table of Contents

Through a set of core security requirements for Web services, they discuss and compare several mechanisms available for addressing those challenges, from current standards to specifications under review. In addition, their attempt to address future trends in the domain of Web service security makes this chapter a very valuable contribution.

Shrideep Pallickara, Geoffrey Fox et al. discuss how service-oriented architectures are envisaged using Web services. They address a number of specifications and as such provide a valuable insight into some of the core elements of this book.

Barbara Carminati et al. address the issue of Web service composition and discuss the challenges in building large applications from modular pieces of software (Web services). Focusing on dependability, the authors provide an overview of the main security requirements that must be taken into account when composing Web services. In addition, a detailed survey of the related literature and standards relevant to Web services are outlined. Finally, the authors present a proposal for a brokered architecture to support secure Web services composition.

Nick Cook et al. tackles a specific security requirement; that of nonrepudiation, and provides a thorough discussion of the problem of making high-value business-to-business (B2B) interactions nonrepudiable. The chapter presents the design and implementation details of the authors' novel Web services-based middleware that addresses nonrepudiable interactions using existing Web service standards.

The subject of access control sets off with the contribution of David Chadwick and his chapter on dynamic delegation of access control rights. David enumerates the requirements for delegation of authority, discusses the various implementation and architectural models, and finally highlights the essential elements of such an approach. David's authority and expertise in the field make this chapter one of the most valuable contribution of the book.

Rafae Bhatti et al., from IBM's Almaden Research Center, describe, and at the same time defend their effort at defining a new access control policy description language for Web services. They make use of some of the current Web services standards and show how their effort can be integrated with existing technologies such as WS-Policy to provide a robust, fine grained mechanism for access control.

Clemente et al. provides an evaluation of the ongoing efforts to use semantically rich ontological languages to represent policies for distributed systems, while at the same time highlighting the architectural considerations and implementation aspects of those efforts.

Asuman Dogac et al. concludes the access control part of the book with what is probably the most widely used of the Web Service standards, namely XACML and SAML. The authors demonstrate how they can be combined to provide an overall authentication and authorization mechanism and at the same time discuss their pros and cons.

Kostantin Beznosov presents an experience report on designing and implementing an architecture for protecting enterprise-grade Web service applications hosted by ASP.NET. Kosta deployes his invaluable insight into .NET security mechanisms to discuss design patterns and best practices for constructing flexible and extensible authentication and authorization logic for .NET Web Services.

Kaliontzoglou et al. discusses a particular domain, that of e-government, and in this light the authors outline specific requirements for e-government services, interoperability, and security. Their chapter presents three innovative e-government architecture and implementation strategies based on Web service technologies technologies, focusing on their security and interoperability aspects.

Asif Akram presents an industrial-based case study that provides a pragmatic test bed for evaluating Web service technologies against emerging GRID scenarios. The author discusses issues such as state-full interactions, interoperability, integration, and others.

Aisha Naseer and Lampros Stergoulias discuss infrastructural aspects of GRID computing and argue that Grids should be developed using the underlying Web infrastructure, and GRID services should be integrated with Web Services using inheritance techniques to produce Grid-supported Web services.

David Meredith addresses message level reliability by providing a lot of valuable technical details on WSDL interface style, strength of data typing, and approach to data binding and validation to demonstrate how these have important implications on application security (and interoperability). David shows how these Web service styles and implementation choices must be carefully considered and applied correctly by providing implementation examples and best practice recommendations.

Chapter XIV
Enhancing Web Service Discovery and Monitoring with Quality of Service Information /
Christian Platzer, Florian Rosenberg, and Schahram Dustdar.. 345
Christian Platzer et al. raise quality of service-related concerns. Focusing on general Web services dependability issues while leveraging his expertise and experience in distributed computing, his chapter deals with the various ways of describing, bootstrapping, and evaluating QoS attributes. The chapter addresses a way to bootstrap the most important performance and dependability values.

Compilation of References 364

About the Contributors 382

Index... 389

Foreword

The context of this book is the shared effort going back almost a decade to achieve standards for programmatic access to data on the Web. Dave Winer introduced the original concept of "RPC over HTTP via XML" in what we would now call a blog post in February 1998. From the outset, the aim has been to build a vendor-neutral, Internet-scale, software platform.

The Internet is a platform. A platform is made up of tools and runtimes. Internet tools run on all kinds of operating systems, as do the runtimes. The beauty of the net is its simplicity, its ubiquity and its lack of a controlling vendor. TCP is the runtime environment of the Internet. It's deeply competitive with Microsoft, and it's larger than Microsoft. The stronger TCP is, the more outside of Microsoft's control it is, the more powerful everyone else will be. The Unix people have been in a struggle with everyone else over who owns the Internet. I've been writing about this for a long time. It would be great if they could let go of the struggle and realize that the Internet is owned by the universe, no single operating system or flavor of operating system can contain it. This is important because there is another layer coming on the Internet, a very simple one, that can build on COM, on Windows and elsewhere, and provide a flat playing field for everyone. It's RPC over HTTP via XML. I believe it's the next protocol for runtimes. (Dave Winer, http://davenet.smallpicture.com/1998/02/27/rpcOverHttpViaXml.html, February 1998)

Since 1998, the WS-* stack of specifications—including the core message format SOAP—has been developed at standards bodies such as W3C and OASIS. Moreover, robust implementations of these specifications are widely available, supporting probably all major programming languages and platforms. There have been criticisms, on grounds of the inefficiency of XML as a message format, and the combinatorial complexity of compositional specifications. Nonetheless, almost 10 years on, SOAP-based Web services are widely used, both within enterprises and on the public Web.

This book concerns security aspects of SOAP-based Web services. The core of SOAP security is a set of WS-* specifications—including WS-Trust and WS-SecureConversation—built on the security header defined by WS-Security. This core was introduced by IBM and Microsoft in a 2002 white paper. Again, from the outset the emphasis is on interoperability.

This document ... defines a comprehensive Web service security model that supports, integrates and unifies several popular security models, mechanisms, and technologies (including both symmetric and public key technologies) in a way that enables a variety of systems to securely interoperate in a platform- and language-neutral manner. (IBM and Microsoft, Security in a Web Services World: A Proposed Architecture and Roadmap, http://msdn2.microsoft.com/en-us/library/ms977312.aspx, April 2002)

Since this proposal there has been great progress in achieving secure, interoperable implementations of these security mechanisms. There are many implementations of WS-Security. Security is hard to get right, though, and there were vulnerabilities in some of the early specifications and implementations. Researchers found that some classic man-in-the-middle and impersonation attacks were possible. For example, in the Samoa Project (http://research.microsoft.com/projects/samoa) we used formal methods to identify such vulnerabilities in early versions of some Microsoft implementations of WS-Security. Although much progress has been made, the formal verification of Web services security protocols and their implementations remains a challenging research problem. Still, pragmatic engineering guidelines now exist, at least for basic security—based on experience in practice, a recent specification (the WS-I Security Profile Version 1.0, March 2007) advises on how to achieve basic security guarantees when using WS-Security.

In the past 5 years, in parallel with the development of basic security standards for Web services, there has been a good deal of research on using and extending the basic security mechanisms, as well as investigating their benefits and limitations. This book is the first to present a selection of this Web services security research as a single collection.

The book includes critical experience reports of implementing WS-* security mechanisms on various platforms. It includes research on combining architectural styles such as model-driven design and grid computing with Web services. Several chapters report research on authorization policies and mechanisms for Web services, and in particular on the need for flexible, fine-grained delegation. The chapters cover a wide range of application areas of Web services including health information systems, financial services, and aspects of e-government such as taxation, virtual organizations in the chemical industry, and grid computing for science.

In keeping with the emphasis on interoperability and platform neutrality of the original Web service proposals, this book itself includes work using a variety of software platforms—including both Java and .NET—and development models—both open source and commercial.

I commend this book as an excellent overview of recent research on a variety of topics in Web services security.

Andrew D. Gordon, Microsoft Research

Preface

Editing this book is the outcome of several years of research and publishing in the areas of dependability and security, which are both fields of high importance that are constantly expanding. The application domain is that of Web services, and my most recent work has been targeted toward making sense of the standards and specifications available in this new arena, while at the same time providing security solution for various distributed applications. Web services are a business driven technology, as they have arisen out of a need for services on demand and just-in-time integration, to enable the rapid exploitation of market opportunities. The Web service ideology of late binding seems to present the ideal solution, as it enables loosely coupled organizational services to collaborate without any prior transactional history. Integration is abstracted to a new level; that of XML and dependability mechanisms that stem from such specifications are targeted at this particular level of abstraction. This abstracted approach to integration does have drawbacks however, rooted in the trust and security issues that arise from doing business in such a manner. The security and dependability requirements themselves in the Web Services arena are not new. They have in fact been accompanying distributed computing since its beginnings. There have been more than 30 standards and specifications proposed to address security issues and provide mechanisms for authorization, authentication, confidentiality, integrity, and nonrepudiation. Each of these proposed specifications span across a number of security and dependability related issues. However, despite such a large number of specifications, there appears to be no clear consensus regarding the overall architectural framework. This book is a contribution toward this need.

I received a large number of proposals, which consequently resulted in a large number of potential chapters. I conducted a highly skilled reviewing team composed largely of fellow academics and IT professionals that helped me through the selection process and eventually to narrow it down to the 14 chapters included in the book. Let us have a quick look at the structure of the book.

The book kicks off with the chapter contribution of Padmanabhuni and Adarkar. Through a set of core security requirements for Web services, they discuss and compare several mechanisms available for addressing those challenges from current standards to specifications under review. In addition, their attempt to address future trends in the domain of Web service security makes this chapter a very valuable contribution.

Shrideep Pallickara, Geoffrey Fox, et al. discuss how service-oriented architectures are envisaged using Web services. They address a number of specifications and as such provide a valuable insight into some of the core elements of this book.

Barbara Carminati et al. address the issue of Web service composition and discuss the challenges in building large applications from modular pieces of software (Web services). Focusing on dependability, the authors provide an overview of the main security requirements that must be taken into account when composing Web services. In addition, a detailed survey of the related literature and standards relevant to Web services are outlined. Finally, the authors present a proposal for a brokered architecture to support secure Web services composition.

Nick Cook et al. tackle a specific security requirement, that of nonrepudiation, and provide a thorough discussion of the problem of making high-value business-to-business (B2B) interactions nonrepudiable. The chapter presents the design and implementation details of the authors' novel Web services-based middleware that addresses nonrepudiable interactions using existing Web service standards.

The subject of access control sets off with the contribution of David Chadwick and his chapter on dynamic delegation of access control rights. David enumerates the requirements for delegation of authority, discusses the various implementation and architectural models, and finally highlights the essential elements of such an approach. David's authority and expertise in the field make this chapter one of the most valuable contribution of the book.

Rafae Bhatti et al., from IBM's Almaden Research Center, describe and at the same time defend their effort at defining a new access control policy description language for Web services. They make use some of the current Web services standards and show how their effort can be integrated with existing technologies, such as WS-Policy, to provide a robust, fine grained mechanism for access control.

We continue our discussion on policies and see how these can potentially govern Web service interactions with the contribution by Clemente et al. Felix provides an evaluation of the ongoing efforts to use semantically rich ontological languages to represent policies for distributed systems, while at the same time highlighting the architectural considerations and implementation aspects of those efforts.

Asuman Dogac et al. conclude the access control part of the book with what is probably the most widely used of the Web service standards, namely XACML and SAML. The authors demonstrate how they can be combined to provide an overall authentication and authorization mechanism and at the same time discuss their pros and cons.

Kostantin Beznosov presents an experience report on designing and implementing an architecture for protecting enterprise-grade Web service applications hosted by ASP.NET. Kosta deploys his invaluable insight into .NET security mechanisms to discuss design patterns and best practices for constructing flexible and extensible authentication and authorization logic for .NET Web Services.

Kaliontzoglou et al. discuss a particular domain, that of e-government, and in this light the authors outline specific requirements for e-government services, interoperability, and security. Their chapter presents three innovative e-government architecture and implementation strategies based on Web service technologies, focusing on their security and interoperability aspects.

Asif Akram presents an industrial-based case study that provides a pragmatic test bed for evaluating Web service technologies against emerging GRID scenarios. The author discusses issues such as state-full interactions, interoperability, integration, and others.

Aisha Naseer and Lampros Stergoulias discuss infrastructural aspects of GRID computing and argue that Grids should be developed using the underlying Web infrastructure and GRID services should be integrated with Web Services using inheritance techniques to produce Grid-supported Web Services.

David Meredith addresses message level reliability by providing a lot of valuable technical details on WSDL interface style, strength of data typing, and approach to data binding and validation to demonstrate how these have important implications on application security (and interoperability). David shows how these Web service styles and implementation choices must be carefully considered and applied correctly by providing implementation examples and best practice recommendations.

The book concludes with Christian Platzer et al. raising quality of service-related concerns. Focusing on general Web services dependability issues while leveraging his expertise and experience in distributed computing, their chapter deals with the various ways of describing, bootstrapping, and evaluating QoS attributes. The chapter addresses a way to bootstrap the most important performance and dependability values.

My main aim is to address both sides of the spectrum; namely, developers that face security requirements in the arena of Web services on a day-to-day basis, as well as academics. As such, I worked tirelessly to maintain the balance between academic research and industrial practice. As a result, the book includes chapters with engaging technical details, as well as thought provoking ideas from several major IT companies and world renowned academics.

Acknowledgment

During this editorial I was lucky to have the support of my colleagues at IGI, who helped me review, produce, and market this book. My thanks go especially to Lynley Lapp, who provided invaluable feedback and advice during the first half of the editorial process. I would also like to thank Meg Stocking, who managed the process of transforming a set of individual chapters into a book. I am also grateful to Professor Andy Gordon of Microsoft Research, who wrote the foreword to the book. I would finally like to thank my review team for their contribution.

Dr. Panos Periorellis
Newcastle University, UK

About the Editor

Panos Periorellis is a computing scientist specializing in security and dependability matters for distributed computing and he has been at the forefront of the development of concepts such as systems of systems and virtual organizations. He currently holds a senior research position at the University of Newcastle upon Tyne in the UK, while at the same time is consulting on security issues for major IT companies. He has written numerous papers in the areas of Web services, and this book constitutes his first editorial effort. In addition, he acts as a reviewer for several journals and participates in various conference and workshop program committees. He maintains strong links with several industrial partners in telecommunications, transactional technologies, and software engineering. As a brief biographical note, he joined the Department of Computing Science at the University of Newcastle upon Tyne in June 2000 as a research associate, shortly after successfully completing his PhD in the area of enterprise modeling, under the supervision of Professor John Dobson. Working on several research projects, he carried out novel and innovative research into areas such as systems integration and security for distributed systems. He was promoted to senior member of academic staff in March 2004, and started researching into issues of security and trust for Web services. Since 1997, he has published over 40 papers on distributed computing, Web and Internet programming, peer-to-peer networks, organizational aspects of software engineering, complex systems, and natural language processing. His research interests remain in the areas of distributed computing, dependability, and complex systems. He holds a PhD in computing science, and an MSc and a BSc (Hons) in information systems.

About the Author of the Foreword

Andrew D. Gordon was a Royal Society University research fellow at the University of Cambridge Computer Laboratory, before joining Microsoft in 1997. He holds degrees in computer science from the University of Edinburgh and the University of Cambridge. As a postdoc, he was a member of the Programming Methodology Group at Chalmers University in Gothenburg. Gordon's research interests are in the general area of computer programming languages. He's published and lectured on operational semantics, type theory, concurrency theory, automated reasoning, program logics, and functional and object-oriented programming. He is the co-inventor of two popular process calculi: the spi calculus (with M. Abadi) and the ambient calculus (with L. Cardelli). His recent work focuses on applying type theory and other formal techniques to problems of computer security. One project is an analysis (with D. Syme) of the type system underlying the bytecode verifier of the Microsoft .NET Common Language Runtime. Another is Cryptyc (with A. Jeffrey), a type-checker for cryptographic protocols. The Samoa Project (with K. Bhargavan and C. Fournet) is developing formal tools for the security of XML Web Services. Gordon regularly serves on conference programme committees, teaches at graduate summer schools, examines doctoral dissertations, and delivers invited lectures at scientific meetings.

Chapter I
Security in Service-Oriented Architecture:
Issues, Standards, and Implementations

Srinivas Padmanabhuni
Software Engineering and Technology Labs, Infosys Technologies Limited, India

Hemant Adarkar
Ness Technologies, India

ABSTRACT

This chapter covers the different facets of security as applicable to Service-Oriented Architecture (SOA) implementations. First, it examines the security requirements in SOA implementations, highlighting the differences as compared to the requirements of generic online systems. Later, it discusses the different solution mechanisms to address these requirements in SOA implementations. In the context of Web services, the predominant SOA implementation standards have a crucial role to play. This chapter critically examines the crucial Web services security standards in different stages of adoption and standardization. Later, this chapter examines the present-day common nonstandard security mechanisms of SOA implementations. Towards the end, it discusses the future trends in security for SOA implementations with special bearing on the role of standards. The authors believe that the pragmatic analysis of the multiple facets of security in SOA implementations provided here will serve as a guide for SOA security practitioners.

INTRODUCTION

Security is a fundamental issue of concern in computing systems. With the recent trends in distributed computing, primarily the emergence of World Wide Web (WWW) as a universal medium for conducting business, security has become critical in IT architectures. Successful

Web security mechanisms like Secure Sockets Layer (SSL) have played a critical role in the emergence of WWW as a mainstream technology with wide acceptance.

In the context of distributed systems, SOA has caught the critical attention of both technology and business champions alike because of its promise in removing some of the hurdles in earlier models of distributed computing. Though SOA as a concept is not new, this promise is based on the open and loosely coupled nature of the newer SOA implementations.

In this chapter, we are concerned with multiple dimensions of security in loosely coupled SOA implementations. Web services, the most prevalent SOA implementation, represent an extension of the paradigm of Web. Web services represent applications that can be invoked over open networks using standard Web-based protocols. Other upcoming SOA implementations include Jini (Jini Spec, 2003), Open Grid Services Architecture (OGSA) (OGSA Spec, 2003), and so forth. We shall cover the various security requirements in SOA implementations, highlighting the differences from security requirements in generic online systems. We shall proceed to cover the different solution mechanisms to address these requirements in SOA implementations. Later, we shall explore the Web services security standards in detail. We shall then proceed to explore the common nonstandard security mechanisms of today, addressing Web services security. Towards the end, we shall present the future trends in security for SOA implementations including Web services.

BACKGROUND

Since we are concerned with security of loosely coupled SOA implementations, we shall cover the generic security requirements and solutions in online systems, alongside the core concepts in SOA.

While online systems have been in use for the past few decades, the advent of the Web as a commercial medium has posed significant security challenges due to its public and open nature. Further, e-business and e-commerce has placed stringent security requirements due to the online transactions involved. Current security technologies in Web are able to handle and manage the expectations for e-commerce and e-business transactions. Security, in effect, broadly reflects a collection of security requirements to be satisfied. In this section, we point out the primary security requirements in online systems. Some of the typical security requirements of online systems are outlined below:

- *Confidentiality:* The confidentiality requirement states that any piece of information should not be understood by anyone other than the person for whom it was intended. Message privacy is a key requirement here.
- *Data Integrity:* The integrity requirement states that information should not be altered in storage or transit between a sender and the intended receiver without the alteration being detected.
- *Authentication*: The authentication requirement states that the sender and receiver should be able to confirm each other's identity and the origin/destination of the information.
- *Authorization*: The authorization requirement ensures that the sender has the required authority to perform the operation. This may range from permission to perform some action to permission for viewing some content.
- *Non-repudiation*: The nonrepudiation requirement ensures that the creator/sender of the information cannot deny at a later stage his or her intentions in the creation or transmission of the information.

- *Privacy:* The privacy requirement is more general than the confidentiality requirement above. It also deals with the question of whether to trust the personal information with a Web site.
- *Trust:* This refers to the confidence in a person or a partner doing the transaction. This concept extends beyond trust in a person accessing an online service to even include participants in business-to-business transactions where trust may be used to refer to the adherence to the contractual agreements between the partners.
- *Auditing:* The ability to know who did what, when and where. This is a key requirement when it comes to detection of possible security breaches.
- *Availability*: The computing resources should be available for genuine users when they wish to access the resource. Denial of Service (DoS) attacks may cause lack of availability, and hence, there is a need to protect against such attacks.
- *Intrusion Detection:* The ability to detect when an unwanted user of an online system has entered the system and done some damage to the system.

Security Solution Mechanisms in Online Systems

Diverse security solutions and mechanisms have been designed and implemented for tackling online security requirements. In this section, we cover the different relevant solutions. This list is not meant to be exhaustive, however it will serve as the base for the discussion in the context of security solutions and standards for SOA implementations. The primary mechanisms of security employed in online systems are enumerated below:

- *Passwords:* A password refers to a unique secret series of characters which allows a user to access a computing resource. Ideally a password should be difficult to guess to prevent access to unauthorized users. It is the most common authentication mechanism in online systems.
- *Encryption:* Encryption is the most common security technique to ensure confidentiality in online systems. Essentially it refers to the process of taking a piece of data (called ***cleartext***) and a short seed string (a *key*) and producing an altered piece of data referred to as ***ciphertext,*** which is not understood by anybody who does not know the key. Decryption is the reverse process of converting the ciphertext to cleartext. Typically, encryption process relies on hard to emulate mathematical algorithms involving the key and the cleartext.

  Encryption algorithms can be divided into symmetric and asymmetric encryption algorithms. In symmetric algorithms, both the encryption and decryption keys are the same. Hence, they function on the basis of shared secret. In asymmetric algorithms, the encryption and decryption keys form a key pair, in which one key is a private key (which shall be kept a secret) and the other is a public key. If a piece of data is encrypted with the public key, it needs the private key to decrypt. Asymmetric methods distribution of the keys is easy, and hence, public key infrastructure relies on asymmetric methods. Encryption of messages ensures confidentiality by making it difficult to deduce the content of the original message from the encrypted message.
- *Access Control Lists:* These are generic formats of security information concerning permissions to access certain resources or to perform certain tasks. Most often, authorization is provided by usage of access control lists (ACL).
- *Hashing:* Hashing is another important technique used to ensure data integrity in online systems. The idea is to take an

arbitrary-sized input data (referred to as a ***message***) and generate a fixed-size output, called a ***digest*** (or hash), such that it is nearly impossible to compute or guess the message from the hash. The hash of a piece of data can be used to verify the integrity after an online transfer by comparison with the recomputed hash of the transferred data.

- *Digital Signature:* Digital Signature is an important technique to ensure data integrity and nonrepudiation. Typically, the hash of a message is encrypted with the private key of an entity and is termed as the signature of the data. To ensure that the message received by the receiver is actually sent by the person who signed the message, the signature after decryption with the public key of sender should match the hash.
- *Digital Certificate:* Usage of digital signature in sending a message requires that the receiver knows *a priori* the sender's public key. This is a big constraint, and hence, it becomes important to make the public key available of the sender as part of the message to achieve flexibility. However, that opens up the requirement of the trust of the public key sent by the sender, whether it is genuine or not. Hence, to overcome these problems, specialized entities termed as certification authorities are entrusted with the task of signing the public key of senders and generate a special form that can be sent along with a message. This signed form of representation of a public key is termed as a digital signature. By leveraging a third-party certification authority (CA), the problem of public keys is reduced to the receivers having to know the public key of the CA. Popular ways of broadcasting this information of public keys of CA entities include integrating them into the popular browsers or other online systems. Digital certificates are stored in standard formats like the popular X.509 Certificate format. Digital certificates are used for authentication and data integrity in public networks.
- *SSL:* SSL (Secure Sockets Layer) is a Web-based protocol that enables a secure connection between the client and the server. It is based on a series of exchange of keys (and the server digital certificate) between the server and the client to generate a session key that is used to encrypt all the following messages in the session. Typically as part of the protocol, the server certificate is requested by the client allowing the client to ensure communication with the right Web server. Thus, SSL enables channel encryption between the client and the server. Client-side SSL uses digital certificates of clients enabling them to prove their identity to the Web server. This personal certification attribute, or the client identification, is not very common at the moment due to the cumbersome process involved in maintenance of huge numbers of client certificates.
- *PKI:* Public Key Infrastructure (PKI) refers to a collection of authorities and a system for exchange of digital certificates to entities. A PKI set up typically includes a CA for generating, revoking, or maintaining the digital certificates. It also includes a registration authority (RA) for physically verifying the identity of a certificate requester using physical means like checking against an identity card before directing the CA to issue a certificate. CA uses the concept of Certificate Revocation Lists (CRL) for revoking inactive certificates.
- *Firewalls:* Firewalls are specialized security tools designed to protect an enterprise typically against attacks from the external network. All network traffic between the internal and external network is channeled through it, and the firewall allows only desired traffic as configured. Traffic from

internal network to external network can also be filtered in the firewall. The conventional firewalls are typically based on the concept of packet filtering, and they operate on the network layer of the stack.

- *Code Signing:* A popular concept for ensuring security of downloadable code on the network is code signing. Any piece of code including Applets, Jar files, ActiveX controls, and so forth are signed before download is allowed. Thus, digitally signed code after download guarantees that the code really comes from the publisher who signs it and ensures that the content has not been corrupted or altered, so it is safe to run.
- *Sandbox model:* An alternative to code signing, the sandbox model, also applies to downloaded code on the network. Unlike the requirement of signing of every piece of code, it places restrictions on the capabilities of the downloaded code to limit the harm it can do on the client machine. Thus, the sandbox model ensures safety to the client machine by restricting the capabilities of the untrusted code; for example, it is not allowed to look at the file system on the client machine.

Service-Oriented Architecture

Research and development over the past few decades in distributed computing has resulted in the current day ideas in SOA implementations. SOA implementations revolve around the basic idea of a service. A service, unlike other previous concepts in distributed computing like objects or components, is more modular and self-contained. In raw terms, a service refers to a modular and self-contained piece of software, which has a well-defined functionality expressed in abstract terms independent of the underlying implementation that is accessible at a network point. Basically, any implementation of Service-Oriented Architecture has three fundamental roles: Service provider, Service requester, and Service registry and three fundamental operations: Publish, Find, and Bind (Figure 1). The service provider *publishes* details pertaining to service invocation with a service registry. The service requester *finds* the details of a service from the service registry. The service requester then invokes (*binds*) the service on the service provider. The role of service registry is sometimes also referred to as the service broker because it acts as a service broker between the requesters and providers.

Figure 1. Service-oriented architecture

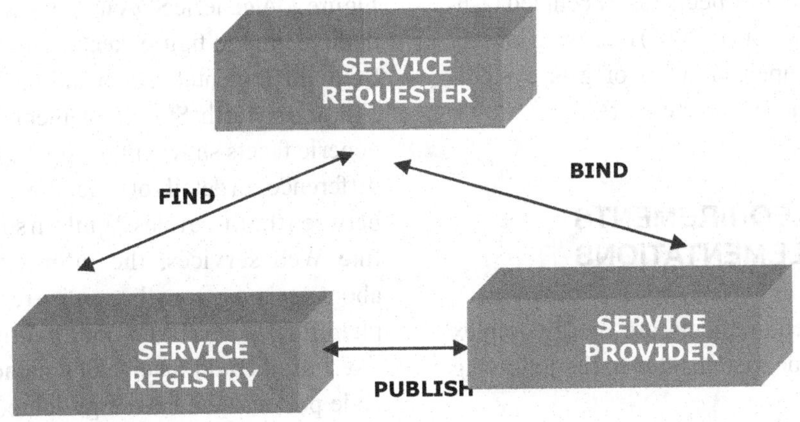

SOA as a concept is not new to distributed computing. Earlier distributed architectural models based on CORBA, DCOM, Java RMI, and so forth had their basis in the SOA concept. However, these implementations were based on *tight coupling* between the service requesters and service providers. In these systems, there was a strict requirement of matching of data and protocol formats on both sides in order for the systems to interoperate. Further, tight coupling required significant changes in any dependent system when one system was changed, and hence, maintenance of systems in tightly coupled SOA implementations was costly.

On the other hand, a loosely coupled SOA implementation offers independence between the different participants so that each can act independently without requiring significant changes when one participant undergoes any change. This independence further extends the removal of strict matching requirements of data and protocol between the two systems. Such independence enables creation of flexible and adaptive distributed environments. Examples of such implementations of SOA include Web services, Jini, and OGSA. Unless otherwise mentioned, we shall use the term SOA implementations to refer to loosely coupled SOA implementations only. Web services represent standards-based functions accessible over a network with XML-based protocols. Jini (Jini Spec, 2003) is an architecture recommendation from Sun Microsystems for networks of devices interacting in a peer-to-peer loosely coupled fashion. OGSA (OGSA Spec, 2003) is an open loosely coupled SOA implementation of grid systems based on the concepts in Web services.

SECURITY REQUIREMENTS IN SOA IMPLEMENTATIONS

SOA security requirements are more complex than that of online systems due to the following factors:

- Heightened security threats on account of easier access to implementations.
- Loosely coupled nature of interaction, requiring flexible ways of handling heterogeneous implementations.
- Dynamic interaction between services necessitates dynamic security mechanisms.
- Need to reuse existing security mechanisms in distributed systems because services are essentially wrappers over implementations.

Loose coupling security requirements in SOA will essentially translate to decentralization of conventional security mechanisms so that the interactions between service requesters and service providers carry the security information. These increased requirements necessitate additional security features including message level security, distributed credential management functions like single sign-on, message content inspection, interoperability of diverse security systems, and federation cum delegation requirements for trust and policies. Some SOA implementations like Web services advocate a recasting of the conventional security strategies and implementations for XML, and others reuse existing security concepts (for example, Jini uses Java RMI concepts).

Figure 2 lists some of the basic security requirements of an SOA implementation.

The primary security requirements in SOA implementations can be outlined as shown in Figure 2. A generic SOA implementation has been depicted in the figure, keeping in view different SOA implementations including Web services, Jini, and so forth. SOA implementations share the generic facets shown in the figure barring minor differences in details of execution of the processes between the three roles. While in some paradigms like Web services, the information retrieved about a service from the service registry could be plain interface information. In other paradigms like Jini, it could involve downloading of actual code proxies. We have highlighted the role of a

Figure 2. A bird's eye view of security requirements in service oriented architecture

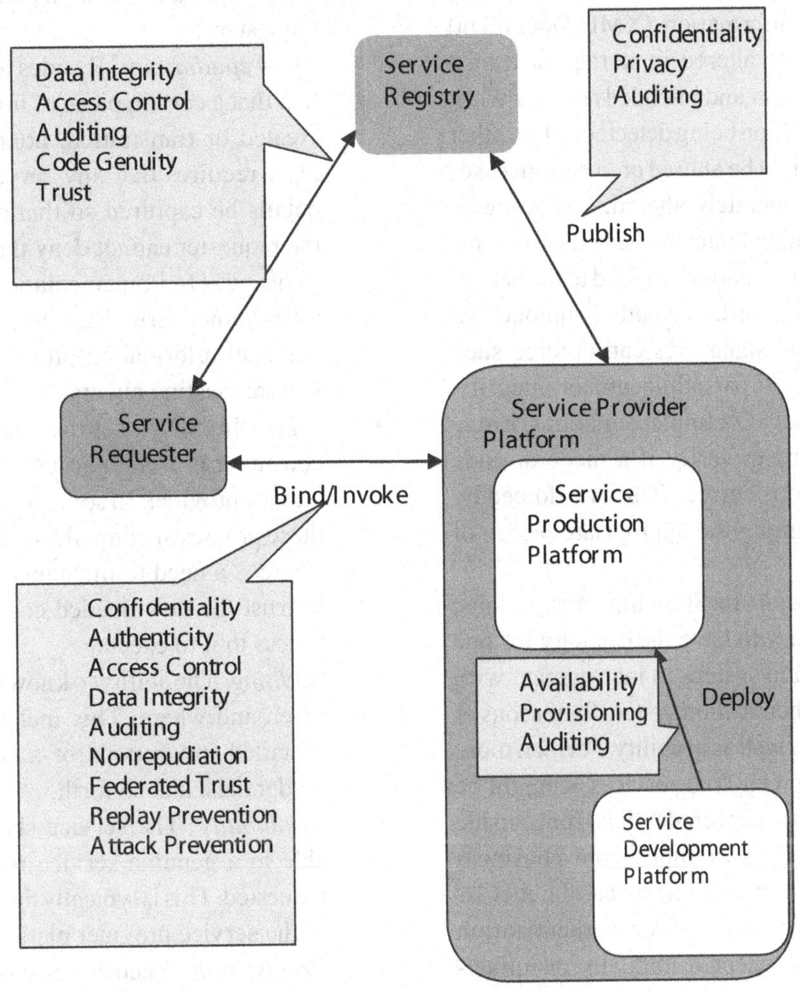

service provider platform typically consisting of a development platform, combined with a deployment platform because the deployment platform is responsible for some of the enterprise grade requirements for service providers.

Online Security Requirements As Mapped to SOA

The primary security requirements in SOA implementations include the following:

- *Confidentiality:* The confidentiality requirement for Web services pertains to the requirement that a certain piece of information (XML Document) should not be understood by anyone other than the person for whom it was intended, while the rest of the document is left untouched. In conventional terms, this requirement applied to the whole of a piece of information. This necessitates partial encryption of the document.

- *Data Integrity*: The integrity requirement in Web services mandates that a portion of a piece of information (XML Document) should not be altered in storage or transit between sender and intended receiver without the alteration being detected, while other portions might be altered or in certain cases even be deliberately altered. For example, in a value added intermediary it is possible that extra information is added to the header of a message while the body is untouched. XML digital signatures can enforce such requirement of partial document integrity. In some other SOA implementations, it may be necessary to verify if a piece of code downloaded is correct. This is enforced by digitally signing the appropriate pieces of code.
- *Authentication:* In SOA implementations, it is necessary to have the capacity for one authentication system to interoperate with another authentication system for reasons of efficiency as well as usability. Further, more specifically with Web services, it might be necessary to accept credentials from outside an enterprise, for example, from a business partner. Such requirements can be met by standardized formats for authentication information accepted mutually or universally.
- *Authorization and Access Control:* The basic authorization mechanisms in online systems commonly prescribe static access control information where permissions are provided for static resources like file systems, systems, and so forth. In SOA implementations, there is a need to further specify operation level access privileges (like permission to execute) dynamically because it may require invocation of operations by different kinds of clients at different times. Further, SOA implementations also need fine-grained specification of access control information related to restricting permissions to specific methods in a service, or a specific data item within a method, depending upon the requester.
- *Non-repudiation:* Besides capturing the fact that a certain piece of information was created or transmitted, nonrepudiation in SOA requires that any service invocation details be captured so that at a later time the requester cannot deny the invocation.
- *Privacy:* SOA implementations should have well-defined formalisms to use and disclose personal information provided by the service-requesting clients.
- *Trust:* In SOA, a proxy on the service consumer is used to access services on the service provider. In some implementations, these proxies are downloaded dynamically. There is a need to implement mechanisms to trust the downloaded code and provide access to it to execute.
- *Auditing:* The ability to know who did what, when and where. This includes capturing of failed invocations of a service, faulty credentials, and so forth.
- *Availability:* The service should be available to a genuine service requester when requested. This is typically the responsibility of the service provider platform.
- *Provisioning*: Security provisioning refers to the process of administering the security information as part of the deployment. In SOA implementations, it is essential that devices or a hosting environment of a service be appropriately provisioned with the appropriate security credentials.

Additional Security Requirements for SOA

SOA poses additional security requirements that can be outlined below:

- *Single Sign-On:* Diverse service providers and service consumers have different authentication and authorization systems, and it is impractical for each system to maintain each other's authentication rights and access control lists. Single sign-on solutions remove the necessity of a universal credential by allowing credential mapping among many diverse systems. When one system authenticates a user, the state of authentication can be used by other systems without reauthenticating and with no change in the authentication mechanisms at other systems. Single sign-on can be implemented by standards for interoperating of security credentials.

- *Malicious Invocations:* The invocations of services may be done with malicious data, which may otherwise appear to be harmless to conventional solutions like firewalls, as input to the service. This malicious data may be in the form of spurious code being sent as part of a Web service request, or it can be a piece of untrusted code downloaded in a Jini environment. Appropriate code inspection technologies are required to identify the appropriate malicious code segments before it is acted on. Another approach to tackle the same is by secluding the running environment for the code execution, as followed by the sandbox model.
- *Repeated Invocations:* Owing to the ease of invocation of services with exposed interfaces, a repeated set of attacks on a service can occur leading to denial of service and loss of availability. This requires a specialized kind of firewalls with the capacity to diagnose the content of the request and examine method invocations in isolation. Code inspection of service requests can provide a clue about repeated requests and appropriate mechanisms can be used to avoid such attacks.
- *Delegation and Federation:* Delegation refers to the capability of a service or an organization to transfer security rights and policies to another trusted service or organization. Federation is a special case when the transferee service is a peer, not a child. Delegation is a crucial component in SOA implementations like OGSA, where failure of a service should not let the whole federation collapse; instead, a delegation is done to another service. A related requirement is federated identity where users can single sign-on across heterogeneous hosts and Web services beyond one's enterprise. Standards and mechanisms to describe appropriate policies for federation and delegation are crucial to perform proper delegation and federation.

SECURITY STANDARDS AND SOLUTIONS FOR SOA

Standards have special relevance to SOA security implementations, primarily Web services, as they form the crucial backbone for implementation of security solutions. Standards are crucial in any discussion of Web services security solutions. A plethora of security standards are being worked on at different standards bodies to enable faster adoption of Web services and grid technologies. Since Web services represent the predominant SOA implementation, we shall first cover the standards and implementations of Web services security before proceeding to discuss more generic SOA security solutions.

Web Services Security Standards

Web services security standards extend standard mechanisms like encryption, digital signature, and public-key infrastructure to handle XML and Web services specific nuances and problems. Some of the protocols are work in progress, and some have been standardized already. A top-level hierarchy of Web services standards is presented in Figure 3, and a detailed listing of the relevant key standards

Figure 3. Web services security standards stack

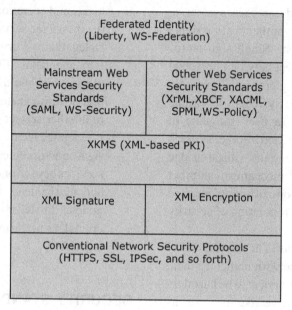

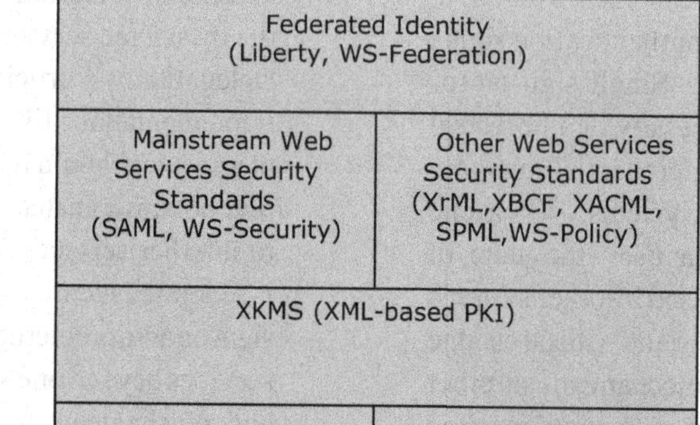

is shown in Table 1. In the hierarchy shown in Figure 3, we have tried to highlight the fact that solutions to Web services security fall above the application layer in the conventional networking stack. Conventional network security protocols have been clubbed for the purpose of simplicity as the bottom-most layer. SSL, the predominant standard for Web security, provides point-to-point confidentiality and, hence, fails to address the situation where intermediaries are involved. Thus, SSL is not ideal for Web services.

Above this layer lies the layer of XML Signature (XML-Signature Spec, 2002) and XML Encryption (XML-Encryption Spec, 2002). Encryption and Digital Signature are key solution mechanisms for security in online systems. XML-Signature and XML Encryption are attempts to remap existing concepts in Web-based security to XML message level security. In that sense, these protocols stress message-level security in contrast to session-level protocols in Web-based world. All the protocols at this level specify how to carry security data as part of XML documents. The ability to encrypt/sign only parts of XML documents is a critical part of security requirements for Web services as mentioned in the previous section.

Above this layer is XKMS (XKMS Spec, 2003), an attempt at extending PKI for XML-based Web services in order to promote widespread acceptability of XML-based security mechanisms. XKMS leverages the XML-Signature and XML-Encryption specifications.

Above this layer are the Web services security standards that leverage the lower level XML security specifications. An overlap is also observable between some key standards in this layer. The two standards of SAML and WS-Security are poised to become the popular *de facto* Web services security standards with wide acceptance. Other standards have not seen widespread acceptance. At the top lie the standards for federated identity

Table 1. A listing of key Web service security standards

Web Service Standard	Security Requirements Addressed	Proposed By	Status of Web Service Standard
XML Encryption	Message level Confidentiality	W3C	W3C approved
XML Signature	Message level Integrity, Nonrepudiation	W3C	W3C approved
XML Key Management System	XML-based PKI	W3C	W3C deliberations on
Security Assertions Markup Language	Single Sign-on, Authentication, and Authorization Interoperability	OASIS	OASIS approved
WS-Security	SOAP Message Security, Security credentials Interoperability	Microsoft, Verisign, and IBM	OASIS Spec. recently approved
XACML	Access Control and Policy Management	OASIS	OASIS approved
WS-Trust	Trust Management	Microsoft	No standardization
WS-Policy	Policy Management	Microsoft	No standardization
WS-SecureConversation	Secure Session Management	Microsoft	No standardization
XBCF	Biometrics	OASIS	OASIS approved
SPML	Service Provisioning	OASIS	OASIS approved
Project Liberty	Federated Identity	Sun and others	Project Liberty approved
WS-Federation	Federated Identity	Microsoft and IBM	None

of Web services. Federated identity is key to promote widespread acceptance of customer-focused dynamic Web services. In this section, we shall cover the key Web services security standards in greater detail.

XML Signature: In Web services, there is a need to partially encrypt the body or parts of a SOAP request to enable transmission with authenticity and integrity assured. Because of the involvement of such multi-hop data transfers in Web services, the original concept of digital signatures will not extend to XML-based content as it is based on the idea of getting signatures from the message digests of the entire document. Hence, intermediaries need mechanisms for development of complete trust of the handling of the content of messages keeping partial content intact. Such mechanisms have been provided in the XML Signature (XML-Signature Spec, 2002) specification.

XML Signature defines an XML-compliant syntax for representing signatures over Web resources and portions of protocol messages and procedures for computing and verifying such signatures.

Such signatures will be able to provide data integrity, authentication, and/or nonrepudiation. In real-life scenarios, it is necessary that in the transmission route of the XML message, different parties sign different parts. XML Signature specification allows for this kind of signing. XML Signature validation requires that the data object that was signed be accessible. The XML Signature itself will generally indicate the location of the original signed object. This reference can:

- Be referenced by a URI within the XML Signature;
- Reside within the same resource as the XML Signature (the signature is asibling);
- Be embedded within the XML Signature (the signature is the parent-*enveloping* form); and
- Have its XML Signature embedded within itself (the signature is the child-*enveloped* form).

Typical computation of XML Signature of an XML document involves computing of the message digest of the given XML document. However, it is often necessary to understand there are many cases where seemingly dissimilar XML documents and nodes actually refer to the same document/node. A typical example is shown in Listing 1 (all listings are at the end of the chapter): All three of the above represent the same basic structure, that is, the structure 1. Thus, the idea in canonical XML is to obtain the core of any XML structure so that any two structurally equivalent XML documents are identical byte for byte in their core form. This core form is termed as the *canonical form* of an XML document. Canonicalization refers essentially to the process of conversion of any XML documents to its canonical form and is necessary for XML Signature computation. An example of enveloped XML Signature is shown in Listing 2. This example uses the DSAwithSHA1 algorithm to compute the signature, and the XML Signature also provides details of key values used to compute the signature.

XML Encryption: XML Encryption (XML-Encryption Spec, 2002) is a W3C standard for storing results of an encryption operation performed on XML data in XML form. XML Signature supports the concept of encrypting only specific portions of an XML document. This minimizes the encryption processing and leaves non-sensitive information in plain text form such that general (i.e., non-security-related) processing of the XML can proceed. This addresses the necessity of partial encryption of an XML document in case of involvement of intermediaries. A typical example of an XML-Encryption output is shown in Listing 3. It shows that only the credit card component is encrypted.

XKMS: This standard (XKMS Spec, 2003) is being developed to handle the infrastructure requirements for capturing the security information (values, certificates, and trust data) related to public Web services. It defines protocols for distributing and registering public keys suitable for use in conjunction with XML Signature. Essentially, it is attempting to extend concepts in PKI to XML-based interactions. It is being designed to support the key management functionalities including registrations, trust, and delegation when XML documents are involved. XKMS is critical for large-scale deployments of Web services for public consumers.

SAML: Security Assertions Markup Language (SAML) (SAML Spec, 2003) is a standard ratified by OASIS as a high level XML-based standard for exchanging security credentials (assertions) among online business partners. The assertions could be authentication assertions (identity), attribute assertions (user limits and so forth), or authorization decision assertions (access control like read/write permission and so forth). It also specifies different protocols and profiles governing structure of SAML requests, responses, and mode of retrieval of assertions, for example, using SOAP over HTTP.

SAML does not prescribe a standard for authentication or authorization; instead, it offers a universal language to specify the information on authentication or authorization. Hence, heterogeneous authentication mechanisms can interoperate using SAML. This way, SAML addresses the requirement related to single sign-on of Web services, too. SAML assertions can be signed using XML Signature. SAML is also the base for the federated identity system developed by Project Liberty. A sample SAML Response is shown in Listing 4. This example shows an authentication assertion and an attribute assertion which indicates the *membership* attribute as having the value *Gold.*

WS-Security: WS-Security (IBM-MS WS-Security Roadmap, 2002) is an overall framework for security for Web services. As part of the framework, the initial spec has been submitted to OASIS for ratification. Currently, WS-Security is in the final stages of public review and will be ratified soon. WS-Security has support from a critical mass of Web services vendors and will be a key standard for Web services security.

WS-Security provides a generic mechanism to attach a generic security token (public certificate, X.509 certificate and so forth) to SOAP messages in the header. The token takes care of many special variations including public certificates, shared tickets, and so forth. WS-Security defines how to attach signature and encryption headers to SOAP messages. Leveraging XML Signature in conjunction with security tokens provides message integrity, and leveraging XML Encryption in conjunction with security tokens provides message confidentiality. WS-Security allows interoperation of different existing security mechanisms like Kerberos, PKI, username-passwords, and so forth. A sample WS-Security SOAP message for passing username-password information is as given in Listing 5.

Federated Identity Standards: Federated identity is the ability to securely recognize and leverage user identities enabling single sign-on across disparate applications and hosts. Federation also allows an organization to securely share its confidential user identities with other trusted organizations with a single sign-on. Enterprises of today use multiple sources of identities including NT Domains, LDAP servers, RADIUS, and so forth, but none of them qualify for the federated identity system because of the heterogeneous nature of each of these protocols. There have been multiple attempts at creation of such a federated infrastructure by multiple vendors. The prominent among them are WS-Federation and Project Liberty. WS-Federation is a proposition from Microsoft/IBM combination based on the WS-Security specification. WS-Federation (WS-Federation Spec, 2003) describes how to manage the trust relationships in a heterogeneous federated environment including support for federated identities. Project Liberty (Project Liberty Spec, 2003) is a consortium of companies formed to provide a simplifying standard for federated identity, which will allow consumers to share credentials and enable single sign-on to disparate applications and Web sites. Its vision is to enable choice and convenience for consumers to access business services using any device connected to the Internet in a secure manner. Project Liberty has based its federated identity implementation on SAML as the core of the identity management system in combination with XACML, XKMS, and XML Signature. Project Liberty released its first functional specs in August 2002.

Current Web Services Security Implementations

In spite of the fact that all standards required for Web services security have not converged, most Web services security implementations have embraced the crucial Web services standards discussed in the previous section. We shall explore briefly the broad categories of Web services security solutions not necessarily based upon Web services standards.

XML Firewalls: In Web services environments, malicious attacks and DoS attacks present new challenges. XML firewalls (Quadrasis Firewall, 2003; Reactivity Firewall, 2003; Vordel Firewall, 2004; Westbridge Firewall, 2004) are a new generation technology, which operate above the conventional application layer unlike conventional firewalls that operate on the network layer. XML firewalls have the capability of examining an incoming SOAP request and taking an appropriate action based on the message content. Such content inspection is vital to prevention of malicious as well as DoS attacks. Further, XML firewalls can offer nonrepudiation mechanisms by providing audit trails of all service accesses.

XML Networks: Some Web services management vendors view that a network-based solution is better suitable for Web services, owing to the peer-to-peer nature of the paradigm. These solution vendors (Blue Titan Network, 2004; Flamenco Network, 2004) provide solutions that cater to various QoS parameters and sit at various network endpoints where the requests and responses from service consumers/providers respectively pass through in Web services invocations. Security is also a crucial function performed by these Web services networks.

Extension of EAI and Application Server Technologies: Existing enterprise application integration (EAI) products are enabling Web services today. They are able to provide security by extending their current security infrastructure, as it exists today. These vendors use some of the key existing Web-based technologies like SSL and X.509 certificates.

J2EE application server vendors base the Web services on current security infrastructures provided by J2EE platform itself. A leading number of J2EE application server vendors are working towards Web services standards like SAML, WS-Security, and so forth but have not come out with J2EE-based standard implementations of these standards due to the corresponding Java Specification Requests for Standardization (JSRs) that are still incomplete.

The .NET application server suite has been incrementally offering security support for Web services as outlined in IBM-MS WS-Security Roadmap (2002). Current versions fully support the WS-Security specification.

Security Infrastructure Vendors: Existing market leaders for Web-based security and PKI have made moves for extending their current implementations for Web services. These vendors have come up with suites of software products for securing Web services. Some of these products are offering support for SAML, WS-Security, and other standards. SAML is being adopted by a majority of identity management vendors (SAML Interop, 2002), while WS-Security is being adopted for Web services security. In the long run, all vendors will offer entirely standards-based products once the dust on standards gets cleared.

Web Services Management Vendors: Many pure play and enterprise management vendors have jumped into the Web services management space. Some of these vendors are providing implementations based on the new Web services standards, while some are based on proprietary implementations. Most pure play or mainstream Web services management vendors have security as part of their management suite.

Security Solutions in Other SOA Implementations

Each SOA implementation has its own specialized security requirements, which may require specialized solutions.

Jini is essentially based on the idea of transfer of code from one entity to another. Hence, security of mobile code is important for Jini. Jini relies on the basic Java Security model and its extensions to fulfil the security requirements. The basic idea is to define a mechanism of trust for dynamically downloaded code and use it in combination with code-signing mechanisms. While code signing provides the integrity check, trust mechanism enables a decision point for execution of the dynamically downloaded code on the client.

OGSA has prescribed a standard for implementation of security in a service-oriented fashion. The recommended architecture for security in OGSA (Nataraj Nagartnam et al., 2002) is based around core Web services security standards. While it leverages SAML spec for the authorization service, it leverages WS-Security as the base for message-level security. The core recommendation of the security model for OGSA endorses the view of security requirements being provided by OGSA-compliant services. In that sense, certain core OGSA-compliant services form the infrastructure-level OGSA security services and are invoked for security needs. This model furthers the notion of a loosely coupled security model for the security requirements of a loosely coupled architecture model like OGSA.

FUTURE TRENDS

SOA being a relatively recent trend in enterprise architecture, SOA implementations are still in infancy and have not matured yet. However, it is fast capturing the mindshare of enterprise architects with many enterprises announcing long term plans for migration to SOA. In due course of time, SOA implementations involving loose coupling will be pervasive across enterprises. In terms of trends in security for SOA implementations, we envisage the following trends in the future.

Standards Convergence and Maturity

The current standards stack in Web services security is a mix of standards under various stages of standardization: some (like XML Encryption) are fully ratified as standards; some (WS-Security) are nearing the end of the standardization process, while some (like WS-Federation) are proprietary and yet to be submitted to a standards body. Also, there is a clash in some competing security standards addressing the same requirements (for example, WS-Federation and Project Liberty both address federated identity).

Over time, it can be envisaged that the standards will converge to a core set of standards addressing Web services security. It is likely that two competing standards may be present for the same functionality with ways of interoperating. An example of such competing standards can be seen in SAML and WS-Security where there is some amount of overlap with each other, and WS-Security is working on a profile for including SAML assertions in WS-Security tokens. Some of the current security requirements like nonrepudiation, auditing, and so forth, which have not seen any standardization process yet, will be tackled by standards in the long run.

Standards Compliance for Security Products

Over time, the majority of Web services security offerings will be based on standards. This will lead to decreased cost of security administration. This is already evident from some category of products like identity management products, a majority of which have provided compliance with SAML (SAML Interop, 2002). In case of availability of multiple standards for the same implementation, products will offer interoperability support for multiple standards.

WS-I (Web Services Interoperability Organization) will have a key role in promoting standards adoption in products and vendors. WS-I is working on a security profile for Web services. This will be a key step in increasing standards compliance awareness among security vendors.

Federated Identity

Even though vendors and standards bodies have been quick in coming up with standards for federated identity in view of lack of convergence in standards and the enhanced skepticism, there is a lesser chance of federated identity-based business models being successful. Hence, federated identity as a concept will take more time to make inroads into enterprises.

XML-Based PKI

In view of the increased role of XML in SOA implementations in distributed systems, dealing with public keys will become a major scalability issue for SOA implementations. The current PKI constituents like Registration Authorities and Certification Authorities will evolve to be compliant with XML-based PKI. Hence, in due course of time, XKMS will play a key role for the development of PKI.

New Generation Security Products

On account of the peer-to-peer nature of SOA implementations, specialized security intermediaries will be vital to managing the complexity of security requirements in enterprise grade and highly distributed environments. These specialized intermediaries will offload the security-related services away from the service consumers and service providers, thereby increasing scalability.

As part of this trend, some of the current day innovative SOA security products like XML networks and XML gateways will be commoditized owing to standardization of these innovative technologies as part of security best practices in enterprise architecture.

Component Security Models

Current component models like J2EE and .NET have varying levels of support for different Web services standards. The Java Community process (JCP) has currently admitted various specification requests to include various Web services security standards as part of J2EE spec. Until these are approved in the JCP, J2EE products will base their implementations of Web services security standards on proprietary mechanisms and APIs. In the .NET platform, the current support for WS-Security is proprietary, as the standard is only recently ratified. In the long run, it will be standards compliant.

CONCLUSION

In this chapter, we have examined the various security requirements as applicable to SOA implementations. As part of this exercise, we have seen how generic online security requirements map to SOA implementations. Further, the paradigm of SOA introduces new categories of security requirements.

Towards identifying potential solutions to the security requirements in SOA implementations, we have examined in detail the various standards and implementation mechanisms in Web services. Web Services being the predominant SOA implementation, these solution mechanisms guide us to appropriate security solutions for SOA implementations. We have shown the vital role of standards in Web services security implementations.

We also attempted a brief summary of different solution mechanisms in other SOA implementations. Since the SOA requirements for these implementations are varied, some of the concepts in Web services cannot be applied directly to these models. OGSA-based grid solutions being based on Web services, solutions for OGSA security are directly dependent upon Web services security solutions.

Towards the end, we have tried to outline the future trends in SOA security on multiple dimensions, primary among them being the trends in standards. Over time, we feel that standards compliance will be commonplace among all the implementations.

We can see that standards have a key role to play in driving Web services security implementations. Over time, we feel that Web services security standards of WS-Security and SAML will occupy center stage for message-level security and identity management, respectively. These standards will provide flexibility as desired in Web services applications.

OGSA security architecture by its dependence upon core Web services architecture will be directly dependent upon the success of Web services security standards. Hence, the full realization of the security architecture for OGSA will take a somewhat longer time. A lot of work in security for Jini is still at a research stage, especially on requirements of trust management in networked computing and security of mobile code.

Further, we have seen that the loosely-coupled nature of SOA implementations necessitates a loosely-coupled approach to security, as is evident by the necessity of message-level security in Web services instead of the conventional channel-level security. We have also seen how SOA security implementation mechanisms advocate reuse of existing security infrastructure instead of fresh investment. All the standards for Web services security leverage existing security mechanisms and techniques in online systems and handle the extra requirements owing to usage of XML as the language.

Overall, security in SOA implementations is vital for success of SOA as a futuristic enterprise architecture paradigm.

REFERENCES

Blue Titan Network. (2004, January 3). *Blue Titan Network Director*. Retrieved August 18, 2004, from http://www.bluetitan.com/products/btitan_network.htm

Flamenco Network. (2004, January). *Flamenco Networks*. Retrieved August 18, 2004, from http://www.flamenconetworks.com/solutions/nsp.html

IBM-MS WS-Security Roadmap. (2002, April 7). *Security in a Web services world: A proposed architecture and roadmap*. Retrieved August 18, 2004, from http://msdn.microsoft.com/library/en-us/dnwssecur/html/securitywhitepaper.asp

Jini Spec. (2003, September 12). *Jini technology specification*. Retrieved August 18, 2004, from http://wwws.sun.com/software/jini/jini_technology.html

Nataraj Nagaratnam, Jason Philippe, Dayka John, Nadalin Anthony, Siebenlist Frank, Welch Von, et al. (2002, July). *OGSA security roadmap*. Retrieved August 18, 2004, from http://www.cs.virginia.edu/~humphrey/ogsa-sec-wg/OGSA-SecArch-v1-07192002.pdf

OGSA Spec. (2003, April 5). *Open grid services infrastructure*. Retrieved August 18, 2004, from http://www.gridforum.org/ogsi-wg/drafts/draft-ggf-ogsi-gridservice-29_2003-04-05.pdf

Project Liberty Spec. (2003, January 15). *Project Liberty specification*. Retrieved August 18, 2004, from http://www.projectliberty.org/specs/archive/v1_1/liberty-architecture-overview-v1.1.pdf

Quadrasis Firewall. (2004, January 2). *Quadrasis EASI SOAP content inspector*. Retrieved August 18, 2004, from http://www.quadrasis.com/solutions/products/easi_product_packages/easi_soap.htm

Reactivity Firewall. (2004, January 2). *Reactivity XML firewall.* Retrieved August 18, 2004, from http://www.reactivity.com/products/solution.html

SAML Spec. (2003, September 2). *Security Assertions Markup Language (SAML).* Retrieved August 18, 2004, from http://www.oasis-open.org/committees/download.php/2949/sstc-saml-1.1-cs-03-pdf-xsd.zip

SAML Interop. (2002, July 15). *SAML interoperability event.* Retrieved August 18, 2004, from http://xml.coverpages.org/ni2002-07-15-a.html

Vordel Firewall. (2004, January 2). *Vordel XML security server.* Retrieved August 18, 2004, from http://www.vordel.com/products/xml_security_server.html

Westbridge Firewall. (2004, January 2). *Westbridge XML message server.* Retrieved August 18, 2004 from http://www.westbridgetech.com/products.html

WS-Federation Spec. (2003, July 18). *WS-Federation specification.* Retrieved August 18, 2004, from http://www-106.ibm.com/developerworks/webservices/library/ws-fed/

WS-Policy Spec. (2002, December 18). *WS-Policy Specification.* Retrieved August 18, 2004, from http://msdn.microsoft.com/library/default.asp?url=/library/en-us/dnglobspec/html/wspolicyspecindex.asp

WS-Security Spec. (2002, April 5). *Web services security (WS-Security).* Retrieved August 18, 2004, from http://msdn.microsoft.com/library/en-us/dnglobspec/html/ws-security.asp

XACML Spec. (2003, February 18). *eXtensible Access Control Markup Language (XACML).* Retrieved August 18, 2004, from http://www.oasis-open.org/committees/download.php/2406/oasis-xacml-1.0.pdf

XKMS Spec. (2001, March). *XML Key Management Specification (XKMS).* Retrieved August 18, 2004, from http://www.w3.org/TR/xkms/

XML-Encryption Spec. (2002, December 10). *XML Encryption Syntax and Processing.* Retrieved August 18, 2004, from http://www.w3.org/TR/xmlenc-core/

XML-Signature Spec. (2002, February 12). *XML-Signature Syntax and Processing.* Retrieved August 18, 2004, from http://www.w3.org/TR/xmldsig-core/

SOURCE CODE LISTINGS

Listing 1. Canonical form inputs

```
1.   <node>b &amp; c</node>
2.   <node> b &#x26; c</node>
3.   <node><![CDATA[b&c]]></node>
```

Listing 2. Enveloped digital signature

```
<!-- Comment before -->
<apache:RootElement xmlns:apache="http://www.apache.org/ns/#app1">SOME
SIMPLE TEXT
<Signature xmlns="http://www.w3.org/2000/09/xmldsig#">
<SignedInfo>
    <CanonicalizationMethod Algorithm="http://www.w3.org/TR/2001/REC-xml-c14n-
20010315"></CanonicalizationMethod>
<SignatureMethod Algorithm="http://www.w3.org/2000/09/xmldsig#dsa-
sha1"></SignatureMethod>
<Reference URI="">
<Transforms>
<Transform Algorithm="http://www.w3.org/2000/09/xmldsig#enveloped-
signature"></Transform>
<Transform Algorithm="http://www.w3.org/TR/2001/REC-xml-c14n-
20010315#WithComments"></Transform>
</Transforms>
<DigestMethod
Algorithm="http://www.w3.org/2000/09/xmldsig#sha1"></DigestMethod>
<DigestValue>YNvvmanolyMNI+33mqiZuJe9WIE=</DigestValue>
</Reference>
</SignedInfo>
<SignatureValue>TrTeerc9ddqStQ0X/0XO/6G5k48kgUQtvRQofcbOZrJnYKyTJG9PX
Q==</SignatureValue>
<KeyInfo>
<X509Data>
<X509Certificate>
..........................................(Contents Shortened..)
</X509Certificate>
</X509Data>
<KeyValue>
<DSAKeyValue><P>
....(Contents Shortened).</P>
<Q>l2BQjxUjC8yykrmCouuEC/BYHPU=</Q>
<G>9+GghdabPd7LvKtcNrhXuXmUr7v6OuqC+VdMCz0HgmdRWVeOutRZT+ZxBxC
BgLRJFnEj6EwoFhO3
zwkyjMim4TwWeotUfl0o4KOuHiuzpnWRbqN/C/ohNWLx+2J6ASQ7zKTxvqhRklmog9
/hWuWfBpKL
Zl6Ae1UlZAFMO/7PSSo=</G>
<Y>
45T+wNtzv+XRinm6c/D/xb4DCcndZUtGeHva+0BbLBrlYHO2VN1mV1Sk1R4ThcPrjtx
Oa2Q4F6+O
MKlwSVleCsk/2gUhHPNdBTEt+wEG7GpvO1QEE7i1k+AK8BhEzEAr7mUEh/7QhS6/
Kd+H0ZkLD/ZK
pTmYZnSP0EGVmscK0sY=</Y>
    </DSAKeyValue> </KeyValue> </KeyInfo> </Signature></apache:RootElement>
<!-- Comment after -->
```

Listing 3. Example of XML encryption

```
<?xml version='1.0'?>
 <PaymentInfo xmlns='http://example.in/payments'>
   <Name>Srini<Name/>
   <CreditCard Limit='2,000' Currency='INR'>
     <Number>
       <EncryptedData xmlns='http://www.w3.org/2001/04/xmlenc#'
        Type='http://www.w3.org/2001/04/xmlenc#Content'>
          <CipherData><CipherValue>A213C45D79</CipherValue>
          </CipherData>
       </EncryptedData>
     </Number>
     <Issuer>Online State Bank of the India</Issuer>
     <Expiration>03/04</Expiration>
   </CreditCard>
 </PaymentInfo>
```

Listing 4. Example of SAML response with embedded authentication and attribute assertions

```
<Response xmlns="urn:oasis:names:tc:SAML:1.0:protocol"
xmlns:samlp="urn:oasis:names:tc:SAML:1.0:protocol" IssueInstant="2003-10-
16T13:04:03Z" MajorVersion="1" MinorVersion="0" Recipient="ravi"
ResponseID="7ea17dd3-655a-40e9-a890-ab548c0d71c1">
<Status>
<StatusCode Value="samlp:Success">
</StatusCode></Status>
<Assertion xmlns="urn:oasis:names:tc:SAML:1.0:assertion" AssertionID="dab9ae6d-
01a2-4122-a3a0-a2da221907e8" IssueInstant="2003-10-16T13:04:08Z"
Issuer="Srinivas" MajorVersion="1" MinorVersion="0">
<Conditions NotBefore="2003-10-16T13:04:03Z" NotOnOrAfter="2003-10-
16T13:06:03Z">
</Conditions>
<AuthenticationStatement AuthenticationInstant="2003-10-16T13:04:03Z"
AuthenticationMethod="urn:oasis:names:tc:SAML:1.0:am:unspecified">
<Subject>
<NameIdentifier>
Gold
</NameIdentifier>
<SubjectConfirmation>
<ConfirmationMethod>urn:oasis:names:tc:SAML:1.0:cm:bearer</ConfirmationMethod
>
</SubjectConfirmation>
</Subject>
</AuthenticationStatement>
<AttributeStatement xmlns:xsd="http://www.w3.org/2001/XMLSchema"
xmlns:xsi="http://www.w3.org/2001/XMLSchema-instance">
<Subject>
<NameIdentifier>Gold</NameIdentifier>
</Subject>
<Attribute AttributeName="Membership" AttributeNamespace="namespace">
<AttributeValue>Gold</AttributeValue>
</Attribute>
</AttributeStatement>
</Assertion>
</Response>
```

Listing 5. WS-Security example with username password credentials


```
<?xml version="1.0" encoding="utf-8"?>
<S:Envelope
 <S:Header>
  <wsse:Security>
  <wsse:UsernameToken wsu:Id="MyID">
    <wsse:Username>Sam</wsse:Username>
    <wsse:Password>MyPassword</wsse:Password>
    <wsse:Nonce>FKJh...</wsse:Nonce>
    <wsu:Created>2001-10-23T09:00:00Z</wsu:Created>
  </wsse:UsernameToken> ..... </wsse:Security>
 </S:Header>
  <S:Body wsu:Id="MsgBody"> ..... </S:Body>
   </S:Envelope>
```


This work was previously published in Service-Oriented Software System Engineering: Challenges and Practices, edited by Z. Stojanovic and A. Dahanayake, pp. 292-316, copyright 2005 by IGI Publishing, formerly known as Idea Group Publishing (an imprint of IGI Global).

Chapter II
A Retrospective on the Development of Web Service Specifications

Shrideep Pallickara
Community Grids Lab, Indiana University, USA

Mehmet S. Aktas
Community Grids Lab, Indiana University, USA

Beytullah Yildiz
Community Grids Lab, Indiana University, USA

Sima Patel
Community Grids Lab, Indiana University, USA

Damodar Yemme
Wheaton Van Lines Inc., USA

Geoffrey Fox
Community Grids Lab, Indiana University, USA

Harshawardhan Gadgil
Community Grids Lab, Indiana University, USA, & Amazon.com, USA

Marlon E. Pierce
Community Grids Lab, Indiana University, USA

Sangyoon Oh
SK Telecom, Korea

ABSTRACT

In this chapter, we present a discussion on our experiences with the development of Web service specifications. Web services, and the service oriented architecture model engendered therein, have gained significant traction in recent years with deployments in ever increasing domains. In this chapter, we describe our experiences with several Web service specifications. In general lessons learned, and design decisions made, during these implementations would be applicable to several other specifications. The authors hope that their insights and experiences with the development of Web service specifications would be beneficial to other researchers in this area in formulating a strategy for the development of systems based on Web services.

INTRODUCTION

Web services have gained considerable traction over the past several years, and are being increasingly leveraged within the academic, business, and research communities. The service oriented architecture (SOA) model engendered within Web services provides a simple and flexible framework for building sophisticated applications. A slew of specifications addressing several core areas, such as reliable messaging, addressing, security, and so forth, within distributed systems have emerged recently. The term WS-* is used as an umbrella term to collectively refer to these specifications. The use of XML throughout the Web services stack of specifications facilitates interactions between services implemented in different languages, running on different platforms, and over multiple transports. This use of XML distinguishes Web services from previous efforts such as CORBA (common object resource broker architecture) to simply building distributed systems.

In this chapter, we describe our experiences with several Web service specifications. In general lessons learned, and design decisions made, during these implementations would be applicable to several other specifications. We begin this chapter with some observations regarding Web service specifications. This includes a discussion on the SOAP-centric (simple object access protocol) (Gudgin, 2003) nature of the specifications, their reliance on one-way asynchronous message exchanges, how a specification can itself leverage other specifications, and, finally, how these specifications are intended to be stackable to facilitate use in tandem with each other. Several specifications leverage the WS-addressing (Box, 2004a) specification, and this specification has, in recent years, become the de facto standard to target Web service instances; we also include a brief description of this specification.

WS-* specifications are XML-based and have schemas associated with them. In the section on Processing XML Schemas we describe the choices available to designers for processing these schemas. In subsequent sections, we describe the implementation strategy for various specifications that we have implemented. These include WS-reliable messaging (Bilorusets, 2004) (hereafter WSRM), WS-reliability (Oasis-WSR, 2004) (hereafter WSR), WS-eventing (Box, 2004b) (hereafter WSE), WS-Context [7], the universal description, discovery and integration (UDDI) (Bunting, 2003), WS-management (Arora, 2005) and WS-transfer (Alexander, 2004a). Depending on the interactions and exchanges that are part of these specifications, the complexity of the implementation and corresponding deployments varies.

The WSRM and WSR specifications pertain to providing support for reliable messaging between Web service endpoints. These aforementioned specifications guarantee delivery of messages in the presence of failures and disconnects; endpoints can also retrieve lost messages after a failure. The WSE specification provides a mechanism for routing notifications from the producers to the registered consumers. Consumers can register their interest in specific messages using XPath queries; only messages that satisfy the previously specified constraint are routed to a consumer. Implementation of the WSRM, WSR, and WSE specifications are outlined in a separate section.

WS-management facilitates the efficient management of distributed systems; this specification identifies a core set of Web service specifications and usage requirements to expose a common set of operations central to all systems management. Our implementation is described in the section on management within distributed systems.

WS-context models session metadata as an external entity where more than two services can access/store highly dynamic shared metadata. Extensions to the WS-context specification and implementation are described in the section on Extending WS-context specifications. The UDDI specification defines a searchable repository of Web service description language (WSDL) (Christensen, 2001) specifications of Grid/Web services. We have designed and implemented a hybrid information service that provides semantics for both types of information that are defined by the WS-Context and UDDI Specifications; this is described in the section on modified UDDI. Issues related to the use of Web services in power and compute constrained devices such as mobile devices are described in the section on Web services and mobile devices.

In the section on Deployment Related Issues within Axis, we discuss issues within a dominant Web service container—Apache Axis—vis-à-vis support for interactions mandated within Web service specifications. We also describe deployment strategies to cope with the constraints imposed within the container. In the section on use cases for various specifications, we describe use cases for these specifications. Specifically, we outline how we leveraged implementations of various WS-* specifications in various projects and settings. Finally, we outline our conclusions.

SOME OBSERVATION ABOUT WS-* SPECIFICATIONS

WS-* specifications typically tend to address cores areas or areas where the demand is sufficiently high enough that it makes sense to eschew proprietary solutions. In some cases, if there is a common thread among several specifications, this needs to be abstracted into a specification in its own right. Exemplars of this include WS-addressing, which provides a scheme to address Web service endpoints, and WS-policy, which provides a framework for exchanging policy information between the service endpoints.

Most of these specifications are developed such that they can be leveraged by other specifications. The specifications also provide a framework to facilitate the incremental addition of capabilities at a given service endpoint. In some cases, these specifications are stackable and when used together provide capabilities available in the stacked specifications.

The specifications also specify a WSDL document, which describes message formats and message exchange patterns associated with them. However, all communications and exchanges outlined within these specifications are to be encapsulated within stand-alone SOAP messages. SOAP is an XML-based protocol, and provides a framework for building self-contained messages that can reference elements from other schemas. This extensibility mechanism allows a given SOAP message to contain elements from schemas related to different specifications (such as WS-addressing, WS-security, etc.) at the same time, should the need arise. SOAP messages are also used by service endpoints to report faults and errors related to processing messages. The extensibility framework in SOAP allows a given SOAP message to contain elements from schemas related to different specifications.

Here, we also note that SOAP-based asynchronous interactions and the stackable nature of these specifications are particularly well-suited for one-way messaging. However, most Web service containers (at least for Java) are designed around the RPC-style request-response model as its primary mode of interaction.

WS-ADDRESSING

WS-addressing is a way to abstract, from the underlying transport infrastructure, the addressing needs of an application. WS-addressing is thus central to most Web service specifications. WS-Addressing incorporates support for end point references and message information headers. End point references standardize the format for referencing (and passing around references to) both a Web service and Web service instances. The message information headers standardize information pertaining to message processing, related to replies, faults, and actions, and the relationship to prior messages. This is especially useful in cases where there would be multiple dedicated entities dealing with these different cases. The message information headers elements comprise the following:

- **To (mandatory element):** This specifies the intended of receiver of message. If there are end point references contained in the SOAP header element, this identifies the node that is responsible for routing the message to the final destination.
- **From:** This identifies the originator of a message.
- **ReplyTo:** Specifies where replies to a message will be sent.
- **FaultTo:** Specifies where faults generated as a result of processing the message should be sent to. If this element is not present, faults will be routed to the element identified in the replyTo element. If both the replyTo and faultTo elements are missing, the faults are issued back to the source of the message.
- **Action:** This is a URI that identifies the semantics associated with the message. WS-Addressing also specifies rules on the generation of Action elements from the WSDL definition of a service. In the WSDL case, this is generally a combination of **[target namespace]/[port type name]/[input/output name]**. For example, http://schemas.xmlsoap.org/ws/2004/08/eventing/Subscribe is a valid Action element.
- **MessageId:** This is typically a UUID which uniquely identifies a message. This is also used to correlate previous messages. For example, in WSRM if you have requested the creation of sequence, the response to the creation of the sequence would include the MessageId of the request in the relatesTo element.
- **RelatesTo:** This identifies how a message relates to a previous message. This field typically contains the MessageId of a previously issued message.

PROCESSING THE XML SCHEMAS

One of the most important decisions while developing Web service specifications is the choice of the tool to use while processing the XML schema related to the specification being implemented (along with those that are leveraged within the aforementioned specification) and SOAP. We were looking for a solution that allowed us to process XML from within the Java domain. Here, there were four main choices.

First, we could develop these Java classes along with the parsing capabilities ourselves. This is the approach that was used in Apache's Sandesha project, which provides an implementation of WSRM. This approach is error-prone and is generally quite difficult. Furthermore, this approach quickly becomes infeasible as the complexity of the schema increases, and also as the number of leveraged specifications increases. Another possible approach is to process these messages based on the DOM (Document Object Model) model; here, the development process would be quite complicated; presently, we are not aware of any system that leverages this scheme.

Second, we could use the Axis Web service container's *wsdl2java* compiler. Issues (in version 1.2) related to this tool's support for schemas have been documented in Ref (Gibbs & Goodman, 2003). Specifically, the problems related to insufficient (and, in some cases, incorrect) support for complex schema types, XML validation, and serialization issues. This precludes the use of this tool in several settings.

The third approach was to use the JAXB specification, a specification from Sun to deal with XML and Java data-bindings. The classes generated through JAXB, though better than what is generated using Axis' *wsdl2java,* still does not provide complete support for the XML Schema. One may thus run into situations where one may find inaccessible data elements. We looked into both the JAXB reference implementation from Sun and JaxMe from Apache (which is an open source implementation of JAXB) before deciding not to use this approach for processing the WS-* schemas.

The final approach involves utilizing tools which focus on complete schema support. Here, there were two candidates—XMLBeans and Castor—which provide good support for XML Schemas. We settled on XMLBeans for two reasons. First, it is an open-source effort. Originally developed by BEA, it was contributed by BEA to the Apache Software Foundation. Second, in our opinion, it provides the best and most complete support for the XML schema of all the tools currently available. It allows us to validate instance documents and also facilitates simple but sophisticated navigation of XML documents. Finally, the XML generated by the corresponding Java classes is true XML that conforms to, and can be validated against, the original schema.

WSRM, WSR, and WSE

In this section, we describe our scheme for the implementation of the WSRM, WSR, and the WSE specifications. One thing to note about these specifications is that they are intended to provide incremental addition of capabilities at a given service endpoint. The WSRM and WSR specifications pertain to providing reliable delivery of messages between service endpoints, while the WSE specification provides a framework for routing notifications from a source to registered sinks. We first provide an overview of these systems before we describe the implementation strategy for these specifications. Here, we note that these implementations are available as part of the NaradaBrokering project (http://www.naradabrokering.org/). Furthermore, implementation strategies for WSRM and WSR are identical, and we have chosen to describe only WSRM in this section.

The Base Framework for Implementing the Specifications

In order to facilitate incremental addition of capabilities at an endpoint, functionality related to the specification should be encapsulated in a *processor* which processes these SOAP messages. We first developed the most generic version of this processor—the WsProcessor—which can be leveraged by the implementations. Furthermore, in the specifications that we consider there are multiple roles that have been outlined within the same specification; in this case, each role needs to extend this basic processor with additional functionality.

The basic WsProcessor serves the following functions. First, it provides a framework for funneling interactions in a manner that is suitable for incrementally adding capabilities to the service endpoint. Second, it provides a framework for delegating the networking requirements to another interface; this enables the developer to simply focus on implementing the specification without having to focus on developing a scheme to transporting SOAP messages. Finally, the WsProcessor also provides a framework for reporting a variety of exceptions related to deployments and faults that have been outlined within the specification being implemented.

The WsProcessor contains a method processExchange() which can be used by the endpoint to funnel all inbound and outbound messages to and from the endpoint. By funneling all messages through the processors we also have the capability of shielding the Web service endpoints from some of the control messages that are exchanged as part of the routine exchanges between WS-* endpoints. For example, a Web service endpoint need not know about (or cope with) control messages related the acknowledgements and the creation/termination of Sequences in WSRM.

Included below is the definition of the processExchange() method. Using the SOAPContext it is possible to retrieve the encapsulated SOAP message. The logic related to the processing of the funneled SOAP messages is different depending on whether the SOAP message was received from the application or network. Exceptions thrown by this method are all *checked* exceptions and can thus be trapped using appropriate try-catch blocks. Depending on the type of the exception that is thrown, either an appropriate SOAP Fault is constructed and routed to the relevant location, or it triggers an exception related to processing the message at the node in question. A processor decides on processing a SOAP message based on one of three parameters:

- The contents of the WSA action attribute contained within the SOAP Header
- The presence of specific schema elements in either the Body or Header of the SOAP Message
- If the message has been received from the application or if it was received over the network

```
public boolean
processExchange(SOAPContext soapContext,
 int direction)
throws UnknownExchangeException,
 IncorrectExchangeException,
 MessageFlowException,
 ProcessingException
```

If the WsProcessor instance does not know how to process a certain message, it throws an UnknownMessageException. An example of this scenario is a WSRM processor receiving a control message corresponding to a different Web service specification, such as a WSE Subscribe request. An IncorrectExchangeException is thrown if the WsProcessor instance should not have received a specific exchange. For example, if a WSRM sink receives a wsrm:Acknowledgement it would throw this particular exception because acknowledgements are processed by the source. MessageFlowException reports problems related to networking within the container environment within which the WsProcessor is hosted. The ProcessingException corresponds to errors related to processing the received SOAP message. This is typically due to errors related to the inability to locate protocol elements within the SOAP message, the use of incorrect (or different versions of) schemas and no values being supplied for some schema elements.

If the ProcessingException was caused due to a malformed SOAP message received over the network, an appropriate SOAP Fault message is routed back to the remote endpoint. If a ProcessingException was thrown due to messages received from the hosting Web service endpoint, or if networking problems are reported in the MessageFlowException, processing related to the SOAP message is terminated immediately.

Another class of interest is the WsMessageFlow class. This interface contains two methods, enrouteToApplication() and enrouteToNetwork(), which are leveraged by the WsProcessor to route SOAP messages (requests, responses, or faults) *en route* to the hosting Web service or a network endpoint, respectively. The WsProcessor has methods which enable the registration of WsMessageFow instances. Because the WsProcessor delegates the actual transmission of messages to Web service container-specific implementations of the WsMessageFlow, it can be deployed in a wide variety of settings within different Web service containers, such as Apache Axis and Sun's JWSDP, by registering the appropriate WsMessageFlow instance with the WsProcessor. The capabilities within the WsProcessor and the WsMessageFlow enable the developer to focus only on the logic related to the respective roles within the specifications being implemented.

The WSRM & WSR Specifications

The specifications—WSR and WSRM—both of which are based on XML, address the issue of ensuring reliable delivery between two service endpoints. In this section, we outline the similarities in the underlying principles that guide both these specifications. The similarities that we have identified are along the six related dimensions of acknowledgements, ordering and duplicate eliminations, groups of messages and quality of service, timers, security, and fault/diagnostic reporting.

Both the specifications use positive acknowledgements to ensure reliable delivery. This in turn implies that error detections, initiation of error corrections, and subsequent retransmissions of "missed" messages can be performed at the sender side. A sender may also proactively initiate corrections based on the nonreceipt of acknowledgements within a predefined interval.

The specifications also address the related issues of ordering and duplicate detection of messages issued by a source. A combination of these qualities-of-service (QoS) can also be used to facilitate exactly once delivery. Both the specifications facilitate guaranteed, exactly-once delivery of messages, a very important quality of service that is highly relevant for transaction-oriented applications, specifically banking, retailing, and e-commerce.

Both the specifications also introduce the concept of a *group* (also referred to as a *sequence*) of messages. All messages that are part of a group of messages share a common group identifier. The specifications explicitly incorporate support for this concept by including the group identifier in protocol exchanges that take place between the two entities involved in reliable communications. Furthermore, in both the specifications the QoS constraints specified on the delivery of messages are valid only within a group of messages, each of which has its own group identifier.

The specifications also introduce timer-based operations for both messages (application and control) and groups of messages. Individual and groups of messages are considered invalid upon the expiry of timers associated with them. Finally, the delivery protocols in these specifications also incorporate the use of timers to initiate retransmissions and to time out retransmission attempts.

In terms of security both the specifications aim to leverage the WS-Security specification, which facilitates message level security. Message level security is independent of the security of the underlying transport and facilitates secure interactions over insecure communication links.

The specifications also provide for notification and exchange of errors in processing between the endpoints involved in reliable delivery. The range of errors supported in these specifications can vary from an inability to decipher a message's content to complex errors pertaining to violations in implied agreements between the interacting entities.

WSRM Implementation

In our implementation (Java-based) functionality related to the sink and sink roles in WSRM are encapsulated within the WSRMSourceProcessor and WSRMSinkProcessor, respectively. Both these processors extend the WsProcessor base class. It should be noted that a given endpoint may be a source, sink, or both for the reliable delivery of SOAP messages. In the case that the endpoint is both a source and a sink, both the WSRM-SourceProcessor and the WSRMSinkProcessor will be cascaded at the endpoint.

Upon receipt of an outgoing SOAP message, the WSRMSourceProcessor checks to see if an active Sequence currently exists between the hosting endpoint and the remote endpoint. If one does not exist, the WSRMSourceProcessor automatically initiates a create sequence exchange to establish an active Sequence. For each active Sequence, the WSRMSourceProcessor also keeps track of the Message Number last assigned to ensure that they monotonically increase, starting from 1. The WSRMSourceProcessor performs other functions as outlined in the WSRM specification which includes *inter alia* the processing of acknowledgements, issuing retransmissions, and managing inactivity-related timeouts on Sequences. The WSRMSinkProcessor responds to the requests to create a sequence, and also acknowledges any messages that are received from the source. The WSRMSinkProcessor issues acknowledgements (both positive and negative) at predefined intervals and also manages inactivity timeouts on Sequences. Finally, both the WSRMSourceProcessor and WSRMSinkProcessor detect any problems related to malformed SOAP messages and violations of the protocol, and throw the appropriate faults as outlined in the WSRM specification.

Because WSRM leverages capabilities within WS-addressing and WS-policy, we also had to implement processors which incorporate support for rules and functionalities related to these specifications. While generating responses to a targeted Web service, WS-addressing rules need to be followed in dealing with the elements contained within a service's end point reference. Similarly, responses and faults are targeted to a Web service or designated intermediaries based on the information encapsulated in other WS-addressing elements such as wsa:ReplyTo and wsa: FaultTo elements. The WS-policy specification is used to deal with policy issues related to sequences. An entity may specify policy elements from an entire range of sequences. The WSRM processors leverages capabilities available within these WS-addressing and WS-policy processors to enforce rules/constraints, parsing, and interpretation of elements, and the generation of appropriate SOAP messages (as in WS-addressing rules related to the creation of a SOAP message targeted to a specific endpoint).

Upon receipt of a SOAP message, at either the WSRMSourceProcessor or the WSRMSink-Processor, the first set of headers that need to be processed are those related to WS-Addressing. For example, the first header that is processed in typically the wsa:From element which identifies the originator of the message. The wsa:To element is also checked to make sure that the SOAP message is indeed intended for the hosting Web service endpoint. In the case of control exchanges, the semantic intent of the SOAP message is conveyed through the wsa:Action element in WS-Addressing. Similarly, the relationship between a response and a previously issued request is captured in the wsa:RelatesTo element.

WSRM requires the availability of a stable storage at every endpoint. The storage service leverages the JDBC API, which allows interactions with any SQL-compliant database. Our implementation has been tested with two relational databases—MySQL and PostgreSQL. Comprehensive details, and results, pertaining to the WSRM implementation can be found in (Pallickara, 2005).

Several WS-* specifications (such as WSE) require a lot of input from the users to facilitate interactions between entities. However, to facilitate reliable messaging between two endpoints, using FIRMS' implementation of WSRM, all an entity needs to do is to ensure that the message flows through the appropriate processors. There are two distinct roles within the WSRM, the source and the sink. The WSRM specification facilitates the reliable delivery of messages from the source to the sink. Thus, if we were to consider two endpoints **A** and **B** (depicted in Figure 1), and if we were required to ensure reliable messaging from **A** to **B**, we need to ensure that messages generated at **A** flow through the source processor that is configured at endpoint **A** and the sink processor that is configured at endpoint **B**. If one needs to ensure bidirectional reliable communications, a source processor needs to be configured at endpoint **B** and a sink processor needs to be configured at endpoint **A**.

Let us now look closely at communications between endpoints **A** and **B**. Furthermore, for the purposes of this discussion let us assume that we are interested in reliable messaging for messages issued from **A** to **B**. In this case, we first configure a source-processor at endpoint **A** and a sink-processor at endpoint **B**. Second, all messages issued by the application at endpoint **A** are funneled through the source-processor. Third, all messages received from the network are funneled through the sink processor at endpoint **B**.

When endpoint **A** is ready to send a message to endpoint **B**, it creates a SOAP Message with the appropriate WS-Addressing element [wsa:To] indicate the endpoint to which the message is targeted. Because all messages are funneled through the source processor, the source-processor at endpoint A receives this message. This source processor then proceeds to initiate the following series of actions.

1. The source-processor at **A** checks to see if a Sequence (essentially a group of messages

Figure 1. Example scenario for WSRM communications

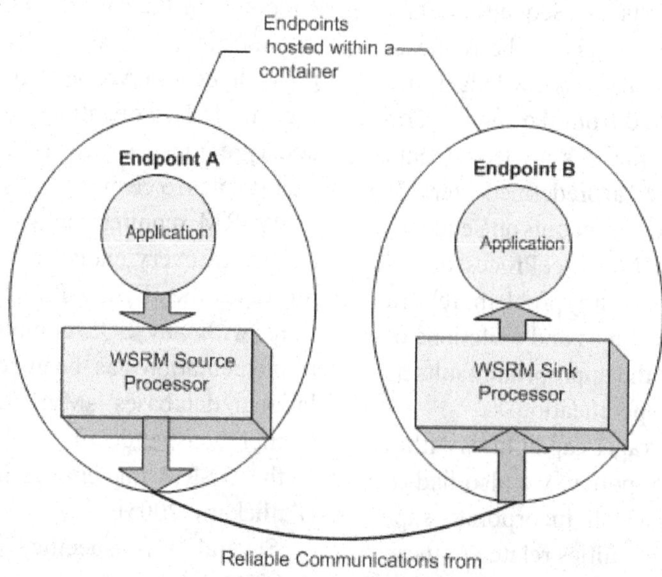

identified by a UUID) has been established for messages originating at **A** and targeted to **B**.

  a. If a Sequence has not been established, the source-processor at endpoint A initiates a CreateSequence *control message* to initiate the creation of sequence. In WSRM the creation of a Sequence is within the purview of the sink processor at the target endpoint. Upon receipt of this CreateSequence request, the sink-processor at the target endpoint **B** generates a CreateSequenceResponse, which contains the new established Sequence information. In case there are problems with the CreateSequence request, an error/fault may be returned to the originator.
  b. If a Sequence exists (or if one was established as outlined in item 1.a), the source-processor at the originator endpoint **A** will associate this Sequence with the message. Additionally, for every Sequence, a source-processor also keeps track of the number of messages that were sent by the source endpoint **A** to the target sink-endpoint **B**. For every unique application message (retransmissions, control messages, and so forth, are not within the purview of this numbering scheme) sent from **A** to **B**, the source-processor at **A** increments the message number by 1. This message number is also included along with the Sequence information.

2. Upon receipt of such a message at the sink endpoint **B**, the sink-processor checks to see if there were any losses in messages that were sent prior to this message (the numbering information reveals such losses). If there were no losses and the message order is correct, the sink-processor releases the message to the application at **B**.
  a. If there are problems with the received message, such as unknown Sequence Information or if the Sequence was terminated, an error message is returned to the source.
  b. If there are no problems, the message is stored onto stable storage and an acknowledgment is issued based on the acknowledgement interval.
  c. If a message loss has been detected, the sink will initiate retransmissions by issuing a negative acknowledgement to the source endpoint **A**. This negative acknowledgement will include the message numbers and the Sequence information about the messages that were not received.

WS-Eventing

WSE is an instance of a tightly-coupled notification system. Here there is no intermediary between the source and sink. The source is responsible for the routing of notifications to the registered consumers. WSE, however, introduces another entity—the subscription manager—within the system. This subscription manager is responsible for operations related to the management of subscriptions. Subscriptions within WSE have an identifier and expiration times associated with them. The identifier uniquely identifies a specific subscription, and is a UUID. The expiration time corresponds to the time after which the source will stop routing notifications corresponding to the expired subscription. Every source has a subscription manager associated with it. The specification does not either prescribe or prescribe the colocation of the source and the subscription manager on the same machine. The subscription manager performs the following operations:

- It is responsible for enabling sinks to retrieve the status of their subscriptions; these subscriptions are the ones that the sinks had previously registered with the source

- It manages the renewals of the managed subscriptions
- It is responsible for processing unsubscribe requests from the sinks

Please note that sinks include their subscription identifiers in ALL their interactions with the subscription manager.

Figure 2 depicts the chief components in WSE. When the sink subscribes with the source, the source includes information regarding the subscription manager in its response. Subsequent operations—such as getting the status of, renewing, and unsubscribing—pertaining to previously registered subscriptions are all directed to the subscription manager. The source sends both notifications and a message signifying the end of registered subscriptions to the sink.

WSE Implementation

There are three distinct roles within WSE viz. source, sink, and subscription manager. In our implementations, we have a processor corresponding to each of these roles. These processors contain methods to generate appropriate SOAP requests, responses, and faults as outlined in the specification.

The source is responsible for generating notifications. No restrictions have been imposed on the type or the content of these notifications. Source functionality such as managing subscription requests from the subscriber, coping with the expiry of subscriptions, and dissemination of notifications to registered sinks are all accessible through the WseSourceProcessor class. Care must be taken to ensure that all incoming and outgoing messages for a given endpoint be funneled through this class. Depending on the SOAPMessage (and the information encapsulated therein) and whether the message was received from the application or over the network, this processor deals with exchanges as outlined by the specification.

The functions performed by the WseSourceProcessor are enumerated below:

1. It manages subscription requests received over the network. It can also check this subscription request to see if it is well-formed and conforms to the constraints/rules within the WSE specification.

Figure 2. WSE: Chief components

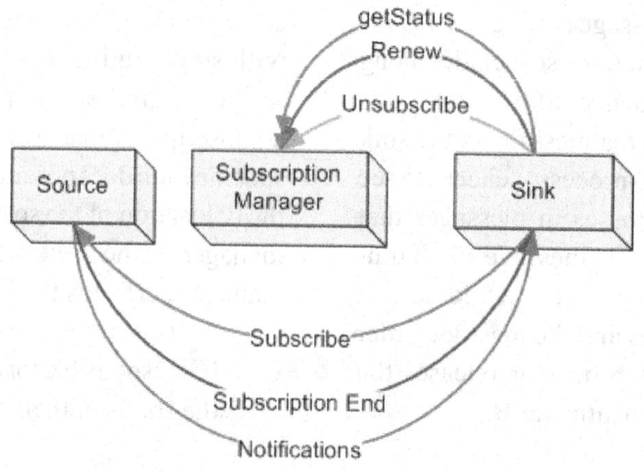

2. Matching Engines: This class automatically loads matching engines related to various subscription dialects. Matching engines related to XPath, String Topics, Regular Expression, and XQuery are loaded by this class.
3. Management of disseminations: This class is responsible for ensuring the dissemination of notifications to the right entities.

By ensuring that all messages from the network and from the application are funneled through this class, the WSE source functionality available within this class is accessible to the application. A source thus needs to be only concerned with its primary role, generation of notifications.

Next, the WseSubscriptionManagerProcessor needs to be deployed. A subscription manager could be associated with multiple sources at the same time. Once a sink has subscribed with the source, all subsequent actions such as GetStatus, Renew, and Unsubscribe should be directed at the Subscription Manager specified in the source's response to the original subscribe request.

Development of the application sink is a little more involved than on the source side. This is because the sink is responsible for the generation of several different request types. We, however, have a class—WseSinkProcessor—which encapsulates the sink's capabilities and simplifies the generation of requests. An application sink thus need not worry about the generation of well-formed requests because all processing related to this is handled by the WseSinkProcessor. We now briefly enumerate the different types of requests that are issued by the sink:

1. **Subscribe:** This register's a sink's interest with the source. GetStatus: This allows a sink to check for the status of a previously registered subscription. Specifically, this allows a sink to know when exactly its subscription is scheduled to expire.
2. **Renew:** This exchange allows a sink to renew previously registered subscriptions, so that they expire at a later time.
3. **Unsubscribe:** This indicates that a sink is no longer interested in the receipt of notifications corresponding to a previously registered subscription.

Upon receipt of a SubscribeResponse to the Subscribe request, the WseSinkProcessor keeps track of both the subscription identifier (a UUID) and the SubscriptionManager information contained in the received response. When an endpoint needs to perform actions such as GetStatus, Renew, and Unsubscribe all that it needs to specify is the subscription identifier, and the WseSinkProcessor constructs the corresponding SOAP message targeted to the appropriate Subscription Manager.

The WSE specification mandates support only for XPath subscriptions. We have included additional support for String Topics, Regular Expressions, and XQuery-based subscriptions. It is entirely possible that a given application may need to support additional subscription formats. We have built a very easy extensibility mechanism into the system so that users can develop and register their own matching engines so that they can support additional filter/subscription dialects.

For example, suppose one is interested in incorporating support for an SQL-based subscription dialect. In this case, there is only one class that needs to be implemented—SQLMatchingCapability—which extends a base class that all matching engines extend: cgl.narada.wsinfra.wse.matching.MatchingCapability. Here, we need to implement only one method, performMatching(), which is related to the actual matching operation. The signature of this method has been included for the reader's perusal.

```
public abstract boolean
 performMatching(EnvelopeDocument
envelopeDocument, FilterType filter)
 throws ProcessingException;
```

Once, this method has been implemented, the availability of this SQL matching engine needs to be made known to the source-processor, which performs the matching operations for the SOAP messages received from the application. This can be done by leveraging the cgl.narada.wsinfra.wse.matching.MatchingCapabilityFactory class. The code snippet below demonstrates how this is done.

```
SQLMatchingCapability sqlMatchingCapability = new
SQLMatchingCapability();
MatchingCapabilityFactory matchingCapabilityFactory
= MatchingCapabilityFactory.getInstance();
matchingCapabilityFactory.registerMatchingCapability
(sqlMatchingCapability)
```

MANAGEMENT WITHIN DISTRIBUTED SYSTEMS

As application complexity grows, the need for efficient management of system arises. Various system specific management architectures have been developed previously, and have been quite successful in their areas. Examples include SNMP (simple network management protocol) (Case, Fedor, Schoffstall, & Davin, 1990) and CMIP (Warrier, Besaw, LaBarre, & Handspicker, 1990). The chief drawback in these management systems is interoperability. To address interoperability, the distributed systems community has been orienting toward the Web services framework, and the corresponding WS-* suite of specifications that defines rich functions while allowing services to be composed to meet varied QoS requirements.

A crucial application of the Web services architecture is in the area of systems management. WS management (Arora, 2005) and WS distributed management (WSDM) (HP, 2005) are two competing specifications in the area of management using Web services architecture. Both specifications focus on providing a Web service model for building system and application management solutions specifically focusing on resource management. This includes basic capabilities such as creating and deleting resource instances, setting and querying service specific properties, and providing an event-driven model to connect services based on the publish/subscribe paradigm.

WSDM, on the other hand, breaks management in two parts, management using Web services (MUWS) and management of Web services (MOWS). MUWS focuses on providing a unifying layer on top of existing management specifications such as CIM from DMTF, SNMP, and OMI models. MOWS presents a model where a Web service is itself treated as a manageable resource. Thus, MOWS will serve to provide support for the management framework and support varied activities such as service metering, auditing, SLA management, problem detection and root cause failure analysis, service deployment, performance profiling, and life-cycle management.

WS-management, on the other hand, attempts to identify a core set of Web service specifications and usage requirements to expose a common set of operations central to all systems management. This minimum functionality includes ability to discover management resources, CREATE, DELETE, RENAME, GET, and PUT individual management resources, ENUMERATE contents of containers and collections, SUBSCRIBE to events emitted by managed resources, and EXECUTE resource-specific management methods. Thus, the majority of overlapping areas with the WSDM specification are in the MUWS specification.

IMPLEMENTATION OF WS-MANAGEMENT

In this section, we describe our implementation of the WS-management specification. Our choice of leveraging WS-Management was mainly motivated by the simplicity of WS-Management and also the ability to leverage WSE. We have been using the management architecture for modeling the management of a distributed brokering infrastructure (Gadgil, Fox, Pallickara, & Pierce, 2006).

The WS-management framework only defines the minimum required interactions; the application thus is free to extend beyond this minimum specification. Furthermore, a manageable endpoint is not required to support all interactions specified (such as GET, PUT, CREATE, DELETE, RENAME) but only those that make sense in the particular context of the application. Not all manageable resources would provide enumeration or the eventing model; however, it is required that if an application intends to support these models, then it must leverage the WS Enumeration and WSE specifications, respectively.

LEVERAGED SPECIFICATIONS

WS-management leverages the following specifications:

1. WS-addressing (Box, 2004a) for referencing resource endpoints.
2. WS-transfer (Alexander, 2004a) for providing the common minimum set of actions, namely GET, PUT, CREATE, and DELETE. WS-management defines an additional verb RENAME to allow renaming or resources.
3. WS-enumeration (Alexander, 2004b) for retrieving contents of large containers, collections, logs, and so forth.
4. WS-eventing to serve as a notification model on the publish/subscribe paradigm; and
5. SOAP version 1.2.

We implemented WS-Transfer and WS-Enumeration while WSE (whose implementation was described in section 4) was leveraged from NaradaBrokering.

Implementation

WS-management relies heavily on the SOAP 1.2 specification, specifically for modeling faults. SAAJ (Soap Attachments API for Java) version 1.3 supports SOAP 1.2; however, to maintain compatibility with other leveraged software, we implemented our own SOAP marshalling and unmarshalling framework using XMLBeans.

We also implemented our own prototype Web service Engine that processes SOAP messages. Although the most commonly used method of transport is SOAP over HTTP, we plan to use the NaradaBrokering messaging substrate for delivering SOAP messages between endpoints. Our Web service engine can use HTTP as well as NaradaBrokering's publish/subscribe mechanism for delivering and receiving events. We believe this to be a novel characteristic of our architecture because this allows us to seamlessly leverage a variety of features provided by the NaradaBrokering messaging substrate such as reliable delivery, exactly-once delivery, and message-level security. Furthermore, NaradaBrokering supports a variety of transport protocols and tunneling through firewalls, which allows us to apply the management architecture to remote resources.

Processing Messages

The message processing flow in our framework is depicted in Figure 3. In our architecture, the actual message transport is handled by the message received and send response units, which provide multiple ways of delivering messages. In the future, additional processing elements may be plugged in here to meet QoS requirements, such as reliable delivery and security, by utilizing appropriate Web service specifications.

The processing begins by checking the maximum envelope size for the response. WS-Management specifies that if such an element is present and a size is specified, the minimum size must be 8192 octets to reliably encode all possible faults.

Figure 3. Flow chart for processing WS management messages

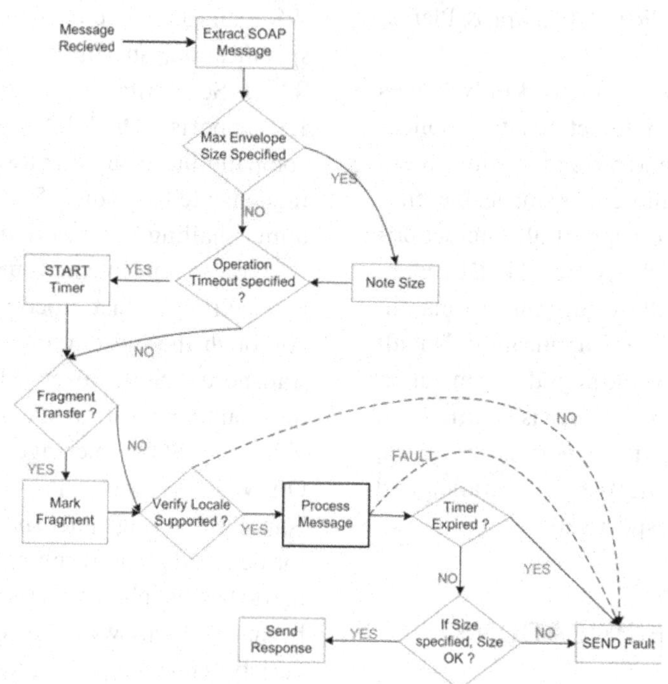

This element may be discarded if mustUnderstand is set to FALSE; when this is TRUE and if the value is less than 8192, a fault is thrown.

An operation timeout may be specified to indicate that a response is desired within the specified timeframe. If specified, a timer is started. If a response is indeed generated (success OR failure) the timer is cancelled. However, if the timer expires before the processing has finished, a TimedOut fault is sent back to the requestor. WS-Management states that any state changes that may have occurred during the processing are later inspected by the requestor by making one or more GET requests to retrieve the service state.

Finally, the process message block is invoked. Depending on the characteristics of a particular resource, only a subset of operations may be supported. We describe each of the three main operations below.

WS-Transfer

Application developers can provide the ability to GET, PUT, CREATE, DELETE, and RENAME individual management resources by providing implementation for the abstract operation methods of the WS-management processor. For example, to support a GET operation the developer simply implements the following method:

```
public abstract void
processWxfGet(EnvelopeDocument
envelopeDocument,
MessageHeaders headers,
XmlFragmentDocument xmlFrag)
throws WSManServiceException;
```

If a resource supports GET and PUT operations but does not support CREATE, DELETE, and RENAME, then the developer has to throw an UnsupportedFeature fault for the unsupported verbs.

In our architecture, WS-enumeration and WSE have been implemented by a completely different set of abstract classes. Thus, if a service wishes to provide an enumeration capability, it can provide an implementation of Enumeration and register itself with the WS-management processor. An UnsupportedFeature fault is immediately thrown if the WS-enumeration/WSE processor is not registered and a corresponding request is received.

WS Enumeration

WS-enumeration processing requires the system to do bookkeeping of enumeration requests, which are referred to as enumeration context. The WS-enumeration processor maintains the context info (which could be a simple UUID). A service is free to extend the basic enumeration processor to provide additional service specific features. Every time a PULL or any other request is received, the WS-enumeration processor checks the enumeration context and validates it. The validation process checks for expiry of the enumeration context and an `InvalidEnumerationContext` fault is automatically thrown.

LOOKING AHEAD

As part of the future work in this area we plan to investigate how we can incorporate WS security in our present architecture. Service policies dictate the service requirements and capabilities and define the handling of management related requests. WS policy (Bajaj, 2006) provides a general purpose model and corresponding syntax to describe such policies. We are currently investigating the use of WS Policy in our work. Typically, a client may need to list available resources, obtain XML schemas or WSDL definitions, or perform other discovery tasks. WS Management recommends WS Metadata Exchange (Ballinger, 2004) for these tasks. In the future, we will investigate incorporating a discovery processor to facilitate discovery of service-specific metadata. Recently, the Web services community announced the merger (Cline, 2006) of WS-Management and WSDM specifications. We plan to investigate how to support the upcoming management specification within our current implementation.

EXTENDING THE WS-CONTEXT SPECIFICATION

Often Web services are assembled into short-term service collections that are gathered together into a meta-application (such as a workflow) and collaborating with each other to perform a particular task. For example, an airline reservation system could consist of several Web services, which are combined together to process reservation requests, update customer records, and send confirmations to clients. As these services interact with each other they generate session state, which is simply a data value that evolves as a result of Web service interactions and persists across the interactions. As the applications, employing Web service-oriented architectures, need to discover, inspect, manipulate state information in order to correlate the activities of participating services a need arises for specifications that would standardize the management of distributed session state information.

The Web service context (WS-context) specification (Bunting, 2003) was introduced to define a simple mechanism to share and keep track of common context information shared between multiple participants in Web service interactions. A participating application can also discover results (which is stored as context) of other participants' execution. The context here has information such as unique ID and shared data. It allows a collection of actions to take place for a common outcome. The WS-context specification also defines a Web service interface, the context manager, which in turn allows applications to retrieve and set data associated with a context.

There are other specifications, such as the Web service resource framework (WSRF) (Czajkowski, Ferguson, Foster, Frey, Graham, Sedukin et al., 2004) and WS-metadata exchange (WS-ME) (Ballinger, 2004), that have been introduced to define stateful interactions among services. Among these existing specifications, which standardize service communications, we chose WS-context specifications to tackle the problem of managing the distributed session state. Unlike the other service communication specifications, WS-context models a session metadata repository as an external entity where more than two services can easily access/store highly dynamic, shared metadata.

We find various limitations in WS-context specification in supporting stateful interactions of Web services. First, the context manager, a component defined by WS-context to provide access/storage to state information, has limited functionalities, such as the two primary operations: Gontext and Sontext. However, Grid applications present extensive metadata needs, which in turn requires advanced search, access, and store interfaces to distributed session state information. Second, the WS-context specification does not define an information model for the context manager component. So, there is a need for a data model to store the state information in persistent data structures. Third, the WS-context specification is only focused on defining stateful interactions of Web services. However, there is a need for a specification which can provide an interface for not only stateful interactions but also the stateless and interaction-independent information associated with Web services. In order to address these limitations, we have investigated XML metadata services that can be used as the context manager and that can provide a uniform programming interface to both stateless and stateful service metadata.

We designed and built a hybrid WS-Context compliant metadata catalog service (Aktas, Foz, & Pierce, 2005) supporting both handling and discovery of not only quasi-static, stateless metadata, but also session related metadata. We based the information model and programming interface of our system on two widely used specifications: Web services context, and universal description, discovery, and integration (UDDI) (Bellwood, Clement, & Riegen, 2003).

We utilized Xerces software (http://xerces.apache.org/xerces-j/) as the XML schema processor to process the extended version of WS-context specification schema. Xerces is an open-source, high-performance XML parser component developed by the Apache XML Project. We have focused on the two base elements of the semantics and implementation of the proposed system: (a) information model (data semantics), (b) XML programming interface (semantics for publication and inquiry, security, and proprietary XML API). The information model is composed of various entities, such as session, service, and context entities. These entities are the information holders; in other words, directories where distributed session state information is stored.

The programming interface of the hybrid WS-context service introduces various additional publishing/discovery and information security capabilities. The additional XML API capabilities may broadly be categorized as: (a) functions operating on dynamic, session-related metadata space, (b) functions operating on static, stateless metadata space, (c) hybrid functions operating on both metadata spaces, and d) information security related functions. The dynamic metadata functions are used to enable the system to track the associations between sessions and contexts by expanding on primary functionalities of WS-context XML API set. The static, interaction-independent metadata functions are used to provide a programming interface to the static metadata space. These functions simply forward the incoming SOAP messages to the extended

UDDI XML metadata service for handling of query and publishing requests. The hybrid functions provide publishing/discovery capabilities supporting both dynamic and static service metadata. These functions integrate results coming from the two separate metadata spaces. The information security related functions provide an authentication and authorization mechanism, as the shared information may not be open to anyone. Further design documentations are also available at http://www.opengrids.org/wscontext.

EXTENDING THE UDDI SPECIFICATION

As SOA principles have gained importance, there is a need for methodologies to locate desired services that provide access to their capability descriptions. Geographical information systems (GIS) provide very useful problems in supporting "virtual organizations" and their associated information systems. These systems are composed of various archival data services (Web feature services), data sources (Web-enabled sensors), and map generating services. Organizations like the Open Geospatial Consortium (OGC) define the metadata standards. All of these services are metadata-rich, as each of them must describe their capabilities (What sorts of features do they provide? What geographic bounding boxes do they support?) This is an example of the very general problem of managing information about Web services.

One approach to service-metadata management problem is the universal description, discovery, and integration (UDDI) specification. UDDI is a domain-independent standardized method for publishing/discovering information about Web services. It offers users a unified and systematic way to find service providers through a centralized registry of services. As it is WS-Interoperability (WS-I) compatible, UDDI has the advantage being interoperable with most existing Grid/Web service standards.

We observed that the adoption of UDDI specification in various domains such as GIS is slow, because existing UDDI specification has the following limitations. First, UDDI introduces keyword-based retrieval mechanism. It does not allow advanced metadata-oriented query capabilities on the registry. Second, UDDI does not take into account the volatile behavior of services. Because Web services may come and go, and because the information associated with services might be dynamically changing, there may be stale data in registry entries. Third, because UDDI is domain-independent, it does not provide domain-specific query capabilities, in particular for GIS domain such as spatial queries. There is a need for integration between the OGC metadata standards and the UDDI Service information model.

In order to provide solutions to these limitations, various solutions have been introduced. UDDI-M (Dialani, 2002) and UDDIe (ShaikhAli, Rana, Al-Ali, & Walker, 2003) projects introduce the idea of associating metadata and lifetime with UDDI Registry service descriptions where retrieval relies on the matches of attribute name-value pairs between service description and service requests. UDDI-MT (Miles, 2003; Miles, Papay, Payne, Decker, & Moreau, 2004) improves the metadata representation from attribute name-value pairs into RDF triples. A similar approach to leveraging UDDI Specifications was introduced by the METEOR-S (Verma, Sivashanmugam, Sheth, Patil, Oundhaker, & Miller, 2003) project, which identifies different semantics when describing a service such as data, functional, quality of service, and executions.

As an alternative solution, we designed an XML metadata service to provide a solution to the general problem of managing static, stateless information about Web services. The prototype was implemented as a domain-independent metadata service to meet the information requirements of the different application domains. To support the specific metadata requirements of geographical information systems, this prototype implementation was further extended to support geospatial queries on the metadata associated to service entries. We used the UDDI specifications in our design. We also designed extensions to existing UDDI Specifications, as outlined earlier. Similar to previous solutions, we too extend UDDI's Information Model, by providing an extension where we associate metadata ((name, value) pairs and life-time with service descriptions. Apart from the existing methodologies, we provide various advanced capabilities such as domain-independent and GIS-domain-specific query/publishing capabilities, as well as dynamic aggregation and searching of geospatial services. We based the implementation of our design on jUDDI (http://ws.apache.org/juddi, version 0.9r3), a free, open source, and Java-based implementation of the UDDI specification. We used Xerces as the default XML Schema Processor.

We have expanded on the two base elements of the existing semantics of UDDI Specifications: (a) information model (data semantics) and (b) XML programming interface (semantics for publication and inquiry XML API). The extended UDDI information model included service attribute and service entities. Its programming interface provides metadata-oriented publishing/discovery capabilities by expanding on the existing UDDI XML API set. The additional XML API set introduced various capabilities such as (a) publishing additional metadata associated with service entries, and (b) posing metadata-oriented, geospatial, and domain-independent queries on the extended UDDI service. The domain-independent search capability is a more general purpose extension to the UDDI data model that allows us to insert arbitrary XML metadata into the repository. This may be searched using XPATH queries, which is a standard way of searching XML documents. This allows us to support other XML-based metadata descriptions developed for other classes of services besides GIS. The Globus/IBM-led WSRF effort is an important example.

WEB SERVICES AND MOBILE DEVICES

In this section, we address issues related to the use of Web services in mobile computing. Despite the fact that there have been several advances in the area of mobile computing in recent years, applying current Web service communication models to mobile computing may result in unacceptable performance overheads. Two main factors contribute to these problems. First, the encoding and decoding of verbose XML-based SOAP messages consumes scare CPU resources on the device. Second, the performance and quality gap between wireless and wired communication will not close quickly. These issues are depicted in Figure 4.

The use of XML to describe data invariably results in increases in the size of the final representation. This size increase can be as high as an order of magnitudes, if the document structure is especially redundant; for example, in the case of arrays. Encoding data into a SOAP message requires a text-conversion, where the in-memory representation is converted into a textual format. The decoding process does the reverse work; if the data is nontextual, such as a floating point number, the conversion is very expensive in terms of performance overhead, which is especially significant for relatively low-powered mobile devices. We have designed a framework—*Handheld Flexible Representation (or HHFR)*—that addresses these issues in the context of mobile computing.

HHFR works best for Web services, where the two participating nodes exchange a series of messages, which we define as a stream. For applications using a specific service repeatedly, messages in the stream have the same structure and the same data-type for information items. Most of the message headers are unchanged in the

Figure 4. Potential problems in using conventional Web services on mobile devices

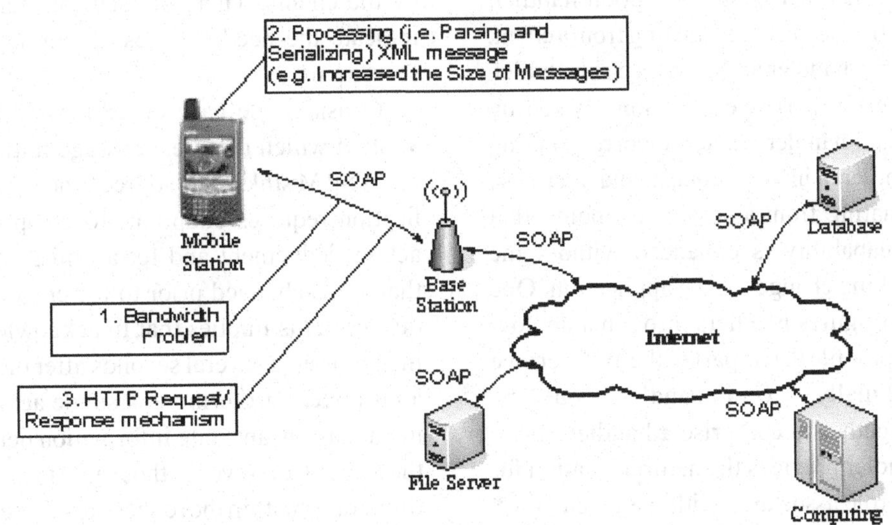

stream. Therefore, the structure and type of SOAP message contents and unchanging SOAP headers may be transmitted only once, and the rest of the messages in the stream have only payloads.

The HHFR implementation leverages the data format description language (DFDL) for negotiation representations and message streaming, and uses a metadata repository to store redundant or unchanging static data. A normal session[1] of the runtime system is as follows. First, an HHFR-capable endpoint sends a negotiation request to the intended endpoint. The negotiation request is a conventional SOAP message that includes characteristics of the stream to be used for communications. The negotiation decides on the optimal representation of messages within the stream. Subsequent stream messages are then exchanged based on this negotiated representation. The unchanging parts (static metadata) of the streamed messages are stored into a dynamic metadata repository during the session. If the service endpoint is not HHFR-capable communications revert to conventional SOAP messaging. This strategy where only the fragments of data that have changed for successive messages are exchanged accrues several benefits in the utilization of CPU and networking resources at the mobile device.

DEPLOYMENT RELATED ISSUES WITHIN AXIS

Axis is the most dominant Web services container within the Java domain, and is used within most Java-based Web services. In this section, we describe issues within the Axis container vis-à-vis interactions mandated within Web service specifications. These issues pertain to Axis version 1.2RC3. A comprehensive discussion of these issues, and results related to the workarounds to these problems, can be found in Yildiz, Pallickara, and Fox (2006).

In addition to the services themselves, several containers (including Axis) incorporate support for handlers or filters which facilitate incremental addition of capabilities at a service endpoint. An example of a handler is an encryption handler, which encrypts messages originating from a client, and an inverse-handler at the service side, which performs the appropriate decryption. By setting up appropriate handlers (and the corresponding inverse handlers) in the request and response flows originating from a service endpoint, that endpoint's capability is enhanced without the need for making changes to the application. One typically configures handlers through a deployment descriptor file that is part of the Web service container. Finally, several handlers could be cascaded together to comprise a handler chain. A given handler provides the natural location for setting up a role associated within a given WS-* specification. The WSRM sink role can be configured in a handler within the handler-chain at the destination service endpoint. Although the Axis architecture provides very good functionalities, there are several areas where we see a need for improvement. We enumerate this below:

1. Within Axis, currently only the clients are allowed to inject (or initiate) messages.
2. In Axis, every message is considered a request, which should have its accompanying response within a predefined period of time. This does not fit very well with interactions where no responses are issued.
3. No ability to gracefully terminate processing related to a message within the handler chain associated with a service.
4. Handlers cannot initiate messages on their own.
5. Static configuration of the handler chain.

Message Initiation

Clients are the only entities that are able to initiate messages as requests. Server-side components, either a handler in the handler-chain or the target service, do not have this capability. The only message initiation is via a request/response mechanism where requests can be initiated only by the clients. There are several scenarios that indicate the need for message initiation in the server part.

Consider the case of acknowledgements in WSRM which requires message initiation from the WSRM sink to the source. The WSRM specification requires endpoints to comply with the acknowledgement and retransmission intervals that are exchanged prior to the creation of a sequence. This implies that in acknowledgements may be issued several seconds after the receipt of a message. Furthermore, a single acknowledgement may encapsulate information pertaining to the receipt of several thousand messages. The limitations within the request-response paradigm are clear in such scenarios. It is clear that one-way messaging and message-initiation would resolve this particular problem. The problems outlined here also arise during retransmissions initiated by a WSRM source. WSE is another case where message initiation is needed. A message may need to be reproduced to send the copies to multiple subscribing endpoints.

Other Request-Response-Based Problems

Sometimes an entity may need to send a message to another entity without the need to receive a response. For example, when we issue a WSRM acknowledgement, we are not looking for an acknowledgement to the WSRM-acknowledgement.

Ability to Terminate Processing Related to Message within a Handler Chain

Currently, there is no ability to gracefully terminate processing related to a message within the handler chain associated with a service. This implies that once a message has been received within a handler chain there is no graceful way to prevent this message from reaching the service. A good example of the need for this feature would be the case of acknowledgments in WSRM. Only the WSRM handler needs to know whether the WSRM sink has received the message that was previously sent; there is no need to inundate the application with every acknowledgement that has been received. Also, because most WS specifications are aimed at incrementally adding functionality to a service, situations may arise where similar such handshakes/control-messages should be stopped from reaching the actual service. In most cases, such messages end up causing problems at the service. Currently, the only way to terminate processing is to throw an exception. Furthermore, there is no way to correctly access or interact with the handler-chain managing a specific handler.

Handlers Cannot Inject Messages

This issue was mentioned earlier too, but needs to be clarified in the case of handlers, too. Most WS specifications are naturally implemented as handlers that can augment a service's capabilities. However, such handlers need to be able to initiate control-messages on their own accord. While there is access to the handler chain, there is no access to message propagation features. This feature may be made available through the AxisEngine class or through the handler chain itself.

Static Handler Chains

In Axis handlers are currently statically configured, the configuration being made when a service is being deployed. A handler cannot be added or removed from a service. Current Axis architecture allows cloning the handler chain, and the cloned chain can then replace the current one after required changes have been applied; however, this is not sufficient. Dynamic configuration of handler chains will be very useful. A deployment may have lots of handlers, but a user/handler should be able to select a group of handlers that a message would need to go through.

This is especially true in cases of retransmissions where the handler may have already processed the message, resulting in duplicate processing, which may or may not lead to errors. Similarly, security requirements may result in a message be passed through a different set of handler chains. Here, handlers related to message digest, encryption, and signing may be added to the outgoing path in the handler chain.

Solutions to Some of the Problems

We have workaround solutions for some issues above; instead of blocking a message, a message can be set to a dummy task. We had to choose this method because we wanted to stop the propagation of the message without getting an exception. By letting the message arrive at the endpoint, we have prevented an exception being thrown. On the other hand, there exists a downside to this solution. This adds to performance costs because of the processing overheads for the dummy task. The costs are acceptable within the current Axis architecture.

Although messages cannot be initiated by the server part, we can bypass this restriction by using an Axis client wherever a message initiation is required. In this architecture, service endpoints will have client and server capability. This results in both the endpoints being maintained within a container.

Next, we developed a sender thread which is responsible for sending any message to the other node. Because we are using one-way messaging, we assign the responsibility of sending messages to this thread instead of dealing with the Axis message response mechanism. The thread enables us to send messages in a nonblocking fashion.

We did not use a response chain because we decided on building our own chain structure. After some point in the response handler chain, we diverted the massage path to the sender thread and added our own handler chain. This allowed us to do one-way messaging without breaking any of the already deployed handler structure at the service; this can easily support dynamic handler chains.

USE CASES FOR VARIOUS SPECIFICATIONS

In this section, we provide examples of the deployments of several of the specifications that have been discussed in this article.

WSE, WSRM, and WSR

The WSE, WSRM, and WSR specifications are part of the OMII Container (3.0.0) available for download from http://www.omii.ac.uk/. All of these specifications leverage the WS-addressing specification. Furthermore, to support exchanges outlined within these specifications, while coping with the constraints within several containers, we deployed strategies outlined in sections 9.6.

WSE, WS-Management, WS-Transfer

As discussed previously, the WS-management leverages the WSE specification for its notification needs. We have leveraged the WS-Management specification implementation as a framework for managing distributed resources. Our specific use case consists of managing the NaradaBrokering messaging middleware, which consists of a large number of dynamic peers, or messaging brokers.

The messaging brokers require resource-specific configuration, such as ports, and a global configuration, such as interconnections, that make a specific broker topology. Run-time metrics are gathered via monitoring techniques or obtained via runtime events generated by the resource. We measure various aspects of the system that enable us to understand the performance of the system and, in some cases, provide hints on improving the performance. This naturally leads to redeployment of the brokering network with a different configuration. To summarize, we need an architecture that enables us to rapidly bring up and tear down a broker network. It is also required to set specific configuration settings for every broker and have the ability to change the configuration on-the-fly. We term these actions collectively, as management of the brokering infrastructure.

To aid the management of brokers and broker networks, we have modeled several resource specific operations, which have been summarized in Table 1.

Table 1. Broker network management: Summary of operations and specifications leveraged

Operation/ Event	Functionality provided	What part of specification has been leveraged
Get/Set Configuration	Reads/Writes the broker specific configuration	WS Transfer – GET/PUT
Create/Delete Broker	Instantiates a new instance of the Broker/Shuts down an existing instance of broker	WS Transfer – CREATE/ DELETE
Create/Delete Link	Creates a link between two brokers/Deletes an existing Link	WS Transfer – CREATE/ DELETE
Link Lost Exception	If a broker detects that an outgoing link was broken, this exception is thrown	WS Eventing – Event notification

Extended UDDI and Hybrid WS-Context

Extended UDDI and hybrid WS-context services have been used as the metadata management components of various application use domains. The first example is a workflow session metadata manager, a vital component of workflow-style Grid applications. A workflow session metadata manager is responsible for providing store/access/search interface to metadata generated during workflow execution. The second example is a metadata catalog service. A catalog service is a metadata service that stores both prescriptive and descriptive information about Grid/Web services. The third example is a third-party metadata repository, also called as Context-store. This component is used in a fast Web service communication model in collaborative mobile computing environments where the redundant parts of the exchanged messages are stored.

The Workflow Session Metadata Manager

The hybrid WS-context service is being used as the workflow session metadata manager in two practical example usage domains: pattern informatics and the interdependent energy infrastructure simulation system (IEISS). Pattern informatics, a technique to detect seismic activities and make earthquake predictions, was developed at University of Southern California at Davis. The pattern informatics GIS Grid (Aydin, 2005) integrates the pattern informatics code with publicly-available, Open GIS Consortium (OGC)-compatible, geo-spatial data, and visualization services. The interdependent energy infrastructure simulation system is a suite of analysis software tools developed by Los Alamos National Laboratory (LANL). IEISS provides assessment of the technical, economic, and security implications of the energy interdependencies (LANL, 2006). The IEISS GIS Grid, a workflow-style GIS Grid application developed at LANL, supports IEISS analysis tools by integrating them with openly available geo-spatial data sources and visualization services. Both pattern informatics and IEISS systems need an information service, which can be utilized as the workflow session metadata manager. In these applications, participants of a workflow must know about the state of the system, so that they can perform their assigned tasks within a specific sequence.

The hybrid WS-context service is used as a workflow session metadata manager, which is responsible for storing transient metadata, needed to describe distributed session state information in a workflow. The hybrid WS-context service allows users to access session state information by either pull- or push-based approaches. In pull-based approach, each participant continuously checks with the system if the state is changed. For instance, some application domains may employ various browser-based applications; here, pushing the states to the Web-applications through the HTTP server is rather complicated. So, the pull-based approach can be used in those domains to interact with the service to get the state updates. In push-based approach, participants are notified of the state changes. The push-based approach is mainly used to interact with the workflow session metadata manager in order to reduce the server load caused by continuous information polling.

The Metadata Catalog Service

The two applications: pattern informatics and IEISS GIS systems are composed of various GIS compatible data and map generating Grid/Web services. Thus, both of these application domains need a metadata catalogs service, which would provide a unified and systematic way to find service through a registry of services. The extended UDDI metadata service is used as the Metadata Catalog Service, which is responsible for providing access/store interface to both prescriptive and descriptive metadata about services. GIS-based Grid applications are composed of various archival services, data sources, and visualization services. Services such as the Web Map (OpenGIS, 2006a) and Web Feature (OpenGIS, 2006b) service, because they are generic, must provide additional, descriptive metadata in order to be useful. The problem is simple: a client may interact with two different Web Feature Services in exactly the same way (the WSDL is the same), but the two Web Feature Services may hold different data. One, for example, may contain GPS data for the Western United States, while the other has GPS data for Northern Japan. Clients must be able to query information services that encode (in standard formats) all the necessary information, or metadata, that enables the client to connect to the desired service. Thus, we see the need for a metadata catalog service, which would manage metadata associated to all these Grid/Web services, and make them discoverable. A client should be able to get "capabilities" metadata file either from the service itself or from the metadata catalog. Thus, these metadata catalog services are also expected to have a dynamic metadata retrieval capability, which enables the system to dynamically retrieve the capability metadata file from the service under consideration. The extended UDDI service introduces capabilities addressing the metadata management requirements of the GIS domain.

The Context-Store for High Performance SOAP

The handheld flexible representation (HHFR) is an application designed to provide efficient and optimized message exchange paradigm in mobile Web service environment (Oh, 2005). The HHFR architecture provides layers, which optimize and stream messages to achieve high performance mobile Web service communication. The HHFR system utilizes the hybrid WS-Context services as a third-party repository (i.e., context-store), to store the redundant/unchanging parts of the messages exchanged between services. This way the size of the exchanged messages can be reduced to achieve optimized Web service communication. A Context-store component is a metadata service responsible for storing redundant/unchanging parts of SOAP messages exchanged in service communication.

CONCLUSION

In this chapter, we provided a discussion of the various Web service specifications that we have implemented. We are hopeful that the strategies (and implementations) outlined in this chapter can be leveraged by other developers. In this chapter, we have touched upon several aspects of building distributed applications using Web services: these include targeting (WS-addressing), content distribution (WSE), guaranteed messaging (WSR and WSRM), the management of resources (WS-management and the suite of specifications it leverages), context (modified WS-context), and discovery (extended UDDI). To leverage Web services within compute and power constrained devices such as PDAs, we included a discussion of HHFR. We have also summarized use cases for these various specifications in the preceding section.

Although these specifications serve different functions, it is possible to build systems that leverage several of these specifications. For example, in the case of managing a distributed messaging system, we leveraged several Web service specifications such as WSE, WS-management, WS-addressing, WS-enumeration, and WS-transfer. This work shows how software services can be managed using a Web service management protocol. This is important, as it lays the groundwork for applications to be very adaptive to changing needs. For example, one may dynamically switch protocols (e.g., TCP, UDP, ParallelTCP) at runtime depending on the application being managed, such as audio-video conferencing or GIS-based Grid applications.

While implementing these WS-* specifications, we found that in some cases the dominant containers have not kept pace with some of the specifications; specifically, this pertained to processing SOAP messages within a container. Here, workarounds had to be developed to cope with the constraints within the containers.

One of the problems that we encountered while developing these specifications was that they would change quite often: sometimes, this resulted in us chasing moving targets with the specification evolving every few weeks. Each new specification has its own unique schema, so an architect has to decide which schema to settle on and proceed from there. There have been significant improvements in this area as specifications have matured. Another area which needs to be addressed very soon is the presence of multiple specifications in the same domain. The functionality provided in these competing specifications tends to be more or less the same. This makes it particularly difficult for a systems designer to decide which specification to bet on. Having to cope with multiple specifications in the same domain increases *complexity* and raises *interoperability* issues, problems which Web services started out to solve in the first place.

Problems with WS-* specifications notwithstanding, Web services have immense potential and offer significant benefits. Web services facilitate the development of loosely-coupled, asynchronous, and interoperable systems. WS-* specifications can be looked upon as a building blocks for the development of distributed applications. Using implementations of these WS-* specification, a systems designer is able to quickly put together a robust, distributed application.

REFERENCES

Aktas, M.S., Fox, G.C., & Pierce, M.E. (2005). Managing dynamic metadata as context. In *Proceedings of the Istanbul International Computational Science and Engineering Conference (ICCSE2005).* Retrieved June 11, 2007, from http://www.iccse.org/

Alexander, J. et al. (2004a). *Web service transfer (WS – Transfer).* Retrieved June 11, 2007, from http://msdn.microsoft.com/library/en-us/dnglobspec/html/ws-transfer.pdf

Alexander, J. et al. (2004b). *Web service enumeration (WS–Enumeration).* Retrieved June 11, 2007, from http://msdn.microsoft.com/library/en-us/dnglobspec/html/ws-enumeration.pdf

Arora, A. et al. (2005). *Web service management (WS – Management).* Retrieved June 11, 2007, from https://wiseman.dev.java.net/specs/2005/06/management.pdf

Aydin, G. et al. (2005). SERVOGrid complexity computational environments (CCE) integrated performance analysis. In *Proceedings of the 6th IEEE/ACM International Workshop on Grid Computing.*

Bajaj, S. et al. (2006). *Web services policy framework (WS-Policy).* Retrieved June 11, 2007, from http://specs.xmlsoap.org/ws/2004/09/policy/ws-policy.pdf

Ballinger, K. et al. (2004). *The Web services metadata exchange specification.* Retrieved June 11, 2007, from http://specs.xmlsoap.org/ws/2004/09/mex/WS-MetadataExchange.pdf

Bellwood, T., Clement, L., & Riegen, C. (2003). *UDDI Version 3.0.1: UDDI spec technical committee specification.* Retrieved June 11, 2007, from http://uddi.org/pubs/uddi-v3.0.1-20031014.htm

Bilorusets, R. et al. (2004). *Web services reliable messaging protocol (WS-ReliableMessaging).*

Retrieved June 11, 2007, from http://www-128.ibm.com/developerworks/library/specification/ws-rm/

Box, D. et al. (2004a). *Web services addressing (WSAddressing).* Retrieved June 11, 2007, from http://www.w3.org/Submission/ws-addressing

Box, D. et al. (2004b). *Web services eventing.* Microsoft, IBM, & BEA. Retrieved June 11, 2007, from http://ftpna2.bea.com/pub/downloads/WS-Eventing.pdf

Bunting, B. et al. (2003). *Web services context (WS-Context)* version 1.0. Retrieved June 11, 2007, from http://www.arjuna.com/ library/specs/ws_caf_1-0/WS-CTX.pdf

Case, J., Fedor, M., Schoffstall, M., & Davin, J. (1990). *Simple network management protocol.* Network working group request for comments 1157. Retrieved June 11, 2007, from http://www.ietf.org/rfc/rfc1157.txt

Christensen, E. et al. (2001). *Web services description language (WSDL) 1.1.* Retrieved June 11, 2007, from http://www.w3.org/TR/wsdl

Cline, K. et al. (2006). *Toward converging Web service standards for resources.* Events, and Management. Retrieved June 11, 2007, from http://msdn.microsoft.com/library/en-us/dnwebsrv/html/convergence.asp

Czajkowski, K., Ferguson, D., Foster, I., Frey, J., Graham, S., Sedukhin, I. et al. (2004). *The WS-resource framework.* Retrieved June 11, 2007, from http://www.globus.org/wsrf/specs/ws-wsrf.pdf

Dialani, V. (2002). *UDDI-M Version 1.0 API specification.* University of Southampton, UK.

Gadgil, H., Fox, G., Pallickara, S., & Pierce, M. (2006). *Managing grid messaging middleware challenges of large applications in distributed environments.* Paris, France.

Gibbs, K., & Goodman, B.D. (2003). *IBM Elias Torres.* Create Web services using Apache Axis and Castor. IBM Developer Works. Retrieved June 11, 2007, from http://www-106.ibm.com/developerworks/webservices/library/ws-castor/

Gudgin, M. et al. (2003, June). *SOAP Version 1.2, Part 1: Messaging framework.* Retrieved June 11, 2007, from http://www.w3.org/TR/2003/REC-soap12-part1-20030624/

HP. (2005). *Web service distributed management (WSDM).* Retrieved June 11, 2007, from http://devresource.hp.com/drc/specifications/wsdm/index.jsp

Los Alamos National Laboratory (LANL). (2006). *The Interdependent Energy Infrastructure Simulation System (IEISS) Project.* Retrieved June 11, 2007, from http://www.lanl.gov/orgs/d/d4/interdepend

Miles, S. et al. (2003). Personalized grid service discovery. In *Proceedings of the Nineteenth Annual UK Performance Engineering Workshop (UKPEW'03),* University of Warwick, Coventry, England.

Miles, S., Papay, J., Payne, T., Decker, K., & Moreau, L. (2004). Towards a protocol for the attachment of semantic descriptions to grid services. In *Proceedings of the Second European across Grids Conference*, Nicosia, Cyprus.

OASIS. (2004). *Web services reliability TC WS-Reliability.* Retrieved June 11, 2007, from http://www.oasis-open.org/committees/download.php/5155/WS-Reliability-2004-01-26.pdf

Oh, S. et al. (2005). Optimized communication using the SOAP infoset for mobile multimedia collaboration applications. In *Proceedings of the International Symposium on Collaborative Technologies and Systems 2005.*

OGC. *The Open Geospatial Consortium.* Retrieved June 11, 2007, from http://www.opengis.org

Open Geospatial Consortium. (2006a). *OpenGIS Web map service (WMS) Specification.* Retrieved June 11, 2007, from http://www.opengeospatial.org/standards/wms

Open Geospatial Consortium. (2006b). *OpenGIS Web feature service (WFS) Specification.* Retrieved June 11, 2007, from http://www.opengeospatial.org/standards/wfs

Pallickara, S. et al. (2005). On the costs for reliable messaging in Web/grid service environments. In *Proceedings of the 2005 IEEE International Conference on E-science and Grid Computing* (pp. 344-351), Melbourne, Australia.

ShaikhAli, A., Rana, O., Al-Ali, R., & Walker, D. (2003). UDDIe: An extended registry for Web services. In *Proceedings of the Service-oriented Computing: Models, Architectures, and Applications, SAINT-2003,* Orlando, FL, USA. IEEE Computer Society Press.

Verma, K., Sivashanmugam, K., Sheth, A., Patil, A., Oundhakar, S., & Miller, J. (3003). METEOR–S WSDI: A scalable P2P infrastructure of registries for semantic publication and discovery of Web services. *Journal of Information Technology and Management.*

Warrier J., Besaw L., LaBarre L., & Handspicker, B. (1990). *The common management information services and protocols for the Internet. Network Working Group request for comments 1189.* Retrieved June 11, 2007, from http://www.ietf.org/rfc/rfc1189.txt

Yildiz, B., Pallickara, S., & Fox, G. (2006). Experiences with deploying services within the Axis container. In *Proceedings of the 2006 IEEE International Conference on Internet and Web Applications and Services,* French Caribbean.

ENDNOTE

1 We use this term to refer to an application session which may have one or more streams in it. In HHFR, the session includes a conventional SOAP message exchange for a negotiation and flexible representation message exchanges through high performance channel stream.

Chapter III
Secure Web Service Composition:
Issues and Architectures

Barbara Carminati
University of Insubria, Italy

Elena Ferrari
University of Insubria, Italy

Patrick C. K. Hung
University of Ontario Institute of Technology (UOIT), Canada

ABSTRACT

Web service security is today receiving growing attention, and enterprises are realizing that effective security management is essential for earning and maintaining trust in their services. One of the major benefits of Web services is that it is possible to dynamically combine different services together to form a more complex service. Also, in this case, security issues are a primary concern. In this chapter, we focus on security issues that arise when composing Web services. We first provide an overview of the main security requirements that must be taken into account when composing Web services. Then, we survey literature and standards related to Web services composition. Finally, we present a proposal for a brokered architecture on support of the secure composition of Web services.

INTRODUCTION

Current trends in information and communication technology are accelerating widespread use of Web services in supporting a service-oriented architecture consisting of services, their compositions, interactions, and management (Papazoglou, & Georgakopoulos, 2003). A Web service is a software system designed to support interoperable application-to-application interactions over the Internet. Using a standardized XML messaging system and with the essential characteristic of not being committed to a specific platform or programming language, Web services have achieved, among others, easy communication through the Internet and reduction of cost and time in the framework of enterprise applications. Web services rely on a set of XML standards, such as Universal Description, Discovery, and Integration (UDDI) (OASIS, 2002), Web Services Description Language (WSDL) (World Wide Web Consortium (W3C), 2002b), and Simple Object Access Protocol (SOAP) (World Wide Web Consortium (W3C), 2003). Each service makes its functionalities available through well-defined or standardized interfaces.

One of the major benefits of Web services is that it is possible to dynamically combine different services together to form a more complex service. The result of this approach is a service-oriented architecture (SOA), in which services are fundamental elements that can be independently developed and evolved over time. A SOA consists of services, their compositions, and interactions. Each service is a self-describing, composable, and open software component. In SOA, we typically deal with layers of services, each with a well-defined goal and functionalities. Sometimes a service can be composed as a workflow of other services. In particular, Grid technologies and infrastructures increase the need for sharing and coordinating the use of Web services for different business processes in a loosely coupled execution environment. A business process contains a set of activities that represent both business tasks and interactions between Web services. This feature is very relevant because in the real-world, business processes are often integrated in both intra- and inter-corporate environments. To this purpose, many emerging languages (e.g., BPEL4WS (IBM Corporation, 2002), WSBPEL (OASIS. *Web Services Business Process Execution Language*) and BPML (Arkin, 2002)) have been proposed for coordinating Web services into a workflow. Additionally, some proposals exist (Kagal, Finin, & Joshi, 2003; Maamar, Mostefaoui, & Yahyaoui, 2005; Milanovic & Malek, 2004) to deal with the composition of Web services, that we survey in the third section. However, security concerns arising during Web service composition have yet to be widely investigated, despite their relevance. In fact, enterprises are realizing that effective security management is essential for earning and maintaining trust in their services. Thus, many enterprises are still having security concerns around adapting and implementing Web services to support their businesses. For this reason, in this chapter, we focus on the security requirements that both Web service requestors and providers may have and that must be taken into account when composing Web services. For instance, a Web service provider may not want to accept requests issued by a specific IP address, or a Web service may require the use of a particular authentication mechanism to participate to the composition. Such constraints must be carefully considered when composing Web services. Constraints are used to specify configurations of the composition that violate specific security requirements of both Web services and Web services requestors.

More precisely, we first discuss security requirements that must be taken into account when composing Web services. Then, we survey related work on Web Service composition, and provide an overview of standards related to Web service composition. Then, the last part of the chapter presents a proposal of a brokered architecture to compose Web services according to the specified security requirements.

SECURITY REQUIREMENTS OF WEB SERVICE COMPOSITION

SOA is built on an insecure, unmonitored, and shared environment, which is open to events such as security threats. This may result in conflicts because the open architecture of Web services makes it available to many parties, who may have competing interests and goals (Ratnasingam, 2002). For example, a party's commercial secrets may be released to another competing company via the Web services execution. As is the case in many other applications, the information processed in Web services might be commercially sensitive, so it is important to protect it from security threats such as disclosure to unauthorized parties. Because security is an essential and integral part of many business processes, Web services have to manage and execute the activities in a secure way. However, the research area of Web services security is challenging, as it involves many disciplines, from authentication/encryption to access management/security policies. Security concerns and the lack of security conventions are the major barriers that prevent many business organizations from implementing or employing Web services.

Such security concerns are also crucial when composing Web services. Usually, Web services composition is only driven by the requested service and the Web service component functionalities. However, besides these obvious criteria to be followed during Web service composition, we believe that an important dimension is related to the security requirements arising during the composition. Here and in the following, we refer to the composition of Web services driven by security requirements as *secure conscious composition* (Carminati, Ferrari, & Hung, 2006). In this respect, we can classify security requirements into two broad categories: security requirements specified by the service requestor and security requirements specified by Web services themselves. This last class of requirements refers to constraints that a Web service may impose to take part to the composition. For instance, consider a request for a trip planning that may require composing several Web services (e.g., air ticket reservation, hotel reservation, car rental, etc.). An example of the first class of security requirements is the following: "*The service requestor requires that the Web service making hotel reservations uses X.509 authentication.*" By contrast, an example of Web services security constraints can be that "*a Web service accepts only requests from Web services using P3P to express privacy policies*" (World Wide Web Consortium (W3C), 2002c).

Therefore, a framework for secure conscious composition of Web services should provide suitable mechanisms to express the above-mentioned security requirements. One of the most intuitive approaches for their modeling is in the form of security constraints, expressing the security characteristics that a Web service should possess to take part into the secure conscious composition. With respect to the classification introduced above, we call *requestor constraints* those security constraints specified by Web service requestors, whereas we call *compatibility constraints* the security constraints specified by Web services themselves. Moreover, requestor constraints can be defined for all the Web services taking part into the composition, referred to as *general constraints*, or only for some of them, referred to as *specific constraints*. Therefore, a framework for secure conscious composition should provide suitable mechanisms to specify all these classes of constraints and to represent them in a way compatible with the Web service architecture (WSA) (World Wide Web Consortium (W3C), 2002a).

Another important requirement is the ability to model the security characteristics of a Web service to be matched against security constraints. For instance, in order to verify whether a constraint asking for the use of P3P policies is satisfied or not by a Web service, we must be able to assess whether a Web service makes use of P3P or not. Therefore, a further requirement is the ability to model the *security profile* of a Web service. A security profile consists of a set of *security capabilities,* each one referring to a particular security characteristic of the Web service (e.g., authentication or encryption techniques used). Such capabilities should be certified by some certification authority attesting the authenticity and the correctness of the information they convey.

From the architectural point of view, we believe that an important requirement is to implement the service on support of secure conscious composition in a way that is as much as possible independent from already existing standard services for Web service discovery and matchmaking, or services for standard Web service composition (i.e., without considering security requirements). The service on support of secure conscious composition can make use of the above-mentioned services, but should not change their application logic. In that way, we can reuse already existing implementations and build on top of them the component in charge of verifying security requirements. Additionally, because the relevance of security strictly depends on the application domain, we believe that it is important to have a modular architecture in which the security component can be easily plugged in only when needed.

Finally, another important issue is related to the efficiency of the composition. Indeed, checking security constraints causes an additional overhead with respect to standard composition. Therefore, there is the need of devising suitable techniques, and related data structures to make security constraints verification efficient.

LITERATURE REVIEW

Workflow management is the specification, decomposition, execution, coordination, and monitoring of workflows. A workflow management system (WFMS) is the middleware to support workflow management (WFMS, 2007). In general, a workflow includes many different entities such as activities, humans, agents, events, and flows. Here, an agent can be considered as a Web service. An activity is a logical unit of work that may be performed by a Web service. An event is an atomic occurrence of something interesting to the system itself or user applications. Events arise during the execution phase of an activity by a Web service.

The combination of workflow technologies and Web services has become more popular in both the research community and industry (Bonner, 1999). For example, Charfi and Mezini present a framework for securing BPEL4WS/WSBPEL (BPEL) compositions using WS-Security and WS-Policy with AO4BPEL, an aspect-oriented extension to BPEL (2005). Charfi and Mezini also introduce the notion of policy-based process deployment to check the compatibility of the security policies of the composition and its partners at deployment time. The security policy specifies which authentication mechanisms (username/password pairs, binary certificates), encryption algorithms, digital signatures, and so forth, are supported by a partner Web service. Next, Koshutanski and Massacci also present a theoretical access control framework for business processes in BPEL (2003). Shi et al. use automata to describe behaviors of Web services in the composition conversation. Each of the underlying Web services can interact with others through asynchronous messages passing according to its interaction role (client or server) (Shi, Zhang, Liu, Liu, Lin, & Shi, 2005). In addition, Milanovic and Malek discuss different approaches for Web services composition in the context of BPEL, OWL-S, Web components, algebraic composition process, Petri nets, model checking, and finite state machine. As what Milanovic and Malek summarize in the paper, most approaches neglect quality of service (QoS) properties such as security, dependability, or performance (Milanovic & Malek, 2004). Security properties, such as capabilities and requirements, are the research focus of this chapter.

Further, Maamar et al. discuss the security of the computing resources on which Web services are executed (2005). Maamar et al. also present a framework for Web service composition management (WSCM) in the context of peer-to-peer service discovery, classes of service management, composition verification, and trust management reputation propagation. In this context, DAML-S (Ankolekar, Burstein, Hobbs, Lassila, Martin, McIlraith et al., 2001) provides the capability to semantically annotate Web services based on an ontology that provides classes and properties to describe content and capabilities of the Web services. Another relevant effort carried on in this field is the one proposed in Kagal, Paolucci, Srinivasan, Denker, Finin, and Sycara (2004), where authors extend OWL-S, the new emerging standard for semantic Web service description, by proposing ontology for annotating input and output parameters of a Web service with respect to their security characteristics (e.g., encryption and digital signature requirements). In Kagal et al. (2004) they also consider privacy and authorization policies expressed by means of the REI language (Kagal et al., 2003). A basic difference between the approach reported in Kagal et al. (2004) and the one discussed in this chapter is that we exploit a syntactic approach to model security requirements of a Web service (i.e., the WSDL document), whereas in Kagal et al. (2004) they use a semantic annotation-based approach. A further relevant difference is that in Kagal et al. (2004) authors only consider the enforcement of security constraints of a single Web service requester. By contrast, in the proposed approach, we consider the security requirements of both Web service requestors and Web services taking part in the composition.

Other major related work is those exploiting AI planning techniques for Web service composition. Among them, we recall the work by McIlraith and Son (2002) that extends the logic programming language Golog for automatic composition of Web services, and the one by Medjahed, Bouguettaya, and Elmagarmid (2003), which proposes a technique for generating composite Web services from high-level declarative descriptions. A framework for composing Web services, based on the use of Mealy machines, has also been proposed by Bultan, Fu, Hull, and Su (2003). However, such frameworks do not address security issues, which is the focus of the work described at the end of this chapter.

There are also XML languages proposed for describing security assertions. These XML languages restrict access to Web services to authorized parties only, and protect the integrity and confidentiality of messages exchanged in a loosely coupled execution environment. Specifically, there is a well-known format for XML-based security tokens, that is, the Security Assertions Markup Language (SAML) (OASIS. SAML 1.0 Specification), which is used to define authentication and authorization decisions in Web services. Web services providers submit SAML tokens to security servers for making security decisions. WS-Security describes enhancements to SOAP messaging to provide quality of protection through message integrity, message confidentiality and single message authentication (IBM, Microsoft & VeriSign, 2002). Based on WS-security, WS-policy provides a grammar for expressing Web services security policies (IBM, BEA, Microsoft, SAP, Sonic Software, & VeriSign, 2004). WS-policy includes a set of security policy assertions to support WS-Security specification defined in WS-security policy (IBM, BEA, Microsoft, SAP, Sonic Software, & VeriSign, 2004). However, none of these works present any formal theoretical model to support the languages.

On the other hand, Channa, Li, Shaikh, and Fu (2005) present a constraint driven Web service composition tool in METEOR-S, which allows process designers to bind Web Services to an abstract process, based on business constraints in QoS ontologies, and generate an executable Web service composition. Though security requirements can be described by constraints, Channa et al. do not discuss how to describe Web service's security capabilities. Next, Aggarwal, Verma, Miller, and Milnor (2004) present the selection and optimization of the services as a constraints satisfaction problem (CSP) to satisfy the customers' requirements in the context of semantic Web process. However, Aggarwal et al. do not discuss any security constraints. Yang, Papazoglou, Orriens, and van Heuvel (2003) illustrate the ReServCom project by introducing a rule-based approach for Web service composition. Again, Yang et al. do not discuss any security rules for supporting service composition. Chun, Atluri, and Adam (2004) present a coherent service flow by using rules and Web services expressed as a knowledge base and topic ontology in OWL, DAML-S, RuleML, and RDF standards. In summary, none of these related work focuses on security capabilities and requirements in Web service composition.

Furthermore, scientific workflow implementation has focused on Web service-based architectures. For example, Ludascher, Altintas, and Gupta (2003) separate the abstract and concrete executable workflows and use database mediation techniques to automatically translate abstract workflows to executable ones. The abstract ones are more scientist-friendly, while the executable ones are more feasible in implementation with Web services. Altintas, Jaeger, Lin, Ludaescher, and Memon (2004) present a Web services framework for scientific workflows, which uses the concept of Web services actors and Web services harvesters to interact with existing Web services. However, none of these two works take into account any security requirement.

STANDARDS FOR WEB SERVICE COMPOSITION

In this section, we overview the main standards related to Web service composition. In doing that, we will focus on standards providing both a syntactic and semantic description of Web services and their composition.

Syntactic-Based Standards

The technical details of Web services are described by the Web services description language (WSDL) (World Wide Web Consortium (W3C), 2002b). A WSDL document describes the Web service interface, such as what operations the Web service supports, what protocols to use, and how the data exchanged should be packed. From another point of view, the WSDL document can be seen as a contract between the Web services requestor and provider. Basically, a WSDL document contains the following technical details:

- **Definitions:** Declares the name of the Web service and the namespaces used to define the elements found throughout the remainder of the document
- **Message:** For all input, output, and fault messages, it specifies message name and message parts (parameters)
- **Operation:** It is a description of a Web method in terms of the messages that are sent and received
- **PortType:** It is a group of operations
- **Binding:** It describes the transport protocols, message formats, and message styles supported by a given Web service
- **Port:** It maps a binding to a network location
- **Service: It** defines the address for invoking the specified service

The Web services provider may publish the WSDL document to the Web services broker, via UDDI registries. Once a Web service is found at the UDDI registries, the Web services requestor gets the corresponding WSDL document and tries to bind with the Web service via a simple object access protocol (SOAP) message. SOAP is an XML-based messaging protocol that is independent of the underlying transport protocol (e.g., HTTP, SMTP, and FTP). SOAP messages are used both by services requestors to invoke Web services, and by Web services to answer to the requests. Therefore, the Web service receives the input SOAP message from the Web services requestor and generates an output SOAP message to the Web services requestor. This model is called the publish-find-bind model.

In the past few years, business process or workflow proposals relevant to Web services are proliferating in the business and academic world. Most of the proposals are XML-based languages to specify Web services interactions and compositions. All of the proposed XML languages are based on WSDL service descriptions with extension elements. For example, Thatte (2001) describes XLANG as a notation for the specification of message exchange behavior (i.e., interactions) among Web services participating in business processes. XLANG is based on the WSDL service description with an extension element that describes the behavior of the services as a part of a business process. In XLANG, the behavior of each Web service is specified independently, and the interaction between Web services is only through message exchanges expressed as operations in WSDL. However, XLANG does not specify security issues of Web service activities. On the other hand, Leymann (2001) describes Web services flow language (WSFL) that is also layered on top of WSDL. WSFL is an XML language for the description of Web services compositions. WSFL specifies the appropriate usage pattern of a collection of Web services in order to achieve a particular business goal (i.e., business processes), and it also specifies the interaction pattern of a collection of Web services.

The business process modeling language (BPML) defines a formal model for expressing abstract and executable processes that addresses all aspects of enterprise business processes (Arkin, 2002). BPML provides an abstracted execution model for collaborative and transactional business processes based on the concept of a transactional finite-state machine. The Business Process Execution Language for Web Services (BPEL4WS) is a formal specification of business processes and interaction protocols. The OASIS WSBPEL Technical Committee is now established to continue working on the BPEL4WS 1.1 specification within the OASIS Consortium OASIS (Web Services Business Process Execution Language). BPEL4WS/WSBPEL (BPEL) defines a model and a grammar for describing the behavior of a business process based on interactions between the process and its Web service interfaces. In short, a BPEL business process definition can be thought of as a template for creating business process instances. Each of the activities in a flow model must be executed by an appropriate Web service. Basically, a BPEL document contains the following technical details:

- **partnerLinks:** Defines the different parties that interact with the business process in the course of processing the order
- **variables:** Defines the data variables used by the process, providing their definitions in terms of WSDL message types
- **flow:** Specifies one or more activities to be performed concurrently
- **links:** Can be used within concurrent activities to define arbitrary control structures
- **received:** Allows the business process to do a blocking wait for a matching message to arrive
- **invoke:** Allows the business process to invoke a one-way or request-response operation on a portType offered by a partner
- **assign:** Can be used to update the values of variables with new data. An <assign> construct can contain any number of elementary assignments
- **reply:** Allows the business process to send a message in reply to a message that was received through a <receive>

The combination of a <receive> and a <reply> forms a request-response operation on the WSDL portType for the process.

Further, van der Aalst, Dumas, and ter Hofstede (2003) discuss the future research topics for BPEL with more fundamental issues such as semantics, expressiveness, and adequacy. In this chapter, we use BPEL to model Web services compositions.

Another relevant standard language to Web service composition is Web services choreography (WS Choreography) (World Wide Web Consortium (W3C), 2004b). WS choreography defines the sequence and conditions in which messages are exchanged for all the involved Web services. Each Web service can then use the definition to build and test solutions that conform to the global definition. The choreography definition can generate a behavioral interface that conforms to a BPEL document to describe the sequence and conditions in which one of the Web services in choreography sends and receives messages. It can also verify that a BPEL document conforms to behaviors defined by a choreography definition. In general, the WS choreography model contains the following components:

- **Participants, roles, and relationships:** Messages are exchanged between participants, such as Web services acting in one or more roles in a relationship of trading partners.
- **Choreography structure, composition, and import:** The choreography can be created by performing other, pre-existing choreographies and importing content from other choreographies.
- **Types, variables, and tokens:** Variables contain information about messages in the choreography. Tokens are aliases that can be used to reference parts of a variable. Both variables and tokens have types that define the structure of variables or tokens.
- **Interactions:** They are the basic building blocks of the choreography that model the results in the sending of messages between roles in either a "one-way" or "request-response" message pattern.
- **Activities and control structures:** Activities are the lowest level components of the choreography model. Control structures combine activities with other control structures in a nested structure.
- **Choreography exceptions and transactions:** Choreography exceptions handle the situation in which a choreography model behaves in an abnormal way. Choreography transactions describe what additional interactions should occur to reverse the effect of a completed choreography.
- **Semantics:** Semantics describes the semantic definitions of every component in the model.

Semantic-Based Standards

In the recent years, it has emerged that to support automated interactions between Web services, there is the crucial need of providing a semantic description of services. In particular, as pointed out by the Semantic Web services language (SWSL) committee of the Semantic Web services initiative (SWSI), it is necessary to define a standardized language for conceptualizing and organizing semantic information about Web services. With this aim, OWL-S (previously DAML-S) (OWL-based Web service ontology, http://www.daml.org/services/owl-s/) is the first Web Services Ontology that has been proposed, and receives a great attention both from industries and academy.

OWL-S is an OWL-based ontology (World Wide Web Consortium (W3C), 2004a) designed to provide a core set of constructs for describing properties and capabilities of Web services in an unambiguous, computer-interpretable way. More precisely, OWL-S has been designed to provide ontologies able to supply essential knowledge about a service. The OWL-S framework consists of three main ontologies, briefly described in what follows.

- **ServiceProfile:** It is the ontology by which it is possible to describe what is provided by a service. It supplies information about the organization that provides the service (i.e., its contact information), a functional description of the service (i.e., required inputs, generated outputs, possible required preconditions), and several other features that specify characteristics of the service. All this information can be exploited by service-seeking or matchmaking agents to determine whether a service meets their needs.

- **ServiceModel:** It is the ontology that describes how to use a service. In particular, it provides concepts able to describe how to require a service and what the expected results are. These concepts are, for instance, the semantic content of requests, the conditions under which particular results will be outputted, and so forth. The description provided by means of the ServiceModel ontology can be used by service-seeking or matchmaking agents to perform a more in-depth search. Moreover, this ontology plays a key role in service composition, because, by means of this ontology, it is possible to coordinate the activities of different participants and monitor the execution of the composed service.
- **ServiceGrounding Ontology:** It is used to provide details on how an agent can access a service. Thus, it supplies information needed to interact with the service, like, for instance, the communication protocol, message formats, port-number, and so forth.

Some of researchers involved in the OWL-S project have focused their attention on security, by proposing a set of security-related ontologies able to describe security characteristics of Web resources, services, and agents. The goal of these security-related ontologies is to define a layer of abstraction on top of the several well-known security standards (e.g., XML signature, WS-security). In order to do that, the OWL-S team designed ontologies able to represent characteristics of well-known security techniques. A brief summary of the proposed security-related ontologies is given in what follows:

- **Credential Ontology:** This ontology has been designed to manage those authentication mechanisms that exploit tokens (i.e., credentials) to identify a user. By means of this ontology, it is possible to describe a simple credential, that is, a credential consisting of a single token, which could be, for instance, a cookie, login, key, certificate, biometric information, and so forth. Moreover, the Credential ontology is also able to describe more complex credentials, that is, credentials (called composed credentials) that consist of several simple credentials.
- **Security Mechanism Ontology:** It provides an abstract description of the most well-known security mechanisms. More precisely, by means of this ontology it is possible to describe the required syntax for a security mechanism (e.g., ASCII, DAML-OIL, OWL, XML), the encryption and signature algorithm (e.g., SMIME-ENC, OpenPGP-ENC, XML-ENC, XML-SIG, SMIME-SIG), as well as the required credentials, for instance, in case of an authentication mechanism. Moreover, the Security Mechanism ontology supports the description of the exploited protocols (e.g., SAML, Kerberos, HTTP) and information about the format of the keys.
- **Service Security Extensions Ontology:** This ontology exploits the credential and security mechanisms ontologies to model security properties of Web services. By means of this ontology, it is possible to describe security capabilities of a Web service, as well as its security requirements.
- **Agent Security Extensions Ontology:** This ontology has the same role as the service security extensions ontology, but with respect to agent.

- **Privacy Ontology:** It has been devised with the goal of describing privacy policies as well as the protocols for privacy policies matching. Privacy policies defined by this ontology can consist of several rules, specifying the actions that should take place if some conditions are satisfied. The Privacy ontology supports different types of rules, that is: *authorization rules*, stating actions preventing unauthorized accesses; *capability rules*, describing actions that should be performed by the service itself to satisfy other Web services privacy policies; and *obligation rules*, stating the actions that the service itself will (or will not) perform when some conditions are satisfied.

SECURE WS-BROKER: AN APPROACH TO SECURE CONSCIOUS COMPOSITION

In this section, we introduce a framework on support of secure conscious Web service composition, which satisfies all requirements discussed in the second section. More precisely, we present the brokered architecture proposed in Carminati et al. (2006), that supports both requestor constraints, that is, security requirements of the requestor of a composition (i.e., users or Web services) as well as compatibility constraints of Web services taking part into the composition. Moreover, a Web service can describe its security characteristics that must be evaluated in order to verify whether compatibility constraints of the other participants to the Web service composition are satisfied. The requestor can also state constraints to be satisfied by all the Web services taking part in the composition (i.e., general constraint), as well as only by those performing a specified activity in the composition (i.e., specific constraint).

In the proposed brokered architecture, depicted in Figure 1, Web services composition is carried out by a Web service, called *secure WS-broker* (SWS-Broker, for short), which receives from the requestor a service request and a set of security requirements and returns it the WSBPEL document representing the secure conscious composi-

Figure 1. A framework for secure conscious Web services composition

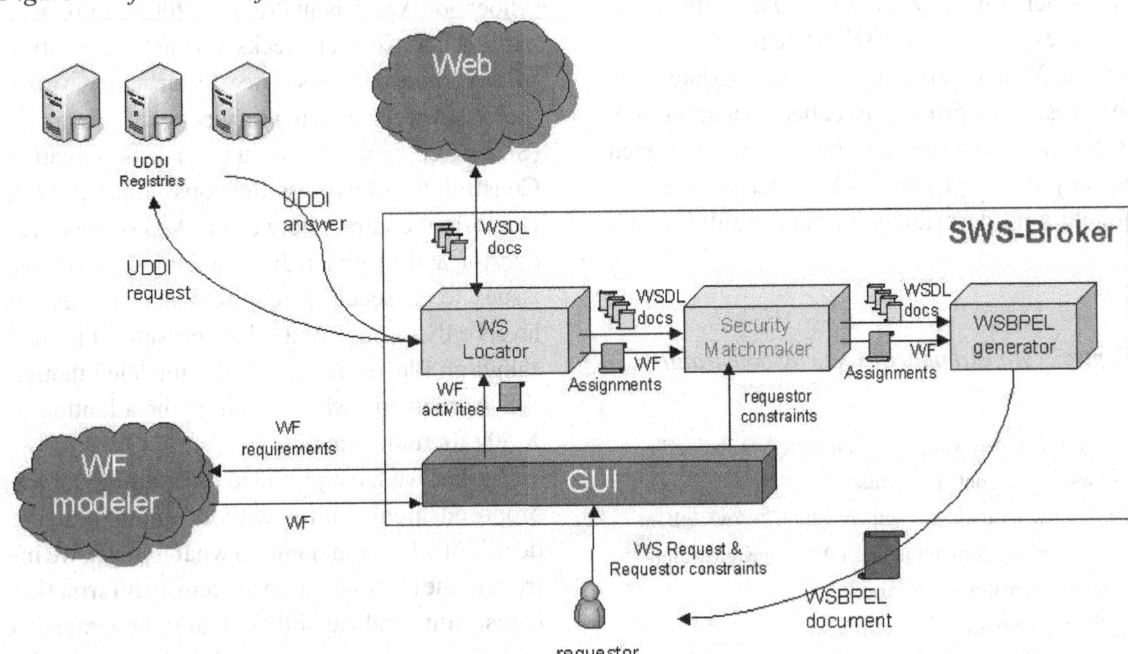

tion for that service, or an error message if it is not possible to find any composition satisfying both the request and the specified constraints. As depicted in Figure 1, the SWS-Broker consists of different components. A first component is the Graphical User Interface (GUI), helping the requestor to search for a service, possibly requiring the composition of several Web services, and to state its security constraints to be satisfied by the resulting composition.

Because the requestor does not supply any information on how and which Web services must be involved in the composition, as a first step the SWS-Broker searches for an appropriate workflow (WF) modeling the business process implementing the required service. This step is performed by means of one or more external Web services, called *WF-modelers*, whose goal is to retrieve from libraries of well-known business processes patterns a suitable workflow, that is, a workflow whose global process implements the required service. Once the appropriate workflow has been returned, for each WF activity the SWS-Broker selects one or more Web services able to carry out the activity. As reported in Figure 1, this task is performed by the *WS-locator* component, which exploits several UDDI registries to find out the WSDL documents of appropriate Web services. This process is called matchmaking. In the workflow returned by *WF-modeler* each activity is complemented by a set of semantic annotations describing its functionalities and capabilities. These annotations help the *WS-locator* to properly inquiry UDDI registries. Thus, the *WS-locator* retrieves for each WF activity a list of Web services simply considering their functionalities, not their security characteristics. These are considered by the *security matchmaker*, which is the core component of the SWS-Broker. For each WF activity the *security matchmaker* selects, among the Web services identified by the *WS-locator*, the Web services satisfying the specified security constraints, obtaining thus the secure conscious composition. Finally, the last step of the process is the translation of the results returned by the *security matchmaker* into a WSBPEL document. This task is done by the *WSBPEL-Generator*, which receives from the *security matchmaker* the Web services assigned to each WF activity. Given this information, the *WSBPEL-generator* is able to generate a WSBPEL document describing the process derived by the WF. Moreover, it inserts into the resulting WSBPEL document further information about security constraints considered during the security conscious composition. Such information is modeled by means of WS-Agreement (Grid Resource Allocation Agreement Protocol, 2005), and can be exploited for further checks during the execution of the composed Web service. In particular, we use the WS-Agreement, as a service-level agreement (SLA), free-form constraint assertions "Creation Constraints" to express the constraints. A SLA is a formal contract between a Web services requestor and provider guaranteeing quantifiable issues (e.g., security requirements) at defined levels only through mutual concessions. Figure 2 shows an illustrative constraint modeled though WS-Agreement, which requires the adoption of X.509 for authentication.

Figure 2. An example of security constraint

```
<wsag:template xmlns:sv="#securityVocabulary">
<wsag:CreationConstraints>
    <wsag:Item>sv:"authentication"></wsag:Item>
    <wsag:Constraint> X.509</wsag:Constraint>
</wsag:CreationConstraints>
</wsag:template>
```

So far, we have provided an overview of the proposed architecture, without going into the details of any component. In what follows, we introduce the representation of security information (constraints and capabilities), and the strategies underlying the *security matchmaker*, that is, the core-component of the SWS-broker.

Figure 3. An example of security capability

```
<saml:AttributeStatement xmlns:sv#securityVocabulary ">
   <saml:Attribute Name =”sv:privacyAccessControl”>
      <saml:AttributeValue>
         P3P
      </saml:AttributeValue>
   </saml:Attribute>
</saml:AttributeStatement>
```

Security Information

In order to implement a system on support of secure conscious composition, the first issue to be addressed is the definition of a language able to model security constraints imposed by the requestor of a Web service composition, as well as those constraints specified by Web services participating in the Web service composition, referred to as compatibility constraints. Moreover, in order to check whether a security or compatibility constraint is satisfied, there is the need also of a language able to specify security characteristics of a Web service (referred to as security capabilities). In what follows, we summarize the representation proposed in Carminati et al. (2006) for both security capabilities and constraints.

Security Capabilities. We assume the existence of a secure capability authority (SCA) in charge of evaluating Web service security capabilities and, based on this evaluation, of issuing signed declarations that certify such capabilities. Such declarations are expressed through security assertions markup language (SAML) (OASIS. SAML 1.0 Specification*)* assertions. SAML defines a standard way to represent authentication, attribute, and authorization information that may be used in a distributed environment by disparate applications. Because a SAML assertion consists of pairs of attribute name and value, it can be easily exploited to model security characteristics of a Web service. More precisely, the attribute name denotes the security feature, whereas the corresponding attribute value provides information on how the security feature is enforced by the Web service.

Figure 3 presents a security capability stating that the Web service adopts P3P to tackle privacy issues. Security capabilities are inserted into the WSDL document of the corresponding Web service. This can be done because SAML assertions are encoded into XML and WSDL specification (World Wide Web Consortium (W3C), 2002b) designed an “extensibility element” as support for possible extensions, that is, an XML element where additional XML nodes can be inserted.

Requestor and Compatibility Constraints. As introduced before, the SWS-Broker is able to handle both requestor and compatibility constraints. In Carminati et al. (2006) we have proposed a uniform notation to model both these kinds of constraints. According to this notation, a security constraint is represented as a Boolean formula defined over security capabilities. More precisely, the disjunctive normal form (DNF) of the formula is encoded into an XML element, called SecCnstr, which contains a different subelement, called Clause, for each clause of the DNF. The Clause element contains the name of the capability to which the condition refers to (AttributeName element), the operator of the condition, and the values to be evaluated on that capability

Figure 4. An example of security constraint encoding

```
<SecCnstr xmlns:sv="#securityVocabulary">
  <Clause>
    <AttributeName name="sv:authentication"/>
    <Oper op="="/>
    <Values>
      <Value val="sv:SAML "/>
    </Values>
  </Clause>
  <Clause>
    <AttributeName name=" sv:privacyAccessControl"/>
    <Oper op="="/>
    <Values>
      <Value val="sv:P3P"/>
    </Values>
  </Clause>
</SecCnstr>
```

Figure 5. An illustrative security vocabulary

```
<owl:Ontology rdf:about="#securityVocabulary">
<owl:versionInfo>v 1.00 2005/06/15 23:59:59</owl:versionInfo>
<rdfs:comment>Security Vocabulary</rdfs:comment>
...
<owl:Class rdf:ID="#privacyAccessControl">
  <owl:unionOf rdf:parseType="Collection">
  <owl:Class rdf:about="#P3P"/>
  <owl:Class rdf:about="#EPAL"/>
  <owl:Class rdf:about="#XACML"/>
</owl:unionOf>
</owl:Class>
...
<owl:Class rdf:ID="#authentication">
<owl:unionOf rdf:parseType="Collection">
  <owl:Class rdf:about="#WS-Security"/>
  <owl:Class rdf:about="#SAML"/>
  <owl:Class rdf:about="#X.509"/>
</owl:unionOf>
</owl:Class>
...
</owl:Ontology>
```

(oper and values element, respectively). Figure 4 shows an example of security constraint requiring adopting SAML as authentication mechanism or P3P to tackle privacy issues.

Similar to security capabilities, there is the need to make compatibility constraints specified by a Web service available to the Security Matchmaker to make it able to perform the appropriate checks. For this reason, compatibility constraints are stored into the WSDL document describing a Web service. As the security capabilities, they are stored into the extensibility element. By contrast, requestor constraints are specified directly by the requestor when it requires the composition to the SWS-Broker. The GUI component is in charge of gathering the requestor constraints and translating them into the corresponding SecCnstr element.

Because security constraints must be matched against capabilities issued by a SCA, the broker and the SCAs have to adopt a common ontology to express security capabilities and constraints. To this purpose, in Carminati et al. (2006) we have defined a Security Vocabulary/Ontology by using the Web ontology language (OWL). An OWL ontology includes descriptions of classes, properties, and their instances, as well as a formal semantic for deriving logical consequences in entailments. Figure 5 shows a simplified OWL Ontology that describes a security vocabulary and related Web services standards.

Security Matchmaker

For each WF activity, the security matchmaker receives as input the Web services selected by the WS-locator, together with the corresponding WSDL documents. The main goal of the security matchmaker is to select among all these Web services, those, if any, whose security capabilities satisfy both the constraints specified by the requestor and the compatibility constraints specified by the Web services with which it has to cooper-

Figure 6. The Security Matchmaker architecture

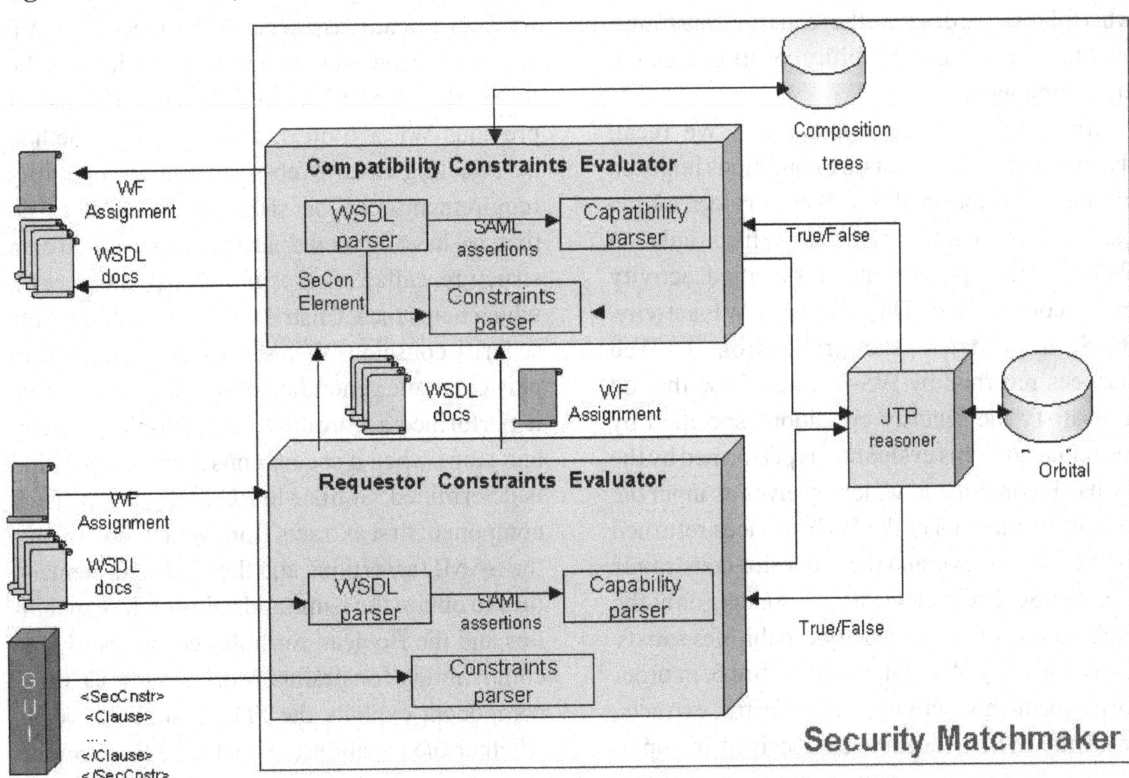

ate. In general, for each WF activity, the Security Matchmaker has to verify the requestor and compatibility constraints. As reported in Figure 6, constraints evaluation is performed by means of two main components, namely, the *requestor constraints evaluator* (RCnstrE, for short) and the *compatibility constraints evaluator* (CCnstrE, for short). In particular, both these components make use of a reasoner in order to verify requestor and compatibility constraints. More precisely, we use the Java theorem prover (JTP) (Richard, Jenkins, & Frank, 2003), which is a Java-based reasoner developed at Stanford University. The main feature of JTP engine is that its object-oriented modular architecture is able to support several libraries of general purpose reasonings. We exploit the Orbital library (Orbital Library, http://www. functologic. com/orbital.), which provides an object-oriented representation of logical and mathematics algorithms. By means of Orbital, the JTP engine is used to evaluate whether a Boolean formula representing a requestor or compatibility constraint is satisfied by security capabilities. In what follows, we describe the requestor constraints evaluator and the compatibility constraints evaluator components.

Security Constraints Evaluator. We recall that requestor constraints are conditions imposed by the requestor on all the Web services taking part into the composition, as well as only on Web services performing a specified activity in the composition. Thus, for each WF activity, the Security Matchmaker prunes from the Web services returned by WS-Locator those that do not satisfy the security conditions specified by the requestor. This evaluation is performed by the RCnstrE component, which receives as input the WSDL documents of the Web services returned by the *WS-Locator* and the requestor constraints (i.e., the SecCnstr element), and selects only the Web services whose security capabilities satisfy the constraints. As depicted in Figure 6, in order to perform this activity, the RCnstrE extracts, from the WSDL documents received in input, the SAML assertions modeling the capabilities of the corresponding Web services, which are further elaborated to obtain the name and value of the capabilities. Moreover, by means of a document object model (DOM) parser, it evaluates the SecCnstr element passed by the GUI to gain the Boolean formula representing the requestor constraint. In order to state whether a set of security capabilities associated with a Web service satisfies a requestor constraint, the RCnstrE component exploits the JTP reasoner, which receives as input the Boolean formula and the set of capabilities, and returns true if the formula is verified.

Compatibility Constraints Evaluator. Once the requestor constraints have been evaluated, the Security Matchmaker tests compatibility constraints. This task is more complex than requestor constraints evaluation, in that it implies several run time evaluations. Indeed, in selecting a Web service to be associated with an activity, the CCnstrE component has to choose a Web service whose security capabilities satisfy the compatibility constraints specified by Web services already assigned to the preceding WF activities. However, if no Web service can be found, the CCnstrE component has to reconsider previous WF activities, thus to verify whether, by selecting other Web services, compatibility requirements can be satisfied. In order to do that, we have defined a particular tree-based data structure, called *composition tree* (see Figure 6), which helps the CCnstrE to generate all possible security conscious Web service compositions. In particular, the generation of the composition tree is performed according to a depth-first strategy and stops when a secure conscious composition is determined. Similar to RCnstrE, the CCnstrE component first extracts from WSDL documents the SAML assertions and the SecCnstr element, thus to obtain the name and value of the capabilities and the Boolean formulas corresponding to compatibility constraints. Moreover, the CCnstrE component exploits the JTP reasoner to verify whether the capabilities satisfy the Boolean formulas.

An Illustrative Example

In this section, we present an example to clarify how a secure conscious composition is generated by the SWS-Broker. Let us assume that a user requires to the SWS-Broker a "travel plan" service, by which to plan a complete travel consisting of flight, hotel, and car reservations. Moreover, let us assume that the user specifies a set of security constraints. More precisely, he or she requires that all Web services participating to the composition exploit X.509 for authentication (i.e., a general constraint). Additionally, the Web service carrying out hotel reservation must adopt P3P to tackle privacy issues (i.e., a specific constraint). In order to generate the secure conscious composition, the SWS-Broker first inquires the WF Modeler (cfr. Figure 1) for modeling such a service.

Assuming that the workflow returned by the modeler is the one reported in Figure 7, the SWS-Broker has to find out, for each of the activities depicted in Figure 7, one or more Web services able to carry out them. This task is performed by the WS-locator, which returns, for each WF activity, the WSDL documents of those Web services able to perform it. In our example, we assume that the WS-Locator found out Web services WS1, WS2, and WS3 for activity A1, Web services WS4 and WS5 for activity A2, and Web services WS6, and WS7 for A3.

Once the Web services have been located, the SWS-Broker can evaluate the security constraints, that is, requestor constraints and compatibility constraints of the discovered Web services. As introduced in a previous section, this task is

Figure 7. The workflow for a travel planning

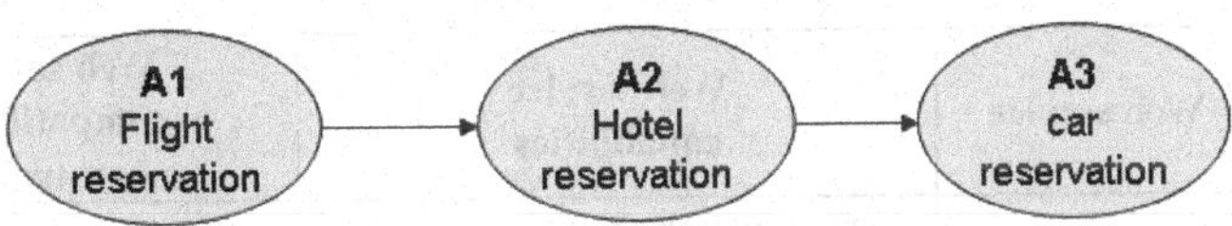

Table 1. Security capabilities of the Web services returned by the WS-Locator

Activity	Web services	Web services capabilities
A1	WS1	Authentication=SAML
	WS2	Authentication=X.509
	WS3	Authentication=SAML
A2	WS4	Authentication=X.509 PrivacyAccessControl=P3P
	WS5	Authentication=X.509 PrivacyAccessControl=P3P Signature=XML-SIG
A3	WS6	Authentication=X.509
	WS7	Authentication=SAML

performed by the security matchmaker, which separately evaluates both kinds of security requirements. In particular, it starts to evaluate requestor constraints.

From each WSDL document returned by the WS-locator, it extracts the security capabilities of the corresponding Web service. Table 1 shows the results of this step, where each Web service is associated with its security capabilities.

During the evaluation of requestor constraints, the security matchmaker prunes from the Web services returned by the WF-locator those that do not satisfy the specified constraints. This implies pruning all the Web services that do not adopt X.509. Moreover, only from the Web services associated with activity A2 (i.e., Web services WS4 and WS5 carrying out the hotel reservation), it has to remove those Web services that do not adopt P3P as privacy technique. Because both WS4 and WS5 support P3P, the final result of the requestor constraints evaluation is presented in Table 2, which also reports the corresponding compatibility constraints.

In the second step, the security matchmaker evaluates compatibility constraints. To do that, it extracts compatibility constraints from the WSDL documents of the selected Web services. As reported in Table 2, there is only one Web service having a compatibility constraint, that is, WS2, who requires to the consequent Web services to adopt the XML-SIG standard as signature mechanism. In order to satisfy this constraint, the SWS-broker prunes from Web services with which WS2 has to cooperate (i.e., Web services associated with activity A2) those that do not adopt XML-SIG.

Table 2. Security capabilities and compatibility constraints of Web services after the evaluation of requestor constraints

Activity	**Web service**	**Web service capabilities**	**Web service compatibility constraints**
A1	WS2	Authentication=X.509	Signature=XML-SIG
A2	WS4	Authentication=X.509 PrivacyAccessControl=P3P	-
	WS5	Authentication=X.509 PrivacyAccessControl=P3P Signature=XML-SIG	-
A3	WS6	Authentication=X.509	-

Table 3. The secure conscious composition

Activity	Web service	Web service capabilities	Web service compatibility constraints
A1	WS2	Authentication=X.509	Signature=XML-SIG
A2	WS5	Authentication=X.509 PrivacyAccessControl=P3P Signature=XML-SIG	-
A3	WS6	Authentication=X.509	-

Table 3 reports the result of the evaluation of compatibility constraints, which basically represents the secure conscious composition. Finally, the secure conscious composition resulting after the evaluation of compatibility constraints is translated into a WSBPEL document (see Carminati et al., 2006, for more details).

CONCLUSION AND RESEARCH ISSUES

Composition of Web services is a very important issue because one of the major benefits of Web services is that it is possible to dynamically combine them together to form more complex services. Among the many research challenges related to Web service composition, one of the most relevant that has not been deeply investigated so far is related to security. In this chapter, we focused on how to express and enforce the security requirements of both Web service requestors and Web services taking part in the composition. After presenting the main security requirements arising when composing Web services, we have discussed some of the related literature in the field. Then, a part of the chapter has been devoted to standards related to Web service composition. In particular, we have reviewed both standards for modeling composite Web services (e.g., BPEL4WS) as well as standards for semantic description of Web services (e.g., OWL). We believe that this last class of standards is fundamental in composing Web services because it allows one to give a semantic description of those characteristics of Web services that must be taken into account when composing them. Finally, in the last part of the chapter we have presented a proposal for a brokered architecture on support of secure conscious Web service composition, able to fulfill most of the identified security requirements.

The area of secure Web service composition is just in its infancy and this leaves room for many research issues. One of the most important issues is how to develop a more comprehensive framework able to consider in an integrated manner other classes of constraints (such as, for instance, quality of services constraints) besides security constraints. Another important issue is related to the protection of security constraints and capability. For instance, Web service capabilities may contain sensitive information, and as such their release should be governed by proper access control policies, that must be checked before the matching against security constraints can take place. From an architectural point of view, it is important to devise efficient techniques and related data structures to perform the secure conscious composition, in that when the number of constraints and Web services increases, efficiency may become a primary concern. In this respect, a related issue is how to move from a centralized architecture, like the one discussed in this chapter, in which the SWS-Broker is the only one in charge of generating secure conscious compositions, to a more decentralized solution in which this task may be shared by several Web services, possibly also by the ones taking part into the composition.

REFERENCES

Aggarwal, R., Verma, K., Miller, J., & Milnor, W. (2004). Constraint driven Web service composition in METEOR-S. In *Proceedings of the 2004 IEEE International Conference on Services Computing* (pp. 23-30). Shangai, China.

Altintas, I., Jaeger, E., Lin, K., Ludaescher, B., & Memon, A. (2004). A Web service composition and deployment framework for scientific workflows. In *Proceedings of the 2004 IEEE International Conference on Web Services* (p. 814). San Diego, CA.

Ankolekar, A., Burstein, M., Hobbs, J.R., Lassila, O., Martin, D.L., McIlraith, S.A. et al. (2001). DAML-S: Semantic markup for Web services.

In *Proceedings of the International Semantic Web Working Symposium (SWWS)*. Standford University, CA.

Arkin, A. (2002). Business Process Modeling Language (BPML), Version 1.0. Retrieved June 3, 2007, from www.BPMI.org

Bonner, A.J. (1999). Workflows, transactions, and datalog. In *Proceedings of the 18th ACM Symposium on Principles of Database Systems (PODS)* (pp. 294-305). Philadelphia.

Bultan, T., Fu, X., Hull, R., & Su, J. (2003). Conversation specification: A new approach to design and analysis of e-service composition. In *Proceedings of 12th International World Wide Web Conference*, Budapest, Hungary.

Carminati, B., Ferrari, E., & Hung, P.C. K. (2006). Security conscious Web service composition. In *Proceedings of the 2006 IEEE International Conference on Web Services* (pp. 489-496). Chicago.

Charfi, A., & Mezini, M. (2005). Using aspects for security engineering of Web service compositions. In *Proceedings of the 2005 IEEE International Conference on Web Services* (pp. 59-66). Växjö, Sweden.

Channa, N., Li, S., Shaikh, A.W., & Fu, X. (2005). Constraint satisfaction in dynamic Web service composition. In *Proceedings of the Sixteenth International Workshop on Database and Expert Systems Applications* (pp. 658-664). Copenhagen, Denmark.

Chun, S.A., Atluri, V., & Adam, N.R. (2004). Policy-based Web service composition. In *Proceedings of the 14th International Workshop on Research Issues on Data Engineering: Web Services for E-commerce and E-government Applications* (pp. 85-92). Boston.

Grid Resource Allocation Agreement Protocol (GRAAP) WG. (2005). *Web Services Agreement Specification (WS-Agreement)*, Version 2005/09, GWD-R (Proposed Recommendation).

IBM, BEA, Microsoft, SAP, Sonic Software, & VeriSign. (2004, September). *Web Services Policy Framework (WS-Policy)*.

IBM Corporation. (2002). *Business Process Execution Language for Web Services (BPEL4WS)*, Version 1.0.

IBM, Microsoft, & VeriSign. (2002, April 5). *Specification: Web Services Security (WS-Security)*, Version 1.0.

Kagal, L., Finin, T., & Joshi, A. (2003). A policy based approach to security on the semantic Web. In *Proceedings of the 2nd International Semantic Web Conference,* Sanibel Island, FL.

Kagal, L., Paolucci, M., Srinivasan, N., Denker, G., Finin, T., & Sycara, K. (2004). Authorization and privacy for semantic Web services. In *Proceedings of the AAAI Spring Symposium, Workshop on Semantic Web Services*, Stanford University, Palo Alto, CA.

Koshutanski, H., & Massacci, F. (2003). An access control framework for business processes for Web services mechanisms. In *Proceedings of the ACM Workshop on XML Security*, Fairfax, VA.

Leymann, F. (2001). *Web Services Flow Language (WSFL 1.0).*

Ludascher, B., Altintas, I., & Gupta, A. (2003). Compiling abstract scientific workflows into Web service workflows. In *Proceedings of the 15th International Conference on Scientific and Statistical Database Management*, Cambridge, MA.

Maamar, Z., Mostefaoui, S.K., & Yahyaoui, H. (2005). Toward an agent-based and context-oriented approach for Web services composition. *IEEE Transactions on Knowledge and Data Engineering, 17*(5), 686-697.

McIlraith, S., & Son, T.C. (2002). Adapting Golog for composition of semantic Web services. In *Proceedings of the 8th International Conference on Knowledge Representation and Reasoning*, Toulouse, France.

Medjahed, B., Bouguettaya, A., & Elmagarmid, A.K. (2003). Composing Web services on the semantic Web. *The VLDB Journal, 12*(4), 333-351.

Milanovic, N., & Malek, M. (2004). Current solutions for Web service composition. *IEEE Internet Computing, 8*(6), 51-59.

OASIS. *SAML 1.0 Specification.*

OASIS. *Web Services Business Process Execution Language (WSBPEL).*

OASIS 2002, *Universal Description, Discovery and Integration UDDI v. 3.0,* UDDI Spec Technical Committee Specification.

Orbital Library. Retrieved June 3, 2007, from http://www.functologic.com/orbital

OWL-based Web Service Ontology. Retrieved June 3, 2007, from http://www.daml.org/services/owl-s/

Papazoglou, M. P., & Georgakopoulos, D. (2003). Service-oriented computing. *Communications of ACM, 46*(10), 24-28.

Ratnasingam, P. (2002). The importance of technology trust in Web services security. *Information Management & Computer Security, 10*(5), 255-260.

Richard, F., Jenkins, J., & Frank, G. (2003). JTP: A system architecture and component library for hybrid reasoning. *In Proceedings of the Seventh World Multiconference on Systemics, Cybernetics, and Informatics.* Orlando, FL.

Semantic Web Services Initiative (SWSI). Retrieved June 3, 2007, from http://www.swsi.org/

Semantic Web Services Language (SWSL) Committee. Retrieved June 3, 2007, from http://www.daml.org/services/swsl/

Shi, Y., Zhang, L., Liu, B., Liu, F., Lin, L., & Shi, B. (2005). A formal specification for Web services composition and verification. In *Proceedings of the Fifth International Conference on Computer and Information Technology* (pp. 252-256). Shanghai, China.

Thatte, S. (2001). *XLANG - Web services for business process design.* Microsoft Corporation.

van der Aalst, W.M.P., Dumas, M., & ter Hofstede, A.H.M. (2003). Web service composition languages: Old wine in new bottles? In *Proceedings of the 29th Euromicro Conference* (pp. 298-305). Belek, Turkey.

WFMC. (2007). Workflow Management Coalition (WfMC). Retrieved June 3, 2007, from http://www.wfmc.org

World Wide Web Consortium (W3C). (2002a). *Web Services Architecture Requirements.*

World Wide Web Consortium (W3C). (2002b). *Web Services Description Language (WSDL) Version 2.0 Part 0: Primer,* W3C Candidate Recommendation, 27 March 2006.

World Wide Web Consortium (W3C). (2002c). The *Platform for Privacy Preferences 1.1 (P3P1.1) Specification,* W3C Working Group Note, 13 November 2006.

World Wide Web Consortium (W3C). (2003). *SOAP Version 1.2 Part 0: Primer (Second Edition,* W3C Proposed Edited Recommendation, 19 December 2006.

World Wide Web Consortium (W3C). (2004a). *OWL Web Ontology Language Overview,* W3C Recommendation, 10 February 2004.

World Wide Web Consortium (W3C). (2004b). Web Services Choreography Description Language Version 1.0, W3C Candidate Recommendation, 9 November 2005.

Yang, J., Papazoglou, M.P., Orriens, B., & van Heuvel, W.J. (2003). A rule based approach to the service composition life-cycle. In *Proceedings of the Fourth International Conference on Web Information Systems Engineering* (pp. 295-298). Rome, Italy.

Chapter IV
High-Value B2B Interactions, Nonrepudiation, and Web Services

Nick Cook
Newcastle University, UK

Paul Robinson
Arjuna Technologies, UK

Santosh K. Shrivastava
Newcastle University, UK

ABSTRACT

This chapter provides an overview of the problem of making high-value business-to-business (B2B) interactions nonrepudiable, where nonrepudiation is the property that no party to an interaction can subsequently deny their involvement in the interaction. Existing approaches are discussed in the context of fundamental work on fairness and nonrepudiation. The existing work suffers from a lack of flexibility both in terms of the mechanisms that can be deployed to achieve nonrepudiation and of the interactions to which nonrepudiation can be applied. The authors contend that it is necessary to be able to render arbitrary Web service interactions nonrepudiable and to optionally invoke application-level validation of business messages at run-time. The chapter presents the design and implementation of a novel Web services-based middleware that addresses these requirements. The middleware leverages existing Web service standards. It is sufficiently flexible to adapt to different regulatory regimes and to provide security guarantees that are appropriate to different business contexts.

INTRODUCTION

It is increasingly common to structure business-to-business (B2B) functions in terms of well-defined business message exchanges between loosely coupled services. This has led to the development of open standards for business conversations. For example, the RosettaNet Partner Interface Process standards (RosettaNet, 2005) define observable B2B interactions in terms of the XML messages that business partners should exchange in order to perform functions such as product line querying and order processing. Business partners use such standards as the basis for agreement on the syntax, semantics and sequencing of messages; and on the B2B processes that they should execute. A problem that then arises is how to ensure that an executing interaction complies with these business agreements. Monitoring for, and enforcement of, compliance implies that interacting parties must be held to account for their actions. That is, it should not be possible to deny participation in a B2B interaction. In this context, nonrepudiation services provide protection against false denial of involvement in communication. A related concern is that honest parties should not suffer disadvantage due to the misbehaviour, or noncooperation, of others.

A typical business message exchange between organisations A and B is shown in Figure 1a. There are two types of message flow: solid lines show the flow of business logic messages and dashed lines the flow of signal messages for acknowledgement of receipt. Party A sends a business message to party B and B provides an acknowledgement of receipt (*ack*) in return. Figure 1b shows an extended interaction where B both acknowledges A's business message and, in step 3, asserts its validity, or otherwise, with respect to agreements governing the interaction. Message validity may relate to some business specific constraints on the content of messages or may be with respect to some contract that governs a cross-organisational business process composed of a number of message exchanges. Essentially, if B signals the validity of a message, they confirm that the message is acceptable for continued processing in the business context. As shown, A is expected to provide an

Figure 1. Typical B2B interactions

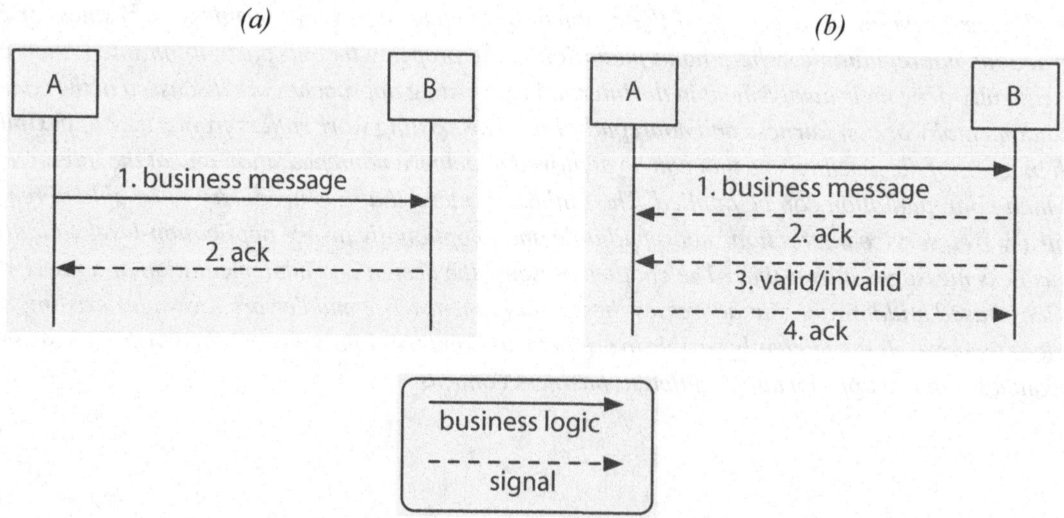

ack for the validation message in step 4. Standards such as RosettaNet define processes in terms of message exchanges that can be mapped to one of the types shown in Figure 1. Now, consider the scenario in which A and B do not unguardedly trust each other and either party may misbehave in some way. For example, B may receive the business message from A but decline to provide the *ack*. This is the selective receipt problem and places A at a disadvantage. Also, unless there is irrefutable evidence of the origin of A's message, A is able to subsequently deny their involvement in the exchange. Similarly, irrefutable evidence of the origin of *ack* is required to subsequently demonstrate B's involvement. The same concerns arise in relation to the exchange of B's validation message for A's *ack*. To address these problems and, thereby, safeguard the interests of both A and B, the simple business message exchange should be made both fair and nonrepudiable. Informally, fairness is the property that well-behaved parties are not disadvantaged by the behaviour of misbehaving parties. Nonrepudiation is the property that an action or event cannot subsequently be denied. The RosettaNet standard specifies whether nonrepudiation is mandatory or optional for a given message exchange. It does not specify the mechanism to achieve nonrepudiation or additional properties such as fairness.

Businesses are adopting Web services as a platform for high-value B2B interactions of the above kind. WS-Security specifies how to apply message-level security. The XML key management specification (XKMS) brings PKI functionality to Web services. The digital signature service (DSS) specifies services for signature verification and secure time-stamps. Implementations of these Web service specifications, and others such as WS-ReliableMessaging and WS-Addressing, represent an essential supporting infrastructure. However, this infrastructure is not sufficient to address the regulatory requirements of high-value B2B interactions. We need additional mechanisms to ensure compliance with business agreements. For example, existing standards cannot guarantee that outcomes are fair to honest participants. Such guarantees are necessary to reduce, if not eliminate, the need to resort to costly dispute resolution. This chapter explores the regulatory mechanisms that are necessary to achieve nonrepudiation and fairness in Web service interactions. It also shows how these mechanisms can be used as building blocks for compliance with business agreements.

The chapter provides an overview of existing solutions to the problem of regulation of B2B interactions. The shortcomings of such solutions are discussed in the context of fundamental work on fairness and nonrepudiation. We motivate our work with a real-world scenario that can be reduced to interactions of the type shown in Figure 1. The scenario demonstrates the need for different approaches, with different security characteristics, to making such interactions nonrepudiable. We describe protocols that are representative of these different approaches. We then present our novel middleware for the regulation of interactions. The middleware leverages Web service standards. It is sufficiently flexible to execute different protocols to suit different regulatory regimes and to provide security guarantees that are appropriate to the given business context. The chapter concludes with suggestions for some further work.

BACKGROUND

This section introduces background to our work, concentrating on examples of existing middleware services for nonrepudiable interaction. We identify shortcomings of existing work that are addressed by the Web services solution presented in the remainder of the chapter. First, we briefly discuss fundamental work on nonrepudiation and fairness that is the basis for the protocols for nonrepudiable B2B interactions.

Nonrepudiation and Fairness

Asokan (1998) provides one of the most widely accepted informal definitions of fairness: that a system is fair if it does not discriminate against correctly behaving parties. More recently, Markowitch, Gollmann, and Kremer (2002) provide an overview of the evolution of the notion of fairness in exchange and the various definitions that have been proposed. To clarify the position, they propose a definition of three mandatory properties that must be satisfied for an exchange protocol to be considered secure: viability, timeliness, and fairness. Viability means that it is possible for an execution of the protocol to result in successful exchange, irrespective of the quality of communication channels. Timeliness is the property that, with the quality of the communication channel fixed, there is always a point in the protocol that can be reached in a finite amount of time when parties can stop the protocol without compromising fairness. The definition of the fairness property is that, with communication channel quality fixed, at the end of the exchange protocol run, either all participants obtain their expected items or they receive none of the information to be exchanged with respect to missing items. They define nonrepudiability as the optional property of a secure exchange that it is impossible for any participant to subsequently deny having participated in a part or the whole of the communication. For nonrepudiation of delivery of a single business message, the sender provides the message and nonrepudiation of origin evidence in exchange for nonrepudiation of receipt evidence from the recipient. The fairness guarantee for the sender is that the recipient must provide a valid receipt in order to obtain the message. The corresponding fairness guarantee for the recipient is that the sender must provide valid evidence of origin in order to obtain the receipt.

There is an extensive literature on the problem of fair exchange and its solution. Kremer, Markowitch, and Zhou (2002) provide a detailed survey of fair nonrepudiation protocols. Wang (2005) includes an updated comparison of deterministic protocols.

The role of a Trusted Third Party (TTP) as guarantor of fairness is central to much of the work on fair exchange. Even and Yacobi (1980) provide the fundamental insight that deterministic fair exchange is impossible without a guarantor TTP. This impossibility result is supported by arguments that relate the problem to the Fischer-Lynch-Paterson (FLP) impossibility result for distributed consensus (Ezhilchelvan & Shrivastava, 2005; Fischer, Lynch, & Paterson, 1985; Pagnia & Gärtner, 1999). Deterministic protocols can be characterised by the level of active involvement of the TTP in an exchange in the normal case. An inline TTP is involved in every message exchange, relaying messages between the other participants. An online TTP is typically only involved in protocol set-up. An off-line TTP is not involved in the normal case and is only called up on to recover fairness for honest participants should normal execution fail. This is the optimistic approach to fair exchange. Inline and online TTPs also recover fairness for honest parties. Recovery of fairness means that the TTP (whether inline, online, or off-line) guarantees that an exchange can terminate without disadvantage to honest parties. The TTP ensures either that honest parties can obtain the items they expect from an exchange or that no party gains any useful additional information from the exchange. This recovery is normally achieved through the execution of subprotocols between protocol participants and the TTP.

The impossibility result and the desire to eliminate the potential bottleneck of a guarantor TTP have led protocol developers to concentrate on the reduction of the involvement of the TTP. This is the main motivation for the optimistic approach to deterministic fair exchange. Other developers have adopted a probabilistic approach that eliminates the need for a guarantor TTP altogether ((Markowitch & Roggeman, 1999) presents an early example). The trade-off for elimination of the guarantor TTP is that there is a non-zero probability of a loss of fairness. Probabilistic protocols are also more communication-intensive than the protocols that offer a deterministic fairness guarantee. Implementation of probabilistic protocols is beyond the scope of this chapter and we will not discuss them further.

Nonrepudiation relies on maintaining the integrity of signed evidence beyond the execution of the given exchange. Because it is possible for a key to become compromised before its expiry, most signature schemes allow the owner of a key to revoke the key. Keys are usually revoked by sending a request to revoke the related certificate to some Certificate Authority. Parties who rely on the validity of a signature also refer to the Certificate Authority for key revocation information. In most commonly used signature schemes, such as the X509 PKI (Housley, Ford, Polk, & Solo, 1999), there is no obligation on the owner of a public key to inform relying parties that they have revoked the corresponding private key. The ability to revoke a private key without reference to relying parties can compromise the long-term integrity of evidence signed with the key. A signing party can use their private key to generate a signature and a relying party can verify the signature upon receipt. However, the signing party can subsequently revoke the key. Without evidence of the time of use of the key, a relying party cannot prove that the signature was generated before key revocation and the signing party can repudiate the evidence. For this reason, if a signing key is revocable, a trusted time-stamp must be applied to signed evidence to demonstrate that the key was not compromised at time of use. Given A's signature s on some data x ($s = sig_A(x)$), a TTP time-stamping authority, TSA, can generate the time-stamp: $\{T_g, sig_{TSA}(s, T_g)\}$ as proof of the generation (or existence) of s at time T_g (Zhou & Gollmann, 1997). Assuming A's key was not revoked at time T_g, the trusted time-stamp prevents A from subsequently denying the validity of s. A TSA is an online TTP. A TTP that provides time-stamping services is a candidate for the provision of other third party services (including that of guarantor TTP for fair exchange protocols). For brevity, we do not show trusted time-stamps in the protocol descriptions. However, they are applied to signatures by our middleware framework during protocol execution.

The FIDES Research Project Fair Exchange Service

The FIDES research project (Nenadic, Zhang, & Barton, 2004) provides services, including TTP services, and an associated application for fair exchange of business items (documents). The project addresses two problems: (1) the development of a family of deterministic fair exchange protocols, and (2) the design and implementation of a system for execution of the protocols. Each enterprise hosts a FIDES server and a set of one or more FIDES clients. A TTP service is available for dispute resolution. Within an enterprise, users interact with the system through GUI-based clients that provide secure access to the services hosted by their local FIDES server. The FIDES server at one enterprise executes fair exchange protocols with a peer server at another enterprise. FIDES servers also execute recovery protocols with the TTP service. Items for exchange are stored in a secure database. FIDES services are implemented on a J2EE application server. Java Messaging Service (JMS) is used for both client-to-server and server-to-server communication. Application clients submit documents to their local FIDES system for fair exchange with partners who also have a FIDES client for verifying and receipting the documents they receive. In effect, FIDES offers a standalone service for fair exchange.

A drawback of the approach is that the only interaction with the exchange protocol service is through FIDES application clients. There is no published API for client-side interaction with a FIDES server or for the server-to-server execution of protocols. Users are therefore restricted to an application-specific mechanism for the exchange of items. Other than user agreement to involvement in an exchange, there is no support for run-time validation of the interaction with respect to contract. Any contractual constraints that should be imposed must be dealt with during negotiation of the items to be exchanged, and of the parameters of the exchange. Nevertheless, as far as we are aware, the FIDES project and our work presented in this chapter represent the only service-based implementations of fair exchange.

Typical Commercial Approach

BEA's WebLogic Trading Partner Integration Engine (TPIE) (BEA, 2005) is typical of commercial approaches to the regulation of B2B interactions. As shown in Figure 2, the Trading Partner Integration Engine (TPIE) is integrated with the application server. Nonrepudiation is provided as a component of the TPIE.

In the BEA system, trading partners agree protocol bindings for their business conversations. Currently, they provide bindings for the ebXML (Grangard, Eisenberg, & Nickull, 2001) and RosettaNet PIP standards. The protocol binding to use at run-time is then configured in the B2BDefaultWebApp component of each partner's TPIE. The trading partners have the option to apply signatures to the messages of the given business protocol. The nonrepudiation service handles the application and verification of signatures at run-time. The service also provides secure audit and time-stamping services. Interfaces to these support services have been defined to allow the plug-in of third-party providers. The BEA system is interesting because they provide nonrepudiation of XML-based business message exchanges that are validated with respect to the business protocol binding in use. This is a form of regulated B2B interaction. The nonrepudiation is voluntary. There is no support for fair exchange and there is no mechanism to introduce protocols to provide

Figure 2. BEA WebLogic Trading Partner Integration Engine

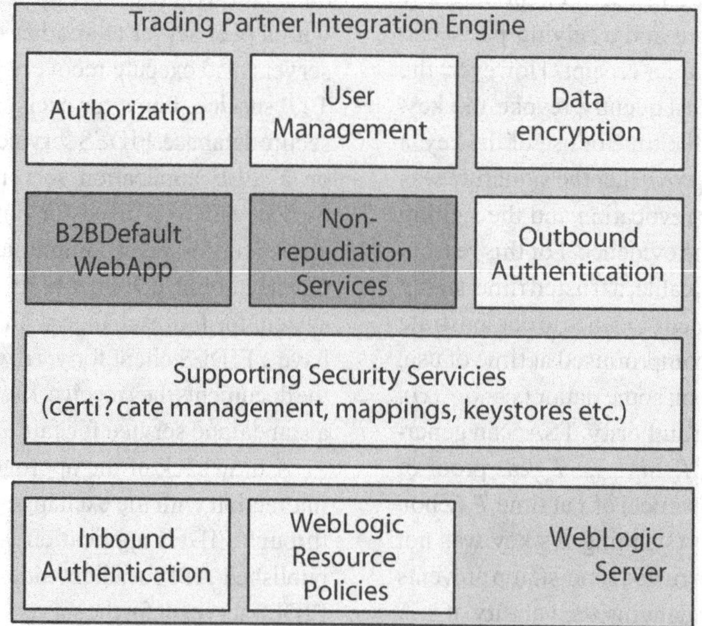

fair exchange. In effect, nonrepudiation of receipt is only available when acknowledgements are specified as part of the run-time business protocol binding. Similarly, validation with respect to contract is only available for the supported business protocol bindings. It is not possible to apply systematic validation with respect to other types of contract or agreement, or to make such validated interactions nonrepudiable. In fact, it is not clear whether it is possible to verify that some agreed composition of PIP exchanges is adhered to correctly.

Summary

In this section, we provided an overview of related background work. The main drawback of these approaches is their inflexibility. FIDES is the only other work we are aware of that takes account of fundamental work on fair exchange and nonrepudiation. They have taken what is in effect a human user centric, proprietary approach. Interorganisational communication is not based on any Web service or other standard for the exchange of business messages. They provide a closed system that is not amenable to interaction with or between Web services.

The state of the art in industry is to provide voluntary nonrepudiation. At the basic level this involves the signing of outgoing messages and the verification of incoming messages, equivalent to voluntary nonrepudiation of origin of messages. Aside from the BEA offering, there are commercial solutions that will provide these operations as part of an XML firewall (see Verisign, 2004; IBM DataPower, 2004). These solutions do not provide the systematic exchange of evidence to achieve nonrepudiation of receipt or to guarantee fairness. However, protocol execution could be built on top of such solutions.

BEA and others in the application server market do provide implementations of standards such as RosettaNet PIP and ebXML that provide a form of validation with respect to business agreement. As noted, voluntary nonrepudiation of receipt is also supported when dictated by the standard being used. There is no provision for general support for validation with respect to contract or the systematic support for nonrepudiable exchange described in this chapter.

The identified drawbacks have led to our systematic and flexible approach to nonrepudiable message exchange and the validation of messages with respect to business agreements. We contend that it is necessary to be able to render arbitrary Web service interactions nonrepudiable and to optionally invoke application-level validation at run-time. This validation must be correctly correlated with the nonrepudiation evidence and, to provide systematic support, the underlying mechanism should be agnostic about the validation process. Further, as will be apparent from the discussion in the following section, different underlying mechanisms may be required even by the same interacting entities in different contexts. The remainder of this chapter presents a middleware solution that addresses these requirements

The ability to invoke arbitrary application-level validation of messages at run-time is a key feature of our approach. This is essentially an extensibility mechanism that allows the middleware to become an enforcement engine not only for business standards such as RosettaNet, but also for other forms of electronic contract. We do not specify how contracts are formulated, verified, or encoded. This is the subject of related but separate research on contract-mediated interaction, of which examples include: (Minsky & Ungureanu, 2000; Milosevic, Gibson, Linnington, Cole, & Kulkarni, 2004; Molina-Jimenez, Shrivastava, & Warne, 2005).

PROTOCOLS FOR NONREPUDIABLE AND VALIDATED BUSINESS MESSAGE DELIVERY

We now present three approaches to achieving the nonrepudiation of interactions of the type described in the introduction to the chapter. The first approach uses voluntary nonrepudiation typical of current commercial solutions. The second approach uses an inline TTP to guarantee the fairness of exchanges. This is a service-oriented approach where the responsibilities of the TTP can be adjusted to suit the capabilities of the exchange endpoints. The third approach involves the direct (optimistic) exchange of items between participants and the involvement of an off-line TTP to guarantee fairness. For each approach, we present protocols for the nonrepudiable exchange of a business message for its receipt (see Figure 1a) and then for nonrepudiation of a validated business message exchange (see Figure 1b). The protocol descriptions are not specific to Web services. We address their execution in our Web services middleware framework, including support for application-level validation of business messages, after discussing the protocols.

First, to provide a concrete context for the subsequent discussion, we present an example of B2B collaboration in chemical manufacturing. The example scenario demonstrates the need for a flexible solution to nonrepudiation with the ability to execute different protocols to meet the requirements of different business relationships and application contexts. From this scenario, we derive a flexible interceptor-based model for protocol-based interactions and summarise the nonrepudiation requirements. Protocol notation and assumptions then precede the protocol descriptions.

The protocols presented in this section are based on existing work published by Coffey and Saidha (1996) and Wang (2005). The various extensions and modifications to the published protocols are based on work published in Cook, Robinson, and Shrivastava (2006). It should be noted that, for brevity, the protocol descriptions in this section do not include the specification of trusted time-stamps. It is assumed that if revocable keys are used to generate signed evidence, then time-stamps of the kind discussed previously will be included in protocol messages. An analysis of the costs of time-stamping is provided in the summary to this section.

An Example Application Scenario

Increasingly, chemical companies are seeking to form alliances, or virtual organisations (VOs), that can rapidly prototype new chemical processes prior to full-scale manufacture of products. These alliances will typically include a lead company that subcontracts work to consultants for process simulation and to equipment manufacturers to design prototype plants. The example presented here is derived from the study of a collaborative B2B process to determine the feasibility of developing a new chemical manufacturing facility (see the Gold project; Periorellis, Cook, Hiden, Conlin, Hamilton, Wu, et al., 2006).

Figure 3 represents a small part of the overall B2B process. In any scenario of this kind, we can distinguish between two types of participant: business partners and TTPs. The consultancy and the manufacturer, represented by white rectangles, are business partners who wish to engage in a mutually advantageous collaboration. To support the process they may agree to use TTP services. The trusted service provider (TSP), represented by a grey rectangle, is a TTP. By definition, TTPs always fulfil the commitments that they make and will cooperate with other correctly behaving parties. In contrast, there is a risk that a business partner may cease cooperation or may be unable or unwilling to fulfil their commitments to the collaboration.

All interactions in Figure 3 are between or with Web services that are hosted either by the business partners or by the TSP that supports the operation of the VO. The lead company (not shown) requires that all project documents (task outputs) must be placed in a shared repository hosted by the TSP that is responsible for managing access to the documents. The subprocess essentially illustrates the end of one task by a consultancy company and

Figure 3. Chemical development WS interaction

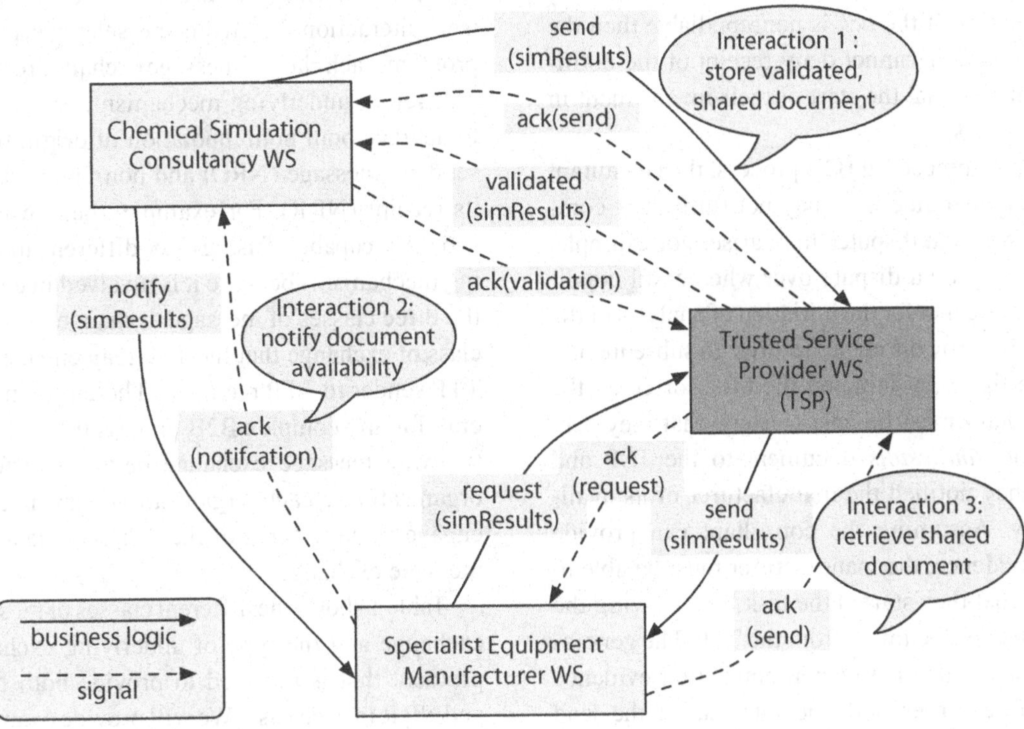

the resulting initiation of a subsequent task at a specialist equipment manufacturer. The consultancy company conducts simulation experiments. The output of these experiments is a simulation results report (*simResults*) that the consultancy stores with the TSP (interaction 1 in Figure 3). Storage of the document requires acknowledgement of receipt by the TSP and validation that the document complies with a structure specified by the lead company. The specialist equipment manufacturer must analyse the *simResults* to determine requirements for construction of a pilot plant for further experimental evaluation of the proposed new chemical manufacturing process. Interaction 2 in Figure 3 shows the consultancy company triggering this task by notifying the manufacturer of the availability of the validated *simResults* document. This task initiation must be acknowledged. Interaction 3 shows the manufacturer starting their task by retrieving the document from the TSP. The request for the document and its provision by the TSP must be acknowledged. As shown, each interaction entails a B2B message exchange of one of the types shown in Figure 1. Interaction 3, is a combination of two of the B2B message exchanges shown in Figure 1a.

The lead company requires that there is an audit trail of the critical interactions between organisations. Critical actions include the storage and retrieval of task outputs and the initiation of tasks. Furthermore, in order to irrefutably bind parties to the actions and commitments that are signified by the interactions, the audit trail must be nonrepudiable. For example, the manufacturer's *ack* in Interaction 2 represents a commitment to start the task triggered by the availability of *simResults*. If the *ack* is nonrepudiable then the manufacturer cannot deny receipt of the notification to signal the start of their involvement in the process.

In the preceding B2B process, the consultant and the manufacturer may not fulfil their commitments and disputes may arise. For example, there may be a dispute over whether all conditions were met for the initiation of analysis of the *simResults* by the manufacturer. To subsequently prove that they initiated the task correctly, the consultant must be able to show that they sent a valid *simResults* document to the TSP and that they notified the manufacturer of its availability. Assuming the consultant can provide this evidence, the manufacturer must be able to show that they started the task by retrieving the *simResults* document from the TSP. The generation and collection of nonrepudiation evidence therefore serves both the interests of the lead company and of well-behaved participants in the process. However, the generation and collection of evidence involves the cooperation of both the TTP and the business partners. Each interaction in Figure 3 is composed from the exchange of a message for an acknowledgement of its receipt. We can group these message exchanges into three classes, characterised by the relationship between the parties: (1) business partner sender to TTP recipient (see phase 1 of Interaction 1 or 3); (2) TTP sender to business partner recipient (see phase 2 of Interactions 1 or 3); and (3) business partner sender to business partner recipient (see Interaction 2). Given the selective receipt problem, each class of message exchange requires a different underlying mechanism, or protocol, to achieve both nonrepudiation of origin of the sender's message (NRO) and nonrepudiation of its receipt (NRR). For example, the consultant should be capable of using three different underlying mechanisms because it is involved in each of the three classes of message exchange. A fourth class of exchange that the TSP may engage in is TTP sender to TTP recipient. Therefore, in general, for any complex B2B process that involves two-way message exchange between different organisations, each organisation may need to engage in up to three of the different classes of message exchange.

Table 1 shows the different classes of message exchange and the type of underlying exchange protocol that is required to provide both NRO and NRR in each case. We will provide examples of each protocol type, starting with voluntary exchange and then fair exchange. Finally, we will consider *receipt-first exchange* where a TTP obtains a receipt for an item before releasing the item. We will show that receipt-first exchange is a simplification of fair exchange. Of the protocol types, fair exchange offers the strongest guarantees. However, fair exchange can also be the most costly in terms of communications, computation and infrastructure. It therefore makes sense for the sender of a message to be able to adopt an

Table 1. Exchange classification

Sender	Recipient	Protocol type
TTP	TTP	voluntary exchange
business partner	TTP	voluntary exchange
TTP	business partner	receipt-first exchange
business partner	business partner	fair exchange

exchange mechanism that is appropriate to their relationship with the intended recipient. Further, different capabilities may lead to the need to use different protocols even within a protocol type. As an example, we will show how to adapt a fair exchange protocol to different endpoint capabilities. That is, even in the context of a single B2B process, organisations may need to be flexible about the mechanisms that they use to achieve non-repudiation. We now describe a model for interaction that can address this need for the flexibility of protocol-based nonrepudiable interaction.

We are interested in business interactions that consist of one or more exchanges of messages for their acknowledgement. Figure 4a presents an abstract view of such interactions between two endpoint participants (A and B) in some B2B process. Our requirements are:

1. To render message exchange between A and B nonrepudiable. That is, the sender of a business message should provide nonrepudiation of origin (NRO) of the message and its recipient should provide nonrepudiation of receipt (NRR).
2. To allow the use of different protocols to exchange nonrepudiation evidence that is appropriate to different application and security contexts.
3. To support business message validation with respect to application-level agreements.

Figure 4. Interceptor-mediated nonrepudiable interaction

(a) Business interaction

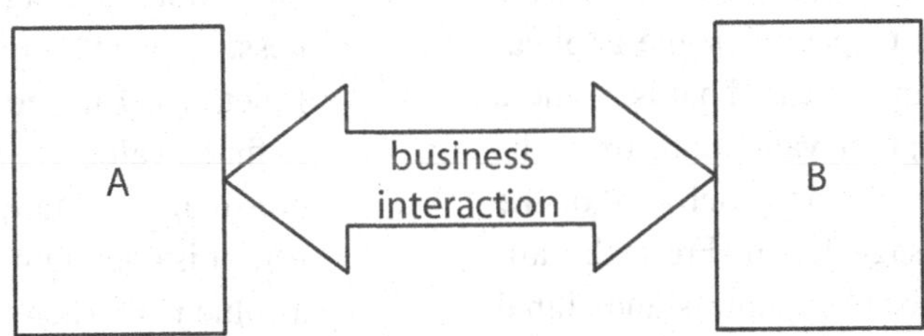

(b) Mediated nonrepudiable interaction

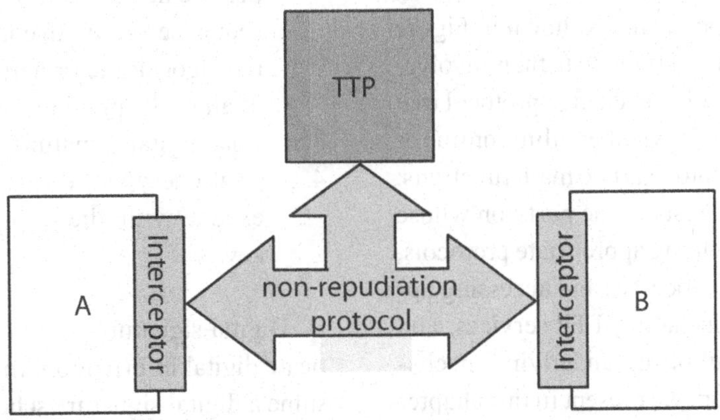

Validation processes must be independent of nonrepudiation mechanism yet validation decisions should be made nonrepudiable. That is, we require nonrepudiation of origin of validation decisions (NROV) and nonrepudiation of receipt of validation decisions (NRRV).

4. To provide the same high-level abstraction of business interaction between A and B shown in Figure 4a regardless of the underlying mechanisms used to achieve the exchange of nonrepudiation evidence. That is, the application processes at either A or B should not be modified to meet the other requirements.

For delivery of a single business message, the precise application-level semantics are that the business message is only processed by the recipient application if the exchange of all related nonrepudiation evidence succeeds. When validation is incorporated in the exchange, the business message is only processed if the message is deemed valid with respect to some application-specific validation process. That is, if there is a failure in exchange or validation, from the application viewpoint it is as if delivery of the related business message failed. From the application viewpoint, for the business and signal messages shown in Figures 1 and 3, either all the messages are valid and are delivered successfully, or the interaction fails.

To address these requirements we adopt an interceptor-based approach. As shown in Figure 4b, interceptors at A and B mediate their involvement in a nonrepudiation exchange protocol that may also involve a TTP (whether inline, online or off-line). The interceptor has two main functions: (i) to protect the interests of the party on whose behalf it acts by executing appropriate protocols, invoking validation processes and accessing appropriate services, including TTP services; and (ii) to hide the detail of the underlying mechanisms. The framework we present in this chapter is a Web services realisation of this model. The following protocol descriptions are an indication of the range of mechanisms that can be deployed in the framework. As we shall see, for business partner to business partner interactions, it is a TTP responsibility to deliver fairness guarantees. The introduction of interceptors allows us to hide such protocol details. For simplicity, in the following protocol descriptions we make no distinction between A and the interceptor that acts on their behalf, or between B and their interceptor.

Protocol Assumptions and Notation

We make the following standard perfect cryptography assumptions (Schneier, 1996).

1. That message digests that are generated by secure hash functions are easy to compute, compress arbitrary length input to a fixed length output (the digest), are first and second pre-image resistant and are collision resistant. First pre-image resistance, or one-wayness, means that given a digest H and hash function $h()$, it is computationally infeasible to find a value x such that $H = h(x)$. Second pre-image resistance means that given x and $h(x)$, it is computationally infeasible to find a value $y \neq x$ such that $h(x) = h(y)$. Collision resistance is the property that if $h(x) = h(y)$ then with effective probability of 1, $x = y$.
2. That it is computationally infeasible to predict the next bit of a secure pseudo-random sequence even with complete knowledge of the algorithmic or hardware generator and of all of the previous bits in the sequence.
3. That digital signatures cannot be forged
4. That encrypted data cannot be decrypted except with the appropriate decryption key.

Digital signatures cryptographically authenticate digital information. In this chapter, we assume a digital signature scheme based on public key cryptography, where each entity has a pair of keys: one public and the other private. Public key cryptography has the following properties: (1) it is computationally infeasible to compute a private key from its corresponding public key; (2) a ciphertext generated using a public key can only be decrypted using the corresponding private key; and (3) a ciphertext generated using a private key can only be decrypted using the corresponding public key. It is this last property that supports digital signatures. Given a key pair and some input x, a digital signature scheme consists of a signing algorithm and a verification algorithm. The signer produces a signature by using their private key to encrypt x. The verifier users the signer's public key to decrypt x and therefore verify the validity of the signature. Without loss of generality, we assume that signature schemes are nonrecoverable. That is, the verifier of a signature over input x can only determine that the signature is valid. They cannot learn any other useful information about x from the signature alone. In practice, a signature is typically created by using a private key to encrypt the digest of inputs as opposed to the inputs themselves. The cryptographic binding between an input x and its digest, $h(x)$, means that it is effectively impossible to modify x and for $h(x)$ to remain valid. Therefore a signature over $h(x)$ is treated as equivalent to a signature over x and, given the fixed length of digests, it is more efficient to sign $h(x)$ than x.

A protocol specifies the correct behaviour of its participants. Well-behaved (honest) parties adhere to a given protocol specification. We make the following assumptions about communications between well-behaved parties and their cooperation in protocol execution.

1. The communication channel between well-behaved parties provides eventual message delivery. That is, there is a known bound on the number of temporary network and computer related failures between well-behaved parties.
2. Each well-behaved party has persistent storage for messages. Minimally, well-behaved parties will ensure that messages are available for as long as is necessary to meet their obligations to other parties. They may require longer-term storage for their own purposes.
3. Well-behaved parties only send messages that meet the specification of the protocol being executed. Similarly, they only process messages that are correct with respect to the protocol specification.

TTPs are well-behaved parties by definition. For the purposes of this discussion, "trusted," "honest," and "correctly behaving" are synonyms of well-behaved.

Table 2 defines the notation used in protocol descriptions. Other, more complex tokens can be generated from the elements indicated. We assume that a protocol run identifier, *id* is unique for an interaction context. That is, *id* need not be globally unique but must be sufficiently unique to unambiguously distinguish between different protocol runs in a given context. The protocol run identifier may be an opaque value that simply satisfies this uniqueness property. Alternatively, it is common in non-repudiation protocols to cryptographically bind a protocol run identifier to other elements of protocol messages. Then, as indicated in Table 2, the identifier may be defined by some generating function. For example, the identifier may be generated from a secure hash of a random number ($id = h(rn)$). In this case, *id* can be used as a commitment to the random number, *rn*, that can in turn act as an authentication token in a protocol. We assume that the protocol initiator is responsible for generation of an identifier. We also assume that if an identifier is not unique then it will be rejected by the recipient, triggering re-start of a protocol with a newly generated identifier.

Table 2. Protocol notation

Notation	Description
$h(x)$	secure hash of x
$sig_P(x)$	principal P's signature over x (using P's private key)
$enc_P(x)$	encryption of x with P's public key
rn	secure pseudo-random number
$id_{[i]}\ [= f()]$	unique protocol run identifier with optional index i to differentiate between 2 or more identifiers and optional generating function
x, y	concatenation of items x and y
payload	arbitrary application data sent as payload of a protocol message (e.g., the original business message)
VAL | *INVAL*	signifies validity or invalidity of application level business message
$P \rightarrow Q : \{x, y \ldots\}$	P sends message containing items $\{x, y \ldots\}$ to Q

Voluntary Nonrepudiable Exchange

In a voluntary nonrepudiable exchange, there is no mechanism to enforce the provision of nonrepudiation information. This is the approach adopted by current commercial solutions (see BEA's WebLogic TPIE) and envisaged by Reactivity's proposed standard for Web services nonrepudiation (Gravengaard, Goodale, Hanson, Roddy, & Walkowski, 2003). In essence, to achieve voluntary nonrepudiation each party simply signs the messages that they send.

Figure 5 shows a voluntary nonrepudiation protocol for the interaction in Figure 1a. In step 1, A sends B the business message *payload* along with a protocol run identifier id_1, the participant identifiers and their NRO token. The NRO token (NRO_A) consists of A's signature over the other items they send. Assuming B verifies the information sent by A, in step 2 they return a receipt message consisting of the protocol run and participant identifiers, and their NRR token. The NRR token (NRR_B) consists of B's signature over the other items they send and A's NRO token.

The preceding protocol is voluntary because there is no guarantee that B will send the receipt to A in step 2, the selective receipt problem. A protocol of this type is suitable if the business message recipient (B in this case) is trusted to provide a receipt. For example, this approach

Figure 5. Voluntary nonrepudiation protocol

$$1 \quad A \rightarrow B : \{id_1, A, B, payload, NRO_A\}$$
$$2 \quad B \rightarrow A : \{id_1, A, B, NRR_B\}$$

where:

$$NRO_A = sig_A(id_1, A, B, payload)$$
$$NRR_B = sig_B(id_1, A, B, NRO_A)$$

could be used for non-repudiation of the storage of the *simResults* document in Figure 3. In that scenario, TSP is a trusted entity that will provide a receipt to A.

Now, recall the validated message exchange shown in Figure 1b. A sends a business message to B for which B returns an *ack*. Subsequently, B signals the validity, or otherwise, of the message and A returns an *ack* for B's validation message. If we treat the validation information generated by B in the same way as business message payload, then we can use two correlated runs of the protocol in Figure 5 to make a validated exchange nonrepudiable. Figure 6 shows this extension. The first run (steps 1.1 and 1.2) is identical to the exchange in Figure 5. In the second run (steps 2.1 and 2.2), B provides their validation information along with nonrepudiation of validation ($NROV_B$) and A provides nonrepudiation of receipt of validation ($NRRV_A$). The protocol run identifier, id_1, is included and signed in steps 2.1 and 2.2 to correlate the two runs of the voluntary protocol. Again, the exchange suffers from the selective receipt problem. That is, A must trust B to provide the receipt in step 1.2 and B must trust A to provide the receipt in step 2.2. If B does not require a receipt, and is able to perform immediate validation of A's original message, then the validated exchange can be simplified to a version of the two-step protocol of Figure 5. In this case, B appends the validation information and $NROV_B$ to the second message. A protocol of this type could be used for validation on storage of the *simResults* document in the example application scenario.

Fair Nonrepudiable Exchange

We now show how to use fair exchange protocols to make business interactions non-repudiable. We describe a family of protocols that use an in-line TTP. The exchange endpoints only communicate through the TTP who is then able to guarantee fairness to well-behaved parties. The protocols are based on a verified fair nonrepudiation protocol developed by Coffey and Saidha (1996) with subsequent improvements by Zhou and Gollmann (1997). After describing this basic protocol, we introduce our modifications to the protocol to support lightweight endpoints and to

Figure 6. Voluntary nonrepudiable exchange with validation

Run 1 of voluntary protocol:

1.1	$A \rightarrow B$:	$\{id_1, A, B, payload, NRO_A\}$
1.2	$B \rightarrow A$:	$\{id_1, A, B, NRR_B\}$

Run 2 of voluntary protocol:

2.1	$B \rightarrow A$:	$\{id_2, A, B, id_1, VAL\|INVAL, NROV_B\}$
2.2	$A \rightarrow B$:	$\{id_2, A, B, id_1, NRRV_A\}$

where:

$NRO_A = sig_A(id_1, A, B, payload)$

$NRR_B = sig_B(id_1, A, B, NRO_A)$

$NROV_B = sig_B(id_2, A, B, id_1, VAL|INVAL)$

$NRRV_A = sig_A(id_2, A, B, id_1, NROV_B)$

integrate application-level message validation. We also define subprotocols for timely termination of an exchange that guarantee fairness in the event of the noncooperation, or misbehaviour, of an endpoint.

Fair exchange with inline TTP is well suited to a service-oriented environment in which there is some trusted hub for communication between business partners. For example, the TSP in the chemical development scenario could provide such a service. However, there will be scenarios in which no sufficiently trusted hub exists or the use of the hub for every nonrepudiable exchange is too costly. In such cases, it is useful to only engage the services of a TTP when the misbehaviour of a business partner (or its endpoint) threatens to compromise fairness for a well-behaved party. There has been significant research on optimistic (off-line TTP) fair exchange protocols that address the preceding requirements. In an optimistic exchange, communicating parties exchange evidence directly and only involve a TTP in the event of noncooperation. After the discussion of fair exchange with inline TTP, we briefly describe the most efficient protocol for optimistic fair exchange. We also explain how to use the protocol to integrate message validation.

Fair Exchange with Inline TTP

The aim of the Coffey-Saidha protocol is for the sender (A) of a business message, or *payload* in the notation, to obtain nonrepudiation of receipt for the message from the recipient (B). Figure 7 shows normal execution of the main protocol. It is followed by a step-by-step commentary.

Step 1: A starts the protocol by sending protocol run and participant identifiers, the business message *payload* and their NRO token to the TTP. All items are encrypted with the TTP's public key to ensure that B does not obtain the items before providing non-repudiation of receipt. At this step, if the TTP finds that the *id* is not unique and is unable to continue with the protocol, an appropriate response is sent to A to prompt restart of the protocol with a newly generated *id*. Otherwise, the protocol proceeds to step 2

Step 2: The TTP provides proof of submission (NRS_{TTP}) to A to signal the TTP's willingness to proceed with protocol execution. We added this step to the protocol to give A an immediate assurance that the exchange will commence. NRS_{TTP} is sufficient for this

Figure 7. Main Coffey-Saidha protocol

1	$A \rightarrow TTP$	:	$\{enc_{TTP}(id, A, B, TTP, payload, NRO_A)\}$
2	$TTP \rightarrow A$	:	$\{id, NRS_{TTP}\}$
3	$TTP \rightarrow B$	:	$\{id, A, B, TTP, h(payload)\}$
4	$B \rightarrow TTP$	:	$\{enc_{TTP}(id, NRR_B)\}$
5	$TTP \rightarrow A$	:	$\{id, NRR_B\}$
6	$TTP \rightarrow B$	:	$\{id, payload, NRO_A\}$

where:

$NRO_A = sig_A(id, A, B, TTP, h(payload))$

$NRS_{TTP} = sig_{TTP}(id, A, B, TTP)$

$NRR_B = sig_B(id, A, B, TTP, h(payload))$

purpose but does not constitute a receipt for the *payload* because only the identifiers are signed. This step may be executed in parallel with step 3.

Step 3: To enable B to construct NRR_B, the TTP sends the identifiers and *h(payload)* to B. This is sufficient information for B to be able to generate a receipt but does not give B access to the *payload.*

Step 4: B responds with NRR_B. It is safe for B to send the receipt to the TTP before obtaining the *payload* because the TTP is trusted to provide the *payload* in return. All items are encrypted with the TTP's public key to ensure that A can only obtain the receipt if the exchange of evidence terminates successfully.

Step 5: The TTP relays NRR_B to A. This step may be executed in parallel with step 6.

Step 6: The TTP sends the *payload* and associated NRO_A to B.

At the end of execution of the protocol, A has acquired NRS_{TTP} and NRR_B, nonrepudiation of submission and receipt. In return, B has acquired *payload* and NRO_A, the business message *payload* and nonrepudiation of its origin. The TTP can guarantee fairness of the exchange because they control the release of information to A and B. On successful completion of the protocol, the TTP sets the termination state of the exchange to *SUCCEEDED*.

Timely Termination of Exchange

In order to achieve timely termination of an exchange, and at the same time preserve fairness, A or B may request that the TTP terminate execution of the main protocol in Figure 7. In this case, an abort or resolve sub-protocol is executed between the endpoint and the TTP. It is the TTP's responsibility to determine from the state of an exchange whether it can be aborted or whether it must be completed (resolved). Step 4 is the pivotal point of the protocol. Once the TTP has received NRR_B in step 4, they have all the information necessary to complete the exchange. Prior to this point, noncooperation by B means that the exchange can only be aborted. After this point, the TTP releases critical information to A and B (in steps 5 and 6) and the TTP must complete the exchange for any well-behaved party. A or

Figure 8. Coffey-Saidha abort subprotocol

1	*P → TTP*	:	$\{id_p, ABORT, id, sig_P(h(id_p, ABORT, id))\}$
2	if *ABORTED* or (not *SUCCEEDED* and *lastStep* < 5) then:		
	TTP → P	:	$\{id_p, ABORTED, id, NRABORT\}$
	else if *P* is *A* then:		
	TTP → *A*	:	$\{id_p, SUCCEEDED, id, NRSUCCEED, NRS_{TTP}, NRR_B\}$
	else:		
	TTP → *B*	:	$\{id_p, SUCCEEDED, id, NRSUCCEED, payload, NRO_A\}$

where:

id_l is a sub-protocol run identifier

NRABORT $= sig_{TTP}(id_p, ABORTED, id)$

NRSUCCEED $= sig_{TTP}(id_p, SUCCEEDED, id)$

B initiate an abort or resolve sub-protocol by sending a request to the TTP. We define the abort sub-protocol in Figure 8.

The abort subprotocol starts with a signed abort request from one of the endpoint participants ($P \in \{A, B\}$). To correlate the request with the exchange to which it relates, the request includes a new protocol identifier, id_P, and the identifier of the associated main protocol, *id*. The TTP checks the local exchange status that consists of the exchange termination state and the number of the last step executed in the main protocol (*lastStep*). As shown, the exchange can be aborted if the exchange termination state is already *ABORTED* **or** the termination state has not already been set to *SUCCEEDED* and the main protocol has not progressed beyond step 4. If the exchange can be aborted, the TTP sends a message that signals aborted exchange to the sub-protocol initiator. This message includes nonrepudiation of abort token (*NRABORT*) signed by the TTP. If not already set, the TTP now sets the termination state to *ABORTED.* If the exchange cannot be aborted (because the termination state is already *SUCCEEDED* or the main protocol has progressed beyond step 4), then the TTP returns a participant-specific resolve message. This message signals successful completion of the exchange with a signed *NRSUCCEED* token and provides the items that the participant expects from the exchange. For A, the expected items are NRS_{TTP} and NRR_B. For B, the expected items are *payload* and NRO_A If not already set, the TTP now sets the termination state to *SUCCEEDED.* The corresponding resolve sub-protocol is the same except that: (i) the initial message is a resolve request (= $\{id_P, RESOLVE, id, sig_P(id_P, RESOLVE, id)\}$) and (ii) the TTP only responds with an abort token if the exchange cannot be completed successfully because termination state is already *ABORTED* or the main protocol has not reached step 4 yet.

Once the TTP has set termination state, either following normal termination of the main protocol or after execution of an abort or resolve subprotocol, the TTP will forever respond in the same way to any subsequent termination request.

Modifications for Lightweight Endpoints

Up to now we have assumed that endpoint processing environments are such that they are able to verify each other's signatures (have access to and can verify each other's public key certificates) and that they have facilities for secure long-term storage of nonrepudiation evidence. However, the TTP's mediator role allows us to adapt the Coffey-Saidha protocol to support more lightweight endpoint environments. The TTP can take on responsibility for endpoint signature verification and long-term storage of evidence. To achieve this, in steps 5 and 6 the TTP does not simply relay the NRO and NRR token provided by A and B. Instead, the TTP produces its own token:

$$NRR_{TTP} = NRO_{TTP} = sig_{TTP}(id, A, B, TTP, h(payload))$$

and sends this to A in place of NRR_A and to B in place NRO_A. This replacement serves as the TTP's guarantee that they have seen, verified and will store all related evidence, including NRO_A and NRR_B, for future reference. It essentially certifies that the TTP can prove both nonrepudiation of origin and nonrepudiation of receipt of the *payload.* This reduces the verification work that A and B have to perform to that of verifying the signature and associated credentials of the TTP. This means that exchange endpoints may only require credential management at the level used by the typical Web browser rather than access to the more comprehensive PKI infrastructure required to verify evidence from all parties that they may interact with. Further, A and B only need provide long-term storage to correlate a business message exchange with nonrepudiation evidence that the TTP holds in long-term secure logs. Of course, a corresponding asymmetric modification to the protocol can be made if only one of A or

B is lightweight and the other is able to process all nonrepudiation evidence.

Corresponding changes are made to abort and resolve subprotocols to provide the items that A and B expect from a lightweight exchange.

Extension for Payload Validation

Neither of the above versions of the Coffey-Saidha protocol provides nonrepudiable validation of *payload*. As with voluntary exchange, we could support nonrepudiation of validation by correlating two runs of the protocol. However, the presence of an inline TTP means that a more efficient extension is possible. The extension adds three extra steps to the protocol to integrate application-level validation of *payload*. A secure pseudo-random number (*rn*), generated by A is used as an authenticator for the TTP to acknowledge B's validation decision. Figure 9 shows the extended protocol. It is followed by a discussion of the modifications to integrate validation.

In step 1, in addition to the items provided in the original protocol, A send *rn* to the TTP. There is now a generating function for the protocol run identifier, *id*. This function is a hash of the participant identifiers with *rn*. Because the TTP receives all the items necessary to verify the integrity of *id* in step 1, B can also rely on its integrity. Thus, *id* can subsequently be used by B to verify the authenticity of *rn*. As shown, because *id* is cryptographically bound to the participant identifiers, it is only necessary to sign *id*, and not the other identifiers, when generating the nonrepudiation tokens. Steps 2 to 6 of the protocol remain the same. Then in step 7, B sends their validation message and $NROV_B$ token to the TTP. In step 8, the TTP acknowledges receipt of the validation message by sending *rn* to B. Up to this point *rn* was only known to A and the TTP and, as noted, it is cryptographically bound to *id*. *rn* therefore represents an authenticated acknowledgement for B's validation message and serves the same purpose as the $NRRV_A$ token

Figure 9. Extended Coffey-Saidha protocol for validation of payload

1	$A \rightarrow TTP$	:	$\{enc_{TTP}(id, A, B, TTP, rn, payload, NRO_A)\}$
2	$TTP \rightarrow A$	:	$\{id, NRS_{TTP}\}$
3	$TTP \rightarrow B$	:	$\{id, A, B, TTP, h(payload)\}$
4	$B \rightarrow TTP$	:	$\{ enc_{TTP}(id, NRR_B)\}$
5	$TTP \rightarrow A$	:	$\{id, NRR_B\}$
6	$TTP \rightarrow B$	:	$\{id, payload, NRO_A\}$
7	$B \rightarrow TTP$	:	$\{ enc_{TTP}(id, VAL\vert INVAL, NROV_B)\}$
8	$TTP \rightarrow B$	:	$\{id, rn\}$
9	$TTP \rightarrow A$	:	$\{id, VAL\vert INVAL, NROV_B\}$

where:

$id = h(A, B, TTP, rn)$

$NRO_A = sig_A(id, h(payload))$

$NRS_{TTP} = sig_{TTP}(h(id))$

$NRR_B = sig_B(id, h(payload)))$

$NROV_B = sig_B(id, VAL\vert INVAL)$

from the protocol shown in Figure 6. In step 9, the TTP relays B's validation message to A. This completes the successful exchange of *payload*, a decision on its validity and associated evidence of the origin and receipt of messages. As for the Coffey-Saidha protocol without validation of payload, this extended version can be adapted to support lightweight endpoints. In this case, the TTP sends $NROV_{TTP} = sig_{TTP}(h(id, VAL|INVAL))$ in place of $NROV_B$.

There are corresponding extensions to the abort and resolve subprotocols to provide fair timely termination of an exchange. Details are published in Cook et al. (2006).

Optimistic Fair Exchange with Off-Line TTP

We now use Wang's protocol (Wang, 2005) as an example of how to perform optimistic, fair, non-repudiable exchange of a message for its acknowledgement. The protocol is of interest because it is the most efficient of the existing deterministic fair exchange protocols. Again, A wishes to send business message *payload* to B and in return B should provide a receipt. In the protocol, A first sends receipt input information for B to sign in order to generate a receipt. B then sends the receipt to A and then A sends the *payload* to B. The key insights behind the protocol are:

1. That A's interests are safeguarded because they obtain a receipt for the *payload* before sending the *payload* to B.
2. B's interests can be safeguarded if the receipt input is cryptographically bound to the *payload* through A's evidence of origin and, in the event of A ceasing cooperation, a TTP, and only the TTP, can enable B to recover the *payload* from the receipt input.

Figure 10 shows the main exchange protocol. To start the protocol A generates two encrypted tokens: *payloadCipher* and *keyCipher*. *payloadCipher* is the encryption of the *payload* using the secret key *kA* that is known only to A. *keyCipher* is the encryption of the secret key with the protocol identifier and a random number using the TTP's public key. The *id* is cryptographically bound to the *payload* through the digest of the *payloadCipher* used in construction of the *id*. Only the TTP can decrypt *keyCipher* but any

Figure 10. Wang's optimistic fair exchange protocol

1	$A \rightarrow B$:	$\{id, A, B, TTP, payloadCipher, h(kA), keyCipher, NRO_A\}$
2	$B \rightarrow A$:	$\{id, NRR_B\}$
3	$A \rightarrow B$:	$\{id, kA, rn\}$

where:

kA is a secret key generated by A to encrypt *payload*

payloadCipher	$= enc_{kA}(payload)$ — the encryption of payload using *kA*
id	$= h(A, B, TTP, h(payloadCipher), h(kA))$
keyCipher	$= enc_{TTP}(id, kA, rn)$
NRO_A	$= sig_A(id, keyCipher)$
NRR_B	$= sig_B(id, keyCipher)$

other party can verify that it is an encryption of *id* and *kA* with some random number. A sends the encrypted items to B along with participant identifiers, including the identifier of the off-line TTP, and NRO_A. NRO_A cryptographically binds *keyCipher* to *id* and therefore to *payloadCipher* and ultimately to *payload*. Given this message, B can generate a receipt by signing the same items as A to produce NRR_B. Now, B knows that either: (1) A prepared *keyCipher* correctly and, therefore, that A or the TTP can recover *kA* and *rn* from *keyCipher* to enable B to verify NRO evidence and obtain *payload*; or (2) A provided an invalid *keyCipher* and therefore NRR_B will not be a valid receipt. That is, B's receipt is only valid if A provides valid input that, if necessary, B can use to recover the *payload* from the TTP. Therefore, it is safe for B to send NRR_B to A in step 2. In the final step, A sends B *kA* and *rn*. These items allow B to verify the integrity of all evidence previously provided by A and to decrypt *payloadCipher* to obtain *payload*.

A full discussion of the security properties of the protocol, how fairness and timeliness are guaranteed, and the specification of abort and resolve subprotocols is presented in Wang (2005). Here we briefly describe protection against cheating by either A or B.

A can attempt to cheat in two ways: (1) they can provide B with an invalid *keyCipher* or invalid *payloadCipher*, or (2) they can decline to send the final message. As discussed previously, invalid input from A will lead to the generation of a useless receipt from B. Therefore, A cannot achieve nonrepudiation of receipt if they provide invalid input to B. If A does not send the final message, then B can obtain *kA* and *rn* from the TTP in return for NRR_B. The TTP will provide *kA* and *rn* unless A has requested that the exchange be aborted. If the exchange has been aborted then the TTP provides B with a signed abort token that can be used to repudiate receipt of *payload*. Therefore, A cannot obtain a valid receipt unless both *payload* and NRO are available to B. B can only attempt to cheat by failing to provide A with a valid receipt *and* requesting that the TTP provide *kA* and *rn*. However, the TTP only provides these items to B if B provides the TTP with NRR_B and all other protocol items for the TTP to verify their consistency and integrity. Further, if the TTP enables B to recover *payload* they also provide A with B's valid receipt.

In conclusion, there is no advantage to either A or B attempting to cheat and therefore the optimistic exchange is only likely to fail because of timeliness constraints. That is, in the normal case the exchange will complete as a direct exchange between A and B without the need to involve the TTP.

As with voluntary exchange, we integrate *payload* validation by executing two correlated runs of the protocol: one to exchange *payload* and NRO for NRR and the other to exchange validation decision and NROV for NRRV. The identifier of the first protocol run is used for correlation with the second.

Summary and Evaluation

In this section, we have described the voluntary and fair exchange approaches to making business interactions nonrepudiable. The voluntary approach is appropriate for interactions between TTPs or when the recipient is a TTP (as in phase 1 of interactions 1 and 3 of Figure 3). Fair exchange is appropriate for interactions between business partners (as in Interaction 2 of Figure 3). In the case of fair exchange with inline TTP, we have also demonstrated how to adapt a protocol for interactions between lightweight participants.

The protocols presented up to now address the following classes of interaction: TTP to TTP, business partner to TTP, and business partner to business partner. The remaining class of interaction is TTP sender to business partner recipient. In this case, to guarantee fairness, it is necessary to ensure that the TTP obtains a receipt regardless of the behaviour of the other party. To achieve this we merge the roles of A and the TTP in the Coffey-Saidha protocol. This reduces the six-step protocol in Figure 7 to the three steps shown in Figure 11. In this protocol, A is a TTP and solicits a receipt for the *payload* before sending the *payload* to B. This protects A's interests because they only release the *payload* if B provides a valid receipt. B's interests are protected by the fact that A is trusted to send message 3. For timely termination, A can unilaterally abort the exchange before B sends the second message. After step 2, the exchange is guaranteed to complete. Validation can be integrated by adding two steps for B to send their validation message and A to return a receipt, which they are guaranteed to do because they are a TTP.

The choice of which exchange mechanism to use will depend on the application context. For example, as discussed up to now, the relationships between protocol participants will have an influence on the choice. When choosing between inline TTP and offline TTP approaches to fair exchange, the availability and the capabilities of TTP services may be significant factors. An obvious consideration is the communication overheads of a protocol in terms of the number of messages needed to achieve the exchange of evidence. However, care must be taken when calculating these overheads. If signing keys are revocable and trusted time-stamps are required for signature verification and the long-term validity of evidence, then the costs of obtaining time-stamps from a TSA must be included in the calculation.

Table 3 compares the costs of three approaches to business partner to business partner fair exchange of a message for its receipt: (1) with an inline TTP, (2) with an inline TTP that is also a TSA, and (3) with an off-line TTP for Wang's optimistic protocol. It should be noted that it is not possible to optimise optimistic fair exchange when a TTP also acts as TSA because there is no TTP involvement in the main exchange. Column 2 shows the number of nonrepudiation protocol messages in each case. In terms of protocol messages, the off-line TTP fair exchange is cheapest with just three messages. Column 3 shows the number of messages required for trusted time-stamping. In each protocol, a time-stamp must be obtained the first time that signed evidence is generated. Two messages are required for each time-stamp, one to send the request to the TSA and the other for the TSAs response. In the first case, three of the inline TTP protocol messages require time-stamping and this leads to an overhead of six messages. As shown, there is no overhead in the second case because the TTP is also a TSA and performs all time-stamping. The off-line TTP protocol requires a time-stamp for two of its three messages, incurring an overhead of four messages. As shown in the final column, fair exchange with an inline TTP/TSA is now cheaper, in terms of total messages required, than the off-line TTP approach. That is, the relative communication

Figure 11. TTP sender to business partner recipient receipt-first exchange

1	$A \rightarrow B$:	*{id, A, B, h(payload)}*
2	$B \rightarrow A$:	$\{id, NRR_B\}$
3	$A \rightarrow B$:	$\{id, payload, NRO_A\}$

where:

$NRO_A = sig_A(id, A, B, h(payload))$

$NRR_B = sig_B(id, A, B, h(payload))$

Table 3. Communication costs of fair exchange

Approach	Protocol messages	Time-stamp messages	Total messages
(ii) Inline TTP fair exchange (Coffey-Saidha — Figure 7)	6	6	12
(iii) Inline TTP/TSA fair exchange (Coffey-Saidha)	6	0	6
(iv) Off-line TTP fair exchange (Wang — Figure 10)	3	4	7

Table 4. Communication costs of fair exchange with application-level validation

Approach	Protocol messages	Time-stamp messages	Total messages
(ii) Inline TTP fair exchange with validation (Coffey-Saidha — Figure 9)	9	8	17
(iii) Inline TTP/TSA fair exchange with validation (Coffey-Saidha)	9	0	9
(iv) Offline TTP fair exchange with validation (Wang)	6	8	14

costs of the different approaches change when time-stamps from a TSA are required.

Table 4 compares communication costs when the exchange includes application-level validation of the business message. As shown, when time-stamping is required, the inline TTP/TSA fair exchange is now significantly cheaper than the off-line TTP approach. In fact, it is cheaper than the voluntary exchange approach shown in Figure 6 that incurs an overhead of eight messages for its four protocol messages (assuming a separate TSA is required and validation cannot be combined with receipting). Clearly, if communication costs are a factor in the choice of mechanism then important considerations include whether trusted time-stamping is required and whether the guarantor TTP can also provide the TSA service. Other factors, such as computational costs, will also inform the choice of mechanism.

The preceding analysis, and the choice of protocols presented in this section, underlines the desirability of being able to choose an appropriate nonrepudiation mechanism to suit the given B2B context. The flexibility necessary to meet this challenge is based on the model of interceptor-mediated interaction described in this section. Our framework for protocol execution between and with Web services is a practical realisation of the model. The execution framework is sufficiently flexible to allow partners to choose to execute a protocol appropriate to the sort of interaction they are engaged in on a per business message basis. It also supports arbitrary, application-level validation of business messages.

WEB SERVICES PROTOCOL EXECUTION FRAMEWORK

In this section, we present our Web services-based implementation of a framework for nonrepudiation protocol execution (WS-NRExchange). A prime requirement on this middleware is that it is able to support the execution of any deterministic non-repudiation protocol. It achieves this flexibility through: (1) a well-defined, generic interface for the exchange of protocol messages between protocol participants, (2) an extensible schema that defines the content of self-describing protocol messages, and (3) a well-defined API for message processing by the middleware that includes the registration of protocol-specific handlers for messages.

As illustrated in Figure 12, the middleware is a realisation of the mediated interaction model described in the previous section. Each protocol participant, including any guarantor TTP, exposes a WS-NRExchange endpoint for protocol execution. At business partners (A and B in Figure 12), the WS-NRExchange middleware intercepts B2B Web service messages. This allows the middleware to adapt to different application requirements, including the execution of different protocols, without disturbing application-level logic. For example, the middleware can execute any of the protocols described in the previous section. We have demonstrated this approach in the context of the Gold project (Periorellis et al., 2006). We successfully applied nonrepudiation and application-level validation to the exchange of SOAP messages between and with existing Web services without modification to the services or their clients. We used AXIS Web services deployed in the Tomcat container (Apache Software Foundation, 2005a, 2005b) as the demonstrator platform. However, apart from some easily isolated AXIS-specific interceptor code, the WS-NRExchange middleware is AXIS-independent and could be redeployed on a range of different Web services platforms. This includes deployment as part of a separate mediation service that is not colocated with the applications to which nonrepudiation is applied.

In this section, we present a general overview of WS-NRExchange interaction and infrastructure services. Then we describe the generic Web service interface to protocol message exchange and the associated message schema. This includes the ability to instantiate protocol-specific handlers at runtime in order to adapt the middleware to the

Figure 12. WS-NRExchange mediated interaction

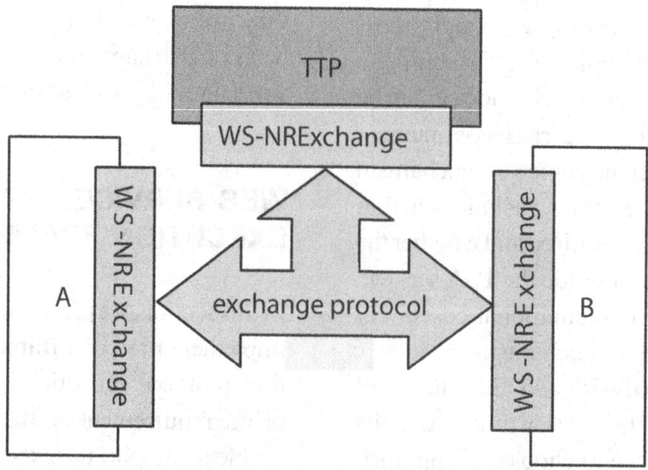

use of different protocols as appropriate for the given interaction. First, we provide an overview of the standards used to support WS-NRExchange and discuss the limitations of the XML Signature standard when expressing certain elements of nonrepudiation protocol message.

Overview of Web Services and Supporting Standards

Figure 13 shows how various XML and Web service standards support WS-NRExchange. SOAP is the basic messaging protocol for communication with and between Web services. We use the SOAP header for message processing information, including non-repudiation protocol elements. The SOAP body carries the business message payload.

The WS-Security standard (Nadalin, Kaler, Hallam-Baker, & Monzillo, 2004) covers the creation of self-protecting messages for Web services. WS-Security applies XML technologies, such as XML Signature (Eastlake, Reagle, & Solo, 2002) and XML Encryption (Eastlake, Reagle, Imamura, Dillaway, & Simon, 2002), to SOAP messages. The XML Signature standard specifies how to generate a signature over some referenced data, how to encode the signature in XML and how to attach the signature, with related information, to XML documents. The standard also specifies how the recipient of a signature should process the XML elements in order to verify the integrity of the signature. XML Encryption is the corresponding standard for encryption. The WS-Security standard specifies a security header for SOAP messages that can convey XML Signature and XML Encryption elements. Other elements carried in the security header include authentication tokens, secure time-stamps, and credentials or certificates.

Digital signature service (DSS) (Perrin, Andivahis, Cruellas, Hirsch, Kasselman, Kuehne et al., 2004) and XML key management specification (XKMS) (Hallam-Baker & Mysore, 2005) are higher level specifications that use WS-Security. DSS specifies a service for the verification and the application of signatures to XML, and for trusted time-stamping of signed information. XKMS concerns public key life-cycle management. It specifies Web service-based PKI functionality such as how to register, locate, verify and revoke the digital credentials that are associated with public keys. XKMS and DSS may be offered as TTP services to support secure Web service interactions, thereby reducing the security infrastructure requirements of user organisations. Organisations may also provide a sub-set of the services in-house as part of their own security

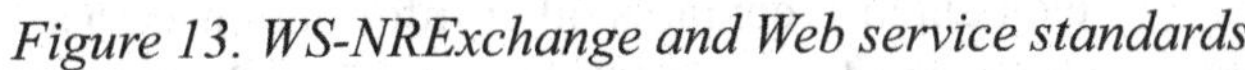
Figure 13. WS-NRExchange and Web service standards

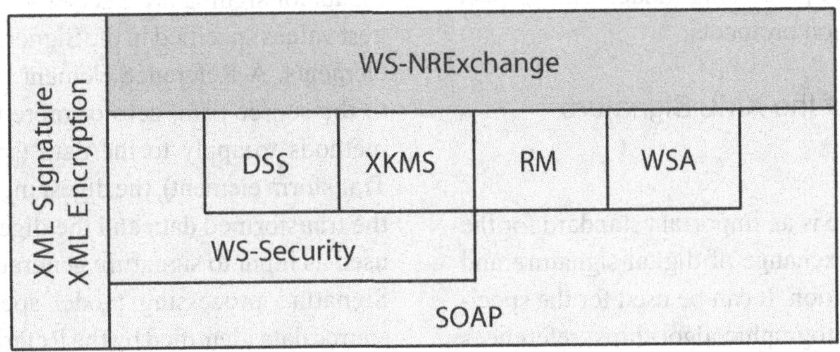

infrastructure. For example, an in-house DSS service can be used to apply corporate signatures to XML messages.

Reliable messaging (RM) specifies the message content, protocols and persistence requirements necessary for Web services to implement various forms of reliable message delivery. To provide at-least-once message delivery, we use an implementation of WS-ReliableMessaging (Bilorusets, 2005).

We use WS-addressing (WSA) (Gudgin, Hadley, & Rogers, 2006) for message routing and for the description of WS-NRExchange Web service endpoints.

Our contribution is to provide the WS-NRExchange middleware that uses the identified standards. The middleware includes the specification of the NRExchange XML schema (Cook & Robinson, 2006) for a nonrepudiation protocol SOAP header, protocol implementations, and protocol message processing services with associated WSDL (Christensen, Curbera, Meredith, & Weerawarana, 2001). As far as possible, we use the XML security standards to encode protocol tokens in XML and include those tokens in the WS-security header. We developed the NRExchange schema to encode tokens that either cannot be expressed using the security standards or whose expression has potential to conflict with the processing model specified by the standards. The NRExchange schema also specifies how to include protocol context and processing information in the SOAP header. Before describing the middleware, we discuss the limitations of the XML Signature standard and its processing model with respect to nonrepudiation protocols.

Limitations of the XML Signature Standard

XML Signature is an important standard for the interoperable exchange of digital signature and related information. It can be used for the specification of cryptographic algorithms, references to source data, and the representation of message digests and of signatures over the digests. As noted in the preceding discussion, and as importantly, the standard also specifies a processing model for the generation and verification of signatures. Digital signatures and message digests are an integral part of nonrepudiation protocols. Therefore, the standard is a fundamental building block for the XML representation of nonrepudiation protocol messages and the processing of those messages. However, the processing model has limitations when it comes to verifying information exchanged in fair exchange protocols. The problem arises because fair exchange protocols rely on the fact that signatures, and digests, provided in one message may reference information that is not made available until a later message. For example, B cannot verify the digest (*h(payload)*) that they receive in message 3 of Figure 7 until they receive the *payload* in message 6. Another example, from the protocol in Figure 9, is that A's signature over *id*, and therefore over the included digest of *rn*, that is sent to B as NRO_A in step 6 is not fully verifiable until B receives *rn* in step 8. But, the core XML Signature processing model specifies that referenced inputs to signatures must be available for verification upon receipt of a signature.

As shown in Figure 14, every Signature element contains at least one SignedInfo element that in turn contains at least one Reference element. The SignedInfo element specifies the input that was used to generate the SignatureValue. A Signature element also contains other information such as the method used and the signer's certificate. The inputs for signing are a sequence of message digest values specified in the SignedInfo Reference elements. A Reference element specifies a URI to the source data, zero or more transformation methods to apply to the data (specified by the Transform element), the digest method applied to the transformed data and the digest value that is used as input to signature generation. The XML Signature processing model specifies that the source data identified by the Reference URI must be available to the processor of the Signature. That is, the recipient processor of a Signature must be able to de-reference all the Reference element URIs, apply the specified transforms to the referenced data and generate the same digest value in order to verify the integrity of the signature. As noted previously, fair exchange protocols achieve fairness by delaying the release of information. However, reference processing will fail if a Reference element that cannot be de-referenced is placed in a SignedInfo element. The XML Signature standard does specify a Manifest element that may contain one or more Reference elements. The standard allows that one or more of the Reference elements contained in a Manifest may not be de-referencable.

Figure 15 illustrates usage of the Manifest element. A SignedInfo element contains a Reference that references a Manifest element. The SignedInfo digest value is the digest over the whole of the Manifest element. In this example, the Manifest element contains three Reference elements that refer to inputs X, Y and Z. As shown, inputs X and Y are available but input Z is not. So, the digest value in the Reference in the SignedInfo element can be verified because it refers to the Manifest element. The Reference elements that refer to inputs X and Y can also be verified. The Reference element that refers to input Z cannot be verified. This level of indirection allows the SignedInfo element to comply with the XML Signature processing model because all references in that element can be verified. The semantics for Manifest processing are application-specific. The standard allows either that the verification process may tolerate the inability to

Figure 14. ds:Signature element

```
<ds:Signature>
 ...
 <ds:SignedInfo>
  ...
  (<ds:Reference URI >
   <ds:Transform>*
   <ds:DigestMethod>
   <ds:DigestValue>
  </ds:Reference>)+
  ...
 </ds:SignedInfo>
 <ds: SignatureValue >...</ds:SignatureValue>
</ds:Signature>

Where:
? = 0 or 1 occurrences
+ = 1 or more occurrences
* = 0 or more occurrences
```

Figure 15. Indirect referencing in XML Signature

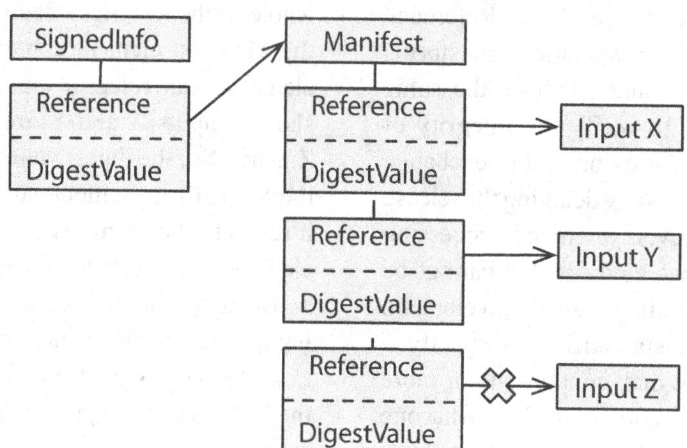

verify one or more Manifest references, or that the verification process may fail after the first failed attempt to dereference a Manifest reference. For the example in Figure 15, it is application-specific whether processing of the Manifest element will succeed or will fail on encountering the reference to input Z.

To address the problem with XML Signature references, we define a MessageReference element in our schema for protocol messages. The MessageReference element supports forward and backward referencing of protocol messages. As with the Manifest element, we exploit reference indirection to preserve processing semantics. Unlike the Manifest element, our MessageReference element has unambiguous processing semantics. In addition, it supports the elegant expression of protocol tokens such as receipts and functions to generate protocol run identifiers. We provide a detailed description of the MessageReference element in the discussion of the NRExchange schema that follows an overview of WS-NRExchange interaction.

WS-NRExchange Interaction

Figure 16 shows the interactions between the main components and services that comprise our implementation. The TTP, A and B each provides an NRExchange Web service that manages their participation in nonrepudiation protocols. Each of these Web service exposes the same interface for non-repudiation protocol execution. At A and B the service is deployed as an interceptor to mediate Web service interactions that require nonrepudiation. This interceptor may be colocated with the local application that uses it or, for example, may be part of a corporate firewall service. The endpoints, A and B, may themselves be Web services or Web service clients, or both. The introduction of the NRExchange services does not require any modification to these application-level processes at A or B. The NRExchange services access additional local services for signing evidence, message persistence and application-level validation. The signing service is required to apply signatures to the parts of messages that have not already been signed. If signatures have been applied at the

Figure 16. WS-NRExchange architecture

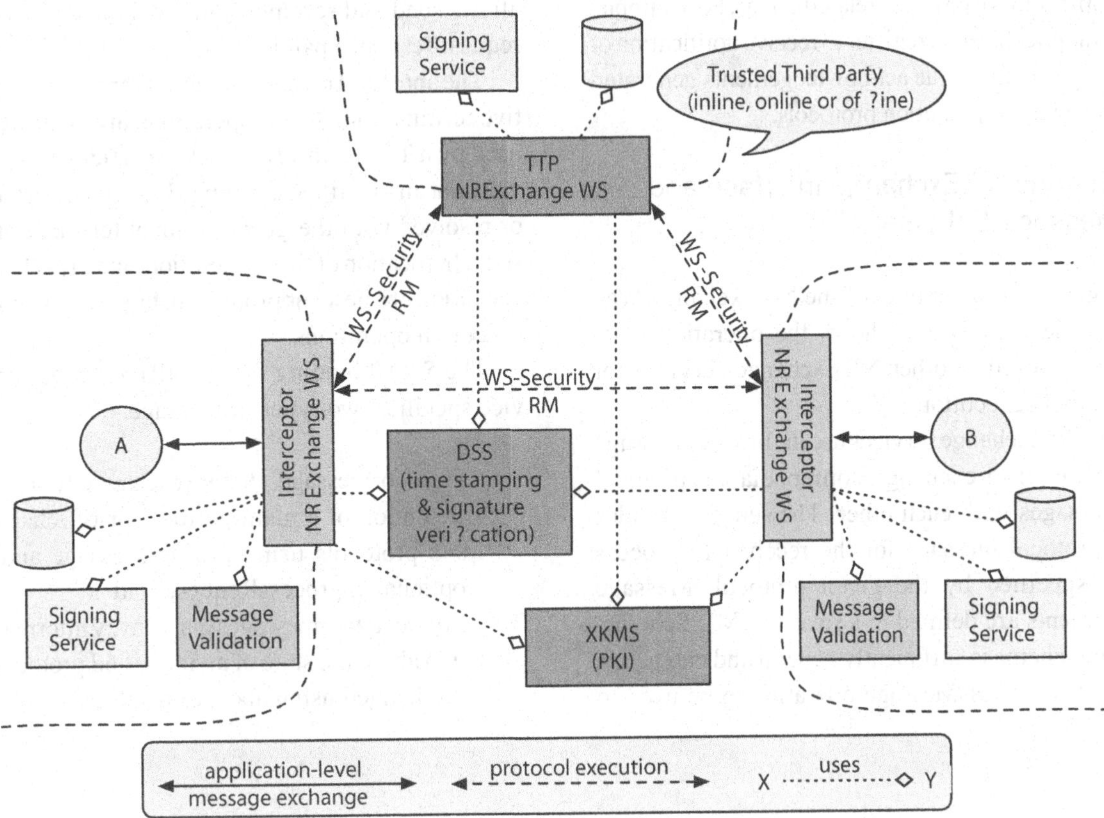

application level, the NRExchange service only needs to countersign the generated signatures and not the message content. This service may be an implementation of DSS or some other mechanism for obtaining private keys to apply signatures as defined by WS-Security. Persistence is required to meet fault tolerance requirements and for audit. The NRExchange services also access trusted time-stamping services and public key management services (e.g., DSS and XKMS services provided by third parties). For protocols that use an inline TTP, trusted time-stamps may optionally be applied by the TTP Web service.

As previously noted, a WSDL interface has been defined for the interaction between NRExchange services. The SOAP messages exchanged comply with the WS-Security specification.

The NRExchange Web service also provides a local interface to allow registration of application-specific listeners for message validation and other events. A message validation listener may trigger arbitrarily complex validation of a business message. If no validation listener is registered, then the NRExchange service assumes that a message is valid with respect to business-specific constraints. Messages that are found to be invalid are logged but are not passed to the target application for processing. Registration of event listeners allows notification of protocol-related events. For example, an application can register to receive notification of zero or more of the acknowledgements generated by the nonrepudiation protocols.

Generic NRExchange Interface and Message Schema

Figure 17 is an extract of the NRExchange Web service WSDL that shows the operations that are exposed to other NRExchange services for protocol execution.

NRExchange services use the processMessage operation to exchange nonrepudiation protocol messages with each other. The sender provides a protocol message for the receiver to process as specified by the given protocol. Message elements are defined in a related XML Schema. The schema is sufficiently general and extensible for the processMessage operation to be used to execute any protocol that participant services support. The processRequest convenience operation allows send and receipt of protocol messages as request/response pairs.

The abort and resolve operations are for proactive termination. These operations are typically used by a TTP to inform another participant service that an identified exchange has been aborted or resolved with the given protocol termination state. Invocation of these operations may result in execution of a new subprotocol using the protocol execution operations.

The SOAP binding for the NRExchange service specifies two types of message:

1. Protocol messages that are exchanged during execution of a main protocol or of related sub-protocols using processMessage and, optionally, processRequest; and
2. Protocol state messages that convey information about the state of an identified protocol (exchanged using abort or resolve).

Figure 17. Extract of NRExchange WSDL

```
<wsdl:portType name="NRExchange">
  <operation name="processMessage">
    <input message="ProtocolMessage"/>
  </operation>
  <operation name="processRequest">
    <input message="ProtocolMessage"/>
    <output message="ProtocolMessage"/>
  </operation>
  <operation name="abort">
    <input message="ProtocolStateMessage"/>
  </operation>
  <operation name="resolve">
    <input message="ProtocolStateMessage"/>
  </operation>
<wsdl:portType>
```

Both types of message use a WS-Security header to carry security tokens such as: signatures over evidence, time-stamps, credential and key information, security context, and access control information.

As shown in Figure 18, protocol messages must have an NRExchangeProtocol header. This is an extensible container for nonrepudiation protocol elements. The elements are defined in the NRExchange XML schema (Cook & Robinson, 2006). The NRExchange schema specifies that any NRExchangeProtocol header must have protocol name, runId, and messageNumber attributes.

The protocol name is a URI that serves to uniquely identify the protocol, or subprotocol, being executed. For example, Table 5 shows names

Figure 18. General form of ProtocolMessage

```
<soapenv:Envelope>
 <soapenv:Header>
  <wsse:Security />
  <nrex:NRExchangeProtocol name runId messageNumber
  purpose? wsu:Id>
   (<nrex:MessageReference protocolName? RunId
    messageNumber wsu:Id?>
     <nrex:MessageList />?
     <ds:Reference />*
   </nrex:MessageReference>)*
   (<nrex:Participant role? URI wsu:Id>
     <wsa:EndpointReference/>*
   </nrex:Participant>)*
   <nrex:RandomNumber />*
   <nrex:ReceiptsRequired />?
   <nrex:RelatedRun />*
   (<nrex:RunIdGenerator baseURI? runId wsu:Id?>
     <ds:Reference/>?
   </nrex:RunIdGenerator>)?
   <xsd:any namespace="##other" />*
  </nrex:NRExchangeProtocol>
 </soapenv:Header>
 <soapenv:Body />
</soapenv:Envelope>

Where:
? = 0 or 1 occurrences
+ = 1 or more occurrences
* = 0 or more occurrences
```

for the set of protocols that together implement the Coffey-Saidha exchange without application-level validation of *payload*. In addition to protocols for the main exchange and abort and resolve, there is a *getStatus* subprotocol. This subprotocol allows one participant to query another's view of current protocol state with the option of requesting missing messages. A getStatus protocol will involve the exchange of evidence to establish that a participant is entitled to the requested information. Implementation of getStatus sub-protocols is optional.

The runId is the protocol run identifier (*id* in the protocol notation). The schema specifies that the runId is a URI. The runId URI may be opaque or it may have a generating function associated with it. For example, the runId in Figure 9 is generated from *h(A, B, TTP, rn)*. In such cases, the RunIdGenerator element can be used to specify the generating function. The RunIdGenerator specifies an optional baseURI and the function over inputs as zero or one digest Reference. A URL-safe Base64 encoding (Josefsson, 2003) of the digest value is used to construct the URI. The runId in Figure 20 is an example of URL-safe Base64 encoding of a digest value where the Base64 character "/" has been converted to a "_". When, for authentication purposes, a runId is constructed from items not available in the current message, we exploit the forward and backward referencing facility provided by the MessageReference element.

The messageNumber is a positive, non-zero value that corresponds to the step of the protocol being executed.

Depending on the protocol being executed, or the step of the protocol, the following optional items may be included in the NRExchangeProtocol header: the purpose of the protocol message (NRR, NRO, etc.), the participants in the protocol, the runIds of any related protocol or subprotocol runs, information related to receipts required, and protocol state information.

The SOAP message body contains the application payload that the business message sender intended for the ultimate recipient.

Protocol state messages do not have an NRExchangeProtocol header. The message body carries protocol state information that is intended for another NRExchange service. The general form of a protocol state message is shown in Figure 19. In addition to identifying the protocol and run to which a message relates, a ProtocolState element may include information such as: the protocol run status; if terminated, the termination state; and the message numbers of any messages seen by the recipient. Protocol messages may be provided as attachments to a protocol state message.

Forward and Backward References to Messages

Now we explain how we address the referencing limitations of the XML Signature standard discussed previously. One approach would be to use the XML Signature Manifest element in a WS-Security header and to restrict the semantics for processing the element to tolerating a failure to dereference. For our purposes, the main problem with this approach is that the

Table 5. Example protocol names

Protocol	Name
Main exchange protocol	*http://www.cs.ncl.ac.uk/nrex/fairex/coffey-saidha/main*
Abort subprotocol	*http://www.cs.ncl.ac.uk/nrex/fairex/coffey-saidha/abort*
Resolve subprotocol	*http://www.cs.ncl.ac.uk/nrex/fairex/coffey-saidha/resolve*
Get status subprotocol	*http://www.cs.ncl.ac.uk/nrex/fairex/coffey-saidha/getStatus*

Figure 19. General form of ProtocolStateMessage

```
<soapenv:Envelope>
  <soapenv:Header>
    <wsse:Security />
  </soapenv:Header>
  <soapenv:Body>
    <nrex:ProtocolState name runId />
  </soapenv:Body>
</soapenv:Envelope>
```

processing semantics for the Manifest element are dependent on the meaning of the element in the context of a nonrepudiation protocol that cannot be inferred from the WS-Security header context. Furthermore, intermediate processors must respect the protocol-specific processing semantics. Therefore, as shown in Figure 18, we have defined our own MessageReference element that is a wrapper for zero or more XML Signature Reference elements.

The MessageReference provides a mechanism to reference both existing and future protocol messages, and a de-referencing context for Reference elements. MessageReference processing semantics are unambiguous: it must be possible for a message processor to dereference the contained Reference elements from the context of any of the messages identified by the MessageReference. A MessageReference must have runId and messageNumber attributes that identify a de-referencing context for the immediate recipient. The runId and messageNumber may identify the current message or another previously received message or some future message. A MessageReference may also contain a MessageList element that specifies the numbers of all the messages in the identified protocol run that can be used as de-referencing contexts for the contained Reference elements. An important feature of the MessageReference element is that it is protocol independent. Given a message identified by the MessageReference it is possible to process the enclosed Reference elements according to core XML Signature processing semantics. We can also express complex protocol tokens with different security properties by exploiting the indirect referencing provided by XML Signature and at the same time preserving our unambiguous processing semantics.

Figure 20 is an extract of an instance of the third message of the Coffey-Saidha protocol from Figure 7. In this message, the sender (the TTP) provides a digest of the *payload* (the SOAP message body) for the recipient to sign. The digest is included in a ReceiptsRequired element that uses a MessageReference element to declare that the *payload* will be available to the recipient in message 6. The MessageList element indicates that the *payload* is available in both protocol messages 1 and 6. The URI in the enclosed Reference element refers the recipient to the "#payload" fragment of message 6. Note that the body of message 3 is empty.

As shown in Figure 21, the recipient includes the MessageReference element from message 3 in the NRExchangeProtocol header of their response. The whole header is signed. The SignedInfo element contains a Reference element that identifies the "#nrexHeader" fragment as input to the signature. Because the MessageReference element contains a digest of the *payload* that will be provided in message 6, the signature over the NRExchangeProtocol header represents the receipt requested in message 3. The TTP relays this information to the original sender in message 5. The inclusion of the MessageList in the MessageReference allows the original sender to verify the receipt with respect to message 1 of the protocol run. Finally, the TTP sends the *payload* to the intended recipient in message 6. Note the nonempty body of message 6 in Figure 22.

The use of the MessageReference element in the preceding examples allows the TTP to explicitly indicate that the recipient is to provide a receipt for the SOAP body of message 6. The element also provides the recipient with the necessary input (*h(payload)*) for the signature and to construct the receipt without requiring access to the *payload*. The inclusion of MessageList indicates to other parties that they can find the same content in any of the other messages in the list to which they have access. In fact, the MessageList is an assertion that the identified input to message digests is identical whichever message in the list is used as a de-referencing context.

Protocol Message Handling

We now describe the processing of an incoming protocol message to illustrate the adaptability of the middleware to different protocols.

As shown in Figure 23, there are two phases to message processing: generic message handling and protocol-specific message handling. Both phases provide the same handler interface to receive incoming messages for processing. In addition, event listeners can be registered in each phase to customise reaction to protocol progress.

In the generic message handling phase, an incoming message is subject to processing that

Figure 20. Example message 3 with forward reference

```
<soapenv:Envelope>
 <soapenv:Header>
  <wsse:Security>
   ...
  </wsse:Security>
  <nrex:NRExchangeProtocol name=".../coffey-saidha/main"
  runId="UrvmUqMES2a08d5ae7v3yZVrum_2livecRVOJxuuC37Q="
  messageNumber="3" wsu:Id="nrexHeader">
   ...
   <nrex:ReceiptsRequired>
    <nrex:MessageReference runId="UrvmUqMES..."
    messageNumber="6">
     <nrex:MessageList>1 6</nrex:MessageList>
     <ds:Reference URI="#payload">...</ds:Reference>
    </nrex:MessageReference>
    ...
   </nrex:ReceiptsRequired>
  </nrex:NRExhangeProtocol>
  ...
 </soapenv:Header>
 <soapenv:Body/>
</soapenv:Envelope>
```

Figure 21. Example message 4 to receipt MessageReference and payload

```
<soapenv:Envelope>
 <soapenv:Header>
  <wsse:Security>
   <ds:Signature>
    ...
    <ds:SignedInfo>
     <ds:Reference URI="#nrexHeader>...</ds:Reference>
    </ds:SignedInfo>
   </ds:Signature>
   ...
  </wsse:Security>
  <nrex:NRExchangeProtocol name="…/coffey-saidha/main"
  runId="UrvmUqMES2a08d5ae7v3yZVrum_2livecRVOJxuuC37Q="
  messageNumber="4" wsu:Id="nrexHeader">
   ...
   <nrex:MessageReference runId="UrvmUqMES…"
    messageNumber="6">
     <nrex:MessageList>1 6</nrex:MessageList>
     <ds:Reference URI="#payload">...</ds:Reference>
   </nrex:MessageReference>
   ...
  </nrex:NRExhangeProtocol>
  ...
 </soapenv:Header>
 <soapenv:Body/>
</soapenv:Envelope>
```

is common to all protocols. First, given access to appropriate keys, any encrypted elements of a message that it is possible to decrypt are decrypted. Then, any signatures contained in the message are verified, along with verification of associated time-stamps and certificates. These first two steps are essentially concerned with processing information in the WS-Security header of a message. Assuming this succeeds, the message is validated against the NRExchange message schema. If any step of generic message handling fails then message processing terminates. This early termination of message processing may indicate an attempt to cheat and, therefore, may trigger dispute resolution (possibly including a request to abort an exchange). One of the uses of event listeners is to allow dispute handling to be triggered at the application-level in response to processing failures. If generic handling completes successfully, the incoming message is passed to

Figure 22. Example message 6 to provide payload

```
<soapenv:Envelope>
 <soapenv:Header>
  <wsse:Security>
   ...
  </wsse:Security>
  <nrex:NRExchangeProtocol name=”.../coffey-saidha/main”
  runId=”UrvmUqMES2a08d5ae7v3yZVrum_2livecRVOJxuuC37Q=”
  messageNumber=”6” wsu:Id=”nrexHeader”>
   ...
  </nrex:NRExhangeProtocol>
  ...
 </soapenv:Header>
 <soapenv:Body wsu:Id=”payload”>
  <!— application payload here -->
  ...
 </soapenv:Body>
</soapenv:Envelope>
```

a protocol-specific handler. The protocol name obtained from the header of the incoming message determines which protocol-specific handler is instantiated.

In the protocol-specific handling phase, the handler first determines the protocol run to which the messages relates and accesses the message log to determine the state of the protocol run. Because protocol messages are self-describing, the state of a protocol run is completely described by the set of messages that have been logged for that run. Given the state of a protocol run, the handler can determine whether the incoming message is in correct sequence. If the message is in correct sequence, the handler can: (1) verify that all expected protocol-specific tokens (message digests, random numbers, etc.) are present; and (2) verify the integrity of the tokens and, in particular, perform any necessary comparisons with tokens from any earlier messages. Assuming the message is valid with respect to the executing protocol, the protocol handler generates and sends any new protocol message(s) that are required to continue protocol execution. If the message is not valid with respect to the executing protocol, then, as for generic handling, processing terminates and dispute resolution may be triggered. As shown in Figure 23, at the appropriate point in protocol execution, the protocol-specific handler invokes application-level message validation via any registered validation listeners.

Both the GenericHandler and the ProtocolHandler provide an interface corresponding to the abort and resolve operations defined in Figure 17. Again, generic processing of a message is followed by instantiation of an appropriate protocol-specific

Figure 23. Message processing overview

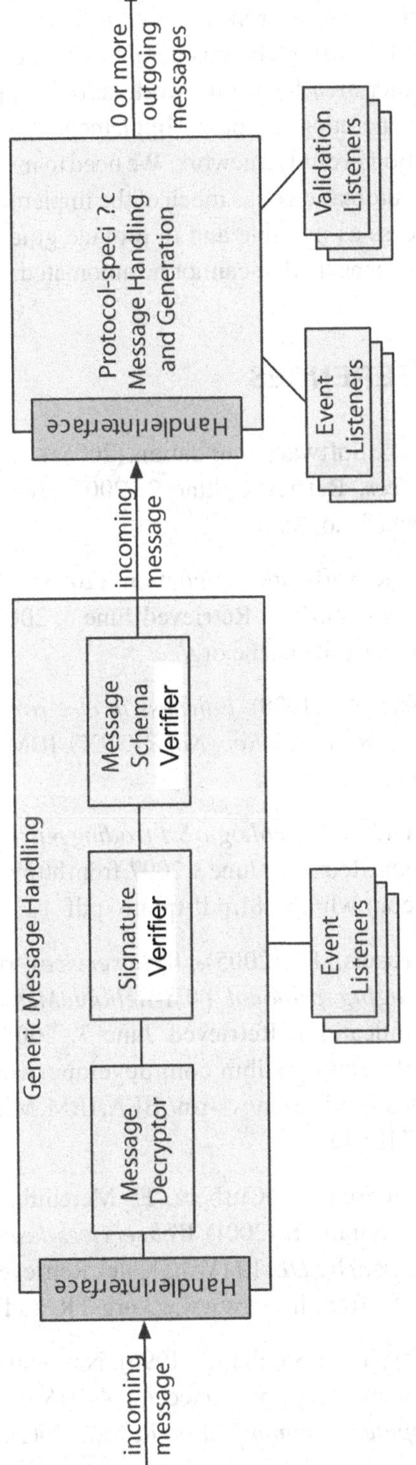

handler from the protocol name obtained from the incoming message.

Validation Listeners

A key requirement is for the middleware to be able to trigger run-time validation of business messages with respect to application-specific constraints (or rules) and, if performed, that this validation is nonrepudiable. As shown in Figure 23, validation is therefore an integral part of message processing and of execution of the protocol chosen to implement run-time monitoring and enforcement. However, if validation logic is application-specific it cannot be fixed for a given protocol and hard-coded as part of the protocol implementation. To address the problem of integrating validation with protocol execution, the middleware supports the configuration of protocol handlers to instantiate one or more validation listeners that are specific to the given business interaction. These listeners are invoked at the appropriate point in protocol execution to obtain a validation decision that can then be incorporated as the payload of a validation message. The application programmer, and not the protocol implementer, is responsible for the implementation and the identification of the validation listeners that the protocol handler should instantiate.

Summary

In this section, we presented our flexible, standards-based middleware for nonrepudiable interactions between and with Web services. The middleware addresses the requirements identified earlier by allowing the "plugging-in" of nonrepudiation protocol implementations to suit the given application context. The middleware also provides a general and systematic mechanism for the validation of business message exchanges with respect to application-specific constraints.

CONCLUSION

In this chapter, we have developed an approach and a reference implementation for the support of non-repudiable B2B interactions. We identified the need for different underlying mechanisms to suit different relationships between participants in a B2B interaction and the need to be able to adapt to the different capabilities of business partners. We described how existing protocols meet some of the identified requirements and presented modifications of the protocols to address others such as incorporation of application-level validation and adaptation for lightweight participants. The description of our Web services-based implementation provided a general overview of the architecture showing how our services interact with existing Web service standards and services. We addressed the limitations of the XML Signature standard with respect to fair nonrepudiation protocols. We described our Web services interface to protocol execution, the protocol message schema, and the message handling process. We are not aware of another middleware system that is capable of rendering arbitrary Web service interactions both nonrepudiable and fair. Further, we know of no other system that provides the flexibility to "plug-in" both the application-level validation of B2B interactions and the mechanism that enforces that validation at run-time.

Our implementation operates a layer above reliable messaging. However, there is duplication of effort between the nonrepudiation protocols and reliable messaging both in terms of acknowledgements generated and message persistence. Further work could investigate tighter integration of the two services. The approach should be modular and configurable. Either the fair exchange service can provide reliable messaging directly (for greater performance) or, as now, it will rely on an existing standards-based implementation to provide a reliable channel.

The correct implementation of nonrepudiation protocols is a challenging task. To gain high confidence in a given implementation, ideally we require both: (1) a formal, verified protocol specification, and (2) tool support to generate an implementation from the specification. The former area has attracted considerable attention. Thus, another area for future work is tool support for the generation of protocol implementations for execution in our framework. We need to investigate the automation of as much of the implementation process as possible and to provide guidance on those aspects that cannot be automated.

REFERENCES

Apache Software Foundation. (2005a). *AXIS Web services*. Retrieved June 3, 2007, from http://ws.apache.org/axis/

Apache Software Foundation. (2005b). *Tomcat servlet container*. Retrieved June 3, 2007, from http://tomcat.apache.org/

Asokan, N. (1998). *Fairness in electronic commerce (Research Rep. No. RZ3027)*. IBM Zurich Research Lab.

BEA. (2005). *WebLogic 8.1 trading partner integration*. Retrieved June 3, 2007, from http://e-docs.bea.com/wli/docs81/pdf/tpintro.pdf

Bilorusets, R. (2005). *Web services reliable messaging protocol (WS-ReliableMessaging)* (Specification). Retrieved June 3, 2007, from http://www-128.ibm.com/developerworks/library/specification/ws-rm/. BEA, IBM, Microsoft and TIBCO.

Christensen, E., Curbera, F., Meredith, G., & Weerawarana, S. (2001). *Web services description language (WSDL)* 1.1 (W3C Note). Retrieved June 3, 2007, from http://www.w3.org/TR/wsdl

Coffey, T., & Saidha, P. (1996). Nonrepudiation with mandatory proof of receipt. *ACM SIGCOMM Computer Communication Review, 26*(1), 6-17.

Cook, N., & Robinson, P. (2006). *NRExchange: XML schema and WSDL for Web service nonrepudiation protocols.* Retrieved June 3, 2007, from http://homepages.cs.ncl.ac.uk/nick.cook/ws-nrex/

Cook, N., Robinson, P., & Shrivastava, S.K. (2006). Design and implementation of Web services middleware to support fair nonrepudiable interactions. *International Journal of Cooperative Information Systems (IJCIS) Special Issue on Enterprise Distributed Computing, 15*(4), 565-597.

Eastlake, D., Reagle, J., Imamura, T., Dillaway, B., & Simon, E. (2002). *XML encryption syntax and processing (W3C Recommendation).* Retrieved June 3, 2007, from http://www.w3.org/TR/xmlenc-core/

Eastlake, D., Reagle, J., & Solo, D. (2002). *XML-signature syntax and processing (IETF RFC 3275 and W3C Recommendation).* Retrieved June 3, 2007, from http://www.w3.org/TR/xmldsig-core/. IETF/W3C

Even, S., & Yacobi, Y. (1980). *Relations among public key signature systems* (Tech. Rep. No. CS175). Haifa, Israel: Technion Israel Institute of Technology.

Ezhilchelvan, P.D., & Shrivastava, S.K. (2005). A family of trusted third party based fair-exchange protocols. *IEEE Transactions on Dependable and Secure Computing, 2*(4), 273-286.

Fischer, M.J., Lynch, N.A., & Paterson, M.S. (1985). Impossibility of distributed consensus with one faulty process. *Journal of the ACM, 32*(2), 374-382.

Grangard, A., Eisenberg, B., & Nickull, D. (2001). *ebXML technical architecture specification v1.0.4 (*OASIS Final Draft). Retrieved June 3, 2007, from http://www.ebxml.org/

Gravengaard, E., Goodale, G., Hanson, M., Roddy, B., & Walkowski, D. (2003). *Web services security: Nonrepudiation (Proposal Draft).* Retrieved June 3, 2007, from http://schemas.reactivity.com/2003/04/web-services-non-repudiation-05.pdf

Gudgin, M., Hadley, M., & Rogers, T. (2006). *Web services addressing (WS-Addressing) (W3C Submission).* Retrieved June 3, 2007, from http://www.w3.org/TR/ws-addr-core/

Hallam-Baker, P., & Mysore, S. (2005). *XML key management specification (XKMS 2.0) (W3C Recommendation).* Retrieved June 3, 2007, from http://www.w3.org/TR/xkms2/

Housley, R., Ford, W., Polk, T., & Solo, D. (1999). *Internet X.509 public key infrastructure: Certificate and CRL profile* (IETF RFC 2459). Internet Engineering Task Force.

IBM DataPower. (2007). *WebSphere DataPower XML security gateway XS40.* Retrieved June 3, 2007, from http://www-306.ibm.com/software/integration/datapower/xs40/

Josefsson, S. (2003). *The Base16, Base32, and Base64 Data Encodings* (IETF RFC 3548): Internet Engineering Task Force.

Kremer, S., Markowitch, O., & Zhou, J. (2002). An intensive survey of fair nonrepudiation protocols. *Computer Communications, 25*(17), 1601-1621.

Markowitch, O., Gollmann, D., & Kremer, S. (2002). On fairness in exchange protocols. In *Proceedings of the 5th International Conference on Information Security and Cryptology (ISISC 2002)*, Seoul, Korea.

Markowitch, O., & Roggeman, Y. (1999). Probabilistic Nonrepudiation without trusted third party. In *Proceedings of the 2nd Workshop on Security in Communication Networks*, Amalfi, Italy.

Milosevic, Z., Gibson, S., Linnington, P. F., Cole, J., & Kulkarni, S. (2004). On design and implementation of a contract monitoring facility. In *Proceedings of the 1st IEEE Workshop on Electronic Contracting*, San Diego, CA.

Minsky, N., & Ungureanu, V. (2000). Law-governed interaction: A coordination and control mechanism for heterogeneous mistributed systems. *ACM Transactions on Software Engineering and Methodology, 9*(3), 273-305.

Molina-Jimenez, C., Shrivastava, S.K., & Warne, J. (2005). A method for specifying contract mediated interactions. In *Proceedings of the 9th IEEE International EDOC Enterprise Computing Conference*, Enschede, Netherlands.

Nadalin, A., Kaler, C., Hallam-Baker, P., & Monzillo, R. (2004). Web Services Security: SOAP Message Security 1.0 (OASIS Standard). Retrieved June 3, 2007, from *http://docs.oasis-open.org/wss/2004/01/oasis-200401-wss-soap-message-security-1.0.pdf*

Nenadic, A., Zhang, N., & Barton, S. (2004). FIDES - A middleware e-commerce security solution. In *Proceedings of the 3rd European Conference on Information Warfare and Security (ECIW),* London.

Pagnia, H., & Gärtner, F. (1999). On the impossibility of fair exchange without a trusted third party (Tech. Rep. No.TUD-BS-1999-02). Department of Computer Science, TU Darmstadt.

Periorellis, P., Cook, N., Hiden, H.G., Conlin, A., Hamilton, M.D., Wu, J. et al. (2006). GOLD infrastructure for virtual organisations. In *Proceedings of the 5th UK E-science All Hands Meeting*, Nottingham, UK.

Perrin, T., Andivahis, D., Cruellas, J.C., Hirsch, F., Kasselman, P., Kuehne, A. et al. (2004). *Digital signature service core protocols, elements and bindings (OASIS Committee Working Draft).* Retrieved June 3, 2007, from http://www.oasis-open.org/committees/dss

RosettaNet. (2005). *E-business standards for the global supply chain.* Retrieved June 3, 2007, from http://www.rosettanet.org/RosettaNet/

Schneier, B. (1996). *Applied cryptography.* John Wiley & Sons.

Verisign. (2004). *Verisign trust gateway: Simplifying application and Web services security (Verisign White Paper).* Retrieved June 3, 2007, from http://www.verisign.com/products-services/security-services/intelligence-and-control-services/application-security/index.html

Wang, G. (2005). Generic fair nonrepudiation protocols with transparent off-line TTP. In *Proceedings of the 4th International Workshop for Applied PKI,* Singapore.

Zhou, J., & Gollmann, D. (1997). Evidence and nonrepudiation. *Journal of Network and Computer Applications, 20*(3), 267-281.

Chapter V
Dynamic Delegation of Authority in Web Services

David W. Chadwick
Computing Laboratory, UK

ABSTRACT

Delegation of authority (DOA) is an essential procedure in every modern business. This chapter enumerates the requirements for a delegation of authority Web service that allows users and services to delegate to other users and services authority to access computer-based resources. The various models and architecture that can support a DOA Web service are described. A key component of the DOA service is the organisation's delegation policy, which provides the rules for who is allowed to delegate what to whom, and which needs to be enforced by the DOA service. The essential elements of such a delegation policy are outlined. The chapter then describes a practical DOA Web service that has been built and piloted in various grid applications. It concludes by reviewing some related research and highlighting where future research is still required.

INTRODUCTION

Delegation of authority is an essential procedure in every modern business. A delegate is defined as "A person authorized to act as representative for another; a deputy or an agent" (www.dictionary.com). Without delegation of authority (DOA), managers would soon become overloaded. DOA allows tasks to be disseminated between employees in a controlled manner. A delegate may be appointed for months, day, or minutes, for one task, a series of tasks, or all tasks associated with a role. DOA needs to be fast and efficient with a minimum of disruption to others. Delegators should not need permission from their superiors for each act of delegation they undertake, or otherwise their superiors would soon become overburdened with delegation requests from subordinates. Instead, a delegation policy should be in place so that delegators know when they are empowered to delegate (i.e., what and to whom) and when they are not.

The recipient (or service provider) who is asked to perform a service for a delegate should be able to independently verify that the delegate has been properly authorized to act as a representative for the delegator, before granting the request. If the delegate has not been properly authorised, the delegate's request should be declined. The recipient will therefore enforce the delegation policy of its organization and deny service requests from unauthorized delegates.

In a computing environment there is also a need for DOA. One computer process may need to delegate to another computer process. One person may need to delegate his privileges to another person in order to allow the later to undertake the computer-based tasks of the former. Similarly, in a service-oriented world, computer services also need the ability to delegate tasks to other services, so that the latter can perform subtasks on the former's behalf. Service providers need to be able to verify that each service requestor is properly authorized. If the service requestor has been dynamically delegated authority by another authorized entity, service providers need to be able to verify that this was done in accordance with their delegation policy.

The objective of this chapter is to present a model for dynamic delegation of authority in a Web services world, in which users can delegate to other users, services to other services, and users to services. This chapter also describes a current implementation of this model and compares and contrasts it with other delegation systems that only partially implement the model.

BACKGROUND

In Grid computing today, which is based on Web services, delegation from a user to his Grid job is enacted via the process of proxy certificates (Tuecke, Welch, Engert, Pearlman, & Thompson, 2004). The purpose of these is two fold. Firstly, it allows a user to start a Grid job, and then leave it to run in his absence for as long as is required, without him needing to be there to continually log in and authorize the use of new Web services by the job. Secondly, it allows the job to migrate around the Grid, and to spawn new subtasks to run on other machines as necessary. These subtasks can themselves authenticate as proxies of the user and consume Web services (or resources) that the user is entitled to have. The process works as follows. The Grid user, who must have an asymmetric key pair and X.509 certificate, initializes his Grid job, and during this process the job creates its own asymmetric key pair. The user then issues an X.509 proxy certificate for the Grid job, which certifies the public key of the job. The proxy certificate also contains the name of the job (which must be subordinate to the user's own distinguished name), the name of the user as the issuer, and the signature of the user. The Grid job can now authenticate to any Web service Grid resource by digitally signing requests using its own newly created private key, and the Web service can authenticate the job using the job's newly created proxy certificate. Because the name of the Grid job is subordinate to that of the user, then the Web service knows that it has to check if the user is authorized to access this service, and if so, then the service is to be consumed on behalf of the user. When a new subtask needs to be spawned, to run elsewhere on the Grid, the spawned subtask can generate its own new asymmetric key pair, and the original Grid job can issue a second proxy certificate for the spawned subtask, with a name that is subordinate to its own. In this way the job can delegate as necessary in order to achieve its aims. In each case, the Web service checks if the user, and not the job itself, is authorized to consume its resources. This is easily achieved because the name of the job is linked to the name of the user by being subordinate to it.

Note that in the basic proxy certificate scheme, determining the user's authorization rights is left to the Web service. In Globus Toolkit, a grid mapfile is used to map the user's authenticated (proxy certificate) name onto a local user account name, and the normal operating system mechanisms are then used to control the access rights of each user account. Proxy certificates do have a field (the Proxy Policy field) to contain authorization information, but no standard mechanisms are currently defined for what this field should contain, other than "inherit all" or "independent." In the basic proxy scheme, the Proxy Policy field is set simply to "inherit all," meaning that the proxy certificate inherits all the user's access rights, whatever they are. The Proxy Policy field may alternatively be set to "independent," meaning that the proxy should be treated as an independent entity that has its own authorization rights issued to it, and it inherits no rights of the issuing user, but we do not believe this latter value is currently being used much, if at all.

A slightly more sophisticated mechanism has recently been engineered in the Virtual Organization Management Service (VOMS) (Alfieri, Cecchini, Ciaschini, Dell'agnello, Frohner, Lorentey, & Spataro, 2005). This allows a user to delegate an explicit subset of his roles to his grid job. The user asks his local VOMS server to issue him with one or more short lived X.509 attribute certificates (ACs) which contain (possibly a subset of) his roles in the virtual organization (VO). These attribute certificates are then placed inside the job's proxy certificate (in a new certificate extension field—called AC Sequence—defined specifically for this) and in so doing, the ACs can be transported around the grid by the job and its spawned subtasks. The purpose of these ACs is to delegate to the job a specific (sub)set of roles held by the user, so that the job only inherits the (sub)set of permissions assigned to these roles. Note that VOMS does not use the Proxy Policy field for this, even though it was designed for this purpose. This is so that service providers which do not understand VOMS ACs and the new AC Sequence certificate extension field, can still utilize the proxy certificate in the basic way, by using the Proxy Policy field and assigning all the user's permissions to the grid job. Whether this is good practice from a security perspective or not is open to debate.

As good as the proxy certificate scheme is, nevertheless there are a number of problems with its approach. Firstly, the delegator must have an asymmetric key pair in order to sign the proxy certificate. Most users today do not have X.509 certificates and signing keys. Thus, we need a delegation process that does not mandate that a delegator has an asymmetric key pair. Secondly, proxy certificates cannot be revoked. Instead, they are designed to be relatively short lived. This means that once the Grid job has started, and its proxy certificate has been issued, it cannot be stopped automatically, and neither can any of the spawned sub tasks. Instead, some form of manual intervention by the Web service administrators will be needed to kill the job. To try to limit the damage, proxy certificates (and VOMS attribute certificates) are given short lifetimes, typically of the order of 24 hours, although the actual duration is application dependent. Ideally, we need a more proactive way of revoking proxy certificates after they have been issued and before they have expired, for example, by re-evaluating their permissions at specific intervals or every time new subtasks are spawned. Finally, the proxy certificate approach only works for DOA from a user to a Grid job and from a job to a spawned subtask, and does not work from user to user. This is a significant limitation in its applicability. In order to overcome all these limitations we need a better approach to DOA, one that is general purpose and can cater for delegation from person to person, person to task, task to task, service to service, and so forth, in which the delegators are not mandated to have PKI key pairs, and in which the act of delegation can be revoked prematurely.

REQUIREMENTS FOR WEB SERVICES DELEGATION OF AUTHORITY

As stated above, the first requirement is for a general purpose delegation of authority service that can delegate from any type of entity to any other type of entity (Requirement 1).

Secondly, we need to be able to independently name the delegator and the delegate. It might be acceptable in person to job delegation that the job takes a name subordinate to that of the person, but in person to person delegation and Web service to Web service delegation we should not have to make the delegate assume a principal name which is subordinate to that of the delegator. For the reason of prudent accountability, if nothing more, every principal should authenticate with its own identity, and not with that of another. So delegation should be from one named entity to another, where their names do not need to bear any relationship to each other (Requirement 2).

In order to build a scalable authorization infrastructure, we need to move toward attribute or role-based access controls, where a principal is assigned one or more attributes, and the holder of a given set of attributes is given certain access rights to certain resources. In this way we can give access rights to a whole group of principals, for example, to anyone with an IEEE membership attribute, or to any member of project X, or any Web service of a specific type, without needing to list all the members individually, as there might be many thousands of them (Requirement 3).

The delegation scheme will benefit from a hierarchical model for roles and attributes so that delegators can delegate a subset of their roles/attributes. With hierarchical roles and attributes, a principal with a superior role (or attribute) inherits all the permissions of the subordinate roles (or attributes), and may delegate a subordinate role rather than the most superior role he holds. For example, a project manager may be superior to a team leader who is superior to a team member who is superior to an employee. Principals should to be able to delegate any of their roles and attributes to other principals, so that the delegate may perform on their behalf only those tasks that are enabled by the delegated attributes. For example, a project manager should be able to delegate the subordinate role of team member to an employee (Requirement 4).

All organizations need to be able to control the amount of delegation that is possible, in order to stop "wrong" delegations from being performed. For example, a project manager should not be able to delegate his age or name attributes to anyone else, nor be able to delegate the team member role to one of his children. So we need to have a Delegation Policy, and an effective enforcement mechanism that will control both the delegation process itself (is this delegator allowed to delegate these attributes to this delegate?) and the verification process by the consuming Web service (is this delegate properly authorized to access this service?) (Requirement 5).

We may want very fine grained delegation, in order to delegate a specific task rather than attributes or roles, because the latter usually confer permissions to perform a set of tasks (Requirement 6).

Users must not be constrained to having a PKI key pair before they can delegate to another entity. Users should be able to authenticate and prove their identity without having to possess a public key certificate (Requirement 7).

A delegator should be able to prematurely revoke an act of delegation, without the delegation lasting for its originally intended period of time. When delegation takes place, its effect should be instantaneous. There are many reasons why premature revocation may be needed, for example, the delegator returns early from vacation or sick leave and wishes to continue in his role himself, or the delegate proves to be untrustworthy or incompetent in the delegated role, or the delegate moves position in the organization and the delegation is no longer appropriate, and so forth (Requirement 8).

Finally, we may wish to make the whole DOA system Web services compliant, so that it will integrate nicely with the service-oriented architectures (SOA) Web services world that is the subject of this book. (Note, however, that this last requirement is not a functional requirement of DOA, because we can map the concepts and designs onto any underlying infrastructure, such as IPv6 protocols, CORBA, and so forth. Rather, it is an implementation requirement to facilitate integration with the Web services world.) (Requirement 9).

The rest of this chapter is structured as follows. The next section describes the hierarchical role/attribute-based access control model, where principals are given any attributes rather than simply roles, and these attributes are used to gain access to resources which are identified by their attributes. The section after that describes a Web services-based architecture of a DOA infrastructure that will allow any principal to delegate any attribute to any other principal, providing it is in accordance with the organisation's Delegation Policy. The following section describes the features that are needed in an organisation's Delegation Policy in order to allow principals to delegate their attributes to other principals. The penultimate section describes one practical implementation of this DOA Web services infrastructure, and shows screen shots of a browser interface that allows humans to delegate attributes to and revoke attributes from other humans. The final section concludes with a comparison of several other schemes and indicates where further research is still needed.

THE HIERARCHICAL RBAC/ABAC MODEL

Role-based access control (RBAC), our Requirement 3, was standardised by NIST and is now published as an American National Standard (ANSI, 2004). Figure 1 shows the ANSI RBAC model. Users are assigned roles via user assign-

Figure 1. The NIST/ANSI RBAC model

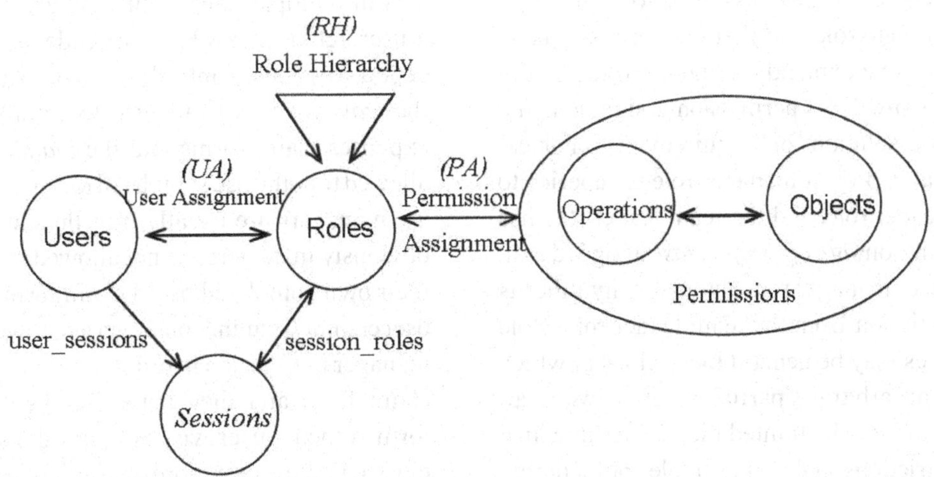

ments (UAs). A user may be assigned zero, one, or more roles. A user with zero roles currently assigned will not be able to access any protected objects.

A role may have zero, one, or more users assigned to it at any time, in order to cater for the natural migration of users between roles in an organisation. Roles are assigned permissions via Permission Assignments (PAs). A permission is the ability to perform an operation on a protected object or resource, for example, print to a laser-jet printer, or invoke a Web service. A role may have zero, one, or more permissions assigned to it. A permission may also be assigned to a set of roles, for example, in order to read certain files of project X, the roles of employee and member of project X are needed. A user obtains the permission to perform an operation on an object by being assigned the role or roles that has (have) the required permission(s) assigned to it (them). Users are statically constrained from having certain permissions by not being assigned the required roles. For example, in a bank the same person cannot usually audit transactions and be a teller, so static constraints will forbid the same user from being assigned both the teller and auditor roles.

In the ANSI RBAC model, roles may be organised in a hierarchy to suit the particular needs of an organisation. The reason for having a hierarchy is that senior or superior roles inherit the permissions assigned to their junior or subordinate roles, so that the permissions do not need to be explicitly assigned to the senior role. This simplifies permission assignment and provides a solution for Requirement 4. For example, say a project manager role is superior to a team leader role, and the team leader role has the permission *sign off project task* assigned to it. The project manager role automatically inherits this permission from the team leader role. Role hierarchies may be general hierarchies in which there is an arbitrary partial order between all the roles, or may be limited hierarchies in which some restrictions apply, for example, the hierarchy forms a tree structure or inverted tree structure. An organisation's general role hierarchy can be a disjoint set of several hierarchies, in which there is no single most superior role or most subordinate role. This allows limited permission inheritance to propagate between the roles.

By extending the ANSI RBAC model to include attributes of a user, such as age, name, and qualifications, in the role hierarchy, we can assign permissions to attributes as well as to roles, and migrate toward an attribute based access control (ABAC) model. Furthermore, by extending RBAC so that permissions can refer to operations on classes of objects identified by their attributes instead of operations on specifically named objects, we extend the migration to ABAC. Also by supporting resource class hierarchies, in which subordinate resource object classes inherit the attributes of their superior more generic object classes, we allow permission assignments to be inherited by subordinate object classes. For example, a permission assignment that says that users with the employee role can print on printers, through the process of role and resource object class inheritance we simultaneously allow managers (who are superior to employees) to print on laser jet printers (which are subordinate to printers).

In order to cater for dynamic constraints, in which a conflict of interest might arise if a user acts in multiple roles simultaneously, but not if a user acts in the roles independently, the concept of sessions is introduced. For example, say the *traveller* role is allowed to complete travel expenses claim forms and the *manager* role is allowed to authorise completed forms. People who are managers are usually travellers as well, but obviously managers are not allowed to authorise their own completed travel claim forms. Thus, a user cannot simultaneously act as a traveller and a manager in a session in order to complete a travel claim form and then authorise the completed form. When a user wishes to use the system he must activate one or more of his roles in a session, and the dynamic constraint will not allow him to activate conflicting roles in the same session. In the case of the travel claim request scenario, the user session starts when the travel claim form is opened and finishes when the user has finished accessing it.

Applying ABAC to Distributed Web Services

The ANSI RBAC standard says nothing about how roles are assigned to users or permissions are assigned to roles. In this chapter, we assume that each role and attribute has an administrative authority that controls the assignment of roles and attributes to users. We further assume that in a distributed environment there will be many such attribute authorities (AAs) that reside in different domains from each other and from the Web service that is being accessed. Consequently, it must be the Web service provider itself that decides who are the attribute authorities that it trusts to assign which roles and attributes to which users, and furthermore, what permissions to confer on each attribute and role. In this way, each Web service remains autonomous and in direct control of who is authorised to access its resources.

Roles (or attributes) are assigned to users in the form of attribute assertions, or attribute certificates (ACs), in which an issuer (an AA) asserts that a holder has a particular attribute. An AC is a digitally signed or "certified" attribute assertion. Each attribute assertion should contain: the name (or identity) of the holder, the attributes that have been assigned to the holder by the issuer, the name (or identity) of the issuer that is, the AA, and the period of time the assertion is valid. Attribute assertions may also optionally contain the policy rules of the issuer, for example, limiting the resources that the assertion may be presented to. The assertion may be digitally signed by the issuer to prove or certify that the contents are authentic. In a distributed environment the digital signature will always be necessary, unless a trusted path exists between the issuer and the consuming Web service. Examples of ACs are: a degree certificate issued to a graduate by a university, a state registered nurse certificate issued to a nurse by the Royal College of Nursing, an employee certificate issued to a member of staff by the employing organisation, and a project manager certificate issued to a person by a VO manager.

There are two standard formats for attribute assertions, or ACs. The first is the ISO/ITU-T X.509 Attribute Certificate format (ITU-T, 2005), and the second is the OASIS SAML attribute assertion format (OASIS, 2005). The primary difference between the two formats is that the former is a binary encoding of the assertion, while the latter is an XML text encoding; furthermore, the digital signature is mandatory in the X.509 AC format, and optional in the SAML attribute assertion format. Both formats are infinitely extensible to allow for bespoke tailoring by applications and issuers, for example, to add application specific policy rules. Both of these token formats can be used as authorisation credentials by users, and a Web services infrastructure should be able to cater for both of these formats as a minimum. If a user presents an X.509 AC or SAML attribute assertion to a Web service, the service should be able to determine from the attribute authorities that it trusts if the user has sufficient attributes (or roles) to be granted access to its resources.

A WEB SERVICES-BASED DELEGATION OF AUTHORITY ARCHITECTURE

The ISO Standard 10181-3 (ITU-T, 1995) provides a general architectural model for controlling access to networked resources (see Figure 2). In this model, the access control enforcement function (AEF) or policy enforcement point (PEP)—the terms are synonymous—intercepts an initiator's access request and asks the application independent access control decision function (ADF) or policy decision point (PDP)—again the terms are synonymous—if the initiator is allowed to perform the requested action on the target resource. The PDP examines the authorisation credentials of the initiator and consults its policy—which can be an ABAC or RBAC policy—to determine if the initiator has sufficient attributes (or roles) to be granted access to the target resource. From this evaluation it returns a granted or denied response to the PEP. The initiator's credentials may be provided by either the initiator in its access request, or the PDP can retrieve them itself from the issuer or a credential repository.

The architectural model (Figure 2) is ideal for controlling access to Web services. The Web service endpoint reference is the PEP that traps the user's service request. It then forwards the user's request to the PDP asking for an authorisation decision. The PEP and PDP can be collocated, or distributed, and communicate via an open protocol such as in Welch, Ananthakrishnan, Siebenlist, Chadwick, Meder, and Pearlman (2006). If the PDP returns granted, the user is allowed to consume the resources of the Web service, but if the PDP returns denied, the user's request will be rejected by the PEP. The complex task of deciding if the user has the correct set of attributes for the requested service is handed over to the application independent PDP to determine. It is the PDP that will decide if the user has been properly assigned or delegated the attributes that are asserted in the user's credentials according to the authorisation policy that is written by the Web service administrator.

Interestingly, we can also utilise the above model when creating a delegation of authority (DOA) Web service (see Figure 3). The DOA Web service will receive a delegation request from a delegator to delegate an attribute or attributes to a delegate. The delegator can be any Web ser-

Figure 2. X.812/ISO 10181-3 access control framework

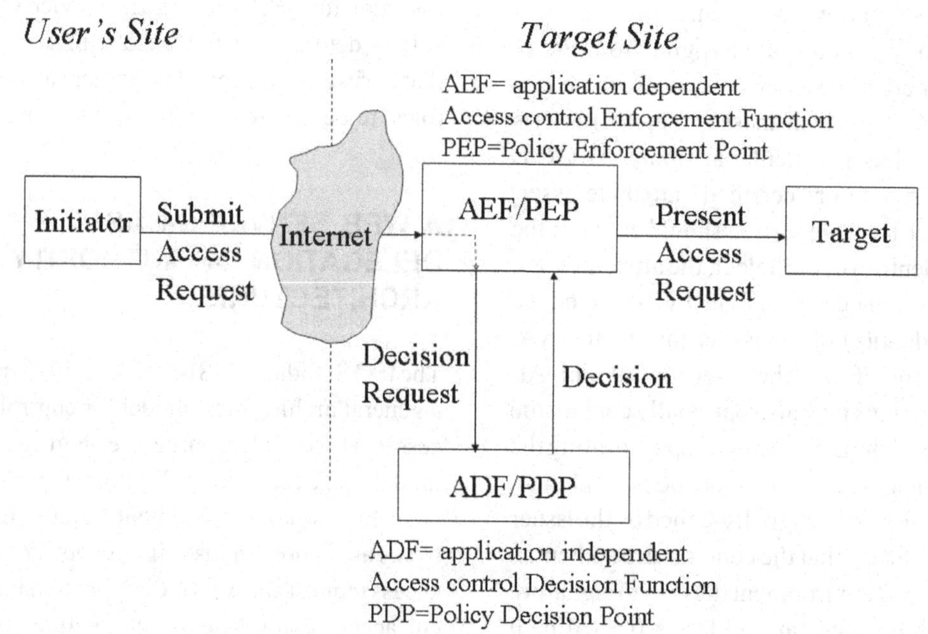

Figure 3. The delegation of authority Web service architecture

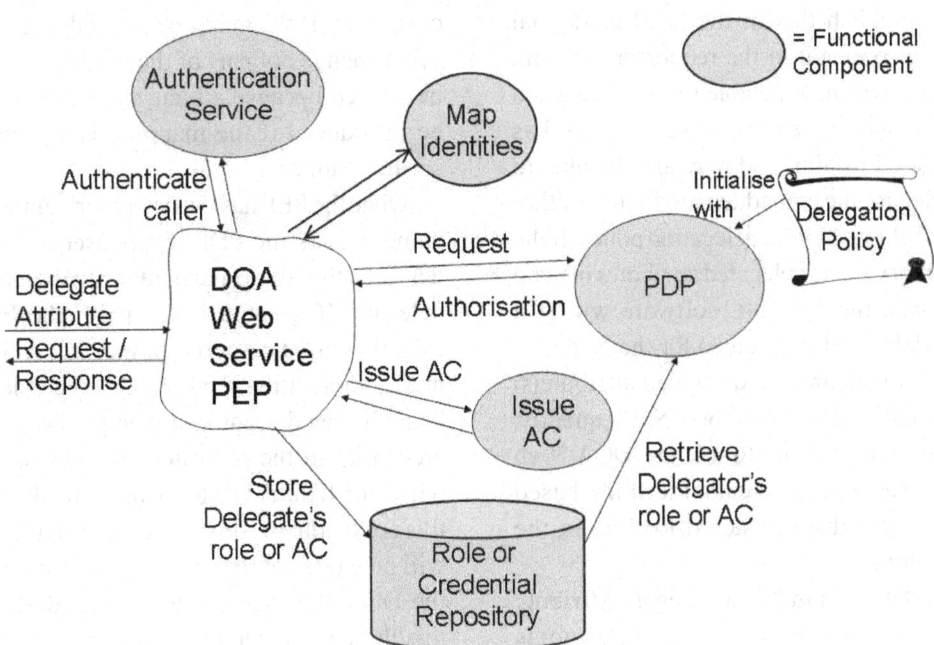

vice, or a human being acting via a Web services user interface. The delegate can be another Web service or another human being. In this way, we achieve the desired objective of person to person, service to service, person to service, and service to person delegation of authority (Requirement 1). The target resource is the Web service software that is able to issue an authorisation credential, in the form of an AC, for the delegate, on behalf of the delegator. This *issue AC* software should be capable of creating the attribute certificate in either X.509 AC or signed SAML attribute assertion format. This *issue AC* software should have its own digital signing key pair for this task, so that future credential recipients can verify that the issued credential is authentic. Because most users do not have their own PKI key pairs, they cannot issue their own ACs. This is why we require the DOA Web service to sign the credential on the delegator's behalf. This solves Requirement 7.

The delegator's request will be intercepted by the PEP, and passed to the PDP to ask if this user is allowed to delegate this/these particular attribute(s) to this delegate, according to the organisation's delegation policy (Requirement 5). The PDP retrieves the delegator's current set of authorisation credentials or roles/attributes from the local repository, and consults the delegation policy to see if the requested delegation is allowed or not. If the policy allows the delegator and delegate to be independently named, then this solves Requirement 2. As a result of evaluating the policy, the PDP replies granted or denied to the PEP. If granted, the PEP will ask the *Issue AC* software to issue a delegated authorisation credential to the delegate on behalf of the delegator, and will then either publish this in the local credential repository or return it to the requestor, or both. The delegate will now be able to use the issued credential to gain access to the service that has been delegated to him, and may also be able to further delegate the embedded attribute to other delegates, if allowed by the delegation policy. If the local repository stores delegated attributes instead of credentials, the *Issue AC* software will still create the delegated attribute(s) for the delegate, but not sign them, and the delegated attribute(s) will be stored in the repository. Subsequently, the delegate will be able to ask the DOA Web service to issue a new credential for him, based on the attributes that are stored for him in the local repository.

When a delegator makes a Delegate Attribute request to the DOA Web service, the delegator is first authenticated to determine who he or she is. Delegator authentication can be by any suitable means, and can be via an internal authentication service or external Web service. This model does not dictate any particular authentication scheme (Requirement 7). It is up to an implementation to determine the most appropriate authentication mechanism to use. That being said, digital signatures would be the most appropriate and secure mechanism for Web service to Web service authentication, but for authenticating a human user that is accessing the DOA Web service via a Web services user interface, a username and password stored in the local LDAP directory might be appropriate.

The next step is to optionally map the requestor's authenticated name into the authorisation name that is held in the authorisation credentials. This step is only needed if the two names are different, for example, when proxying is used (this will be described in more detail in the Implementation Section) or when the authentication mechanism uses a different name form to that stored in the issued credentials. Ideally this step should not be needed in the latter case, because the authenticated name should be held in the authorisation credential. If the mapping is needed, how this is performed is not part of the model, but care will be needed because a security vulnerability will be introduced if the mapping is not made in a secure manner.

Once the PEP has the delegator's authorisation name, it asks the PDP if this user is allowed to delegate this/these particular attribute(s) to the delegate. If granted is returned, the PEP then asks the target resource (*Issue AC*) to issue the new authorisation credential to the delegate, on behalf of the delegator. It then publishes the new credential in the repository or returns it to the requestor. If the delegate wishes to further delegate this credential to someone else, then the delegate will now take on the role of delegator and access the DOA Web service to request delegation of this/these attribute(s) to someone else. In this way, delegation can continue automatically from one user to another, providing, of course, that each delegation is in accordance with the organisation's delegation policy.

The model supports two different modes of operation, depending upon whether the repository stores credentials or attributes/roles. In both cases, delegation only takes places once, but credential issuing may take place zero, one, or more times. When the repository stores credentials, they are only issued once by the DOA Web service, they will typically have a relatively long lifetime (the period of the delegation), and they can be retrieved at will from the repository by users or by Web services that wish to validate the authority of a user to access its service. When the repository stores attributes/roles, the DOA Web service can be called repeatedly to issue typically short lived credentials based on the attributes/roles that have been delegated and stored in the repository. When the DOA Web service is only issuing already delegated attributes, the delegator's name is not required, only the name of the delegate. In both modes of operation the repository will need to record the validity period of the delegation and any policy conditions that are attached to it. If credentials are stored, this information is embedded in the issued credentials, if attributes are stored, separate fields will be needed in the repository to record it. When the repository stores attributes, it has to be strongly secured to prevent tampering with its contents and an attacker inserting false attributes. When the repository stores credentials, because the latter are digitally signed, it is not possible for an attacker to insert false credentials into the repository without first gaining access to the private signing key of the *Issue AC* service. Even if the repository is only weakly protected, the worst an attacker could do would be to remove a user's credentials, a denial of service attack.

The Advantages of a DOA Web Service

Here, we summarise the benefits of using a DOA Web service instead of each delegator issuing their own delegated credentials. Firstly, the DOA Web service can support a fully secure audit trail and a repository, so that there is an easily accessible record of every authorization credential/attribute that has been issued and revoked throughout the organization. If each delegator were allowed to independently issue their own credentials, then this information would be distributed throughout the organization, making it difficult or impossible to collect, being possibly badly or never recorded or even lost.

Secondly, the DOA Web service can be provided with the organization's delegation policy, and apply control procedures to ensure that a delegator does not overstep her authority by issuing greater permissions to delegates, or even to herself, than the organization's policy allows. For example, a delegator may have an attribute that they are allowed to delegate to others, but not allowed to assert themselves. Without proper controls a delegator may delegate the attribute to himself so that he is then allowed to assert the attribute. A well constructed delegation policy and PDP enforcement mechanism can ensure that this does not happen.

Thirdly, we don't get cascading revocations. In a traditional certificate chain, such as a PKI certificate chain, if any superior certificate in the chain is revoked, then all the subordinate certificates are also automatically revoked. Thus, if a delegator issued her own ACs, and her delegates then issued their own ACs, then if her AC was subsequently revoked, then all the delegates' ACs would also become immediately invalid. We typically don't want this to happen in an organization. For example, if a manager delegates various roles to members of staff in her department, and is then replaced and her role is revoked, we don't want all the delegated roles to be immediately revoked as well, or the department might grind to a halt. This does not happen with a DOA Web service. Because all the ACs are issued and signed by the DOA Web service, then a delegator's AC can be revoked without causing any of the delegate's ACs to be automatically revoked. Note however, if we record the name of the delegator in each issued AC, we are still able to implement cascading revocations if we require them.

Fourthly, the complexity of AC chain validation is significantly simplified. When delegators issue the ACs themselves, the AC chains can become arbitrarily long. When the DOA Web service issues the ACs to delegates, the AC chain length will always be a maximum of two, depending upon who the relying party trusts. If the relying party trusts the administrative authority that operates the DOA Web service and the former has delegated the issuing of ACs to the latter, then the chain length will always be two (trusted authority) ← (AC of DOA Web service) ← (AC of delegate). If the relying party trusts the DOA Web service as a root of trust, then AC chain lengths are reduced to just one, the AC of the delegate issued by the trusted DOA Web service.

Finally, a delegator does not need to hold and maintain her own private signing key, which would be needed if the delegator were to issue and sign her own ACs. Only the DOA Web service (the *Issue AC* component) needs to have an AC signing key.

The only disadvantage of using a DOA Web service is that the AC signing key must be permanently online and ready to be used to sign ACs when requested. In some highly secure systems and applications, this will be unacceptable.

Revocation of Authority

There are several different approaches that have been taken to the complex issue of revocation of authority, and of informing remote relying parties when revocation has taken place. Relying parties in our context refers to Web service providers who consume the issued credentials. The primary objective of revocation is to remove a credential (and all its copies, if any) from circulation as quickly as possible, so that relying parties are no longer able to use it. If this is not possible, a secondary objective is to inform the relying parties that an existing credential in circulation has been revoked and should not be used or trusted. The latter can be achieved by requiring either the relying parties to periodically check with the credential issuer, or the credential issuer to periodically notify the relying parties. Of these, requiring the relying parties to periodically check with the credential issuer is preferred, because it places the onus on the relying parties rather than on the issuer, because in general an issuer may not know who all the relying parties are, but the latter will always know who the issuer is.

The simplest approach, that used by X.509 proxy certificates (Tuecke et al., 2004), VOMS ACs (Alfieri et al., 2005), and SAML attribute assertions (OASIS, 2005), is to never revoke a credential, and instead to issue short lived delegation/ authorisation credentials that will expire after a short period of time and thus be effectively and automatically removed from circulation within a fixed period. The assumption in this case is that it is unlikely that authorisations will need to be revoked immediately after they have been issued and before they have expired. Because they are only valid for a short period of time, the opportunity to inflict damage through the illegitimate use of the authorisation credentials is short lived. Of course, the amount of damage that can be done in a short period of time can be huge, so short lived credentials are not always the best solution. Consequently, SAML attribute assertions also have the optional feature of containing a "one time use" element, which means that the consuming Web service can only use the attribute assertion once to grant access, and then it should never be used again. Instead, a new attribute assertion should be obtained from the attribute authority each time the user requests access to the Web service. This feature could be used in our DOA architecture, either at delegation time, in which case it would allow a delegator to delegate an attribute for one time use only by the delegate, or at issuing time (if attributes are stored in the repository) in which case the short lived ACs would be flagged for one time use.

An advantage of short lived credentials is that they effectively remove a credential from circulation after a short period of time, and consequently they mandate that users or service providers must frequently contact the credential issuer in order to obtain new freshly minted credentials.

The main disadvantage of short lived credentials is knowing how long to issue them for. They should be valid for the maximum time that anyone is likely to need them for, or otherwise one of the later steps of a user's task may fail to be authorised before the task has been completed, which could lead to the task being aborted and all the processing lost. This is a current well-known problem with proxy certificates. On the other hand, the longer they are valid, the greater their period of vulnerability to misuse without any direct way of withdrawing them from circulation. This has caused some researchers to suggest that proxy certificates should be revocable!

A second disadvantage of short lived credentials is that the bulk of the effort is placed on the issuer, who has to keep reissuing the short lived credentials. This could become a bottleneck to performance. A better solution should put the bulk of the processing effort onto the relying parties, because these are the ones who want to use the issued credentials.

A different approach to achieving the secondary objective of revocation is to notify the relying parties when revocation has taken place by issuing revocation lists. A revocation list is a digitally signed list of revoked credentials, usually signed by the same authority that issued the original credentials. Revocation lists have an expiry time and are updated and issued periodically. Relying parties are urged to obtain the next issue of the revocation list before the current one has expired, in order to keep as up to date as possible. The latest revocation list can be sent by the user along with his credentials, to prove that his credentials have not been revoked, or the relying party can independently download them from the issuer's repository. The use of certificate revocation lists (CRLs) is the approach standardised in X.509 (ITU-T, 2005) and is most frequently used by X.509 public key infrastructures. Revocation lists ensure that relying parties are eventually informed when a credential has been revoked, no matter how many copies of the credential there are in circulation, but revocation lists have several big disadvantages. Firstly, there is always some delay between a user's credential being revoked and the next issue of the revocation list appearing. This could be 24 hours or even longer, depending upon the frequency of issue of the CRLs. Thus, in order to reduce risk to a minimum, a relying party would always need to delay authorising a user's request until it had obtained the latest CRL that was published *after* the user issued his service request, which of course is impractical for most scenarios. If the relying party relies on the current revocation list, then the risk from using a revoked credential equates, on average, to half that of using a short lived credential, assuming the validity period of a short lived credential is equal to the period between successively issued CRLs. This reduced risk comes at an increased processing cost.

CRLs can put a significant processing load on both the issuer and the relying party. CRLs have to be issued at least once every time period, regardless of whether any credentials have been revoked or not during that period. In a large system the lists can get inordinately long containing many thousands of revoked credentials. These have to be reissued every time period, distributed over the network, and read in and processed by the relying parties. Delta revocation lists (ITU-T, 2005) have alleviated this problem, but again by increased processing complexity. Consequently, few people, if any, today are using revocation lists with authorisation credentials.

An alternative approach to notifying relying parties is to use the online certificate status protocol (OCSP) (Myers, Ankney, Malpani, Galperin, & Adams, 1999). Rather than a relying party periodically retrieving the latest revocation list from the issuer's repository, the OCSP allows a relying party to ask an OCSP responder in real time if a certificate (i.e., credential) is still valid or not. The response indicates if the certificate is good, or has been revoked, or its status is unknown. Because most OCSP responders base their service on the latest published revocation lists, the revocation status information is no more current than if the relying party had consulted the latest revocation list itself; thus the risk is not lessened. But what an OCSP responder does do is reduce the amount of processing that a relying party has to undertake in order to validate a user's credential/certificate. This reduced cost to the relying parties is offset by the cost of setting up and running the OCSP service.

We can see that none of the above approaches to revocation is ideal. Delegation of authority might last for a long period of time, especially when humans delegate roles that are meant to last for months or even years. We could issue long lived credentials, but the use of CRLs for revocation has many disadvantages. We could issue short lived credentials, but there is an inherent conflict between long lived delegation and short lived credentials that needs to be resolved. In the proposed architectural model this can be resolved by storing delegated attributes in the repository, along with the validity period of the delegation, and then repeatedly issuing short lived credentials as and when they are required until the delegation period has expired. Early revocation of the delegation is then achieved by removing the user's attributes from the repository. This approach is viable, but we are still left with the problem of determining the validity period of the short lived credentials.

Consequently, we propose an alternative scheme that we believe is superior to short lived credentials, CRLs, and OCSP servers. We believe that the optimum approach to credential issuing should have the following features. A user's credential should be issued just once and stored in the issuer's repository with its own unique URL. The credential should be valid for as long as the delegation is required, which can be a relatively long or short period of time. This minimises the effort of the credential issuer (and the delegator). A credential should be able to be used many times by many different service providers, according to the user's wishes, without having to be reissued. This mirrors the situation today with our plastic credit cards and other similar types of credential. A credential should be capable of being revoked at any time, and the revocation should be instant. This can be achieved by the issuer simply deleting the credential from its repository and requiring relying parties to contact the issuer's repository periodically, using the URL of the credential, to check if the credential is still present or has been revoked. This period can be determined by the relying party according to its risk mitigation strategy. This period can vary per application or per user request, and is set by the relying party as appropriate, and not by the issuer, which is putting the responsibility where it belongs. Ideally, a relying party should contact the repository when the credential is first used, and then periodically during the life of the authorisation session according to its own risk assessment. In order to strongly bind the repository to the credential, the credential's URL is embedded in the credential, so that the relying party knows where to go to check for the revocation status of the credential. This design minimises the processing effort of the issuers and the relying parties, because issuers do not need to continually mint new credentials, and relying parties do not need to process potentially large revocation lists. A secure network lookup, for example using TLS (Dierks & Allen, 1999) to bind to the repository URL, is all that is needed to ensure that a credential is still valid and has not been revoked. A simple bitwise comparison of the initial validated credential with subsequently retrieved copies is all that is needed to ensure that the credential is still the same one. Finally, there is little possibility of the credential expiring before the user's task has been completed, because it is likely to be long lived, which is not the case with short lived nonrevocable credentials.

THE DELEGATION POLICY

In essence, the delegation policy needs to say who (i.e., the delegator) is entitled to delegate what (i.e., which roles and attributes and if fine grained delegation is also required, which tasks or permissions as well) to whom (i.e., the delegate), and under what constraints. The process of delegation forms a directed acyclic graph (DAG), with the initial attribute holders that is, initial delegators, as the sources of the graph (see Figure 4). Intermediate nodes in the graph represent delegates who subsequently act as delegators and further delegate their attributes (or permissions) to others. Sink nodes represent delegates who have not further delegated their attributes (or permissions) to others. Edges in the graph represent the attributes or permissions that have been delegated from the delegator to the delegate. Successor edges must always represent the same or less attributes and permissions than the union of their predecessor edges; otherwise a delegator will have delegated more privileges than he himself possessed. The graph is acyclic because a delegator should not be able to delegate to herself or to a predecessor (e.g., edges 14 and 17 in Figure 4). Rationally, there is a reason for this; a delegate should never *need* to delegate to an entity that previously delegated directly or indirectly to it. But there is also a security reason for this. There is a potential security loophole if a delegator, who is allowed to delegate a privilege but not to assert it, does subsequently delegate it to herself, as then she would be able to assert the delegated privilege (see later).

The delegation policy specifies the schema for this directed acyclic graph, thereby controlling which entities can be sources, sinks, and intermediate nodes, and what the attribute relationships between the nodes are.

A simplified form of the directed graph is a delegation tree, in which there is only one source or root node which holds all the attributes that can be delegated, and each act of delegation creates a separate delegate subordinate node. If a delegate receives attributes from two or more delegators in separate acts of delegation, such as edges 7 and 12 in Figure 4, then these are represented as separate edges and nodes in the tree, without merging the delegate nodes together. The purpose of this is

Figure 4. An example delegation directed acyclic graph

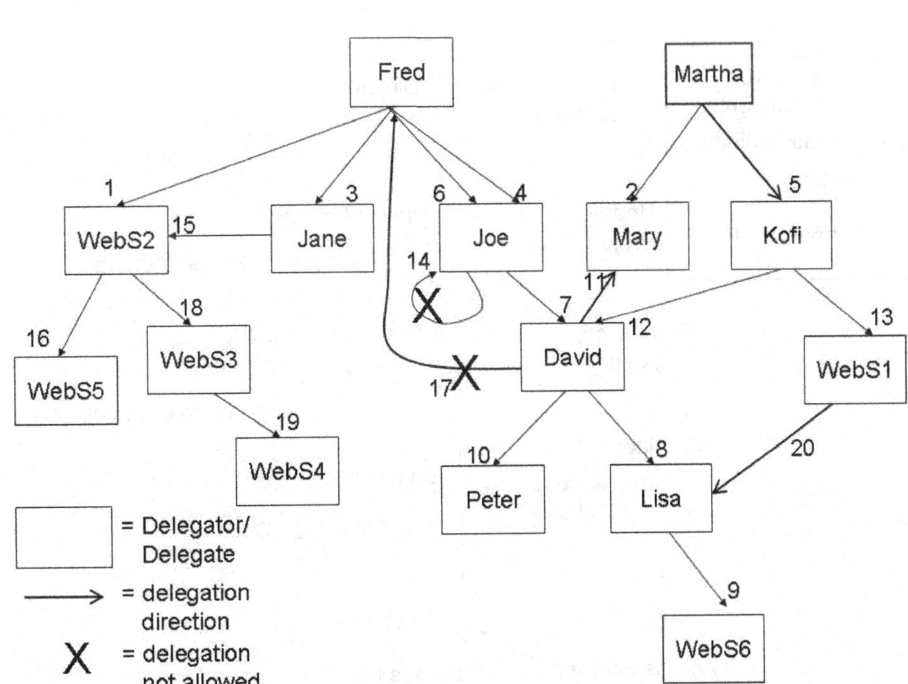

to forbid such a delegate from combining their various attributes together and delegating them to another delegate in a single act of delegation, such as in edges 8, 10, or 11 of Figure 4. Instead, multiple separate acts of delegation must take place, thereby maintaining the tree structure. The reason for this is that subsequent delegation and revocation become cleaner and easier to determine. In the case of delegation it is easier to prevent cycles from occurring. For example, in Figure 4, should the delegation from David to Fred take place in edge 17? The answer is no if it contains attributes from edges 6 or 4, but yes if it only contains attributes from edge 12. Consequently, determining which delegation is allowed and which is not can be quite complex in a DAG, but it is much easier in a tree. The process of revocation is to remove a delegation edge from the DAG and any consequential edges dependent upon the revoked edge. When delegation forms a tree, revoking an edge simply removes the whole subtree in a single act of revocation. With a DAG, there may be multiple incoming edges to a delegate node (from the same or different delegator nodes, as in edges 4 and 6 to Joe or 7 and 12 to David, respectively), and multiple outgoing edges to further delegates. If one of the incoming edges is revoked, the process of determining which outgoing edges and further delegate nodes should be deleted and which should remain becomes much more complicated. Thus, delegation trees significantly simplify delegation DAGs.

Concerning what can be delegated from a delegator to a delegate, this can be determined by reference to the role hierarchy. A delegator should be allowed to delegate any of the roles or attributes that he possesses or any of their junior roles from the role hierarchy. We have already described the role hierarchy in the fourth section, which specifies the partial order relationship

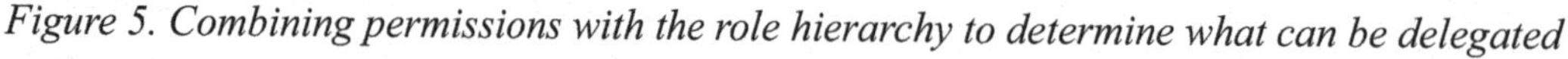

Figure 5. Combining permissions with the role hierarchy to determine what can be delegated

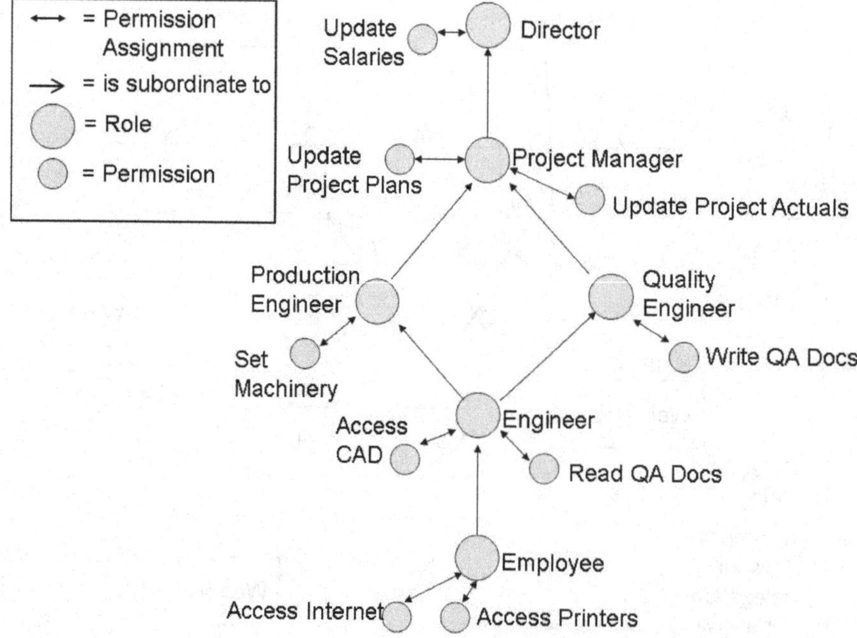

between the attributes and roles, but we can also add the permissions that each role or attribute has been granted into this hierarchy as well, making them the leaves of the delegation role hierarchy (see Figure 5). In this way the holder of an attribute (represented by a large circle in Figure 5) can delegate this particular attribute or any of its subordinate attributes from the role hierarchy or any of their associated permissions (represented by small circles in Figure 5), to a delegate in the DAG or delegation tree. For example, referring to Figure 5, a person holding the project manager role should be able to delegate this role, or any of its subordinate roles, for example, Quality Engineer, or any of the associated permissions, for example, Update Project Plans, to a delegate. This gives the delegator fine grained control over what he is able to delegate (Requirement 6). In the delegation DAG, a successor edge in the delegation graph must contain the same or less attributes/permissions than the union of its predecessor edges, with reference to the role and permissions hierarchy.

Note, however, that there is one significant difference between the roles and the permissions in Figure 5. The roles are assigned by the attribute authorities in one domain, while the permissions are assigned to the roles by the service providers in possibly different domains. Furthermore, different service providers may assign different permissions to the same role/attribute. For example, you might posses an American Express credit card, and find that it is not valid in one shop, is valid for any purchases in another shop, and is only valid for purchases over £5 in a third shop. The attribute has not changed, but the permission assigned to it has, according to the policy of the service provider. Thus, in order to achieve fine grained authorisation at the permission level, the attribute authority will need to closely liaise with the various service providers in order to add these permissions to its delegation role hierarchy. Note that we can achieve the same fine grained control over delegation if we create new uni-permission roles as the leaves of the role hierarchy, where each new uni-permission role is assigned just one of the permissions of the superior "real" role, for example, we can create an AccessPrinter role subordinate to the Employee role in Figure 5 to replace the Access Printer permission. This uni-permission role will not be assigned to a person initially, but it may be delegated to another entity dynamically. However, for this dynamic fine grained delegation of authority to work in a Web services world, the service provider that has assigned the permission to the role, for example, Access Printer to the Employee role, will now need to update its access control policy and add the new uni-permission role, for example, AccessPrinter to its role hierarchy. Service providers may be reluctant to make these changes to their RBAC policies, in which case permissions instead of uni-permission roles will need to be delegated.

There are additional policy rules that may need to be included in the delegation policy, such as: is a delegate allowed to delegate the credential again, that is, is the delegation process recursive or not, and if it is recursive, how many times can the delegation recurse, an infinite number of times or a limited number of times? We also need to consider if a delegator is empowered to assert the attributes and tasks that he is delegating, or is only allowed to delegate them, and if an attribute can be asserted, is there a control on where it can be asserted, that is, with only a subset of service providers? Consider, for example, an airline manager who is assigning a duty roster to pilots. The manager is delegating permission to fly an aircraft (say the "on flight duty" attribute) during certain periods of the day to pilots (the delegates). Clearly, the manager should not be able to invoke this permission himself, and empower himself to fly one of the aircraft, and thus the role (or task) may be delegated but not asserted by the airline manager. (Note that there is an alternative way of modeling this, by requiring a person who is authorised to fly an aircraft to have two attributes, say "on flight duty" and "qualified pilot," and to only give the airline manager permission to delegate the "on flight duty" attribute. Then, the airline manager would only be able to fly the aircraft if he was a qualified pilot. But in order to make our model flexible enough, we see that it is an advantage to have an assertion flag in our delegation policy.) A delegation policy may also contain conditions that a candidate delegate must fulfil before delegation can take place. For example, before a person can be delegated the fire officer role they must first have obtained a first aid certificate. Many of these conditions can be expressed in terms of attributes or roles a candidate delegate must possess before the new attribute or role can be delegated to them.

A flexible delegation policy language will allow the policy writer to specify the delegators and delegates by their attributes or roles, as well by specifically naming them. For example, we should be able to say "heads of department may delegate the fire officer role to members of staff within their department" as well as "Joe can delegate the fire officer role to David." The former allows whole groups of users to be delegators and delegates, the latter only allows specifically named individuals. In order for a person to delegate the fire officer role under the first policy rule, this person must have been assigned the assertable head of department role and the assertable or nonassertable fire officer role (depending upon whether he can act as a fire officer himself or only delegate this role) and the delegate must have been assigned the member of staff role and have the same department attribute as the delegator. In order for the latter policy rule to take effect, user Joe only needs to have been assigned the fire officer role and user David needs to exist. Note that the first policy rule on its own does not constitute a complete delegation policy. In order to be complete, a delegation policy must always specify which users are the delegation sources of authority in the DAG, that is, named individuals or services, and what attributes they are allowed to assign to whom. Otherwise, the PDP will not be able to determine if a particular delegation is allowed or not. For example, if we only have the former policy rule, and Joe attempts to delegate the fire officer role to Fred, then the PDP will not know if Joe is a head of department or not, or who is allowed to say that Joe is a head of department and who is allowed to say that Fred is a member of staff. If we only have the latter policy rule, the PDP will not know who is allowed to say that Joe is a fire officer. Without additional policy rules the PDP will not be able to determine if the delegator or possibly the delegate are bona-fide. Thus, delegation source of authority (SoA) policy rules are needed. These SoA rules may be completely general, and say, for example, that Person X is the trusted source of authority who may issue any credentials to anyone containing any attributes or permissions, or they may be much more specific and say, for example, that Person X is trusted to assign the head of department attribute to anyone in the organisation, but may not assert this attribute himself. With these SoA rules in place the PDP is then able to make authorisation decisions.

To summarise, a delegation policy needs to be able to:

1. Specify the delegation process in terms of a delegation directed acyclic graph (or a simplified delegation tree). This is done by specifying the rules for the delegation relationships that can exist between pairs of nodes in the DAG.
2. Identify the delegator and delegate nodes in the DAG by their attributes or roles or unique names/identifiers.
3. Specify trusted sources of authority of the DAG by their unique names/identifiers.
4. Specify what can be delegated in terms of an attribute/role hierarchy.
5. For very fine grained delegation optionally include the various attribute permissions as the leaf nodes in the attribute/role hierarchy.

6. Specify whether delegator nodes in the DAG can or cannot assert the attributes that they are allowed to delegate.
7. Control the depth of the delegation graph (length of delegation chains).
8. Optionally specify other policy rules that can control when, where, or how delegates may assert the privileges that have been delegated to them.
9. Optionally place conditions on candidate delegates that must be fulfilled before delegation can take place.

IMPLEMENTING A PRACTICAL DOA WEB SERVICE

One can see that building a dynamic DOA Web service is reasonably complex and many competing choices have to be made. Primary choices are: should the DOA Web service repository store attributes or credentials? Should the issued credentials be short lived or long lived? If long lived, then how should revocation be performed? As stated in the fifth section, there are two main modes of operation that can be envisaged for the DOA Web service.

In the first mode of operation, the repository is an internally trusted component of the system and stores attributes rather than credentials. It is assumed that the repository cannot be tampered with by attackers, and therefore the attributes within it are safe. The DOA Web service issues short lived credentials to clients on demand. Consequently, no revocation is necessary. Users can delegate their attributes to other users according to the delegation policy. Clients can make repeated requests to the service for short lived credentials to be issued to users based on the attributes held by the users.

In the second mode of operation, the repository is accessible to the outside world in read mode

Figure 6. A practical delegation of authority Web service

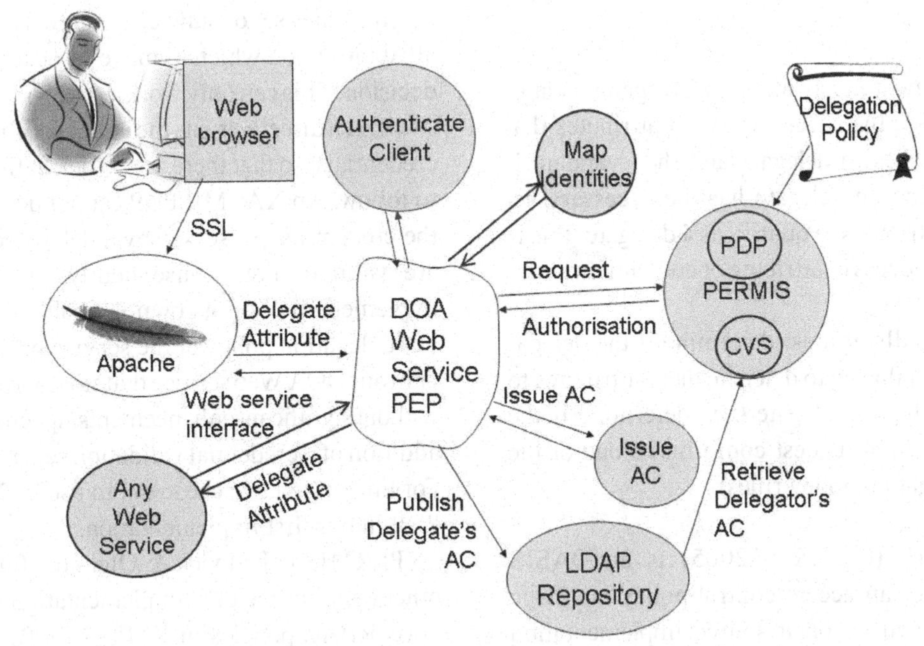

via secure links and stores relatively long lived credentials which are tamperproof. Users delegate these credentials to other users, and the DOA Web service has write access to the repository. Clients retrieve the credentials by contacting the repository directly using the URLs of the credentials. Credentials are revoked by removing them from the repository. Relying parties (service providers) must periodically check the repository to see if a credential is still there or not, according to their own risk assessments.

We have chosen to implement the second mode of operation because of its various advantages given in the fifth section. In our first version, we have used an LDAP server as the credential repository, and in the second version we are adding an Apache WEBDAV server (Goland, Whitehead, Faizi, Carter, & Jensen, 1999; Chadwick & Anthony, 2007).

Delegation Policy Enforcement

The most complex and crucial component in a DOA Web service is the PDP that can support the organisation's delegation policy. The PDP essentially has two complementary functions to perform.

- Firstly, it must validate a delegator's claim to have the necessary set of attributes that it wishes to delegate and then validate if the chosen delegate has the necessary set of attributes to qualify as a delegate (this is the process of attribute or credential validation).
- Secondly, it must determine if the delegator is allowed to delegate these attributes to the chosen delegate (i.e., determine if the delegation request conforms to one of the delegation policy rules).

XACML (OASIS-2, 2005) is an OASIS standard for an access control policy language in XML, and an open source implementation of an XACML PDP exists, written by Sun, and available from http://sunxacml.sourceforge.net/. XACML provides a rich language for specifying who is allowed to do what. Access control subjects, resources, and actions are specified in terms of their attributes. If we make *the delegator* the access control subject and *the delegate* the access control resource, while *to delegate* is the access control action of an XACML access control rule, then an XACML PDP can decide if a delegator with a given set of attributes is allowed to delegate some of these attributes to a potential delegate who possesses another set of attributes. This is the second of the functions described above. Consequently, an XACML PDP should work very well in the first mode of operation where the repository stores user attributes, and the attributes do not need to be validated (because their presence in the trusted repository is sufficient to say they are valid).

However, XACML does not support credential validation, and therefore on its own cannot be used by either service providers that receive delegated credentials, or a DOA Web service that stores credentials instead of attributes. An XACML PDP works on the assumption that it is given a valid set of subject, resource, and action attributes upon which to make its access control decision. This can only work at a service provider site which directly trusts the issuers of all received credentials, so that there are no delegation chains to follow. An XACML PDP cannot determine if the credentials possessed by a delegated subject are valid or not. Consequently, an XACML implementation on its own is unable to enforce our delegation policy at the service provider site or in our DOA Web service that stores credentials, without significant enhancements, specifically the addition of a credential validation service (CVS). For this reason, we chose not to use an XACML PDP in our first implementation.

PERMIS (Chadwick & Otenko, 2003) is another open source PDP implementation that supports RBAC policies in XML. A PERMIS PDP comprises two components, a credential validation service (CVS) that validates users credentials, and a PDP that makes access control decisions. The PERMIS policy says who is entitled to assign which attributes to whom and whether delegation is allowed or not, as well as which attributes are needed to access which resources. Furthermore, PERMIS policies have an integer to control the depth of delegation. Thus, a PERMIS policy can be used to create an organisation's delegation policy, as well as enforce it as a service provider's site. PERMIS can be configured to either pull a user's credentials from an external repository, or to have them presented by the PEP, and so is ideal for our delegation scenario where the user does not have to present his existing credentials in order to request the delegation of attributes to a delegate. The credential format primarily supported by PERMIS is the X.509 attribute certificate, and so this is the format we adopted for our delegated credentials. LDAP repositories support the storage and retrieval of X.509 attribute certificates, and so we chose to use LDAP as our credential repository. PERMIS also supports the no assertion flag and does not allow delegators to delegate attributes to themselves.

One of the limitations of PERMIS is that its delegation policy does not support the specification of delegators and delegates by any of their attributes, but rather only by the naming domains of which they are members. Naming domains are specified using LDAP/X.500 distinguished names. This means that we cannot specify a delegation policy such as "heads of department can delegate the fire officer role to senior members of staff in their department." Instead, we have to name the individual heads of department, and specify the naming domain that potential delegates reside in, for example, cn=John Smith,o=myorg,c=gb can delegate the fire officer role to principals who are from the naming domain "ou=deptA,o=myorg, c=gb." This means our PERMIS delegation policies will be more restrictive or less efficient than ones we could write in the XACML language, but we are able to fully enforce them, while with XACML we can write richer delegation policies but we are not able to fully enforce them because XACML cannot validate (delegated) credentials. Consequently, in our first DOA Web services implementation we chose to use PERMIS on its own, but in the next implementation we plan to investigate the combination of the PERMIS CVS functionality with the XACML policy decision functionality.

Client Access

Our implementation of the DOA Web service is written in Java, and runs inside a Tomcat application server and Apache AXIS SOAP server. Consequently, it can be invoked through SOAP calls. The DOA Web service (actually the containing Tomcat server) has its own X.509 public key certificate, and requires the requesting Web service to have one as well. These certificates are used to open a secure SSL (https) connection with the DOA Web service using mutual authentication. All other types of authentication method or connection are rejected. We chose to use SSL certificate-based mutual authentication rather than XML signed SOAP messages due to SSL's superior performance and ubiquity. The SSL client must either be the entity directly making the request (i.e., the requestor), or a trusted proxy acting on its behalf. In the latter case the name of the requestor is taken from the first parameter of the Web services operation (except the storeACforMe and revokeACforMe operations, which cannot come from a trusted proxy). The names of the trusted proxies are read in at initialisation time from a configuration file. We have implemented an Apache server as a trusted proxy, using LDAP username-password authentication of the users, and this will be described later.

The DOA Web service publishes a standard WSDL file that allows other Web services to determine how to access its services. It supports five operations:

- *delegateForMe*, whose arguments are: the distinguished name (DN) of the requestor (the delegator), the DN of the delegate, the attributes to be delegated, the validity time of the delegation (from and to), whether the delegated attributes can be asserted or not (yes/no), and how many more times the attributes can be delegated (the delegation depth, an integer). If the delegator is allowed to delegate this attribute to this delegate, an X.509 AC is created, with the DOA Web Service set as the credential issuer and the delegator's name placed in the IssuedOnBehalfOf field. The latter is a standard X.509 AC extension defined in the 2005 edition of X.509.
- *revokeForMe*, whose arguments are: the distinguished name (DN) of the requestor and the set of credentials that should be revoked. Each credential is identified by the DN of the holder, the DN of the issuer, and the serial number of the credential. This method allows the requestor to revoke many credentials at the same time (in one request). The DOA Web Service has built in rules for who is allowed to request the revocation of a credential. The allowed revokers are: the holder of the credential (i.e., the delegate himself), the issuer of the credential (which is usually the DOA Web Service but could be the delegator), who the credential was issued on behalf of (usually the delegator but could be blank), the source of authority of the delegation graph, or anyone who could have issued this credential. The rationale for allowing the latter category of revocation requestor was purely one of expediency. It was reasoned that if revocation was deemed to be necessary, then it should be able to be done fast by anyone in authority, in order to minimise the risk of damage from use of an unauthorised credential. If a user has the authority to issue a credential, and could have issued it, even though she did not actually issue it, then she should still be allowed to revoke it. While this does provide a minimal chance for a denial of service attack by a person in authority, the risk from this was deemed to be less than allowing a credential that should be revoked to remain in circulation longer than it should have been, say because the actual delegator was not available to revoke it.
- *storeACforMe*, whose argument is a fully formed digitally signed X.509 AC, sent as a base64 encoded string. This is a repository service for an external user who has the ability to sign and issue credentials herself, but does not have write access to the credential repository. The requestor must be authenticated via SSL client authentication and have the same name as the issuer of the credential. The DOA Web Service checks if the issuer is allowed to delegate this credential according to the delegation policy, and if so, stores the credential in the delegate's LDAP entry in the repository and reports success to the requestor. Otherwise, it reports unauthorised to the requestor and discards the credential.
- *revokeACforMe*, whose argument is the X.509 AC that is to be revoked, encoded as a base64 string. The DN of the requestor is taken from the client certificate of the established SSL connection and must be one of the allowed revokers, according to the rules presented in *revokeForMe* above; otherwise the revocation request is rejected. If the requestor is allowed to revoke the credential, then the AC is removed from the delegate's LDAP entry.
- *searchRepository*, whose arguments are the DN of the requestor and the DN of the delegate. The authenticated SSL client must be the trusted proxy or the requestor. This service searches through the repository for credentials issued to the delegate. The service then checks if the requestor is authorised

to view the retrieved credentials. This is determined from a configuration parameter, which can be set to either *anyone* or *revokers*. If *anyone*, all the retrieved credentials are returned, and there is no privacy protection on viewing a user's credentials. If *revokers*, each credential is checked to see if the requestor is allowed to revoke it, using the same rules as in *revokeForMe* above. The procedure removes from the result all those credentials that the requestor is not authorised to revoke. In this way, the privacy of the delegate's credentials is protected, because only those requestors who are authorised to revoke the credentials are allowed to search for them and retrieve them.

When Apache is acting as a trusted proxy on behalf of a human delegator, the human is presented with the Web page shown in Figure 7. In order to access this page, the user must first be authenticated by Apache. Any type of authentication supported by or plugged into Apache can be used. We have chosen to use standard Apache LDAP authentication, using usernames and passwords stored in our organisation's LDAP server, because this is the authentication mechanism used by all our users to access the university's network and services. The displayed delegation page invites the user to search through the organisation's LDAP service to find the user he wishes to delegate to, for example, be entering the surname. A picking list of users who match the entered criteria is displayed, and the user chooses the correct person. The user then selects the attributes that he wishes to delegate to this person, fills in the validity time of the delegation (from and to), and can then choose if the person should be allowed to further delegate these attributes or not. If further delegation is selected, the user can set the depth of further delegation and choose between allowing or forbidding the user to assert the roles that have just been delegated to him. Finally, the user presses the Issue Attribute button and if everything is in accordance with the delegation policy, the delegation is allowed. If the user has tried to do something counter to the delegation policy, one of two things might happen, according to the *downgradeable* configuration parameter of the delegation service. If the infringement is minor, for example, setting the validity period too long, and *downgradeable* is true, the delegation is still allowed to go ahead but the user's parameters are overridden by ones that conform to the policy. If *downgradeable* is false, or the infringement cannot be downgraded, for example, the delegator is trying to delegate to someone not allowed by the policy, then the delegation is rejected.

The delegator (and all other allowed revokers) can revoke the issued credential at any time by entering the Revocation Service Web page. Again, the requestor must be authenticated by Apache before the revocation page is displayed. Upon entering the revocation page, the requestor is again invited to search through the organisation's LDAP service to find the delegate he wishes to revoke an attribute from. After entering the search criteria, a list of users is displayed. Upon choosing one of them, the system invokes the *searchRepository* Web service and one of three responses will be displayed, either: a list of the user's credentials that are visible to the requestor, or a message saying that this user does not have any attributes, or an error message saying that the requestor is not allowed to search and view this user's attributes.

This DOA Web service has been piloted in various grid applications by the National e-Science centre at the University of Glasgow, and details of these trials can be found in Sinnott, Stell, Chadwick, and Otenko (2005), Sinnott, Watt, Jiang, Stell, and Ajayi (2006), and Watt, Sinnott, Jiang, Ajayi, and Koetsier (2006).

Figure 7. Web-based front end to our delegation service

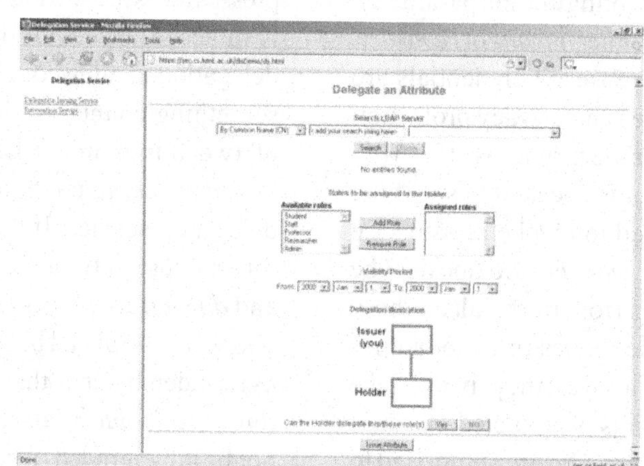

CONCLUSION AND FUTURE TRENDS

Comparison with Other Work

VOMS (Alfieri et al., 2005) is a Web services-based credential issuing service, but it is not a delegation service. It only implements part of the model specified in the fifth section, specifically the *Issue AC* and repository services. A user can make repeated requests to a VOMS service, for it to issue short lived X.509 attribute certificates derived from a subset of the attributes held in the user's repository entry. The user must be in possession of an X.509 public key certificate (PKC) in order to utilise the VOMS service, because the holder field of the credential points to the public key certificate of the user (PKC issuer and serial number) rather than the distinguished name of the user. The repository holds the various attributes of the users, but these can only be inserted into the repository by the VO manager. Users are not able to delegate their attributes to other users. They must ask the VO manager to insert attributes into other user's entries for them. The VOMS service therefore places a high administrative and maintenance load on the VO manager, because he is responsible for all delegations and revocations, and this task cannot be dynamically delegated to the VO users.

Signet (McRae, Nguyen, Cohen, & Vine, 2004) and Grouper (see *http://middleware.internet2.edu/dir/groups/grouper/*) from the Internet2 consortium are developing software that will allow users to assign permissions and delegate privileges between each other. The system is architecturally much simpler than the one depicted in Figure 3. It is designed for human users and is Web server rather than Web services based. The user interface is any standard Web browser, and the server functionality is written as Java servlets and jsp which can run in any container such as Tomcat. The repository is a RDBMS with SQL interface which stores a user's group memberships (or roles) and individual permissions (for fine grained control) along with their validity times and other policy related information such as prerequisites before a privilege can be granted and conditions on its use after it has been granted. Consequently, there is no PDP holding the delegation policy as a separate entity. Rather, the policy is distributed throughout the repository in the various tables. Signet does not issue credentials, and this functionality has to be provided by an external plugin that retrieves and packages the data from the repository in an appropriate way, for example, as a SAML assertion.

Work has been on going since 2004 in OASIS to add support for delegation of authority to XACMLv2 (OASIS, 2007). This work is designed to allow the setting of access control policies to be delegated between administrators, and is complementary to the DOA work described here. Unfortunately, the DOA work in XACML has progressed rather more slowly than originally anticipated, and at the time of writing it is not clear what the outcome will be. In parallel with the OASIS work, we devised a mechanism whereby the PERMIS CVS could be incorporated with a XACMLv2 PDP at a service provider site, in order to provide valid attributes to the PDP from delegated credentials. The valid attributes can then be fed into the XACML PDP for it to make access control decisions. This work is described fully in Chadwick, Otenko, and Nguyen (2006).

Future Work

We have developed a secure audit Web service (SAWS) which allows events to be securely audited in a tamperproof log (Xu, Chadwick, & Otenko, 2005). We propose to incorporate this into a future version of the DOA Web service so that every delegation decision can be securely logged for future reference. This might be important, for example, when trying to retrospectively trace how a person became authorised, or when he was revoked and by whom.

We are currently building a WEBDAV repository to replace the existing LDAP repository, so that individual credentials can be uniquely identified by their URLs (Chadwick & Anthony, 2007). A disadvantage of using LDAP repositories is that a URL can only usually refer to all the credentials of a particular user, rather than to individual credentials. This is because a set of ACs are usually all held together as a set of values within a single LDAP attributeCertificate attribute. This makes it impossible to retrieve a single credential of a user.

We are currently adding the ability to perform fine grained delegation based on individual permissions rather than attributes. As pointed out above, a number of complexities are introduced when this occurs in a multiple domain environment, due to the fact that a permission that is understood and valid in one domain may not be recognised in another domain. We are addressing this problem at the attribute level by adding role/attribute mappings to our service provider PDP policies (Nguyen, Chadwick, & Nasser, 2007). This will allow an attribute that is issued in one domain to be recognised in a service provider domain. Extending this mapping to permissions would allow fine grained authorisations to be understood between domains.

While our system currently only supports credentials in X.509 attribute certificate format, it will be relatively easy to add signed SAML attribute assertions as well due to the modular construction of PERMIS. Once the performance of signed SAML assertions improves, this addition will be made.

Finally, we are investigating how best to combine the PERMIS CVS functionality with the XACML policy decision functionality to allow richer delegation policies to be specified through the identification of delegators and delegates by their attributes rather than by their membership of a specific domain.

As a general trend, we expect to see more Web-based interfaces being gradually introduced to allow users to delegate authority to other users, and more willingness on the side of administrations to empower users to delegate among themselves, providing they can specify adequate delegation policies to control this. We also expect to see users and Web services dynamically delegating authority to subordinate Web services to do work on their behalf, so that work flows can be automated and distributed throughout and between organisations. We also expect to see much richer functionality to be gradually introduced into the Web front ends and the back end delegation policies. We have taken the first tentative steps along this path, by allowing dynamic delegation of authority between users and Web services, and we fully expect more sophisticated and richer mechanisms to follow.

ACKNOWLEDGMENT

We would like to thank the UK JISC for funding this work under the DYVOSE project.

REFERENCES

Alfieri, R., Cecchini, R., Ciaschini, V., Dell'Agnello, L., Frohner, A., Lorentey, K., & Spataro, F. (2005). From gridmap-file to VOMS: Managing authorization in a Grid environment. *Future Generation Computer Systems, 21*(4), 549-558.

ANSI (2004). Information technology: Role-based access control. ANSI INCITS 359-2004.

Chadwick, D.W., & Anthony, S. (2007, June). Using WebDAV for Improved Certificate Revocation and Publication. In *LCNS 4582, Public Key Infrastructure. Proceedings of 4th European PKI Workshop,* Palma de Mallorca, Spain. 265-279

Chadwick, D.W., & Otenko, A. (2003). The PERMIS X.509 Role-based privilege management infrastructure. *Future Generation Computer Systems, 19*(2), 277-289.

Chadwick, D.W., Otenko, S., & Nguyen, T.A. (2006, October 19-21). Adding support to XACML for dynamic delegation of authority in multiple domains. In *Proceedings of the 10th IFIP TC-6 TC-11 International Conference, CMS 2006,* Heraklion, Crete, Greece (pp. 67-86). Springer-Verlag.

Dierks, T., & Allen, C. (1999). The TLS Protocol Version 1.0, RFC 2246.

Goland, Y., Whitehead, E., Faizi, A., Carter, S., & Jensen, D. (1999). HTTP extensions for distributed authoring – WEBDAV. RFC 2518.

ITU-T. (1995). Security frameworks for open systems: Access control framework. ITU-T Rec X.812 | ISO/IEC 10181-3:1996.

ITU-T. (2005). The directory: Public-key and attribute certificate frameworks. ISO 9594-8 (2005) /ITU-T Rec. X.509.

McRae, L., Nguyen, M., Cohen, A., & Vine, J. (2004). Signet functional requirements. Retrieved June 3, 2007, from http://middleware.internet2.edu/signet/docs/signet_func_specs.html

Myers, M., Ankney, R., Malpani, A., Galperin, S., & Adams, C. (1999). X.509 Internet public key infrastructure: Online certificate status protocol – OCSP, RFC 2560.

Nguyen, T.A., Chadwick, D.W., Nasser, B. (2007, September 3-7). Recognition of Authority in Virtual Organisations. Presented at *4th International Conference onTrust, Privacy & Security in Digital Business*, Regensburg, Germany.

OASIS. (2005). Assertions and protocol for the OASIS Security Assertion Markup Language (SAML) V2.0, OASIS Standard.

OASIS. (2007). XACML v3.0 Administrative Policy Version 1.0, working draft 15. Retrieved June 3, 2007, from http://www.oasis-open.org/committees/tc_home.php?wg_abbrev=xacml

OASIS-2. (2005). eXtensible Access Control Markup Language (XACML), Version 2.0. OASIS Standard.

Sinnott, R.O., Stell, A.J., Chadwick, D.W., & Otenko, O. (2005). Experiences of applying advanced grid authorisation infrastructures. In *Proceedings of the European Grid Conference (EGC),* Amsterdam, Holland.

Sinnott, R.O., Watt, J., Jiang, J., Stell, A.J., & Ajayi, O. (2006). Single sign-on and authorization for dynamic virtual organizations. In *Proceedings of the 7th IFIP Conference on Virtual Enterprises, PRO-VE 2006*, Helsinki, Finland.

Tuecke, S., Welch, V., Engert, D., Pearlman, L., & Thompson, M. (2004). Internet X.509 Public Key Infrastructure (PKI) proxy certificate profile. RFC3820.

Watt, J., Sinnott, R.O., Jiang, J., Ajayi, O., & Koetsier, J. (2006). A Shibboleth-protected privilege management infrastructure for e-science education. In *Proceedings of the 6th International Symposium on Cluster Computing and the Grid, CCGrid2006*, Singapore.

Welch, V., Ananthakrishnan, R., Siebenlist, F., Chadwick, D., Meder, S., & Pearlman, L. (2006). Use of SAML for OGSI Authorization, GFD.66. Retrieved June 3, 2007, from http://www.ggf.org/documents/GFD.66.pdf

Xu, W., Chadwick, D., & Otenko, S.(2005). A PKI-based secure audit Web service. IASTED Communications, Network and Information Security CNIS, November 14 - November 16, Phoenix, AZ.

Chapter VI
A Policy-Based Authorization Framework for Web Services: Integrating X-GTRBAC and WS-Policy

Rafae Bhatti
IBM Almaden Research Center, USA

Daniel Sanz
Carlos III University of Madrid, Spain

Elisa Bertino
Purdue University, USA

Arif Ghafoor
Purdue University, USA

ABSTRACT

This chapter describes a policy-based authorization framework to apply fine-grained access control on Web services. The framework is designed as a profile of the well-known WS-policy specification tailored to meet the access control requirements in Web services by integrating WS-policy with an access control policy specification language, X-GTRBAC. The profile is aimed at bridging the gap between available policy standards for Web services and existing policy specification languages for access control. The profile supports the WS-PolicyAttachment specification, which allows separate policies to be associated with multiple components of a Web service description, and one of our key contributions is an algorithm to compute the effective policy for the Web service given the multiple policy attachments. To allow Web service applications to use our solution, we have adopted a component-based design approach based on well-known UML notations. We have also prototyped our architecture in a loosely coupled Web services environment.

INTRODUCTION

Access control in Web services is a neglected frontier that has not seen the development and adoption of many standards, as opposed to the number of current and emerging specifications for authentication aspects of Web services security (WS Security, 2002; WS Trust, 2004; SAML, 2004). Several methods of authentication for Web services (such as SAML, WS-Security) have been proposed, which only help in authenticating the users, but do not differentiate between users in terms of fine-grained access privileges. This results in an *all-or-nothing* access which is not flexible enough for modern day business processes using Web services to execute. In this chapter, we address this requirement and present a policy-based authorization framework to apply fine-grained access control on Web services.

At the very onset, we would like to motivate the problem addressed in this chapter with a typical Web services scenario, which is depicted in Figure 1. It illustrates a health information system Web application that uses multiple Web services to offer a variety of services to its clients. It offers a top level service called patient track service (PTService) which allows physicians to track all patients in the system based on the authorization of the physician. This service returns a list of patients and the location of their records. Subsequently, the physician can choose to view a specific patient record from a given location (USA and Spain in this example), for which the system will invoke the appropriate Patient Record Service (PRService). The authorization credentials of the requesting physician will again be required to obtain this new service. The level of access that the physician is allowed will depend on his or her authorization credentials, and several instances of this Web service with a different set of operations corresponding to various levels of authorization may be defined to accommodate this requirement.

In this example, one would like to specify and enforce rules such as "a physician can access records generated in his/her own hospital, unless he/she obtains an authorization credential to view the records generated in other hospitals," "physicians can only write records related to their specialization area," or "nurses can read records representing prescriptions for patients that are under their care, when the system load is not high." The specific service instance to invoke can be predefined or dynamically discovered (using, for instance, UDDI), but in both cases Web services description language (WSDL) specification (WSDL, 2001) is required to initiate the interaction. Clearly then, the task of interaction between

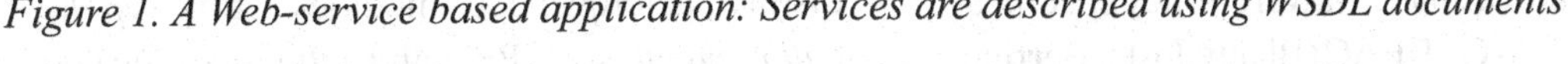
Figure 1. A Web-service based application: Services are described using WSDL documents

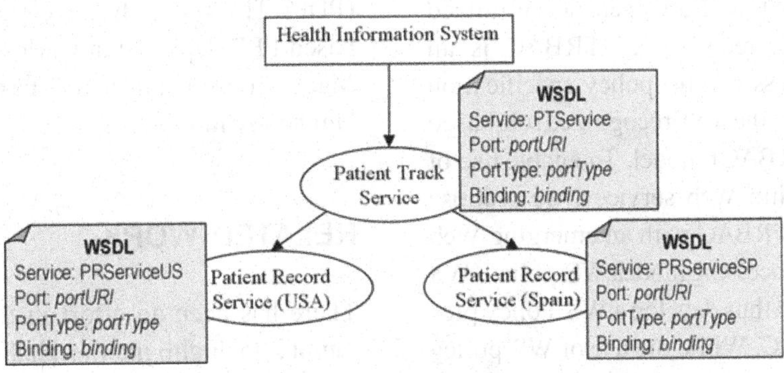

Web services requires a fine grain of control on what components of a service can be invoked and under what circumstances.

This example serves to illustrate the following two requirements for Web service access control: *fine granularity*, and *context-awareness*. The requirement for fine grain is a service design issue, which can be addressed by creating differentiated service instances (with different sets of operations) at distinct ports and associating an access control policy with those instances, and with the components that make up those instances (services, ports, port types, and bindings). The requirement for context-awareness is a policy design issue, and can be addressed by using a policy specification language that can adequately capture the context-aware access control requirements in a dynamic Web services environment. Both these aspects need to be tied together in a seamless manner and included with the service definition so that the WSDL file can be a self-contained description of the service and its applicable access control policies. The focus of our current work is to present an authorization architecture that specifically achieves this objective.

CONTRIBUTIONS AND ORGANIZATION

In this chapter, we propose a policy-based authorization framework for Web services. The framework consists of a context-aware policy specification language, X-GTRBAC (Bhatti, Joshi, Bertino, & Ghafoor, 2005), and an open decentralized enforcement architecture. X-GTRBAC is an XML-based access control policy specification language based on the well-recognized role based access control (RBAC) model. To enable use of X-GTRBAC within Web services, we propose to integrate X-GTRBAC with an emerging Web services policy processing model, WS-policy (WS Policy, 2006), and thus develop a WS-Policy profile of X-GTRBAC. While the use of WS-policy specification alone is sufficient to encode policy rules, it is not a policy language specific to access control, and therefore lacks the semantics necessary to meet the requirements for fine grained and context-aware access control. In other words, while WS-policy provides the alphabet to encode the policy, the WS-policy profile for X-GTRBAC provides the vocabulary. The design of the profile aims at bridging the gap between available policy standards for Web services and existing policy specification languages for access control.

The profile supports the WS-policy attachment specification (WS Attachment, 2006), which allows attaching, retrieving, and combining policies associated with various components of a Web service in the WSDL document. We have identified key integration challenges involving the design of the profile, and also developed a solution to address them. The most notable challenge addressed by our work is the design of an algorithm to compute the *effective access control policy* of a Web service available to a role, where *effective policy* is the policy that is obtained by combining the *relevant* policies attached to various components of the Web service. To allow Web service applications to use our solution, we have adopted a component-based design approach based on well-known UML notations. We have also prototyped our architecture, and implemented it in a Web services environment. In fact, the authorization system itself is also implemented as a loosely coupled Web service, with logically distinct, heterogeneous modules acting as *policy enforcement point* (PEP) and *policy decision point* (PDP). The system has been tested with a PHP-based PEP deployed at Carlos III University of Madrid in Spain and a Java-based PDP at Purdue University in USA.

RELATED WORK

There has been an effort in the research community to highlight the challenges associated with Web-based access control. Many of these mechanisms provide specification of context-aware access control languages (Bhatti, Joshi, Bertino, & Ghafoor, 2004; Hu & Weaver, 2004; Kaminsky, 2005; Sirer & Wang, 2002). They, however, do not provide a mechanism for policy processing in a Web services environment to allow fine-grained access control on individual Web service components defined in WSDL.

A fair amount of related research in the area of Web services security is due to the industry, with standards such as security assertion markup language (SAML) (SAML, 2004) and extensible access control markup language (XACML) (XACML, 2005) having been recently adopted. SAML defines an XML framework for exchanging authentication and authorization information for securing Web services, and relies on third-party authorities for provision of "assertions" containing such information. However, SAML itself is not designed to provide support for specifying authorization policies; it is in fact a complementary specification, and we use it in our work. XACML is an XML framework for specifying context-aware access control policies for Web-based resources. The Web service policy language (WSPL) (WSPL, 2003) is an XACML profile for Web services that can be used to publish the access control requirements of a Web service using XACML. Please note that WSPL is not related to the WS-Policy and WS-Attachment specifications. Being derived from XACML, WSPL can be used for policy specification to satisfy one of the requirements for Web service access control identified above. It, however, does not support a generalized policy processing mechanism and must be bound to an XACML target to be used in a Web service. Unlike WS-Policy, XACML does not provide a formal mechanism to associate policies with individual components of a Web service definition.

The most notable set of emerging specifications are the ones outlined in WS security roadmap (Security in a Web Services World, 2002). The roadmap consists of a number of component specifications, the relevant among them being WS-Security (WS Security, 2002) and WS-Policy (WS Policy, 2006). WS-Security is a specification for securing whole or parts of an XML message using XML encryption and digital signature technology, and attaching security credentials thereto. WS-Policy is used to describe the security policies in terms of their characteristics and supported features (such as required "security tokens," encryption algorithms, privacy rules, etc.). In fact, WS-Policy is a metalanguage which can be used to create various policy languages for different purposes. As mentioned earlier, while the use of WS-Policy specification alone is sufficient to encode policy rules, it is not a policy language specific to access control, and therefore lacks the semantics necessary to meet the fine-grained access control requirements. This is exactly where our current work fits in; we use X-GTRBAC to provide support for expressing authorization policies within the WS-Policy model. To reiterate, our proposed integration of X-GTRBAC and the WS-Policy processing model provides two-fold benefits: the use of a policy attachment mechanism of WS-Policy provides the possibility of fine-grained policy specification and reuse of access policies at different levels of Web service component definitions, and the use of WS-Policy profile of X-GTRBAC actually provides the expressive power required to specify and evaluate complex context-aware constraints for role-based access control policies for the Web service. To the best of our knowledge, the design of a policy-based authorization framework for Web services addressing these requirements remains a novel contribution.

BACKGROUND

This section provides an overview of the key elements of our framework.

X-GTRBAC

Our authorization framework uses the X-GTRBAC policy specification language (Bhatti et al., 2005). X-GTRBAC is based on an XML-based Generalized Temporal extension of the RBAC model (Sandhu, Coyne, Feinstein, & Youman, 1996). RBAC uses the notion of *role* to embody a collection of permissions; permissions are associated with roles through a permission-to-role assignment, and users are granted access to resources through a user-to-role assignment.

X-GTRBAC extends RBAC to provide an expressive and flexible constraint specification mechanism to define temporal and nontemporal contextual constraints. An (user-to-role or permission-to-role) assignment constraint in X-GTRBAC comprises of a set of assignment conditions, where each condition has associated with it an optional temporal constraint expression and an optional set of nontemporal logical expressions. The syntax of an assignment constraint is described in Table 1.

An assignment constraint is satisfied if all included assignment conditions are satisfied, where an assignment condition is satisfied if (i) the associated temporal constraint expression, if any, is satisfied, and (ii) the associated set of logical expressions, if any, is satisfied. A logical expression defines rules on the credential attribute of the constraint subject (user or role). As an example, an assignment constraint can state that "role r can access resource o if (a) the access occurs between 9AM and 5PM during the month of January in year 2006, and (b) the value of location attribute of role is "London" and the value of system load attribute of role is "low." Here, (a) is an example of a temporal constraint, represented as a temporal

Table 1. X-GTRBAC assignment constraint expression

<table>
<tr><th>Syntax</th><th>Description</th></tr>
<tr><td><AssignConstraint op="AND|OR">
[<AssignCondition [cred_type=""]
[pt_expr_id=""]>
[<!--<Logical Expression>-->]*
</AssignCondition>]+
</AssignConstraint></td><td>AssignConstraint: represents a set of constraints to apply to the assignment. The attribute op defines the evaluation mode of the included conditions.
AssignConstraint/AssignCondition: represents a contextual condition. It may specify a credential type and a periodic time expression. The former indicates that the subject of the constraint (user or role) must present a credential, the attributes of which must satisfy the rules defined in this condition. The latter represents a temporal constraint expression (see Bhatti et al., 2005).</td></tr>
<tr><td><!--<Logical Expression>-->::=
<LogicalExpression op="
AND|OR">
[<!--<Predicate Block>-->]+
<LogicalExpression></td><td>AssignConstraint/AssignCondition/LogicalExpression: represents a logical expression. It contains one or more predicates. The attribute op defines the evaluation mode of the predicates.</td></tr>
<tr><td><!--<Predicate Block>--> ::=
<!--<Logical Expression>--> |
<!--<Predicate>--></td><td>AssignConstraint/AssignCondition/LogicalExpression/{PredicateBlock}: represents either another logical expression or a simple predicate.</td></tr>
<tr><td><!--<Predicate>--> ::=
<Predicate>
<Operator/>
<FuncName/>
<ParamName/>
<RetValue/>
</Predicate></td><td>AssignConstraint/AssignCondition/LogicalExpression/Predicate: a simple predicate defines rules on credential attributes of the constraint subject (user or role). It includes a comparison using an (Operator) between the value of the credential attribute computed using a function (FuncName) having one or more arguments (ParamName) and the expected (RetValue).</td></tr>
</table>

constraint expression in X-GTRBAC, and (b) is an example of a nontemporal constraint represented as a set of logical expressions. To evaluate this logical expression, the role r must supply a credential having the attributes location and system load. Similarly, the constraints can also be associated with permission-to-role assignments, such that roles are assigned permissions subjected to the evaluation of the associated credential-based or context-based constraints.

WS-Policy

WS-policy (WS Policy, 2006) defines an abstract model for expressing the capabilities, requirements, and general characteristics of entities in Web services as policies. These properties are expressed as policies. WS-Policy does not specify how policies are discovered or attached to a Web service, but only focuses on defining them. A *policy* is a collection of *policy alternatives*, where each policy alternative is a collection of *policy assertions*. An assertion can express requirements or capabilities that will manifest in the wire, while some others will refer to service usage or selection. For the purposes of this work, we will use the term assertion to indicate assertions used in the authorization policies. A policy is represented by its corresponding policy expression. While many policy expressions are possible according to the model, the *normal form policy expression* is the canonical form, and is described in Table 2.

For the purposes of this work, we will use normal form policy expression to integrate with X-GTRBAC. The specification does not impose any restriction on the kind of XML policy expressions that may be used for assertions. Therefore, the normalized policy expression can be used to convey assertions related to any domain specific policy. It is this flexibility of the specification that will allow us to integrate WS-Policy with X-GTRBAC.

WS-Policy Attachment

WS-policy attachment (WS Attachment, 2006) defines a general purpose mechanism for associating policies to subjects to which they apply, as well as how to apply the mechanism to attach policies to WSDL 1.1 descriptions. A *policy subject* is an entity with which the policy is associated, which in our case is a Web service component defined in the WSDL document Please note that in WS-attachment terminology, the term *subject* refers to a Web service component, as opposed to the traditional RBAC notions of user and role. A given service may have associated policies by means of multiple attachments associated with the various components defined in the WSDL file. The WS-policy attachment specification states that these multiple policy attachments must be combined to obtain the effective policy for the service. We will focus our analysis on WSDL 1.1 meta-model (WSDL 1.1, 2001), because this

Table 2. WS-Policy normal form policy expression

<wsp:Policy> <wsp:ExactlyOne> [<wsp:All> [<*assertion*> ... </*assertion*>]* </wsp:All>]* </wsp:ExactlyOne> </wsp:Policy>	wsp:Policy: represents a policy wsp:Policy/wsp:ExactlyOne: represents a collection of policy alternatives wsp:Policy/wsp:ExactlyOne/wsp:All: represents a policy alternative wsp:Policy/wsp:ExactlyOne/wsp:All/*: XML expressions for assertions, all of which must be satisfied

is the target of current WS-Policy Attachment specification.

An important notion in computing the effective policy is that of *policy scope*. A policy scope is a collection of policy subjects to which a policy may apply, and a *policy attachment* is the mechanism to associate a policy with a policy scope. WS-Policy Attachment defines four types of policy subjects in WSDL 1.1: *Service Policy Subject*, *Endpoint Policy Subject*, *Operation Policy Subject* and *Message Policy Subject*. The *effective policy* for a given subject is defined to be the combination of all policies attached to policy scopes that contain that subject. The subject types must be considered nested, due to the hierarchical nature of WSDL. Table 3 relates policy scopes with their corresponding subject types in WSDL 1.1.

This information has an important consequence in our framework; it tells us which policies need to be merged to compute the effective policy of a service, for which there are multiple policies attached to its various components. The *merge* operation takes all relevant policy expressions, replaces their <wsp:Policy> with a <wsp:All> element, and places them as children of a wrapper <wsp:Policy>. The resulting policy expression is the combined policy of all attachments of the subject. The result is equivalent to normalize all policies and do the cross product among all alternatives of each policy, yielding alternatives that consider all possibilities.

Our architecture currently supports policy specification at the granularity of service, port, port type, and binding elements of a service definition. Referring to Table 3, this comprises the Service and Endpoint policy subjects.

WS-POLICY PROFILE OF X-GTRBAC

This section provides a discussion of the key issues that are required to be considered for carrying out the integration proposed in our framework, as well as an outline of our solution to the identified problems.

Problem Space

The profile has been designed to be used in a scenario, as depicted in Figure 1, where Web applications need to invoke (potentially unknown) Web services. Each service publishes its usage policy, in the form of WS-Policy, attached to its component definitions in its WSDL. These policies include contextual constraints that must be satisfied to invoke the service instances, such as role membership, user location or system load.

Table 3. WSDL 1.1 policy scopes and subject types

Policy scope	Policy Subject Type
wsdl:service	Service policy subject
wsdl:port wsdl:binding wsdl:portType	Endpoint policy subject
wsdl:binding/wsdl:operation wsdl:portType/wsdl:operation	Operation policy subject
wsdl:message wsdl:binding/wsdl:operation/wsdl:input wsdl:portType/wsdl:operation/wsdl:input	Message policy subject

The profile defines the nature and semantics of permission, and the representation of WS-Policy Assertions as X-GTRBAC constraints. To keep our exposition simple, assignment policies we use shall only include the nontemporal constraints modeled by logical expressions, because the treatment of temporal constraint expressions requires more detail than can be provided in this chapter.

Integration Issues

Figure 2 shows the basic elements of the framework and their relationships. It also indicates as numbered boxes the key integration issues that need to be addressed, enumerated below:

1. **Constraint representation:** WS-policy expressions, including assertions and operators, need to be represented as X-GTRBAC constraints. Because X-GTRBAC has its own constraint language which includes operators, a mapping between WS Policy expressions and X-GTRBAC constraints needs to be defined.
2. **Assignment policy:** As discussed before, user assignment is constrained by credential expressions that define which credentials need to be presented by users in order to be assigned to a given role. Because the services that can be invoked may not be known in advance, a mechanism is needed to provide such credentials in order for a user in a given role to access available permissions at run time.
3. **Constraint interpretation:** X-GTRBAC constraint expressions may be used to restrict user-role and permission-to-role assignments. WS-Policy expressions when attached to WSDL description are intended to express constraints on service access. As part of the design of the profile, a careful configuration is required to apply the role-based constraint model of X-GTRBAC onto the WSDL-based WS-Policy processing model.
4. **Permission nature:** Another key issue concerning the application of RBAC to WSDL-based WS-Policy processing model is to define the notion of permission, taking into

Figure 2. Integration issues in the design of the WS-Policy profile of X-GTRBAC

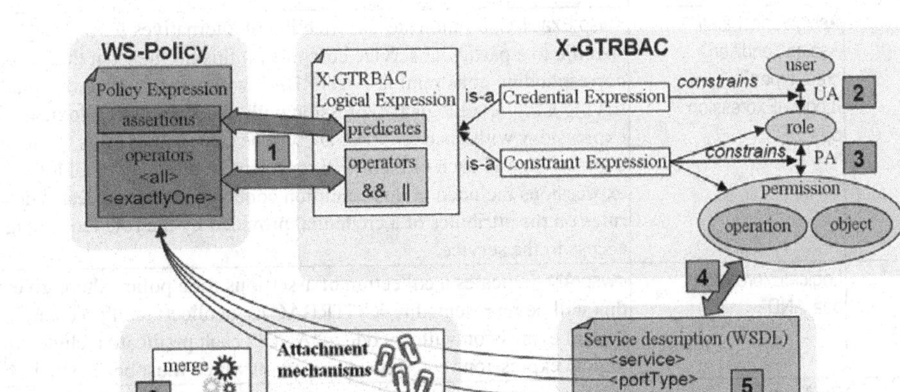

account the balance between fine-grained access and simplicity of administration. A permission may range between an operation for a service instance to a set of operations specified by an interface deployed at several network locations.

5. **Policy applicability:** Derived from the previous two issues, it is crucial to determine the relevant policy applicable to a given service access, because a service may represent a collection of operations on different ports, each having its own access control policy. This issue requires the definition of an algorithm to compute the effective permission policy, described later.
6. **Policy merging:** The particular nature of constraints on the service usage may require special care in order to produce correctly merged policies, even after the applicable policy has been determined. This issue may arise when merging policies attached to different components of a Web service description.

Following subsections explain how our framework provides solutions to the issues identified above.

Constraint Representation

We define a mechanism to represent WS-Policy assertions as X-GTRBAC constraints. As already indicated, we will only consider normal form WS-Policy expressions, and nontemporal X-GTRBAC constraints modeled by logical expressions. Our analysis proceeds as described in Table 4. Table 5 shows an example of the mapping between a normal form WS-Policy and X-GTRBAC constraint. It may be observed that the credential type associated with an assignment condition is predefined based on the role that is accessing the service. This credential type must be registered with the PDP in order to evaluate the condition. In practice, this can be done by either a prior arrangement between the PDP and the Web application invoking the PDP, or registering it dynamically using a SAML-based protocol.

Table 4. WS-Policy and X-GTRBAC integration analysis

Normal Form Expression Element	Contextual Constraint Element	Analysis
<wsp:ExactlyOne>	AssignConstraint/ AssignCondition cred_type="" /LogicalExpression op="OR"	<wsp:ExactlyOne> indicates a collection of alternatives for a policy specific to a particular service component; this implies that the corresponding constraint in X-GTRBAC will comprise of one condition having a top-level logical expression with opcode = "OR"; logical expressions with opcode = "AND" will be nested inside this top level expression, and each of them will represent an alternative; all logical expressions included in this condition contain a set of predicates defining rules on the attributes of a credential provided by the role requesting access to the service.
<wsp:All>	LogicalExpression op="AND"	<wsp:All> indicates a collection of assertions for a policy alternative; this will be represented in X-GTRBAC as a collection of predicates in a logical expression with opcode = "AND"; each predicate included in this logical expression represents an assertion which must be satisfied.
<assertion ...>	Predicate	<assertion> represents a system-specific assertion; this will be represented in both policies using the Predicate element of X-GTRBAC.

Table 4. Example of mapping WS-Policy/X-GTRBAC

WS-Policy	X-GTRBAC Constraint
<wsp:ExactlyOne> <wsp:all> <Predicate>predicate </Predicate> <Predicate>predicate </Predicate> </wsp:All> </wsp:All> <Predicate>predicate 3</Predicate> <Predicate>predicate 4</Predicate> </wsp:All> </wsp:ExactlyOne>	<AssignConstraint> <AssignCondition cred_type = "role_cred_type"> <LogicalExpression op = "OR"> <LogicalExpression op = "AND"> <Predicate>predicate 1</Predicate> <Predicate>predicate 2</Predicate> </LogicalExpression> <LogicalExpression op = "AND"> <Predicate>predicate 3</Predicate> <Predicate>predicate 4</Predicate> </LogicalExpression> </LogicalExpression> </AssignCondition> </AssignConstraint>

Assignment Policy

As described and shown in Tables 4 and 5, an assignment constraint in X-GTRBAC involves the use of credential types. Recall that a subject (user or role) in our framework possesses a credential (set of <attribute, value> pairs) having a given credential type. The logical expression in an assignment constraint may encode predicates defined on the attributes of the credential type, and an assignment succeeds if the constraints are satisfied. The point worth noting here is that assignment depends on the credential type definition, and not on the definition of the role. This means that the roles need not be shared globally by multiple services, and users can still be assigned locally to roles defined within a service according to an acceptable credential presented by the users. A user credential will be acceptable if it has the same credential type as the role credential, and satisfies any applicable constraints.

We mentioned before that credentials are also used by roles for permission-to-role assignment. As a result, permissions can be assigned to roles defined within a service if the role possesses a credential having a credential type as required by the permission-to-role assignment policy, and the credential satisfies any applicable constraints.

Constraint Interpretation

Once a mechanism to represent constraints is defined, the impact of interpreting them in the profile needs to be defined. We are particularly interested in expressing contextual constraints on service usage, which can be modeled in X-GTRBAC as a permission-to-role assignment policy. The only assumption we need to make is that the service access policy is designed based on the RBAC model, which is realistic in practice given the popularity of RBAC. Therefore, user authorization levels are modeled as roles, and services are modeled as permissions associated with roles. A permission in this model refers to the service instance represented by the <service> element in the WSDL. Access to a service instance will represent a permission which is assigned to a given role, subject to the permission-to-role assignment policy in X-GTRBAC.

Permission Nature

A permission in the WS-Policy profile of X-GTRBAC represents access to a service instance. It is identified by the "name" attribute of the <service> element in the WSDL. Because a conventional permission in RBAC is a combination of an object and an associated operation, we now need a special interpretation for the purposes of the profile. We interpret the object and operation of a permission defined in the profile as follows:

- **An object:** Because a given service instance is identified in a WSDL by a unique port, the object the permission belongs to is the value of "portURI" attribute of the <service> element in the WSDL. Each service instance implements an interface via this unique port, and access to the service at this portURI implies access to all the operations provided by that interface.
- **An operation:** It is currently fixed to be HTTP:GET; it indicates that access to the service will be through an HTTP binding and will use the GET verb, which implies the ability to invoke any operation available through the service instance. For the sake of simplicity, this chapter does not address the SOAP binding.

Table 6. Merging process at different levels in WSDL

Type of Merge	Example	Explanation
XML Element Merges individual policies	<wsdl:service PolicyURI= uriPol > <wsp:Policy> inlinePol </wsp:Policy> </wsdl:service> uriPol + inlinePol = XMLPol	WS-Policy Attachment allows a policy to be attached either by using a URI or including it inline. Merge is needed to compute the XML element policy from different fragments attached to it, when more than one attachment mechanism is used. This applies to XML elements representing different WSDL components such as services or port types.
Policy Subject Merges XML Element Subject policies	<wsdl:port/> → XMLPPol + <wsdl:portType/> → XMLPTPol + <wsdl:binding/> → XMLBPol = endpSubjectPol	WS-Policy Attachment defines an Endpoint Subject as combination of port, port type, and binding elements, each of which may have an attached policy. In turn, the Service Subject is defined by the WSDL service element. Merge is needed to compute the effective policy for an Endpoint Subject and for a Service Subject.
Permission (Service usage) Merges WSDL Subject policies	Endpoint Subject → endpSubjectPol + Service Subject → serviceSubjectPol = PermissionPol	WS-Policy Attachment specifies that Service Subject includes the Endpoint subject (due to the hierarchical nature of WSDL). Merge is needed to compute the *effective permission policy* from effective policies of Endpoint and Service subjects. This *effective permission policy* represents the overall policy for the Web service.

Note that our strategy suggests the definition of different interfaces according to the access control requirements, and make those interfaces accessible via service instances. Therefore, fine-grained service access control policies can be composed by associating multiple roles with multiple differentiated instances of a Web service defined by the same WSDL.

Computing Effective Service Access Policies

The computation of effective policy in our system uses the *merge* operation defined in WS-Policy. Because access to a service is equivalent to the existence of a permission for that service, we define the *effective permission policy* as the policy that must be enforced in order to invoke a given service provided at a given port.

We define and illustrate in Table 6 the three different levels where merging occurs in our system. Note that the + symbol denotes the use of the merge operation as described in the WS-Policy specifications (Nolan, 2004; WS Policy, 2006). The processing is independent of the semantics of the assertions and alternatives, and results in a *normal form expression*, where different assertions (<Predicate> tags) will appear grouped within in <All> tags as alternatives. In turn, all alternatives are enclosed within one top-level <ExactlyOne> tag.

The normalized policy expression covers all alternatives of each individual policy, and yields alternatives that consider all possibilities. The normalized policy produced this way therefore has a lot of alternatives (because it is equivalent to a cross product of alternatives). Note that we assume nonconflicting policy alternatives which yield a conflict-free normalized policy.

Algorithm and Termination Proof

We now provide a formal algorithm for computing the effective permission policy.

Algorithm (ComputeEffectivePermissionPolicy):

1. Let *perm* be a permission in the WSPolicy profile of XGTRBAC. *perm* is related to a service *s* provided by a WSDL port, whose effective policy should be calculated from the two types of *policy subjects* involved, namely endpoint subject and service subject.
2. Let $PS_{perm} = \{e, s\}$ be the set of *policy subjects* involved in the invocation of any operation in *s*, as defined in the WS-Policy Attachment specification (where elements *e, s* represent the endpoint and service, respectively). For every possible PS_{perm} in a WSDL file, we have that *e* □ *s* (here □ can be seen as "defined in," as follows from the WSDL 1.1 schema). Note that all PS_{perm} sets must have these two elements, because every WSDL service is implemented at a given port, from which the rest of WSDL elements in the hierachy are accesible. Therefore, from <wsdl:service name="*s*" > tag in the WSDL file one can construct PS_{perm}.
3. Let $EP_{perm} = \{p_e, p_s\}$ be the set of normalized *effective policies* associated with PS_{perm}, whose elements represent the endpoint and service effective policy, respectively, computed as stated in WS-Policy Attachment. Note that any element of EP_{perm} can be undefined (e.g., you can have policies attached only at the service level), but we assume that there are no empty or null policies, see Nolan (2004) for a discussion on empty and null policies. Computing EP_{perm} and PS_{perm} involves minimal XML processing: fetching and merging the corresponding policy fragments (see Table 4) and transforming the resulting policy to the normal form expression.
4. Let EPP_{perm} be the *effective permission policy* for a permission *perm*. We define EPP_{perm} as the merging of all policies in EP_{perm}: EPP_{perm} = merge $(p_i) \mid p_i$ □ EP_{perm}

The *ComputeEffectivePermissionPolicy* algorithm terminates, provided that there are no cyclic policy references. Step 1 determines the service implied by the permission supplied as input to the algorithm, and retrieves the WSDL document describing the service. Step 2 retrieves the service *chain*, made up by the service, port, binding, and portType elements implied in the service description. According to the WSDL and WS-Policy Attachment metamodels, there is no possibility of deadlock in well-formed service descriptions, due to the hierarchical nesting of the four *Policy Subject Types*. Step 3 computes the effective policy of each policy subject. A policy subject exists in one or more policy scopes, which in turn can make use of one or more attachment mechanisms, as exemplified in first row of Table 6. If the attachment is done using the policy inclusion mechanism (WS Policy, 2006), which uses URL references to point to a policy, and if these references are circular, the policy retrieval will enter an infinite loop. Assuming no circular references, the retrieval phase will always terminate. Once the policies are retrieved, they are merged. Because any policy has a finite number of alternatives, the computation of the cross product will terminate. This also applies to step four, where all policies are merged.

ARCHITECTURE/IMPLEMENTATION

This section presents the software architecture and implementation of our authorization framework.

Software Architecture

Architecture Components

Figure 3 shows the component-based software architecture of our framework. We use the well-known UML notation to show the various components of the architecture and their interactions to allow our solution to be used by Web Services applications.

The architecture has three main actors:

- **Web services (right):** These are the PatientTrack, PatientRecordUS, and PatientRecordSP services described in Figure 1. All three of them publish their usage policies using WS-Policy, which are processed using WS-Policy Attachment. According to our requirement for context-aware and fine-grained access control policies, the policy for the port, port type, binding, or service component is individually specified for each service.
- **Web application (PEP) (bottom middle):** This is the Web application hosted at a Web server, and is the policy enforcement point (PEP) in the architecture. It provides its clients with secure access to health care services and makes Web service invocations to determine their authorizations to access the services.
- **X-GTRBAC PDP (left):** This is the X-GTRBAC system which acts as the Policy Decision Point (PDP). It implements the WS-Policy profile for X-GTRBAC, accepting access control requests from the Web application and returning authorization decisions. It provides a SAML-based Web service interface for message exchange.

Policy Repository

A policy repository resides in the PDP. This repository, called the XML policy base, comprises of a set of XML files representing the RBAC policy. The policy base represents the core of the system, and contains the policy files necessary to evaluate the service access request. It consists of the following files: XML user sheet (XUS), XML role sheet (XRS), XML permission sheet (XPS), XML credential type definition (XCredTypeDef), XML user-to-role assignment sheet (XURAS), and XML permission-to-role assignment sheet (XPRAS). All files in the policy base are created at the time of registering the service (i.e., the service designer configures the PDP for future service access request evaluations).

The details of the policy files are as follows:

- A permission *P* is created in the XPS corresponding to the registered service. *P* represents access to the service at the defined port using a given HTTP verb, as defined in section Permission Nature, and is built from the port URI and the <Action> element indicated in the SAML query.
- A credential type *CTu* is added to the XCredTypeDef. *CTu* is a user credential, and includes a set of attributes used by the X-GTRBAC system for a user-to-role assignment.
- A credential type *CTr* is added to XCredTypeDef. *CTr* is a role credential, and includes a set of attributes belonging to the role *R* which are used to define rules on permission-to-role assignment, as discussed above.
- A role *R* is created in the XRS. *R* is an internal role created specifically to access a specific service, and has an associated credential type *CTr* with a set of attributes.
- A user-to-role assignment policy is added to the XURAS. To assign a user to a role *R*, a credential of type *CTu* must be presented and evaluated against the set of rules included in the user assignment policy. In our system, this occurs at two stages: (i) the user is initially authenticated into a role by the Web application to access PatientTrack service, and (ii) the user is subsequently assigned another role by the PatientTrack service to

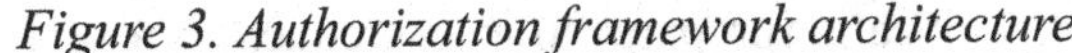

Figure 3. Authorization framework architecture

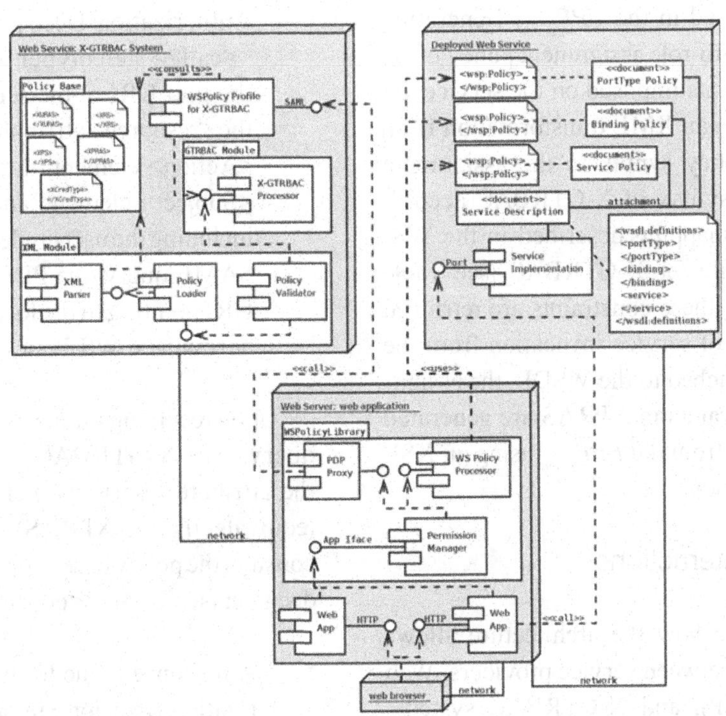

access either of PatientRecordUS or PatientRecordSP service. This is actually a single sign-on scenario, where the authorization by the secondary service depends on the authorization provided by the first service. In case (i), the user provides the credentials at the time of login to the Web application, and in case (ii), the credentials are forwarded by the PatientTrack service, and includes an attribute that specifies the role currently assigned to the user. The information from primary user-to-role assignment then becomes the criterion of secondary user-to-role assignment. Overall, the assignment of a user to a role *R* (whether primary or secondary) is done based on the credentials of a user supplied as an assertion in the SAML query. The PDP is aware of the role and credential definitions, and uses them to automate the user-to-role assignment.

- A permission-to-role assignment policy is added to the XPRAS. To assign *P* to the role *R*, a credential of type *CTr* must be presented and evaluated against the set of rules included in the EPP_{perm}. Generating the service-to-role assignment policy using the constraints imposed on the service usage requires an XML transformation from the WS-Policy syntax to the assignment constraint syntax of X-GTRBAC according to the mapping described in the WS-Policy profile for X-GTRBAC (see Table 4). Because these constraints are retrieved at the time of service invocation from the policies attached to the WSDL, the assignment constraints in XPRAS are generated at run time from the EPP_{perm} using an XSL transformation.

Component Interactions

We now describe how the architecture allows communication between service providers, Web applications (PEP), and X-GTRBAC systems (PDP). The communication uses the SAML profile for X-GTRBAC described in an earlier work (Bhatti, Bertino, & Ghafoor, 2007). The sequence diagram is depicted in Figure 4, and consists of following steps:

1. The Web application accesses the WSDL URI (see UML <<use>> stereotype) to register the service. Then, using the Permission Manager, it creates a permission corresponding to the service based on the WSDL description
2. The application creates a session object including the user credentials, and invokes it.
3. From the permission, the Policy Processor retrieves the service usage policy via attachments (see the UML "attachment" association), merges them, and computes EPP_{perm}.
4. When a user issues a request to access a service, the PDP proxy within the Web application prepares an access request to be sent to the actual PDP, encoding it using a SAML Authorization Decision Query (see UML <<call>> stereotype). The request includes the port URI of the service as the value of the <resource> attribute, HTTP "get" as the <Action> element, the user login id as the <Subject> element, and a set of assertions including the user credential. Along with the SAML query, the PDP proxy also sends a URI pointing to the location of the effective normalized WS-Policy file (i.e., EPP_{perm}).

Upon receiving the access request as a SAML query, the X-GTRBAC Processor evaluates the attribute assertions included in the EPP_{perm} (equivalently, the XPRAS). For this purpose, it consults the policy base to make the authorization decision (see UML <<consults>> stereotype).

5. A response in the form of a SAML Authorization Decision Statement is prepared by

Figure 4. Simplified sequence diagram

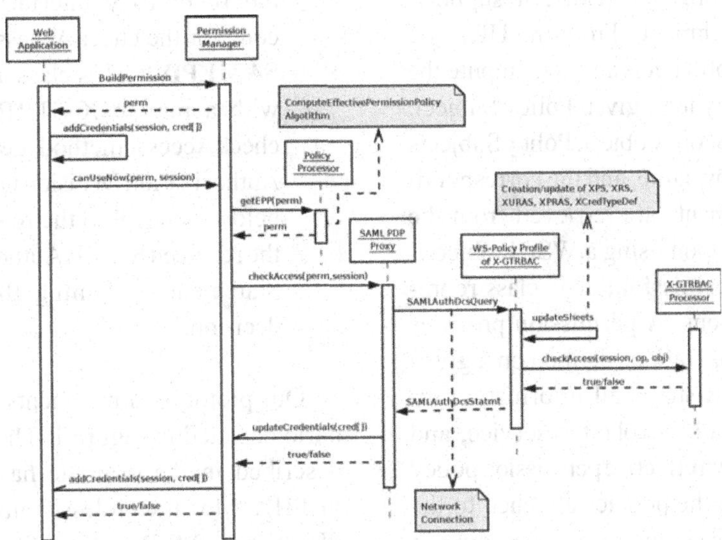

the X-GTRBAC Processor, including either the "permit" or the "deny" value, and sent to the Web application. This response may include new credentials from the PDP.

6. The PDP proxy inside the Web application reads the authorization decision. If it is "permit," it returns true; otherwise it returns false. It also updates the set of credentials for the current session.

The Web application enforces the policy: if the PDP returned true, the service invocation is performed and the requested resource is accessed using an HTTP:GET operation.

Implementation

We have prototyped our framework using Web services architecture. The WS-Policy profile of X-GTRBAC has been implemented as a Java-based PDP Web service at Purdue University in the United States, whereas the policy processing model of WS-Policy supported by WS-Policy Attachment has been implemented as a PHP-based class library deployed at Carlos III University of Madrid in Spain. The most important classes of the WS-Policy package are depicted in Figure 5.

- **WSDL:** This class encapsulates access to Web service descriptions. Given the URI of the WSDL file, it provides methods to retrieve XML nodes representing services, ports, port types, and bindings. All these elements are Policy Scopes that contain Policy Subjects (Service, Endpoint, Operation, and Message).
- **WSPolicy:** This class represents policies. It is able to load a policy from a URI or from an XML document containing it, perform merge between two WSPolicy objects, and return the resulting normalized policy expression.
- **WSAttachment:** This class works with all attachments specified in a service descrip-

tion. It can extract policies by using attachment mechanisms (currently, it supports the XML attachment). From the URI of a WSDL description, it is able to compute the Effective Policy for a given Policy Subject, returning a WSPolicy object. Policy Subjects are identified by name, and the corresponding XML elements are retrieved from the service description using a WSDL object.

- **XGTRBACPermission:** This class represents permissions. A permission provides access to the operations defined on a given port. This class stores all information required to actually invoke the service, and computes its own effective permission policy (EPP_{perm}) from the policies attached to the different service components according to the algorithm given above.
- **PermissionPool:** This class manages all permissions used by an application. It serves as front end to Web applications that use the pool as a factory to create new permissions (corresponding to services) by specifying the service invocation data, and ask the pool for permission usage.
- **PDPManager:** This class is responsible to instantiate the PDP that will take a decision about the usage of a given permission (i.e., a service). All PDPs implementations (whether local or remote) have to implement the IPDPProxy interface, thus providing code for the checkAccess method.
- **SAMLPDP:** This class acts as PDP proxy with a remote X-GTRBAC system. The checkAccess method generates a SAML Authorization Decision Query, as discussed before, sends it to the real PDP, and parses the received SAML Authorization Decision Statement containing the access control decision.

Our prototype implements the example scenario depicted in Figure 1. The Web application described in the example has been developed in PHP, which seamlessly integrates with the PHP-based WS-Policy profile class library. In the current prototype, a basic underlying Web system interface is assumed, and is used as a mechanism to glue together contents provided by different services, perform application-dependent computations, and present the information to the user, as explained next.

- **PatientTrack:** This service provides a patient list to the authorized physician. For each entry in the list, it includes a patient identification, together with the name of institution that has created a medical re-

Figure 5. Class diagram for the WS-Policy package

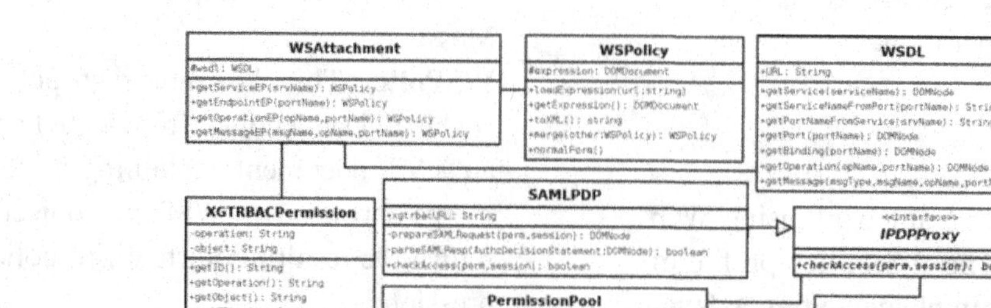

cord for the patient. For each institution, the service also maintains a port URI for the PatientRecord service from where the medical record may be obtained (see Figure 6). This service defines a parameter-less operation, and the authorization is based on the requesting physician's credentials encoded in the SAML query itself.

- **PatientRecord:** This set of services (PatientRecordUS and PatientRecordSP) provides medical records for a patient given the patient identification. The records have a very simple structure. We assume that both services in this set share the same PatientRecord interface, though each one will provide at least one concrete implementation at a given port for that interface using an HTTP binding. The records are accessed through an HTTP: GET operation and displayed in the client browser (See Figure 7).

Figure 6. View of the patient list as result of Patient Track service invocation

Patient selection

Welcome dsanz. Please select a patient to review:

Name	Treated in	Medical Records
Daniel Sanz	Lafayette Health Center	See records
Rafae Bhatti	NY Medical Center	See records
	Lafayette Health Center	See records

Figure 7. View of the patient record as result of Patient Record service invocation

Patient records

Patient Name		Clinic	
Daniel Sanz		Lafayette Health Center.	
Date	**Symptoms**	**Diagnosis**	**Prescription**
10/28/2004	Headache	Stress and anxiety	Prozac
9/23/2005	Vomits	Bad digestion	Chicken and rice diet

Back

The key functionalities of the Web system are the following:

- **Service discovery:** The Web system discovers the WSDL URI of all required services (currently available at a predefined well-known location).
- **Authentication:** The Web system provides authentication through a simple login page to access the top-level PatientTrack service. Users are authenticated by providing their authenticating credentials (containing a set of <attribute, value> pairs). For our current prototype, we do not deal with mechanisms of credential creation and dissemination. In our current architecture, credential types are assumed to be created and disseminated in advance. In practice, new credentials may be obtained by either registering with a certification authority, or simply by the system administrator of the local site.
- **Role assignment:** Each user is assigned a role within the system based on the supplied attributes. It is worth pointing out that role assignment is handled by the Web system at two stages: (i) the user is initially authenticated into a role by the Web application to access PatientTrack service, and (ii) the user is subsequently assigned another role by the PatientTrack service to access either of PatientRecordUS or PatientRecordSP service. This is actually a single sign-on scenario, where the authorization by the secondary service depends on the authorization provided by the first service, and the state between the sessions is maintained by the Web system. In case (i), the user provides the credentials at the time of login to the Web application, and in case (ii), the credentials are provided by the PatientTrack service, and includes an attribute that specifies the role currently assigned to the user. The information from primary user-to-role assignment then becomes the criterion of secondary user-to-role assignment. Overall, the assignment of a user to a role (whether primary or secondary) is done based on the credentials of a user supplied as an assertion in the SAML query.
- **Policy collection:** With the help of WSPolicy profile class library, the Web system gathers all policies from the corresponding attachments and prepares a SAML query including the user credentials. It then submits the query and the link to the merged policy URI to the X-GTRBAC PDP.
- **Policy enforcement:** Web system enforces the policy according to the decision returned by the X-GTRBAC PDP. Thus, the Web service invocation only occurs if the access control decision so allows.
- **Content presentation:** The result of the request (if allowed) is rendered in the browser using HTML.

Appendix A shows the policy files and the XML policy based created by the Web system on behalf of the Web application to provide access to the PatientTrack service (PatientRecordUS and PatientRecordSP are similar). It includes the service WSDL files (Figure A.1), the policies attached to the service components (Figure A.2), and the corresponding XML files that comprise the policy base for the X-GTRBAC system (Figure A.3). The overall Web application and the associated application and Web service files can be accessed at *http://arce.dei.inf.uc3m.es/src/websystem/index.php*. The X-GTRBAC PDP and associated policy files used by the system can be accessed at *http://mmpc3.ecn.purdue.edu:8090/index-wspolicy.html*.

CONCLUSION

In this chapter, we have proposed a policy-based authorization framework for Web services. Our framework consists of a fine-grained, context-aware policy specification language, X-GTRBAC, and an open decentralized enforcement architecture. To enable use of X-GTRBAC within Web services, we integrate X-GTRBAC with an emerging Web services policy processing model, WS-Policy, and thus develop a WS-Policy profile of X-GTRBAC. The profile supports the WS-Policy Attachment specification, which allows attaching, retrieving, and combining policies associated with various components of a Web service in the WSDL document. We have identified key integration challenges involving the design of the profile, most notable among them the design of an algorithm to compute the effective access control policy of a Web service based on its description, and also presented our solution strategy. To allow Web service applications to use our solution, we have adopted a component-based design approach based on well-known UML notations. We have also prototyped our architecture, and implemented it as a loosely coupled Web service providing health care information services to physicians subject to applicable authorization policies.

REFERENCES

Bhatti, R., Bertino, E., & Ghafoor, A. (2007). An integrated approach to federated identity and privilege management in open systems. *Communications of the ACM, 50*(2), 81-87.

Bhatti, R., Joshi, J. B. D., Bertino, E., & Ghafoor, A. (2004). XML-based specification for Web services. *IEEE Computer, 37*(4), 41-49.

Bhatti, R., Joshi, J.B.D., Bertino, E., & Ghafoor, A. (2005). X-GTRBAC: An XML-based policy specification framework and architecture for enterprise-wide access control. *ACM Transactions on Information and System Security (TISSEC), 8*(2), 187-227.

Bhatti, R., Sanz, D., Bertino, E., & Ghafoor A. (2006). A policy-based authorization system for Web services: Integrating X-GTRBAC and WS-policy (Tech. Rep. No. 2006-03). CERIAS. Retrieved June 4, 2007, from https://www.cerias.purdue.edu/tools_and_resources/bibtex_archive/archive/2006-03.pdf

Extensible Access Control Markup Language (XACML). (2005). Retrieved June 4, 2007, from http://www.oasis-open.org/committees/tc_home.php?wg_abbrev=xacml

Hu, J., & Weaver, A.C. (2004). Dynamic, context-aware security infrastructure for distributed healthcare applications. In *Proceedings of the First Workshop on Pervasive Security, Privacy and Trust (PSPT).*

Kaminsky, D. (2005). An introduction to policy for autonomic computing. Retrieved June 4, 2007, from http://www-128.ibm.com/developerworks/autonomic/library/ac-policy.html

Nolan, P. (2004). Understand WS-policy processing. Retrieved June 4, 2007, from http://www-128.ibm.com/developerworks/webservices/library/ws-policy.html

Sandhu, R., Coyne, E.J., Feinstein, H.L., & Youman, C.E. (1996). Role-based access control models. *IEEE Computer, 29*(2), 38-47.

Security Assertions Markup Language (SAML). (2004). Retrieved June 4, 2007, from http://xml.coverpages.org/saml.html

Security in a Web services world: A proposed architecture and roadmap. (2002). Retrieved June 4, 2007, from http://www-128.ibm.com/developerworks/webservices/library/ specification/ws-secmap/

Sirer, E., & Wang, K. (2002). An access control language for Web services. In *Proceedings of the Seventh ACM Symposium on Access Control Models and Technologies*, Monterey, CA.

Web Services Description Language (WSDL 1.1). (2001). Retrieved June 4, 2007, from http://www.w3.org/TR/2001/NOTE-wsdl-20010315

Web Services Policy Attachment (WS Attachment). (2006). Retrieved June 4, 2007, from http://www-128.ibm.com/developerworks/webservices/library/specification/ws-polatt/

Web Services Policy Framework (WS Policy). (2006). Retrieved June 4, 2007, from http://www-128.ibm.com/developerworks/webservices/library/specification/ws-polfram/

Web Services Security (WS Security). (2002). Retrieved June 4, 2007, from http://www-128.ibm.com/developerworks/webservices/library/specification/ws-secure/

Web Services Trust Language (WS Trust). (2004). Retrieved June 4, 2007, from http://www-128.ibm.com/developerworks/library/specification/ws-trust/

XACML Profile for Web Services (WSPL). (2003). Retrieved June 4, 2007, from http://www.oasis-open.org/committees/download.php/3661/draft-xacml-wspl-04.pdf

APPENDIX A

Figure A.1. WSDL excerpt for the PatientTrack service

```
<?xml version="1.0"?>
<definitions
 name="PatientTrack" targetNamespace="http://arce.dei.inf.uc3m.es/src/services/PTService/PTService.wsdl.xml"
 xmlns:tns="http://arce.dei.inf.uc3m.es/src/services/PTService/PTService.wsdl.xml"
 xmlns="http://schemas.xmlsoap.org/wsdl/"
 xmlns:wsp="http://schemas.xmlsoap.org/ws/2004/09/policy"
 xmlns:http="http://schemas.xmlsoap.org/wsdl/http/"
 xmlns:mime="http://schemas.xmlsoap.org/wsdl/mime/">
 <wsp:UsingPolicy Required="true"/>
 <types>
  <schema targetNamespace="http://arce.dei.inf.uc3m.es/src/services/PTService/PTService.wsdl.xml" xmlns="http://
www.w3.org/2000/10/XMLSchema">
   <element name="patients">
    <complexType>
          <!-- here goes the patient list schema. -->
    </complexType>
   </element> <!-- end patients -->
  </schema>
 </types>
 <message name="GetPatientListResponse">
  <part name="body" element="patients"/>
 </message>
 <portType name="PTPortType"
      wsp:PolicyURIs="http://arce.dei.inf.uc3m.es/src/services/PTService/PTPortTypePolicy.xml">
  <operation name="GetPatientList">
   <output message="GetPatientListResponse"/>
  </operation>
 </portType>
 <binding name="PTHttpBinding" type="PTPortType">
  <http:binding verb="GET"/>
  <operation name="GetPatientList">
   <!-- location is the operation relative URI, which base uri is port uri -->
   <http:operation location="PTService.php"/>
   <output>
          <!-- this should be a MIME type representing XML documents -->
          <mime:content type="text/xml"/>

   </output>
  </operation>
 </binding>
 <service name="PTService" wsp:PolicyURIs="http://arce.dei.inf.uc3m.es/src/services/PTService/PTServicePolicy.
xml">
  <port name="PTPort" binding="PTHttpBinding"
     wsp:PolicyURIs="http://arce.dei.inf.uc3m.es/src/services/PTService/PTPortPolicy.xml">
   <!-- port base addres, all operations are provided from this URI -->
   <http:address location="http://arce.dei.inf.uc3m.es/src/services/PTService/"/>
  </port>
 </service>
</definitions>
```

Figure A.2. Individual policies attached to PatientTrack service definition (left) are merged to produce the normalized WS-Policy (EPPperm) for the service (right)

Policy attached to the <port>

```
<wsp:Policy>
 <wsp:ExactlyOne>
  <wsp:All>
   <Predicate>
    <Operator>eq</Operator>
    <ParamName>system_load</ParamName>
    <FuncName>hasCredAttributeValue</
FuncName>
    <RetValue>low</RetValue>
   </Predicate>
  </wsp:All>
 </wsp:ExactlyOne>
</wsp:Policy>
```

Policy attached to the <portType>

```
<wsp:Policy>
 <wsp:ExactlyOne>
  <wsp:All>
   <Predicate>
    <Operator>eq</Operator>
    <ParamName>location</ParamName>
    <FuncName>hasCredAttributeValue</
FuncName>
    <RetValue>NewYork</RetValue>
   </Predicate>
  </wsp:All>
 </wsp:ExactlyOne>
</wsp:Policy>
```

Policy attached to the <service> tag

```
<wsp:Policy>
 <wsp:ExactlyOne>
  <wsp:All>
   <Predicate>
    <Operator>eq</Operator>
    <ParamName>priority</ParamName>
    <FuncName>hasCredAttributeValue</
FuncName>
    <RetValue>high</RetValue>
   </Predicate>
  </wsp:All>
  <wsp:All/>
 </wsp:ExactlyOne>
</wsp:Policy>
```

Merged policy: EPP_{perm}

```
<wsp:Policy>
 <wsp:ExactlyOne>
  <wsp:All>
   <Predicate>
    <Operator>eq</Operator>
    <ParamName>system_load</ParamName>
    <FuncName>hasCredAttributeValue</FuncName>
    <RetValue>low</RetValue>
   </Predicate>
   <Predicate>
    <Operator>eq</Operator>
    <ParamName>location</ParamName>
    <FuncName>hasCredAttributeValue</FuncName>
    <RetValue>NewYork</RetValue>
   </Predicate>
   <Predicate>
    <Operator>eq</Operator>
    <ParamName>priority</ParamName>
    <FuncName>hasCredAttributeValue</FuncName>
    <RetValue>high</RetValue>
   </Predicate>
  </wsp:All>
  <wsp:All>
   <Predicate>
    <Operator>eq</Operator>
    <ParamName>system_load</ParamName>
    <FuncName>hasCredAttributeValue</FuncName>
    <RetValue>low</RetValue>
   </Predicate>
   <Predicate>
    <Operator>eq</Operator>
    <ParamName>location</ParamName>
    <FuncName>hasCredAttributeValue</FuncName>
    <RetValue>NewYork</RetValue>
   </Predicate>
  </wsp:All>
 </wsp:ExactlyOne>
</wsp:Policy>
```

Figure A.3. X-GTRBAC policies for the Patient Track service. Note that XPRAS is a result of XSL transformation on EPP_{perm} in Figure A.2.

```
<?xml version=”1.0” encoding=”UTF-8” ?>
<XCredTypeDef xctd_id=”LibElseXCTD”>
<CredentialType cred_type_id=”LEResPT” type_name=”LibElseResPT”>
<AttributeList>
 <Attribute name=”role” type=”string” usage=”mand” />
</AttributeList>
</CredentialType>
<CredentialType cred_type_id=”LERolePTP” type_name=”LibElseRolePTP”>
<AttributeList>
<Attribute name=”system_load” type=”string” usage=”mand” />
<Attribute name=”location” type=”string” usage=”mand” />
<Attribute name=”priority” type=”string” usage=”opt” />
</AttributeList>
</CredentialType>
</XCredTypeDef>
```

```
<?xml version=”1.0” encoding=”UTF-8” ?>
<XURAS xuras_id=”LibElseXURAS”>
 <URA ura_id=”uraPTP” role_name=”PTPhysician”>
 <AssignUsers>
 <AssignUser user_id=”any”>
  <AssignConstraint>
  <AssignCondition cred_type=”LibElseResPT”>
   <LogicalExpr>
   <Predicate>
    <Operator>eq</Operator>
    <FuncName>hasCredAttributeValue</FuncName>
    <ParamName order=”1”>degree</ParamName>
    <RetValue>MD</RetValue>
   </Predicate>
   <Predicate>
    <Operator>eq</Operator>
    <FuncName>hasCredAttributeValue</FuncName>
    <ParamName order=”1”>affiliation</ParamName>
    <RetValue>USAMed</RetValue>
   </Predicate>
   </LogicalExpr>
  </AssignCondition>
  </AssignConstraint>
 </AssignUser>
 </AssignUsers>
 </URA>
</XURAS>
```

```
 <?xml version=”1.0” encoding=”UTF-8” ?>
 <XPS xps_id=”LibElseXPS”>
 <Permission perm_id=”LEPTService”>
 <Object object_type=”port”
 object_id=”http://arce.dei.inf.uc3m.es/src/services/PTService/” />
 <Operation context=”saml:ghpp”>GET</Operation>
 </Permission>
 </XPS>
```

```
<?xml version=”1.0” encoding=”UTF-8” ?>
<XRS xrs_id=”LibElseXRS”>
 <Role role_id=”rPTP” role_name=”PTPhysician”>
 <CredType cred_type_id=”LERolePTP”
     type_name=”LibElseRolePTP”>
 <CredExpr>
  <Attribute name=”location”>NewYork</Attribute>
  <Attribute name=”system_load”>low</Attribute>
  <Attribute name=”priority”>low</Attribute>
 </CredExpr>
 </CredType>
 </Role>
</XRS>
```

```
<?xml version=”1.0” encoding=”UTF-8”?>
<XPRAS xpras_id=”LibElseXPRAS”>
<PRA role_name=”PTServiceCustomer”
    pra_id=”praPTServiceCustomer”>
 <AssignPermissions>
 <AssignPermission perm_id=”LEPTService”>
 <AssignConstraint>
  <AssignCondition cred_type=”LibElseRolePT”>
  <LogicalExpr op=”OR”>
   <Predicate>
   <LogicalExpr op=”AND”>
    <Predicate>
    <Operator>eq</Operator>
    <FuncName>hasCredAttributeValue</FuncName>
    <ParamName order=”1”>priority</ParamName>
    <RetValue>high</RetValue>
    </Predicate>
    <Predicate>
    <Operator>eq</Operator>
    <FuncName>hasCredAttributeValue</FuncName>
    <ParamName order=”1”>system_load</ParamName>
    <RetValue>low</RetValue>
    </Predicate>
    <Predicate>
    <Operator>eq</Operator>
    <FuncName>hasCredAttributeValue</FuncName>
    <ParamName order=”1”>location</ParamName>
    <RetValue>NewYork</RetValue>
    </Predicate>
   </LogicalExpr>
   </Predicate>
   <Predicate>
   <LogicalExpr op=”AND”>
    <Predicate>
    <Operator>eq</Operator>
    <FuncName>hasCredAttributeValue</FuncName>
    <ParamName order=”1”>system_load</ParamName>
    <RetValue>low</RetValue>
    </Predicate>
    <Predicate>
    <Operator>eq</Operator>
    <FuncName>hasCredAttributeValue</FuncName>
    <ParamName order=”1”>location</ParamName>
    <RetValue>NewYork</RetValue>
    </Predicate>
   </LogicalExpr>
   </Predicate>
  </LogicalExpr>
  </AssignCondition>
 </AssignConstraint>
 </AssignPermission>
 </AssignPermissions>
</PRA>
</XPRAS>
```

Chapter VII
Description of Policies Enriched by Semantics for Security Management

Félix J. García Clemente
University of Murcia, Spain

Gregorio Martínez Pérez
University of Murcia, Spain

Juan A. Botía Blaya
University of Murcia, Spain

Antonio F. Gómez Skarmeta
University of Murcia, Spain

ABSTRACT

Policies, which usually govern the behavior of networking services (e.g., security, QoS, mobility, etc.) are becoming an increasingly popular approach for the dynamic regulation of Web information systems. By appropriately managing policies, a system can be continuously adjusted to accommodate variations in externally imposed constraints and environmental conditions. The adoption of a policy-based approach for controlling a system requires an appropriate policy representation regarding both syntax and semantics, and the design and development of a policy management framework. In the context of the Web, the use of languages enriched with semantics has been limited primarily to represent Web content and services. However the capabilities of these languages, coupled with the availability of tools to manipulate them, make them well suited for many other kinds of applications, as policy representation and management. In this chapter, we present an evaluation of the ongoing efforts to use ontological (Semantic Web) languages to represent policies for distributed systems.

INTRODUCTION

The heterogeneity and complexity of computer systems is increasing constantly, but their management techniques are not changing and so system configuration processes are getting more complicated and error-prone. Therefore, there is a clear need for standardized mechanisms to manage advanced services and applications. Policy-based management (PBM) frameworks (Verma, 2000; Kosiur, 2001; Strassner, 2003) define languages, mechanisms and tools through which computer systems can be managed dynamically and homogeneously.

One of the main goals of policy-based management is to enable service and application control and management on a high abstraction level. The administrator specifies rules that describe domain-wide policies independent of the implementation of the particular service and/or application. It is then the policy management architecture that provides support to transform and distribute the policies to each node and thus to enforce a consistent configuration in all involved elements, which is a prerequisite for achieving end-to-end security services, or consistent access control configuration in different Web servers, for example.

The scope of policy-based management is increasingly going beyond its traditional applications in significant ways. The main functions of policy management architectures are:

- **Enforcement:** to implement a desired policy state through a set of management commands.
- **Monitoring:** ongoing active or passive examination of the information system, its services and applications for checking its status and whether policies are being satisfied or not.
- **Decision-taking:** to compare the current state of the communication system to a desired state described by a policy (or a set of them) and to decide how the desired state can be achieved or maintained.

In the information systems security field, a policy (i.e., security policy) can be defined as a set of rules and practices describing how an organization manages, protects, and distributes sensitive information. The research community, the industry, and standardization bodies have proposed different secure policy specification languages (Martínez Pérez, 2005) that range from formal policy languages that can be processed and interpreted easily and directly by a computer, to rule-based policy notation using *if-then* rules to express the mandatory behavior of the target system, and to the representation of policies as entries in a table consisting of multiple attributes. There are also ongoing standardization efforts toward common policy information models and frameworks such as CIM (Common Information Model) from the DMTF (Distributed Management Task Force, 2005).

In the Web services world, standards for SOAP-based message security and XML-based languages for access control are now appearing, as it is the case of XACML (OASIS, 2004). However the immaturity of the current tools along with the limited scope and total absence of explicit semantics of new languages make them less than-ideal candidates for sophisticated Web-based services or applications.

Ontological languages like OWL (Connolly et al., 2003) and others can be used to incorporate semantic expressiveness into the management information specifications and some reasoning capabilities which definitely would help in handling the management tasks aforementioned (i.e., enforcement, monitoring, and decision-taking). For example, in this kind of systems it is an important improvement to allow simple operations on different policies like testing equality, inclusion, equivalency and so. Ontological languages allow this kind of operations for the entities expressed with them.

This chapter provides some initial concepts related with policy management and their formal representation complemented with a case study and specific examples in the field of Web systems security where the reader can see the requirements regarding syntax and semantics that any policy representation should satisfy.

This analysis also provides a comparative study of main semantic security policy specification languages against a set of "traditional" non-semantic policy languages, such as Ponder (Damianou et al., 2001), XACML and XML/CIM. Some of the criteria used for this analysis include their ability to express semantic information, the representation technique they use, and the concepts they are able to express.

Then, this chapter examines the main existing policy-related technologies based on specifications with semantics. In particular, it presents the results of our in-depth analysis of four candidates: KaoS (Uszok et al., 2003), RuleML (The Rule Markup Initiative, August 2004), Rei (Kagal et al., 2003) and SWRL (The Rule Markup Initiative, May 2004) along with their associated schemas and ontology specifications. The analysis focuses on the expressiveness of each language, and is presented along several dimensions and summarized in a comparison table. Moreover, the chapter shows the implementation of our case study by the four languages analyzed and, to some extent, a criticism of each of the resulting specifications.

The state-of-the-art vision is also complemented with some future trends in semantic-based policy languages, mainly the open issues that should be resolved as a prerequisite to widespread adoption. Some new designs and developments from the research community considered of relevance for the reader are also being presented.

BACKGROUND AND RELATED WORK

This section is intended to provide the reader with an overview of the main elements and technologies existing in semantic security policy specifications and frameworks from both a theoretical and a practical perspective. It starts by describing some useful concepts around policy management paradigm and formal representation techniques. Then, it presents a case study related with Business-to-Consumer (B2C) Web-based e-commerce systems, which will be used throughout this chapter to illustrate different concepts like, for example, how different security policy languages enriched by semantics express the same high-level policy. Next, it describes two of the main policy languages in use today. Finally, this section provides a comparative study between these two "traditional" non-semantic policy languages and other semantic security policy languages; it is based on our own research work, but also incorporating the view of others. This study is intended to help the reader to understand the need of semantic policy languages.

Policy-Based Management: A Brief Overview

Introduction

Policy rules define in abstract terms a desired behavior. They are stored and interpreted by the policy framework, which provides a heterogeneous set of components and mechanisms that are able to represent, distribute, and manage policies in an unambiguous, interoperable manner, thus providing a consistent behavior in all affected policy enforcement points (i.e., entities where the policy decisions are actually enforced when the policy rule conditions evaluate to "true").

Security policies can be defined to perform a wide variety of actions, from IPsec/IKE management (example of network security policy) to access control over a Web service (example of application-level policy). To cover this wide range of security policies, this chapter aims to examine the current state of policy engines and policy languages, and how they can be applied to both Web security and information systems security to protect information at several levels. Some future directions of interest for the reader are provided as well.

Requirements of a Policy Language and Policy Framework

Administrators use policy languages assuring that the representation of policies will be unambiguous and verifiable. Other important requirements of any policy language are:

- **Clear and well-defined semantics.** The semantics of a policy language can be considered as well-defined if the meaning of a policy written in this language is independent of its particular implementation.
- **Flexibility and extensibility.** A policy language has to be flexible enough to allow new policy information to be expressed, and extensible enough to allow new semantics to be added in future versions of this language.
- **Interoperability with other languages.** There are usually several languages that can be used in different domains to express similar policies, and interoperability is a must to allow different services or applications from these different domains to communicate with each other according to the behavior stated in these policies.

Once the policy has been defined for a given administrative domain, a policy management architecture is needed to transfer, store, and enforce this policy in that domain. The main requirements for such policy management architecture are:

- **Well-defined model.** Policy architectures need to have a well-defined model independent of the particular implementation in use. In it, the interfaces between the components need to be clear and well-defined.
- **Flexibility and definition of abstractions to manage a wide variety of device types.** The system architecture should be flexible enough to allow addition of new types of devices with minimal updates and recoding of existing management components.
- **Interoperability with other architectures (inter-domain).** The system should be able to interoperate with other architectures that may exist in other administrative domains.
- **Conflict detection.** It has to be able to check that a given policy does not conflict with any other existing policy.
- **Scalability.** It should maintain quality performance under an increased system load.

Introduction to Formal Representation Techniques

The Concept of Ontology

An ontology consists on a number of terms precisely defined. It is actually a vocabulary which can be shared between humans and/or applications. The concepts in the vocabulary are usually arranged as a hierarchy of elements. Moreover, each element, called a concept, comes with a set of properties and another set of instances pertaining to the concept. A simple definition of what is really an ontology can be found in Gruber et al. (1993) and says "an ontology is an explicit specification of a conceptualization". From the point of view of knowledge representation in computers, what is represented is what exists, in a declarative way. And what is represented is done by using an abstract model of a concrete phenomenon, in where the model represents the most relevant concepts of the phenomenon.

Traditionally, ontologies have been used for knowledge sharing and reuse in the context of knowledge-based systems like distributed problem solvers (Avouris et al., 1992) and more recently multi-agent systems (Wooldridge, 2001). In turn, this kind of systems has been used for intelligent information integration, cooperative information systems, information gathering, electronic commerce, and knowledge management.

In the classification of the different ontologies introduced by Fensel et al. (2004) and using as a dimension for classification the kind of phenomenon they try to represent, we are interested, in the context of this work, in the *domain ontology*. A domain ontology represents the knowledge extracted from a particular application domain like the one we are working on this chapter: policy management for securing Web services and environments.

The Role of Formal Logics in Semantic Web Technologies

Ontology technology finds its roots in traditional logic. Formal logic provides us with two important things used in ontological research:

- Languages for knowledge representation, and
- Functional models for the implementation of reasoning processes.

Knowledge representation is half of the story with respect to ontology technology. The other part of the story gets to do with reasoning. With a proper reasoning mechanism, we can use an ontological specification to infer interesting details about our model of the world, in other words, deduce or discover properties or relations between concepts that we did not explicitly define.

There are three different and important logics for representing knowledge. Two basic logics: propositional and first order logic. The third one, description logic, is considered as an extension of first order logic, and nowadays is seen as the most suitable to manage ontologies in the context of the Semantic Web.

They all are distinct kind of logics for representing distinct kind of conceptualizations. If we talk about semantics in propositional logic, it has to be understood in terms of truth values. The semantic of each well formed formula depends of how the truth values are evolved with using the above mentioned connectives. With respect to reasoning, in the context of propositional logic it is of deductive nature. In this kind of process, there are some premises which in turn are well-formed formulae, and a conclusion. In order to deduce the conclusion from the premises, these must imply the conclusion.

Propositional logic compound a very poor expressiveness language as it does not allow for properties-based or general-relations-based reasoning. As general knowledge can not be represented, no general reasoning can be performed. As the reader may have supposed, this kind of logic is not suitable for representing policy specifications. For a more detailed explanation, please see Russell et al. (1995) and Genesereth et al. (1986).

First order predicate logic is a more advanced kind of logic, in the sense that the basic representational element is a predicate. With a predicate, we can represent properties of an entity or relations between different entities. This is accomplished by using variables inside predicates for representing objects of individuals. Moreover, we can specify the scope of variables by using quantifiers like the universal quantifier (i.e., for all) and the existential one (i.e., it exists at least one).

If semantics in propositional logic were based on a truth value for the propositions, in first order predicate logic we have the interpretation for giving meaning to expressions. Talking about reasoning, predicate logic is consistent with the appropriate inference rules and it is semi-decidable, in other words, if a logic expression can be deduced from a set of other logic expressions, then a demonstration of the first one exist but you can not always find the demonstration that a logic expression can not be deduced from a set of logic expressions.

A more advanced logic is description logic (DL). This kind of logic uses concepts (or classes) instead of predicates. If predicate logic is oriented to truth values of true and false, descriptive logic is oriented to concepts and concept belonging relations. For example, we can represent the fact that someone has a child with the binary predicate:

$$\{x|(\exists y)(hasChild(x,y) \land Person(y))\}$$

but in descriptive logic the approach is slightly different as we use properties for that and represent it with:

$$\exists hasChild.Person.$$

Other of the interesting features of DL is the availability of a number of constructors to build more complex classes from basic and other complex classes.

Languages for Ontology Representation

Ontology can be, in principle, considered as independent of the language used to serialize it. As argued in Gruber et al. (1993), in systems where knowledge must be shared between different and independent entities, it is needed a common agreement at three different levels: format of languages for knowledge representation, knowledge sharing communication protocol and specification of the knowledge to be shared. In this way, the task of defining an ontology is totally decoupled of the task of using a concrete language for representing knowledge outside of the entity using it internally. That is why we can use languages like XML or RDF, which can be seen as not related to ontologies at all, for knowledge exchanging.

RDF results in an interesting approach because it offers a direct and easy way to state facts (W3C, 1999). On the other hand, RDFS (Brickley et al., 2004), the schema of RDF, organizes the modeling elements in a very convenient way through classes and properties. For example, you can define a hierarchy of classes in terms of subsumption of classes inside other. You can also add semantics by means of adding ranges, domains, and cardinality to properties. OWL (Connolly et al., 2003) is the cutting edge language nowadays for dealing with semantics, more specifically in the context of the Web. With OWL we will be able of doing things like:

- State that two different kinds of policies are disjoint classes.
- Declare a new policy as the inverse for other policy.
- State new policies by adding restrictions to the properties of other policies.

A Case Study

Once we have described the basic concepts of policy management and formal representation techniques and the requirements of policy languages and frameworks, this background analysis will be complemented with one case study, which will be used throughout the chapter to show the advantages, and also some of the current open issues of using policy specification languages with semantics.

Business-to-consumer (B2C) e-commerce systems are an example of Web Information System (WIS) where security is a fundamental aspect to be considered. A secure e-commerce scenario requires transmission and reception of information over the Internet such that:

- It is accessible to the sender and the receiver only (privacy/confidentiality).
- It cannot be changed during transmission (integrity).
- The receiver is sure it came from the right sender (source authenticity).
- The sender can be sure the receiver is genuine (authenticity of the destination).
- The sender cannot deny he/she sent it (non-repudiation).

As stated before, security policies can be specified at different levels of abstraction. The process starts with the definition of a business security policy. This can be the case of the next authorization security policy, which is defined in natural language: "*Permit the access to the e-payment service, if the user is in the group of customers registered for this service.*"

Next, the security policy is usually expressed by a policy administrator as a set of IF-THEN policy rules as, for example:

IF ((<Requester> is member of Payment Customers) AND (<Server> is member of Payment Servers)) THEN (<Requester> granted access to <Server>)

Policy languages to be analyzed in this chapter (both semantic and non-semantic) will be used to represent this specific policy, so the reader will be able to understand their descriptions and compare them.

Non-Semantic Security Policy Languages

This section describes two of the most relevant "traditional" non-semantic policy languages in use nowadays: Ponder and XACML (eXtensible Access Control Markup Language), together with their main advantages and disadvantages.

Ponder

Ponder (Damianou et al., 2001) is a declarative, object-oriented language developed for specifying management and security policies. Ponder permits to express authorizations, obligations (stating that a user must or must not execute or be allowed to execute an action on a target element), information filtering (used to transform input or output parameters in an interaction), refrain policies (which define actions that subjects must not perform on target objects), and delegation policies (which define what authorizations can be delegated to whom).

Figure 1 presents an example of policy expressed in Ponder using our case study.

It shows how to express with an authorization policy the business level security policy and IF-THEN rules defined in our case study. The positive authorization policy defines that the subject PayCustomer is permitted to access to the target PayServer.

Ponder can describe any rule to constrain the behavior of components in a simple and declarative

Figure 1. Example of policy representation in PONDER

```
inst auth+ PaymentAuthPolicy1 {
        subject s = people/PayCustomer ;
        target t = servers/PayServer ;
        action t.access (s);
}
```

way. However, it does not take care of the description of the content of the policy (e.g., description of the specified components, the system, etc.). The adoption of a Semantic Web language can clearly overcome this limitation.

XACML

The eXtensible Access Control Markup Language (XACML) (OASIS, 2004) describes both an access control policy language and a request/response language. The policy language provides a common means to express subject-target-action-condition access control policies and the request/response language expresses queries about whether a particular access should be allowed (requests) and describes answers to those queries (responses).

Figure 2 presents an example of policy expressed in XACML using our case study.

From our point of view, the main failing of XACML is that the policy is rather verbose and not really aimed at human interpretation. In addition, the language model does not include any way of grouping policies.

Figure 2. Example of policy representation in XACML

```
<Policy PolicyId="PaymentAuthPolicy1">
  <Target>
      <Subjects><AnySubject/></Subjects>
      <Resources> <Resource>
            <ResourceMatch MatchId="function:anyURI-equal">
             <AttributeValue>
                        http://payserver.ourcompany.com
             </AttributeValue>
            <ResourceAttributeDesignator/>
            </ResourceMatch>
      </Resource> </Resources>
      <Actions><AnyAction/></Actions>
  </Target>
  <Rule RuleId="ReadRule" Effect="Permit">
      <Target>
            <Subjects><AnySubject/></Subjects>
            <Resources><AnyResource/></Resources>
            <Actions> <Action>
             <ActionMatch MatchId="function:string-equal">
               <AttributeValue>access</AttributeValue>
               <ActionAttributeDesignator/>
             </ActionMatch>
            </Action></Actions>
      </Target>
      <Condition FunctionId="function:string-equal">
            <Apply FunctionId="function:string-one-and-only">
             <SubjectAttributeDesignator AttributeId="group"/>
            </Apply>
            <AttributeValue>PayCustomer</AttributeValue>
      </Condition>
  </Rule>
</Policy>
```

DISCUSSION

Now the basic concepts of policy-based management and formal representation techniques have been presented, a case study for WIS security has been introduced, and two of the main "traditional" non-semantic languages have been introduced and generally compared with semantic languages, this section shows how the administrator models business security policies using a policy representation based on ontology to create a formal representation of the business policy, and which are the frameworks allowing the management of such policies.

Although many semantic security policy specifications exist, we have selected four of them as they are considered nowadays as the most promising options: KAoS, RuleML, SWRL, and Rei. They are now described in detail, while a comparison of their main pros and cons is presented at the end of this section.

Semantic Policy Languages and Frameworks for Managing System Security

KAoS

KAoS (Uszok et al., 2003) is a collection of services and tools that allow for the specification, management, conflict resolution, and enforcement of policies within domains describing organizations of human, agent, and other computational actors. While initially oriented to the dynamic and complex requirements of software agent applications, KAoS services are also being extended to work equally well with both general-purpose grid computing and Web service environments.

KAoS uses ontology concepts encoded in OWL to build policies. The KAoS Policy Service distinguishes between authorization policies (i.e., constraints that permit or forbid some action) and obligation policies (i.e., constraints that require some action to be performed when a state- or event-based trigger occurs, or else serve to waive such a requirement). The applicability of the policy is defined by a set of conditions or situations whose definition can contain components specifying required history, state and currently undertaken actions. In the case of the obligation policy the obligated action can be annotated with different constraints restricting possibilities of its fulfillment.

The current version of the KAoS Policy Ontologies (KPO) defines basic ontologies for actions, conditions, actors, various entities related to actions, and policies, as depicted in Figure 3. It is expected that for a given application, the ontologies will be further extended with additional classes, individuals, and rules.

Figure 4 shows an example of the type of policy that administrators can specify using KAoS. It is related with the case study described earlier.

KAoS defines a Policy Framework (see Figure 5) that includes the following functionality:

- Creating/editing of policies using KAoS Policy Administration Tool (KPAT). KPAT implements a graphical user interface to policy and domain management functionality.
- Storing, deconflicting and querying policies using KaoS Directory Service.
- Distribution of policies to Guard, which acts as a policy decision point.
- Policy enforcement/disclosure mechanism, i.e., finding out which policies apply to a given situation.

Every agent in the system is associated with a Guard. When an action is requested, the Guard is automatically queried to check whether the action is authorized based on the current policies and, if not, the action is prevented by various enforcement mechanisms. Policy enforcement requires the ability to monitor and intercept actions, and allow or disallow them based on a given set of policies. While the rest of the KAoS architecture

Figure 3. KAoS policy ontology

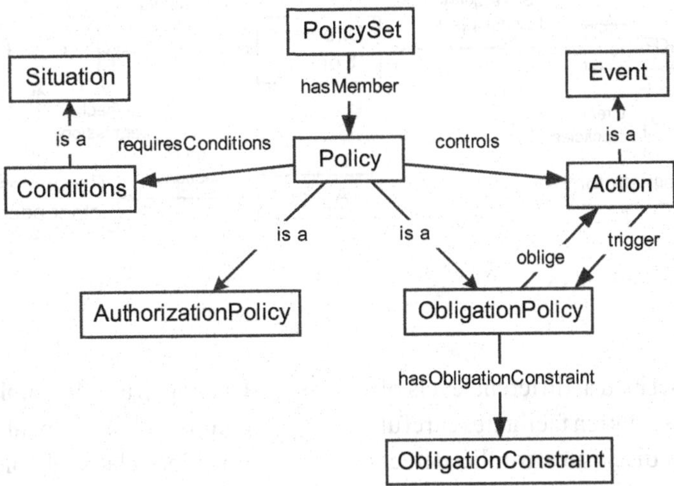

Figure 4. Example of policy representation in KAoS

```
<owl:Class rdf:ID="PaymentAuthAction">
<owl:intersectionOf rdf:parseType="owl:collection">
   <owl:Class rdf:about="&action;AccessAction"/>
   <owl:Restriction>
   <owl:onProperty rdf:resource="&action;#performedBy"/>
   <owl:toClass rdf:resource="&domains;MembersOfPayCustomer"/>
   </owl:Restriction>
   <owl:Restriction>
   <owl:onProperty rdf:resource="&action;#performedOn"/>
   <owl:toClass rdf:resource="&domains;MembersOfPayServer"/>
   </owl:Restriction>
</owl:intersectionOf>
</owl:Class>
<policy:PosAuthorizationPolicy rdf:ID="PaymentAuthPolicy1">
   <policy:controls rdf:ID="PaymentAuthAction"/>
   <policy:hasSiteOfEnforcement rdf:resource="#TargetSite"/>
   <policy:hasPriority>1</policy:hasPriority>
</policy:PosAuthorizationPolicy>
```

is generic across different platforms, enforcement mechanisms are necessarily specific to the way the platform works.

The use of OWL as a policy representation enables runtime extensibility and adaptability of the system, as well as the ability to analyze policies

Figure 5. KAoS framework

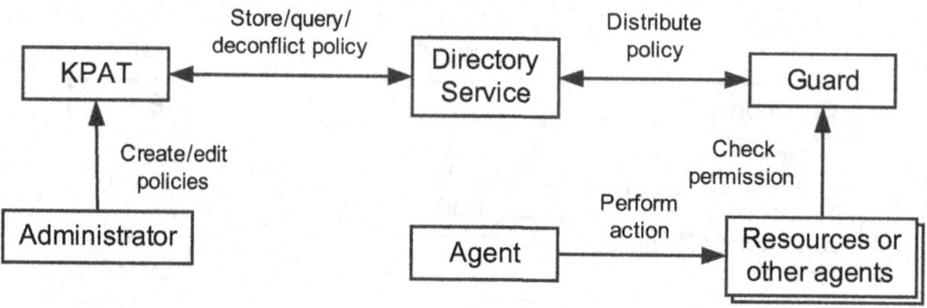

relating to entities described at different levels of abstraction. The representation facilitates careful reasoning about policy disclosure, conflict detection, and harmonization about domain structure and concepts.

RuleML

The Rule Markup Language (RuleML) initiative defines a family of XML-based rule languages (The Rule Markup Initiative, 2004 August). The model of the RuleML family of sublanguages is shown in Figure 6.

For these families, XML Schemes are provided. The main RuleML sublanguages are described as follows:

Figure 6. RuleML family of sublanguages

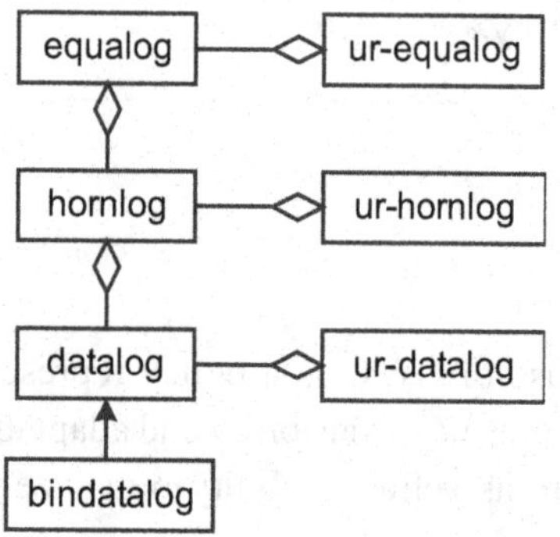

- Datalog RuleML sublanguage is entirely composed of element modules: core, description, clause, boolean, atom, role, and data. Each module declares a set of XSD elements.
- Binary Datalog RuleML sublanguage redefines Datalog so that atoms are binary.
- Horn-Logic RuleML sublanguage adds the Horn elements module.
- Equational-Logic RuleML sublanguage adds the equation elements module to Hornlog.
- 'UR' Datalog RuleML sublanguage redefines datalog to permit href attributes. The same way is used to define the 'UR' Horn-Logic RuleML sublanguage and the 'UR' Equational-Logic RuleML sublanguage.

RuleML encompasses a hierarchy of rules, including reaction rules (event-condition-action rules), transformation rules (functional-equation rules), derivation rules (implicational-inference rules), also specialized to facts ("premise-less" derivation rules) and queries ("conclusion-less" derivation rules), as well as integrity-constraints (consistency-maintenance rules). A graphical view of RuleML rules is a reduction tree rooted in general rules is showed in the Figure 7.

RuleML permits both forward (bottom-up) and backward (top-down) rules and facts in XML to describe constrains. We distinguish between the following facts/rules for policy representation:

Figure 7. Graphical view of RuleML rules

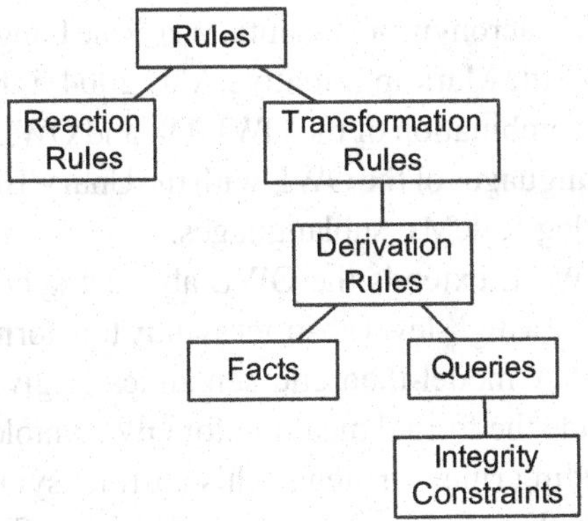

- **Structural/organizational** facts and rules. These rules are used to encode domain specific ontologies.
- **Service definition** facts and rules, provided with links to the structural rules and facts.
- **Task-specific** rules and facts, provided by the service clients.

The benefit of categorizing the policy rules in this way is that an organization can utilize a common ontology that can be shared amongst services and service clients. The rules/facts (i.e., policies) inform to clients about the usage of services in achieving business objectives.

Let consider an example to illustrate the policy representation in RuleML with the ur-datalog sublanguage. It is related with the case study described earlier (see Figure 8).

Figure 8. Example of policy representation in RuleML

```
<rulebase direction="backward">
<imp>
  <_head>
     <atom>
      <_opr href="#GrantedAccess"/>
      <var>requester</var>
      <var>server</var>
     </atom>
  </_head>
  <_body>
    <and>
     <atom>
      <_opr href="#isMember"/>
      <var>requester</var>
      <ind>PayCustomer</ind>
     </atom>
     <atom>
      <_opr href="#isMember"/>
      <var>server</var>
      <ind>PayServer</ind>
     </atom>
    </and>
  </_body>
</imp>
</rulebase>
```

One or more rule engines will be needed for executing RuleML rulebases (Friedman-Hill, 2004; Spencer, 2004). RuleML provides tools for deduction, rewriting, and further inferential-transformational tasks. However, the main motivation is to employ RuleML as a semantic interoperable vehicle for heterogeneous policy languages, standards, protocols, and mechanisms. RuleML provides intermediate markup syntax, with associated deep knowledge representation semantics for interchange between those languages, standards, and mechanisms. For interchange between policy languages/standards/protocols/mechanisms that are already XML-based, this can, for instance, be achieved using XSL transformations (XSLT), e.g., to translate into and then out of RuleML.

SWRL

SWRL, acronym of Semantic Web Rule Language (The Rule Markup Initiative, May 2004) is based on a combination of the OWL DL and OWL Lite sublanguages of the OWL with the Unary/Binary Datalog RuleML sublanguages.

SWRL extends the OWL abstract syntax to include a high-level abstract syntax for Horn-like rules. A model-theoretic semantics is given to provide the formal meaning for OWL ontologies including rules written in this abstract syntax.

In the same way that in RuleML, SWRL rules are used for policy representation. Atoms in SWRL rules can be of the form C(x), P(x,y), sameAs(x,y) or differentFrom(x,y), where C is an

Figure 9. Example of policy representation in SWRL

```
<ruleml:imp>
 <ruleml:_head>
      <swrlx:individualPropertyAtom
      swrlx:property="GrantedAccess">
            <ruleml:var>requester</ruleml:var>
            <ruleml:var>server</ruleml:var>
      </swrlx:individualPropertyAtom>
</ruleml:_head>
 <ruleml:_body>
      <swrlx:classAtom>
            <owlx:Class owlx:name="User" />
            <ruleml:var>requester</ruleml:var>
      </swrlx:classAtom>
      <swrlx:classAtom>
            <owlx:Class owlx:name="Server" />
            <ruleml:var>server</ruleml:var>
      </swrlx:classAtom>
      <swrlx:individualPropertyAtom swrlx:property="Member">
            <ruleml:var>requester</ruleml:var>
            <owlx:Individual owlx:name="#PayCustomer" />
      </swrlx:individualPropertyAtom>
      <swrlx:individualPropertyAtom swrlx:property="Member">
            <ruleml:var>server</ruleml:var>
            <owlx:Individual owlx:name="#PayServer" />
      </swrlx:individualPropertyAtom>
 </ruleml:_body>
</ruleml:imp>
```

OWL description, P is an OWL property, and x,y are either variables, OWL individuals or OWL data values.

SWRL is defined by an XML syntax based on RuleML and the OWL XML Presentation Syntax. The rule syntax is illustrated with the following example (see Figure 9) related with the case study described earlier.

A useful restriction in the form of the rules is to limit antecedent and consequent classAtoms to be named classes, where the classes are defined purely in OWL. Adhering to this format makes it easier to translate rules to or from existing or future rule systems, including Prolog.

Rei

Rei (Kagal et al., 2003) is a policy framework that integrates support for policy specification, analysis, and reasoning. Its deontic-logic-based policy language allows users to express and represent the concepts of rights, prohibitions, obligations, and dispensations. In addition, Rei permits users to specify policies that are defined as rules associating an entity of a managed domain with its set of rights, prohibitions, obligations, and dispensations.

Rei provides a policy specification language in OWL-Lite that allows users to develop declarative policies over domain specific ontologies in RDF, DAML+OIL, and OWL.

A policy (see Figure 10 for the Rei Ontology) primarily includes a list of grantings and a context used to define the policy domain. A granting associates a set of constraints with a deontic object to form a policy rule. This allows reuse of deontic objects in different policies with different constraints and actors. A deontic object represents permissions, prohibitions, obligations, and dispensations over entities in the policy domain. It includes constructs for describing what action (or set of actions) the deontic is described

Figure 10. Rei ontology

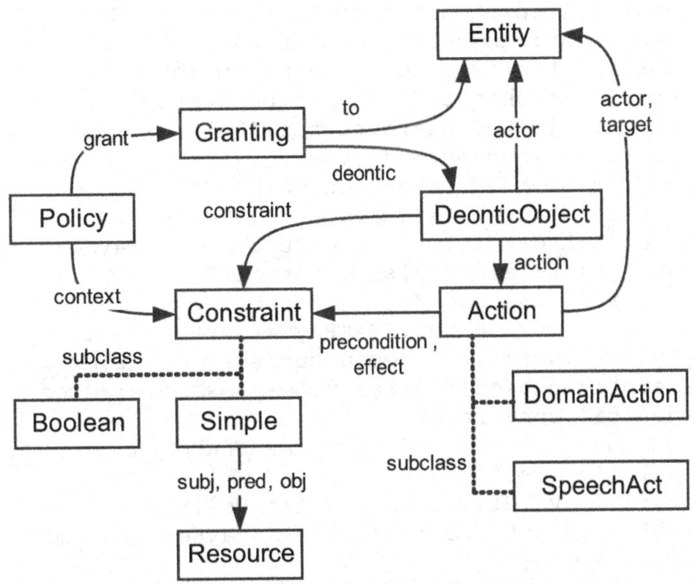

over, who the potential actor (or set of actors) of the action is and under what conditions is the deontic object applicable.

Actions are one of the most important components of Rei specifications as policies are described over possible actions in the domain. The domain actions describe application or domain specific actions, whereas the speech acts are primarily used for dynamic and remote policy management.

There are six subclasses of SpeechAct: Delegate, Revoke, Request, Cancel, Command, and Promise. A valid delegation leads to a new permission. Similarly, a revocation speech act nullifies an existing permission (whether policy based or delegation based) by causing a prohibition. An entity can request another entity for a permission, which if accepted causes a delegation, or to perform an action on its behalf, which if accepted causes an obligation. An entity can also cancel any previously made request, which leads to a revocation and/or a dispensation. A command causes an obligation on the recipient and the promise causes an obligation on the sender.

To enable dynamic conflict resolution, Rei also includes meta-policy specifications, namely setting the modality preference (negative over positive or vice versa) or stating the priority between rules within a policy or between policies themselves.

Figure 11 shows an example illustrating the policy representation in Rei. It is related with the case study described earlier.

The Rei framework provides a policy engine that reasons about the policy specifications. The engine accepts policy specifications in both the Rei language and in RDFS, consistent with the Rei ontology. Specifically, the engine automatically translates the RDF specification into triplets of the form (subject, predicate, object). The engine also accepts additional domain-dependent information in any semantic language that can then be converted into this recognizable form of triplet.

Figure 11. Example of policy representation in Rei

```
<constraint:SimpleConstraint rdf:ID="IsPayCustomer"
    constraint:subject="#RequesterVar"
    constraint:predicate="&example;memberOf"
    constraint:object="&example;payCustomer"/>
<constraint:SimpleConstraint rdf:ID="IsPayServer"
    constraint:subject="#PayServerVar"
    constraint:predicate="&example;memberOf"
    constraint:object="&example;payServer"/>
<constraint:And rdf:ID="ArePayCustomerAndPayServer"
    constraint:first="#IsPayCustomer"
    constraint:second="#IsPayServer"/>
<deontic:Permission rdf:ID="PayServerPermission">
    <deontic:actor rdf:resource="#RequesterVar"/>
    <deontic:action rdf:resource="&example;access"/>
    <deontic:constraint
      rdf:resource="#ArePayCustomerAndPayServer"/>
</deontic:Permission>
<policy:Policy rdf:ID="PaymentAuthPolicy1">
    <policy:grants rdf:resource="#PayServerPermission"/>
 </policy:Policy>
```

The engine allows queries according to the Prolog language about any policies, meta-policies, and domain dependent knowledge that have been loaded in its knowledge base.

The Rei framework does not provide an enforcement model. In fact, the policy engine has not been designed to enforce the policies but only to reason about them and answer to queries.

Comparative Analysis Between Semantic and Non-Semantic Security Policy Languages

A comparative analysis between PONDER, Rei, and KAoS is presented in Tonti et al. (2003). In this analysis, it is discussed the differences between PONDER, a non-semantic policy language, and Rei, KAoS that are based on OWL. Based on this work and our research, which includes an extensive analysis of XACML, RuleML, and SWRL, we can identify the next topics as the most relevant ones for the comparison:

- **Abstraction.** Levels of abstraction (high, medium, and low) that a policy specification can represent.
- **Extensibility.** The capability to include new concepts and elements of the system in the representation.
- **Representability.** Types of environments (complex or specific) that the specification can represent.
- **Readability.** The quality of specification that makes it easy to read and to understand.
- **Conflict Detection.** A policy framework should be able to check that a given policy does not conflict with any other existing policy.
- **Policy Access.** A policy framework has to be able to access to policy repositories.
- **Interoperation.** A policy framework has to be able to interoperate with other policy frameworks.
- **Enforcement.** A policy framework has to be able to enforce a given policy.

Table 1 shows a summary of the comparison between semantic and non-semantic policy languages using these criteria, and how the first ones provide some really interesting features to be used in policy-based management frameworks.

Semantic approaches have the ability to analyze policies related with entities described at a high level of abstraction, while in non-semantic ones, such as Ponder and XACML, it is necessary the identification of resources and therefore, in some cases, they have to pay attention to some implementation details. For example, in the policy

Table 1. Comparative analysis between semantic and non-semantic policy languages

	Semantic Languages	Non-Semantic Languages
Abstraction	Multiple levels	Medium and low level
Extensibility	Easy and at runtime	Complex and at compile-time
Representability	Complex environments	Specific environments
Readability	Specialized tools	Direct
Conflict Detection	Easy, directly supported	Complex
Policy Access	Querying the ontology	By API
Interoperation	By common Ontology	By Interfaces
Enforcement	Complex	Easy

expressed in XACML using our case study (see Figure 2) the tag <Resources> is used to identify the resources, whereas in SWRL (see Figure 9) the entities are described at a high level using an ontology. On the contrary, this capability to express policy at multiples levels of abstraction makes automation mechanisms for policy enforcement more complex in the case of semantic languages.

The use of ontologies permits the extensibility at runtime and the representability of complex environments in the semantic languages, although it is necessary the use of specialized tools for the policy specification. For example, the reader can compare the readability of the Ponder policy in Figure 1 with the Rei policy in Figure 11. Moreover, the use of ontologies facilitates the reasoning over the policies; therefore it makes easy the detection of conflicts.

In addition, the access to policy information and its sharing between different entities is easier when using ontologies than when using APIs and exchange interfaces in traditional non-semantic languages. For example, the interoperability between two heterogeneous applications, one using Ponder and other one using XACML should be based on the creation of complex interfaces to permit the exchange of policies between them, whereas one application using KAoS and another one using SWRL just need a common ontology for being interoperable between them.

Comparative Analysis of the Semantic Policy Languages Described

Table 2 shows a comparison of the aforementioned policy languages. Many aspects can be identified as part of this comparison, although the most relevant are:

- Approach. Two types of approaches have been identified: Rule-based and deontic logic-based.
- Specification language. It can be XML, RDFS, or OWL.
- Tools for policy specification.
- Reasoning engine for policy analysis and verification.
- Enforcement support to the policy deployment.

KAoS presents a full solution that includes from the policy language to the policy enforcement, while the rest of approaches lack some components (e.g., tools for policy specification).

On the other hand, OWL has a limited way of defining restrictions using the tag *owl:Restriction*.

Table 2. Comparative analysis between KAoS, RuleML, SWRL, and Rei

	KAoS	RuleML	SWRL	Rei
Approach	Deontic Logic	Rules	Rules	Deontic Logic + Rules
Specification language	DAML/OWL	Prolog-like syntax + XML	RuleML + OWL	Prolog-like syntax + RDF-S
Tools for specification	KPAT	No	No	No
Reasoning	KAoS engine	External Engine	External Engine	Prolog engine
Enforcement	Supported	External Engine	External Engine	External Functionality

Figure 12. Operational security policy in SWRL

```
<ruleml:imp>
 <ruleml:_head>
      <swrlx:individualPropertyAtom
      swrlx:property="Status">
             <ruleml:var>server</ruleml:var>
             <owlx:Individual owlx:name="#Stopped" />
      </swrlx:individualPropertyAtom>
 </ruleml:_head>
 <ruleml:_body>
      <swrlx:classAtom>
             <owlx:Class owlx:name="Server" />
             <ruleml:var>server</ruleml:var>
      </swrlx:classAtom>
      <swrlx:individualPropertyAtom swrlx:property="Intrusion">
             <ruleml:var>server</ruleml:var>
             <owlx:Individual owlx:name="#Detected" />
      </swrlx:individualPropertyAtom>
 </ruleml:_body>
 </ruleml:imp>
```

This limitation also appears in KAoS, but SWRL overcomes it by the extending the set of OWL axioms including horn-like rules.

Moreover, SWRL is not limited to deontic policies as it happens in Rei and KAoS. For example, in the case of the next operational security policy, which is defined in natural language as "*If an intrusion is detected in the e-payment service, stop this service*", it cannot be described in KAoS or Rei, but it can in SWRL as it is illustrated in Figure 12.

CONCLUSION AND FUTURE WORK

This chapter has provided the current trends of policy-based management enriched by semantics applied to the protection of information systems. It has described some initial concepts related with policy management and formal representation techniques complemented by a case study where the reader can see the advantages and also some of the current open issues of using this approach to management versus traditional "non-semantic" languages and frameworks.

This chapter has also provided some discussions of the most relevant security aware semantic specification languages and information models. Our perspective on the main issues and problems of each of them has also been presented, based on different criteria such as their approach or the specification technique they use.

According to our analysis KAoS presents a full collection of services and tools allowing the specification, reasoning, and enforcement of policies, whereas Rei lacks in the definition of a full framework with tools and enforcement mechanisms. RuleML and SWRL (which is based on RuleML) are ideal as interoperable semantic language formats; in fact, they can be integrated in other external frameworks with a compatible engine.

In the field of security policy languages enriched by semantics the future work is focused on its application in different contexts such as grid-computing environments, coalition search and rescue, and semantic firewalls. More specifically, and regarding the policy languages analyzed in this chapter, currently a graphical user interface is being developed to specify policies for Rei (UMBC eBiquity, 2005), and KAoS services are being adapted to general-purpose grid computing and Web services environments (Institute of Human and Machine Cognition, 2005).

Regarding our future work, it is being devoted to investigate how the Common Information Model (CIM) defined by DMTF can be expressed in OWL and used as common ontology for SWRL or other specific-purpose semantic security policy languages.

ACKNOWLEDGMENT

This work has been partially funded by the EU POSITIF (Policy-based Security Tools and Framework) IST project (IST-2002-002314) and by the ENCUENTRO (00511/PI/04) Spanish Seneca project.

REFERENCES

Avouris, N. M., & Gasser, L. (1992). *Distributed artificial intelligence: Theory and praxis*. Kluwer Academic Publishers.

Brickley, D., & Guha, R. V. (2004, January). *Rdf vocabulary description language 1.0: Rdf schema.* Technical Report, W3C Working Draft.

Connolly, D., Dean, M., van Harmelen, F., Hendler, J., Horrocks, I., McGuinness, D. L., et al. (2003, February). *Web ontology language (owl) reference version 1.0.* Technical Report, W3C Working Draft.

Damianou, N., Dulay, N., et al. (2001). *The ponder policy specification language.* Policy 2001: Workshop on Policies for Distributed Systems and Networks. Springer-Verlag.

Distributed Management Task Force, inc. (2005). *Common Information Model (CIM), Version 2.9.0.*

Fensel, D. (2004) *Ontologies: Silver bullet for knowledge management and electronic commerce.* Springer-Verlag.

Friedman-Hill, E. (2004, December). *Jess Manual, Version 7.0.* Distributed Systems Research, Sandia National Labs.

Genesereth, M. R., & Nilsson, N. (1986) *Logical foundation of artificial intelligence.* Morgan Kaufmann.

Gruber, T. R. (1993). *A translation approach to portable ontology specifications.* Knowledge Acquisition.

Institute of Human and Machine Cognition. (2005). *IHMC ontology and policy management.* University of West Florida.

Kagal, L., Finin, T., & Johshi, A. (2003). *A policy language for pervasive computing environment.* Policy 2003: Workshop on Policies for Distributed Systems and Networks. Springer-Verlag.

Kosiur, D. (2001). *Understanding policy-based networking.* John Wiley & Sons.

Martínez Pérez, G., García Clemente, F. J., & Gómez Skarmeta, A. F. (2005) *Policy-based management of Web and information systems security: An emerging technology.* Hershey, PA: Idea Group.

OASIS. (2004, November). *Extensible Access Control Markup Language (XACML), Version 2.0.*

Russell, S., & Norvig, P. (1995). *Artificial intelligence: A modern approach.* Prentice Hall.

Spencer, B. (2004). *A Java deductive reasoning engine for the Web (jDREW), Version 1.1.*

Strassner, J. (2003). *Policy-based network management: Solutions for the next generation.* Morgan Kaufmann.

The Rule Markup Initiative. (2004, May). *SWRL: A Semantic Web rule Language combining OWL and RuleML, Version 0.6.*

The Rule Markup Initiative. (2004, August). *Schema specification of RuleML 0.87, Version 0.87.*

Tonti, G., Bradshaw, J. M., Jeffers, R., Montanari, R., Suri, N., & Uszok, A. (2003). Semantic Web languages for policy representation and reasoning: A comparison of KAoS, Rei, and Ponder. *The Semantic Web — ISWC 2003. Proceedings of the Second International Semantic Web Conference.* Springer-Verlag.

UMBC eBiquity. (2005). *Project Rei: A policy specification language.* University of Maryland, Baltimore County (UMBC).

Uszok, A., Bradshaw, J., Jeffers, R., Suri, N., et al. (2003). *KAoS Policy and domain services: Toward a description-logic approach to policy representation, deconfliction, and enforcement.* Policy 2003: Workshop on Policies for Distributed Systems and Networks. Springer-Verlag.

Verma, D. C. (2000). *Policy-based networking: Architecture and algorithms.* Pearson Education.

W3C. (1999, February). *Resource Description Framework (RDF), data model and syntax.* W3C Recommendation.

Wooldridge, M. (2001). *An introduction to multiagent systems.* John Wiley & Sons.

This work was previously published in Web Semantics and Ontology, edited by D. Taniar, pp. 364-390, copyright 2006 by IGI Publishing, formerly known as Idea Group Publishing (an imprint of IGI Global).

Chapter VIII
Using SAML and XACML for Web Service Security and Privacy[1]

Tuncay Namli
Middle East Technical University, Turkey

Asuman Dogac
Middle East Technical University, Turkey

ABSTRACT

Web service technology changes the way of conducting business by opening their services to the whole business world over the networks. This property of Web services makes the security and privacy issues more important because the access to the services becomes easier. Many Web service standards are emerging to make Web services secure and privacy protected. This chapter discusses two of them; SAML (OASIS, 2005) and XACML (OASIS, 2005). SAML is an XML-based framework for communicating user authentication, entitlement, and attribute information. In other words, SAML handles the user authentication and also carries attribute information for authorization (access control). XACML is the complementary standard of OASIS to make the access control decisions. This work is realized within the scope of the IST 027074 SAPHIRE Project which is an intelligent health care monitoring and decision support system.

INTRODUCTION

Web service technology changes the way of conducting business by opening their services to the whole business world over the networks. This property of Web services makes the security and privacy issues more important because the access to the services becomes easier. Furthermore, the privacy and security issues are indispensable for Web service technology in order to make them acceptable in more sensitive business transactions.

Many Web service standards are emerging to make Web services secure and privacy protected. Some of the available standards are WS-Security (OASIS, 2004), WS-Policy (W3C, 2006), WS-Trust (IBM, BEA Systems, Microsoft, Layer 7 Technologies, Oblix, VeriSign, Actional, Computer Associates, OpenNetwork Technologies, Ping Identity, Reactivity, RSA Security, 2005), and WS-SecurityPolicy (IBM, Microsoft, RSA Security, VeriSign, 2005).

In this chapter, we discuss two security and privacy related standards for Web services, namely, SAML (OASIS, 2005) and XACML (OASIS, 2005). SAML is an XML-based framework for communicating user authentication, entitlement, and attribute information (OASIS, 2006, http://www.oasis-open.org/committees/tc_home.php?wg_abbrev=security). In other words, SAML handles the user authentication and also carries attribute information for authorization (access control). XACML is the complementary standard of OASIS to make the access control decisions. For example, once the identity of a physician is confirmed by the system using SAML, whether this physician in the role he plays has the right to access the particular data of a particular patient can be decided by using XACML mechanisms.

Generally, the clients of the Web services are the software, not the direct users in B2B systems. Therefore, usually access control decisions may not be needed and only the authentication of the requestor software is enough. However, there are cases where authorization of the user becomes important. In this chapter, we give a real life Web service example from the health care domain where a medical institute serves access to medical documents. Because a patient's medical data is sensitive information, the Web service needs an authentication mechanism to authenticate the user. Furthermore, an authorization decision is necessary to decide if the user is allowed to access to the Web service and the resource that it has requested.

This chapter describes the use of SAML and XACML technologies to provide for the security and privacy of Web services. This work is realized within the scope of the IST 027074 SAPHIRE Project, which is an intelligent health care monitoring and decision support system. SAPHIRE System is a platform integrating the wireless medical sensor data with hospital information systems. The patient monitoring is achieved by using agent technology where the "agent behaviour" is based on computerized clinical practice guidelines. The patient medical history stored in medical information systems is accessed through semantically enriched Web services. In this way, not only the observations received from wireless medical sensors, but also the patient medical history, is used in the reasoning process. The security and the privacy architectures described in this chapter are developed for the SAPHIRE system.

The chapter is organized as follows; In Section 3, OASIS standard XACML, the policy language, the processing environment, and the request/response context are described. Section 4 describes the Web Service profile of XACML. Section 5 and Section 6 provide the details of the XACML's SAML profile. This profile describes how to use SAML to carry XACML instances and Role Based Access Control (RBAC) profile of XACML. Section 7 describes the SAML token profile for Web Service Security and subject confirmation methods. Finally, Section 8 presents a comprehensive real life example from the medical domain which uses all the given profiles described in this chapter.

ACCESS CONTROL AND SINGLE SIGN-ON

In order to provide a strong access control mechanism, a system should deal with several class types. For example, the system should be able to deal with the properties of participating entities such as principals (subjects), access control policies, documents (resources), and subject roles. In addition to these, the system should also provide some functionality like policy management, authentication, audit, access control management, and privilege management.

To provide such functionalities several access control management models are proposed. One of them is the "Control Model" which illustrates how control is exerted over access to operations on protected objects. In this model, there are five actors: the Claimant, the Verifier, the Target, the Access Control Information, and the Access Control policy. The Claimant provides identity information (e.g., attribute certificates or SAML Assertions, etc.) about the subject to the Verifier. The Target actor obtains information about the resource (e.g., sensitivity level, resource ID) and environment (e.g., time) and gives to the Verifier. In this model, the Verifier may be owner of the Target or may be an independent entity. Then, the Verifier gets the applicable policies from the Target and evaluates the policy with the information obtained from both the Target and the Claimant. In this model, the communication between the Claimant and Verifier can be performed in two ways. In the first alternative, the Push model, the Claimant provides the identity information along with the request in a security token. In the second alternative, Pull model, the Verifier gets the identity information from a trusted party. The ASTM E31.20 Working Draft - Privilege Management Infrastructure (ASTM, 2006) describes the factors that should be considered before choosing the push or pull methodology. In the push model, it is stated that the token holding the identity and authentication information must be sufficiently secure (token lifetime, validation, and encryption). In the pull model, the authentication service and attribute authority service must be accessible, and a trusted communication should be established with the trusted party.

This communication is better defined in the "Delegation model." The model defines a new actor called the Source of Authority in addition to the Verifier and Claimant. In this model, there should be a strong trust relationship with the Source of Authority and the Verifier. The Source of Authority assigns privilege to Claimants by issuing attribute credentials (e.g., attribute certificates or SAML attribute assertions). Then, the Claimant asserts its delegated privilege by demonstrating its identity.

It is very hard to manage the access control model when the access rules are based on the real identities of the subject. In this case, for each subject different access control policy should be defined. Therefore, role-based access control is more suitable for real life systems.

Figure 1 presents an adapted Role-Based Access Control Schema from the ANSI RBAC standard. Structural Roles are directly assigned to the principals. However, Functional Roles are assigned to Principal over a session. Then permissions are assigned to the roles that are currently active across all the user's sessions. There are several ways to represent the Role credentials for a user. For example, SAML Attribute Assertions attribute certificates, public-key certificates, entries in a directory service, or XACML attributes can be used.

In this document, we describe how the XACML Role model can be used for the RBAC systems. However, other alternatives also exist, such as X509 Role Based infrastructure. In this model, attribute certificates (AC) described in the X509 standard are used to represent role credentials. The certifcates are obtained from the Attribute Authority (AA). The Attribute Authority signs the attribute certifcates in order to provide the trust. In X.509 role based infrastructure, Role-specification ACs, Role-assignment ACs, and Policy ACs can be used. However, this infrastructure needs a policy language. In addition to XACML, Ponder (Imperial Collage, 2000), Keynote (Keynote, 1999), and IBM Enterprise Privacy Authorization Language (EPAL) (IBM, 2003) can be used as the policy language.

Figure 1. Role-based access control schema

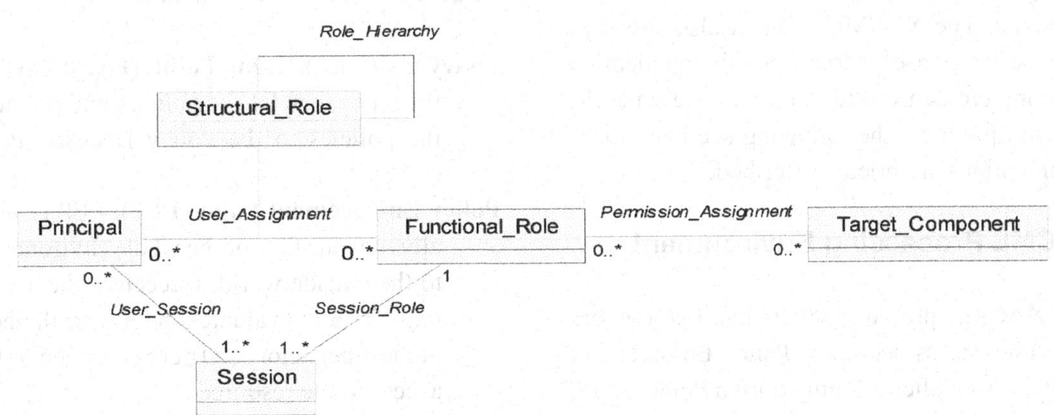

In addition to role attributes, several type of information may be needed to implement access control systems. Such information is named as Access Control Information (ACI) in the Control model. ISO defines possible ACI as follows:

- **User ACI:** Individual access control identities, organizational position, membership of a project or task group, sensitivity markings to which access is allowed, integrity markings to which access is allowed, security attributes of delegates, location (e.g., sign-on workstation);
- **Target ACI:** Target access control identities, individual initiator access control identities and the actions on the target allowed or denied them, hierarchical group membership access control identities and the actions on the target allowed or denied them, functional group membership access control identities and the actions on the target allowed or denied them, role access control identities and the actions on the target allowed or denied them, sensitivity markings, integrity markings;
- **Action ACI:** ACI associated with operating zoning action (e.g., Sensitivity markings, integrity markings, originator identity, owner identity), ACI associated with the action as a whole (e.g., initiator ACI, permitted initiator and target pairs, permitted targets, permitted initiators, allowed class of operations: read, write, and so forth, required integrity level); and
- **Contextual ACI:** Time periods, route, location, system status (e.g., emergency), strength of authentication.

EXTENSIBLE ACCESS MARKUP LANGUAGE (XACML)

XACML is an XML-based markup language for the policy management and access decisions. It was approved and became an OASIS standard in February 2003. It provides an XML schema for a general policy language, which is used to protect any kind of resource and make access decisions over these resources. XACML standard not only gives the model of the policy language, but also proposes a processing environment model to manage the policies and to conclude the access decisions. The XACML Context also specifies Request/Response protocol that the application environment can use to communicate with the decision point. In the following sections, these specifications are briefly described.

XACML Processing Environment

The XACML profile specifies five main actors to handle access decisions: Policy Enforcement Point (PEP), Policy Administration Point (PAP), Policy Decision Point (PDP), Policy Information Point (PIP), and a context handler.

Policy Administration Point (PAP): PAP is the repository for the policies and provides the policies to the Policy Decision Point (PDP).

Policy Enforcement Point (PEP): PEP is actually the interface of the whole environment to the outside world. It receives the access requests and evaluates them with the help of the other actors and permits or denies the access to the resource.

Figure 2. XACML actors [OASIS, 2005. eXtensible Access Control Markup Language (XACML) Version 2.0.]

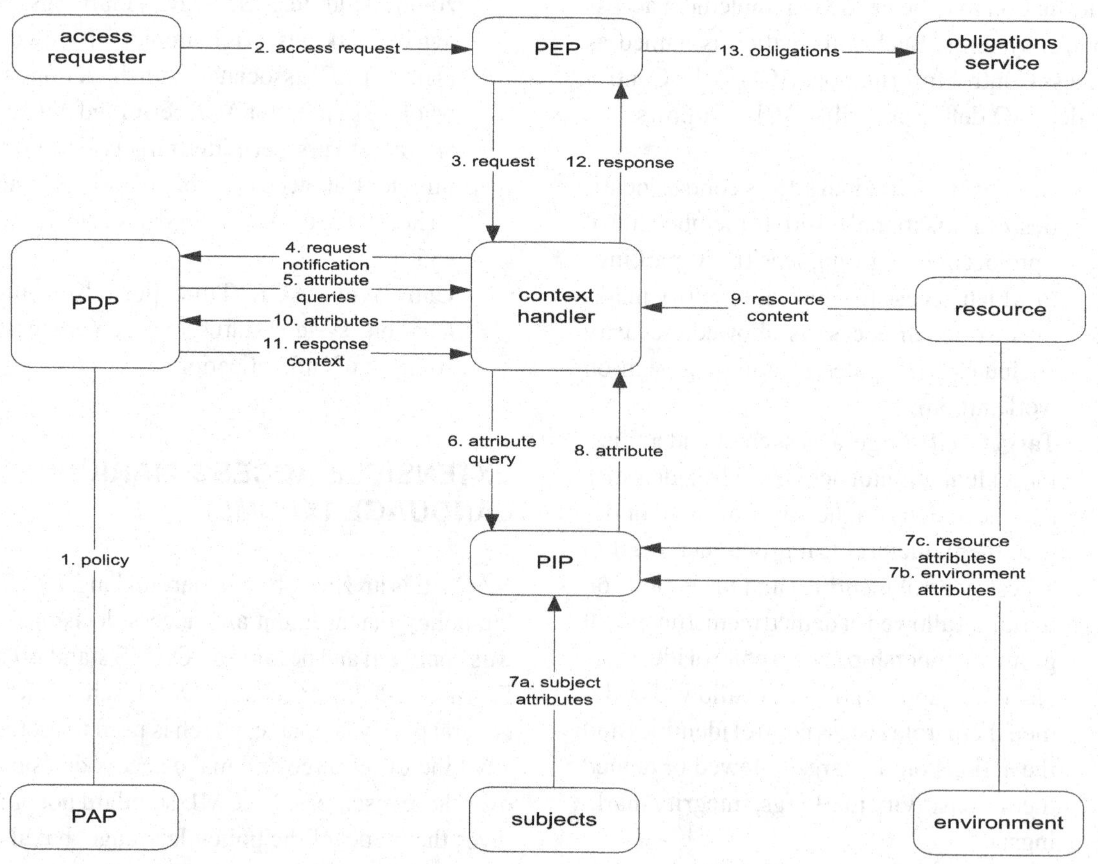

Policy Decision Point (PDP): PDP is the main decision point for the access requests. It collects all the necessary information from other actors and concludes a decision.

Policy Information Point (PIP): PIP is the point where the necessary attributes for the policy evaluation are retrieved from several external or internal actors. The attributes can be retrieved from the resource to be accessed, environment (e.g., time), subjects, and so forth.

Figure 2 illustrates these actors and information flow. As can be seen in the figure, the Policy Enforcement Point (PEP) is the component where the request is received. In this part, the attributes in the request may be in the format of the application environment (e.g., SAML, etc.). The Policy Enforcement Point (PEP) sends the request to the Context Handler. Context Handler maps the request and attributes to the XACML Request context and sends the request to the Policy Decision Point (PDP). While evaluating the request, the Policy Decision Point (PDP) needs some attributes and sends the attribute queries to the Context Handler. The Context Handler collects these attributes by the help of the Policy Information Point (PIP) from the resources, subjects, and the environment. After evaluation, the Policy Decision Point (PDP) sends the XACML Response to the Policy Enforcement Point (PEP) via the Context Handler. The Policy Enforcement Point (PEP) fulfills the obligations if they exist and applies the authorization decision that Policy Decision Point (PDP) concludes.

XACML Model

The language model is composed of three main components, which are PolicySets, Policies, and Rules.

Rule: A Rule element is the basic element of the policy. It defines the target elements to which the rule is applied and gives conditions to apply the rule. It has three components, namely, target, effect, and condition. The target element defines the resources, subjects, actions and the environment to which the rule is applied. As an example, assume that a physician is willing to access a patient's clinical summary data. If an XACML rule is defined for such a case, the resource target element can be the clinical summary data type, target action can be the retrieval of this data, and the environment can restrict the access time. To apply the rule, all these entities should match the defined subjects, resources, actions, and environment in the request context. The "Condition" element gives the conditions to apply the rule. Continuing with the example, the condition can be that the physician number accessing the patient's record should match the physician number on the clinical summary data. "Effect" is the consequence of the rule as either "permit," or "deny."

Policy: Policies are the set of rules which are combined with some algorithms. The algorithms used are called Rule-combining algorithms. For example, "Permit Override" algorithm allows the Policy to evaluate to "Permit" if any rule in the policy evaluates to "Permit." If a rule evaluates to "Deny" and all others are "Not Applicable," the result is "Deny." If all the rules are "Not Applicable" then the policy is "Not Applicable." Policies have also "target" elements which give the subjects, resources, actions, and environment that policy is applied. For example, a policy's subject can be a user role to indicate that the policy restricts the access rights related with that user role.

Another component is the obligations which define necessary actions if the policy is evaluated to "Permit" before giving access to resource. For example, a possible obligation is to send an e-mail to the patient when his clinical summary data is accessed.

PolicySet: A set of policies compose the policy sets by policy-combining algorithm as in the policy. It has also "target" and "obligations" components with the same semantics.

XACML Context

The request and response context used by the Policy Decision Point (PDP) are also defined in the standard. This context is actually the interface to the application environment to insulate the core XACML language. Therefore, applications can use other representations like SAML, which is the most suitable one for the attributes. Then, the Policy Enforcement Point (PEP) applications convert these attribute representations to the XACML context attributes.

The top level element of the context schema is the "Request" element. It includes four components as "Subject," "Resource," "Action," and "Environment." For example, the "Subject" element contains subject's details such as name, e-mail, role, and so forth, and can occur more than once. Furthermore, each "Subject" element may describe the entity associated with the request. "Resource" elements specify the resources for which access is requested, such as a patient's clinical summary data. The requested action to be performed on resource is specified by "Action" element such as "read" or "write." Finally "Environment" element contains attributes of the environment.

The "Response" element is the authorization decision information produced by the Policy Decision Point (PDP). It includes one or more "Result" elements. The "Result" element includes the "Decision" element which can be "Permit," "Deny," "Indeterminate," or "NotApplicable." "Indeterminate" means that the Policy Decision Point (PDP) is somehow unable to evaluate the Request. "NotApplicable" is produced when there is no applicable policy to the request. Another element in the "Response" is the "Status" element which gives the errors occurred and their descriptions while evaluating the request. The last element is the "Obligations" element. This element includes the obligations specified in the "PolicySet" and "Policy" elements in the policy description which should be fulfilled before giving permit to the request.

XACML PROFILE FOR WEB SERVICES

The motivation behind this profile is to manage the optional features and parameters of the technical aspects like reliable messaging, privacy, authorization, security, authentication, and so forth. Therefore, this profile can be used as complementary to Web service standards, such as WS-ReliableMessaging, WS-Security, WS-Trust, and so forth. The two end points of the Web service, the provider and consumer, determine their preferences and mandatory features related with these aspects and may define them in XACML. During the service invocation these policies are combined, and either a successful invocation is realized which fulfills the requirements of both parties or invocation fails because a requirement is not satisfied.

XACML Web Service profile (OASIS, 2003) is restrictions over the core model to apply the XACML concepts over the Web service data model. The first restriction is actually specifying the target of the "PolicySet" as the Web service port which binds the "PolicySet" to Web Service endpoint definition. In addition to this, if it is desired to bind a "PolicySet" to Web service operations rather than to bind them to a port, a second level "PolicySet" is used inside in which target element refers to the Web service operations. The Policy elements in the "PolicySet" elements correspond to the aspects of the end-point policy. For example, it can define a security policy for an operation of a Web service port, which should be fulfilled in order to achieve successful invocation of the operation.

The profile also gives bindings of "PolicySet" elements to WSDL 1.1 and SOAP 1.1 in order to facilitate distribution of the policies by these standards. The WSDL 1.1 schema is extended by adding an extension element "PolicySetIdReference" to "port" element. For the SOAP binding the "PolicySet" elements are carried in the SOAP headers.

SAML 2.0 PROFILE OF XACML V2.0

The contents of the messages exchanged between the XACML actors are specified in the XACML standard. For example, the Policy Enforcement Point (PEP) sends the request to the Policy Decision Point (PDP) with the "Request" element defined in the XACML context. However, the protocol and transport mechanisms for these messages are not set. SAML by its nature is designed for carrying the security and authorization related information and have the bindings to basic transportation mechanisms. Therefore, OASIS publishes a SAML profile for the XACML (OASIS, 2005) to carry the XACML messages between the XACML actors. This profile defines the usage of SAML 2.0 to protect, transport, and request XACML instances and other information. It defines six types of queries or statements:

AttributeQuery: This query may be used by the Policy Information Point (PIP)s to request attributes from Attribute Authorities or Attribute Repositories (e.g., LDAP, etc.). It is a standard SAML Request. For example, this query can be used to retrieve patient's e-mail address to satisfy an obligation that requests the patient to be notified each time his clinical data is accessed.

AttributeStatement: The statement is the response to the attribute query giving one or more attributes;

XACMLPolicyQuery: This query is used for requesting policies from the Policy Adminstration Point (PAP). The element is extension of SAML Request element. For example, this query can be used to retrieve policies specific to a patient;

XACMLPolicyStatement: This element is an extension to SAML Statement. It carries the policies requested from the Policy Adminstration Point (PAP);

XACMLAuthzDecisionQuery: This element is also extension for SAML Request element. It carries the XACML Request that the Policy Enforcement Point (PEP) sends to the Policy Decision Point (PDP) to request authorization decision; and

XACMLAuthzDecisionStatement: XACMLAuthzDecisionStatement is an extension for SAML Statement element. It carries the XACML Response message sent from the Policy Decision Point (PDP) to Policy Enforcement Point (PEP).

CORE AND HIERARCHICAL ROLE-BASED ACCESS CONTROL (RBAC) PROFILE OF XACML V2.0

Most applications use role-based authorization and access control system rather than authorize individual subjects. ANSI-RBAC is the well-known role-based access control standard. XACML RBAC profile (OASIS, 2005) defines the usage of XACML to meet the requirements in the ANSI RBAC "core" and "hierarchical" standards. Mainly, it can handle the access control decisions for a given subject having specific roles. In addition, it can be answered if a subject is allowed to have a specific role. Another capability of this profile is related with the hierarchical roles. From the subjects existing roles, it can be deduced that if the subject has the permissions on another role by determining if the role is the junior role of the existing roles subject have.

XACML express roles as attributes with "AttributeId" equals to "&role." Then, role values are set as attribute values. In order to provide the role-based control, the profile defines four types of policy sets. The first one is the Role <PolicySet> (RPS), which defines the role and has reference to Permission <PolicySet> (PPS). For each role, a Role <PolicySet> should be defined. Permission <PolicySet> defines the actual permission on the resource. These policy sets are not directly used and only referenced from Role <PolicySet>s. The following example illustrates these policies.

Figure 3 gives the "RolePolicy" of the role "DirectCareProvider." It matches the subject role and includes a reference, the "PermissionPolicy," which states the rules about the role over the resources. Figure 4 illustrates the "PermissionPolicy" for the "DirectCareProvider" role. As seen from the figure, the <Policy> element has the permit-overrides as the rule-combining algorithm. Therefore, if any of the rules are evaluated to "Permit," then the whole policy is evaluated as "Permit." The rules inside the policy state the actions that the role is allowed to take on the resources. The first rule states that this permission policy gives permission to read the resources, which has the resource identification "Sensitive Clinical Information." In fact, in this example, we use the types of resources as the resource identification.

WEB SERVICE SECURITY SAML TOKEN PROFILE

This profile defines the extensions to use SAML together with the Web Service Security standard. According to this profile, SAML assertions can be carried in the wsse:Security headers or in the other parts of the SOAP message. Therefore, references to SAML assertions may be in several contexts. For example, a SAML assertion can be referenced directly from wsse:Security header or <KeyInfo> element of digital signature. These referencing issues are described clearly in the profile.

Figure 3. Role <Policy>

```
<PolicySet xmlns="urn:oasis:names:tc:xacml:2.0:policy:schema:os" PolicySetId="RPS:DCP:role" PolicyCombiningAlgId="&policy
-combine;permit-overrides">
  <Target>
    <Subjects>
      <Subject>
        <SubjectMatch MatchId="&function;anyURI-equal">
          <AttributeValue DataType="&xml;anyURI">&roles;DirectCareProvider </AttributeValue>
          <SubjectAttributeDesignator AttributeId="&role;" DataType="&xml;anyURI"/>
        </SubjectMatch>
      </Subject>
    </Subjects>
  </Target>
  <!—Give Reference to Permission Policy for DirectCareProvider role-->
  <PolicySetIdReference>PPS:DCP:role</PolicySetIdReference>
</PolicySet>
```

Figure 4. Permission <Policy>

```
<PolicySet xmlns="urn:oasis:names:tc:xacml:2.0:policy:schema:os" PolicySetId="PPS:DCP:role" PolicyCombiningAlgId="&policy-
combine;permit-overrides">
  <!-- Permissions for the Direct Care Provider-->
  <Policy PolicyId="Permissions:DirectCareProvider " RuleCombiningAlgId="&rule-combine;permit-overrides">
  <Rule RuleId="Permission:read:SensitiveClinicalInformation " Effect="Permit">
    <Target>
      <Resources>
        <Resource>
          <ResourceMatch MatchId="&function;string-equal">
              <AttributeValue DataType="&xml;string">Sensitive Clinical Information </AttributeValue>
              <ResourceAttributeDesignator AttributeId="&resource;resource-id"  DataType="&xml;string"/>
          </ResourceMatch>
        </Resource>
      </Resources>
      <Actions><Action>
          <ActionMatch MatchId="&function;string-equal">
            <AttributeValue DataType="&xml;string">read</AttributeValue>
            <ActionAttributeDesignator AttributeId="&action;action-id" DataType="&xml;string"/>
          </ActionMatch>
      </Action></Actions>
    </Target>
  </Rule>
  <Rule RuleId="Permission:read:BillingInformation " Effect="Permit">
    <Target>
      <Resources>
        <Resource>
          <ResourceMatch MatchId="&function;string-equal">
              <AttributeValue DataType="&xml;string">Billing Information </AttributeValue>
              <ResourceAttributeDesignator AttributeId="&resource;resource-id"  DataType="&xml;string"/>
          </ResourceMatch>
        </Resource>
      </Resources>
      <Actions>
        <Action>
          <ActionMatch MatchId="&function;string-equal">
            <AttributeValue DataType="&xml;string">read</AttributeValue>
            <ActionAttributeDesignator AttributeId="&action;action-id" DataType="&xml;string"/>
          </ActionMatch>
        </Action>
      </Actions>
    </Target>
  </Rule>
  </Policy>
</PolicySet>
```

Another important issue in this profile is subject confimations of SAML assertions. The <Subject> element in the SAML assertion identifies the subject of the assertion by giving some of the subject attributes. The subject of the assertion should be confirmed by some mechanism when the relying party wants to be sure about the requests or messages coming from the entity associated with the subject. SAML has defined three methods for the subject confirmation.

Holder-of-Key

The URI of this method in SAML is *urn:oasis:names:tc:SAML:2.0:cm:holder-of-key*. This method establishes the subject confirmation by giving information about a public or secret key that the subject holds. To achieve this, SubjectConfirmation element includes one or more <KeyInfo> element which can either have the key value or some information about how to access to the key. The attesting entity (associated subject of the assertion) should use digital signatures and sign the message it sends by the confirmation key to accomplish subject confirmation. Then the receiver (relying party) use the SubjectConfirmation content (KeyInfo elements) to verify the digital signature of the message or request.

Sender Vouches

The URI of this method is urn*:oasis:names:tc:SAML:2.0:cm:sender-vouches*. In this method, no information exists about the use of assertions and the relying party should use other methodologies for subject confirmation.

Bearer

The URI is *urn:oasis:names:tc:SAML:2.0:cm:bearer*. In this method, the bearer (carrier) of the assertion is assumed to be the subject of the assertion.

This profile requires that either holder-of-key or sender-vouches methods be used for subject confirmation. The profile also gives the processing rules for receiver and sender to process the SubjectConfirmation element.

EXAMPLE: IHE RETRIEVE INFORMATION FOR DISPLAY (RID) WEB SERVICE

In this section, the use of the described technologies is explained through an example Web service, called IHE-RID, employed in the health care domain. IHE is an initiative by health care professionals and industry to improve the way computer systems in health care share information (IHE, 2006). IHE publishes Integration Profiles in order to provide interoperability between health care enterprises for specific use cases. The IHE Retrieve Information for Display Integration Profile (IHE-RID) provides simple and rapid read-only access to patient-centric clinical information that is located outside the user's current application, but is important for better patient care (e.g., access to lab reports from radiology department) (IHE, 2005). It supports access to existing persistent documents in well-known presentation formats such as CDA (Level 1), PDF, JPEG, and so forth. It also supports access to specific key patient-centric information such as allergies, current medications, summary of reports, and so forth, for presentation to a clinician. The technology used in this profile is the Web services. A simplified version of the description of the Web service is given in the Appendix A. Some of the messages and operations are removed for the sake of simplicity. We describe the issues involved through a scenario.

Scenario

John Doe is a patient who has several health care records and documents in the Ankara Hospital. Ankara hospital implements IHE-RID profile and opens the IHE-RID Web service over the Internet. The hospital has an access policy in order to restrict the access to patient's records. The hospital system implements "Role Based Access Control (RBAC)" model and have a specific list of health care roles such as "Direct Care Provider" or "General Care Provider" whose access can either be permitted or denied over the resources according to the policy. The Ankara hospital has integrated this model to the IHE-RID Web service. The hospital has also a policy about the authentication and security issues.

Mr. Bob Barry is a general practioner, in the role "General Care Provider," looking after John Doe. He accesses the IHE-RID Web service from his office. At a certain point in time, he needs the "Discharge Summary" records of John Doe after the surgery that John went through at the Ankara hospital.

XACML RBAC Policy over RID Web Service

The consent that John Doe signed for the hospital includes the following rules about the summary types SUMMARY-SURGERY, SUMMARY-DISCHARGE, SUMMARY-EMERGENCY;

1. Anyone can access SUMMARY-EMERGENCY.
2. Only General Care Provider and Direct Care Provider can access SUMMARY-DISCHARGE and an e-mail has to be sent to the patient e-mail address.
3. Only Direct Care Provider can access SUMMARY-SURGERY. Also access time should be between 8:00 am and 6:00 pm.

The required XACML policies to enforce these rules are illustrated in the following figures.

Figure 5 shows the XACML Policy of the IHE-RID Web service which includes three role policy sets: one for the role Direct Care Provider; one for General Care Provider; and one for any role for this example. The resource of the root policy set matches with the port address of the Web service. The <PolicySetIdReference> elements reference to Permission Policy Sets in which the rules for access controls exist.

Figure 6 illustrates the Permission Policy Set for any role. In this example, anyone can access SUMMARY-EMERGENCY type of information through the IHE-RID Web service. <ActionMatch> element states that the "action-id" attribute in the request context should be equal to "read." <ResourceMatch> element restricts the rule to SUMMARY-EMERGENCY documents. The "requestType" element of the Web service input carries what type of information the subject wishes to access about the patient. This element value should be placed in the resource-id attribute in the request context.

Figure 7 shows the Permission Policy Set for GeneralCareProvider who can access SUMMARY-DISCHARGE type of information. As in the case above, <ResourceMatch> element restricts the rule to SUMMARY-DISCHARGE type of information.

In this policy, there is also an obligation that an e-mail should be sent to patient about the person who accesses his SUMMARY_DISHARGE information. Policy Enforcement Point (PEP) processes this obligation. The attributes that is used while sending the e-mail are taken from the request context's resource and subject attributes. At the end of the policy, by using <PolicySetIdReference> element, we give reference to Permission Policy Set for anyone. This allows the GeneralCareProvider role to access SUMMARY-EMERGENCY.

Figure 8 illustrates the Permission Policy Set for DirectCareProvider role. Like others, this policy restricts the rule to apply on a specific type, which is SUMMARY-DISCHARGE. <Apply> element in the <Condition> element states that time should be between 08:00 and 18:00. Giving

Figure 5. RID XACML policy

```
<PolicySet xmlns="urn:oasis:names:tc:xacml:2.0:policy:schema:os" PolicySetId="Policy-for-RID" PolicyCombiningAlgId="urn:oasis:
names:tc:xacml:2.0:policy-combining-algorithm:deny-overrides">
 <!--PolicySet for RID Web Service-->
 <Target>
  <Subjects>
   <AnySubject/>
  </Subjects>
  <Resources>
   <ResourceMatch MatchId="urn:oasis:names:tc:xacml:2.0:function:string-equal">
         <AttributeValue DataType="anyURI">
           <!--serviceX:portX-->
           IHERetrieveForDisplay:IHERetrieveForDisplayHttpGet
         </AttributeValue>
   </ResourceMatch>
   <ResourceAttributeDesignator AttributeId="urn:oasis:names:tc:xacml:2.0:attribute:portId" DataType="anyURI"/>
  </Resources>
  <Actions>
   <AnyAction/>
  </Actions>
 </Target>
 <!--Role Policy for Direct Care Provider-->
 <PolicySet xmlns="urn:oasis:names:tc:xacml:2.0:policy:schema:os" PolicySetId="RPS:DCP:role" PolicyCombiningAlgId="urn:oasis:
names:tc:xacml:2.0:policy-combining-algorithm:permit-overrides">
  <Target>
   <Subjects>
         <Subject>
          <SubjectMatch MatchId="urn:oasis:names:tc:xacml:2.0:function:anyURI-equal">
                   <AttributeValue DataType="anyURI">urn:example:roles:DirectCareProvider</AttributeValue>
                   <SubjectAttributeDesignator AttributeId="urn:example:attribute:role" DataType="anyURI"/>
          </SubjectMatch>
         </Subject>
   </Subjects>
  </Target>
  <!--Give Reference to Permission Policy for DirectCareProvider role-->
  <PolicySetIdReference>PPS:DCP:role</PolicySetIdReference>
 </PolicySet>
 <!--Role Policy for General Care Provider-->
 <PolicySet xmlns="urn:oasis:names:tc:xacml:2.0:policy:schema:os" PolicySetId="RPS:GCP:role" PolicyCombiningAlgId="urn:
oasis:names:tc:xacml:2.0:policy-combining-algorithm:permit-overrides">
  <Target>
   <Subjects>
         <Subject>
          <SubjectMatch MatchId="urn:oasis:names:tc:xacml:2.0:function:anyURI-equal">
                   <AttributeValue DataType="anyURI">urn:example:roles:GeneralCareProvider</AttributeValue>
                   <SubjectAttributeDesignator AttributeId="urn:example:attribute:role" DataType="anyURI"/>
          </SubjectMatch>
         </Subject>
   </Subjects>
  </Target>
  <!--Give Reference to Permission Policy for DirectCareProvider role-->
  <PolicySetIdReference>PPS:GCP:role</PolicySetIdReference>
 </PolicySet>
 <!--Reference to Permission Policy for any role-->
 <PolicySetIdReference>PPS:anyone:role</PolicySetIdReference>
</PolicySet>
```

Figure 6. Permission policy set (PPS) for any role

```
<PolicySet xmlns="urn:oasis:names:tc:xacml:2.0:policy:schema:os" PolicySetId="PPS:anyone:role" PolicyCombiningAlgId="urn:
oasis:names:tc:xacml:2.0:policy-combining-algorithm:permit-overrides">
  <!-- Permissions for anyone in emergency case-->
  <Policy PolicyId="Permissions:anyone" RuleCombiningAlgId="urn:oasis:names:tc:xacml:2.0:rule-combining-algorithm:permit-
overrides">
    <Rule RuleId="Permission:read:SUMMARY-EMERGENCY" Effect="Permit">
     <Target>
            <Resources>
             <Resource>
              <ResourceMatch MatchId="urn:oasis:names:tc:xacml:2.0:function:string-equal">
               <AttributeValue DataType="http:www.w3.org/2001/XMLSchema#string">SUMMARY-EMERGENCY</
AttributeValue>
               <ResourceAttributeDesignator AttibuteId=urn:"oasis:names:tc:xacml:2.0:resource:resource-id" DataType="http:
www.w3.org/2001/XMLSchema#string"/>
              </ResourceMatch>
             </Resource>
            </Resources>
            <Actions>
             <Action>
              <ActionMatch MatchId="urn:oasis:names:tc:xacml:2.0:function:string-equal">
               <AttributeValue DataType="http:www.w3.org/2001/XMLSchema#string">read</AttributeValue>
               <ActionAttributeDesignator AttributeId="urn:oasis:names:tc:xacml:2.0:action:action-id" DataType="http:www.
w3.org/2001/XMLSchema#string"/>
              </ActionMatch>
             </Action>
            </Actions>
     </Target>
    </Rule>
  </Policy>
</PolicySet>
```

reference to PPS:GCP:role the DirectCareProvider role has gained all the rights of the GeneralCare-Provider role.

User Authentication with SAML

Before handling the access control, authentication of the user should be handled. By using the SAML Token profile for Web Services, we may authenticate the user to the IHE-RID Web service and get some attribute information to be used in the access control. Figure 9 illustrates the SOAP message for Web service invocation in our scenario. Dr. Bob Barry, using the system: example.clinic.com tries to access SUMMARY-DISCHARGE information of the patient with 123456 as patientID (the patient John Doe) by invoking the RID Web service.

The SAML Assertion and related digital signature details are inserted into the <wsse:Security> header. <Assertion> element has the "ID" attribute which identifies the assertion in the message.

Figure 7. PPS for GeneralCareProvider

```
<PolicySet xmlns="urn:oasis:names:tc:xacml:2.0:policy:schema:os" PolicySetId="PPS:GCP:role" PolicyCombiningAlgId="urn:
oasis:names:tc:xacml:2.0:policy-combining-algorithm:permit-overrides">
  <!-- Permissions for the General Care Provider-->
  <Policy PolicyId="Permissions:GeneralCareProvider" RuleCombiningAlgId="urn:oasis:names:tc:xacml:2.0:rule-combining-
algorithm:permit-overrides">
    <Rule RuleId="Permission:read:SUMMARY-DISCHARGE" Effect="Permit">
     <Target>
           <Resources>
            <Resource>
             <ResourceMatch MatchId="urn:oasis:names:tc:xacml:2.0:function:string-equal">
              <AttributeValue DataType="http:www.w3.org/2001/XMLSchema#string">SUMMARY-DISCHARGE</
AttributeValue>
              <ResourceAttributeDesignator AttibuteId=urn:"oasis:names:tc:xacml:2.0:resource:resource-id" DataType="http:
www.w3.org/2001/XMLSchema#string"/>
             </ResourceMatch>
            </Resource>
           </Resources>
           <Actions>
            <Action>
             <ActionMatch MatchId="urn:oasis:names:tc:xacml:2.0:function:string-equal">
              <AttributeValue DataType="http:www.w3.org/2001/XMLSchema#string">read</AttributeValue>
              <ActionAttributeDesignator AttributeId="urn:oasis:names:tc:xacml:2.0:action:action-id" DataType="http:www.
w3.org/2001/XMLSchema#string"/>
             </ActionMatch>
            </Action>
           </Actions>
    </Target>
   </Rule>
   <Obligations>
    <Obligation ObligationId="urn:oasis:names:tc:xacml:2.0:obligation:email" FulfillOn="Permit">
          <AttributeAssignment AttributeId="urn:oasis:names:tc:xacml:2.0:attribute:mailto" DataType="http://www.w3.org/2001/
XMLSchema#string">
           <ResourceAttributeDesignator AttributeId="urn:oasis:names:tc:xacml:2.0:resource:mailto" DataType="http:www.
w3.org/2001/XMLSchema#string"/>
          </AttributeAssignment>
          <AttributeAssignment AttributeId="urn:oasis:names:tc:xacml:2.0:attribute:mailsubject" DataType="http://www.
w3.org/2001/XMLSchema#string">
           <SubjectAttributeDesignator AttributeId="urn:oasis:names:tc:xacml:2.0:subject:subject-id"/>
          </AttributeAssignment>
    </Obligation>
   </Obligations>
  </Policy>
  <PolicySetIdReference>PPS:anyone:role</PolicySetIdReference>
</PolicySet>
```

Figure 8. PPS for DirectCareProvider

```
<PolicySet xmlns="urn:oasis:names:tc:xacml:2.0:policy:schema:os" PolicySetId="PPS:DCP:role" PolicyCombiningAlgId="urn:
oasis:names:tc:xacml:2.0:policy-combining-algorithm:permit-overrides">
 <!-- Permissions for the Direct Care Provider-->
 <Policy PolicyId="Permissions:DirectCareProvider" RuleCombiningAlgId="urn:oasis:names:tc:xacml:2.0:rule-combining-
algorithm:permit-overrides">
  <Rule RuleId="Permission:read:SUMMARY-SURGERY" Effect="Permit">
   <Target>
        <Resources>
         <Resource>
          <ResourceMatch MatchId="urn:oasis:names:tc:xacml:2.0:function:string-equal">
           <AttributeValue DataType="http:www.w3.org/2001/XMLSchema#string">SUMMARY-SURGERY</
AttributeValue>
           <ResourceAttributeDesignator AttibuteId=urn:"oasis:names:tc:xacml:2.0:resource:resource-id" DataType="http:
www.w3.org/2001/XMLSchema#string"/>
          </ResourceMatch>
         </Resource>
        </Resources>
        <Actions>
         <Action>
          <ActionMatch MatchId="urn:oasis:names:tc:xacml:2.0:function:string-equal">
           <AttributeValue DataType="http:www.w3.org/2001/XMLSchema#string">read</AttributeValue>
           <ActionAttributeDesignator AttributeId="urn:oasis:names:tc:xacml:2.0:action:action-id" DataType="http:www.
w3.org/2001/XMLSchema#string"/>
          </ActionMatch>
         </Action>
        </Actions>
   </Target>
   <Condition>
        <Apply FunctionId="urn:oasis:names:tc:xacml:2.0:function:time-in-range">
         <Apply FunctionId="urn:oasis:names:tc:xacml:2.0:function:time-one-and-only">
          <EnvironmentAttributeDesignator AttributeId="urn:oasis:names:tc:xacml:2.0:environment:current-time"
DataType="http:www.w3.org/2001/XMLSchema#time"/>
         </Apply>
         <AttributeValue DataType="http:www.w3.org/2001/XMLSchema#time">08:00:00</AttributeValue>
         <AttributeValue DataType="http:www.w3.org/2001/XMLSchema#time">18:00:00</AttributeValue>
        </Apply>
   </Condition>
  </Rule>
 </Policy>
 <PolicySetIdReference>PPS:GCP:role</PolicySetIdReference>
</PolicySet>
```

Figure 9. SAML Assertion and SOAP message

```
<?xml version="1.0" encoding="UTF-8"?>
<S12:Envelope
 xmlns:xsi="http://www.w3.org/2001/XMLSchema-instance"
 xmlns:xsd="http://www.w3.org/2001/XMLSchema">
 <S12:Header>
  <wsse:Security>
   <!--Assertion by the system (example.clinic.com) that Dr. Bob Barry uses -->
   <saml:Assertion ID="12135464" IssueInstant="2006-07-12T12:32:41.162Z" Issuer="example.clinic.com" xmlns:saml="urn:
oasis:names:tc:SAML:2.0:assertion">
        <!--It is stated that this assertion is not valid after 2006-07-12T12:37:41.162Z -->
        <saml:Conditions NotOnOrAfter="2006-07-12T12:37:41.162Z"/>
        <!--States subject name and subject confirmation of method-->
        <saml:Subject>
         <saml:NameID NameQualifier=»example.clinic.com»>
          Bob Barry
         </saml:NameID>
         <saml:SubjectConfirmation Method=»urn:oasis:names:tc:SAML:2.0:cm:holder-of-key»>
          <saml:SubjectConfirmationData xsi:type=»saml:KeyInfoConfirmationDataType»>
           <ds:KeyInfo>
                <ds:KeyValue>...</ds:KeyValue>
           </ds:KeyInfo>
          </saml:SubjectConfirmationData>
         </saml:SubjectConfirmation>
        </saml:Subject>
        <saml:AttributeStatement>
         <!--States the functional role about the patient-->
         <saml:Attribute AttributeName=»role» AttributeNamespace=»urn:example:roles»>
          <saml:AttributeValue>urn:example:roles:GeneralCareProvider</saml:AttributeValue>
         </saml:Attribute>
         <saml:Attribute AttributeName=»patientId» AttributeNamespace=»urn:example»>
          <saml:AttributeValue>123456</saml:AttributeValue>
         </saml:Attribute>
        </saml:AttributeStatement>
        <!--The example.clinic.com system signs the assertion with its own private key-->
        <ds:Signature xmlns:ds="http://www.w3.org/2000/09/xmldsig#">
         ...
          <ds:Reference URI=»#12135464» xmlns:ds=»http://www.w3.org/2000/09/xmldsig#»>
                ...
          </ds:Reference>
         ...
        </ds:Signature>
   </saml:Assertion>
  <!--Signature of the Dr. Bob Barry which is used to prove subject's identity (subject confirmation)-->
   <ds:Signature>
        <ds:SignedInfo>
         <ds:CanonicalizationMethod Algorithm=»http://www.w3.org/2001/10/xml-exc-c14n#»/>
         <ds:SignatureMethod Algorithm=»http://www.w3.org/2000/09/xmldsig#rsa-sha1»/>
         <ds:Reference URI=»#MsgBody»>
          <ds:DigestMethod Algorithm="http://www.w3.org/2000/09/xmldsig#sha1"/>
          <ds:DigestValue>...</ds:DigestValue>
         </ds:Reference>
        </ds:SignedInfo>
```

Figure 9. continued

```
            <ds:SignatureValue>...</ds:SignatureValue>
            <ds:KeyInfo>
             <wsse:SecurityTokenReference wsu:Id="STR1" wsse11:TokenType="http://docs.oasis-open.org/wss/oasis-wss-
samltoken-profile-1.1#SAMLV2.0">
              <wsse:KeyIdentifier wsu:Id="..." ValueType="http://docs.oasis-open.org/wss/oasis-wss-saml-tokenprofile-
1.1#SAMLID">12135464</wsse:KeyIdentifier>
             </wsse:SecurityTokenReference>
            </ds:KeyInfo>
    </ds:Signature>
   </wsse:Security>
  </S12:Header>
 <S12:Body>
   ...
   <!--Web Service Input-->
   <!--requestType: type of the information requested-->
   <RetrieveSummaryInfoHttpGetIn>
    <requestType>SUMMARY-DISCHARGE</requestType>
    <patientID>123456</patientID>
    <lowerDateTime>...</lowerDateTime>
    <upperDateTime>...</upperDateTime>
    <mostRecentResults>...</mostRecentResults>
   </RetrieveSummaryInfoHttpGetIn>
   ...
  </S12:Body>
 </S12:Envelope>
```

"IssueInstant" attribute gives the time when the assertion is constructed at the example.clinic.com site. "Issuer" attribute gives the owner of the assertion. Inside the assertion, we can state conditions regarding the assertion. In this example, <Conditions> element states that this assertion is not valid after some specific time in order to prevent message replay attacks. The <Subject> element specifies the subject of the assertion. In our example, the subject's name is stated to be Bob Barry. The <SubjectConfirmation> element gives the method and key info used to confirm the subject, which is discussed in the sixth section. In the <AttributeStatement> element example .clinic.com states that the functional role of the subject on the patient is the role of "GeneralCareProvider". The <ds:Signature> element inside the assertion is the signature of the example.clinic.com system on the Assertion.

The other <ds:Signature> element outside the assertion is the signature of Dr. Bob Barry (subject) to use for subject confirmation. The signature applies to message body and the <KeyIdentifier> element gives reference to ID of assertion, which includes the <KeyValue> inside the <SubjectConfirmation> element. This <KeyValue> is used to verify the signature.

The authentication implementation of the Web service should first verify the assertion signature (signature of example.clinic.com) in order to be sure about integrity of the assertion. In this example, we assume that Web service implementation trusts the example.clinic.com. Some mechanisms can be implemented which use trust lists. After verification of the signature related with the assertion, the system should confirm the subject's identity by the method defined through <SubjectConfirmation> element. In our example, holder-of-key method is used. Therefore, the <ds: Signature> element, which is used to sign the message body with subject's private key, should be verified with the <KeyValue> element given in the <SubjectCOnfirmationData> element in the assertion.

Figure 10. XACML request

```
<?xml version="1.0" encoding="UTF-8"?>
<XACMLAuthzDecisionQuery>
 <Request xmlns="urn:oasis:names:tc:xacml:2.0:context:schema:os"
  xmlns:xsi="http://www.w3.org/2001/XMLSchema-instance"
  xsi:schemaLocation="urn:oasis:names:tc:xacml:2.0:context:schema:os
  http://docs.oasis-open.org/xacml/access_control-xacml-2.0-context-schema-os.xsd">
  <Subject>
   <Attribute AttributeId="urn:oasis:names:tc:xacml:1.0:subject:subject-id" DataType="http://www.w3.org/2001/
XMLSchema#string" Issuer="example.clinic.com">
        <AttributeValue>Bob Barry</AttributeValue>
   </Attribute>
   <Attribute AttributeId="urn:example:attribute:role" DataType="anyURI" Issuer="example.clinic.com">
        <AttributeValue>GeneralCareProvider</AttributeValue>
   </Attribute>
  </Subject>
  <Resource>
   <ResourceContent>
        <!--The web service input can be inserted into the ResourceContent if necessary-->
        <rid:RetrieveSummaryInfoHttpGetIn>
         <rid:requestType>SUMMARY-DISCHARGE</rid:requestType>
         <rid:patientID>123456</rid:patientID>
         ...
        </rid:RetrieveSummaryInfoHttpGetIn>
   </ResourceContent>
   <Attribute AttributeId="urn:oasis:names:tc:xacml:1.0:resource:resource-id" DataType="http://www.w3.org/2001/
XMLSchema#anyURI">
        <AttributeValue>SUMMARY-DISCHARGE</AttributeValue>
   </Attribute>
   <Attribute AttributeId="urn:oasis:names:tc:xacml:2.0:resource:mailto" DateType="http://www.w3.org/2001/
XMLSchema#anyURI">
        <AttributeValue>john.doe@example.com</AttributeValue>
   </Attribute>
  </Resource>
  <Action>
   <Attribute AttributeId="urn:oasis:names:tc:xacml:1.0:action:action-id" DataType="http://www.w3.org/2001/
XMLSchema#string">
        <AttributeValue>read</AttributeValue>
   </Attribute>
  </Action><Environment/>
 </Request>
</XACMLAuthzDecisionQuery>
```

XACML Request

Until now, we have authenticated the user, obtained some SAML attributes related with subject, and we have the XACML policies. Now, we need to evaluate the policies according to the inputs. However, first of all, the XACML Request should be constructed by some mechanism.

In the processing environment of XACML, this part is called the Policy Enforcement Point (PEP) as previously. Figure 10 illustrates the XACML Request that the Policy Enforcement Point (PEP) sends to the Policy Decision Point (PDP) inside the SAML <XACMLAuthzDecisionQuery> element. As seen from the Request, the Policy Enforcement Point (PEP) maps the SAML attributes to XACML attributes for the <Subject> and <Resource> elements. The input of the Web service is inserted in the ResourceContent, which is not needed for this example. The "requestType" element in the Web service input is mapped to "resource-id" attribute of <Resource>. The Policy Enforcement Point (PEP) somehow use the patient-id and get the mail address of the patient to insert it into the "urn:oasis:names:tc:xacml:2.0:resource:mailto" attribute in this example.

XACML Response

Policy Decision Point (PDP) produces the result "Permit" because the subject has the role "GeneralCareProvider" and he wants to access SUMMARY-DISCHARGE, which is allowed for this role in the policies. However, there is an obligation that should be fullfilled in order to give "Permit" decision. Figure 11 illustrates

Figure 11. XACML response

```
<XACMLAuthzDecisionStatement>
  <Response xmlns="urn:oasis:names:tc:xacml:2.0:context:schema:os"
   xmlns:xsi="http://www.w3.org/2001/XMLSchema-instance"
   xsi:schemaLocation="urn:oasis:names:tc:xacml:2.0:context:schema:os
   http://docs.oasis-open.org/xacml/xacml-core-2.0-context-schema-os.xsd">
   <Result>
    <Decision>Permit</Decision>
    <Obligations>
         <Obligation ObligationId="urn:oasis:names:tc:xacml:2.0:obligation:email" FulfillOn="Permit">
          <AttributeAssignment AttributeId="urn:oasis:names:tc:xacml:2.0:attribute:mailto" DataType="http://www.
w3.org/2001/XMLSchema#string">
             <ResourceAttributeDesignator AttributeId="urn:oasis:names:tc:xacml:2.0:resource:mailto" DataType="http:www.
w3.org/2001/XMLSchema#string"/>
          </AttributeAssignment>
          <AttributeAssignment AttributeId="urn:oasis:names:tc:xacml:2.0:attribute:mailsubject" DataType="http://www.
w3.org/2001/XMLSchema#string">
             <SubjectAttributeDesignator AttributeId="urn:oasis:names:tc:xacml:2.0:subject:subject-id"/>
          </AttributeAssignment>
         </Obligation>
    </Obligations>
   </Result>
  </Response>
</XACMLAuthzDecisionStatement>
```

the XACML Response message wrapped into <XACMLAuthzDecisionStatement> element. The Policy Enforcement Point (PEP) handles the obligation by obtaining the "mailto" and "subject-id" attributes and sending the e-mail to patient address (mailto) which says that "Dr. Bob Barry had accessed his record."

REFERENCES

ASTM. (2006, September). ASTM E31.20 working draft 0.9k, privilege management infrastructure.

IBM. (2003). Enterprise privacy authorization language (EPAL). Retrieved June 4, 2007, from http://www.zurich.ibm.com/security/enterprise-privacy/epal/Specification/index.html

IBM, BEA Systems, Microsoft, Layer 7 Technologies, Oblix, VeriSign, Actional, Computer Associates, OpenNetwork Technologies, Ping Identity, Reactivity, RSA Security. (2005). Web services trust language (WS-Trust). Retrieved June 4, 2007, from ftp://www6.software.ibm.com/software/developer/library/ws-trust.pdf

IBM, Microsoft, RSA Security, VeriSign. (2005). Web services security policy language

(WS-SecurityPolicy). Retrieved June 4, 2007, from ftp://www6.software.ibm.com/software/developer/library/ws-secpol.pdf

IHE. (2005). IHE IT infrastructure technical framework (vol. 1), Integration profiles. Retrieved June 4, 2007, from http://www.ihe.net/Technical_Framework/upload/ihe_iti_tf_2.0_vol1_FT_2005-08-15.pdf

IHE. (2005). IHE IT infrastructure technical framework (vol. 2), Transactions. Retrieved June 4, 2007, from http://www.ihe.net/Technical_Framework/upload/ihe_iti_tf_2.0_vol2_FT_2005-08-15.pdf

IHE. (2006). Integrated health care enterprise. Retrieved June 4, 2007, from http://www.ihe.net/

Imperial Collage. (2000). Ponder: A language for specifying security and management policies for distributed systems. Retrieved June 4, 2007, from http://www-dse.doc.ic.ac.uk/Research/policies/ponder/PonderSpec.pdf

Keynote. (1999). The keynote trust-management system, Version 2, Matt Blaze, Joan Feigenbaum, John Ioannidis, and Angelos D. Keromytis. Request for comments (RFC) 2704, http://www1.cs.columbia.edu/~angelos/Papers/rfc2704.txt

OASIS. (2003). XACML profile for Web services. Retrieved June 4, 2007, from http://www.oasis-open.org/committees/download.php/3661/draft-xacml-wspl-04.pdf

OASIS. (2004). WS-security 1.1 core specification. Retrieved June 4, 2007, from http://www.oasis-open.org/committees/download.php/16790/wss-v1.1-spec-os-SOAPMessageSecurity.pdf

OASIS. (2005). eXtensible access control markup language (XACML) Version 2.0. Retrieved June 4, 2007, from http://docs.oasis-open.org/xacml/2.0/access_control-xacml-2.0-core-spec-os.pdf

OASIS. (2005). Assertions and protocols for the OASIS security assertion markup language (SAML) V2.0. Retrieved June 4, 2007, from http://docs.oasis-open.org/xacml/2.0/access_control-xacml-2.0-saml-profile-spec-os.pdf

OASIS. (2005). Core and hierarchical role based access control (RBAC) profile of XACML v2.0. Retrieved June 4, 2007, from http://docs.oasis-open.org/xacml/2.0/access_control-xacml-2.0-rbac-profile1-spec-os.pdf

OASIS. (2005). SAML 2.0 profile of XACML v2.0. Retrieved June 4, 2007, from http://docs.oasis-open.org/xacml/2.0/access_control-xacml-2.0-saml-profile-spec-os.pdf

OASIS. (2005). Web service security SAML token profile 1.1. Retrieved June 4, 2007, from http://www.oasis-open.org/specs/index.php#wssprofilesv1.0

SAPHIRE. (2006). Intelligent health care monitoring based on semantic interoperability platform. Retrieved June 4, 2007, from http://www.srdc.metu.edu.tr/Web page/projects/saphire/

W3C. (2006). Web service policy 1.2-framework (WS-Policy). Retrieved June 4, 2007, from http://www.w3.org/Submission/WS-Policy/

ENDNOTE

* This work is supported by the European Commission, DG Information Society and Media, eHealth Unit (*http://ec.europa.eu/information_society/activities/health/index_en.htm*) through the IST 027074 SAPHIRE Project (*http://www.srdc.metu.edu.tr/Web page/projects/saphire/*) and in part by the Scientific and Technical Research Council of Turkey (TUBITAK) through the EEEAG-105E133 Project.

APPENDIX A: WSDL OF RID WEB SERVICE

```
<?xml version="1.0" encoding="utf8"?>
<definitions xmlns:http="http://schemas.xmlsoap.org/wsdl/http/"
        xmlns:s="http://www.w3.org/2001/XMLSchema"
        xmlns:s0="http://rsna.org/ihe/IHERetrieveForDisplay"
        xmlns:tm="http://microsoft.com/wsdl/mime/textMatching/"
        xmlns:mime="http://schemas.xmlsoap.org/wsdl/mime/"
        targetNamespace="http://rsna.org/ihe/IHERetrieveForDisplay"
        xmlns="http://schemas.xmlsoap.org/wsdl/">
        <types>
                <s:schema elementFormDefault="qualified"
                        targetNamespace="http://rsna.org/ihe/IHERetrieveForDisplay">
                        <s:simpleType name="summaryRequestType">
                                <s:restriction base="s:string">
                                        <s:enumeration value="SUMMARY" />
                                        <s:enumeration value="SUMMARY-RADIOLOGY" />
                                        <s:enumeration value="SUMMARY-CARDIOLOGY" />
                                        <s:enumeration value="SUMMARY-LABORATORY" />
                                        <s:enumeration value="SUMMARY-SURGERY" />
                                        <s:enumeration value="SUMMARY-EMERGENCY" />
                                        <s:enumeration value="SUMMARY-DISCHARGE" />
                                        <s:enumeration value="SUMMARY-ICU" />
                                </s:restriction>
                        </s:simpleType>
                        <s:simpleType name="ReturnedResultCount" type="s:positiveInteger" />
                        <s:simpleType name="SearchString" type="s:string" />
                </s:schema>
        </types>
        <message name="RetrieveSummaryInfoHttpGetIn">
                <part name="requestType" type="summaryRequestType" />
                <part name="patientID" type="SearchString" />
                <part name="lowerDateTime" type="s:dateTime" />
                <part name="upperDateTime" type="s:dateTime" />
                <part name="mostRecentResults" type="ReturnedResultCount" />
        </message>
        <message name="RetrieveSummaryInfoHttpGetOut">
                <part name="Body" element="s0:string" />
        </message>

        <portType name="IHERetrieveForDisplayHttpGet">
                <operation name="RetrieveSummaryInfo">
                        <input message="s0:RetrieveSummaryInfoHttpGetIn" />
                        <output message="s0:RetrieveSummaryInfoHttpGetOut" />
                </operation>
        </portType>
```

```
<binding name="IHERetrieveForDisplayHttpGet" type="s0:IHERetrieveForDisplayHttpGet">
                <http:binding verb="GET" />
                <operation name="RetrieveSummaryInfo">
                        <http:operation location="/IHERetrieveSummaryInfo" />
                        <input>
                                <http:urlEncoded />
                        </input>
                        <output>
                                <mime:content type="text/html" />
                        </output>
                </operation>
        </binding>
        <service name="IHERetrieveForDisplay">
                <port name="IHERetrieveForDisplayHttpGet" binding="s0:IHERetrieveForDisplayHttpGet">
                        <http:address location="http://localhost/" />
                </port>
        </service>
</definitions>
```

Chapter IX
Protecting ASP.NET Web Services

Konstantin Beznosov
University of British Columbia, Canada

ABSTRACT

This chapter reports on our experience designing and implementing an architecture for protecting enterprise-grade Web service applications hosted by ASP.NET. Security mechanisms of Microsoft ASP.NET container—a popular hosting environment for Web services—having limited scalability, flexibility, and extensibility. They are therefore inadequate for hosting enterprise-scale applications that need to be protected according to diverse or complex application-specific security policies. To overcome the limitations of ASP.NET security, we developed a flexible and extensible protection architecture. Deployed in a real-world security solution at a financial organization, the architecture enables integration of ASP.NET into the organizational security infrastructure with reduced effort on the part of Web Service developers. Throughout this report, we discuss our design decisions, suggest best practices for constructing flexible and extensible authentication and authorization logic for Web Services, and share lessons learned.

INTRODUCTION

Although Web Services security standards and technologies are close to being ready for wide implementation, there is little feedback in the literature from those who are starting to use these building blocks to make Web Service applications fully secured and trusted. This chapter provides such feedback by reporting on our experience of designing an architecture for protecting enterprise-grade distributed applications hosted by the popular Web Services container, ASP.NET. The chapter also contributes the best practices on constructing flexible and extensible authentication and authorization logic for Web Services by employing Resource Access Decision (RAD)

(Beznosov, Deng, Blakley, Burt, & Barkley,1999; Beznosov, Espinal, & Deng, 2000; Object Management Group [OMG], 2001), and Attribute Function (AF) (Beznosov, 2002a) architectural styles. We implemented our architecture in just over 4 KLOCs of C#.

ARCHITECTURE OVERVIEW

ASP.NET container is a popular hosting environment for Web Services built and run on Microsoft Windows and .NET platforms. However, the ASP.NET security architecture (Microsoft, 2001, 2002), as provided "out-of-the-box," lacks sufficient flexibility and extensibility to be adequate for enterprise applications (Beznosov, 2002b). As we describe in Hartman, Flinn, Beznosov, and Kawamoto (2003), ASP.NET supports limited authentication and group/user-based authorization, both being bound to Microsoft proprietary technologies (Windows domains and Passport). If a Web Service application needs to be protected via a third-party authentication or authorization services available in the enterprise security infrastructure, the real-world developers have two options. The first is to develop home-grown container security extensions, which are hard for average application developers to get right. The second is to program the security logic into the Web Service business logic, making the resulting application expensive to maintain and modify. In both cases, the development of security-specific components by average application developers is commonly believed to result in high vulnerability rates, due to security-related bugs that are hard to avoid and catch.

Due to its flexibility and extensibility, our protection architecture enables integration of ASP.NET into the organizational security infrastructure with reduced effort on the part of Web Service developers. The architecture is flexible because it allows configuring machine-wide authentication and authorization functions, and overriding them for a subtree of the Web Services (up to an individual application) in the directory-based ASP.NET hierarchy. Its extensibility is revealed through the support of a wide variety of authentication and authorization (A&A) logic, provided that the logic can be translated into a .NET class or accessed (possibly via a proxy) through a predefined .NET API. Furthermore, one can reuse instances of such logic by combining authorization decisions from them according to predefined or custom rules.

We achieved these by:

1. separating custom SOAP (World Wide Web Consortium [W3C], 2002a, 2002b, 2002c, 2002d) extension modules (which act as ASP.NET-specific A&A enforcement logic) from the A&A decision logic;
2. following the RAD architecture style (Beznosov et al., 1999; Beznosov et al., 2000; OMG, 2001), which makes customization of access control decision logic easier and avoids the need for a generic policy evaluation engine;
3. taking advantage of the extensibility, inheritance, and caching features of ASP.NET web.config configuration mechanism; and
4. separating the logic of retrieving attributes of Web Service implementations from the authorization and business logic by following the AF approach (Beznosov, 2002a).

In the next section, we discuss the requirements that drove the design, and present the architecture. To illustrate the architecture's capabilities, we also present two examples of policies and configurations for supporting these policies. Intertwined with the requirements and the architecture descriptions in the preceding two sections, our reflections on designing the architecture, and the lessons we learned, are mentioned in the discussion and summarized at the end of the chapter.

REQUIREMENTS

The design of the architecture was driven by its requirements and the underlying technology, ASP. NET. The functional objectives of the architecture were to allow flexible authentication and authorization for ASP.NET Web Service applications. It also needed to support the following types of data (i.e., security tokens) "out-of-the-box" for client and message authentication:

- user name and password found in the HTTP message header, a.k.a., HTTP Basic Authentication (HTTP-BA);
- ASP.NET Session state object with a preconfigured name; and
- "stringified" SAML-like (Hallam-Baker, Moses, Morgan, Adams, Krouse, Orchard et al., 2001) or other credentials token found in any of the following: the custom field of the HTTP header, or an HTTP cookie with a preconfigured name, or the header block of the SOAP message carrying the request to the ASP.NET Web Service, similar to WS-Security (Atkinson, Della-Libera, Hada, Hondo, Hallam-Baker, Klein et al., 2002).

One of the lessons we learned from the requirements analysis exercise was that end users do not care about compliance with SAML, Liberty Alliance, or WS-Security specifications as long as the design is in the spirit of these standards and therefore enables eventual compliance at some point in the future. The likely reason for this attitude was the lack of plans for mixing heterogeneous (i.e., produced by different development teams) Web Services. That is, no cross-enterprise Web Service deployments were required.

The other conclusion we drew from the work on the architecture concerned the difficulty of determining a practical set of compliance criteria. Taking into account the flexibility of the information architectures for both SAML and WS-Security specifications, it was hard to define what a compliant implementation is expected to do and not do. Furthermore, without prior agreement between application owners on the specific SAML and WS-Security profiles, two compliant applications would not necessarily interoperate in a useful manner.

Flexible and meaningful interpretation of multiple tokens was a difficult issue to address. A Web Service might receive a message containing more than one security token from the above list, for example, a SAML-like token in the SOAP header, a token in an HTTP cookie, or an HTTP-BA token. Therefore, we also needed to provide a means for selecting which tokens should be used for message authentication, and which principal each token should represent.

We found SAML and WS-Security to be insufficiently expressive for the cases when more than one token is received; how, for example, to interpret three security tokens in a single wsse: Security header block? If all the tokens are valid, which one should be used for authorization? If one token is not authorized, should others be tried or not? Should two out of three be tried? One might argue that implementing monotonic policies, where "extra" invalid or unauthorized tokens do not decrease the privileges of the message sender, should suffice. This approach, however, would mean that a Web Service becomes vulnerable to a new type of denial of service (DoS) attack: SOAP messages containing a large number of security tokens that are expensive to (in)validate.

Another issue that we left unresolved is the flexible support for *composite principals*. How should the WSS-Security or SAML information models be used to express the "speaks for" relation (Abadi, Burrows, Lampson, & Plotkin, 1993; Lampson, Abadi, Burrows, & Wobber, 1991)? Neither specification seems to provide a standard means for supporting this relation. The problem exacerbates when transport-layer security tokens (e.g., X.509 certificates from the underlying SSL/TLS session, HTTP-BA) and session or request attributes (e.g., IP addresses) are required to represent principals. How should a message sender be permitted to specify (in an interoperable form) that the SAML token *speaks for* the HTTP-BA token, which speaks for the SSL client certificate? We had to resort to a configuration-driven selection of the tokens to be validated and separate them into two groups: "user" and "sender" credentials. Our crude model was that "users" are human beings that use programs, acting as "senders," to send their requests in the form of SOAP messages. We designed the authorization logic to make decisions using either "user's" or "sender's" credentials, or both, based on configuration. However, deeper chains of invocation (e.g., an originator and an intermediary with communication channels between them as principals) could not be supported. We can identify two prime obstacles: lack of support in WS-Security and SAML information architectures, and a possible exponential increase in the complexity of security policies if the support for composite principles is implemented in a naïve way.

In regard to authorization, the architecture was required to support:

- third-party enterprise-wide A&A products, such as Policy Director (Karjoth, 2003), SiteMinder (Netegrity, 2000), and GetAccess (Encommerce, 1999), and so forth;
- selective availability of some Web Service methods for public (i.e., anonymous) access; and
- simple variants of authorization logic.

The architecture also needed to be extensible enough to accommodate new types of A&A logic that application developers would like to support in the future, for example, access restriction based on the (range of) IP addresses of the Web Service clients or the day and time of access. Because it was impossible to envision all probable instances of A&A policies, the extension mechanisms had to be sufficiently generic. We also anticipated a need for composing new authorization policies out of existing ones (where developers could reuse much of the existing A&A logic), for example, a subset of publicly accessible methods with the remainder controlled by the enterprise-wide authorization. Due to space constraints and our focus on A&A, we omit the discussion of other requirements, such as audit.

THE ARCHITECTURE

To integrate with ASP.NET run-time, the architecture takes advantage of the ASP.NET generic interception mechanism, SOAPExtension (Microsoft, 2002), intended for additional processing of SOAP messages. As shown in Figure 1, our custom version of SOAPExtension (labeled "interceptor") performs initial extraction, formatting, and other preparation of HTTP and SOAP messages contained therein, passing the data to the decision A&A logic and enforcing authorization decisions.

It was surprising to discover that not all the requests to a Web Service application "go" through the ASP.NET SOAPExtension interception point. Because an ASP.NET Web Service can be accessed with the HTTP-GET mechanism, which generates "SOAP-less" requests, we had to handle such requests using another interception point, HTTP Module, in ASP.NET container, which allows preprocessing of all HTTP traffic regardless of its payload.

Because the purpose of the architecture is A&A, SOAP messages are processed on their way in and only after ASP.NET run-time has successfully parsed all SOAP-specific XML and HTTP formatting. If the protection of data in transit were a requirement, then additional processing of the SOAP messages on their way out would be necessary. Using the terminology of

Figure 1. General organization of the architecture into an interceptor, which acts as a PEP, and A&A logic, which performs credentials authentication, permission construction, and authorization

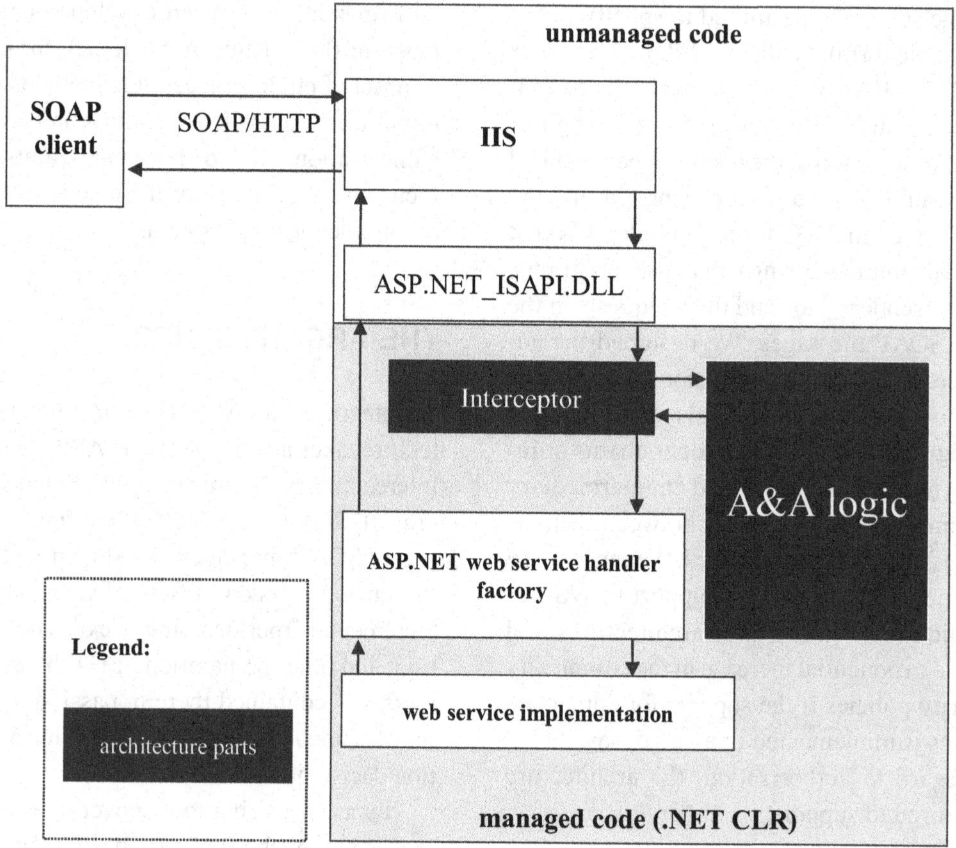

XACML (XACML Technical Committee, 2003), our interceptor acts as a policy enforcement point (PEP). The policy decision point (PDP) comprises different instances of several other elements of the architecture, described in the following sections. The protocol between our PEP and PDP, however, does not follow the XACML specification, as both points are parts of the same security subsystem, and thus no interoperability with other PDPs is necessary.

AUTHENTICATION

Authentication is commonly divided into two phases: retrieving authentication data and validating it. Following this same division, our *CredentialsRetriever* objects specialize in retrieving authentication data. Each retriever implementation is responsible for extracting particular data types (e.g., user name and password encoded as HTTP-BA, SAML-like credentials token found in the header block of the SOAP message, etc.) from appropriate locations. To achieve the required extensibility of the architecture, retrieved authentication data and retrievers themselves are represented in a uniform fashion as implementations of *Credential* and *CredentialsRetriever* interfaces, accordingly. This representation allows adding new modules of retrieving logic to the architecture by application developers, owners, or third-party vendors. For instance, the use of new types of authentication data, such as a client's public key certificate in requests over HTTPS, could be accommodated by developers through the creation of a new implementation of *CredentialsRetriever* that retrieves the corresponding attributes of the HTTPS connection and packages them into a new instance of *Credential.* Before retrieved credentials can be used in authorization decisions, they need to be validated.

There are several reasons why credentials validation is separated from the retrieval phase and delayed until authorization. First, some credentials could be computationally expensive to validate. For instance, the validation of credentials signed by a private key requires public key operations, as well as potentially unbound delays, due to checking certificates against revocation lists. Second, it is only during the authorization step that the credentials to be used for access control decisions are determined. Third, some useful policies might call for the evaluation of the same credential (e.g., user name and password) with more than one authentication authority. The fourth reason stems from the frequent collocation of authentication and authorization servers in enterprise security infrastructures based on such commercial products as SiteMinder (Netegrity, 2000). Lumping authentication and authorization steps in one batch and sending it to a remote security server allows substantial reduction of the communication overhead in such cases.

AUTHORIZATION

The structure of the authorization-related elements follows RAD and AF architectural styles, described briefly in Appendices A and B, respectively. An authorization decision is reached through the following three-step process.

Initial decisions are made by zero or more predefined or custom authorization modules, each referred to as *PolicyEvaluator* (PE). The simplest PE is one that always returns the same decision, for example, "deny," or "permit," depending on its static configuration. Clearly, it ignores any credentials or other attributes of the request or target in question, the environment, and the history of previous requests. Despite these limitations, the PE turned out to be very handy for testing, debugging, and deploying Web Service applications and the architecture itself. More interesting PEs, supplied with the architecture implementation, grant access based on the IP address of the request sender, the name of the Web Service target and its methods, and decisions provided by an enterprise authorization server. The strength of RAD architectural style is in the support of fairly sophisticated authorization policies (see Barkley, Beznosov, & Uppal, 1999, for an example) without the need for complex authorization engines. The support is achieved by combining various run-time decisions from several simple PEs into one at the second step, performed by a *DecisionCombinator* (DC).

Similar to PEs, common variations of combination logic are provided in prebuilt DCs with the ability for developers to "plug" custom implementations. Inspired by XACML, we implemented several basic types of DC in our architecture:

- *All Permits Required*—permits access only if every single PE granted access. As a PE could return not only "deny" or "permit," but also "indeterminate" or "not applicable"

Figure 2. Configuration after adding the PE, which restricts access based on the sender's IP address

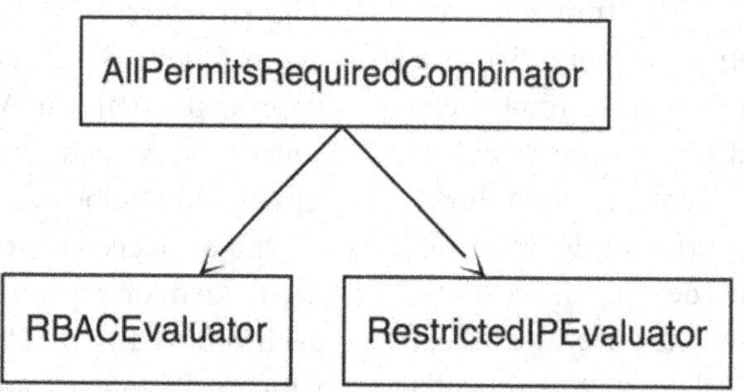

decisions, the semantics of this DC is different from the following DC.

- *Deny Overrides*—permits access only if at least one PE permitted access and no PE denied.
- *Permit Overrides*—permits access as soon as any PE decided so, and otherwise denies.

To appreciate the power of the DC&PEs approach, consider the composition of an "All Permits Required" DC with a role-based access control (RBAC) (Sandhu, Coyne, Feinstein, & Youman, 1996) PE. Both implement authorization based on user roles and their hierarchies. If the application owner decides to further restrict access to a particular range of IP addresses, they can do so by adding a PE that authorizes IP addresses, instead of modifying the fairly complex logic of the RBAC PE. The result is shown in Figure 2. Support for policies in which PEs might have different priorities is enabled through the use of PE names, so that custom DC logic can discriminate them.

The first two DC types in the above list are required because of the potential ambiguity of the decisions returned by PEs. Because of communication and other failures, a PE might not complete evaluation. Instead of supporting only *closed world* authorization policies, which mandate that any access should be denied unless explicitly permitted, the decision was to let PEs report their inability to complete evaluation to the respective DC. Application owners can therefore tune the handling of undesirable situations by implementing custom DCs, instead of reimplementing possibly complex PEs. Similarly, we let PEs report back to the DC those situations where they have no authorization policies applicable to the request in question.

While another key property of RAD architecture, support for authorizations based on request-specific attributes of the subject, requires the presence of dynamic attribute service (DAS), we have not implemented this component. Request-specific subject attributes are necessary for supporting relationship-based access control policies (Barkley et al., 1999) (Rel-BAC) in which access control decisions depend on the relationship between the subject and the object to be accessed, for example, "attending physician" in the case of access to a patient record, or "account owner" for access to a bank account. We found that the weak support for dynamic Web Service instantiation in ASP.NET makes it almost impossible for developers to use DAS for implementing such policies. Request-specific attributes of subjects can be determined effectively by DAS implementations only if the target represents a fine-grained object in a system, for example, patient medical record or

Figure 3. Elements of the permission generated by the default permission factory

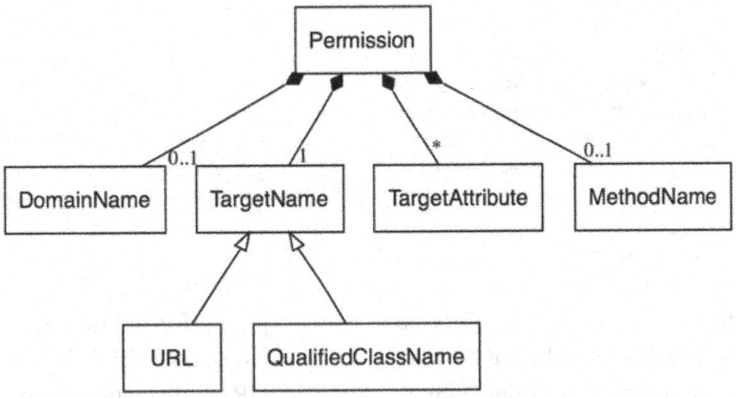

Permission
0..1 DomainName
1 TargetName
* TargetAttribute
0..1 MethodName
URL
QualifiedClassName

bank account. For an application to be scalable in the presence of fine-grained objects, the underlying technology has to support efficient life-cycle management of objects, that is, dynamic object creation, deletion, activation, and deactivation. Some middleware architectures and technologies (e.g., CORBA, COM+, EJB) do provide mechanisms for efficient object life-cycle management. Although in theory the Web Services architecture defined by SOAP does not preclude efficient life-cycle management of Web Service instances, ASP.NET (and possibly other implementations) lacks it. What, then, are application developers left with if their ASP.NET (and possibly other) applications have to enforce Rel-BAC? Unfortunately, the only currently available option we could find is to mix application and authorization logic "inside" of Web Service applications.

The authorization process continues to its third stage in order to achieve *fail-safe defaults*, when a DC experiences a failure and, due to a design or implementation error, does not come to a binary decision, During this stage, the interceptor, which originally delegated the process to the corresponding DC, renders any decision (except "permit") received from the DC to "deny" and thus reaches the authorization verdict. If access has been denied, the corresponding exception with the configurable explanation message is thrown to the ASP.NET run time, which translates it into an appropriate SOAP exception message.

Besides credentials, obtained from the SOAP message, the corresponding HTTP request, or the underlying communication channel, PEs are supplied with other information related to the request: name and attributes of the Web Service, its policy domain, and the method to be invoked. All of this information is constructed into a *permission*. Thus, the authorization process results in a decision whether a permission should be granted to a (potentially compound) subject, given the subject's credentials. If so, then the interceptor passes control to ASP.NET, which activates the corresponding Web Service implementation and passes to it the request contained in the SOAP message. It is the construction of the permission that furthers the flexibility and extensibility of the architecture.

PERMISSION CONSTRUCTION

To support the flexibility and extensibility of the architecture, we designed permission construction from four distinct elements, as shown in Figure 3 and detailed below.

Figure 4. The association among Web Services, their implementations, directories, and configuration files

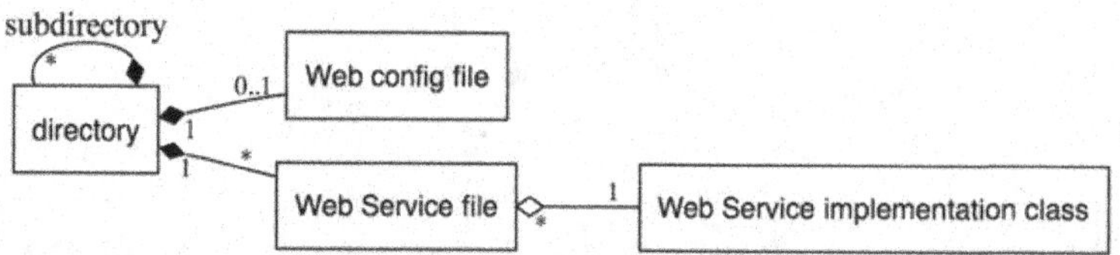

1. *Name*—the name of the target Web Service can be represented by either the URL or the .NET class name of the service implementation. The URL represents the Web server's interpretation of the target URL from the corresponding HTTP request. It may have been modified from that which the Web Service client sent to reflect load-balancing, failover, or other request routing actions. Clearly, URL-based naming, however appropriate, it may be for uniquely identifying Web Service endpoints, makes security administration in the face of environmental changes labor-intensive. For example, each time the host name or the directory of the Web Service application changes, the URL very likely changes too. This could also be a source of vulnerabilities in situations where several distinct URLs could refer to the same instance of a Web Service but not all have been "secured."

   The use of URLs for naming Web Services is even less attractive in ASP.NET, because the same .NET class can be reused for creating separate instances of Web Services. In the ASP.NET environment, a single file hosts each target Web Service, as illustrated in Figure 4. Multiple different virtual Web addresses can be used to invoke the methods of the same underlying implementation class. The presence of these synonyms can pose a challenge to the security administrator's primary goal, maintaining proper security policy for the deployed Web Services. By using the .NET class name instead of the URL, all instances of a Web Service application can share the same authorization policy rules. The use of class names reduces maintenance cost and allows the same application logic to be protected no matter under at how many URLs it is deployed on a machine. When used together with the domain capability, several instances of the same Web Service can be treated the same, or distinctly, as appropriate for the application structure.
2. *Domain*—the use of a domain classifier is borrowed from CORBA Security (Blakley, 1999; OMG, 2001a) architecture, whose policy domains support different security requirements for implementations of the same interfaces. In our architecture, optional domains allow discrimination between the same implementations of a Web Service that have different access control requirements. Another intended purpose of domains is to allow a logical grouping of several Web Services, perhaps so that they can share an authorization server or its policy database. Because the means of determining the domain of a Web Service is highly specific to the application and its authorization policies, our architecture provides a simple version of a domain retriever and a means for replacing it with custom implementations.

Table 1. Examples of permissions

Permission Example	Explanation
http://foobank.com/bar.asmx	Only the URL is used
com.foobank.ws.Sbar/m1	Class and method names
D1/com.foobank.ws.Sbar /m1	Same but in domain "D1"
com.foobank.ws.Sbar/owner=smith	Class name and attribute
D1/com.foobank.ws.Sbar/owner=smith/m1	Domain, class, attribute, method

3. *Target attributes*—further differentiation among Web Service instances is achieved through an optional list of one or more name-value pairs holding target attributes. For example, a Web Service representing a bank account manager could have attributes that identify the branch to which all the managed accounts belong, provided the partitioning of the accounts among such managers is based on the branches. As Beznosov (2002a) argued, the use of target attributes reduces the need for mixing authorization and other security logic with business logic. These application-specific attributes and the mechanism for obtaining them at run time are directly based on our prior work on Attribute Function (Beznosov, 2002a; OMG, 2001c), an overview of which is provided in Appendix B. The extensible retrieval mechanism is designed as a replaceable *TargetAttributeRetriever* interface, with a simple implementation provided by the architecture's implementation.
4. *Method*—because ASP.NET, at the time of our work on the architecture, supported only RPC semantics for interactions with hosted Web Service implementations, acceptable SOAP messages had to specify the method of the .NET implementation class responsible for processing the request. As with other RPC-based middleware technologies, it was important to support authorization decisions based on method name. We made inclusion of the method name in the constructed permission optional to accommodate types of applications that did not require authorization policy granularity at the method level.

Table 1 shows examples of permissions.

The construction of permissions is done by a default permission factory, which can be replaced by a custom implementation, possibly producing permissions of a different format and content. Which permission factory, DC&PEs, credential retrievers, and other replaceable parts of the architecture are used for serving requests for each Web Service instance is determined by the configuration.

REPLACEABLE PARTS

As stated previously, the flexibility and extensibility of the architecture is achieved by designing most of its elements to be replaceable. Any of the black boxes in Figure 5 can be replaced by a version that comes with the implementation or by a version produced by Web Service developers or owners. Custom versions of the grey boxes are subject to control by those modules that create them. Other architectures, for example, CORBA Security (Blakley, 1999; OMG, 2001a), also make some of their parts replaceable. The novelty of our approach is the level of granularity of the replaceable parts. In CORBA Security, for instance, authorization logic (encapsulated in the *AccessDecision* interface) has to be replaced as a whole, whereas in our architecture, one can selectively replace specific PEs or a DC. Even more, each Web Service in the same container can be protected by a different set of replaceable elements, which is not the case with CORBA Security, COM+, or EJB implementations. Flexible and manageable configuration turned out to be critical in making fine-grained, yet scalable, replaceability work.

CONFIGURATION

Flexible and scalable configuration is critical in order for our architecture to be extensible and, at the same time, carry low administration or run-time overhead. Because an ASP.NET container might host many Web Services, each with its own security requirements, deployment and maintenance life cycles, the run-time changes to the configuration should not result in restart of the container or its lasting performance degradation. We determined that ASP.NET configuration architecture, with settings defined in web.config files, had most of the features we were looking for.

The use of simplified XML in web.config files enables a flexible hierarchy of configuration elements, as shown in Figure 6. By leveraging web.config's ability to delegate handling of new configuration sections to custom handling logic, we developed a simple hierarchical language for defining and configuring various elements of the A&A decision logic, as well as the protection policies they comprise.

A protection policy can simply be considered as a collection of specific credential retrievers, PEs, a DC, attribute and domain retrievers, and a permission factory, which are referenced by name in the policy, but are defined in other sections of the configuration. Because all these ele-

Figure 5. Key elements of the architecture, with replaceable elements shown in black, modifiable through their creators, shaded in grey

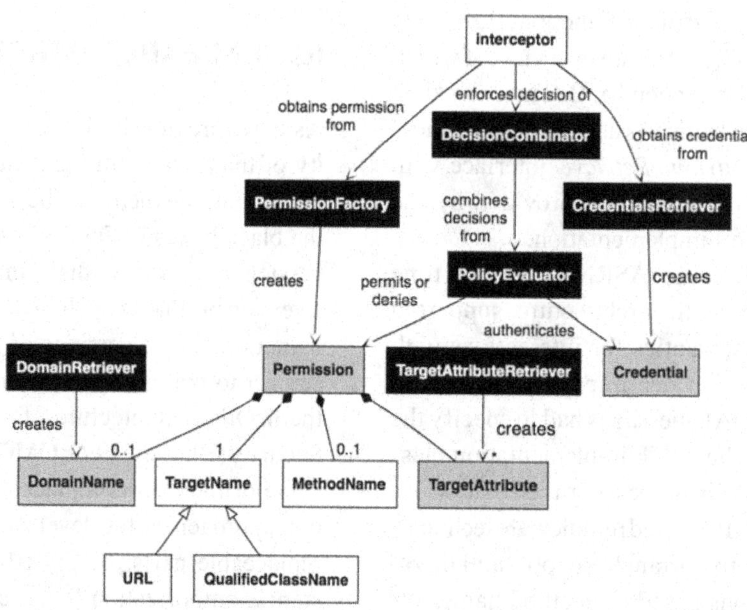

Figure 6. Simplified model of the configuration elements with default cardinality "0..."*

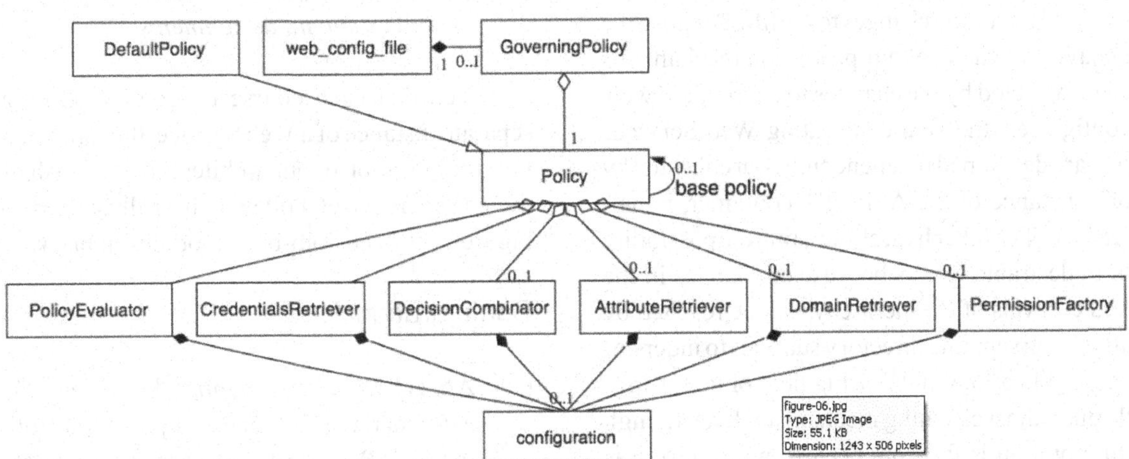

ments are defined independently of the policies and have unique names, they can be referenced by more than one protection policy. A singleton in the scope of a web.config instance, *Governing Policy* (GP), specifies which particular policy is used for controlling access to a Web Service in question. Thus, one can prepare and test a protection policy, and perform a quick switch to the new policy by just changing the *name* attribute of the GP, a reference to a specific protection policy. Multiple policies can be prepackaged and used for altering the behavior of the protection mechanisms in response, for example, to threat level changes.

Illustrated in Figure 4, the hierarchal nature of web.config parsing semantics enables good scalability without losing the fine level of granularity in the control over subsets of (or individual) Web Services. The GP defined in the web.config of the ASP.NET root determines the protection of all those Web Services with no overriding web.config file between the service file and the root directory. Thus, developers can deploy their Web Services, which could be administered by changes to the root web.config file. This approach, though, does not address the question of scalable administration for multiple ASP.NET containers, which is an issue for COM+ and standard EJB containers as well. Similar to product-specific solutions on the EJB market, one could remedy the problem by synchronizing web.config files or their specific sections across multiple containers.

Configuration flexibility is achieved through two design decisions. First, any web.config file down in the ASP.NET directory hierarchy can override GP, or define any new element, including new policies, as long as the name of this element has not been used in an ascendent web.config. By "ascendent web.config" we mean a web.config file located down in the directory hierarchy. Unfortunately, the freedom of overriding GP comes with the loss of control over GPs used for protecting the Web Services located down in the directory hierarchy. However, this loss can be compensated for by the OS file system controls, if necessary. Second, to reduce the amount of effort required for creating policy variations, we also implemented a single inheritance mechanism for protection policy definitions. This way, a policy could reuse most of the other policy's definitions and override just a few elements, such as a *DomainRetriever*, or a specific PE.

The performance overhead due to storing all configuration information in web.config seems to be relatively small, because ASP.NET caches web.config files and invalidates the cache when the OS detects any changes to the file. Because the behavior or cache of our protection mechanisms is not affected by the changes to descendent web. config files, the goal of isolating Web Services that are developed independently, but cohosted by one instance of the ASP.NET container, is half reached. The other half, eliminating the possibility of undesirable effects because of changes in the higher levels of the hierarchy, can be reached by allocating separate directory subtrees to independent applications and sharing little or no settings through the web.config mechanism. Even though this solution is far from perfect, we believe it is good enough for the majority of environments.

EXAMPLES

To demonstrate the ability of our architecture to be customized through different compositions of black-box implementations, we provide examples of implementing two different policies.

Example 1: University Course Web Service

Consider a simplified hypothetical application that enables online access to university courses as Web Services. Let us assume that the following criteria are relevant to the example fragment of the application security policy to be enforced:

Policy 1:

1. All users should authenticate using HTTP-BA.
2. **Anybody** can look up course descriptions.
3. **Registration clerks** can *list students* registered for the course and *(un)register* them.
4. The **course instructor** can *list registered students* as well as *manage course assignments* and *course material.*
5. **Students registered** for the course can *download assignments* and *course material*, as well as *submit assignments.*

Given that each course is represented by a separate instance of a Web Service, the following is a configuration of our architecture that enables the enforcement of Policy 1. It is illustrated in Figure 7, with custom-built modules in black.

Configuration 1:

- An HTTP-BA *CredentialsRetriever* CR_1 extracts the user name and password from the HTTP request that carried the corresponding SOAP request.
- A custom *TargetAttributeRetriever* provides the course number in the form of an attribute, for example, CourseId=EECE412.
- The default *PermissionFactory* is configured to compose permissions with the qualified class name of the .NET class, as a *TargetName*, the corresponding method name, and the attributes provided by the custom retriever. Here is an example: 'ca.ubc.CourseManagment.SimpleCourse/CourseId=EECE412/GetDescription'. No domain name is used in this configuration.
- A prebuilt *PolicyEvaluator* PE_1 grants permissions to any request on publicly accessible methods. In the case of Policy 1, there is one public method, GetCourseDescription.
- A custom *PolicyEvaluator* PE_2 is programmed and configured to make authorization decisions according to the rules informally described as follows:
    1. Permit users in role "registration clerk" to access methods "ListStudents," "RegisterStudent," and "Unregister-Student."
    2. Permit users in role "instructor" whose attribute "CourseTaught" contains the

Figure 7. Configuration 1. Custom-built components have a black background

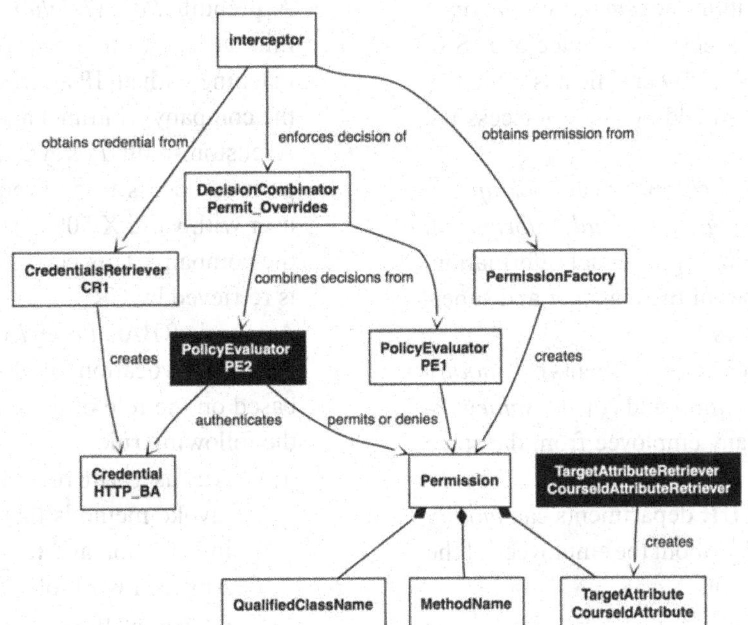

course listed in Permission.TargetAttributes.CourseId to list registered students, and manage course assignments and material.

3. Permit users in role "student" whose attribute "RegisteredCourses" contains the course listed in Permission.TargetAttributes.CourseId to list registered students, and manage course assignments and material.

Note that user roles and other attributes are retrieved by the PE during or after it validates the credential received from the HTTP-BA *CredentialsRetriever.* We refrain from discussing this step because it is highly specific to the particular student and employee databases used by the university and is irrelevant to the discussion.

- A prebuilt *DecisionCombinator* of type *Permit Overrides*, which grants access if either PE grants access.

Example 2: Human Resource Web Service for an International Organization

Consider now a multinational company with divisions in Japan, Canada, Austria, and Russia. Each division has its own department of human resources (HR). The company rolls out a Web Service application in all of its divisions to provide online access to employee information. Each division has one or more Web Services providing the HR information for that division. The company establishes the following security policy for accessing this application.

Policy 2:

1. Only users within the *company's intranet*, or those who access the service over SSL and have valid X.509 certificates issued by the company, should be able to access the application.
2. **Anybody** in the company can *look up* any employee and *get essential information* about her or him (e.g., contact information, title, and names of the manager and supervised employees).
3. **Employees of HR** departments can *modify contact information* and *review salary information* of any employee from the same division.
4. **Managers of HR** departments can *modify any information* about the employees of the same department.

Configuration 2:

- Same *CredentialsRetriever* CR_1 as in Example1.
- Another *CredentialsRetriever* CR_2 obtains an SSL client certificate from the corresponding HTTPS connection.
- A prebuilt simple *DomainRetriever* that always returns the same statically configured domain name. The domain name designates the division for which HR information is served by the Web Service instance, for example, "Japan."
- The default *PermissionFactory* is configured to compose permissions with the domain name, qualified class name of the .NET class as a target name, and the corresponding method name. No target attributes are used in this case. Here is an example: "Japan/com.mega-foo.EmployeeInfo/GetContactInfo."
- Same prebuilt *PolicyEvaluator* PE_1 as in Example 1. In the case of Policy 2, there are four public methods: FindEmployee, GetEmployeeInformation, GetEmployeeManager, GetSupervisedEmployees.
- A prebuilt *PolicyEvaluator* PE_3 that permits access to any request made from a machine with an IP address in the range of the company's intranet addresses.
- A custom-built *PolicyEvaluator* PE_4 that permits access to any request made by a user with valid X.509 certificate issued by the company. This certificate, if available, is retrieved by CR_2.
- A generic RBAC *PolicyEvaluator* PE_5 that permits invocation of different methods based on the role of the user, according to the following rules:
    1. Any user with role "hr employee" can invoke methods that modify contact information and review salary.
    2. Any user with role "hr manager" can invoke methods permitted to users with role "hr employee," as well as methods that modify employee's salary, title, and names of the manager and supervised employees.
- A custom-built *PolicyEvaluator* PE_6 that permits access to any authenticated user whose attribute "Division" has the same value as the domain in the permission.
- A custom-built *DecisionCombinator* DC_2 that grants access according to the following formula: $(PE_3 \vee PE_4) \wedge (PE_1 \vee (PE_5 \wedge PE_6))$. That is, a request is permitted only to intranet users or those with a valid company's certificate $(PE_3 \vee PE_4)$, provided that either the requested method is public (PE_1) or an authorized HR person is accessing a record of the employee from the same division $(PE_5 \wedge PE_6)$.

The high degree of composability of the architecture allows reusing two prebuilt (PE_1 & PE_3) PEs. Even though Configuration 2, shown in Figure 8, has three more PEs and one more

Figure 8. Configuration 2. Custom-built components have a black background. Generic components from third-party vendors have a gray background.

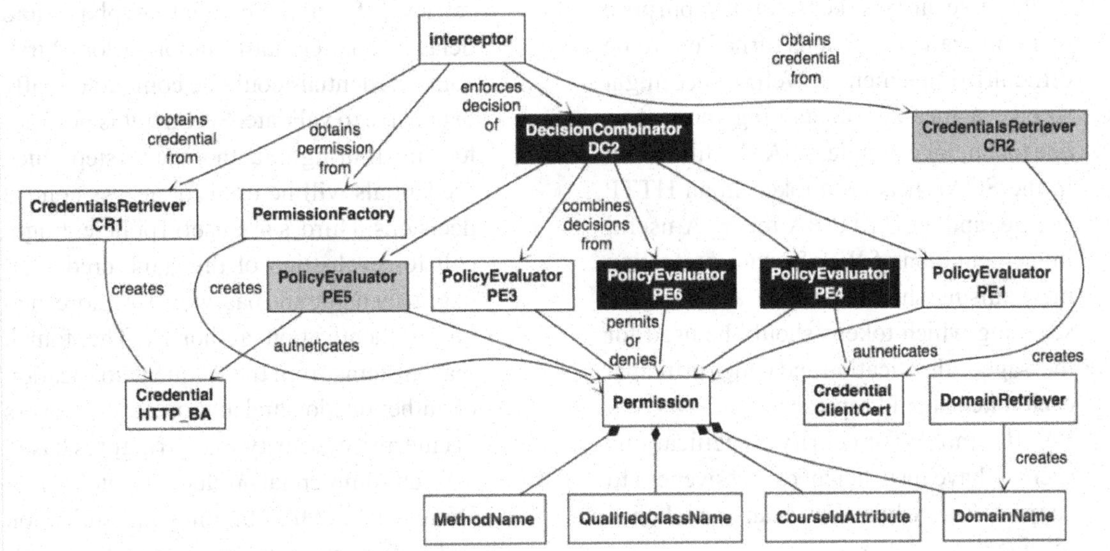

CredentialsRetriever than Configuration 1, there are only three components (DC_2, PE_4, and PE_6) that have to be custom built. Among them, PE_4 is simple to build using certificate validation tools and libraries, and PE_6 requires marginal effort. DC_2 can be implemented in one "if" structure. Two other PEs (PE_5 and CR_2) are generic and can be supplied by third-party vendors.

SUMMARY OF REFLECTIONS LESSONS LEARNED

To ground the discussion in its proper context, we've interspersed our description of the architecture in the previous section with our reflections on the process and the lessons we learned from it. To make clear what exactly we've learned through designing and implementing the architecture, we summarize the discussion in this section. We begin with general remarks and conclude with ASP.NET-specific ones.

General Remarks

- The end users did not require compliance with SAML or WS-Security specifications as long as the design was in the spirit of those standards and therefore enabled eventual compliance with them in an undetermined future. The likely reason they did not was the lack of plans for mixing heterogeneous (i.e., produced by different development teams) Web Services, possibly due to the lack of cross-enterprise deployments.
- Even if compliance were required, it would be difficult to determine a practical set of compliance criteria for SAML and WS-Security. Taking into account the flexibility of the information architectures for both SAML and WS-Security specifications, it was hard to define what a compliant implementation is expected to do and not do. Furthermore, without prior agreement between application owners on the specific SAML and WS-Security profiles, two compliant applications

would not necessarily interoperate in a useful manner.

- Flexible and meaningful interpretation of multiple security tokens for the purpose of authorization decisions turned out to be difficult to implement. A Web Service might receive a message containing more than one token, for example, a SAML-like token in the SOAP header, a token in an HTTP cookie, and an HTTP-BA token. A useful implementation of Web Service protection mechanisms should provide a means for selecting which tokens should be used for message authentication and which principal each token should represent.
- SAML and WS-Security specifications seem to have insufficient expressiveness to support cases when more than one token is received.
- Implementing monotonic policies, where "extra" invalid or unauthorized tokens do not decrease the privileges of the message sender, could make a Web Service vulnerable to a new type of denial-of-service attack: SOAP messages containing a large number of security tokens that are expensive to (in)validate.
- Deep chains of invocation (e.g., an originator and an intermediary with communication channels between them, with a total of four principals connected via a "speaks for" relation (Abadi et al., 1993; Lampson et al., 1991) are hard to support because of two key obstacles: lack of necessary support in WS-Security and SAML information architectures, and an exponential increase in the complexity of security policies if the support for composite principles is implemented in a naïve way. The former obstacle is accidental and can be addressed by revising the specifications. The latter, however, is incidental and cannot be addressed by incremental revisions and redesign.
- When integrating protection mechanisms with third-party enterprise security products, it is beneficial to separate credentials retrieval from the validation phase and delay the latter until authorization. First, some credentials could be computationally expensive to validate. Second, it is only determined during the authorization step which credentials will be used for access control decisions. Third, some useful policies might call for evaluation of the same credential (e.g., user name and password) by more than one authentication authority. The fourth reason stems from the frequent collocation of authentication and authorization servers in enterprise security infrastructures based on such commercial products as SiteMinder (Netegrity, 2000). Lumping authentication and authorization steps in one batch and sending it to a remote A&A server allows substantial reduction of the communication overhead in such cases.

Specific to ASP.NET

- ASP.NET out-of-the-box A&A mechanisms are tied to the Windows OS or ASP.NET and do not have enough flexibility and extensibility to support enterprise-grade Web Service applications.
- The weak support for dynamic Web Service instantiation in ASP.NET makes it almost impossible for developers to use dynamic retrieval of request-specific attributes of subjects for implementing relationship-based access control (Barkley et al., 1999).
- By using the .NET class name instead of the service URL for identifying the protected target, all instances of a Web Service application can share the same authorization policy rules. This feature reduces the cost of maintenance and allows the same application logic to be protected no matter under how many names it is deployed. When used

together with the domain capability, several instances of the same Web Service can be treated the same, or distinctly, as appropriate for the application structure.

- Not all the requests to a Web Service application "go" through the ASP.NET *SOAP Extension* interception point. Those created using HTTP-GET syntax result in "SOAP-less" requests and have to be handled using another interception point, *HTTP Module*.
- The use of simplified XML in web.config files enables a flexible hierarchy of configuration elements.
- On the one hand, the hierarchal nature of web.config parsing semantics enables good scalability without losing the fine level of granularity in the control over subsets of (or individual) Web Services. On the other hand, this flexibility comes with the cost of increased interdependencies between configuration settings at the different levels of the web.config hierarchy. A possible way of reducing the risk of inadvertent misconfigurations is to ensure that all Web Services hosted by the same ASP.NET container are in the jurisdiction of the same administrator.
- The performance overhead resulting from storing all configuration information in web.config seems to be relatively small, because ASP.NET caches web.config files and invalidates the cache when the OS detects any changes to the file.
- Unlike its predecessors (DCOM, ASP, COM+), ASP.NET has sufficiently extensible architecture, with a reasonable number of replaceable parts, to allow mixing and matching Microsoft products with third-party or home-grown ones. It remained an open question for us whether the points of extension and replacement and the corresponding interfaces in ASP.NET were sufficient for fully supporting such security-related standards as SAML, XACML, and WSS-* from OASIS, as well as ID-* from Liberty Alliance.

SUMMARY

In this chapter, we reported on our experience of designing a flexible and extensible architecture for protecting enterprise-grade ASP.NET Web Services. The architecture has been implemented in a real-world security solution deployed at a financial organization. We have described requirements, presented the architecture, and explained our design decisions, as well as the lessons we learned from this work.

REFERENCES

Abadi, M., Burrows, M., Lampson, B., & Plotkin, G. (1993). A calculus for access control in distributed systems. *ACM Transactions on Programming Languages and Systems*, *15*(4), 706-734.

Atkinson, B., Della-Libera, G., Hada, S., Hondo, M., Hallam-Baker, P., (Ed.), Klein, C.K. et al. (2002). *Web services security (WS-Security) v1.0.* IBM, Microsoft, Verisign.

Barkley, J., Beznosov, K., & Uppal, J. (1999). Supporting relationships in access control using role based access control. In Proceedings of the *Fourth ACM Role-based Access Control Workshop* (pp. 55-65), Fairfax, VA.

Beznosov, K. (2002a). Object security attributes: Enabling application-specific access control in middleware. In *Proceedings of the 4th International Symposium on Distributed Objects & Applications (DOA)* (pp. 693-710). Irvine, CA: Springer-Verlag.

Beznosov, K. (2002b). Overview of .NET Web services security. In *Proceedings of the OMG Distributed Object Computing Security Workshop*, Baltimore, MD.

Beznosov, K., Deng, Y., Blakley, B., Burt, C., & Barkley, J. (1999). A resource access decision service for CORBA-based distributed systems. In *Proceedings of the Annual Computer Security Applications Conference* (pp. 310-319). Phoenix, AZ: IEEE Computer Society.

Beznosov, K., Espinal, L., & Deng, Y. (2000). Performance considerations for CORBA-based application authorization service. In *Proceedings of the Fourth IASTED International Conference Software Engineering and Applications*, Las Vegas, NV.

Blakley, B. (1999). *CORBA security: An introduction to safe computing with objects.* Reading, MA: Addison-Wesley.

Encommerce. (1999). *GetAccess design and administration guide.*

Hallam-Baker, P., Moses, T., Morgan, B., Adams, C., Knouse, C., Orchard, D. et al. (2001). *Security assertions markup language: Core assertion architecture.* OASIS.

Hartman, B., Flinn, D.J., Beznosov, K., & Kawamoto, S. (2003). *Mastering Web services security.* New York: John Wiley & Sons.

Karjoth, G. (2003). Access control with IBM Tivoli Access Manager. *ACM Transactions on Information and Systems Security, 6*(2), 232-257.

Lampson, B., Abadi, M., Burrows, M., & Wobber, E. (1991). Authentication in distributed systems: Theory and practices. In *Proceedings of the ACM Symposium on Operating Systems Principles* (pp. 165-182), Asilomar Conference Center, Pacific Grove, CA.

Microsoft. (2001). Securing XML Web services created using ASP.NET. *.NET framework developer's Guide.* Microsoft Press.

Microsoft. (2002a). *Altering the SOAP message using SOAP extensions.* Microsoft.

Microsoft. (2002b). *Building secure ASP.NET applications: Authentication, authorization, and secure communication.* Microsoft Press.

Netegrity. (2000). *SiteMinder concepts guide.* Waltham, MA: Netegrity.

Object Management Group. (2001a). *CORBAservices: Common object services specification, Security Service Specification v1.7.* Object Management Group, document formal/01-03-08.

OMG. (2001b). *Resource access decision facility.* Object Management Group.

OMG (2001c). *Security domain membership management service.* Final Submission, Object Management Group.

Sandhu, R., Coyne, E., Feinstein, H., & Youman, C. (1996). Role-based access control models. *IEEE Computer, 29*(2), 38-47.

World Wide Web Consortium [W3C]. (2002a). *SOAP Version 1.2 Part 0: Primer*, W3C.

W3C. (2002b). *SOAP Version 1.2 Part 1: Messaging Framework*, W3C.

W3C. (2002c). *SOAP Version 1.2 Part 2: Adjuncts*, W3C.

W3C. (2002d). *SOAP Version 1.2 Usage Scenarios*, W3C.

XACML-TC. (2003). *OASIS eXtensible access control markup language (XACML) version 1.0*, OASIS.

APPENDIX A. OVERVIEW OF RESOURCE ACCESS DECISION ARCHITECTURE

With the RAD architecture, an application requests an authorization decision from a RAD authorization service and enforces the decision. The flow of interactions between application client, application system, and the authorization server is depicted in Figure 9.

A RAD service is composed of the following components (Figure 10). The *AccessDecisionObject* (ADO) serves as the interface to RAD clients and coordinates the interactions between other RAD components. Zero or more *PolicyEvaluators* (PEs) perform evaluation decisions based on certain access control policies that govern the access to a protected resource. The *DecisionCombinator* (DC) combines the results of the evaluations made by potentially multiple PEs into a final authorization decision by applying certain combination policies. The *PolicyEvaluatorLocator* (PEL), for a given access request to a protected resource, keeps track of and provides references to a DC and potentially several PEs, which are collectively responsible for making the authorization decision to the request. The *DynamicAttributeService* (DAS) collects and provides dynamic attributes about the client in the context of the intended access operation on the given resource associated with the provided resource name.

Figure 10 shows interactions among components of the authorization service:

Figure 9. High-level view of RAD role in authorization decisions

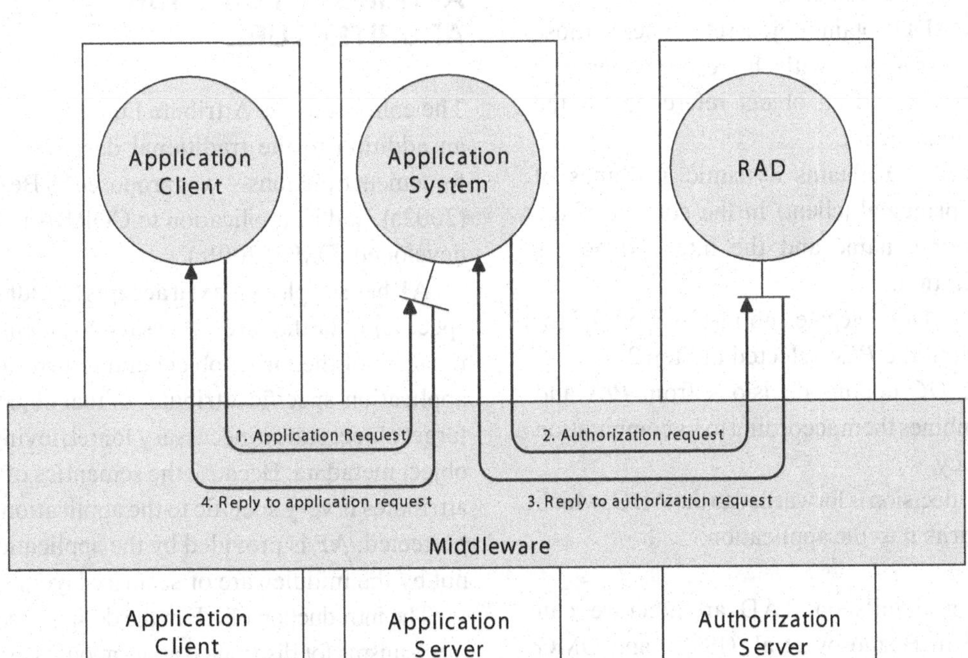

Figure 10. RAD interaction diagram

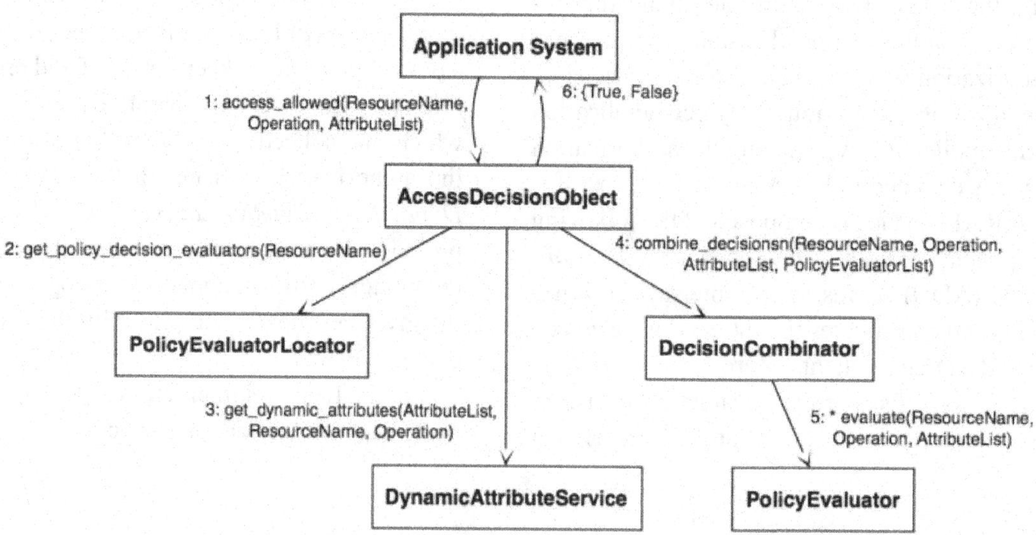

1. The authorization service receives a request via the ADO interface.
2. The ADO obtains object references to those *PEs* associated with the resource name in question and an object reference for the responsible *DC*.
3. The ADO obtains dynamic attributes of the principal (client) in the context of the resource name and the intended access operation.
4. The ADO delegates an instance of *DC* for polling the *PEs* (selected in Step 2).
5. The *DC* obtains decisions from *PEs* and combines them according to its combination policy.
6. The decision is forwarded to the ADO, which returns it to the application.

Further details on RAD architecture can be found in Beznosov et al. (1999), and OMG (2001b).

APPENDIX B. OVERVIEW OF ATTRIBUTE FUNCTION ARCHITECTURE

The concept of the Attribute Function (AF)—as an addition to the traditional decision and enforcement functions—was proposed by Beznosov (2002a), and its application to CORBA has been developed (OMG, 2001c).

AF has simple syntax: it accepts (middleware-specific) data that are necessary for identifying the state of the target object and returns a set of application-specific attributes of that object. The target object state is necessary for retrieving such object metadata. Because the semantics of object attributes is very specific to the application being protected, AF is provided by the application and not by the middleware or security layers.

The introduction of AF in the design of security mechanisms for distributed applications is expected to enable the use of application-specific factors in security policy decisions without coupling enforcement and decision functions with the application code.

Figure 11. Attribute Function and its relationship to enforcement and decision functions

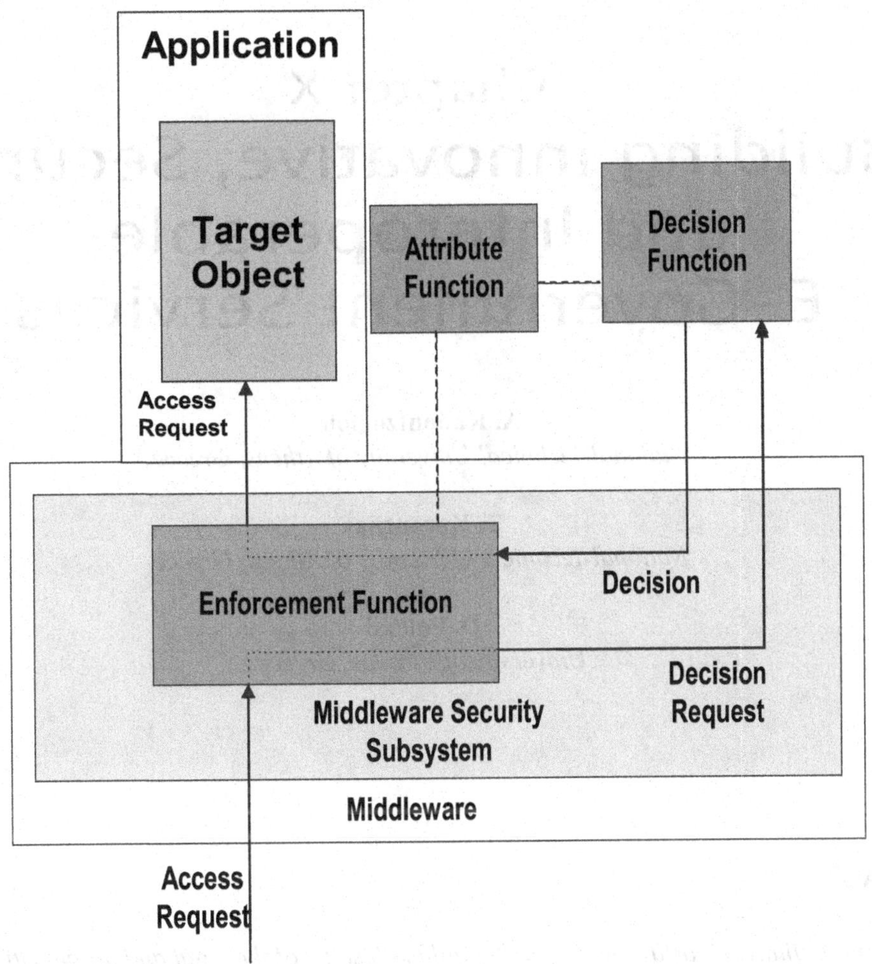

Chapter X
Building Innovative, Secure, and Interoperable E-Government Services

A. Kaliontzoglou
National Technical University of Athens, Greece

T. Karantjias
National Technical University of Athens, Greece

D. Polemi
University of Piraeus, Greece

ABSTRACT

Research into initiatives worldwide shows that although some of the legal and organizational barriers for the adoption of new technologies in e-government have been lifted, there are still not many implementations of actual e-government services that have been designed based on a common and systematic approach. The prevailing requirements for e-government services, interoperability and security, pose major challenges to e-government architects and it is now being slowly understood that Web services in combination with public key infrastructures may provide the necessary solutions. In this context, this chapter presents three innovative e-government services based on these technologies, focusing on their security and interoperability aspects. The goal of the chapter is to demonstrate the services' specifications and use cases so that they may act as examples for further research and development.

INTRODUCTION

Nowadays it has become evident from the existing e-government initiatives and best practices that although most of the legal and organizational barriers for the wide adoption of e-government services have been lifted, there is still a lack for actual e-government services implementations.

Services that make appropriate use of new and already established technologies, such as Web services and PKI, are considered promising in the sense that they satisfy the important e-government requirements of interoperability and security, respecting at the same time the business goals of public organizations and the expectations of citizens that interact with them.

Designing, building, and delivering e-government services that share a set of common requirements demands at first the introduction of a generic e-government architecture that fulfils those requirements, and then the change of focus to the specific requirements posed by each service to be deployed. Those special requirements might stem from the policies of the specific organizations wishing to deploy the service, or even by the legal framework set up by the state or country where the service is to be offered.

This chapter initially presents the major requirements of e-government services and references an existing e-government architecture that satisfies them. It then goes further into analyzing three distinct service implementations that rely on the architecture and leverage its common functionalities. These services include the issuance and distribution of public certification documents, such as birth certificates, electronic invoicing, and electronic ticketing. Their selection has been based on desk study and worldwide research results that demonstrate they are among the top services demanded by governmental organizations and citizens. Their implementation is based on Web services and PKI filling the gap of successful deployments of those technologies and demonstrating use cases that can be further consulted in the future for similar endeavours.

The chapter is structured as follows: "Generic E-Government Requirements and Architecture" focuses on the most important requirements that need to be satisfied by an e-government service and references a generic e-government architecture that has been already designed and has already been built in the European e-mayor project. "Three Innovative Secure and Interoperable E-Government Services" investigates in detail one by one the use cases of the three aforementioned innovative e-government services: issuance of public certification documents, e-invoicing, and e-ticketing. Finally, "Conclusion" draws conclusions.

GENERIC E-GOVERNMENT REQUIREMENTS AND ARCHITECTURE

This section describes firstly the basic requirements that need to be taken into account when building an e-government service and then goes on to give an overview of an e-government architecture that may host e-government services that satisfy the requirements.

It should be noted that in the rest of the chapter when we refer to an e-government service, we specifically mean an enterprise service operated by a public organization that performs one instance of a business function, as for example the issuance of a certification document etc. The terms "enterprise service" and "e-government service" are therefore interchangeable in this context.

E-Government Requirements

Interoperability is a primary goal of an e-government service. Lack of interoperability amongst services is mainly due to the unhomogeneity of technical solutions deployed in the infrastructures that support the service itself, as well as the lack of well-defined service business functions.

The interconnection of governmental organizations that use various platforms and systems is a difficult task requiring easily identifiable and publishable e-services, as well as clear interfaces for the establishment of secure and reliable connection points.

Interoperability is satisfied by using widely deployed standards and technologies during the services' design and implementation phases.

Current practices indicate that in order for an e-government service to succeed in its business goals, it should be secure in all aspects so that the entities involved trust it. An e-government service should make use of security services and mechanisms supported by the environment or architecture where it is deployed.

There are five critical security requirements that need to be satisfied (Hartman, Flinn, Beszosov, & Kawamoto, 2003):

- **Authentication:** The method with which an entity is uniquely identified and its identity verified.
- **Integrity:** The method that ensures that every system, resource, file, and information in general can be modified only by authorized entities.
- **Privacy and confidentiality:** The method by which access to the content of information is available only to authorized recipients.
- **Non-repudiation:** The method that produces cryptographic data that ensure that an entity cannot repudiate its actions.
- **Availability:** The method that ensures that a system can fulfil its purpose with a given degree of success.

An e-government service can satisfy the security requirements by making use of a set of *security mechanisms* and a set of *security services*. Security mechanisms are stand-alone instances of components that are directly embedded within an e-government enterprise service and that address a security requirement based on a policy. Security services on the other hand, are independent services within an e-government architecture that are available to any enterprise service wishing to perform a security goal as part of a policy. Security services integrate security mechanisms, and may interact with other security services as part of their operation. Security mechanisms may also interact with security services to send and receive information.

Yet another important requirement that an e-government service has to take into account is the friendliness towards users and respect to the way a user perceives the service itself.

This requirement is usually satisfied in two ways:

- With the support of applications with which most users are already accustomed and do not pose additional training requirements.
- With the provision of a high level of transparency for complex processes that the service entails, so that a user does not perceive the lower level technical details, without nevertheless losing the meaning of what process they are involved in and why.

Therefore, an e-government service should be supporting standard browsing facilities common in most computers nowadays and a high level of abstraction with respect to technical details.

Finally, a major requirement of e-government services is the compliance with the underlying legal and policy framework as dictated by the laws and directives of the states where the service is to be deployed and operated. The legal specificities are tightly coupled on one hand with the business functions of the service itself, and on the other with the security functions that it has to support, such as the restrictions posed by law regarding digital signatures and their equation with hand written ones under specific constraints. Furthermore, an e-government service has to abide by the organizational policies of the organization hosting it.

A Generic Secure E-Government Architecture

The study of previous e-government requirements has lead to the design of a new e-government architecture that on one hand is generic enough to accommodate them and on the other hand offers an adequate framework for the implementation and deployment of e-government services that achieve specific governmental business goals. This architecture is part of the work that has occurred in the E.C. funded "e-mayor project" (e-mayor, 2004) which has the purpose of building and evaluating a platform that is an instance of the architecture.

The architecture is depicted in Figure 1.

As can be seen in Figure 1, the architecture is divided into specific areas of services that perform core functions of an e-government architecture. These are the basic services, administration and orchestration services, security services, enterprise services, and existing infrastructure support services. A short description of these groups follows. The main concepts behind the systematic design approach of the architecture are based on the RM-ODP standard (e-mayor Consortium D3.1, 2004; Kaliontzoglou, Sklavos, Karantjias, & Polemi, 2004; Meneklis, Kaliontzoglou, Polemi, & Douligeris, 2005) for a more detailed analysis).

- **Administration and orchestration services:** These services perform two very important functions within the architectural framework: they manage all other services and orchestrate the enterprise services so that they successfully achieve the business goals. They are divided into access services, process coordination services, and user management services.
- **Basic services:** These provide the basic functions that are used by the architecture as a whole to perform primitive tasks.

Figure 1. A generic secure e-government architecture

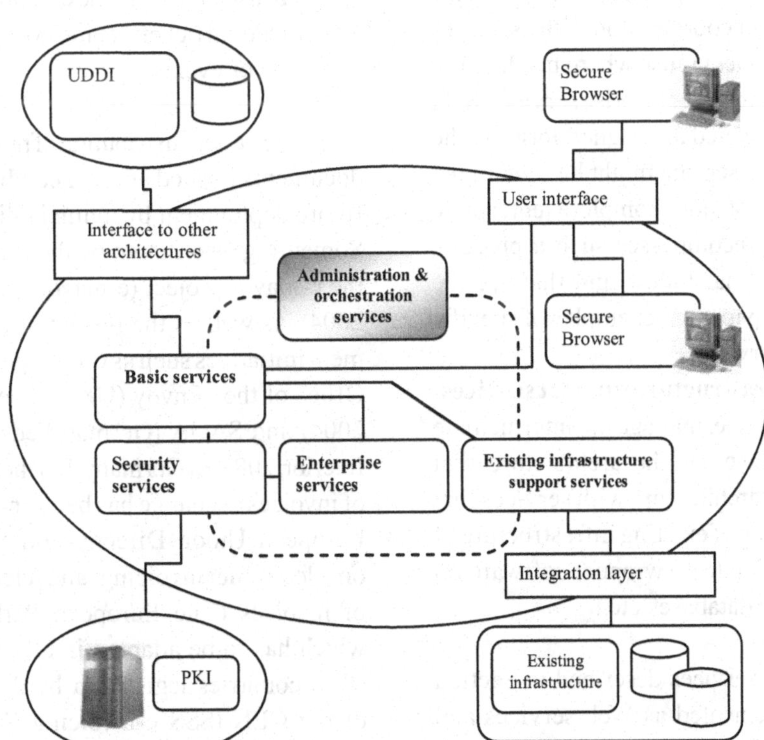

Basic services are user interface services, message transformation services, message forwarding services, publication and query services, notification services, and printing services.

- **Security mechanisms and services:** These address the security requirements of Section 2. Security mechanisms that are supported are the following: digital signatures, advanced electronic signatures, and encryption. Security mechanisms are encapsulated into distinct components that are in turn, embedded into any other component that needs them, based on the policies that govern the services. The security services that the e-government architecture comprises are the following: identity management, access control, time stamping and keys, and certificates management.
- **Enterprise services:** These are the actual e-government services. Enterprise services are divided into a set of atomic sub-processes and each one is mapped into a service. This achieves better coordination of the services and more efficient reuse where needed. For example, an atomic enterprise service might accept a completed and signed form by the user. This sub-service might be used in the composition of any complete enterprise service that encompasses such a process. The services that follow and that are the focus of this paper are examples of specific enterprise services.
- **Existing infrastructure support services:** These, in essence, manage the intermediate integration layer of the architecture that connects the architecture with services that operates on top of existing infrastructure of an organization (e.g., wrapper software on top of legacy databases etc.)

The enterprise services described in Section 3 have been implemented as Web services and incorporated into the previous architecture. Each enterprise service utilizes the previous services and resources of the e-mayor architecture appropriately in order to carry out its intended business purpose.

THREE INNOVATIVE SECURE AND INTEROPERABLE E-GOVERNMENT SERVICES

This section presents the three new services that are the focus of this chapter:

- **Issuance and distribution of public certification documents:** Involving the generation of digital certificates requested by citizens, bearing the proper credentials of public authorities
- **E-invoicing:** Involving the secure issuance and distribution of digital invoices among commercial partners
- **E/m-ticketing:** Involving the setup of an infrastructure for the creation and validation of digital tickets related to public transportation or events

Issuance and distribution of public certification documents is rated as a top candidate service for future deployment by municipalities worldwide. Something also shown by the research results of the e-mayor project (e-mayor Consortium D2.1, 2004), as well as the results of major e-government initiatives such as e-Gif operated by the UK Office of the eEnvoy (UK Office of the eEnvoy, 2004) and SAGA (German Federal Ministry of Interior, 2003) in Germany. Furthermore, the value of invoices exchange has been emphasized by the European Union Directive on VAT legislation on electronic invoicing and electronic storage of invoices (The European Parliament, 2001), which has to be adapted in all European Union (EU) countries legislation by 2008. The report of the CEN/ISSS e-invoicing Focus Group on standards and developments on electronic invoicing (CEN/ISSS e-invoicing Focus Group, 2003) demonstrates the needs for electronic invoice implementations. Electronic ticketing has been receiving attention the last years mainly because buying and collecting tickets produces crunch times. Being competitive means changing business models from paper passed tickets to keep up with customers' changing habits and needs, adopting mobile for one. Electronic tickets enabled by mobile phones comprise an important class of everyday consumer transactions, fulfilling the requirement of governmental organizations to easily provide tickets to events, public museums, public transportation, and so forth.

In the sections that follow, each service is described in terms of what its business goals are in the context of e-government, what are the more specific requirements it poses in addition to the common e-government requirements described in the section "E-Government Requirements," which are its main actors and components, and which are its functional and operational phases and characteristics.

Issuance and Distribution of E-Certification Documents

Description and Purpose

This service deals with the secure issuance and distribution of certification documents. Example certification documents that can be reported are birth, death, or marriage certificates (we use the term certification document in this section in order to avoid any confusion with security certificates such as those complying with the X509 standard). In this section, we present a particular enterprise service that can be deployed in the reference architecture of section "A Generic Secure E-Government Architecture," in which municipalities (a representative governmental organization) are able to generate, issue. and deliver securely (to citizens or other municipalities) digitally signed birth certificates. The functionality and initial implementation aspects of the service are provided here where as a full implementation occurred as part of the e-mayor project.

Figure 2. Certification document issuance

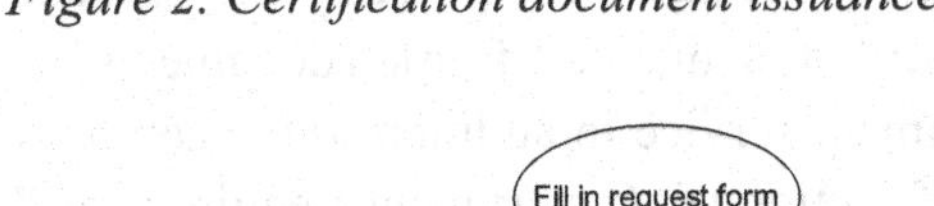

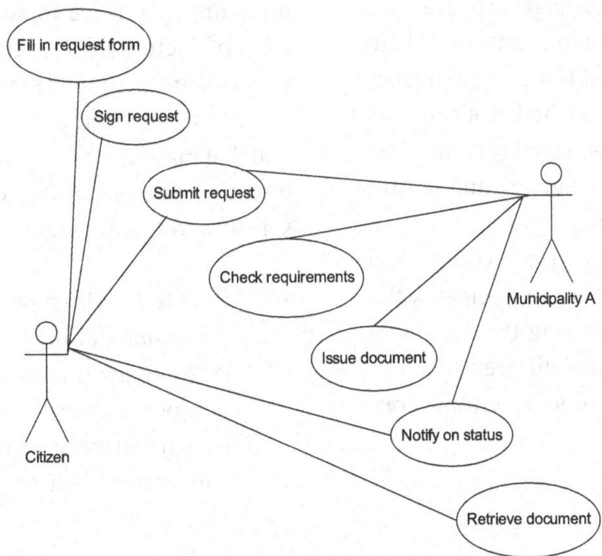

Figure 3. Certification document issuance with propagation

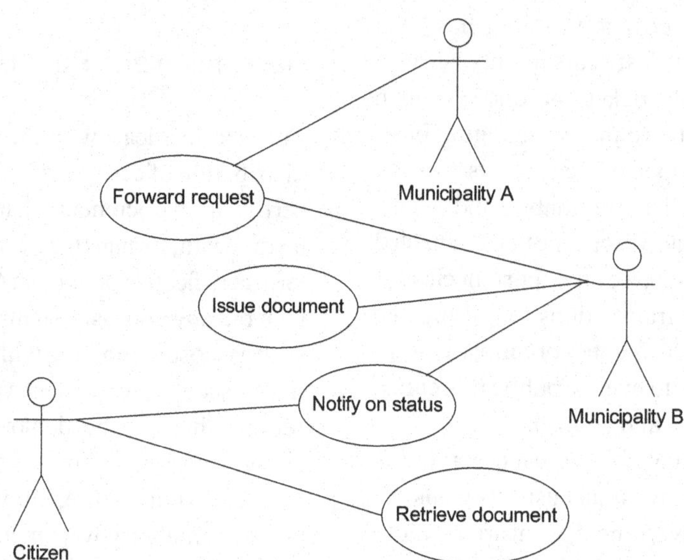

The purpose of this service is to enable a citizen to interact with the intended municipality, regardless of the citizen's location, in order for him to make a secure request for a specific certification document that the municipality can provide.

As shown in the use case diagram of Figure 2, the citizen has to fill in certain forms, sign them, and then submit the request to the municipality. The municipality checks on whether it can issue the desired document. If yes, a civil servant issues the certification document, signs it, and notifies the citizen that he or she may retrieve it.

If not, as shown in the diagram of Figure 3, the request is propagated to the municipality that is indeed responsible for issuing the document, which may reside even on a different country, therefore requiring cross-border electronic communication.

Additional/Specific Service Requirements

There are two requirements posed by the "issuance and distribution of e-certification documents" e-government service in addition to the common ones of section "E-Government Requirements" and they are attributed to the fact that municipalities are small sized governmental organizations and that may have to interact with each other over country borders in order to deliver the requested services to their citizens.

- **Limited trained personnel:** Smaller sized governmental organizations suffer from a lack of personnel that is adequately trained to cope with the technologies introduced by IT. Furthermore, training the personnel has a greater impact on smaller governmental organizations because of the limited funds it usually has available

- **Cross border communication:** An ever increasing number of citizens change their location to work and live in other countries. This means that there is a definite demand to support them in everyday administrative procedures that include cross-border communication. In cross-border services, there is exchange of information, data, or documents between citizens and public administrations in an international context and across administrative boundaries

The enterprise service described in the following paragraphs has to take into account these additional requirements.

Main Service Components

The certification document issuance service operates as an enterprise service within the architecture. The WSDL description of the endpoint of the service can be published in a UDDI directory through the publication and query service. This allows searching for the specific enterprise service and comprehension of the messages this service understands so that messages can be sent to and received from it.

The enterprise service is running as a Web service in the architecture and it is managed by the orchestration service. It communicates with the following architecture services:

- With secure browsers through the access service
- With any required databases through an existing infrastructure support service
- The forwarding service of the architecture, in order to securely dispatch the certification document to its final destination
- The key and certificate management service for validation of key and certificates

An important part of the service is the format of the data that is being exchanged. It is evident from the fundamental e-government requirements of section "E-Government Requirements" that this format has to be XML to ensure interoperability. Further interoperability nevertheless has to be ensured with respect to the exact structure supported specifically for data related for example to address information or birth details, etc. Therefore, the messages have to be based on widely adopted e-government standards that define such XML data such as the following:

- The schemas produced under the UK eGif initiative (Hunter, 2004; Kent, 2003)
- The OASIS Universal Business Language (UBL) Schemas (Meadows & Seaburg, 2004)
- Schemas derived from the e-gov project–GovML (Kavvadias, Spanos, & Tambouris, 2002)
- The IDA e-procurement XML schemas initiative (IDA BC, 2004)

Transformations between formats and languages respecting semantic differences may be performed by using the message transformation services of the architecture.

Entities and Actors

This section presents the entities involved in a typical certification document issuance and delivery and their roles. All entities and their relationships are depicted in Figure 4.

The actors that take part are:

- **The citizen:** The citizen is the consumer of any e-government service supported by the architecture. It has to communicate with the TTP to get the proper security credentials
- **Municipalities and personnel:** The municipalities are the governmental organizations

Figure 4. Certification document issuance and delivery transaction scheme

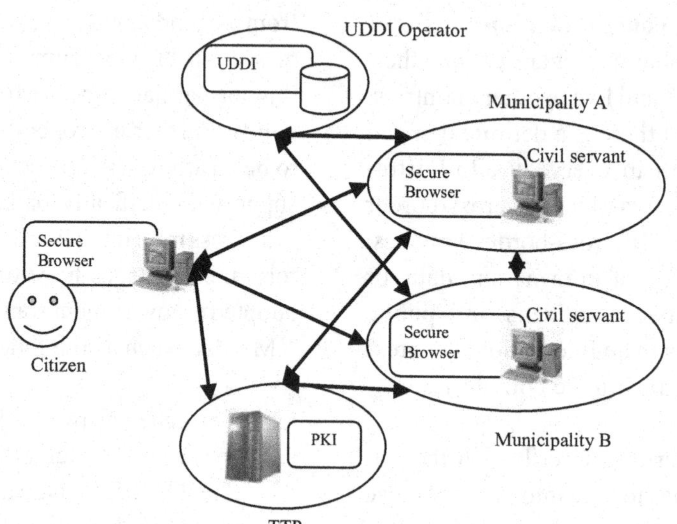

that are part of the e-government architecture and host the services. Their personnel (civil servants, administrators etc.) are the internal users of the e-government services. They too have to communicate with the TTP to receive credentials. The service does not pose a limit to the number of municipalities that may participate in a transaction. This means that a citizen may request a certification document for which a number of municipalities shall have to cooperate to complete the service

- **The trusted third party (TTP):** Before any secure messaging can take place, all participants need to have established an adequate security framework. Such a framework may be an infrastructure based on TTP technologies (Nash, Duane, Brink, & Joseph, 2001). In our case, the required TTPs are at a minimum a certification authority (CA) and a registration authority (RA) offering the PKI services of registration, certification, and revocation status information with OCSP, as well as a time stamping authority (TSA) offering standard based time stamping services
- **Universal description, discovery, and integration (UDDI) directory operator:** This operator hosts a public UDDI directory where Web services can be published and thus become publicly available

Functional and Operational Description

This section presents the functional description of a typical transaction that is supported by the enterprise service. More specifically, the section describes the sequences of operations that are carried out in order for a citizen in city A to receive a birth certificate from a municipality that is located in city B. In the paper world, a citizen would have to sign a formal request form in the premises of the municipality B and wait for a few days for the civil servant there to fill in and sign the birth certificate.

Supposing that an implementation of the e-government architecture of the section "A Generic Secure E-Government Architecture" has been deployed at both the municipalities A and B along with the enterprise service described here, the citizen may acquire the certificate in a more efficient manner.

The service execution has two main phases. The first one involves the actions that take place at the premises of municipality A and the second the actions that take place at municipality B. The first phase is depicted in the sequence diagram of Figure 5.

A description of the process is the following:

- **Selection of service, authentication, and submission of request:** The citizen logs on directly to the site of municipality A where he or she currently resides and selects the certification document issuance enterprise service. This is performed through a secure browser. The access service of the architecture authenticates the user utilizing proper calls to the keys and certificates management service. If authentication is successful, the citizen goes on to complete the specific form, declaring whether he would like to receive a signed paper document in municipality A, or a purely digital birth certificate in case this was acceptable. The citizen has the option to sign the form he completes. A user signature may be optional at this point, according to the active municipality policy.
- **Authorization:** The access service propagates the request to the actual enterprise service that runs as a Web service in the architecture. This enterprise service consults the access control service to take the necessary actions to authorize the citizen's request and provide him or her with a success or failure result. In case of success, the citizen is also provided with an estimation of time within which his or her request will be completed and served. More specifically, the enterprise service retrieves the form, checks its destination, and checks whether it adheres to a policy permitting it to exchange securely documents with the municipality B and whether it knows where to find corresponding services of the architecture at

Figure 5. Birth certificate service operation on municipality A

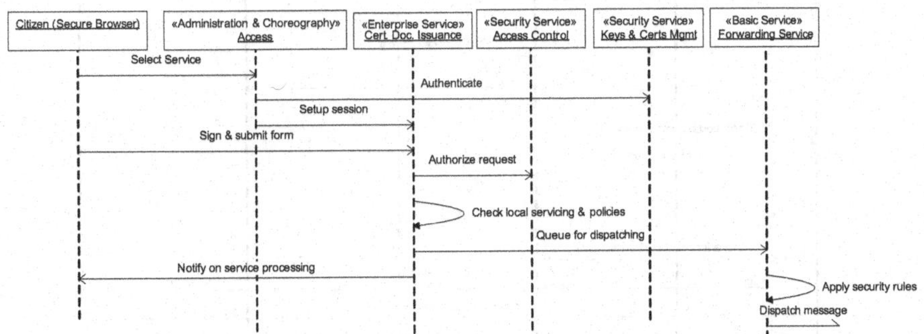

municipality B (based on new or previous queries on known UDDI registries).

- **Confirmation whether request can be served locally and request propagation:** According to this information and local database information, the enterprise service checks whether it can serve the request locally, or the request has to be propagated to another municipality. Since the citizen requested a birth certificate from municipality B, the request needs to be propagated. The enterprise service takes the appropriate steps to wrap the request into a SOAP message, and send over to the forwarding service. The forwarding service checks what security rules must be applied to the message (e.g., apply WS-Security extensions), applies those rules and forwards the message to platform B.

The next part of the process takes place at platform B, as depicted in Figure 6. The steps of the second phase are the following:

a. **Request retrieval, credentials validation, and request storage:** A corresponding enterprise service at platform B receives and parses the message and validates any security credentials applied to it by the service of platform A. This is performed with information acquired by the keys and certificates service in the architecture of municipality B. This security service will perform credentials validation, as is for example the validation of an X509 certificate through an OCSP or XKMS interface. If this process is successful, the citizens' request is extracted from the message and stored as pending.

Figure 6. Birth certificate service operation at platform B

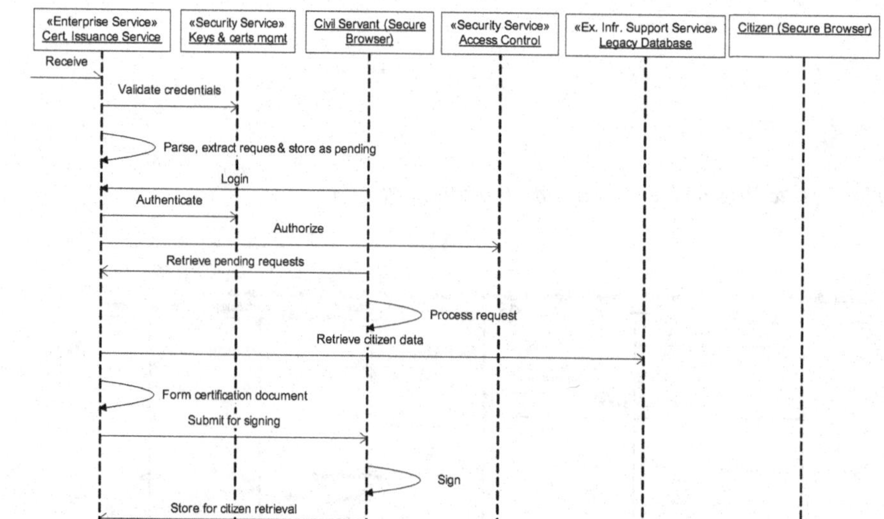

b. **Civil servant authentication and access to pending requests:** The procedure continues from the point where a civil servant at the municipality responsible for processing requests and serving them, accesses through a secure browser the citizens pending request. The civil servant first has to strongly authenticate himself to the platform, based on deployed policies and credentials.

c. **Service processing and issuance of XML birth certificate:** As part of normal processing, the civil servant checks whether the local database contains an entry verifying that the citizen is a person indeed born in municipality B. The database consulted may be a new one which is part of the platform or a legacy system which is contacted via an existing infrastructures support service. The next step is to transparently formulate a proper XML document with all the required information and present it to a proper official at municipality B to be signed, which may be the same civil servant or another person.

d. **Signing of birth certificate with XAdES and storage of signed birth certificate:** The official uses the proper cryptographic token (smart card) to sign the document using the secure browser with the proper advanced electronic signature mechanism embedded on it. The electronic signature will be based on the XAdES standard (ETSI, 2002) and will have to abide by a signature policy used in the municipality which enables cross-border exchange of such electronic information with other public organizations. Finally, the signed document is stored for further retrieval by the citizen.

e. **Retrieval of signed birth certificate:** Depending on the citizen's choice on the form in which he wants the document (paper or digital) the platform will employ different notification mechanisms:

- **Paper form:** The XML document is forwarded by the corresponding services from platform B back to platform A, which utilizes the printing service of the architecture to be printed under the supervision of a responsible civil servant. Platform A automatically contacts the citizen by e-mail and/or a message to his mobile phone to retrieve the paper document at the municipality A premises.
- **Digital form:** The platform B notification service notifies the citizen directly by e-mail and/or message to a mobile device that his digital birth certificate is ready to be collected. The citizen uses his secure browser to authenticate at platform B and retrieve his birth certificate.

The operation can alternatively be realized by having the citizen log on directly to the services at municipality B first to request the same data. The services at platform B would take the appropriate steps to contact platform A and automatically again receive the birth certificate.

The same architecture implementation could be operated on several other municipalities forming a network. The fact that it is based on XML and Web services enables other municipalities deploying their own solutions to find the platform's interfaces and use them. This would also ideally suit more complex cases where people are married to foreigners and are living and working abroad, where getting a valid birth or marriage certificate from their hometown may be an extremely cumbersome process. Furthermore, businesses building proprietary Web services software to also access specific services provided by municipalities (for example services related to taxes).

Electronic Invoicing

Description and Purpose

A commercial invoice is the most important document exchanged between trading partners. In addition to its commercial value, an invoice is an accounting document that has legal implications to both transacting parties and constitutes the basis for value added tax (VAT) declaration, VAT reclamation, statistics declaration for intra community trade, and export and import declaration for extra community trade. Nevertheless, in order for e-invoicing implementations to be successful, they need to be in compliance with the EU Directive requirements (i.e., acceptable, interoperable, secure, and affordable by the majority of businesses and organizations operating in EU Member states).

As shown in CEN/ISSS E-Invoicing Focus Group (2003) and The European Parliament (2001), most contemporary e-invoicing implementations are based on EDI, which is an option covered by the Directive. The usage of advanced eSignatures is the other option suggested in the Directive, but their adoption in e-invoicing systems is not widespread at the moment. The following sections present an alternative to EDI enterprise service of electronic invoicing that is an open, practical, cost-effective, and secure solution in accordance to EU legislation. This e-invoicing service has been presented so far as a reference implementation of a stand-alone e-invoicing service (CEN/ISSS e-invoicing Focus Group, 2003; Kaliontzoglou, Boutsi, Mavroudis, & Polemi, 2003; Kaliontzoglou, Boutsi, & Polemi, 2005), while in this chapter we present how it is embedded and deployed as an enterprise service in the architecture of section "A Generic Secure E-Government Architecture," further leveraging its interoperability and security features.

At an abstract business level, e-invoicing is about the exchange and storage of e-invoices.

Figure 7. A typical e-invoice transaction

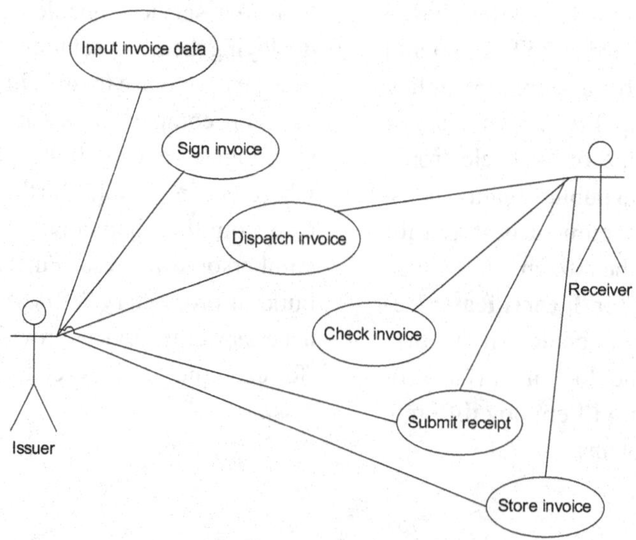

As shown in the use case diagram of Figure 7, electronic invoicing starts with the completion of the invoice data by an employee of the organization that issues the invoice and the signing of the invoice based on a specific signature policy. The signed electronic invoice is then forwarded to the recipient organization that checks its content and cryptographic validity. The transaction is finalized by the submission of a confirmation receipt back to the issuing organization and storage of the invoice.

Additional/Specific Service Requirements

Council Directive 2001/115/EC of December 20, 2001 amends Directive 77/388/EEC with a view of simplifying, modernizing, and harmonising the conditions laid down for invoicing in respect of value added tax. This Directive clarifies the implementation of e-invoicing through the Member States and aims to introduce harmonized procedures for invoicing (paper or electronic invoicing) across Member State borders in a homogeneous home market. The Directive additionally promotes the use of PKI by obligating EU countries to accept digitally signed electronic documents.

As shown in Kaliontzoglou, Boutsi, and Polemi. (2005), this directive poses certain requirements to e-invoicing implementations. In addition to the common e-government requirements presented in the section "E-Government Requirements" that are indeed enforced by the Directive, further requirements are the following:

- **Electronic storage of e-invoices:** The conditions for electronic storage of e-invoices and the technical requirements of the electronic storage system are integral components of the security requirements concerning e-invoicing. Authenticity, integrity, and readability should be guaranteed throughout the storage period, according to the e-invoicing Directive.
- Integrity of the *sequence of the invoices* assists in avoiding any gaps occurring in the outgoing invoices and in strengthening company and tax authority control. This requirement is implementation specific and can be fulfilled by enforcing a tight sequence issuance scheme for the reference number embedded in each invoice.

These additional requirements are met by the enterprise service presented in the following paragraphs.

Main Service Components

The e-invoicing service operates as an enterprise service within the architecture. The WSDL description of the endpoint of the service can be published in a UDDI directory through the Publication and query service. This allows searching for the specific enterprise service and comprehension of the messages this service understands so that messages can be sent and received from it.

The enterprise service is running as a Web service in the architecture and it is managed by the orchestration service. It communicates with the following entities:

- With secure browsers through the access service
- The repository for e-invoices and receipts. This communication may be direct (i.e., the repository is a database directly controlled by the enterprise service) or indirect through an existing infrastructure support service of the architecture
- The forwarding service of the architecture, in order to securely dispatch the invoice to its final destination
- The key and certificate management service for validation of key and certificates

The repository for invoices and receipts may take many forms. In case it is part of the enterprise service itself, it may be any database. Due to the requirement imposed by the Directive that the invoices should retain their form while stored, a Native XML database implementation of such a repository is considered ideal. This is in contrast to a relational database that "breaks down" invoice elements to store them in distinct tables. Another option would be to use an existing system that is visible in the architecture through an existing infrastructure support service.

In order to promote interoperability with respect to the exact structure supported specifically for e-invoices, various business XML schemas that represent invoices have to be supported. The most widely adopted standards that define forms for e-invoices are the following:

- XML Common Business Library version 4.0 (xCBL 4.0) (xCBL.org, 2003)
- Business Application Software Developers Association (BASDA) electronic Business Interchange standard using XML (eBis-XML suite) (Business Application Software Developers Association, 2005)
- The Universal Business Language (UBL) (Meadows & Seaburg, 2004).
- The Open Applications Group Integration Specification (OAGIS) (Rowell, 2002)

Transformations between e-invoicing formats may be performed by using the message transformation services of the architecture. The more of this type of standards are supported by the enterprise service, the more increases the level of interoperability it offers.

Entities and Actors

This section presents the entities involved in an e-invoicing transaction with the e-invoicing enterprise service and their roles. As in common invoicing practice, an e-invoicing transaction occurs between the issuer for the invoice who charges for a set of services or products and the receiver who is called to pay for them. Both parties have to be able to view and process e-invoices and be

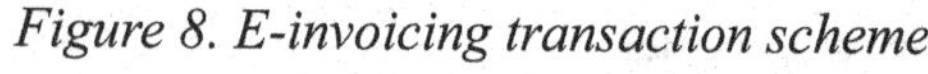

Figure 8. E-invoicing transaction scheme

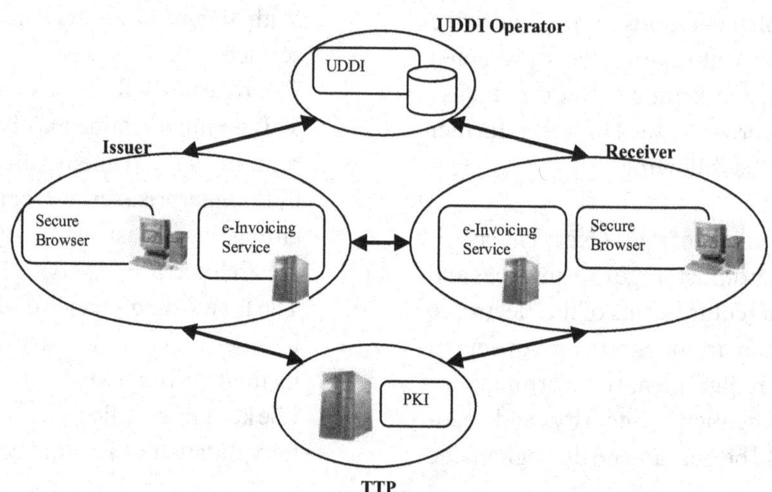

able to understand the security policy applied in a user-friendly manner.

All entities and their relationships are depicted in Figure 8.

The actors that take part are:

a. **The Issuer:** This organization hosts the e-government architecture that operates the enterprise service. It takes the appropriate steps to deploy the service and publish it in the Registry, so that other organizations may find it. It also communicates with the TTP to get the proper security credentials.
b. **The Receiver:** The Receiver organization may be part of the same or similar e-government architecture, or may operate a completely independent e-invoicing service. In the latter case, the two services have to support at least one common e-invoicing schema. The Receiver organization will also have to communicate with the TTP to get its proper security credentials.
c. **The TTP:** Before any secure messaging can take place, all participants need to have established an adequate security framework with Trusted Third Parties (TTPs) as described in the section "Entities and Actors" of the previous service.
d. **UDDI directory operator:** This operator hosts a public UDDI directory where Web services can be published as described in the section "Entities and Actors" of the previous service.

Functional and Operational Description

The e-invoicing process can be divided into three phases: issuing, dispatch/reception, and storage. Credentials and security policy setup, as well as search and discovery in UDDI are considered already in carried out before these phases begin.

A. E-Invoice Issuance Phase

As depicted in the sequence diagram of Figure 9, an employee of the issuer organization (represented by the class user on the figure) initiates the e-invoicing process. He first authenticates himself by means of his smart card and PIN through the user interface. Based on the authentication credentials, the system performs an authorization check. The initial authentication and access control process through the access and access control services of the architecture are performed transparently.

The user interface transparently communicates with the enterprise service to enable the user to create a new invoice and supply the necessary data to complete the invoice or manage existing invoices (e.g., received, drafts etc.). This data input is automatically checked for prevention of errors. According to the user's privileges, the option for signing and dispatching the e-invoice is enabled or disabled. If the user has the right of signing and presses the "Sign and Send" button, the user interface transparently completes a series of steps:

- The form data are gathered and are used to structure an e-invoice
- The time stamps and revocation status information data are gathered from the corresponding time stamping service and keys and certificates management service of the architecture, and
- The XAdES signature is formulated based on the cryptographic primitives in the smart card, the user's certificate, and the invoice data

The distinction between types of users provides flexibility for both the employee that feeds in the data and the person who is responsible for signing the invoices, if they are not the same person.

The singing and authentication certificates might be different or they might be the same,

Figure 9. E-invoice issuance phase

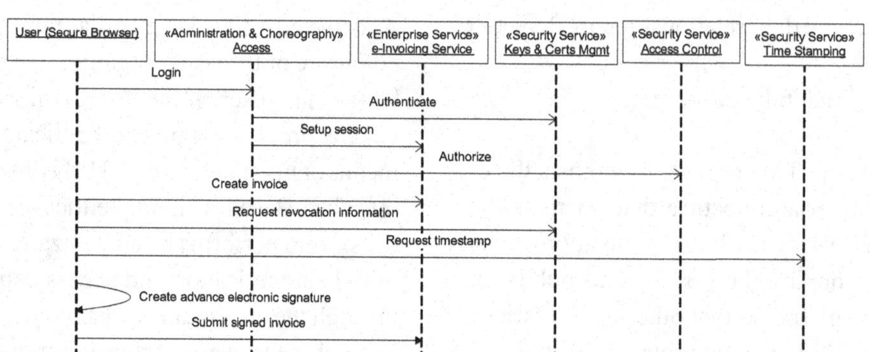

something which is governed by the organizations policies. In case they are different, the user is prompted to use one or the other to according to what he is trying to accomplish at that particular time.

B. E-Invoice Dispatching and Receipt Phase

After the successful creation of the XAdES signature, the invoice is embedded in a SOAP message and sent to the forwarding service of the

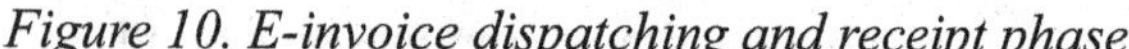

Figure 10. E-invoice dispatching and receipt phase

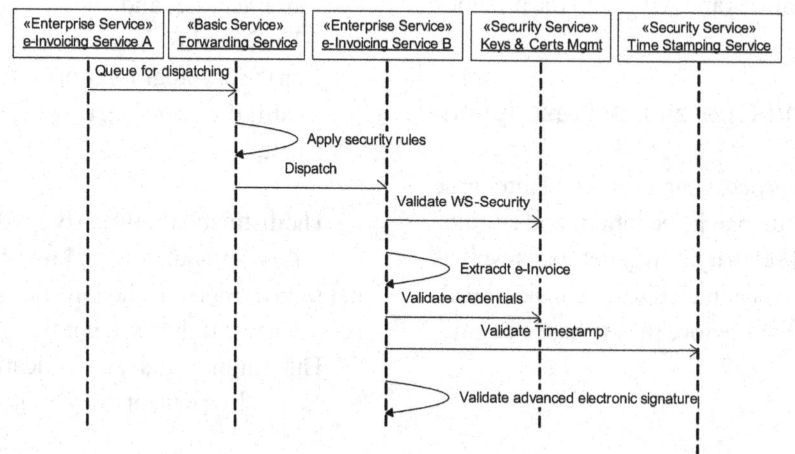

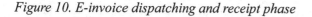

architecture, as shown on Figure 10. The forwarding service is responsible to extract the invoice, and pack it in a new message adding this time the specific security extensions mandated by the WS-Security standard, utilizing the xml digital signatures and encryption security mechanisms. The secure SOAP message is then dispatched to a corresponding e-invoicing/forwarding service on the receiver organization.

The receipt of the invoice is a fully automated process which does not require any human intervention. The SOAP message that contains the invoice is decrypted and the WS-Security based signature verified.

The next step is to extract the invoice itself and verify the credentials information that were used to create the advanced electronic signature along with any timestamps it contains. Finally, the XAdES signature itself is validated. These last steps all utilize the security services of the architecture.

C. E-Invoice Storage Phase

During the last phase, initially the e-invoice is stored in the database of the Receiver, as shown on Figure 11. That makes it available for parsing and further processing by the Receiver's users. The process is finalized by the dispatch of a SOAP reply (receipt), referencing the newly received invoice, and containing the status of the whole process. This reply is signed in a similar way using WS Security extensions by the Receiver's server in order to be valid as a receipt. When the Issuer service receives this signed SOAP reply, it is stored in the Issuer repository along with the sent invoice.

The full automation of the whole process for batch dispatching of the invoices is generally an open area of research, since it is a requirement usually posed by the organizations exchanging electronic invoices due to performance reasons, but it contradicts the related Directive and the application of advance electronic signatures.

Electronic Ticketing

Description and Purpose

Nowadays, the development and adoption of mobile technologies have enabled the introduction of new advanced services. The tremendous development of the Internet and related technologies, the understanding and exploitation of the business potentials that rest behind this trend, the boost of e-government frameworks and technologies, and the impressive growth of wireless mobile networks, are some of the main factors that contributed to this.

Figure 11. E-invoice storage phase

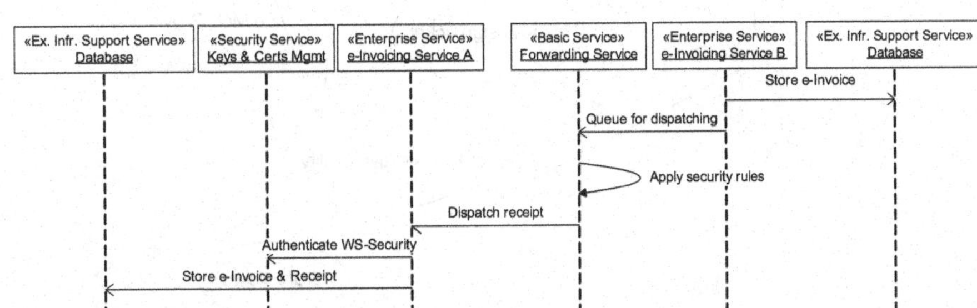

One of the core visions of IT is that the mobile phone has the potential to become the user's Personal Trusted Device, an accessory that is familiar and trusted from a security standpoint that will be used for much else than voice communications. However, mobile payments alone are not sufficient to fully leverage the potential of the mobile phone as an essential and trusted personal accessory. Electronic tickets enabled by mobile phones comprise an important class of everyday consumer transactions, fulfilling the requirement of governmental organizations to easily provide tickets to events, public museums, public transportation, etc.

A ticket is considered as a proof of access or usage rights to a particular service. Electronic ticketing enabled by mobile devices:

- Eliminates paper tickets with digital codes displayed on mobile terminals
- Provides instant delivery
- Allows the usage of direct mobile marketing to offer discounts and promotions
- Offers lower costs such as paper, ink, printers, and manpower
- Adds convenience
- Protects the purchase due to the fact that there is no paper ticket to lose and a virtual record is tried to the user's mobile terminal number
- Provides versatile real-time database to compile reports and track attendance and solutions can be applied to all aspects of theatre or venue, including for example parking, vending machines, and concessions

These tickets exist in two different types (Mobile Electronic Transactions, 2003), regarding the place that each ticket resides:

Figure 12. E-ticketing business process

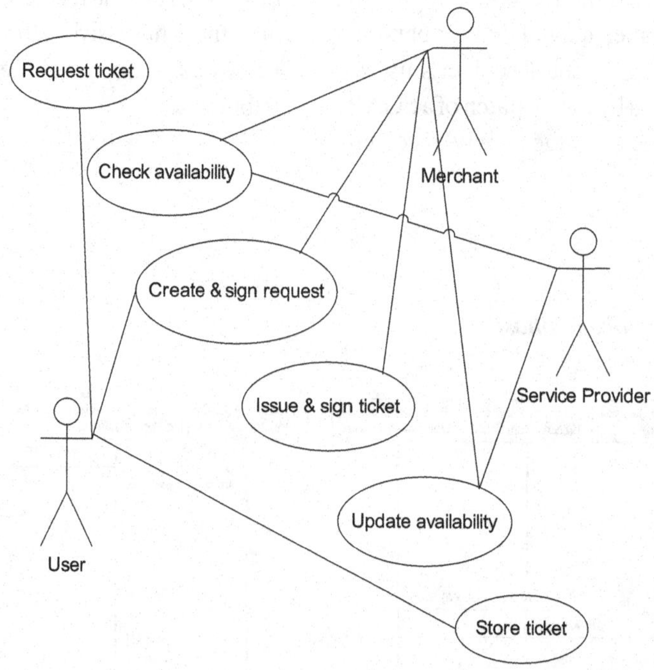

- **Virtual tickets:** Where the proof resides in a ticket issuer's server in which case the redemption of the ticket consists of online connection and user authentication to the server, at the usage point
- **PTD tickets:** Where the proof is an electronic data object carried in a mobile device in which an online connection to the ticket issuer's server is not required at the usage point.
- Actually, the possession of the particular data object is sufficient proof of access rights.

In this chapter, the electronic tickets that are generated are equivalent of physical tickets, as used in our everyday life. In particular, these tickets belong to the second type of tickets, as previously described. The ticketing system accommodates both single and multiple usages. However, the payment aspect of ticketing is not addressed in this chapter as it is considered largely independent of the ticketing aspect. The independence of this mobile ticketing architecture from the particularities of the various payment methods, which are out of the scope or can be themselves electronic services that can be offered from this platform, allows the adoption of multiple alternatives (credit cards, pre-paid cards, Web/mobile banking, or even charge of the user's bill)

As shown in the previous use case diagram, the user-citizen accesses the ticketing service and requests availability through the presented information from the merchant. The merchant checks for availability through the service provider, which is actually the governmental organization, and answers to the citizen.

The user in turn, fills in the request form, signs the form, and requests the specific ticket. The merchant issues the ticket and sends it to the citizen, informing the governmental organization for the previous issuance in order to update availability. The citizen stores the ticket in his or her mobile device and keeps it for further usage.

Additional Requirements

Nowadays, despite that 3G handheld devices provide additional functionality, mobile users have limited capability in changing contexts. Traditional techniques, which sometimes rely on powerful processors and extensive amounts of memory, are not suitable for wireless platforms, creating the need for new, wireless-specific technologies.

Furthermore, in the e/m-ticketing service there is the need to provide strong security mechanisms in the generated content and not only on the transferred messages (Josang & Sanderud, 2003). Indeed, the received ticket has to preserve the security credentials that strongly authenticate the merchant that issued the ticket. Similarly, the request of the citizen may need to preserve its confidentiality and integrity in specific parts that contain sensitive information regarding the payment procedure, which probably should be kept secret from the merchant or other intermediary entities. The enterprise service described in the following paragraphs has to take into account these additional requirements.

Main Service Components

The e/m-ticketing service operates as an enterprise service within the architecture. The WSDL description of the endpoint of the service can be published in a UDDI directory through the publication and query service. This allows searching for the specific enterprise service and comprehension of the messages this service understands so that messages can be sent and received from it.

The enterprise service is running as a Web service in the architecture and it is managed by the orchestration service. It communicates with the following entities:

- Secure mobile browsers through the access service

- The actual service provider hosting the repository for e/m-tickets and receipts. This communication may be direct (i.e., the repository is a database directly controlled by the enterprise service or indirect through an existing infrastructure support service of the architecture)
- The forwarding service of the architecture, in order to securely dispatch the ticket to its final destination
- The key and certificate management service for validation of keys and certificates

In order to promote interoperability with respect to the multiple mobile devices existing today and their different operation platforms, several third-party, lightweight XML parsers are used.

In the presented Web services platform, kXML by Enhydra (Enhydra, 2005) offers both Simple API for XML (SAX) (Megginson, 2005), and limited document object model (DOM) (Le Hégaret, 2004) capabilities. The implementation of the various Web services uses the special utility of kXML, called kSOAP (Enhydra, 2005), for parsing SOAP messages (Table 1). The integration of mobile Web services, using kXML technology, allows business logic and data to reside and be executed at the most appropriate point on the network, as demanded by each service type. As a result, business processes are directly exposed to mobile services in a highly standardised and extensible manner.

However, the proposed platform offers the opportunity, to use other lightweight available technologies for the integration of the required Web services and secondly to interoperate with such implementations. Such a technology is the gSOAP Web services toolkit for C and C++, which is an open source development environment for Web services (Van Engelen, Gupta, & Pant, 2003). gSOAP supports pure C, which makes it essential for many embedded systems kernels and systems-oriented applications developed in C, providing performance that can surpass in some cases the corresponding performance of Java RMI and IIOP. Finally, the RPC compiler (Srinivasan, 1995) generates compact code and the runtime environment of the SOAP/XML engine has a small memory footprint, which is very important for the case of the mobile environment (Van Engelen, 2003).

Additionally, transformations in various e/m-ticketing formats may be performed by using the message transformation services of the architecture. The more ticket formats supported, the higher the level of interoperability.

Furthermore, as mentioned in the previous paragraph regarding the requirements of e/m-ticketing service, the need of an additional security level for the content itself in order for the last to preserve the credentials of the involved entities, is fulfilled with the integration of a mobile module, which provides the following:

Table 1. kSOAP performance (Source: Nokia 9210)

	MIDlet Size	Request Setup	Request	Request Size	Reply Size
SOAP	~ 48 kb	~ 12.0 sec	~ 3 sec	529 bytes	594 bytes
Non-SOAP	~ 5 kb	~ 4.7 sec	~ 2.1 sec	18 bytes	34 bytes
%Overhead of SOAP	960 %	255 %	181 %	2939 %	1747 %

- Generation and validation of XML digital signatures for mobile XML content
- Encryption/Decryption mechanisms for the previous content

This validation procedure is introduced in two different ways. The first involves the downloading of the certification revocation lists (CRLs) from the PKI of the presented platform and the execution of complex cryptographic operations in the mobile device (Karantjias, Kaliontzoglou, Sklavos, & Polemi, 2004). However, in most cases this is not feasible in many mobile devices that are used today. The second solution is the integration and existence of a suitable interface that is used in the mobile device in order to communicate with an XKMS server of the PKI. This second solution suits more in the mobile environment because many complex and heavy functionalities are lifted from the mobile terminal (Kasera, Mizikovsky, & Sundaram, 2003).

Entities and Actors

This section presents the entities that may be involved in a typical ticketing issuance and delivery and their roles. These entities, as well as their relationships are depicted in Figure 13.

The actors that take part are:

a. **The citizen:** The citizen is the consumer of any government service supported by the architecture. It has to communicate with the TTP in order to get the proper security credentials.
b. **The merchant:** The merchant is the entity that hosts the main service platform and offers the required e/m-ticketing service, as well as other services, to mobile citizens. It has to communicate just like the citizen with the TTP to get the proper security credentials, as well as with the actual service provider described next in order to the required info regarding the ticket availability.

Figure 13. E-ticketing actors

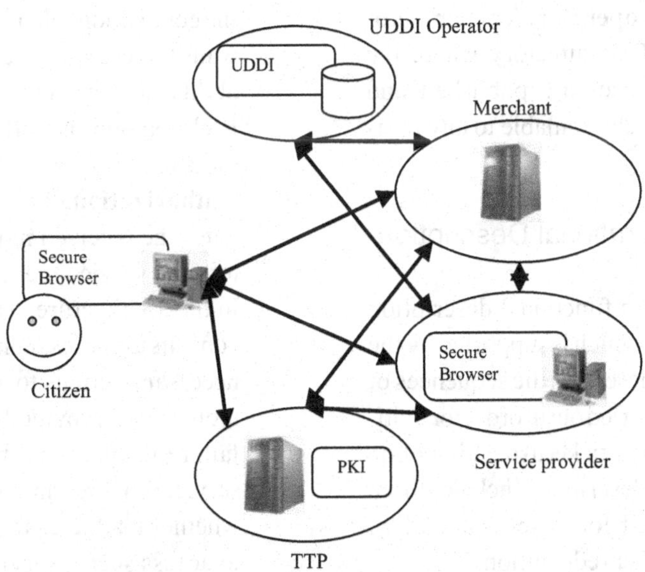

c. **The service provider:** The service provider is the governmental organization that provides the e/m actual service, which in our case is the ticket provider. This entity could represent a public museum, stadium, or any governmental organization wishing to provide tickets to its citizens. The service provider communicates with the TTP to get the security credentials with the merchant in order to provide ticket availability and with the client at the time of ticket usage from the last mentioned. The platform could be hosted by the service provider (and therefore the roles of merchant and provider would be one and the same), but this is not a strong requirement. Some mobile and electronic service modules are needed to complement and communicate with the main components of the Web services platform.
d. **The TTP:** Before any secure messaging can take place, all participants, need to have established an adequate security framework with trusted third parties (TTPs). The required TTPs are at a minimum a CA and a RA offering the PKI services of registration, certification, and revocation status information with OCSP, as well as TSA, offering standard based time stamping services.
e. **UDDI directory operator:** This operator hosts a public UDDI directory where the various Web services are published and thus become publicly available to any user-citizen.

Functional and Operational Description

This section presents the functional description of a typical transaction, which is supported by the enterprise service and describes the sequences of the operations that are carried out in order for a citizen to receive an electronic ticket using his mobile device. This functional description includes three different phases: request for ticket availability, ticket issuance, and ticket redemption.

The main prerequisite for the successful operation of the service is that an implementation of the e-government architecture of section "A Generic Secure E-Government Architecture" has been deployed at both the merchant side and the governmental organization, which is the actual service provider. Additionally, we suppose that the citizen, who wishes to get an electronic ticket using his mobile device, has installed the required applications in order to structure the appropriate Web services for communicating with the e-government architecture, as well as the application module that is required for providing cryptographic mechanisms in the content.

The initial process that takes place is the request for ticket availability as follows:

a. **Selection of service, authentication, and submission of request for availability:** The citizen uses his mobile terminal to log on directly to the e-government architecture of the merchant and submits a signed request for ticket availability. This is performed through a secure browser. The access service of the architecture authenticates the user using utilizing proper calls to the keys and certificates management service. If the authentication procedure ends successfully, the connection remains open and the citizen waits for receiving the requested ticket availability. In every other case, the connection is closed and the citizen receives a failure message.
b. **Authorization:** The access service propagates the received request to the actual enterprise service that runs as a Web service in the architecture. This enterprise service consults the access control service to take the necessary actions to authorize the citizen's request and provide him with a success of failure result. In particular, the enterprise service retrieves the request form and checks whether it adheres to a policy permitting it to access such a service.

Figure 14. Availability request submission and checking

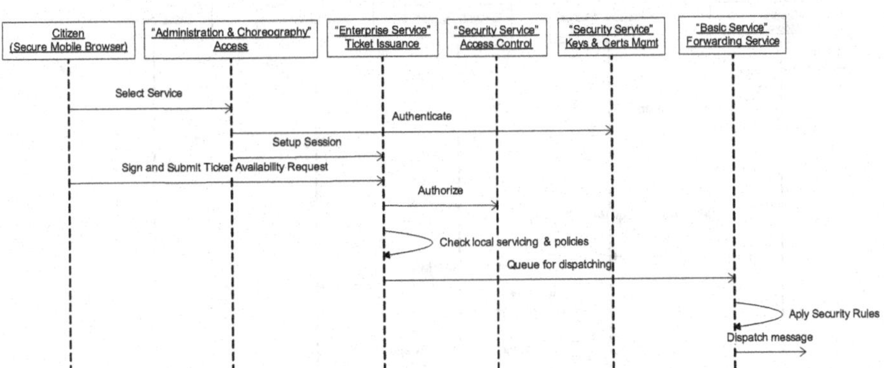

Figure 15. Request validation and availability response

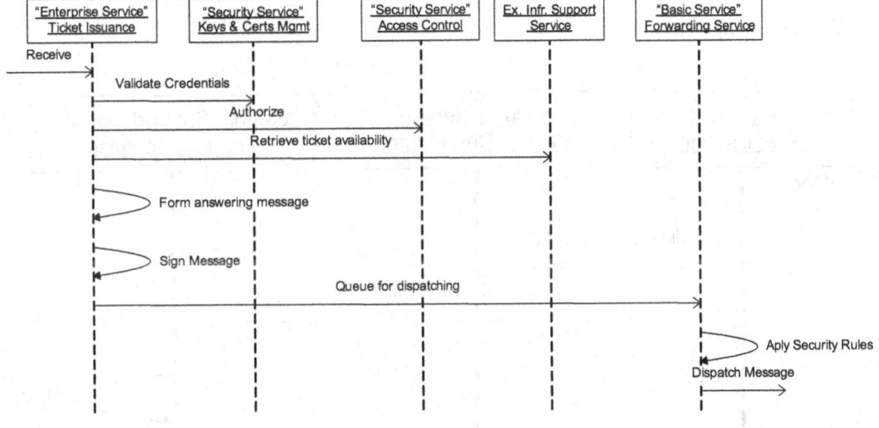

c. **Communication with the actual service provider:** The merchant digitally signs the submitted request for ticket availability and forwards it to the actual service provider. The last entity validates any security credentials applied to the received message, using the information acquired by the keys and certificates service in the architecture. This security service performs credential validation through an XKMS interface. If this process is successful, the forwarded citizens' request is extracted from the message and the service provider checks for ticket availability in its database through the "Existing infrastructure support services" of the architecture, as described in the section "A Generic Secure E-Government Architecture." It then structures an

Figure 16. Service access and ticket formulation

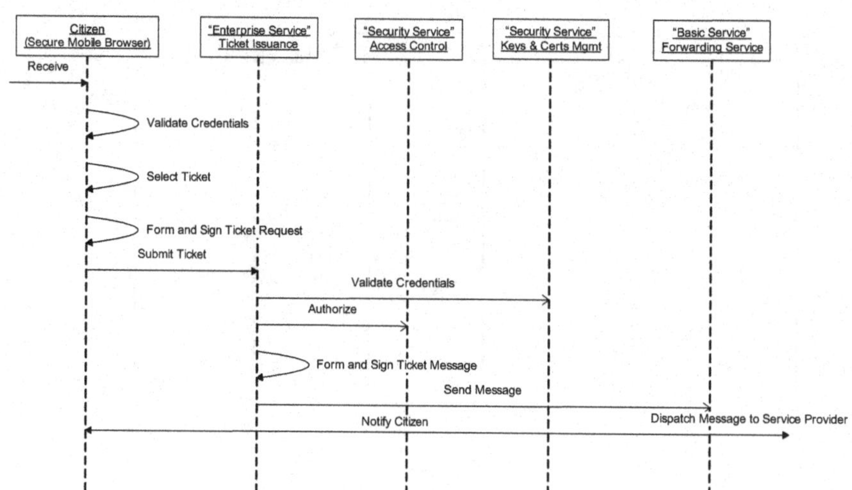

Figure 17. Availability update

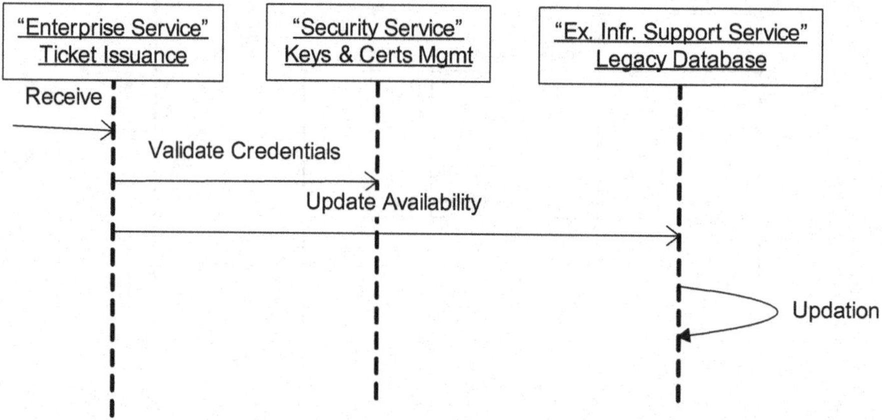

answered message providing the required information, digitally signs it, and sends it to the merchant.

d. **Answer retrieval:** The merchant validates any security credentials applied to the received message following the previously described procedure (through an XKMS interface), digitally signs the received message, and forwards it to the citizen. The citizen following the same validating procedure on the security credentials of the message is now capable of choosing the desirable ticket.

Some of the steps described so far may be optional, especially in cases where the citizen does not have to choose a specific ticket. The

Figure 18. Ticket redemption

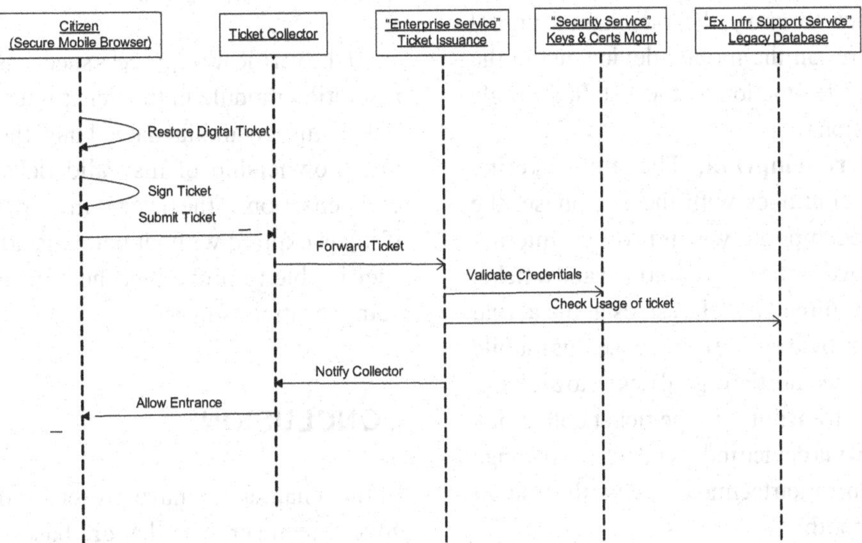

ticketing process continues with the second phase, the issuance of the ticket, as follows:

a. **Selection of desirable ticket and submission of the ticket request:** The citizen, using his mobile device and the advanced browser of it, is able to choose the desirable ticket and automatically structure the appropriate request of the selected ticket. It performs cryptographic mechanisms on the message; digitally signing the message and encrypting the sensitive parts of it, especially in cases where payment info is included (e.g., credit cards info, bank accounts, etc.). The citizen sends the ticket request to the merchant, waiting to receive the final ticket.
b. **Issuance of the ticket and update of ticket availability:** The merchant receives the final ticket request from the citizen and performs cryptographic mechanisms on it, validating the signature of the sender, and decrypting the parts of the message that correspond to his private key. He then initializes the payment procedure, which as previously mentioned is out of the scope of the described service, but it could be another service integrated in the architecture. The successful finish of this procedure is continued from the desirable ticket issuance. The merchant using the additional mobile module that provides security mechanisms on the content, as described in the previous paragraph, adds his secure credentials (his digital signature) on the XML ticket as well as on the message that includes the first, and sends it to the citizen. Simultaneously communicates with actual ticket provider, which in the described case is a governmental organization, informing it for the citizens' ticket final selection, in order for message receiver to update the availability.
c. **Receipt and storage of ticket**: The citizen receives the desirable ticket and validates the security credentials on message as well

as the ticket itself. If the received message is valid, he then stores the XML ticket, which continues to carry the merchant's digital signature, on the mobile device, using the appropriate functions of the installed mobile application.

d. **Ticket redemption**: The e/m-ticketing service continues with the last phase, the ticket redemption, which involves interaction between the mobile citizen and a ticket issuer terminal, which resides at the actual service provider. The citizen uses his mobile device to restore the digital ticket, to digitally sign and transmit it to the ticket collector's terminal via device independent, short-range communication technologies like the Infared or Bluetooth.

In particular, the service provider operates on the ticket issuer's terminal the module that provides security mechanisms on pure content. This module is able to receive the digitally signed XML document and to provide cryptographic mechanisms on it (e.g., in this case verifies the merchant's digital signature on the received message). Any related revocation material (e.g., CRLs) is already preinstalled on the device and is updated periodically in case XKMS has not been adopted for the communication with the corresponding PKI. If the device is connected with the main architecture, the XKMS interface is used instead.

If the signature is valid, the ticket issuer checks whether the ticket has been used again in order to prevent the use of copied tickets, receives clearance from the local server, updates its usage information and makes the mobile citizen able of using the ticket (e.g., entering an event, traveling, etc.).

In the case of disputes where the ticket appears invalid and the mobile citizen claims otherwise, the last has to vindicate that the XML ticket stored in his mobile device is signed with the following two valid signatures:

- The mobile citizens' signature
- The merchants' signature

If the verification process succeeds, the dispute resolution module in the ticket issuer checks the tickets' usage and its data. Thus, the citizen can prove ownership of his valid ticket and claim compensation. If the ticket is invalid (for example, if it has expired without being used) then the issuer is able to prove that the citizen's claim for compensation is false.

CONCLUSION

In this chapter, we have presented three new e-government services that are based on the Web services technology and leverage the functionality of an existing e-government architecture, with the purpose of filling in a gap of the lack of "killer applications" for e-government and presenting useful case study material to similar endeavours of public organizations in the future. Each service respects a set of common e-government requirements as well as some additional requirements imposed by its specific business goals and legal restrictions.

ACKNOWLEDGMENT

The authors would like to thank the E.C. for its support in funding the e-mayor project (IST-2004-507217) and all the members of the project consortium for valuable discussions.

REFERENCES

Business Application Software Developers Association (BASDA). (2005). *eBIS-XML Specifications ver. (3.05).* Retrieved from basda.net/twiki/pub/Core/DownloadTheSuite/eBIS-XML-3.05.zip

CEN/ISSS e-invoicing Focus Group. (2003). *Report and recommendations of CEN/ISSS e-invoicing focus group on standards and developments on electronic invoicing*. Retrieved from www.cenorm.be/isss/Projects/e-invoicing

e-mayor consortium D2.1. (2004). Deliverable D2.1: Municipal services–Analysis, requirements, and usage scenarios. *e-mayor project* (IST-2004-507217).

e-mayor consortium D3.1. (2004). Deliverable D3.1: e-mayor–System design. *e-mayor project* (IST-2004-507217).

e-mayor. (2004). Electronic and secure municipal administration for European citizens. E.C 6th Framework Programme, IST-2004-507217. Retrieved from www.emayor.org

Enhydra. (2005). *Open source for eBusiness*. Retrieved from http://www.enhydra.org

ETSI. (2002). ETSI TS 101 903 V1.1.1 - XML Advanced Electronic Signatures (XAdES). (Technical Specification.)

German Federal Ministry of Interior. (2003). *SAGA—Standards and Architectures for e-government Applications,* (version 2.0.)

Hartman, B., Flinn, D., Beszosov, K., & Kawamoto, S. (2003). *Mastering Web services security*. Indianapolis, IN: Wiley Publishing.

Hunter, R. (2004). E-government schema guidelines for XML. *Office of the eEnvoy,* (v3.1.) Retrieved from http://www.govtalk.gov.uk/documents/schema-guidelines-3_1.pdf

IDA BC. (2004). *IDA eProcurement XML schemas initiative—eOrdering and e-invoicing phases,* (v 2.0.) Retrieved from http://europa.eu.int/idabc/en/document/4721/5874

Josang, A., & Sanderud, G. (2003). Security in mobile communications: Challenges and opportunities. In *Proceedings of the Australasian Information Security Workshop* (AISW2003) Conference on ACSW Frontiers (Vol. 21, pp.43-48).

Kaliontzoglou, A., Boutsi, P., Mavroudis, I., & Polemi, D. (2003). Secure e-invoicing service based on Web services. In *Proceedings of the 1st Hellenic Conference on Electronic Democracy,* Athens, Greece.

Kaliontzoglou, A., Sklavos, P., Karantjias, T., & Polemi, D. (2004). A secure e-government platform architecture for small to medium sized public organizations. *Electronic Commerce Research & Applications, 4*(2), 174-186.

Kaliontzoglou, A., Boutsi, P., & Polemi, D. (2005). E-invoke: Secure e-invoicing based on Web services. Electronic Commerce Research, Kluwer (accepted for publication).

Karantjias, A., Kaliontzoglou, A., Sklavos, P., & Polemi, D. (2004). Secure applications for the Chambers of Commerce: Functionality and technical assessment. In *Proceedings of EUROSEC 2004 15th Forum on Information Systems and Security,* Paris.

Kasera, S., Mizikovsky, S., Sundaram, G. (2003). On securely enabling intermediary-based services and performance enhancements for wireless mobile users. In *Proceedings of the 2003 ACM workshop on Wireless security* (pp. 61-68).

Kavvadias, G., Spanos, E., & Tambouris, E. (Eds.). (2002). Deliverable D2.3.1 GovML syntax and filters implementation. *E-gov project* (IST-2000-28471). Retrieved from http://www.e-gov-project.org/e-govsite/e-gov_D231.zip

Kent, A. (2003). Address and personal details schema. *Office of the eEnvoy,* (v1.3) Retrieved from http://www.govtalk.gov.uk/documents/APD-v1-3.zip

Le Hégaret, P. (2004). *W3C document object model–DOM*. Retrieved from http://www.w3.org/DOM/

Meadows, B., & Seaburg, L. (2004). *Universal Business Language UBL 1.0. Official OASIS Standard.* Retrieved from http://docs.oasis-open.org/ubl/cd-UBL-1.0.zip

Megginson, D. (2005). *Simple API for XML–SAX.* Retrieved from http://www.saxproject.org/

Meneklis, B., Kaliotzoglou, A., Polemi, D., & Douligeris, C. (2005). Applying the ISO RM-ODP standard in e-government. In *Proceedings of E-government: Towards Electronic Democracy: International Conference,* Bolzano, Italy (LNCS 3416, pp. 213). Springer-Verlag GmbH.

Mobile Electronic Transactions. (2003). *MeT white paper on mobile ticketing.* Retrieved from http://www.mobiletransaction.org/

Nash, A., Duane, B., Brink, D., & Joseph, C. (2001). *PKI: Implementing & managing eSecurity.* Emeryville, CA: McGraw-Hill Osborn Media Publishing.

Rowell, M. (2002). OAGIS—A "Canonical" business language. *Open Applications Group, white paper,* (version 1.0.) Retrieved from www.openapplications.org/downloads/whitepapers/whitepaperdocs/20020429_OAGIS_A_Canonical_Business_Langugage-PDF.zip

Srinivasan, R. (1995). *Remote procedure call protocol specification version 2 (RPC) (RFC1831).* Retrieved from http://asg.web.cmu.edu/rfc/rfc1831.html

The European Parliament. (2001, December 20). *Council Directive 2001/115/EC, amending Directive 77/388/EEC with view to simplifying, modernizing, and harmonizing the conditions laid down for invoicing in respect of value added tax.*

UK Office of the eEnvoy. (2004). *UK GovTalk portal.* Retrieved from www.govtalk.gov.uk

Van Engelen, R. (2003). Pushing the SOAP envelope with Web services for scientific computing. In *Proceedings of the International Conference on Web services (ICWS)* (pp. 346-352).

Van Engelen, R., Gupta, G., & Pant, S. (2003). Developing Web services for C and C++. *In IEEE Internet Computing* (pp. 53-61).

xCBL.org. (2003). *XML common business library version 4.00* (xCBL v4.00). Retrieved from www.xcbl.org/xcbl40/xcbl40.html

This work was previously published in Secure E-Government Web Services, edited by A. Mitrakas, P. Hengeveld, D. Polemi, and J. Gamper, pp. 29-62, copyright 2007 by IGI Publishing, formerly known as Idea Group Publishing (an imprint of IGI Global).

Chapter XI
Grid Business Process: Case Study

Asif Akram
CCLRC Daresbury Laboratory, UK

Rob Allan
CCLRC Daresbury Laboratory, UK

Sanjay Chaudhary
Dhirubhai Ambani Institute of Information and Communication Technology, India

Prateek Jain
Dhirubhai Ambani Institute of Information and Communication Technology, India

Zakir Laliwala
Dhirubhai Ambani Institute of Information and Communication Technology, India

ABSTRACT

This chapter presents a "Case Study" based on the distributed market. The requirements of this Grid Business Process are more demanding than any typical business process deployed within a single organization or enterprise. Recently, different specifications built on top of Web service standards have originated from the Grid paradigm to address limitations of stateless Web services. These emerging specifications are evaluated in the first part of the chapter to capture requirements of a dynamic business process, that is, Business Process Grid. In second part of the chapter, a case study with different use cases is presented to simulate various scenarios. The abstract discussion and requirements of the case study is followed by the actual implementation. The implementation is meant for the proof-of-concept rather than fully functional application.

GRID SPECIFICATIONS AND STANDARDS

Web services architecture lacks support for the state, event and notification, and resource lifecycle management to share and coordinate diverse resources of real life in dynamic "virtual organizations" (Foster, 2002). Recent convergence between Web services and the Grid computing community (Czajkowski, Ferguson, Foster, et al., 2004) toward the refactoring and evolution of Grid standards aimed at aligning OGSI functions with the emerging consensus on Web services architecture (Booth, Haas, McCabe, et al., 2004). This effort has produced two important sets of specifications: WS-RF (WS-ResourceFramework, 2005) and WS-Notification (WS-Notification, 2005). These specifications essentially retain all the functional capabilities present in OGSI, and at the same time built on broadly adopted concepts of Web services.

Web Services Addressing

The WS-Addressing specification defines a standard for incorporating message addressing information into SOAP (SOAP, 2000) messages. SOAP does not provide a standard way to specify where a message is going, how to return a response, or where to report an error. WS-Addressing introduces two new constructs for Web services vocabulary: *Endpoint References* and *Message Addressing Properties.*

Endpoint Reference (EPR)

Endpoint References are a new model for describing the Web service destination and service-specific attributes within an address for routing the message to a service or for use by the destination service itself. An endpoint reference is a data structure that is defined to encapsulate all the information required to reach a service endpoint at runtime.

A significant aspect of an endpoint reference is the ability to attach data from any XML namespace via Reference Properties or Reference Parameters. Both of these elements are collections of properties and values used to incorporate elements from different XML namespace into the endpoint reference. The key distinction between a Reference Property and a Reference Parameter is not the format but the intended usage. The reference properties help to identify the resource to be used during service invocation. The reference parameters wrap the information required for successful invocation of the service, which is not required to identify the resource.

The following example shows an endpoint reference for a service that simulates the personal address book. The service's URI is specified in the Address element. A reference property indicates the type of the resource, that is, family, friend, colleague, and so forth. A reference parameter specifies the information required, that is, address, home number, mobile number, and so forth:

Listing 1. Example of endpoint reference

```
<wsa:EndpointReference xmlns:wsa="..." xmlns:
example="...">
 <wsa:Address>http://example.com/contact</wsa:
Address>
 <wsa:ReferenceProperties>
   <example:contactType>Family</example:contactType >
 </wsa:ReferenceProperties>
 <wsa:ReferenceParameters>
   <example:detail>Mobile</example: detail >
 </wsa:ReferenceParameters>
</wsa:EndpointReference>
```

Message Addressing Properties

WS-Addressing introduces a set of message headers providing information about a message by incorporating delivery, reply-to, and fault handler addressing information into a SOAP envelope necessary to support a rich bidirectional and asynchronous interaction. Most of the fields are optional; the only required fields are the "To" and "Action" fields, each of which specifies a URI. The "To" header identify the destination of the message and "Action" header provides additional information on how to process the message. The value of Action URI is related to the WSDL operation to which the message is related. In the absence of Action URI in the WSDL, the Action URI in the EPR is target namespace and the operation called. The following example illustrates a typical SOAP message using WS-Addressing:

Listing 2. SOAP message

```
<S:Envelope xmlns:S="http://www.w3.org/2003/05/soap-envelope"
      xmlns:wsa="http://www.w3.org/2004/12/addressing">
  <S:Header>
    <wsa:MessageID>
     http://......
    </wsa:MessageID>
    <wsa:ReplyTo>
      <wsa:Address>http://client.application</wsa:Address>
    </wsa:ReplyTo>
    <wsa:FaultTo>
      <wsa:Address>http://logging.application</wsa:Address>
    </wsa:FaultTo>
    <wsa:To>http://service.to.invoke</wsa:To>
    <wsa:Action>http:// method.to.invoke</wsa:Action>
  </S:Header>
  <S:Body>
    <!-- The message body of the SOAP request appears here -->
  </S:Body>
</S:Envelope>
```

When a service receives a message addressed using WS-Addressing, it will also include WS-Addressing headers in the reply message. The *Message ID* of the original message becomes a *RelatesTo* element in the reply's address. At present, the only supported relationship type is "Reply." If a client is sending multiple Web services requests and receiving asynchronous responses, possibly over different transports, the *RelatesTo* element provides a standard way to associate incoming replies with their corresponding requests.

Web Service Resource Framework (WS-RF)

Web Service Resource Framework specifies various aspects related to stateful Web services. It defines message exchange pattern as to how stateful Web services should be created, addressed, and destroyed. (Foster, Czajkowski, et al., 2005). WS-RF defines conventions within the context of established Web Services standards for managing "state" so that applications can reliably share changing information, and discover, inspect, and interact with stateful resources in a standard and interoperable way. WS-RF is a collection of four specifications, namely WS-ResourceProperties, WS-ResourceLifetime, WS-ServiceGroup, and WS-BaseFaults. It also refers to two related specifications, namely WS-Notification and WS-Addressing.

WS-ResourceProperties (WS-ResourceProperties, 2006)

WS-ResourceProperties describes properties of stateful resources and its association with Web services as the *Implied Resource Pattern*. In the *Implied Resource Pattern*, SOAP messages include a component that identifies a stateful resource to be used in the execution of the message exchange. The composition of a stateful resource and a Web service under the Implied Resource Pattern is termed as a WS-Resource. The specification standardizes the definition of the properties of a WS-Resource as a part of the Web service interface in terms of a resource properties document. The declaration of the WS-Resource's properties represents a view on the resource's state in XML format.

This specification standardized set of message exchanges for the retrieval, modification, update, and deletion of the contents of resource properties and supporting subscription for notification when the value of a resource property changes. The set of properties defined in the resource properties document associated with the service interface defines the constraints on the valid contents of these message exchanges.

WS-ResourceLifetime (WS-ResourceLifetime, 2006)

The lifetime of a WS-Resource is defined as the period between its instantiation and its destruction. The WS-ResourceLifetime specification standardizes the means by which a WS-Resource can be destroyed either immediately or at a scheduled time. The scheduled destruction of the WS-Resource means that a resource may be destroyed after a certain period of time. When that time expires, the WS-Resource may self-destruct without requiring an explicit destroy request message from a client. The specification also supports extension of the scheduled termination time of a WS-Resource at runtime.

WS-ResourceLifetime defines a standard message exchange by which a service requestor can destroy, query, establish, and renew a scheduled termination time for the WS-Resource. To support the standard message exchange pattern, WS-ResourceLifetime declares different methods which are normally implemented by the WS-RF engine. The specification also supports the notification to interested parties when the resource is destroyed.

WS-ServiceGroup (WS-ServiceGroup, 2006)

The WS-ServiceGroup provides a description of a general-purpose WS-Resource which aggregates information from multiple WS-Resources or Web Services for domain specific purposes. The aggregated information can be used as a directory in which the descriptive abstracts of the individual WS-Resources and Web Services can be queried to identify useful entries. The WS-ServiceGroup itself is a stateful Web Service that is a collection of other Web Services or WS-Resources and the information that pertains to them.

The specification standardized message exchange for registration or addition of new members, membership rules, duration of the membership, contents advertised by the members, and support for notification when a new member is added or when details of the existing member are modified. The membership in the ServiceGroup is flexible and it can be either through ServiceGroupRegisteration defined by specification or through any other means. Details of each member in the ServiceGroup are in the form of WS-ResourceProperties, which wraps the EndpointReference and the contents of the member.

Membership in the group can be constrained and controlled through policies. Controlled membership enables requestors to form meaningful queries against the contents of the WS-ServiceGroup. The membership of the service group can be restricted to only those members which implement any particular interfaces or declare any specific WS-Resource model. The ServiceGroup resource property document may contain zero MembershipContentRule child elements. When no MembershipContentRule elements are specified, the members of the ServiceGroup are unconstrained. The element MembershipContentRule in the resource property document of the ServiceGroup has following two attributes:

MemberInterfaces: This attribute is optional and declares the list of interfaces which must be implemented by each "entry" in the ServcieGroup.

ContentElements: This attribute declares the list of WS-ResourceProperties, which must be part of the WS-Resource model for each entry. ContentElements is a mandatory attribute in the element MembershipContentRule, but can have no value.

```
<wssg:MembershipContentRule
MemberInterface="ns2:X" ContentElements=""/>
<wssg:MembershipContentRule
MemberInterfaces="ns3:Y" ContentElements="ns3:RP1
ns3:RP2" />
```

MembershipContentRule in the first statement expects members to implement "ns2: X" portType; where as second MembershipContentRule expects not only implementation of "ns3:Y," but also exposing two ResourceProperties. Multiple MembershipContentRule elements have the "or" relation, which means the members should fulfil at least one of the membership criteria completely. A member fulfilling different membership criteria can appear multiple times in the ServiceGroup.

WS-BaseFaults (WS-BaseFaults, 2006)

A typical Web services application often uses interfaces defined by others. Fault management in such an application is more difficult when each interface uses a different convention for representing common information in fault messages. Web services fault messages declared in a common way improves support for problem determination and fault management. It is also more likely that common tooling can be created to assist in the handling of faults described uniformly. WS-BaseFaults defines an XML Schema type for a base fault, along with rules for how this fault type is used by Web services. It standardizes the way in which errors are reported by defining a standard base fault type and procedure for use of this fault type inside WSDL. WS-BaseFault defines different standard elements corresponding to the time when the fault occurred (*Timestamp*), the endpoint of the Web service that generated the fault (*OriginatorReference)*, error code (*ErrorCode*), error description (*Description*), the cause for the fault (*FaultCause*), and any arbitrary information required to rectify the fault.

Use of Base Faults in WSDL 1.1

The WS-BaseFaults specification recommends that each custom fault type must extend the base fault. Each distinct type of base fault associated with a WSDL [WSDL 1.1] operation should be listed as a separate fault response in the WSDL operation definition. The extended faults must follow the following rules:

1. There must be a distinct XML Schema complexType that extends WS-RF bf:BaseFaultType, which represents this fault's distinct type. This extended fault complexType can contain additional attributes or elements.
2. An element must be defined for this distinct fault, whose type is the complexType of the distinct fault, as defined in step 1. This is the requirement of Document/literal style Web Services, which are compliant to the WS-I Basic Profile.
3. A WSDL message must be defined for this distinct fault. This message must have one part. The WSDL part must have an "element" attribute and this must refer by fully qualified name to the element of this distinct fault, as defined in step 2. This is once again the requirement of Document/literal style Web Services, which are compliant to WS-I Basic Profile.
4. The WSDL operation must have a fault element for this distinct fault. The value of the WSDL fault element's name attribute should be the same as the NCName of the fault element defined in step 2, although it may ignore this rule (e.g., to avoid NCName collisions between fault elements defined in different namespaces). The value of the WSDL fault element's message attribute must refer by fully qualified name to the WSDL message

element of this distinct fault, as defined in step 3.

Web Services-Notification

The Event-driven, or Notification-based, interaction pattern is a commonly used pattern for interobject communications. Different domains provide this support in varying extent; "Publish/Subscribe" systems provided by Message Oriented Middleware vendors; support for "Observable/Observer" pattern in the programming languages; and "Remote Eventing" in the RMI and CORBA. Due to the stateless nature of Web Services, the Web Service paradigm has no notion of Notifications, which limits the applicability of Web Services for complicated application development. WS-RF defines conventions for managing "state" so that applications can reliably share changing information, discover, inspect, and interact with stateful resources in standard and interoperable ways, bringing Notification-based interaction patterns in Web Services domain. WS-Notification (WSN) [14] is set of three separate specifications (WS-BaseNotification, WS-BrokeredNotification, and WS-Topics), but its usefulness beyond WS-RF is limited.

WS-BaseNotification (WS-BaseNotification, 2006)

The WS-BaseNotification is the base specification on which all the other specifications in the family of WSN depend. It defines the normative Web services interfaces for two of the important roles in the notification pattern, namely, the NotificationProducer and NotificationConsumer roles. Strictly speaking this specification defines many different roles and any single entity can fulfill the criteria of different roles. This specification includes standard message exchanges to be implemented by service providers that wish to act in these roles, along with operational requirements expected of them. Latest WS-BaseNotification specification supports "Pull" based notification for resource constrained devices, yet none of the WS-RF framework supports those recommendations, and it is not discussed.

NotificationProducer: A NotificationProducer is an entity which monitors the state of different resources and detects various types of events. Whenever there is any change in the state of a resource or occurrence of any new event, which may qualify for certain actions, the NotificationProducer notifies the relevant entities. These entities may be only interested in the changes, or may initiate the series of events to accommodate changes.

The NotificationProducer must support any appropriate mechanism that lets a potential Subscriber to discover which resources and events are monitored by a NotificationProducer. These resources and events monitored by the NotificationProducer are called Topics. For this purpose, each NotificationProducer must support resource properties (Listing 3) defined in the specification other than any custom resource properties. Out of these resource properties, the "TopicSet" is the collection of topics supported by the NotificationProducer expressed, as a single XML element as described in WS-Topics.

Listing 3. Resource properties supported by notification producer

```
<xsd:element ref="wsnt:TopicExpression"
minOccurs="0" maxOccurs="unbounded" />
<xsd:element ref="wsnt:FixedTopicSet" minOccurs="0"
maxOccurs="1" />
<xsd:element ref="wsnt:TopicExpressionDialect"
minOccurs="0" maxOccurs="unbounded" />
<xsd:element ref="wstop:TopicSet" minOccurs="0"
maxOccurs="1" />
```

The WS-BaseNotification specification standardized various message exchanges for NotificationProducer to support subscription for notification, querying the last message, renewal, cancellation, pause, and resumption of subscription. These methods heavily rely on Topics declared in the TopicSet.

NotificationConsumer: An entity which may have interest in the elements monitored by the NotificationProducer for appropriate actions is called a NotificationConsumer. A NotificationConsumer can subscribe to receive notifications directly from a NotificationProducer, supporting only direct and point to point notifications. A NotificationConsumer discovers the NotificationProducer and browses the Topics for subscription (i.e., sending Subscribe request or invoking Subscribe operation). A NotificationConsumer must implement the callback methods to receive the notification. Normally, the NotificationConsumer implements *Notify* callback operation, which is invoked by the NotificationProducer. The NotificationConsumer must support one of the two or both NotificationMessage formats, or at least should be in position to handle the form of Notification it has requested for the given Subscription.

NotificationMessage: The NotificationProducer must also clarify the supported formats for the notification messages. When NotificationProducer has a notification to distribute, it matches the notification against the subscription list and issues the notification to the subscriber which is registered for the notification of such event. WS-Notification allows a NotificationProducer to send a NotificationMessage to a NotificationConsumer in one of two ways:

1. The NotificationProducer may simply send the raw NotificationMessage (i.e., the application-specific content) to the NotificationConsumer.
2. The NotificationProducer may send the NotificationMessage data using the Notify message, which means wrapping the application-specific content in the Notify element along with additional information, that is, the source of notificatioin; time, last value, and so forth.

When a Subscriber sends a Subscribe request message, it indicates which form of Notification is required (the raw NotificationMessage or the Notify Message). The NotificationProducer must observe this Subscription parameter, and use the form that has been requested.

WS-Topics (WS-Topics, 2006)

The "WS-Topics" defines a mechanism to organize and categorize items of interest for subscription knows as "topics." WS-Topics defines an XML model for describing metadata associated with topics, and three topic expression dialects that can be sued as subscription expressions in subscribe request messages. The specification aims at categorizing topics in different categories under which the topics are clubbed.

Topics and Topic Namespaces

The WS-Notification specifications allow the use of Topics as a way to organize and categorize a set of Notifications messages that relate to a particular type of information. For example, a stock ticker NotificationProducer application might set the Topic of the NotificationMessages it produces to the stock symbol with which the information is associated - for example "stock/BP." The Topics mechanism provides a convenient means by which subscribers can reason about Notifications of interest. A Topic is the concept used to categorize Notifications and their related Notification schemas. These Topics are used as part of the matching process that determines which (if any) subscribing NotificationConsumers should receive a Notification. When Topic generates a Notification, a NotificationPublisher can associate it with one or more Topics.

The mechanism for achieving this collision avoidance is normally determined by the application developer: in one pattern, an application developer defines a namespace for use by a related group of applications. This leaves the developer free to use whatever topic structure they see fit within that namespace. To continue the example above, the application developer could define one TopicNamespace for notification messages published in French, and a different one for notifications published in English. A subscribing application then specifies the namespace/topic in which they are interested (e.g., "english:stock/BP") to ensure they receive notification messages in the appropriate language. In this way, you can use the "same" topic structure (with different namespaces) to ensure that the application does not receive incompatible notifications. The set of Topics associated with a given XML Namespace is termed a Topic Namespace. Each Topic in a Topic Namespace can have zero or more child Topics, and a child Topic can itself contain further child Topics. A Topic without a parent is termed a root Topic. A particular root Topic and all its descendents form a hierarchy called a Topic Tree.

Topic Expression Dialects

Topics are referred to by TopicExpressions. TopicExpression is a query mechanism to reach one particular Topic in unambiguous manner in the Topic Tree. Section 8 of the WS-Topics specification defines example topic expression dialects that are recommended for use by WS-Notification applications. Note that the WS-Notification specifications provide an extensibility mechanism to allow vendors to define their own topic expression dialects if they wish. The different default topic expression dialects supported by different Application Server are *Simple TopicExpressions, Concrete TopicExpressions, Full TopicExpressions,* and *XPath TopicExpression Dialect.*

Topic Set

The Topic Set is a collection of Topics supported by a NotificationProducer. Topics from a single Topic Namespace can be referenced in the Topic Sets of many different NotificationProducers. Moreover, the Topic Set of a NotificationProducer may contain Topics from several different Topic Namespaces. A NotificationProducer can support an entire Topic Tree, or just a subset of the Topics in a Topic Tree. The set of Topics supported by the NotificationProducer may change over time.

WS-BrokeredNotification (WS-BrokeredNotification, 2006)

The WS-BrokeredNotification specification defines the interface for the NotificationBroker. A NotificationBroker is an intermediary between message Publishers and message Subscribers. A NotificationBroker decouples NotificationProducers and NotificationConsumers and can provide advanced messaging features such as demand-based publishing and load-balancing. A NotificationBroker also allows publication of messages from entities that are not themselves service providers. The NotificationBroker interface specifies standardized message exchange to be implemented by NotificationBroker along with operational requirements expected of service providers and requestors that participate in brokered notifications. A NotificationBroker is capable of subscribing to notifications, either on behalf of a NotificationConsumers, or for the purpose of messaging management. It is also capable of disseminating notifications on behalf of Publishers to NotificationConsumers. Thus, the NotificationBroker aggregates NotificationProducer, NotificationConsumer, and RegisterPublisher interfaces.

Web Service Resource

The WS-Resource represents the state in a Web services context. This state has atomic components, called *ResourceProperties* elements, which can be updated and queried. A set of resource property elements are gathered together into a resource property document: an XML document that can be queried by client applications using XPath or any other query languages. WS-RF supports dynamic insertion and deletion of the resource property elements of a WS-Resource at run time according to the XML Schema of resource property document.

A WS-Resource itself is a distributed object, expressed as an association of an XML document with a defined type attached with the Web service portType in the WSDL. Each WS-Resource has a unique identity and distinguishable handler; which can be serialized in XML format to embed it in the message before sending across the network. Although WS-Resource itself is not attached to any Uniform Resource Locator (URL), it does provide the URL of the Web service that manages it. The unique identity of the resource and the URL of the managing Web service is called an Endpoint Reference (EPR), which adheres to Web Services Addressing. Instances of a resource have a certain lifetime, which can be renewed before they expire, as specified by WS-ResourceLifetime specification. They can also be destroyed prematurely, as required by the application. The lifetime of an instance of a resource is managed by the client itself or any other process interacting as a client, independent of the Web service and its container.

WS-Resources are not bound to a single Web service; in fact, multiple Web services can manage and monitor the same WS-Resource instance with different business logic and from a different perspective. Similarly, WS-Resources are not confined to a single organization and multiple organizations may work together on the same WS-Resource, which leads to the concept of collaboration (Akram, 2006). Resource sharing is extensively used for load balancing. Semantically similar or cloned Web services are deployed independently for multiple client access. At run time, appropriate EPR's of the WS-Resource are generated with the same unique Resource identity, but with different URLs of managing Web services.

Resources are composed of Resource Properties, which reflect their state. These can vary from simple to complex data types and even reference other Resources. Referencing other Resources through Resource Properties is a powerful concept, which defines and elaborates interdependency of the Resources at a lower level.

Implied Resource Pattern

The WSA defines the relationship between Web services and stateful resources, which is the core of the WS-Resource Framework. The WS-RF specifications recommend the use of the Factory/Instance pattern that is, Implied Resource pattern. The term implied is used because the identity of the resource isn't part of the request message, but rather is specified using the reference properties feature of WSA. The endpoint reference provides means to point to both the Web service and the stateful resource in one convenient XML element.

This factory pattern is well understood in computer science: the notion of an entity that is capable of creating new instances of some component. A Factory service is responsible for creating the resource, assigning it an identity, and creating a WS-Resource qualified endpoint reference to point to it. An Instance service is required to access and manipulate the information contained in the resources according to the business logic. Implied Resource Pattern can be extended in various ways to effectively capture the requirements of the application. Different possible extensions are discussed below.

Factory/Instance Pair Pattern

The Factory/Instance Pair Model is the simplest model, in which for each resource there is a Factory Service to instantiate the resource and corresponding Instance Service to manage the resource. In a typical application, different Factory Services are independent of each other and can work in

Figure 1. Various forms of factory/instance pattern (Akram, 2006)

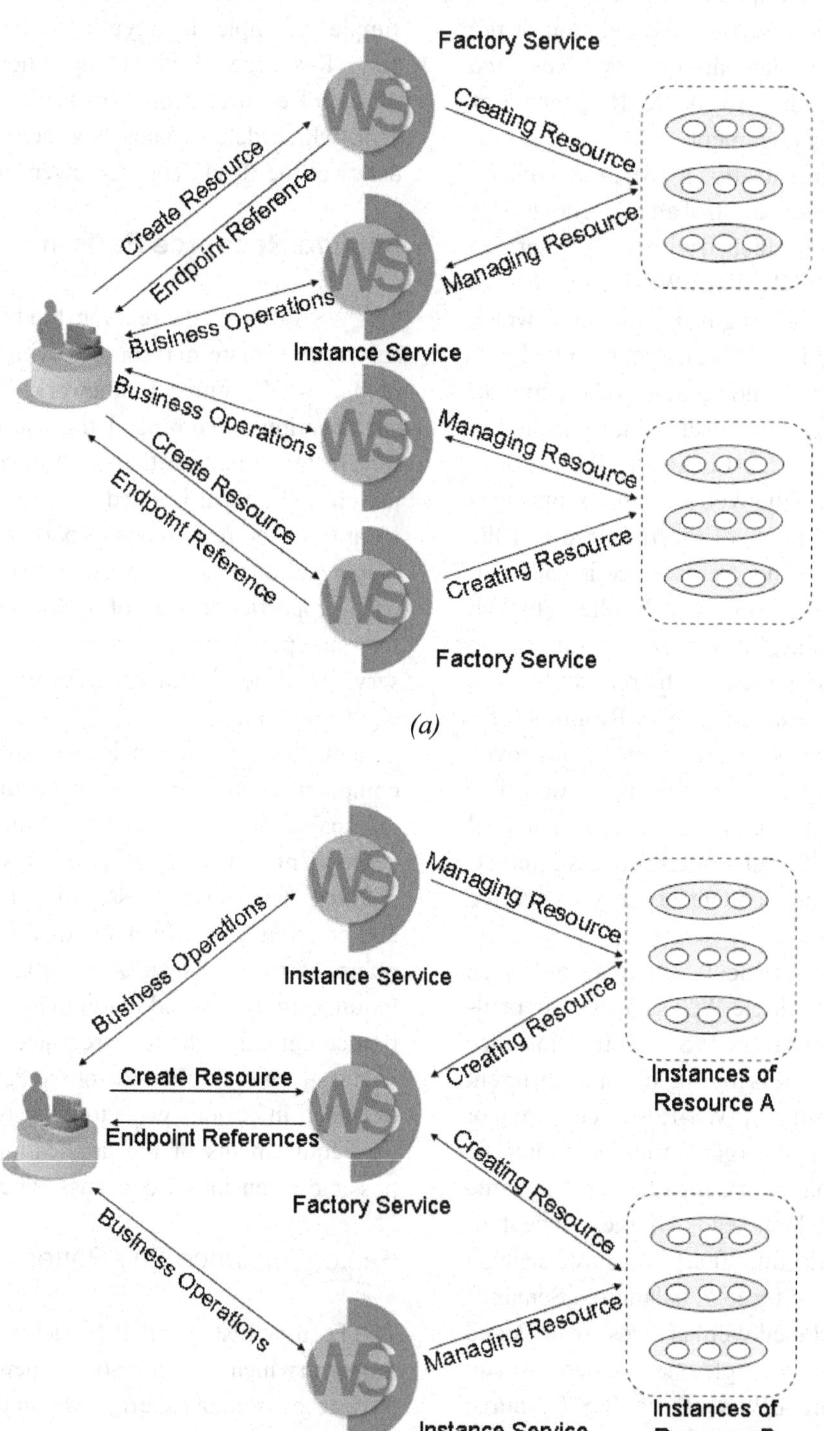

continued on following page

Figure 1. continued (Akram, 2006)

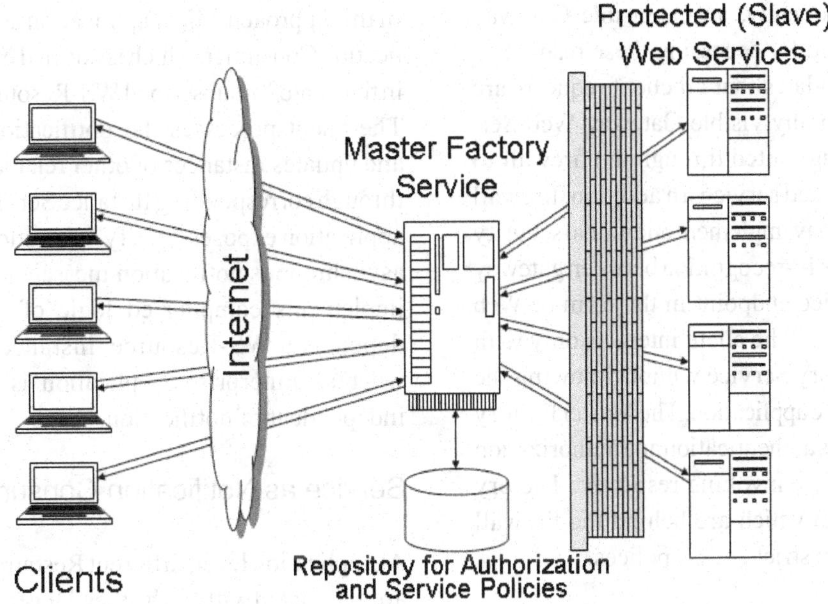

(c)

isolation. This is the simplest approach: repeating the similar resource instantiating logic in multiple Factory Services or even the same Factory Service can be deployed multiple times.

In this model, the user manually interacts with different Factory Services, which instantiates the appropriate resources and return the corresponding EPR's to the client. The client application contains the logic of deciding when and which resources should be instantiated.

Factory/Instance Collection Pattern

The Factory/Instance Collection Model is an extension of the Factory/Instance Pair Model. The difference being that a single Factory Service instantiates multiple WS-Resources managed by different Instance Services. In any Business Process various entities can be tightly coupled and due to this interdependency all of these WS-Resources must coexist before a client may interact with them successfully.

Master-Slave Pattern

In a Grid application with unpredictable request traffic, different security and load balancing measures are required for smooth execution. Business Processes are frequently protected by a firewall. It has to be anticipated that firewall policies will limit direct access from external clients to WS-Resources (i.e., it is most likely that these

Resources will be located inside private firewalls, and can only be accessed via known gateway servers). Consequently, an extensible Gateway model is required for accessing these resources. This model mandates that all client requests are sent to an externally visible Gateway Web Service before being routed through the firewall to the actual requested service. In addition, firewall administrators may implement additional security measures such as IP-recognition between gateway server and service endpoint in the form of Web Services handlers. The client interacts only with the Master Factory Service without knowing the inner details of the application. The Master Factory Service performs authentication and authorization of the client before invoking respective Factory Services (Slaves) which are behind the firewall and restricted by strict access polices.

Hybrid Approach

The best approach for any complicated Business Process is to combine these variations of the Implied Resource Pattern as follows. The client still interacts with a single Factory Service which instantiates all mandatory WS-Resources and returns a single EPR. Subsequent client interactions invoke the "create" operation of the Factory Service with different "parameters" with the Factory Service instantiating the corresponding WS-Resources according to those parameters. Optional WS-Resources are supported using a Factory/Instance Pair model due to their limited usage.

Notification Pattern

The Event-driven or Notification-based interaction pattern is a commonly used pattern for interobject communications. WS-RF and WSN bring notification-based interaction pattern in Web Services domain. This notification pattern can be extended in various ways to meet the application requirements.

Client as Notification Consumer

In this approach, client application acts as a Notification Consumer, which is notified of any change in the "state" of subscribed WS-Resource instance. The client processes the notification messages and updates instances of other related Resources through corresponding Instance Service(s). Client application exposes "notify" operation to receive asynchronous notification messages. Client also implements complicated logic of interrelating dependent WS-Resource instances together, whereas Enterprise Application is simple and independent of notification.

Service as Notification Consumer

At application level, different Resource instances are associated with each other. Due to interdependency of WS-Resources, the managing services have interest in the state of other Resource instances. Thus, handling the notifications at service level is more appropriate without involving client applications. This is the situation where automatic and quick actions are required. The client does not manage actions, and it does not have a role in the decision-making. Actions required are related to the main functionality of the application and not with a specific client.

Resource as Notification Consumer

The two notification approaches discussed above have their own limitations and benefits. A third notification model can provide the best of both approaches with an even cleaner design. In this approach WS-Resource itself is a notification consumer, yet may also act as a producer to have one-to-one associations. Each instance of the WS-Resource can subscribe to "state" changes of specific WS-Resource instances while broadcasting notification messages related to its own "state." Overall, this mechanism gives tighter control on the business logic without interference from the client side.

Implementing a WS-Resource as a notification consumer or a consumer-producer can result in large numbers of messages which can overload the Subscription Manager Service, thus affecting the overall performance of the application. The more interrelated instances, the worse the problem becomes. This model should be applied with caution.

TRADING SCENARIO

To demonstrate the application of WS-RF specifications in the Business Process Grid, an application to demonstrate Agricultural Marketing Process in India has been developed (Sorathia, Laliwala, & Chaudhary, 2005). In any typical Asian Agro-market, wholesale spot markets and derivative markets are emerging hubs of agricultural marketing business. Agro trade in these markets is heavily influenced by local, socio-economic, and cultural characteristics. This leads to variation in the crop prices of same crop in different markets. The producers have little choice to search for the best available price and are forced to sell their products in a local market. Inhibitive transport and storage cost can also play a pivotal role apart from urgency to sell perishable products. Buyers and wholesalers experience difficulties in purchasing desired quality of products at competitive prices. A typical trade in a Business Process Grid can span across different markets located at various places. Privately owned markets, food processing, and other related industries are allowed to trade directly with the farmers. Trading in such a competitive market will be more complex than that in the conventional trading scenario constrained to a single geographical market.

Figure 2. Workflow of marketing of agro-produce

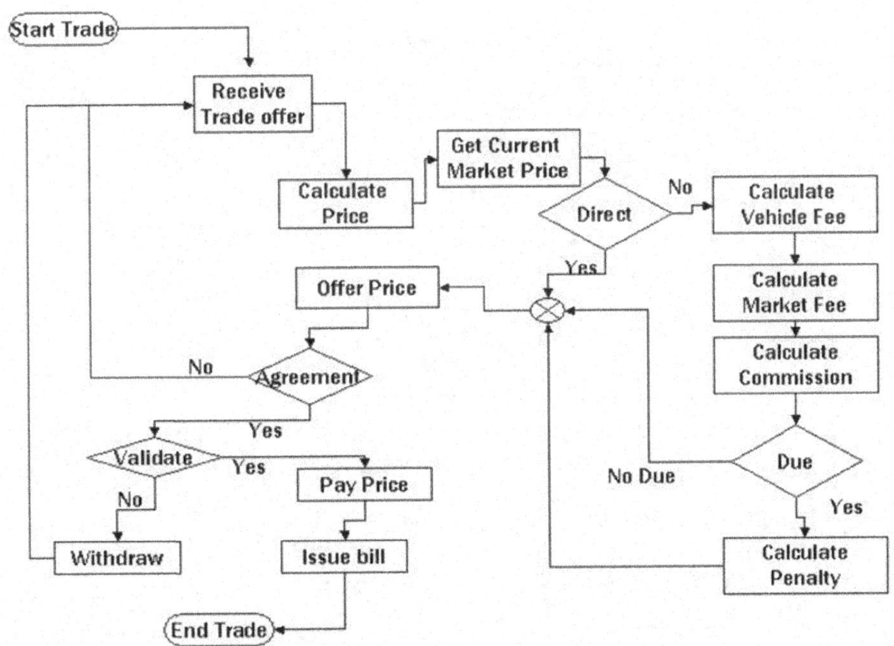

EXECUTION OF TRADE WORKFLOW

A seller or a farmer joins the market place with intentions to start a trade of agricultural produce. An authorized market functionary carries out measurement and grading of the produce and collect fees for any optional service such as transportation or storage. Price of the produce can be set by tender bid, auction, or any other transparent system. In case of direct sale, a seller is exempted to pay any market fee or commission; whereas in case of indirect sale the market fee is imposed on the seller for using different utility services. Once the agreed upon price is received, it is published for the traders. Only license holders are allowed to carry out any trade in the market area. If the trader fails to pay any fees to the Trade Market or fail to pay the agreed-upon price of the purchased good, the system may cancel the license of the trader. This is the situation where management of the whole market is required, independent of the main functionality of the Grid market. If the trade is carried out by license holders in a manner explained above, the bill will be issued and the transaction will be recorded in the Trade Market database. Figure 2 represents a simplified workflow capturing few aspects of a typical trade.

SYSTEM ARCHITECTURE

The Grid computing utilizes the Service Oriented Architecture (SOA) to meet requirements of the Grid Business Process. The goal of SOA is to achieve loosely coupled interoperable integration among scattered and heterogeneous services and clients. Principles of SOA influence the business logic of services by encouraging modular design and component reuse through dynamic discovery

Figure 3. Interaction diagram of agricultural marketing system

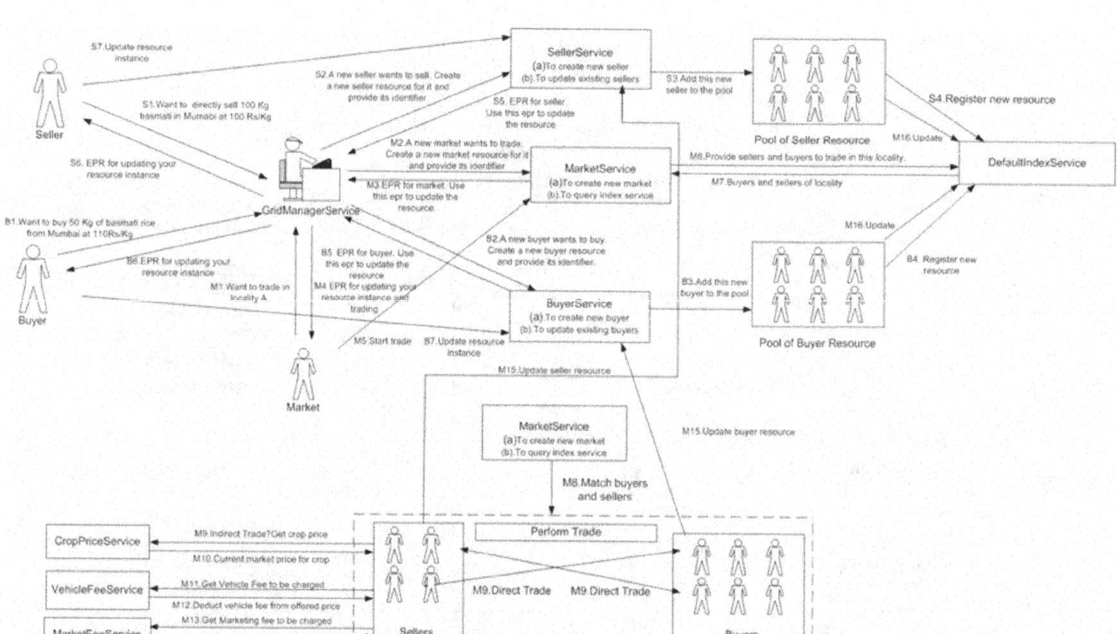

of existing services. Web services have been established as a popular technology for design and implementing SOA (Laliwala, Jain, & Chaudhary, 2006) based business process. A Web service has five essential attributes: (Gottschalk, Graham, Kreger, & Snell, 2002) it can be described using a standard service description language, Web Service Description Language (WSDL) (WSDL, 2005); it can be published to a registry of services, Universal Description, Discovery and Integration (UDDI) (UDDI, 2004) registry; it can be discovered by searching the service registry; it can be invoked, usually remotely, through a declared API; and, it can be composed with other Web services. Interaction Diagram of components of Agricultural Marketing System is shown in Figure 3.

COMPONENTS OF GRID APPLICATION

The case study is designed following the service-oriented grid architecture to provide state, notification, execution and monitoring, and scalability. The role of the targeted system is to automate the business process with interoperable integration of scattered services. The design is upon various WS-* specifications, specifically set of WSRF and WS-Notification (WSN) specifications to achieve required compliance. The distributed architecture implemented in the use case comprises of various components and resources; the role of these resources and components in the application is discussed below:

Grid Manager: Grid Manager Service is implementation of the Factory/Instance Collection Pattern. It initiates different type of resources, that is, Seller, Buyer, Crop, and Market according to the client request; hosted by different Grid Nodes. The Grid Manager orchestrates different components of the system in a predefined manner for smooth working of the whole application. The Grid Manager is the first point of the contact with the system.

Grid Nodes: Grid Nodes are the hosting environment which host different vanilla or stateful Web Services. The services hosted on different nodes are used in various combinations to capture the requirement of the application. Each initialized WS-Resource has Endpoint Reference (EPR) attached to it, which identify the resource itself and the URL of the managing Instance Service. Ideally, these Grid Nodes should be geographically dispersed across various enterprises.

Grid Registry: Grid Registry is a special Service based on the WS-ServiceGroup specification, which keeps track of various resources initialized during the course of application. The Grid Client (seller or buyer) can update and query the Grid Registry to search appropriate resources.

Grid Client: Grid Client is an external application which either request for initialization of the resource/s or interact with the existing resource/s to query, destroy, or modify them. The client adheres with WSA specification to work with WS-Resources and corresponding services through their EPR. In this case study the Grid Client has three flavors, for buyers, sellers, and administrator which instantiate the market instance for the trade.

INTERACTIONS AMONG COMPONENTS

In the Grid architecture for our agrocultural case study, various WS-Resources, that is, Seller, Buyer, Market, and Crop and so forth, are involved. During the lifecycle of a business process there can be various instances of similar WS-Resource instantiated during different phases. For example, at any time there can be various buyers and sellers in a single market, and similarly the same buyer or seller can participate in different transactions initiated in different markets. The following subsections illustrate steps involved in the instantiation of different WS-Resources and interactions among different components through sequence diagram.

Instantiation and Interaction with the Seller Entity

The first interaction of the seller with the system results in the creation of the new seller WS-Resource. This resource captures all details of the specific seller and is used for the future interaction with that seller. Figure 4 shows the sequence of events, which allow registration of the buyer with intention to purchase the required produce in the market.

1. The trading for a seller begins with the expression of intent to sell the available crops by supplying crop name, crop quantity, crop variety, expected price/kg. of crop, and market city for trade by using the GridManagerClient.
2. The GridManagerClient sends a request to GridManagerService, which looks up the instance service of a Seller to create an instance of SellerResource.
3. Newly created Seller resource, registers with the DefaultIndexService (i.e., Grid Registry) exposed by Globus container to register the details of the newly created seller resource.
4. The GridManager returns back the EPR of a newly created SellerResource to the GridManagerClient.
5. The GridManagerClient utilizes the EPR to invoke different operations to update the newly created resource.

Instantiation and Interaction with the Buyer Entity

Similarly, the first interaction of the buyer with the system results in the creation of the new buyer WS-Resource. This resource captures all details of the specific buyer and is used for the future

Figure 4. Seller service sequence diagram

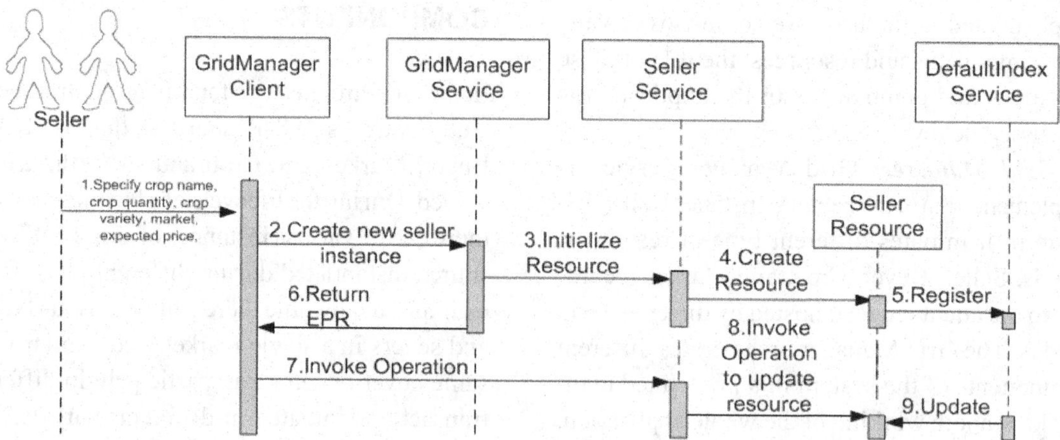

Figure 5. Buyer service sequence diagram

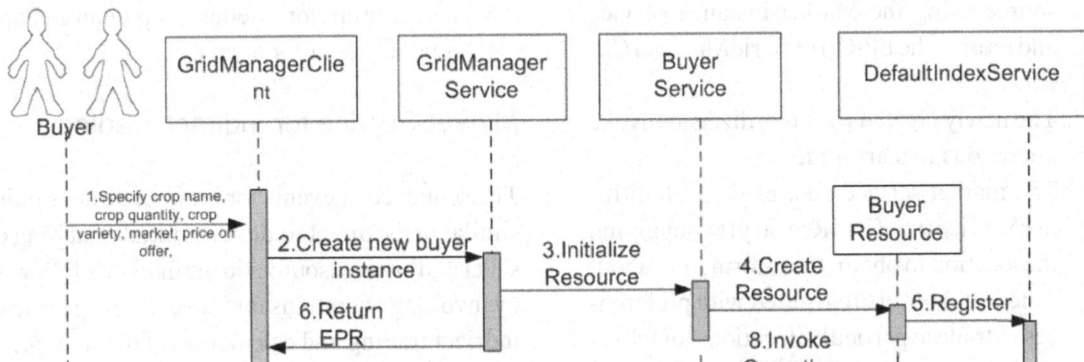

interaction with that seller. Figure 5 shows the sequence of events, which allow registration of the buyer with intention to participate in the trade.

1. The trading for a buyer begins with the expression of intent to buy the available crops by supplying crop name, crop quantity, crop variety, offered price/kg. of crop and market city for trade by using the GridManagerClient.
2. The GridManagerClient sends a request to GridManagerService, which looks up the instance service of a Buyer to create an instance of BuyerResource.
3. Newly created Buyer resource, registers with the DefaultIndexService (i.e., Grid Registry) exposed by Globus container to register the details of the newly created buyer resource.
4. The GridManager returns back the EPR of a newly created BuyerResource to the GridManagerClient.
5. The EPR is utilized by the GridManagerClient to invoke different operations to update the newly created resource.

Market Service for Direct Trading

In Direct Trading the system matches resources for different sellers and buyers which are trading in the same location. Once any such match is found, then it means there is atleast one buyer interested in the produce of a seller. To simulate the successful trade the resource properties for seller and buyers are updated. Below is the sequence diagram of events involved in direct trading.

1. The first step for successful trade is the instantiation of the MarketResource by passing the required location. The market only starts its operation once MarketResource is instantiated through GridManagerClient.
2. The GridManagerClient invokes the GridManagerService to create a new instance of

MarketResource. The GridManagerService triggers the creation of a new MarketResource using the Market instance service and returns the EPR to the GridManagerClient.

3. The newly created EPR is utilized to invoke operations to start trade.
4. The market service queries the DefaultIndexService (i.e., Grid Registry) by supplying the location to obtain the information about sellers and buyers registered with preferences to trade at particular locations for which this market service instance is running.
5. The DefaultIndexService returns the EPR of Buyer and Seller resources interested in trading at a given location.
6. The MarketService compares for the resource properties of the buyer and seller resources by utilizing retrieved EPRs. If the trading mode for a seller is direct and if its resource properties matches with that of required by a buyer, trading is performed by invoking operations on the seller and buyer resources to adjust the crop quantities and earning for a seller, crop quantity, and amount spent for a buyer.

Market Service for Indirect Trading

The sequence of events for indirect trade is quite similar to the direct trade. The initial matching of seller and buyer resources in the market is followed by invoking operations for the services specific to indriect trading and calculation of the final price after deducting appropriate charges. Below is the sequence diagram for the Indirect Trading:

1. The market starts its operation by expressing its intent to trade. Market uses the GridManagerClient and informs about the location where it wants to trade.
2. The GridManagerClient invokes the GridManagerService to create a new instance of MarketResource. The GridManagerService,

Figure 6. Sequence diagram of market service for direct trading

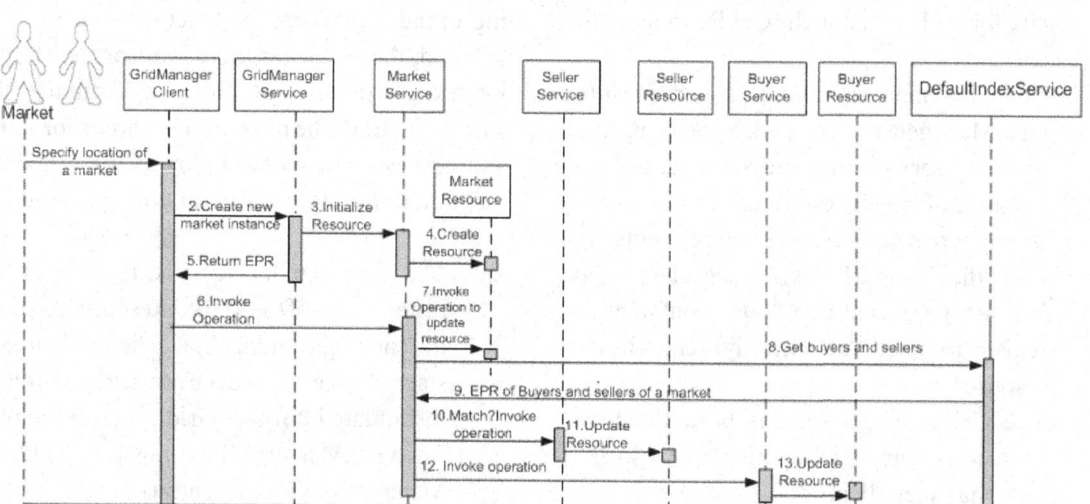

triggers the creation of a new MarketResource using the Market instance service and returns the EPR to the GridManagerClient.

3. The newly created EPR is utilized to invoke operations to start trade.
4. The MarketService queries the DefaultIndexService (i.e., Grid Registry) by supplying the location to obtain the information about sellers and buyers registered with preferences to trade at particular location for which this market service instance is running.
5. The DefaultIndexService, returns the EPR of Buyer and Seller resources interested in trading at a given location.
6. The MarketService, compare for the resource properties of the seller and buyers trading within the same location. On any successful match, the trade preference of the seller is queried for indirect trading. The indirect trading is simulated by deducting transportation and marketing fees from the asked price.
7. As a result of successful transaction, the seller resource is updated to reflect the new values, that is, crop still available to sell and total earnings.
8. Similarly, the buyer resource is updated to reflect new quantity of crop required and amount spent in single year.

IMPLEMENTATION

The dynamic nature of the agro-marketing case study and requirements to monitor the state of different resources during the lifecycle of business process are difficult to manage through vanilla Web services. Different built in features of the WS-RF family specifications naturally maps the demanding requirements of the case study and are

Figure 7. Sequence diagram of market service for indirect trading

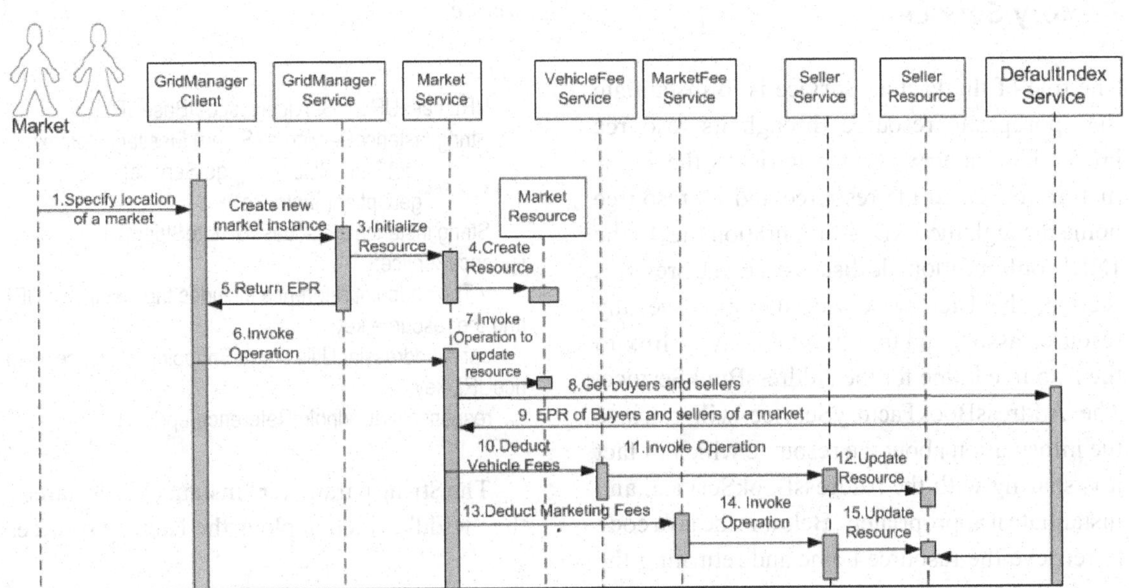

the first choice for the implementation. Different commercial and open source implementation of the WS-RF specifications are available, and selecting any one of them is more or less personal choice. During this development Globus Toolkit 4.0.1 (GT4) on Red Hat Linux 9 is used to develop and deploy different Web services. Globus implementation of WS-RF comes with an embedded container (i.e., Tomcat) and has extensive support for different levels of security. The working details of the GT4 are very specific, and thorough understandings of them are very crucial to develop any real world application. GT4 is based on the Axis SOAP engine and makes maximum use of different tools and feature available in the Axis toolkit.

IMPLIED RESOURCE PATTERN

In the Implied Resource Pattern the Factory service instantiate the appropriate resource and returns the EPR of the resource to the client. The EPR includes the unique ID of the resource and the URL of the Instance service managing the resource.

Factory Service

The role of the Factory service is to instantiate the appropriate resource through its resource home. The Factory service retrieves the information related to the resource and its resource home through the JNDI configuration file. In the JNDI configuration file discussed in the previous section, the Factory service doesn't have any resource associated to it but it do have a link to the resource home for the AddressBookService. The AddressBookFactoryService will retrieve the information about the resource which in fact it is sharing with the AddressBookService, and instantiate it appropriately. Below is the java code to retrieve the resource home and returning the resulting EPR to the client:

Listing 4. Code snippet of Factory Service to retrieve Resource Home

```
try {
    Context initialContext = new InitialContext();
    ctx = ResourceContext.getResourceContext();
    String name = Constants.JNDI_SERVICES_BASE_
NAME + ctx.getService() +
        "/AddressBookHome";
    home = (AddressBookResourceHome) initialContext.
lookup(name);
    key = home.create();   }
```

"/AddressBookHome" is the name of the resource link declared in the Factory service. The above code retrieves the resource home object and calls the create() method of the resource home object. The create() method instantiate the resource and returns the unique ID of the resource. The normal practice is to keep the resource instantiation code in the private utility method of the Factory service and this convention is followed during the implementation of the case study. This unique ID is used to create EPR, which is returned to the client. Below is the remaining code which creates the EPR of the resource:

Listing 5. Code snippet for EPR creation of resource

```
try {
    URL baseURL = ServiceHost.getBaseURL();
    String instanceService = (String) MessageContext
            .getCurrentContext().getService().
            getOption("instance");
    String instanceURI = baseURL.toString() +
instanceService;
    // The endpoint reference includes the instance's URI
and the resource key
    epr = AddressingUtils.createEndpointReference(insta
nceURI, key);
    response.setEndpointReference(epr);   }
```

The String parameter "instance" is declared in the "wsdd" which deploys the Factory service.

Resource Home

The resource home is simple class with only one create(); which initialize the corresponding resource. The resource home normally extends the GT4 specific ResourceHomeImpl class. The ResourceHomeImpl is very useful class which shields user from lot of implementation. This supper class locates the implementation of the resource through the JNDI configuration file and instantiates it appropriately. The ResourceHomeImpl also provides the private hash table to store all the resources created through the custom tailored resource home. The business logic of searching and updating the private hash table is automatically available in the custom resource home by extending the ResourceHomeImpl. Below is the code for the sample resource home.

Listing 6. Code snippet of AddressBookResourceHome

```
public class AddressBookResourceHome extends
ResourceHomeImpl {
        private String instanceServicePath;
        public ResourceKey create(){
        ResourceKey key=null;
        try{
                // Retrieves the resource class from
the JNDI configuration file
                AddressBookResource
addressBookResource = (AddressBookResource) this.
createNewInstance();
                addressBookResource.initialize();
                key=new SimpleResourceKey(this.
getKeyTypeName(),addressBookResource.getID());
                this.add(key, addressBookResource);
}
```

The most important bit in the method is to create the instance of the resource through createNewInstance() method. This method is implemented in the super class, that is, ResourceHomeImpl; which returns an object instance of respective resource by retrieving the implementation details of the resource from JNDI configuration file. Other than instantiating the resource, the resource home creates the instance of the SuperResourceKey. The SuperResourceKey couples the unique ID of the resource with its fully qualified name. This fully qualified unique ID is used in the EPR. At anytime container can be managing many different types of resources which may have the same unique ID; it is the fully qualified name and the unique ID of the resource which makes any specific instance of the resource unique from other instances.

Listing 7. Coupling of unique resource ID and resource

```
key=new SimpleResourceKey(this.getKeyTypeName(),ad
dressBookResource.getID());
this.add(key, addressBookResource);
```

The implementation details of each resource home developed during the course of the case study are very similar and it will not be discussed further with actual implementation details of that Web service.

GRID REGISTRY

The role of the Grid Registry is to monitors all resources instantiated during the life cycle of the application; irrespective of its nature and type. The resource home only monitors and manage resources of specific type, so they can't be used directly as Grid Registry. Although it is possible to develop Grid Registry on the top of all different resource homes; but this requires lot of effort to implement the business logic of searching, querying and modifying these individual resources. The GT4 implementation provides the DefaultIndexService built according to the specifications of WS-ServiceGroup discussed in the section 2.2.3. This Index Service maps to our concept of the Grid Registry; which aggregates the information related to all available resources at one place. The Index Service can be built on top other Index Services and each child Index Service mapping specific type of resources. This concept of child Index Services leads to better management and organization of resources in the hierarchical manner. Each Grid Node, that is, GT4 WS-RF container has one Index Service supporting all the operations required by WS-ServiceGroup specification. By default the resources instantiated through resource homes are not registered with the Index Service. The resource home explicitly registers new creates resource instance with the Index Service; which aggregates all the resources at a single point. The registration process is done through ServiceGroupRegistrationClient. Below is the Java code snippet from the resource home to register the resource with the Index Service:

Listing 8. Code snippet demonstrating registration of resource with Index Service

```
protected void add(ResourceKey key, Resource resource)
{
..................
EndpointReferenceType epr=null;
try {
                URL baseURL = ServiceHost.
getBaseURL();
                String instanceService =
getInstanceServicePath();
                String instanceURI = baseURL.
toString() + instanceService;
                epr = AddressingUtils.createEndpoint
Reference(instanceURI, key); }
......
// Location of the configuration file
String regPath = ContainerConfig.getGlobusLocation()
            + "/etc/org_sws_examples_services_buyer/
registration.xml";

try {
                AddressBookResource
buyerResource = (AddressBookResource) resource;
ServiceGroupRegistrationParameters params =
ServiceGroupRegistrationClient

.readParams(regPath);
params.setRegistrantEPR(epr);
Timer regTimer = regClient.register(params);
addressBookResource.setRegTimer(regTimer);
//regClient.register(params);
} ..................
```

The resources have tight control the amount of information they want to advertise in the Index Service, how frequently the Index Service query their states to update itself, and the polling interval. The Index Service is distributed registry, which keeps on updating itself regularly after specific intervals. Any change in the state of the resource or its deletion results in the notification of Index Service; which adjusts itself accordingly. This information is provided in the form configuration file "*registration.xml*" for each resource. Below is the sample configuration file.

Listing 9. XML code snippet of registration.xml

```
<ServiceGroupRegistrationParameters xmlns:sgc="http://
mds.globus.org/servicegroup/client"
..........
<RefreshIntervalSecs>30</RefreshIntervalSecs>
 <Content xsi:type="agg:AggregatorContent" xmlns:
agg="http://mds.globus.org/aggregator/types">
   <agg:AggregatorConfig xsi:type="agg:
AggregatorConfig">
    <agg:GetMultipleResourcePropertiesPollType
     xmlns:bs="http://www......./AddressBookService" >
     <agg:PollIntervalMillis>20000</agg:PollIntervalMillis>
<agg:ResourcePropertyNames>....</agg:
ResourcePropertyNames
<!—Resource Properties specific to the
AddressBookService -->
         .........................................
</agg:GetMultipleResourcePropertiesPollType>
  </agg:AggregatorConfig>
 <agg:AggregatorData/>
 </Content>
</ServiceGroupRegistrationParameters>
```

WEB SERVICES DEVELOPED

In a previous section, different components required in any Grid applications are discussed. In the agro-marketing use case along with discussed components, different stake holders are also involved such as buyer, seller, market, and so forth. These components and stake holders are implemented are either implemented as stateful Web services or simple stateless Web services based on its role in the overall functioning of the application. Below is the list of different Web services with their role and responsibilities, developed during the prototype.

1. **Seller Service:** The Seller Service implements the business logic necessary for the seller. This service expose different operations related to the seller resource such as instantiation of seller resources, monitoring, and modification of different properties for seller resources. These operations are either executed manually by the seller or invoked automatically by other components during the course of the application as discussed in the different sequence diagrams.
2. **Buyer Service:** The Buyer Service is the implementation of our buyer stake holder. It instantiates the resource for a buyer, and provides different operation on the buyer resources. Instantiation of a buyer resource result in the registration of the Buyer with our system for future interactions. The service after receiving the preferences instantiates a new resource instance for the buyer. The service also registers these preferences with the DefaultIndexService of GT4 and provides operations to be invoked on this resource instance.
3. **Market Service:** This service acts as an intermediary between buyers and sellers. The role of the Market Service is more or less like a broker service among different stake holders. It queries the Grid Registry (i.e., Index Service provided by the Globus Toolkit) to obtain the list sellers and buyers trading in the same city/market and continuously monitors the trading preferences of buyers and sellers to perform trade. Market Service instantiate the new trade and transaction once it successfully matches the seller and buyer preferences. Initiation of the trade triggers sequence of events which results in the update of buyer and seller resources involved in the trade and notification to interested parties.
4. **GridManager Service:** The GridManager Service acts as a common factory service to instantiate different resources involved in the case study. The GridManager Service is implemented according to the Factory/Instance Collection Pattern and Master/Slave Pattern as discussed previously. GridManager Service instantiate different resources through the specific service, that is, seller resource is instantiated through Seller Service Interacting.
5. **VehicleFee Service:** VehicleFee Service is responsible for calculating any transportation charges incurred in case of indirect trade. The transportation charges are deducted from the final selling price and are paid by the seller.
6. **CropPrice Service:** CropPrice Service is used for retrieving the current market price of the crop involved in the trade. The CropPrice Service calculates the price of the crop based on different factors such as the type of the crop, season, its availability in the market, its demand, and so forth. This service is only invoked when the mode of trade is indirect.
7. **MarketingFee Service:** The MarketingFee Service is used for deducting any marketing fee incurred during the course of indirect trade. Similar to the transportation charges, marketing fee is deducted from the final selling price and is paid by the seller.

In the subsequent sections, details about various implemented services are given.

GridManagerService

The "GridManager" service as mentioned above is an interface provided to the Client application to instantiate resources related to different stateful Web services. The GridManager Service is implemented according to the Factory/Instance Collection Pattern and Master/Slave Pattern, which instantiate appropriate resource according to the client preference. The intended service whose resource instance has to be created is specified by the client program.

Implementation of GridManagerService

The WSDL document is a contract between the service and the client. Implementation of the service strictly follows this contract and it has one-to-one mapping of all functionality advertised through the WSDL. The implementation of the GridManager implements the only operation exposed by the WSDL document. The implementation can have any number of utility operations to support the mandatory operation. The mandatory method in the GridManager is the createResource() method, which instantiates the appropriate resource and returns the corresponding EPR. The main points related to the implementation are discussed below with reference to relevant implementation.

1. The createResource operation retrieves the name of the service from the client request for which the resource has to be instantiated. The serviceName is a private attribute of type String in the CreateResource class.
2. The getInstanceResourceHome is a private utility method to obtain the home of an appropriate resource. Each resource is instantiated through its corresponding home.
3. The object of ResourceHome is utilized to invoke create method of resource home object. The create() method creates a new resource instance and returns its unique identifier or the resource key. Notice that key is an object of the ResourceKey class. The properties related to resource key, like the type of key, name of the key, and so forth, are defined in the JNDI file of the instance, as discussed earlier.
4. Once the create method returns a key, then this key is used to construct the EPR of the WS-Resource. Remember
   ```
   EndPointReference=URL of the instance Service + Unique Resource Identifier.
   ```
5. The next step is to create the URL of the instance service. The URL of the instance service is created by adding the name of the instance service to the base URL of the container. The Factory service obtains the name of the appropriate instance service from the "wsdd" (Web service Deployment Descriptor) file.
   ```
   String instanceURI = baseURL.toString() + instanceService;
   ```
   The "wsdd" file of GridManager service has an entry corresponding to the instanceService,
   ```
   <parameter name="buyerInstance" value="sws/examples/BuyerService"/>
   ```
6. Once URL and resource key are obtained, the remaining step is to create the EPR to be return back to the client using the generated stub classes from the WSDL file.
   ```
   epr = AddressingUtils.createEndpointReference(instanceURI, key);
   CreateResourceResponse response = new CreateResourceResponse();
   response.setEndpointReference(epr);
   return response;
   ```

This utility method getResourceInstanceMethod() retrieves the information from the JNDI file associated to locate the appropriate resource home.

Resource Home and Resource

The GridManager service is stateless Web service which only instantiate different resources managed by other services. It doesn't manage any resource, and thus there is no specific resource and resource home attached with the GridManager service.

BuyerService

Once the resource associated with the BuyerService is instantiated and the corresponding EPR is returned to the GridManagerClient, The GridManagerClient invokes different operations of the instance service referenced in the EPR, which may result in modification and update of the resource properties of the resource associated with the instance service.

Implementation of BuyerResource

The resource declared in the WSDL document is implemented as a separate class. It is important that the Factory service can instantiate the resource and the Instance service can locate and update the resource properties of the corresponding resource. The container locates any particular resource through its unique ID and its qualified name as declared in the WSDL document. The namespaces in the Web services are always error prone and these are normally declared in a separate interface for reusability and maintenance purposes.

Listing 10. Code snippet of Java interface for namespace declaration

```
public interface BuyerConstants {
public static final String NS = "http://www...../namespaces/
examples/BuyerService";
public static final QName RP_BUYERCROPNAME = new
QName(NS, "BuyerCropName");
.........
```

Resource properties and resources are referenced by their fully qualified name. The fully qualified name includes the namespace to which the resource property and resource belongs and its local name, as shown in the above code snippet.

The namespace and local name of the resource and resource properties in the interface must be in accordance with the fully qualified name of the resource and resource properties in the WSDL document. It is possible to hard code these qualified names in the Web service and resource implementation class which can lead to unnecessary typo errors. However, use of separate interface is an elegant approach because this allows all declaration in a single place. In case of any change, only interface needs update, which considerably minimize the possibilities of errors.

Each resource is implemented as a separate class and the name of the resource class is declared in the JNDI configuration file. The resource class is very simple class only instantiating different private resource properties and providing corresponding accessor methods.

Listing 11. Code snippet from BuyerResource class

```
// BuyerResource class.
public class BuyerResource implements Resource,
ResourceIdentifier,
                    ResourceProperties,
TopicListAccessor {
private String buyerCropName;
public Object initialize() {
this.key = uuidGen.nextUUID();
this.propSet = new SimpleResourcePropertySet(
                              BuyerConstants.
BUYERRESOURCE_PROPERTIES);
                try {
buyerCropNameRP=new SimpleResourceProperty(Buyer
Constants.RP_BUYERCROPNAME);
setCropName("NULL");
buyerCropNameRP.add(buyerCropName);
this.propSet.add(buyerCropNameRP);
....
```

The code snippet above shows the declaration of a resource property set (i.e., the resource property set wraps all resource properties related to a single resource) and a particular resource property the "buyerCropNameRP". The resource property set maps to the resource declaration in the WSDL document and thus shares the same fully qualified name.

The buyerCropNameRP is declared as an object of a SimpleResourceProperty type, provided by the GT4 implementation of the WS-RF. The SimpleResourceProperty eases the efforts to manage, monitor, and update individual resource properties. The objects of SimpleResourceProperty can also be advertised as WS-Notification topics without extra efforts. The container monitors the states of these WS-Notification topics and generates notification messages on any state change.

The SimpleResourceProperty has two constructors; one takes the qualified name of the resource property and other takes the object of ResourcePropertyMetaData. The ResourcePropertyMetaData is an interface and SimpleResourcePropertyMetaData is its concrete implementation. By default GT4 WS-RF implementation ignores the maximum and minimum occurrence of any element declared in the WSDL. The ResourcePropertyMetaData provides developer tight control on the cardinality of different resource properties within the resource. The utility interface *BuyerConstants* explained earlier is utilized to initialize resource property set and different member resource properties.

As mentioned earlier, the resource property set is the wrapper around different resource properties use of GT4 provided API makes it easy to transform these objects in the corresponding XML document. This XML document is part of SOAP messages exchanged between a client and the service. In the implementation, different resource properties are initialized without any default values. It is possible to assign the default values directly to the resource properties, but the more flexible approach is to declare private variables for each resource property and these variables are used to manage the state of resource properties. Each private variable has corresponding accessor methods which are indirectly used to modify and query values of resource properties at run time. For example, the resource property BuyerCropName declared in the WSDL has corresponding utility variable buyerCropName of type String.

Listing 12. Accessor method for setting resource property

```
private String buyerCropName;
public void setCropName(String cropName) {
  this.buyerCropName = cropName; }
```

The buyerCropNameRP; which is the actual resource property is passed the utility variable buyerCropName. However, it is worth mentioning that the getters and setters are not strictly required when resource properties are instances of SimpleResourceProperty. We can directly assign the value to the resource property but this approach makes it difficult to manage the state of the resource property and the source of change. Below is the code assigning the value to the resource property buyerCropNameRP through the utility variable buyerCropName.

Listing 13. Assignment of Resource Property value using utility variable

```
buyerCropNameRP.add(buyerCropName);
```

Once the resource properties are initialized properly they are added to the resource property set. The same process has to be followed for initialization of all other resource properties, which collectively represent the state of the resource.

Listing 14. Addition of resource property to resource property set

```
this.propSet.add(buyerCropNameRP);
```

Implementation of BuyerResourceHome

The BuyerResourceHome is a typical resource home implemented on the lines discussed earlier and its implementation details are not repeated here. The main functionality of the BuyerResourceHome is outlined below.

- Creates a new instance of BuyerResource and passing the EPR to the GridManager.
- Provides the querying and searching functionality of the resource based on the resource key.
- Registers the newly created resources in the DefaultIndexService of Globus Toolkit 4.

Implementation of BuyerService

The BuyerService provides various operations to manage and alter the state of already created buyer resources through the EPR. The BuyerService is the interface between buyer resources and entities interested in its state, that is, client, GridManager Service, Market Service, and so forth. The BuyerService is a stateful Web service exposing various business operations and few operations related to the management of the resources as specified in the WS-RF specification. The BuyerService does not implement WS-RF specific operations as they are provided by the WS-RF container, but it has to provide the signature of WS-RF specific methods supported by the service in the WSDL file. Any service deployed in the WS-RF container is not stateful service unless it manages any resource and supports few of the WS-RF specific operations. The stateful service does not need to support all of the WS-RF specific operations and it can only support subsets of operations appropriate for its business logic. The implementation details of the BuyerService are pretty trivial, and most of the logical details are related to the deployment descriptor and the WSDL document. The "wsdd" file is specific to the Axis framework. The service informs the WS-RF container of its dependency on the WS-RF specific operations, which are implemented by the container through the parameter "providers." The parameter "providers" take space separated list of Java classes implementing various WS-RF specific operations. These classes are already registered with the WS-RF container and the container knows which class implements which operation. Below is the fragment from the "wsdd" highlighting the use of parameter "providers:"

Listing 15. Usage of WSDL pre processor (wsdlpp)

```
<parameter name="providers" value="GetRPProvider
GetMRPProvider DestroyProvider"/>
```

The GT4 provides extension of the <wsdl:portType> in the form of attribute "wsdlpp." The "wsdlpp" stands for "WSDL pre processor;" which is a precise way to add the details of the WS-RF specific operations in the WSDL supported by the service. Below is the portion of the WSDL document from the BuyerService showing the use of "wsdlpp."

```
<portType name="BuyerPortType"
        wsdlpp:extends="wsrpw:GetResourceProperty
wsrpw:GetMultipleResourceProperties"
   wsrp:ResourceProperties="tns:
BuyerResourceProperties">
```

The developers should remember that this extension property is a utility feature only provided by GT4, for the convenience. In the final flattened file generated by GT4, the actual signature of the (i.e., messages and elements) related to wsrpw:GetResourceProperty will be inserted in the WSDL. It can be understood as a copy paste operation of picking elements from one WSDL file and placing them in another WSDL. The use of "wsdlpp" restricts the reuse of the WSDL document across different implementations of

WS-RF so it should be used with care. The actual signature of the "wsrpw:GetResourceProperty" is shown below:

Listing 16. Signature of the wsrpw:GetResourceProperty

```
<operation name="GetResourceProperty">
   <input name="GetResourcePropertyRequest"
message="wsrpw:GetResourcePropertyRequest"
      wsa:Action="http://docs.oasis-open.org/wsrf/2004/06/
   wsrf-WS-ResourceProperties/GetResourceProperty"/>
   <output name="GetResourcePropertyResponse"
message="wsrpw:GetResourcePropertyResponse"
      wsa:Action="http://docs.oasis-open.org/
   wsrf/2004/06/wsrf-WS-ResourceProperties/
   GetResourcePropertyResponse"/>
   <fault name="InvalidResourcePropertyQNameFault"
message="wsrpw:InvalidResourcePropertyQNameFault"/>
   <fault name="ResourceUnknownFault"
message="wsrpw:ResourceUnknownFault"/>
</operation>
```

The GetResourceProperty and GetMultipleResourceProperties allow the clients to query and retrieve the current values of the resource properties of the resources. These portTypes are also utilized by the Index Service to regularly query the resources for updated information regarding their state.

The business operations implemented by the BuyerService are pretty trivial. Each method looks up the resource referenced in the EPR through the resource home and then after locating the resource it invokes the appropriate action on it. Below is the code for updating the amount spent by the buyer in a single year, which can be used for statistical, accounting, or taxation purposes (not implemented in the case study).

Listing 17. BuyerService operation setAmountSpent()

```
public AmountSpentResponse setAmountSpent(float
amount) throws RemoteException      {
                BuyerResource buyerResource =
getResource();
      System.out.println("Old amount spent:"+
   buyerResource.getAmountSpent());
                amount=amount+buyerResource.
getAmountSpent();
                System.out.println("New amount
spent:"+ amount);
                Float amountSpeant=new
Float(amount);
                buyerResource.setAmountSpent(amo
untSpeant);
                return new AmountSpentResponse();
}
```

The reader can now appreciate the use of accessor methods for the utility private variables corresponding to each resource property, which were implemented in the BuyerResource class. These utility methods provide more elegant solution to update the resource properties. These utility methods can validate the values before assigning to the resource properties. This validation can be of various types, such as the appropriate range for numerical values, decimal rounding for floating points, and regular expressions for the String values.

BuyerProperties is a complex data type which is declared in the WSDL document of the BuyerService. A wrapper Java class is generated for this data type when the tool "wsdl2Java" is used. The object of this class is used within the actual implementation of the case study and by the client application rather than working with raw XML documents through DOM or SAX API.

SellerService

The SellerService manages and monitors the resources related to the seller and its implementation is very similar to the BuyerService. Hence, the explanation of the SellerService is not repeated here. The complete WSDL document and the implementation of the SellerService is included in the downloadable source code.

MarketService

The MarketService is an intermediate between the ByerService and the SellerService. The MarketService provides the required platform to carry out any trade. The MarketService orchestrate different services in the preset manners for successful transactions, updating the involved resources, and notifying the interested parties.

Implementation of MarketResource and MarketResourceHome

The implementation of the MarketResourceHome has exactly the same business logic and nearly the same operations as discussed in the BuyerService section. The MarketResource is instantiating the resource property set and different resource property elements on the same line as discussed in the BuyerResource. The implementation of these classes are not repeated here, but the source code is available for download.

Implementation of MarketService

The MarketService implements few business operations to manage resource, but the most important methods in the MarketService are the fireXpathQuery() and storeEntries() method. In this section, only these two methods are discussed. Familarity of these methods will help to understand the working of IndexService, that is, Grid Registry provided by the GT4.

The fireXpathQuery() Method

The fireXpathQuery() method is used to construct and fire appropriate XPath query, to query the IndexService (i.e., Grid Registry). The main purpose of this operation is to match trading preferences of buyers and sellers registered in the same market.

The fireXpathQuery() operation is a bit complicated method, and good understanding of its implementation is important for the understanding of the role played by the MarketService. Below are the main points related to the fireXpathQuery() operation.

1. Firstly, the fireXpathQuery() operation retrieves the URL of the IndexService. This URL is used to create the EPR of the IndexService. This new created EPR is used to invoke different operations on the IndexService.
2. The fireXpathQuery() invokes different operations on the IndexService through Axis generated utility classes, that is, WSResourcePropertiesServiceAddressingLocator and QueryResourceProperties_PortType, which serialize and de-serialize SOAP request and response messages before transforming down the wire.
3. The next step is to create an appropriate XPath query to be fired. However, the version of XPath query being used is to be specified as there are two different versions of XPath. The XPath version used for the query should match the XPath supported by the WS-ServiceGroup. This purpose is achieved by using the dialect.
4. The XPath query is used to create an appropriate request message. This newly created request message is passed to the queryResourceProperties(..) operation of the QueryResourceProperties_PortType class. The QueryResourceProperties_PortType the local stub for the remote Web service.
5. The queryResourceProperties(..) returns the result of the query wrapped in the QueryResourcePropertiesResponse object.

The storeEntries() Method

After receiving the response from the queryResourceProperties(..) in the fireXpathQuery, the next step is to get the entries matching the query crieria. Remember that the DefaultIndexService of GT4 is actually an Aggregrator Service, that is, its function is to aggregrate several resource properties together according to the WS-Service-Grooup specifications. All entries are retrieved from the response by calling queryResponse. get_any() method; which returns an array of MessageElement type.

```
MessageElement[] buyerEntries = queryResponse.
get_any();
```

The MessageElement is the Axis framework specific Java mapping of data type xsd:any. The data type xsd:any is used to pass raw XML between services, particularly when the contents of the XML are dynamic and changes at run time. Hence, we need to de-serialize the MessageElement entries to invoke different operations on them and particularly to retrieve the EPR of the resources for further point-to-point communication. The business logic of retrieving the information from individual entries is implemented in the storeEntries(..) operation.

First an array of the MessageElements is deserialized into an object of EntryType class. From the object of EntryType different operations are invoked to retrieve information related to that the particular entry, that is, EPR. AggregatorContent class is used to retrieve the aggregated data within a particular "entry" object of EntryType class. Since the actual data, that is, resource properties, are required for match making, which is the key to initiate the trade.

```
AggregatorContent content = (AggregatorContent) entry.
getContent();
AggregatorData data = content.getAggregatorData();
```

The "data" object obtained is actually an array of the information advertised by the resource within the Index Service in the form of String. Hence, each entry in the array is reference to the specific resource property. The registration.xml file is used to set the resource properties to be advertised in the IndexService.

```
String cropName = data.get_any()[0].getValue(); is utilized
```

The data.get_any()[0].getValue() retrieves the very first entry of the array which has been returned, which is of String type. Similarly, the process has to be repeated to obtain the values for other entries. Because the position of the element can change; which requires the appropriate change in the "index" passed to the get_any() operation. Once all entries are retrieved they are stored in a Vector, whose elements are accessed later to mach if the requirements of any buyer are satisfied by any seller. Operation performTrade() uses this Vector in which the buyer and seller entries were stored and then performs the trade contingent on the following conditions being met:

- Crop required by any buyer is being offered by any seller;
- Quantity is appropriate;
- Crop Variety is matching; and
- Offered price of buyer is higher or equal to expected price of seller.

If these conditions are met, then the performDirectTrade0 function is invoked by passing the seller & buyer EPR, the quantity to be purchased and the amount, which will be offered to the seller. Operation performDirectTrade(), is a normal function which utilizes the EPR's of the buyer and the seller to adjust the quantity and the amount spent by buyer and amount earned by the seller. Thus, adjusting these resource properties simulates the successful trade and transaction.

For example, if a seller has 60Kg. of rice offered at 10 Rs./Kg., and its preference match that of a buyer which needs this 60 Kg. at 12 Rs./Kg., the SellerCropQuantity ResourceProperty for this instance will be set to 0 and BuyerCropQuantity will be also set to 0, because the seller has sold as much as it wanted to and buyer has purchased as much as it wanted to. However, the SellerEarning ResourceProperty will be set to Rs. 60 x 12= Rs.

720 and the BuyerAmountSpent ResourceProperty will be set to Rs. 60 x 12 = Rs. 720.

SERVICES FOR INDIRECT TRADING

The market service also takes care of performing trading for sellers interested in indirect trading. This is achieved with the help of simple services by invoking operations on them by passing suitable parameters. These services manipulate a resource properties associated with the EPR of the seller for whom the trade is being performed. Hence, they have functions which are invoked by passing EPR of the seller. Crop quantity, crop name, crop variety, and so forth, are also passed depending upon the provided functionality.

CropPriceService

CropPriceService is a simple Web service, which returns the price to be offered to any farmer which is interested in indirect mode of trade. For any crop name which is provided as input, it provides the price per kg. which is offered. It does not have a resource factory with it, as the function is invoked by passing input parameters. It is based on singleton resource instance pattern. This multiplied by quantiy returns the total amount for this crop variety. The service further invokes the setEarning() method of SellerService to set the earning for this crop. The code of the service is easy to understand and comprises of just one java file namely CropPriceService.java along with other additional files related to container deployment.

MarketFeeService

MarketFeeService is based on a similar pattern as CropPriceService. It deducts the marketing fee, which is imposed on the earning of the seller. As explained above, this also takes seller EPR as input. It utilizes this EPR to obtain the earning of the seller and deducts the market fee as applicable and invokes operation setEarning() of SellerService to set the earning for the seller after deduction of market fee.

VehicleFeeService

VehicleFeeService imposes vehicle fee levied on the seller for using vehicle inside market area for transport of crop. It takes seller EPR and crop quantity transported as input and then invokes setEarning() operation to set the earning for this seller after deducting vehicle fee.

CLIENT

The end user interacts with the developed Web services with the help of a Java-based Client program.The end user executes this client program by providing certain command line arguments. These command line arguments are different for a seller,buyer, and market. Hence, from the common code related to initializing some parameters, the discussion for the client will be dealt in three different sections with perspective for seller, buyer, and market.

Sellers Perspective

a. An end user interested in executing the client as seller has to provide following command line arguments:
   1. URL of GridManager Service;
   2. Trader type namely seller in this case;
   3. Crop name offered for sale;
   4. Crop variety;
   5. Crop quantity;
   6. Expected price;
   7. Trade mode like if seller wants to do direct trading with a buyer or wants to offer crop to amrket service for sale; and

8. Preferred trading location.

b. Using values assigned to these variables, an object of the SellerProperties is created.

```
sp=new SellerProperties(cropName,cq,cropVariety,
op,market,tradeMode);
```

c. Next, a reference to the GridMangerPortType is obtained to create a new instance of the Seller Resource. This is achieved by using the EPR of the GridManager service, which can be created by using the URI of it.

Listing 18. EPR retrieval of GridManagerService

```
GridManagerPortType gridManager;
SellerPortType seller;
gridManagerEPR = new EndpointReferenceType();
gridManagerEPR.setAddress(new Address(gridManager
URI));
gridManager = gridManagerLocator.getGridManagerPortT
ypePort(gridManagerEPR);
```

d. Security related parameters are to be initialized in order to encrypt the exchange of SOAP message between the Client and the GridManagerService. Here, Message Level Security is being utilized. Hence, only the body of the message is encrypted, leaving the header untouched.

Listing 19. Initialization of security related parameters for SOAP message encryption

```
((Stub)gridManager)._setProperty(Constants.GSI_SEC_
CONV,Constants.ENCRYPTION);
((Stub) gridManager)._setProperty(Constants.
AUTHORIZATION, NoAuthorization.getInstance());
```

e. The GridManagerService acts as a common factory for the Seller, Buyer, and Market Service. Its create method will be invoked by passing an object of the stub class CreateResource, which was discussed in the section related to GridManagerService. The constructor of CreateResource class expects a String argument namely serviceType, to identify which stake holders Resource instance has to be created and initialized. In this case, the serviceType argument will have value as "seller" to indicate that a new Seller Resource has to be created.

```
try {
createResponse = gridManager.createResource(new
CreateResource(serviceType));}
```

The EPR of a Resource instance is to be returned after creating it. The EPR returned will be stored in an object of createResponse. The client needs to inform the GridManagerService about the stakeholder of a newly created resource instance, namely, the seller, buyer, or the market.

f. Once the EPR is returned and stored in the object createResponse, operations can be invoked on this Seller Resource to modify the default values and set the trading parameters as indicated by the command line arguments provided by the end user. This is done, by first obtaining a reference to the SellerService port type, setting of security related parameters to secure the conversation, and then invoking operations exposed by the SellerService namely setSellerProperties() by passing the object of SellerProperties class created and initialized above.

Listing 20. Invocation of operation setSellerProperties of SellerService

```
if(serviceType.equals("seller")){
 sellerInstanceEPR= createResponse.
getEndpointReference();
 notificationEPR=sellerInstanceEPR;
seller = sellerInstanceLocator.getSellerPortTypePort(selle
rInstanceEPR);
((Stub)seller)._setProperty(Constants.GSI_SEC_
CONV,Constants.ENCRYPTION);
((Stub) seller)._setProperty(Constants.AUTHORIZATION,
NoAuthorization.getInstance());
```

```
Try {
seller.setSellerProperties(sp); }
```

g. The EPR of the Seller Resource is created and written in a file, will be utilized by a client responsible for providing notification related information when changes take place in the value of SellerResourceProperties; that is, the sellerStatus. After writing EPR in a file, the client NotificationListenerClient responsible for listening to notifications is invoked by invoking its operation startSubscription by passing serviceType and filename, which contains the EPR of this newly created Resource.

Buyers Perspective

a. An end user interested in executing the client as buyer has to provide following command line arguments:
   1. URL of GridManager Service;
   2. Trader type namely buyer in this case;
   3. Crop name interested in purchasing;
   4. Crop variety;
   5. Crop quantity;
   6. Offered price; and
   7. Preferred trading location.

b. Using values assigned to these variables, an object of the BuyerProperties is created.

```
buyerProperties=new BuyerProperties(cropName,c
q,cropVariety,market,op);
```

c. Next, a reference to the GridMangerPortType is obtained to create a new instance of the Buyer Resource. The explanation and the steps are as similar as we have seen for Seller Perspective till step (e), where the serviceType will be "buyer" instead of "seller."

d. The EPR, which will be returned, and will be of Buyer Resource; hence, operations exposed by BuyerService, namely setBuyerProperties() will be invoked to replace the default initialized value of the Buyer Resource with the arguments specified by the end user. After this, the explanation related to writing EPR in a file and notification is the same as that of SellerResource.

Markets Perspective

a. An end user interested in executing the client as market has to provide following command line arguments:
   1. URL of GridManager Service; and
   2. Trading location for which it wishes to trade.

b. Most of the explanation related to execution of a client from Market perspective remains same as Seller Perspective and Buyer Perspective. The only noticible difference being that after obtaining the EPR of the Market Resource, the operation invoked will be setMarketProperties(marketProperties); marketPortType.setMarketProperties(mar ketProperties);

   Once the property is set, then trading will begin for the specified trading location. Sellers and buyers registered with the DefaultIndexService will be matched for similar trading preferences and trade will be done. In case of indirect trade mode for some sellers, suitable amounts will be offered and its Earning Resource Property will be modified to reflect its earning. WS-RF offers functionality related to Notifications using WS-Notification, whereby a client is delivered messages whenever there is a change in the Resource Property to which it subscribes.

NOTIFICATION LISTENER CLIENT

A client to subscribe and receive notification messages is developed.

1. The client is a notification consumer. It will receive notifications, which will be sent by the services, BuyerService, and SellerService. The services acting as notification producer will invoke Notify operation on this client. The client runs in a daemon mode to receive the notifications at any time. Thus, it acts like a server on which operations can be invoked any time. In order to attain this property NotificationConsumerManager class is utilized.

```
NotificationConsumerManager consumer = null;
consumer = NotificationConsumerManager.getInstance();
consumer.startListening();
```

2. The client starts listening to the incoming notifications. In order to identify the end point at which the notification has to be delivered by the Seller or Buyer service, a proper address has to be assigned to this client. This is achieved by creating an EPR of the client.

```
EndpointReferenceType consumerEPR=consumer.
createNotificationConsumer(this);
```

3. Next, we send a request to the services to start sending the notification by using the standard Notify operation. The consumer EPR is passed to identify the end point at which the notification is to be delivered.

```
Subscribe statusRequest = new Subscribe();
statusRequest.setUseNotify(Boolean.TRUE);
statusRequest.setConsumerReference(consumerE
PR);
```

4. The client needs to inform the Topic to which it wishes to subscribe. In this case the client subscribes to different resource properties depending upon the service to which it subscribes. As for example, if the client program is executed as a seller, then the Resource Properties will be SellerStatus.

```
TopicExpressionType statusExpression = new TopicExpressionType();
statusExpression.setDialect(WSNConstants.
SIMPLE_TOPIC_DIALECT);
if(serviceType.equals("seller")) {
statusExpression.setValue(SellerConstants.
RP_SELLERSTATUS);
} else {
statusExpression.setValue(BuyerConstants.
RP_BUYERSTATUS); }
```

5. A reference to the notification producer is obtained for sending subscription request by obtaining reference to the NotificationProducerportType, implemented by the remote service like the BuyerService or SellerService. This is done by using extends tag in the WSDL, where the portType of these service extend the NotificationProducerPortType. The notification to be delievered is for a service based on factory pattern. Thus, EPR of the resource instance to be subscribed is to be obtained. This is achieved by reading from a file, which is created by the Client.java program. After reading EPR subscription a request is sent to the remote service.

```
WSBaseNotificationServiceAddressingLocator notifLocator =
new WSBaseNotificationServiceAddressingLocator();
try {
        FileInputStream fis = new
FileInputStream(fileName);
        File file=new File(fileName);
        file.deleteOnExit();
```

```
            endpoint=null;
endpoint = (EndpointReferenceType)
            ObjectDeserializer.deserialize(new
InputSource(fis),

EndpointReferenceType.class);
            if(serviceType.equals("seller"))
            {
                        endpointString = ObjectSerializer.toString(endpoint,SellerRESOURCE_ENDPOINT);
            }           else
            {
                        endpointString = ObjectSerializer.toString(endpoint,BuyerRESOURCE_ENDPOINT);
            }           System.out.println("\nEND POINT STRING:"+ endpointString);
}
............
producerPort = notifLocator.getNotificationProducerPort(endpoint);
```

6. For every subscription request, a unique EPR is created. This EPR can be used to subscribe, pause, and terminate subscription. This is achieved by

```
EndpointReferenceType statusSubscriptionEPR =
producerPort.subscribe(statusRequest).getSubscriptionReference();
```

7. The client starts listening to subscriptions until the time key is pressed. Incoming notifications are handled by a different method called deliver. The deliver method uses three parameters, namely, the topicPath used for creating subscription, the EPR of a producer of notification, and the message which is sent by the service.
Our Resource classes used ResourcePropertyTopic for notification in ResourceProperties. Hence, the notification messages are of ResourcePropertyValueChangeNotificationType. This further embeds message of ResourcePropertyValueChangeNotificationType in itself. The object of this class contains the new resource property value.

EXECUTION SCENARIO

In this section, the trading process is displayed by execution of various services depending on the preferences indicated by a client.

Execution of Seller Grid Service

Now, when the GridManagerClient is executed for each of the above given entities to perform trade, the following situation will emerge:

- By looking at the data above, it can be inferred that for direct trade, seller and buyers interested in trading in Bhopal will trade with each other. Similarly, trading will take place for sellers interested in indirect trading irrespective of location of their trading.
- A seller expresses his intention to offer his crop for sale by running the client program, Client.java by providing command line arguments.These arguments are in the following order:
    - URL of the GridManager service;
    - seller: This word is provided to indicate client wants to have an instance of a seller service;
    - Crop Name: The crop seller wishes to sell;
    - Crop Quantity: The quantity of a crop, which seller is interested in selling;
    - Crop Variety: The variety of a crop;
    - Trade Location: The location where the seller wishes to trade;
    - Expected Price/Kg.: The amount which a seller wishes to obtain per kg. of a crop; and
    - Trade Mode: If seller directly wants to sell directly to a buyer, then direct

mode is adopted; otherwise, indirect mode is adopted.

In the following example, an intention of a seller is shown, who is ready to sell 50 kg. of wheat at Bhopal location, and expecting minimum of Rs. 60 per kg.

```
$ java -DGLOBUS_LOCATION=$GLOBUS_LOCATION
org.sws.examples.clients.GridManager.Client
http://10.100.64.65:8080/wsrf/services/sws/examples/
GridManager seller wheat 50 kamla Bhopal 60 direct
```

Execution of seller grid service will start and will wait for appropriate offer to come from a potential buyer. Seller grid service will receive notification, once an appropriate offer is floated by a buyer. Initially, following output will be generated:

```
END POINT STRING:<ns1:SellerServiceEndpoint xsi:
type="ns2:EndpointReferenceType" xmlns:ns1="http://
www.securingwebservices.org/namespaces/examples/
SellerService" xmlns:xsi="http://www.w3.org/2001/
XMLSchema-instance" xmlns:ns2="http://schemas.
xmlsoap.org/ws/2004/03/addressing">
 <ns2:Address xsi:type="ns2:AttributedURI">http://10.100
.64.65:8080/wsrf/services/sws/examples/SellerService</
ns2:Address>
 <ns2:ReferenceProperties xsi:type="ns2:
ReferencePropertiesType">
 <ns1:SellerResourceKey>a1662350-1628-11db-9878-
ce21816644d9</ns1:SellerResourceKey>
 </ns2:ReferenceProperties>
 <ns2:ReferenceParameters xsi:type="ns2:
ReferenceParametersType"/>
</ns1:SellerServiceEndpoint>
Waiting for notification. Ctrl-C to end.
Waiting for notification. Ctrl-C to end.
```

Execution of Buyer Grid Service

Similarly, a buyer can express his intention to purchase crop by running Client.java, but with a different set of command line arguments:

- URL of the GridManager service;
- buyer: This word is provided to indicate that a client would like to have an instance of a buyer service;
- Crop Name: The crop buyer wishes to buy;
- Crop Quantity: The crop quantity buyer is interested in purchasing;
- Crop Variety: The crop variety of the crop;
- Trade Location: The location where the buyer wishes to trade; and
- Offered Price/Kg.: The amount which a buyer would like to obtain per kg. of a crop.

As shown in the following screen, one buyer is ready to purchase 10 kg. of wheat at Rs. 70 per kg. Thus, buyer grid service will also wait for an appropriate match to happen in the market located at Bhopal.

```
$java -DGLOBUS_LOCATION=$GLOBUS_LOCATION
org.sws.examples.clients.GridManager.Client
http://10.100.64.65:8080/wsrf/services/sws/examples/
GridManager buyer wheat 10 kamla Bhopal 70
```

Here, execution of buyer grid service will start and it will wait for an appropriate match to be identified in a market located at Bhopal.

```
END POINT STRING:<ns1:BuyerServiceEndpoint xsi:
type="ns2:EndpointReferenceType" xmlns:ns1="http://
www.securingwebservices.org/namespaces/examples/
BuyerService" xmlns:xsi="http://www.w3.org/2001/
XMLSchema-instance" xmlns:ns2="http://schemas.
xmlsoap.org/ws/2004/03/addressing">
 <ns2:Address xsi:type="ns2:AttributedURI">http://10.100
.64.65:8080/wsrf/services/sws/examples/BuyerService</
ns2:Address>
 <ns2:ReferenceProperties xsi:type="ns2:
ReferencePropertiesType">
 <ns1:BuyerResourceKey>3136b260-1629-11db-9878-
ce21816644d9</ns1:BuyerResourceKey>
 </ns2:ReferenceProperties>
 <ns2:ReferenceParameters xsi:type="ns2:
ReferenceParametersType"/>
</ns1:BuyerServiceEndpoint>
```

```
Waiting for notification. Ctrl-C to end.
Waiting for notification. Ctrl-C to end.
```

Execution of Market Grid Service

Whenever the buyers and sellers express their intentions to trade, their resource instances are also registered with the DefaultIndexService. When MarketService start its operations, it will query DefaultIndexService to obtain the buyers and sellers interested in trading. The Client.java program is executed with a different set of command line arguments.

- URL of the GridManager service.
- Market: This word is provided to indicate that the client would like to have an instance of a market service.
- Trade location: The location of a market where the actual trade will occur.

```
$ java -DGLOBUS_LOCATION=$GLOBUS_LOCATION
org.sws.examples.clients.GridManager.Client
http://10.100.64.65:8080/wsrf/services/sws/examples/
GridManager market Bhopal
```

Once market service of a particular location starts executing, it tries to match potential buyers and sellers. If an appropriate buyer is found for a seller, approprate notification is sent to both of them to inform them about success of entering into a trade deal. Otherwise, both of them will wait for a potential purchaser of a crop. In case of indirect trade mode, the seller receives various types of notifications, which are computed for this trade.

NOTIFICATION TO SELLER SERVICE

After initiation of a market service for Bhopal, matching will be performed for buyer(s) and seller(s) having preference for Bhopal. Based on the match found for a seller and a buyer for wheat, following notification will be generated for a seller service:

```
A new notification has arrived
Your crop sold till now is 10.0Kg
A new notification has arrived
Your crop has been sold recently
A new notification has arrived
Your crop quantity still remaining to be sold is:40.0Kg
A new notification has arrived
Amount Offered to you per Kg is Rs70.0
A new notification has arrived
Crop Quantity Which will be purchased by a buyer is
10.0Kg
A new notification has arrived
Your Earning is Rs700.0
Waiting for notification. Ctrl-C to end.
```

NOTIFICATION TO A BUYER SERVICE

The following notification will be generated for a buyer service:

```
A new notification has arrived
The Crop Quantity which you will purchase from a seller
is 10.0Kg
A new notification has arrived
Amount Offered by you per Kg is:Rs70.0
A new notification has arrived
Amount spent by you in current purchase is Rs700.0
```

MANAGEMENT OF GRID MARKET

In the Grid environment, the heterogeneous nature of resources, services, and their functionality makes it difficult to manage them in a uniform way. Querying the functionality of any node and service is one of the hardest processes and Grid management system often relies on the static WSDL documentation available to them even before the start interacting with the node, rather than determining its capabilities on the fly.

In our case study, their can be different types of markets specializing in different domains, sellers, trade scenarios, buyer interests, and so forth, which makes the management very difficult, if not possible. The situation becomes more complicated as the heterogeneity of the system can't be predicted at anytime and it should cope with any future situation. WSDM provides the uniform mechanism to interact with the heterogeneous resources for effective management. As discussed earlier, WSDM specification describes what information any service or node may expose for uniform management. This information can be set of resource property elements, WSDM capabilities, that is, caption, description and version, manageability characteristics specific to its domain, operational status, metrics, notification of WSDM events, metadata for resource properties elements, relationship of different resources, and resource properties elements.

Although we haven't discussed different type of markets and different trade scenarios in our case study, still we have to monitor the activities of sellers and buyers. To manage different stake holders involves exposing new set of resource property elements and corresponding operations. The implementation of these manageable resources and operations is very similar to the any ordinary resource and has not discussed in the case study. The possible manageable resource for the seller is discussed briefly, so that readers can appreciate the usage and role of WSDM in any Grid application. The possible resource properties elements for the seller manageable resource can be which can be modified only by the authentic management client:

- *Number of previous transactions:* This is metric metadata monitored for a certain time period such as the last 6 months. This resource property is updated for each successful transaction.
- *Number of items to be sold:* This is a simple counter which monitors the item still available for sale.
- *Pending Fee:* This resource property is of data type Boolean, which can have a value of false if the user has failed to pay any previous market fee for using any utility service.
- *Ranking:* This resource property indicates the ranking of the seller based on seller's previous activities, that is, successful transactions, activeness in the market, any complaints against the seller, his promptness to pay market fee, and so forth.

Similarly, their can be few management operations for the seller which depends on the manageable resource, update these resources, or take appropriate actions in case of any notification. A few such operations are listed below:

- *suspendMembership:* This operation temporarily suspends the membership of the seller may be due to any on going dispute.
- *resumeMembership:* This operation lets seller to continue trading in the market once the issues related to its suspensions are resolved.
- *cancelMembership:* This operation cancels the membership of the seller permanently.
- *updateRanking:* After any transaction, sellers intentions to sell any new thing or any complaint against seller updateRanking operation is called automatically.

These manageable resources and corresponding operations are important for efficient queries. The buyer can search the seller based on the rankings, and the management system can offer incentives to the seller based on its activeness in market trading. This brings a lot more confidence in the Grid Market, as only management clients have complete access to these resource properties values and only few read-only resource properties are available to users of the system. On the same lines, there will be manageable resource properties for the buyer and market.

SUMMARY

Business processes of large enterprise systems interact with various stack holders, that is, business partners and customers to integrate distributed heterogeneous services. In this chapter, different specifications originating from the Grid paradigm are evaluated to capture the requirements of dynamic business process which is called Business Process Grid. These long running and dynamic business processes require support for state monitoring, transaction management, and event notifications.

We focused our attention toward the utilization and integration of existing technologies to achieve loosely coupled integration of services having support for state, notification, execution monitoring, and scalability. Principles of Grid computing utilizing the Service Oriented Architecture (SOA) are followed and implemented to satisfy the requirements of the business process. To achieve these objectives, WS-RF, WSN, and relevant specifications and standards in this area are followed here. We have shown the use of WS-RF to achieve state in Web Services and WSN for notification and integration of distributed heterogeneous services. We have demonstrated the use of grid services to provide required middleware support. Convergence of grid and Web services standards and specifications for the complete execution of a business process is discussed in this chapter. The future work is diverted into several paths: implementation of policy, agreement, negotiation, and use of semantic Web to provide meaningful integration and coordination of resources in a grid environment.

REFERENCES

Akram, A. (2006). Web services resource framework resource sharing (Tutorial 9 and Tutorial 10). Retrieved June 11, 2007, from http://esc.dl.ac.uk/WOSE/tutorials/

Akram, A., Kewley, J., & Allan, R. (2006, October). Modelling WS-RF based enterprise applications. In *Proceedings of the Tenth IEEE International Enterprise Distributed Object Computing Conference* (EDOC 2006).

Birman, K. (2005). Can Web services scale up? *Computer, 38*(10), 107-110.

Booth, D., Haas, H., McCabe, F. et al. (2004, February). Web services architecture, W3C Working Group Note 11. Retrieved June 11, 2007, from http://www.w3.org/TR/ws-arch/

Czajkowski, K., Ferguson, D., Foster, I. et al. (2004). From open grid services infrastructure to WS-resource framework: Refactoring & evolution.

Foster, I. (2002). The physiology of the grid: An open grid services architecture for distributed systems integration. Retrieved June 11, 2007, from www.globus.org/alliance/publications/papers/ogsa.pdf

Foster, I., Czajkowski, K. et al. (2005). Modeling and managing State in distributed systems: The role of OGSI and WSRF. In *Paper presented at the Proceedings of the IEEE.*

Gottschalk, K.D., Graham, S., Kreger, H., & Snell, J. (2002). Introduction to Web services architecture. *IBM Systems Journal, 41*(2), 170-177.

Joseph, J., & Fellenstein, C. (2003). *Grid computing.* Upper Saddle River, NJ, USA: Prentice Hall.

Junginger, M.O. (2003). *High performance messaging system for peer-to-peer networks.* Kansas: University of Missouri.

Laliwala, Z., Jain, P., & Chaudhary, S. (2006). Semantic based service-oriented grid architecture for business processes. In *Proceedings of the 2006 IEEE International Conference on Services Computing* (SCC 2006), SCC 2006 Industry Track.

Modal Act. (2003). The State Agricultural Produce Marketing (Development & Regulation Act, 2003). Retrieved June 11, 2007, from http://agmarknet.nic.in/reforms.htm

Pallickara, S., & Fox, G. (2005). An analysis of notification related specifications for Web/grid applications. In Paper presented at the ITCC (2).

Papazoglou, M.P. (2003). Web services and business transactions. *World Wide Web, 6*(1), 49-91.

Schmit, B., & Dustdar, S. (2005). *Systematic design of Web service transactions.*

SOAP. (2000). Simple object access protocol (SOAP) 1.1. Retrieved June 11, 2007, from http://www.w3.org/TR/2000/NOTE-SOAP-20000508/

Sorathia, V., Laliwala, Z., & Chaudhary, S. (2005). Towards agricultural marketing reforms: Web services orchestration approach. In *Paper presented at the SCC '05: Proceedings of the 2005 IEEE International Conference on Services Computing*, Washington, DC, USA.

UDDI. (2004). Universal description, discovery and integration, UDDI Version 3.0.2. Retrieved June 11, 2007, from http://uddi.org/pubs/uddi_v3.htm

Vinoski, S. (2004a). More Web services notifications. *Internet Computing, IEEE, 8*(3), 90-93.

Vinoski, S. (2004b). WS-nonexistent standards. *Internet Computing, IEEE, 8*(6), 94-96.

Wang, H., Huang, J.Z., Qu, Y., & Xie, J. (2004). Web services: Problems and future directions. *Journal of Web Semantics, 1*(3).

Wilkes, L. (2005). The Web services protocol stack. Retrieved June 11, 2007, from http://roadmap.cbdiforum.com/reports/protocols/index.php

WS-Addressing. (2004). Web services addressing. W3C Member Submission 10 August 2004. Retrieved June 11, 2007, from http://www.w3.org/Submission/ws-addressing/

WS-BaseFaults. (2006). Web services base faults 1.2. Retrieved June 11, 2007, from http://docs.oasis-open.org/wsrf/wsrf-ws_base_faults-1.2-spec-os.pdf

WS-BaseNotification. (2006). Web services base notification 1.3. Retrieved June 11, 2007, from http://docs.oasis-open.org/wsn/wsn-ws_base_notification-1.3-spec-pr-03.pdf

WS-BrokeredNotification. (2006). Web services brokered notification 1.3. Retrieved June 11, 2007, from http://docs.oasis-open.org/wsn/wsn-ws_brokered_notification-1.3-spec-pr-03.pdf

WS-Eventing. (2006). Web services eventing (WS-Eventing). Retrieved June 11, 2007, from http://www.w3.org/Submission/WS-Eventing/

WS-Notification. (2005). Web services notification. Retrieved June 11, 2007, from www.oasis-open.org/committees/wsn/

WS-ResourceFramework. (2005). Web services resource framework. Retrieved June 11, 2007, from www.oasis-open.org/committees/wsrf/

WS-ResourceLifetime. (2006). Web services resource lifetime 1.2. Retrieved June 11, 2007, from http://docs.oasis-open.org/wsrf/wsrf-ws_resource_lifetime-1.2-spec-os.pdf

WS-ResourceProperties. (2006). Web services resource properties 1.2. Retrieved June 11, 2007, from http://docs.oasis-open.org/wsrf/wsrf-ws_resource_properties-1.2-spec-os.pdf

WS-ServiceGroup. (2006). Web services service group 1.2. Retrieved June 11, 2007, from http://docs.oasis-open.org/wsrf/wsrf-ws_service_group-1.2-spec-os.pdf

WS-Topics. (2006). Web services topics 1.3. Retrieved June 11, 2007, from http://docs.oasis-open.org/wsn/wsn-ws_topics-1.3-spec-pr-02.pdf

WSDL. (2005). Web services description language (WSDL) 1.1. Retrieved June 11, 2007, from http://www.w3.org/TR/2001/NOTE-wsdl-20010315

Chapter XII
Combining Web Services and Grid Services:
Practical Approaches and Implications to Resource Discovery

Aisha Naseer
Brunel University, UK

Lampros K. Stergioulas
Brunel University, UK

ABSTRACT

Web technologies have played a significant role in supporting the global sharing of Internet resources and thereby improving communications. On another front, Grids hold the promise to provide global interoperability and interconnectivity at a level considered impossible a few decades ago. In practice, there is not much difference between the existing Grid and Web infrastructures; in fact, a Grid infrastructure could be built by making minor modifications to a Web infrastructure. The implementation of Web-based Grids or a partially-Gridified Web is one of the potential solutions to Grid infrastructure problems. This can be done by sharing Grid services across the Grid infrastructure, effectively using the underlying Web services as vehicles or transporters of these services. The chapter discusses Grid services as another type of Grid resources, examines possible ways to integrate Grid services and Web services, and explores how this will support Grid resource discovery. It is argued that Grids should be developed using the underlying Web infrastructure and Grid services could be integrated with Web services using inheritance techniques to produce Grid-supported Web services. Furthermore, this approach seems to deal effectively with the problems of resource discovery in such partially-Gridified Web environments. An earlier version of this work has been presented in Naseer and Stergioulas (2006a).

INTRODUCTION

Web technologies have played a significant role in supporting the global sharing of Internet resources and thereby improving communications. On a different front, Grids are expected to power up the next generation of Web and hold the promise to provide global interconnectivity and interoperability, regardless of the geographical and heterogeneity constraints, and at such an advanced and ubiquitous level that was considered impossible a few decades ago. Grids enable the sharing, selection, and aggregation of geographically distributed "autonomous" resources dynamically at run time depending on their availability, capability, performance, cost, policies, or rules which govern them and the users' quality-of-service requirements and reliability. Grids are composed of a global network infrastructure that contains several other networks (local or wide area) and exhibits extensively high synergy among all its units (humans, networks, programs, processes and services, etc.). Cross-communication among the various types of units is needed on a large scale in order to enhance the capabilities and capacities of Grids. Such units or resources are capable of sending and receiving requests/commands and act as independent communicators. This can be made possible by specialized services that are available on the Grids (Grid services).

The trend to use Web-services as wrappers or transporters of Grid services is today becoming more and more popular and is one of the ways to integrate Web services with Grid services. The reason behind this need for integration lies in two crucial facts: (1) Web services alone cannot be directly implemented on a Grid architecture due to constraints such as the requirement for them to have a "stateless appearance" and their persistency, whereas for a service to operate on Grids, it should always have a state and should be transient in nature; (2) Grid services alone cannot be directly implemented on the (successfully deployed) Web infrastructure due to the lack of standardization (standard protocol or standard language). Moreover, Grid technology, being a relatively newly emerged discipline, has neither infrastructural standards nor benchmarks established yet. Therefore, the integration of Grid services with Web services is necessary in order to support a fully- or partially-Gridified Web. The two types of services have to be glued together using some specialized object-oriented techniques. Because Grids, from this perspective can be viewed as the next generation of Web, Grid infrastructure could be built by making minor modifications to the Web infrastructure. The implementation of Web-based Grids or partially-Gridified Web is one of the potential responses to Grid infrastructure needs, which would facilitate the formation of virtual organizations globally. These virtual organizations would then be Grid-like structures residing over the Web.

Grid services provide a means for discovering other Grid resources; the term used for this operation is Resource Discovery. The Grid community has not yet been able to fully resolve the issue of Resource Discovery due to various technical constraints and geographical limitations. However, Grid services can be shared across the Grid infrastructure by using the underlying Web services as vehicles or transporters. Integration of Grid services into Web services can provide an efficient way to pass requests and responses to resource discovery queries, which is a key issue to be addressed. There are two potential ways to address this issue through services integration: (a) by using a Grid-based Web service approach or (b) by using a Web-based Grid service approach. The former supports the development of Web services containing special Grid services' interfaces or behaviors (inherited or encapsulated) to make them operable on the Grids, that is, it encapsulates or *wraps* Grid services into Web services as specialized functions; and the latter supports the development of individual Grid services containing the features and functionalities of the Web services that are inherited or extended from the Web services class, that is, it encapsulates or wraps Grid services into Web services to support the service integration.

Furthermore, there is currently a well-recognized need for both the Grid and Web communities to work in close collaboration and find a Web-based solution to Grid resource discovery problems. This chapter also discusses the main issues of resource discovery in Grids and examines potential solutions. Section 1 offers an introduction to the problem, while section 2 discusses the background of Grid networks and Grid services. Section 3 reviews the challenge of resource discovery in Grids with potential problems and methods. Section 4 defines the notion of a Partially-Gridified Web. Section 5 argues that a potential solution to Grid resource discovery lies in combining the Grid services with Web services by using one of the service integration approaches, namely, the Grid-based Web service approach or the Web-based Grid service approach, depending on the respective viewpoint. In section 6, a review of related work toward achieving this goal is included, the two approaches are examined, and suggestions are made as to the suitability of these approaches if implemented in their respective environments by employing encapsulation or inheritance techniques. An example of service integration is discussed in section 7, and future directions are explored in section 8. Finally, conclusions are drawn in section 9.

BACKGROUND: GRID ARCHITECTURE AND SERVICES

What Are Grids?

Grids are Multipeer to Multipeer network architectures (Naseer & Stergioulas, 2005) on which all the components (resources, protocols, interfaces, services, network layers, etc.) are integrated with each other in a controlled and consistent manner so as to support the functionality of a Grid (Figure 1). The primary purpose of Grids is to globally share resources across various organizational domains,

Figure 1. Grid networks

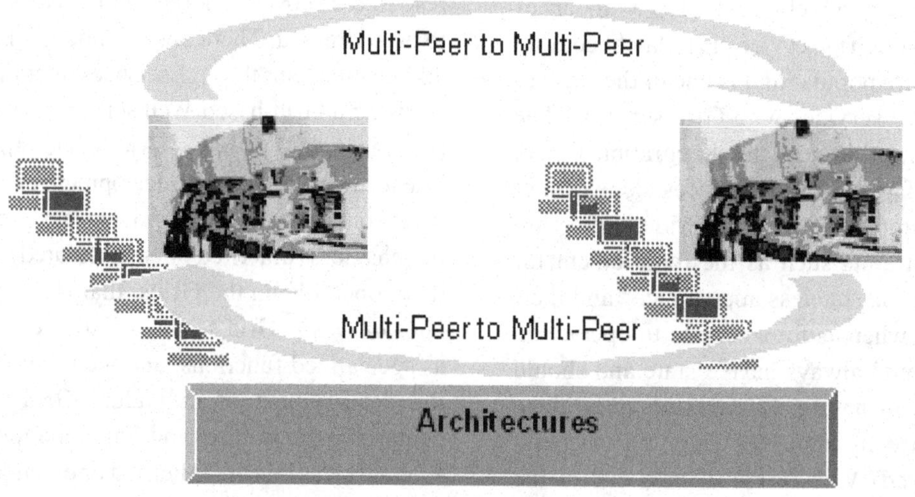

regardless of their geographical dispersion. The Grid infrastructure, being distributed in nature, allows for high variability in user and resource participation. It deploys a decentralized computing environment, which is compatible or interoperable with all sorts of network architectures.

Why Do We Need Grids?

In the face of recent technological advancements in different fields of computer science, there is a need for an infrastructure that would assist all domains of economy and society to cope with and make maximum use of these rapid advancements. The infrastructure known as Grid promises to fulfill these expectations and provides a platform for carrying out remote processing through intensive communicational ability (Naseer & Stergioulas, 2006c). The distributed computing systems of the 1990s did not provide facilities such as on-demand, pick 'n choose, integrated services, and globally shared channels of collaboration. Such enhanced facilities require powerful middleware that resides on a strong infrastructural backbone, which would assist and manage these services in a secure and controlled manner. The emergence of scientific needs for performing joint and collaborative tasks on a large scale has made Grids a necessity. These tasks require access to not only intense computational power resources, but also to massive data storage resources (in the order of peta-bytes). To acquire and own all these resources could be very expensive for a single organization, whereas on Grids one can not only share resources from other people, but can also render their resources available to other people for their use.

Moreover, Grids aim to provide abstraction - at both the user and resource level - that is transparent to the user and relies on a standard-based service infrastructure to share computers, storage space, sensors, software applications and data, and so forth, across organizational boundaries. However, crossing organizational boundaries is one of the main issues of resource sharing, because one has to deal with maintaining security and confidentiality of data and other Grid resources.

The Web can be considered as an "information Grid" and the Grid as an "extended Web" that goes beyond information sharing to allow users to share computer resources (Talia, 2002). In fact, the Web infrastructure is quite similar to the Grid infrastructure in the sense that it aims at interconnecting hardware, software, and users for sharing, via some transmission media, and provides abstraction and transparency at the user level but with limited functionality or accessibility options, whereas Grids provide more functionality than the Web.

Grid Features and Capabilities

In addition to the services provided by the Web, Grids are expected to possess extra capabilities and features, such as:

1. **Self-Management:** Automatic online upgrading of resources at runtime;
2. **Self-Configuration:** Automatic online configuration of settings;
3. **Self-Motivation:** Automatic online scheduling;
4. **Self-Developed Growth:** Automatic dynamic expansion (addition of new nodes);
5. **Self-Maintenance:** Automatic online repairing and elimination of distortion among resources or nodes;
6. **Dynamic Extraction:** Intelligent synthesis of knowledge and creation of security models for Grids dynamically;
7. **Self-Alerting:** Intelligent security system that dynamically generates automatic alerts throughout Grid;
8. **Resource Discovery:** Automatic tracking of resources;
9. **Self-Integration:** Automatic intelligent distributed resource management; and

10. **Self-Resolving:** Automatic resolution of semantic compatibility issues.

Moreover, the types of resources available on a Grid are generally more powerful, more diverse, and better connected than the typical Web resource. The service type resources over the Grids are generally more complex, because they have to support dynamic environments and communities.

Grid Services: A Type of Grid Resource

A resource can be any real or conceptual object that is needed to be accessed by other entities, such as human users of the system or programs that generate requests for accessing particular resources. The two major categories of Grid resources are physical resources (storage, computational, network, and peripheral) and logical (data, knowledge, and application) resources. There are many types of resources in each category. Grid services belong to the logical class of Grid resources (Naseer & Stergioulas, 2005). All the other types of Grid resources are accessed by using the service type Grid resource. Services can be technically defined as lines of code that are packaged into a component to perform a dedicated functionality. In terms of their function, services implemented on a network infrastructure could resemble thread-like neuron structures or impulses in a human body. Thus, the output of one service can serve as an input to another service. We need services with special capabilities and features, which we will from now on call Grid services, to get our tasks successfully accomplished on Grid networks.

There are two types of Grid services. The first type is known as Operational-Level services and the second type is known as Management-Level services (Naseer & Stergioulas, 2006b). Speaking in a broader sense, the former relates to the user operations on a Grid and the latter relates to the management of Operational-Level services and to making them available on Grids. The user operations include data manipulation (storage or retrieval) by using storage resources, compute-intensive calculations, and providing either solutions to complex problems by using extra computational power via computational resources, or access to hardware devices, such as particle accelerators, Magnetic Resonance Imaging (MRI) machines, printers, and so forth. Each of these operations is related to different Operational-Level services, but recruits the same Management-Level services, such as registration and description, management and configuration, scheduling and planning, ubiquitous access and retrieval, and fault tolerance services. These two levels of services are strongly correlated and integrated in order to provide complete service delivery on Grids.

On a Grid infrastructure, multiple services are dispersed or scattered across different regions. Their disparate geographical locations, heterogeneous platforms, and diverse dynamic statuses make these services rather specialized in nature, and while offering much desired versatility, they are difficult to locate, access, and manage. Most importantly, Grid services have changed the vision of Grids from resource-centric to service-centric, and brought forward the widespread adoption of Service Oriented Architecture (SOA) for the implementation of Grid infrastructure.

The many social and scientific disciplines that involve manipulation of massive datasets and need intensive computational power have the tendency to become Gridified. Recently, we have witnessed the emergence of dedicated Grids possessing specialized functionalities and offering customized services, such as accumulation of celestial phenomenon observations in astronomy (Qin, Davenhall, Noddle, & Walton, 2003), earthquake simulation (Peng & Law, 2004), and health care services in Biomedicine (Stewart, 2004), and so forth.

Web Services: Platform Independent Communicators

In the new Internet landscape, Web services are now considered as the most efficient and reliable communicators of messages from one place to another, regardless of geographical or technological heterogeneity. The emerging Web services provide a framework for an application-to-application interaction that grants access to business-to-business, e-science, and e-government services over the Internet. These services will allow a more extensive use of the Web's functionality by supporting automated processes involving machine-to-machine cooperation and interaction (Talia, 2002). Thus, Web services are considered as one of the potential solutions for the practical implementation of Service Oriented Architecture (SOA) in Grid infrastructure. Web services enable interoperability, mainly via a set of open standards to provide information about the data in a document to users on various platforms. Web services are built on service-oriented architecture, Internet/intranet technologies, and other technologies like information security tools, and so forth. Moreover, Web services support Web-based access, easy integration, and service reusability. Using a Web service architecture, everything is a service, encapsulating behavior and making it accessible through an interface that can be invoked for use by other services on the network (Wu, Moslehi, & Bose, 2005). Because Web technology concepts are independent of any programming language, operating systems platforms, or systems software, they can be easily integrated with other technologies and infrastructures to facilitate intratechnology integration at an advanced level. The traditional Grid applications, with their predominantly scientific focus, typically rely on hosting environments provided by native operating system processes. Grid semantics also usually come from the operating system rather than from external services. Web services, however, can be employed in relatively sophisticated component-based hosting environments, such as Sun's J2EE (Goth, 2002). Moreover, Web services can communicate with other Web services regardless of their implementation method in order to make them interoperable. Therefore, Web services technologies and components such as XML, WSDL, UDDI, or SOAP could be integrated with specialized Grid services or Grid functions to provide enhanced extensible functionality over a partially-Gridified Web.

THE CHALLENGE OF RESOURCE DISCOVERY IN GRIDS

Grid services can provide a means for discovering other Grid resources. The Grid community has not yet been able to fully resolve the issue of Resource Discovery due to various technical constraints and geographical limitations, such as autonomous, heterogeneous resources, dynamic nature and status of resources, geographical dispersion of resources, large number of users and large distributed networks, different operating systems/platforms, different administrative domains, lack of portability, availability status of resources, and different technology policies. It is not easy to track or locate the right resource in a vast interconnected environment. The mechanism of resource discovery can be viewed through different lenses in various domains; it is a multidisciplinary task and is one of the most important issues to be dealt with in future Grid technology. For the successful deployment of a Grid infrastructure, it is essential to access and make maximum use of the resources that are available on the Grid and this is possible only if the resources can be tracked effectively and efficiently.

Techniques adopted for resource discovery should be both location and platform independent. When a request is placed for some particular resource, the entire network is first searched to track or locate a suitable resource, and then the resource is matched against the request query and selected (if a sufficient match is established). Upon selection, its availability status is checked and, if available, the desired task is performed.

Resource discovery on Grids is quite similar to the discovery of resources on the Web, because in both cases the user is "blind" to the specific resource location. This difficulty in tracking down the right resource in a vast interconnectivity environment raises the issue of Resource Discovery, that is, the process of gaining access to resources for successful completion of the job at hand. For this purpose, a consistent and controlled relationship among the various resources defined on a Grid is needed. As the cost and time taken to complete a job can vary enormously between applications, it is often useful to monitor the job consumption rate. Successful allocation, aggregation, management, selection and utilization of autonomous, and versatile and distributed resources operating under different authentication policies are issues not resolved yet.

A detailed analysis of many different methods that have been used to address the issue of resource discovery, and many approaches that have been taken can be found in Naseer and Stergioulas (2006c). The three basic resource discovery models, namely centralized, distributed, and semidistributed, could be used with various approaches according to their application environment. The Centralized resource discovery model is the simplest and a centralized architecture is easy to design. Moreover, data management is easy because the entire data is hosted at a single point. However, it is not likely to be recommended as a resource discovery solution in general purpose Grids, because a centralized architecture is entirely different from Grid architecture, which is multipeer to multipeer. Hence, it would be an inappropriate route to follow in the case of ever-growing networks, due to the major issue of poor scalability. Furthermore, poor security and reliability are serious disadvantages of the centralized model. The Distributed resource discovery model can address this problem to some extent, but is not a perfect solution, because even though being distributed in nature, if the network grows it becomes difficult to maintain and track the huge reservoir of resources, reducing the efficiency of a resource discovery mechanism. The issues of scalability and architectural compatibility arise in both the Centralized and Distributed models. The Semidistributed resource discovery model can provide the best option for creating resource/request brokering systems and designing related middleware packages, because overall it seems to be more reliable. However, this model also has some limitations, such as complexity, time, costs and difficulty of managing/maintaining, and so forth. In order to provide optimal service, such systems need to be easily configurable, flexible, and generic. Moreover, a semidistributed network architecture should be modeled in a sophisticated manner, so as to address the scalability issue sufficiently to ensure that its effectiveness and efficiency remain unaltered, regardless of the number of nodes or peers or resources added to or removed from the network. It must also possess load-balancing and fault-tolerance features. There is no definitive or complete solution to this problem. However, because Web services can be used to discover resources on the Grids, one way of achieving successful resource discovery is by integrating the Grid services with Web services or gluing them together under the Semidistributed model and using the hybrid approach for resource discovery.

PARTIALLY-GRIDIFIED WEB

By providing specialized services onto the Web and making it extensible with additional features such as the global provision of computational power, storage space, and intergroup collaboration across various geographically dispersed domains, the building of Grid infrastructure would be possible over existing Web infrastructure, thereby making it a "partially Gridified Web" (see Figure

2). It would possess all the features and functionalities of a Web with some additional and enhanced functionalities to make it "Grid-enabled."

A Web-based Grid infrastructure would transform the basic elements, such as Extensible Markup Language (XML), Web Service Definition Language (WSDL), Universal Description, Discovery, and Integration (UDDI), and Simple Object Access Protocol (SOAP) Web services, and so forth, into extensible carriers of specialized (Grid) services that would be dedicated to dealing with requests for specialized tasks on the Grids.

A partially-Gridified Web has an infrastructure network that is based on the Web, but have a number of small Grid networks (or Grid infrastructures) built on top of it. It would provide a platform for carrying out distributed execution and remote processing of any dataset through intensive computation, for storing peta-bytes of massive data, and for supporting group-wise collaborative analysis. Where group-wise collaborative analysis includes remotely analyzing a particular problem in groups or communities (online), such as groups of pharmacists analyzing the effects of a drug or a group of scientists carrying out disease analysis through performing an online simulation of the body organ. Users of the partially-Gridified Web resources can be human users, such as computer operators, system administrators, programmers, scientists, or some automated processes or computer programs that send commands/requests to use or discover a Grid resource.

Figure 2. Partially-gridified Web

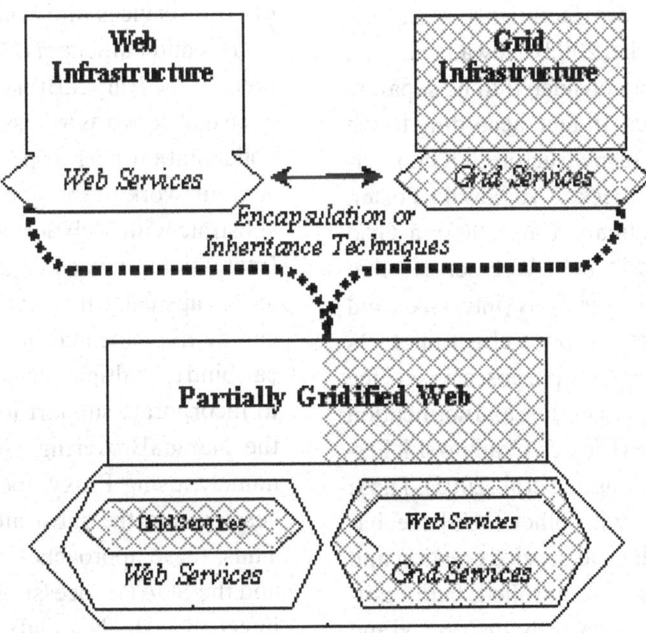

COMBINING GRID SERVICES WITH WEB SERVICES: A SERVICE INTEGRATION APPROACH

Each of the Grid and Web services are specialized so as to provide sophisticated functionalities in their own domains. Web services cannot be directly implemented on Grid architecture due to constraints, such as their stateless nature and persistency, whereas the Grid services should always have a state and are transient in nature. Therefore, the integration of Grid services with Web services is necessary in order to support a fully- or partially-Gridified Web. The two types of services need to be glued together using some specialized object-oriented techniques. The Open Grid Services Architecture (OGSA) defines the Grid service concept, based on principles and technologies from both the Grid computing and Web services communities (Talia, 2002). Moreover, OGSA not only defines the semantics for a Grid service, but also defines standard mechanisms for creating, naming, and discovering transient Grid service instances. It also provides location transparency and multiple protocol bindings for service instances and supports integration with underlying native platform facilities (Foster, Kesselman, Nick, & Tuecke, 2002). Nowadays, Grid services are no longer considered to be separate from the Web services. In fact, according to the Open Grid Services Infrastructure (OGSI) version 1.0 specification (Tuecke, Czajkowski, Foster, Frey, Graham, Kesselman et al., 2003), a Grid service is considered to be a Web service that conforms to a set of conventions (interfaces and behaviours) which define how a client interacts with a Grid service for such purposes as service lifetime management, inspection, and notification of service state changes (Foster, Czajkowski, Ferguson, Frey, Graham, Maguire et al., 2005). These conventions, together with other OGSI mechanisms associated with Grid service creation and discovery, provide for the controlled, fault-resilient, and secure management of the distributed and often long-lived state that is commonly required in advanced distributed applications. Recently, there has been a drift from OGSI to the Web-Services Resource Framework (WSRF) due to potential performance advantage reasons. WSRF (Czajkowski, et al., 2004) is concerned primarily with the creation, addressing, inspection, and lifetime management of state-enabled resources. It codifies the relationship between Web services and state-enabled resources in terms of the implied resource pattern, which is a set of conventions on Web services technologies. A state-enabled resource that participates in the invoked resource pattern is termed a WS-resource. The framework describes the WS-resource definition and its association with the description of a Web service interface and describes how to make the properties of a WS-resource accessible through a Web service interface and to manage a WS-resource's lifetime. Based on industry feedback, the revised and updated WSRF specifications are submitted to two new OASIS technical committees, the WS-Resource Framework (WSRF) TC and the WS-Notification (WSN) TC (Baker, Apon, Ferner, & Borwn, 2005). All these endeavours represent forward steps in the strife toward the integration of Grid services into Web services.

Fox and Pallickara (2005) discuss the deployment of the NaradaBrokering system, which has been developed as a messaging infrastructure for collaboration, peer-to-peer, and Grid applications. A framework to integrate the NaradaBrokering substrate with Web Services has been described. Interactions, invocations, and data-interchange are encapsulated in SOAP messages. The services can be implemented in different languages and can bind to multiple transports. Three approaches to incorporate support for Web Services within the NaradaBrokering substrate are described; namely, using Proxy, incorporating SOAP processing into the substrate, and using Handlers. Thus, these approaches exploit WS-Addressing and the SOAP processing stack to build ways of interfacing the NaradaBrokering substrate with

Figure 3. Building grid-based Web infrastructure

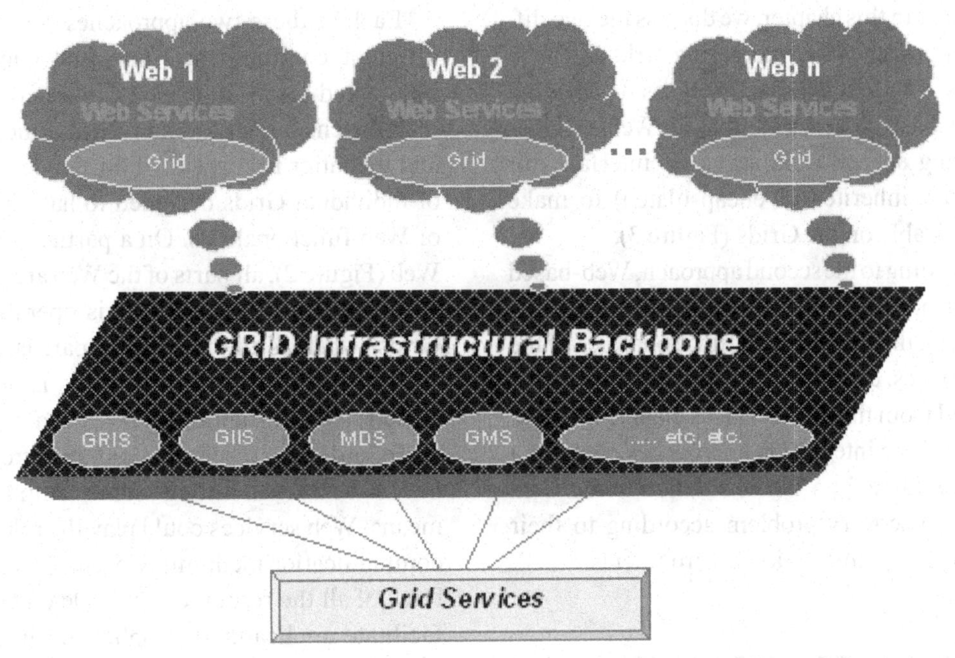

Figure 4. Building a Web-based grid infrastructure

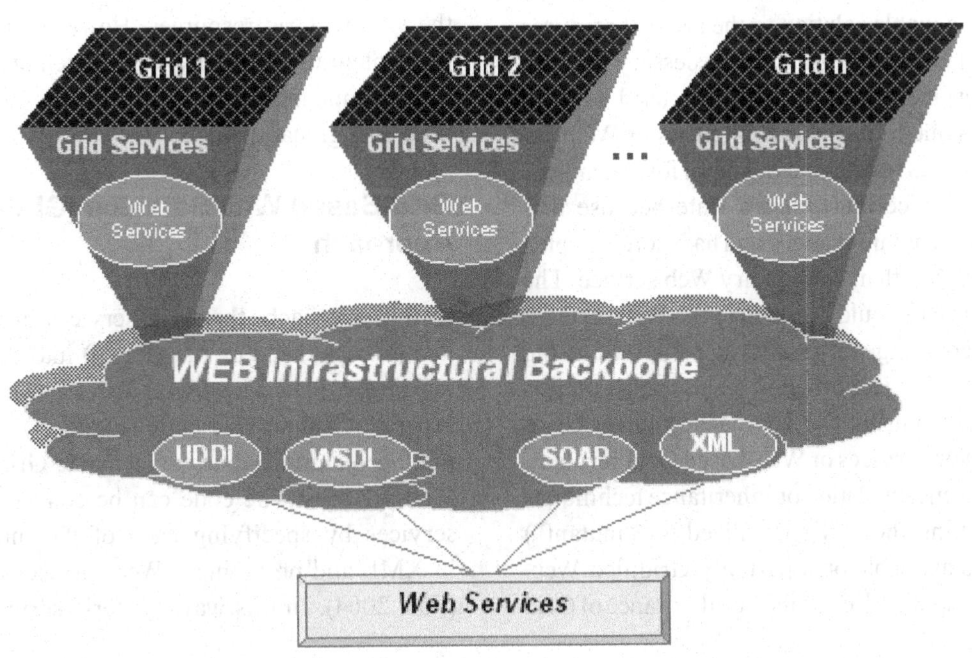

Web services, while imposing no changes to the service implementation themselves.

Further in this chapter, we discuss the two different approaches for integrating Grid and Web services. The first approach focuses on building Grid-based Web services, that is, Web services containing special Grid services' interfaces or behaviors (inherited or encapsulated) to make them operable on the Grids (Figure 3).

According to the second approach, Web-based Grid services, that is, individual Grid services containing the features and functionalities of the Web services, can be built, which are inherited or extended from the Web services class (Figure 4). Either of these integration approaches could be a good candidate for a viable solution to the Grid resource discovery problem according to their respective implementation environments.

SOLUTIONS TO GRID RESOURCE DISCVERY: USING THE SERVICE INTEGRATION APPROACH

So far in this chapter, we have seen that the integration of Grid services into Web services might provide a viable solution to the issue of resource discovery. This integration is necessary because Web services cannot directly be used as Grid services due to intrinsic limitations of Web services such as statelessness, and so forth. whereas a Grid service must have a state because it is prone to dynamic changes and has more complex functionality than an ordinary Web service. The Grid services could be glued to the Web services for discovering various Grid resources using specialized object-oriented techniques, and this can be done using two approaches: either Grid-based Web services or Web-based Grid services, by using encapsulation or inheritance techniques and making the new specialized (or "mutant") services available on a partially-Gridified Web. The first approach exploits the inheritance of Grid services into Web services, and the second one the inheritance of Web services into Grid services.

Each of these two approaches is suitable for different environments. The first approach is best suited for Web (existing Internet) development/extension with some Grid functionality, and the latter is best suited for the development of individual Grids designed to have some sort of Web functionalities. On a partially-Gridified Web (Figure 2), all parts of the Web are not Grid-enabled; rather, a small part is operable under Grids, whereas the remaining part is ordinary Web (no Grid functionality). This is one of the reasons why this approach is needed.

In order to discover Grid resources, they have to be tracked through some communication means. Web services could play the role of these communication mediums, via which we can keep track of all the resources available on Grids and facilitate application-to-application interaction. Therefore, this marriage of Grid services with Web services is an essential step toward efficient resource discovery on a partially-Gridified Web. To achieve resource discovery on Grids, we have to follow the second, Web-based Grid services approach to define, access, and manage the various Grid resources. However, studying both integration approaches is essential for the future implementation of a partially-Gridified Web on a global scale.

Grid-Based Web Services (GbW) Approach

In this approach, the Grid services are inherited (encapsulated or functioned) into the same existing Web service class, instead of having a separate Grid service class (Figure 5). Following this technique, one can generate Grid-based Web services. The code can be converted into services by specifying each of the interfaces in XML and providing a Web service wrapper (Fox, 2004). In this way, the Grid services can be embedded into the Web services as dedicated functions in an XML document, or we can have specific tags for Grid services. The end product is thus specialized Grid-based Web services that are fit to operate on both the standalone Grid environments, as well as on a partially-Gridified Web. Gannon, Alameda, Chipara, Christie, Dukle, Fang et al. (2005) present Web service-based architecture for building specialized Web services and portal clients for Grid applications. The main idea is to wrap Grid application scripts and workflows under a "Grid" Web service that offers the capability to run instances of the workflow or script. In many cases, these specialized application services have implementations that are dynamically generated from a simple XML specification by a persistent factory service. Each dynamically generated object (application service or executing application instance) is associated with a resource which is stored and allocated to the user. For application execution instances, the resource stores everything needed to recreate the execution, including records of execution events and links to the output files. Anane, Chao, and Li (2005) present a hybrid composition of Web services and Grid services in order to develop a compositional framework, which brings together Grid services, Web services and Semantic Web technology within a BPEL4WS platform (Khalaf, Mukhi, and Weerawarana, 2003). It is aimed at enhancing BPEL4WS by allowing for the hybrid composition of Web services and Grid services, and by incorporating dynamic binding through agent mediation.

Zheng, Hu, Yang, Wu, Chen, Ma et al. (2004) use a Web-based approach and presents a fully decentralized Grid system with *graceful* scalability named Construction Platform for Specific

Figure 5. Grid-based Web service

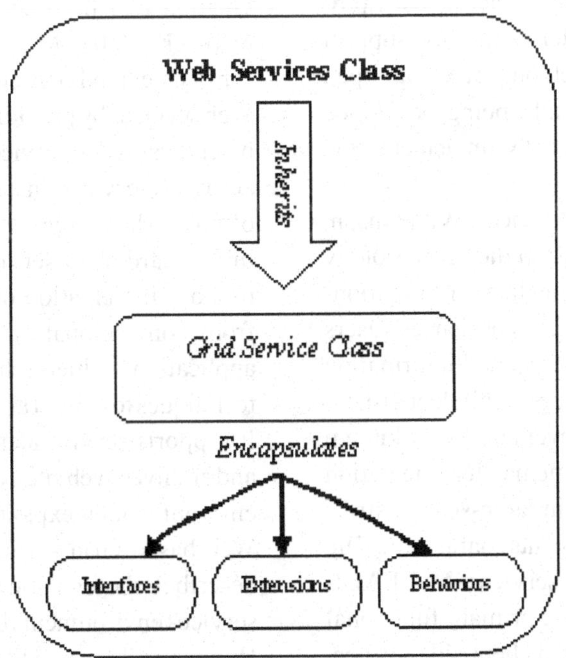

Computing Grid (CPSCG). CPSCG provides tools to wrap shared computational resources and to export them as Web/grid services. Yang, Hayes, Usher, and Spivack (2004) describe how Web services could be developed for Grid applications and used to wrap Grid services. Both of these studies suggest the encapsulation technique for Web-Grid integration.

Fitzgibbons, Fujimoto, Fellig, Kleban, and Scholand (2004) discuss the development of an Interoperable Distributed Simulation (IDSim) framework that builds upon the Open Grid Services Infrastructure (OGSI) to provide distributed simulation services to federated simulators. OGSI and Web technology standards provide novel opportunities for a domain-independent, distributed simulation framework to support extensibility by users of the system. IDSim services can be extended through inheritance to add or extend operations tailored to the needs of specific simulation domains. XML-based documentation of simulation models allows the framework to operate upon the contents of shared events. It uses OGSI as a foundation for providing stateful Web services and utilities for locating, creating, managing, and using those services. OGSI provides a high-degree of interoperability, support for both push and pull methods, and is an open standard. IDSim is currently being developed using the Globus Toolkit 3.0.x implementation of the OGSI.

Finally, Plale, Gannon, Alameda, Wilhelmson, Hampton, Rossi et al. (2005) studies meteorology through MyLEAD, a personalized information-management tool that helps geosciences' users make sense of this vastly expanded information space. MyLEAD extends the general Globus Metadata Catalog Service and leverages a well-known general and extensible schema. Its orientation makes it an active player in large-scale distributed computation environments characterized by interacting Grid and Web services. MyLEAD's architecture consists of three primary functional units: a server-side service, a client-side service, and a user interface. The MyLEAD service is a persistent Grid service built on top of a relational database management system (RDBMS). The MyLEAD service extends the MCS schema and interface. MCS is built on top of the Open Grid Services Architecture Data Access and Integration (OGSA-DAI) Web service, which is a set of generic Grid services that provide access to any database management system. The MCS catalogue service extends OGSA-DAI by providing methods to access particular tables in the database schema.

Web-Based Grid Services (WbG) Approach

In this approach, the Web services are inherited (encapsulated or functioned) into the same existing Grid services class (Figure 6). The Grid services can be used to extend the basic Web services by defining a two-layer naming scheme that will enable support for the conventional distributed system transparencies, by requiring a minimum set of functions and data elements that support discovery, and by introducing explicit service creation and lifetime management (Grimshaw & Tuecke, 2003). Moreover, the Web-based Grid services extend and enhance the capabilities of Web services by providing common and powerful mechanisms that service consumers can rely upon across all services, instead of the service-specific, often ad-hoc approaches typically employed in standard Web services. Li and Yang (2005) propose the creation of state-enabled resources from conventional HTML Web sites, and the application of hierarchical cluster and wrapper techniques to extract and translate Web resources. It supports service identification and packaging and archives Web site evolution into Grid services environment by exploiting WRSF. It follows the Web-based Grid services approach, because it describes the evolution of Web sites into Grid services environments based on WRSF. Zang, Jie, Hung, Lei, Turner, and Cai (2004) present a high level OGSI-compliant hierarchical Information Service built on Globus Toolkit MDS-3. Following the OGSA standard, it integrates with local information suppliers that are implemented as OGSI-compliant Grid services, such as local resource management systems, job Grid service, job queuing Grid service, and so forth, and supports information collection, update, and accessing on a Grid Virtual Organization that consists of multiple administrative domains and resources.

The proposed information model includes job status, computational resources, local resource workload, service metadata, and queue status. This information is further classified into two categories, the static information and the dynamic information.

The stateless nature of Web services, which is a limitation and creates a need for integration, can be addressed by having a separate Grid class that is inherited by the Web class. It will have all the functionalities of a typical Web service and also have some additional functionalities, such as service state, service interfaces, service structure, and so forth.

Aloisio, Blasi, Cafaro, Fiore, Lezzi, and Mirto(2003) present the evolution of Web-services compliant TACWeb, which is a Web-based Grid portal built on top of the Globus Toolkit. It is an interactive environment that deals with complex user requests, regarding the acquisition of biomedical data and the processing and delivering of biomedical images, using the power and security of Grids. The basic capabilities are encapsulated and exposed as Web Services, allowing the development of new health applications as compositions of such services. The use of Grid portal

Figure 6. Web-based grid service

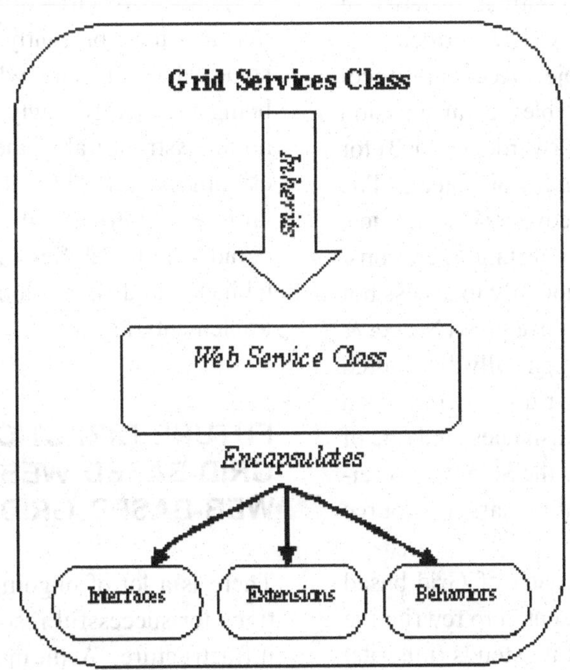

technology is proposed for the development of user-centred applications, such as an Electronic Patient Record system to support the management of biomedical images.

Krishnan and Gannon (2004) describe implementation of the XCAT3 system and discuss the ways it can be used to compose complex distributed applications on the Grid in a modular fashion. XCAT3 is a distributed software component framework. It is compatible with the Common Component Architecture (CCA) and also compliant with the Open Grid Services Infrastructure (OGSI). This allows the combination of benefits from both models, that is, the ability to construct complex distributed applications by composition due to the former, and the ease of use in a Grid-based environment due to the latter.

SOAP-RD: AN INTEGRATION EXAMPLE IN RESOURCE DISCOVERY

An example of integrating Grid services and Web services is discussed here, in which the SOAP Web service technology is fused with an instance of the Grid Resource Discovery (RD) service.

The standard Simple Object Access Protocol (SOAP) was developed to enable the transmission and reception of messages (Twardoch, 2003) for accessing distributed resources or objects. The Grid-specific Resource Discovery (RD) service, which is one of the most important operations/services on Grids, is used not only to access but also to track, match, select, and request (Naseer & Stergioulas, 2005) the geographically distributed resources or objects. This Grid RD service is a set of many subservices or instances, and one of its instances can be glued to the SOAP Web service for the simplification of the larger resource discovery problem.

Following the first approach of Grid-based Web service, it would be essential to rewrite the original SOAP class so that it extends (inherits) the functionalities of the Grid RD service class because, being merely a Web service, SOAP has limited functionalities. This is actually not far from re-engineering the entire protocol, which is an error prone and complicated process.

Whereas, following the second approach of Web-based Grid service, there is no need to modify or rewrite the original SOAP class (re-engineering is not required); rather, this class needs to be simply extended or inherited by a Grid-specific/scripted RD service class performing the basic SOAP operations and possessing extra capabilities that are Grid-specialized (such as service state, etc.). This solution effectively supports the operation of resource discovery in Grid environments or Partially-Gridified Web. Furthermore, it is relatively simple and less prone to errors.

Therefore, instead of recreating (rescripting) the existing Web services to include new Grid functionalities, it is advisable to develop new Grid services and include (encapsulate) in them the existing Web service functionalities.

A further reason why it is beneficial to use the existing Web infrastructure and Web services technologies as the standard platform for the deployment of Grid infrastructure is that Web Services have presently reached a state of high standardization state, whereas Grid technology, being a relatively newly emerged discipline, has no infrastructural standards and benchmarks established yet. Thus, it seems that it is by and large easier to use the existing standardized paradigm of Web Services, which is widely established and with a long history of successful implementations.

FUTURE DIRECTIONS: GRID-BASED WEB VS. WEB-BASED GRID

There is a lot of ongoing work exploring solutions for successful resource discovery in Grid infrastructures. At the meeting of the Global Grid

Forum (GGF) held in March 2004, a proposal for an evolution of OGSI based on a set of new Web Services specifications—WS-Resource Framework (WS-RF) and WS-Notification (WS-N)—was presented (Czajkowski et al., 2004). It supports the extension of Grid services from Web services, which is the Web-based Grid services approach using the inheritance technique of integration. Today, most of the ongoing work involves the use of the WS-RF for the extension and integration of Grid services into Web services.

A solution employing the Grid-based Web service approach for Grid-Web integration would be more complicated to implement (this implementation has to take place in a purely Grid environment), as the extension of dedicated functions defined for the Grid services class into the Web services class can be a task of high complexity. On the other hand, adoption of the Web-based Grid approach in a purely Grid environment may be more effective because in this way we have the entire Web service class packaged and integrated

Figure 7. Implementation architecture for grid applications

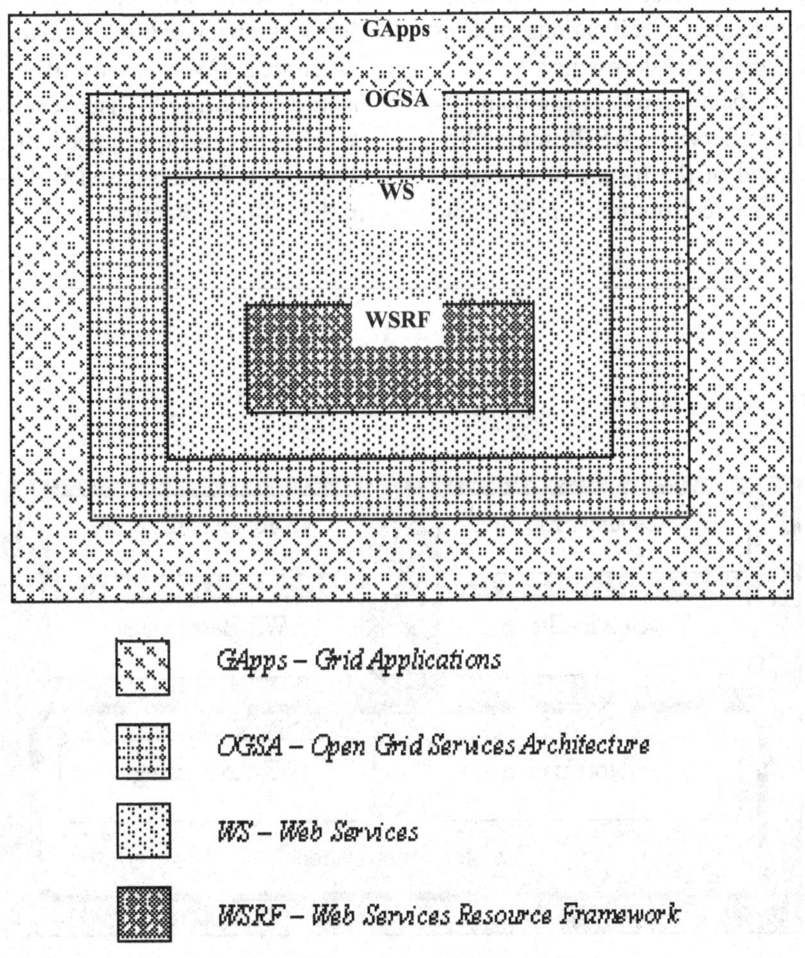

into the Grid service class and each Grid service object, thus instantiated, would have all the capabilities of a Web service and some additional specialized capabilities of its own.

Applications designed based on the Web-based Grid approach are expected to be built on a special architecture for Grid Applications (Figure 7). The core of this architecture is composed of stateful resources within the Web Services Resource Framework (WSRF) that is built using Web Services (WS), which are required by the Open Grid Service Infrastructure (OGSA) standardisation, upon which Grid Applications are built.

As WSRF is the core of this architecture, we further provide a description of its main components. WSRF has five specifications (Figure 8), namely: WS-ResourceProperties, WS-ResourceLifetime, WS-ServiceGroup, WS-BaseFaults, and other related specifications such as WS-Notification and WS-Addressing.

The WSRF specifications relate to the management of stateful Web Services. WS-ResourceProperties is composed of the resource or service attributes, WS-ResourceLifetime is responsible for the lifecycle management of the resources or services, WS-ServiceGroup facilitates group operation of services, and WS-BaseFaults deals with the reporting of all faults occurring during the invocation of a Web Service. Other related collections of specifications, which is not part of WSRF but is quite related to it, includes WS-Notification, which is responsible for notifying changes in a Web Service, and WS-Addressing, which is used to address a Web Service (Borja, 2006). In WSRF, Web Services are considered resources which are stateful Web Services, also known as WS-Resources.

The latest version of Globus Toolkit (GT4) uses the WSRF framework. Although the WSRF infrastructure is only a part of GT4, most of GT4 architecture is built on it. The future releases of Globus Toolkit are expected to be based on Web Services specifications and those components which are not Web-based will be deprecated, such as the Monitoring & Discovery Service (MDS2), which is soon to be dropped in the next release, as there is a new Web-based WebMDS component in the GT4 architecture.

Figure 8. WSRF specifications

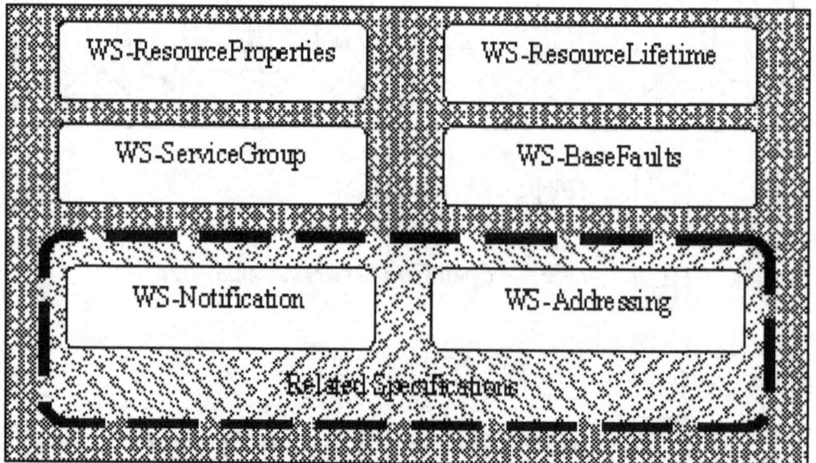

CONCLUSION

The designing and deployment of a Grid infrastructure is the subject of a relatively new area, which has not yet reached a maturity stage of effective standardization. Many of the problems associated with the implementation of Grids could be resolved if the Web is used as the underlying ("backbone") infrastructure for the development of Grids, thus resulting in the formation of a Grid-enabled or a partially Gridified-Web.

The chapter presented Grid services as one type of Grid resources, explored possible ways to integrate Grid services and Web services, and discussed how this will support Grid resource discovery. The two approaches, namely the Grid-based Web service approach and the Web-based Grid service approach, are examined critically, and suggestions are made as to their suitability for implementation in their respective environments. On a partially-Gridified Web, the use the Web-based Grid services approach seems to be more directly applicable and more appropriate for the integration of Grid services and Web services and for addressing the issue of resource discovery. This means that for most applications, it would be best if Grids were developed using the underlying Web infrastructure and Grid services could be integrated with Web services using inheritance or encapsulation techniques to produce Grid-based Web services.

REFERENCES

Aloisio, G., Blasi, E., Cafaro, M., Fiore, S., Lezzi, D., & Mirto, M. (2003). *Web services for a biomedical imaging portal* (pp. 432-436).

Anane, R., Chao, K-M., & Li, Y. (2005). *Hybrid composition of Web services and grid services* (pp. 426-431).

Baker, M., Apon, A., Ferner, C., & Brown, J. (2005). Emerging grid standards. *Computer, 38*(4), 43-50.

Czajkowski, K., Ferguson, D., Foster, I., Frey, J., Graham, S., Maguire, T. et al. (2004, March). *From open grid services infrastructure to WS-resource framework: Refactoring & evolution* (White Paper No. Version 1.1). The Globus Alliance. Retrieved June 11, 2007, from http://www.globus.org/alliance/publications/papers.php#OGSI-to-WSRF

Czajkowski, K., Ferguson, D., Foster, I., Frey, J., Graham, S., Sedukhin, I. et al. (2004, March). *The WS-resource framework* (White Paper No. Version 1.0), The Globus Alliance.

Fitzgibbons, J.B., Fujimoto, R.M., Fellig, D., Kleban, S.D., & Scholand, A.J. (2004). *IDSim: An extensible framework for interoperable distributed simulation* (pp. 532-539).

Foster, I., Czajkowski, K., Ferguson, D.E., Frey, J., Graham, S., Maguire, T. et al. (2005). Modeling and managing state in distributed systems: The role of OGSI and WSRF. *Proceedings of the IEEE, 93*(3), 604-612.

Foster, I., Kesselman, C., Nick, J.M., & Tuecke, S. (2002). Grid services for distributed system integration. *Computer, 35*(6), 37-46.

Fox, G. (2004). Grids of grids of simple services. *Computing in Science & Engineering [see also IEEE Computational Science and Engineering], 06*(4), 84-87.

Fox, G., & Pallickara, S. (2005). Deploying the NaradaBrokering substrate in aiding efficient Web and grid service interactions. *Proceedings of the IEEE, 93*(3), 564-577.

Gannon, D., Alameda, J., Chipara, O., Christie, M., Dukle, V., Fang, L. et al. (2005). Building grid portal applications from a Web service component architecture. *Proceedings of the IEEE, 93*(3), 551-563.

Goth, G. (2002). Grid services architecture plan gaining momentum. *Internet Computing, IEEE, 6*(4), 11-12.

Grimshaw, A. (2003). Grid services extend Web services [Electronic version]. *SOA Web Services Journal, 3*(8).

Khalaf, R., Mukhi, N., & Weerawarana, S. (2003). *Service-oriented composition in BPEL4WS.* In Paper presented at the Budapest, Hungary. Retrieved June 11, 2007, from http://www2003.org/cdrom/papers/alternate/P768/choreo_html/p768-khalaf.htm

Krishnan, S., & Gannon, D. (2004). *XCAT3: A framework for CCA components as OGSA services* (pp. 90-97).

Li, J., & Yang, H. (2005). *Towards evolving Web sites into grid services environment* (pp. 95-102).

Naseer, A., & Stergioulas, L.K. (2005). Resource discovery in computational grids: State-of-the-art and current challenges. In H. Czap, R. Unland, C. Branki, & H. Tianfield (Eds.), *Self-organization and autonomic informatics (I)* (2005th ed., pp. 237-245). Amsterdam, Netherlands: IOS Press.

Naseer, A., & Stergioulas, L.K. (2006a). *Integrating grid and Web services: A critical assessment of methods and implications to resource discovery.* In Paper presented at the IWI-WWW 2006: 2nd Workshop on Innovations in Web Infrastructure, Edinburgh, Scotland, UK. Retrieved June 11, 2007, from http://www.wmin.ac.uk/~courtes/iwi2006/naseer.pdf

Naseer, A., & Stergioulas, L.K. (2006b). Discovering HealthGrid services. In *Proceedings of the IEEE International Conference on Services Computing (SCC'06)* (pp. 301-306). Retrieved June 11, 2007, from http://dx.doi.org/10.1109/SCC.2006.44

Naseer, A., & Stergioulas, L.K. (2006c). Resource discovery in grids and other distributed environments: States of the art. *Multiagent and Grid Systems - An International Journal, 2*(2), 163-182.

Peng, J., & Law, K.H. (2004). *Reference NEESgrid data model* (Tech. Rep. White Paper Version 1.0, No. TR-2004-40). Retrieved June 11, 2007, from http://eil.stanford.edu/publications/NEESgrid/TR_2004_40.pdf

Plale, B., Gannon, D., Alameda, J., Wilhelmson, B., Hampton, S., Rossi, A. et al. (2005). Active management of scientific data. *Internet Computing, IEEE, 9*(1), 27-34.

Qin, C.L., Davenhall, A.C., Noddle, K.T., & Walton, N.A. (2003). Myspace: Personalized work space in astrogrid. In *Proceedings of the UK E-Science all Hands Meeting* (pp. 361-365), University of Southampton.

Sotomayor, B. *The Globus Toolkit 4 Programmer's Tutorial.* Retrieved June 11, 2007, from http://gdp.globus.org/gt4-tutorial/singlehtml/progtutorial_0.2.1.html

Stewart, C.A. (2004). Introduction. *Communications of the ACM, 47*(11), 30-33.

Talia, D. (2002). The open grid services architecture: Where the grid meets the Web. *Internet Computing, IEEE, 6*(6), 67-71.

Tuecke, S., Czajkowski, K., Foster, I., Frey, J., Graham, S., Kesselman, C. et al. (2003). *Open grid services infrastructure (OGSI)* (No. Version 1.0), Global Grid Forum (GGF). Retrieved June 11, 2007, from http://www.globus.org/alliance/publications/papers.php#GSSpec

Twardoch, A. (2003). *Web services technologies: XML, SOAP and UDDI.* Retrieved June 11, 2007, from http://www.twardoch.com/webservices/

Wu, F.F., Moslehi, K., & Bose, A. (2005). Power system control centers: Past, present, and future. *Proceedings of the IEEE, 93*(11), 1890-1908.

Yang, X., Hayes, M., Usher, A., & Spivack, M. (2004). *Developing Web services in a computational grid environment* (pp. 600-603).

Zang, T., Jie, W., Hung, T., Lei, Z., Turner, S.J., & Cai, W. (2004). *The design and implementation of an OGSA-based grid information service* (pp. 566-573).

Zheng, W., Hu, M., Yang, G., Wu, Y., Chen, M., Ma, R. et al. (2004). *An efficient Web services based approach to computing grid* (pp. 382-385).

Chapter XIII
Approaches and Best Practices in Web Service Style, XML Data Binding, and Validation: Implications to Securing Web Services

David Meredith
STFC E-Science Centre, UK

Asif Akram
STFC E-Science Centre, UK

ABSTRACT

This chapter shows how the WSDL interface style (RPC / Document), strength of data typing, and approach to data binding and validation have important implications on application security (and interoperability). This is because some (common) bad-practices and poor implementation choices can render a service vulnerable to the consequences of propagating loosely bound or poorly constrained data. The chosen Web service style and strength of data typing dictate how SOAP messages are constructed and serialized, and to what extent SOAP messages can be constrained and secured during validation. The chosen approach to binding and validation dictates how and where the SOAP-body and SOAP-header (which includes the security constructs) are handled in the application, and also determines the reliability of message parsing. The authors show how these Web service styles and implementation choices must be carefully considered and applied correctly by providing implementation examples and best practice recommendations.

INTRODUCTION: HOW WSDL STYLE, STRENGTH OF DATA TYPING, BINDING, AND VALIDATION ARE IMPORTANT FOR WEB SERVICE SECURITY

In this chapter, we show how the WSDL interface style (RPC / Document), strength of data typing ("loosely typed" or "strongly typed") and method used for data binding and validation have important implications to application security and interoperability, as each play important roles in securing and constraining how the message data is handled (or propagated) by an application. Some common bad-practices and poor implementation styles can cause serious security implications. These Web service implementation styles and choices must be carefully considered and applied correctly in order to ensure; a) The correct choice of Web service style, which dictates how the SOAP message is constructed, serialized, and to what extent messages can be constrained during validation; b) The complete binding and validation of a SOAP payload before the business logic is invoked. This includes both *how* and *where* the SOAP Body and SOAP header (which contains the security constructs) are handled in the application; The chosen binding and validation style also dictates the reliability of data parsing, which is especially important when parsing complex security constructs associated with Web service security specifications; c) Data contract compliance between client and service; and d) Interoperability and robustness.

If implemented incorrectly, a Web service can be vulnerable to the consequences of accepting (or propagating) loosely bound or poorly validated data. For example, a service that defines only "loose" WSDL typing with only a limited or "weak" binding and validation strategy would be vulnerable to routing erroneous, restricted, or even malicious message content to business logic and to third-parties. The potential consequences are similar for the client. These consequences can easily compromise security, hinder reliability, and breach service and consumer trust. In this chapter, we provide some implementation best practices and recommendations based on our experimentation with Web service styles and binding/validation frameworks. Examples are provided using current SOAP standards for Java, including JAX-RPC and JAX-WS. We assess the advantages and disadvantages associated with "loose" verses "strong" data typing and when decoupling the binding/validation framework from the SOAP engine. For the most part, we recommend the use of the Document/ literal wrapped Web service style coupled with a dedicated binding and validation framework. These choices leverage the advanced capabilities of XML schema for precisely declaring/describing, constraining, and validating data and security constructs.

BACKGROUND

At the heart of Web service style, interoperability, and data binding and validation is the Basic Profile 1.0 (Basic Profile Version 1.0, 2004), published by the Web services Interoperability Organization (*http://www.ws-i.org/*). The Basic Profile 1.0 details how to use primary Web service related specifications together, including; XML (Extensible Markup Language, 2006), WSDL (Web Services Description Language, 2001), SOAP (Simple Object Access Protocol, 2000), and UDDI (Universal Description, Discovery and Integration, 2004). In doing this, the Basic Profile provides important guidelines that should be observed in order to create fully interoperable and well defined/constrained services. The recommendations and best-practice examples provided throughout this chapter are WS-I compliant and coverage of the Basic Profile is an important part of this chapter. Of critical importance to both the interoperability and effective binding and validation of data is the chosen Web service style (or WSDL binding style). The Web service style is discussed in the following section.

WEB SERVICE STYLE / WSDL BINDING

It is important to understand how the WSDL binding "style" and "use" attributes dictate how a SOAP message is constructed and formatted into XML when transmitted over the wire. These style choices have serious implications upon security, as they directly influence how the SOAP message is constructed, serialized, and to what extent messages can be constrained during validation. Collectively, the process of generating SOAP messages according to different bindings is referred to as "SOAP encoding" or "WSDL binding."

a. The WSDL binding "style" attribute indicates whether a <wsdl:operation> is RPC-oriented (SOAP messages containing parameters and return values) or document-oriented (SOAP messages containing XML instance documents). The style attribute has the value "document" or "rpc."
b. The "use" attribute dictates how the input and output data of a <wsdl:message> is serialized into XML and has the value "encoded" or "literal."

Table 1. Advantages and disadvantages of each WSDL binding style

Style	Advantages	Disadvantages
RPC Encoded	• Simple WSDL • Operation name wraps parameters	• Complex types are sent as multipart references meaning <soap:Body> can have multiple children • Not WS-I compliant • Not interoperable • Type encoding information generated in soap message • Messages can't be validated • Child elements are not fully qualified
RPC Literal	• Simple WSDL • Operation name wraps parameters • <soap:Body> has only one element • No type encoding information • WS-I compliant	• Difficult to validate message • Sub elements of complex types are not fully qualified.
Doc Literal	• No type encoding information • Messages can be validated • WS-I compliant but with restrictions • Data can be modeled in separate schema	• WSDL file is more complicated • Operation name is missing in soap request, which can create interoperability problems • <soap:Body> can have multiple children • WS-I recommends only one child in <soap:Body>
Doc Wrapped	• No type encoding information • <soap:Body> has only one element • Operation name wraps parameters • Messages can be validated • WS-I compliant	• Request and response wrapper elements may have to be added to the <wsdl:types> if the original schema element name is not suitable for Web service operation name.

For the encoded style, the most common encoding is SOAP encoding, which is a set of serialization rules defined in SOAP, which specify how objects, structures, arrays and object graphs should be serialized into XML. Applications using SOAP encoding focus on RPC. For the literal style, WSDL message parts reference schema defined in the <wsdl:types> using either the "element" or "type" attribute. Using different combinations of the binding style and use attributes, different Web service styles are possible. These are assessed in Table 1. Each style is further discussed in the following sections. It must be stated from the outset, however, that the Document literal (wrapped) style is the recommended style due to the greater functionality for describing, constraining, and validating messages. The encoded styles should be avoided and should be used only for legacy purposes.

RPC BINDING STYLE

The RPC binding style specifies that the <soap:body> of a SOAP request message contains an element named after the service method being invoked (the wrapper element). This element, in turn, contains <part> elements for each parameter (Section 7.1 of the SOAP specification). The wrapper element namespace is defined by the "namespace" attribute of the <soap:binding> element. Each message part is named after the corresponding parameter of the call. Parts are arranged in the same order as the parameters of the call unless specified differently in the WSDL document by the "parameterOrder" attribute. For a SOAP response message, the <soap:body> contains an element named after the service method being invoked with "Response" appended to the

Table 2. The RPC encoded binding style (SOAP)

Style	SOAP Request/Response
RPC Encoded	<soapenv:Body> <getIndex xmlns:="urn:ehtpx-process"> <admin href="#id0"/> <URL xsi:type="xsd:string"> </URL> </getIndex> <multiRef id="id0" ......> <email xsi:type="xsd:string"> </email> <PN xsi:type="xsd:string"> </PN> </multiRef> </soapenv:Body> <soapenv:Body> <ns1:getIndexResponse soapenv:encodingStyle="http://.../" xmlns:ns1="urn:ehtpx-process"> <getIndexReturn xsi:type="soapenc:string" xmlns:soapenc="http://../"> .... </getIndexReturn> </ns1:getIndexResponse> </soapenv:Body>

name. This element contains a <part> element for the return value.

The following summary examines the key features of the RPC WSDL binding style and the format of a resulting SOAP message. Tables 2 to 4 illustrate these key points (schema examples are numbered and referred to in the text).

RPC (Applies to Encoded and Literal)

- An RPC style WSDL file contains multiple <part> tags per <message> for each request/response parameters (10b, 11b).
- Each message <part> tag defines type attributes, not element attributes (10b, 11b) (message parts are not wrapped by elements as in Document style WSDL files).
- The type attribute in each <part> tag can either; a) reference a complex or simple type defined in the <wsdl:types> section, for example, <part name="x" type="tns:myType">, or b) define a simple type directly, for example, <part name="x" type="xsd:int"> (10b, 11b, respectively).
- An RPC SOAP request wraps the message parameters in an element named after the invoked operation (2a). If a namespace is locally declared in the <wsdl:soapBody> element, it overrides the target namespace of the WSDL file (24b); otherwise the WSDL target namespace is applied.
- An RPC SOAP response wraps the message parameters in an element named after the invoked operation with "Response" appended to the element name (12a).
- The difference between RPC encoded and RPC literal styles relates to how the data in the SOAP message is serialized/formatted when sent over the wire. The abstract parts of the WSDL files are similar (i.e., the <wsdl:types>, <wsdl:message> and <wsdl:portType> elements). The difference relates to the definition of the <wsdl:binding> ele-

Table 3. The RPC literal binding style (SOAP)

Style	SOAP Request/Response
RPC Literal	17a <soapenv:Body> 18a <getIndex xmlns="urn:ehtpx-process"> 19a <admin xmlns=""> 20a <email> </email> 21a <PN> </PN> 22a </admin> 23a <URL xmlns=""> </URL> 24a </getIndex> 25a <soapenv:Body> 26a <soapenv:Body> 27a <getIndexResponse xmlns=" urn:ehtpx-process "> 28a <getIndexReturn> .... 29a </getIndexReturn> 30a </getIndexResponse> 31a </soapenv:Body>

ment. The binding element dictates how the SOAP message is formatted and how complex data types are represented in the SOAP message.

Table 4. The RPC WSDL (encoded and literal)

<table>
<tr><th>Style</th><th>WSDL</th></tr>
<tr><td>RPC</td><td><definition ….>
<types>
<complexType name="AdminT">
<sequence>
<element name="email" type="enc:string"/>
<element name="PN" type="enc:string"/>
</sequence>
</complexType>
</types>
<wsdl:message name="getIndexRequest">
<wsdl:part name="admin" type="tns:AdminT"/>
<wsdl:part name="URL" type="enc:string"/>
</wsdl:message>
<wsdl:portType name="IndexService">
<wsdl:operation name="getIndex">
<wsdl:input message="impl:getIndexRequest" name="getIndexRequest"/>
<wsdl:output message="impl:getIndexResponse" name="getIndexResponse"/>
</wsdl:operation>
</wsdl:portType>
<wsdl:binding name="IndexSoapBinding" type="impl:IndexWS">
<wsdlsoap:binding style="rpc" transport="http://schemas.xmlsoap.org/soap/http"/>
<wsdl:operation name="getIndex">
<wsdlsoap:operation soapAction=""/>
<wsdl:input name="getIndexRequest">
<wsdlsoap:body encodingStyle="http://../" namespace=" urn:ehtpx-process" use="<b>encoded | literal</b>"/>
</wsdl:input>
<wsdl:output name="getIndexResponse">
<wsdlsoap:body encodingStyle="http://..if use is encoded only" namespace=" urn:ehtpx-process" use=" <b>encoded | literal</b> "/>
</wsdl:output>
</wsdl:operation>
</wsdl:binding>
<wsdl:service> ......</wsdl:service>
</definition></td></tr>
</table>

RPC/encoded (Depreciated)

- An RPC/encoded WSDL file specifies an "encodingStyle" attribute nested within the <wsdl:binding> (24b). Although different encoding styles are legal, the most common is SOAP encoding. This encoding style is used to serialize data and complex types in the SOAP message. (http://schemas.xmlsoap.org/soap/encoding).

- The use attribute, which is nested within the <wsdl:binding> has the value "encoded" (24b).
- An RPC/ encoded SOAP message has type encoding information for each parameter element. This is overhead and degrades throughput performance (4a, 7a, 8a) and is not strictly required by the server.
- Complex types are SOAP encoded and are referenced by "href" references using an identifier (3a). The "hrefs" refer to "multiref" elements positioned outside the operation wrapping element as direct children of the <soap:Body> (6a). This complicates the message as the <soap:Body> may contain multiple "multiref" elements.
- RPC/encoded is not WS-I compliant, which recommends that the <soap:Body> should only contain a single nested sub element.

RPC/literal

- RPC/literal style improves upon the RPC/ encoded style.
- An RPC/literal WSDL does not specify an encodingStyle attribute.
- The use attribute, which is nested within the <wsdl:binding>, has the value "literal" (24b).
- An RPC/literal encoded SOAP message has only one nested child element in the <soap:Body> (12a). This is because all parameter elements become wrapped within the operation element that is defined in the WSDL namespace.
- Validation can be problematic when using the RPC/literal style because qualification of the operational wrapper element comes from the WSDL namespace definitions, not from the individual schema elements defined in the <wsdl:types>. This introduces additional complexities when integrating nested sub elements with custom schema defined namespaces (i.e., data binding and validation must also account for the RPC element naming conventions and WSDL namespaces, rather than solely binding and validating plain XML instance documents).
- As a result of this (see above bullet), the namespace information for each nested parameter sub element may be dropped in a SOAP message by the SOAP engine implementation (19a, 20a, 21a). Indeed, we have noticed that in most Java SOAP-engine implementations, often only the operational wrapper element remains fully qualified (it must be noted, however, that this is not always the case). This can mean all parts and elements in an RPC/literal SOAP message share the same namespace and lose their original schema namespace definitions. Consequently, validation may only be possible for limited scenarios, where original schema elements have the same namespace as the WSDL file.
- RPC/literal is WS-I compliant, but has validation limitations.

The main weakness with the RPC style is its lack of support for the constraint and validation of complex data. The RPC/encoded style usually adopts the SOAP encoding specification to serialize complex objects, which is far less comprehensive and descriptive when compared to XML schema. Validation can also be problematic when using the RPC/literal style, as data binding must also account for the RPC element naming conventions and WSDL namespaces, rather than solely binding and validating plain XML documents. As previously discussed, this has serious implications for securing the data that is declared and handled by the service.

DOCUMENT BINDING STYLE

Document style encoding provides more effective support for data binding and validation by using standard XML schema as the encoding format. The main feature of a Document style service is that each message part references a concrete schema using the "element" attribute. The schema is defined in the <wsdl:types> section and can be embedded or imported. The contents of the SOAP request/response body can be described completely using the schema without any additional encoding rules or WSDL namespace dependencies. The following summary examines the key features of the Document WSDL binding style and the format of a resulting SOAP message. Tables 5 to 8 illustrate these key points (schema examples are numbered and referred to in the text).

Document (Applies to Literal and Wrapped)

- Document style Web services use standard XML schema for the serialisation of XML instance documents and complex data.
- Document style messages do not have type-encoding information for elements, and each element in the soap message is fully qualified by a Schema namespace by direct declaration (34a, 41a, 54a), or by inheritance from an outer element (35a, 36a, 46a, 47a, 48a).
- Document style services leverage the full capability of XML Schema for data validation.

Document/literal

- Document/literal messages send request (34a, 38a) and response (41a) parameters to and from operations as direct children of the <soap:Body> .
- The <soap:Body> can contain many immediate child sub elements (34a and 38a).
- A Document/literal style WSDL file may contain multiple <part> tags per <message> (37b and 38b).
- Each <part> tag in a message can specify either a type or an element attribute, however, for WS-I compliance, it is recommended

Table 5. The document literal binding style (SOAP)

Style	SOAP Request/Response
(Request)	32a <soapenv:Body> 33a 34a <admin xmlns=”urn:ehtpx-process”> 35a <email xmlns=””> </email> 36a <PN xmlns=””> </PN> 37a </admin> 38a <URL xmlns=””> </URL> 39a </soapenv:Body>
Doc Literal	
(Response)	40a <soapenv:Body> 41a <adminReturn xmlns=”http://paperwstest”> ………. 42a </adminReturn> 43a </soapenv:Body>

that only element attributes be defined in <part> tags for Document style WSDL (37b, 38b).

- This means that every complex type parameter should be wrapped as an element and be defined in the <wsdl:types> section (33b).
- The main disadvantages of the Document/literal Web service style include: a) the operation name is removed from the <soap:Body> request, which can cause interoperability problems (33a), and b) the <soap:Body> will contain multiple children (34a, 38a) if more than one message part is defined in a request/response message (37b, 38b).
- WS-I recommends that the <soap:Body> should only contain a single nested sub element.

Document/literal Wrapped

- An improvement on the Document/literal style is the Document/literal wrapped style.
- When writing this style of WSDL, the request and response parameters of a Web service operation (simple types, complex types, and elements) should be "wrapped" within single all-encompassing request and response elements defined in the <wsdl:types> section (61b - akin to the RPC/literal style).
- These "wrapping" elements need to be added to the <wsdl:types> section of the WSDL file (61b).
- The request wrapper element (61b) should have the same name as the Web service operation to be invoked (this ensures the operation name is always specified in the <soap:Body> request as the first nested element).
- By specifying single elements to wrap all of the request and response parameters, there is only ever a single <part> tag per <message> tag (71b).
- A Document/literal wrapped style WSDL file is fully WS-I compliant, because there

Table 6. The document wrapped binding style (SOAP)

Style	SOAP Request/Response
(Request) Doc Wrapped	44a <soapenv:Body> 45a <getIndex xmlns=" urn:ehtpx-process"> 46a <admin> 47a <email xmlns=""> </email> 48a <PN xmlns=""> </PN> 49a </admin> 50a <URL xmlns=""> </URL> 51a </getIndex> 52a </soapenv:Body>
(Response)	53a <soapenv:Body> 54a <adminReturn xmlns="http://paperwstest"> .... 55a </adminReturn> 56a </soapenv:Body>

is only a single nested element in the <soap: Body> (45a).

- Document/literal wrapped style messages are therefore very similar to RPC/literal style messages because both styles produce a single nested element within a <soap:Body>. The only difference is that for Document/literal wrapped style, each element is fully qualified with a Schema namespace.

The main advantage of the “literal” styles over the “encoded” styles is the abstraction/separation of the type system into a 100% XML Schema compliant data model. This facilitates complete messages description with strong data typing, and increases the extent to which SOAP messages can be constrained and secured during validation.

Table 7. The document literal WSDL

Style	WSDL
Doc Literal	<definition ….> 31b <types> 32b <complexType name=”AdminT”>… </complexType> 33b <element name=”admin” type=”tns:AdminT”> 34b <element name=”URL” type=” enc:string”> 35b </types> 36b <wsdl:message name=”getIndexRequest”> 37b <wsdl:part name=”in0” element=”tns:admin”/> 38b <wsdl:part name=”URL” element=”enc:string”/> 39b </wsdl:message> 40b <wsdl:portType name=”IndexService”> 41b <wsdl:operation name=”getIndex”> 42b <wsdl:input message=”impl:getIndexRequest” name=”getIndexRequest”/> 43b <wsdl:output message=”impl:getIndexResponse” name=”getIndexResponse”/> 44b </wsdl:operation> 45b </wsdl:portType> 46b <wsdl:binding name=”IndexSoapBinding” type=”impl:IndexWS”> 47b <wsdlsoap:binding style=”document” transport=”http://schemas.xmlsoap.org/soap/http”/> 48b <wsdl:operation name=”getIndex”> 49b <wsdlsoap:operation soapAction=””/> 50b <wsdl:input name=”getIndexRequest”> 51b <wsdlsoap:body use=”literal”/> 52b </wsdl:input> 53b <wsdl:output name=”getIndexResponse”> 54b <wsdlsoap:body use=”literal”/> 56b </wsdl:output> 57b </wsdl:operation> 58b </wsdl:binding> <wsdl:service> ……</wsdl:service> </definition>

Table 8. The document wrapped WSDL

Style	WSDL
Doc Wrapped	<definition ….> 59b <types> 60b <complexType name="AdminT"> ...</complexType> 61b <element name ="getIndex"> 62b <complexType> 63b <sequence> 64b <element name ="admin" type ="tns:AdminT"/> 65b <element name =" URL " type ="xsd:string" /> 66b </sequence> 67b </complexType > 68b </element> 69b </types> 70b <wsdl:message name="getIndexRequest"> 71b <wsdl:part name="in0" element="tns:getIndex"/> 72b </wsdl:message> 73b <wsdl:binding name="IndexSoapBinding" type="impl:IndexWS"> 74b <wsdlsoap:binding style="document" transport="http://schemas.xmlsoap.org/soap/http"/> 75b <wsdl:operation name="getIndex"> 76b <wsdlsoap:operation soapAction=""/> 77b <wsdl:input name="getIndexRequest"> 78b <wsdlsoap:body use="literal"/> 79b </wsdl:input> 80b <wsdl:output name="getIndexResponse"> 81b <wsdlsoap:body use="literal"/> 82b </wsdl:output> 83b </wsdl:operation> 84b </wsdl:binding> <wsdl:service> ......</wsdl:service> </definition>

DATA ABSTRACTION

Abstraction of the Web service type system into a 100% XML Schema compliant data model produces several important advantages:

- *Separation of Roles (e.g., segregation of "sensitive" data model)*

The type system can be fully abstracted and developed in isolation from the network protocol and communication specific details of the WSDL file. This allows the development team to be separated into groups with differing concerns, for example, separating those involved with the description/handling of potentially sensitive data. In our experience, this is invaluable for encouraging collaboration and trust between those involved in service development.

- *Data Model Reusability/Extensibilty*
  Existing XML Schema can be reused, rather than redesigning a new type system for each new Web service. This helps reduce development efforts, cost, and time.
- *Isolation of Changing Components*
  In our experience, the data model is the component that is most subject to change, often in response to changing scientific requirements. Its isolation limits the impact on other Web service components, such as the concrete WSDL.
- *Avoid Dependency on SOAP Namespaces and Encoding Styles*
  Manual modeling of XML Schema may constitute extra effort, but this gives the developer the most control and avoids dependencies on SOAP framework namespaces and weak encoding styles. Most of the SOAP frameworks are traditionally RPC-centric and create WSDL based on the RPC/encoding style, which is not WS-I compliant. This also applies to languages other than Java.
- *Full XML Schema Functionality*
  The XML Schema type system leverages the more powerful features of the XML Schema language for description, constraint, and validation of complex data (e.g., XSD patterns/regular expressions, optional elements, enumerations, type restrictions, etc.). In our experience, this has proven invaluable for the description and constraint of complex scientific data. As previously discussed, this is vital for securing and fully describing the data handled by a service and for declaring the message data accurately "upfront" in the WSDL service contract.
- *Can Choose to Use Data Binding/Validation Framework Implemented by SOAP Engine, or Can Choose to Separate Data Binding/Validation from SOAP Engine.*
  Having the choice to either delegate data binding/validation to the SOAP engine or to use a separate binding and validation framework dictates how and where binding and validation is handled in a service. This has important implications related to who has responsibility for binding/validating messages, and for ensuring the correct parsing and validation of data. The following sections provide a detailed discussion of both approaches to data binding and validation and their associated advantages and disadvantages for securing the payload.

LOOSE VS. STRONG DATA TYPES: IMPLICATIONS FOR SECURING MESSAGE CONTENT

A "loosely typed" Web service means the WSDL file does not contain a highly constrained XML schema in the type system to fully define the format and content of the messages. Instead, the WSDL defines generic types to encapsulate data. The main advantage of loose types is that different data formats can be encapsulated without having to update the WSDL interface. The main disadvantage of loose typing is that unconstrained or undefined data (e.g., erroneous or even malicious content) can both penetrate and be routed by the service without prior validation constraint. Furthermore, the WSDL interface, which is the "contract" between service and consumer can be ambiguous, which can lead to data integrity and security concerns. Conversely, a "strongly typed" Web service means the WSDL type system strictly dictates the format and allowed content of the message data from the outset. Strongly typed Web services are less flexible, but fully declare the allowed message data in the WSDL contract, which helps to secure the message. Each style influences the chosen approach to binding and validation and each has its own advantages and disadvantages, as summarized in Table 9.

Table 9. Advantages and disadvantages of loose vs. strong data typing

Modeling Approach	Advantages	Disadvantages
Loose Type	• Easy to develop. • Easy to implement. • Stable WSDL interface (can change the data that is encapsulated by the loose type without updating the WSDL interface). • Flexibility in implementation. • Single Web service may handle multiple types of message. • Can be used as a gateway service which routes to actual services based on contents of message.	• Requires additional/manual negotiation between client and service to establish the format of data wrapped in a generic type • Ambiguous WSDL contract. • Limited or no control on message content (e.g., malicious code can enter business logic). • Prone to message related exceptions due to inconsistencies in the format of data sent and accepted (requires WS to be tolerant in what it accepts).
Strong Type	• Properly defined interfaces. • Message validation with tight control on parameter values helps secure message payload (reject invalid message content before business logic is invoked). • Often more robust (only highly constrained data enters WS business logic). • Benefits from richness of XML.	• Can be more difficult to develop (requires a working knowledge of XML and WSDL). • Resistive to change in data model.

Loosely Typed Web Services

A loosely typed WSDL interface specifies generic data types to encapsulate data for an operation's input and output messages (either string, CDATA, Base64-Encoded, xsd:any, xsd:anyType, or Attachment types). The loosely typed approach requires extra negotiation between providers and consumers in order to agree on the format of the encapsulated data. Consequently, an understanding of the WSDL alone is usually not sufficient to consume the service. As discussed above, the main security concern of loose typing is the potential for ambiguous message content and lack of data validation control.

String Loose Data Type

A string variable can be used to encode markup and complex data allowing the WSDL interface to define simple string input/output parameters for operations (i.e., akin to simple "helloworld" style services). The string input could be an XML fragment or multiple name-value pairs (similar to a query string). An XML document formatted as a string requires extra coding and decoding in order to escape the markup (e.g., XML special characters). This can drastically increase the message size. This approach is generally only suitable only for encoding simple markup fragments that have limited use of namespaces.

The CDATA Section Loose Data Type

A CDATA section can be used to embed markup directly within a SOAP message (data defined within a CDATA section is not parsed by a SOAP engine). This prevents the need to escape data. Listing 1 shows an example CDATA section that is embedded within a SOAP message. Traditionally, few systems wrap encoded data with a CDATA section and this approach introduces limitations related to interoperability.

Listing 1. A CDATA section embedded within a SOAP message fragment

```
<ns3:e3 xmlns:ns3="urn:foo">
  <![CDATA[Text with      Important
    <b> whitespace </b> and tags – no escaping of XML
special chars ! ]]>
  </ns3:e3>
```

xsd:any and xsd:anyType Loose Data Types

An XML schema defined in the WSDL <types> section may define <xsd:any> or <xsd:anyType> elements. These elements make XML documents extensible, allowing instance documents to contain additional elements that are not declared in the schema. Consequently, arbitrary XML can be embedded directly into the SOAP message. Partners receive the actual XML, but no contract is specified regarding what the XML data actually represents. The <xsd:any> element is a "placeholder" that can be directly replaced by an element, whereas <xsd:anyType> can be used to declare elements where the type is unknown. This is shown in Listing 2. Extraction of information requires raw XML manipulation, using the Java SAAJ, DOM, and SAX APIs, for example. The use of these elements is suitable for dynamic environments requiring raw XML handling, and enables schema versioning and flexible polymorphism. It must be noted that extensive use of <xsd:any> and <xsd:anyType> deviates from the intent of a WSDL file in providing a full service interface description.

Listing 2. The <xsd:any> element can be directly replaced by any XML element. The <xsd:anyType> element is used to declare elements where the type is unknown.

```
<types>
  <schema ....>
    <element name="getIndexRequest">
      <complexType> <sequence>
           <any maxOccurs="1"/> <!-- replace with any
element -->
      </sequence> </complexType>
    </element>
    <!-- declare element where type is unknown -->
    <element name="dummy" type="xsd:anyType" />
  </schema>
    </types>
```

Base64 encoding Loose Data Type

Base64 Content-Transfer-Encoding is a two way encoding scheme defined by RFC 1521 that represents data as arbitrary sequences of octets. An XML document can be transmitted as a Base64 encoded string or as raw bytes in the body of a SOAP message. This approach is WS-I compliant, meaning every SOAP engine handles this data in a compatible fashion. This may be useful when the XML contains characters that are not supported by the SOAP message info-set or by the runtime. The encoding and decoding algorithms are simple, but encoded data are consistently about 33% larger than nonencoded data. A WSDL fragment defining Base64 encoding is shown in Listing 3. Listing 4 shows an example of the encoded data that is embedded within a SOAP message. In practical terms, the Base64 loose data type is suitable only for encoding relatively small amounts of data and small files.

Listing 3. WSDL document defining the xsd: base64Binary type

```
   ...
<element name="getIndexRequest" type="xsd:base-64Binary"/>
  .....
<message name="getIndex_Request">
  <part name="getIndex_Request" element="ns1:getIndexRequest"/>
</message>
```

Listing 4. SOAP message with Base64 encoded data

```
          <soapenv:Body>
       <getIndex xmlns="urn:ehtpx-process"> <getIndex_Request>
PD94bWwgdmVyc2lvbj0iMS4wIiBlbmNvZGluZz0iV-VRGLTgiP
z4NCc2RsO.........Dwvd3NkbDpzZXJ2aWNlPg0K-Cjwvd3Nkb
            </getIndex_Request > </ns1: getIndex >
          </soapenv:Body>
```

SOAP Attachment Loose Data Type

SOAP attachments can be used to send multiple files of any format, especially when it is not practical to embed or encode data directly within the SOAP body. Consequently, it is difficult (if not impossible) to impose effective validation and tight controls on the content of attachments. As previously discussed, this can raise security concerns related to the content of messages. Sending data in an attachment is efficient because the SOAP message contains a reference to the data, but not the data itself (this enables faster message processing). SOAP attachments can be implemented using a number of different methods, but none of these are universally accepted. The two most commonly used mechanisms are MIME (Multipurpose Internet Mail Extensions, 1996) and DIME (Direct Internet Message Encapsulation, 2002). Recently however, the WS-I organisation introduced an XML type for attachments 'wsi: swaRef' (Attachments Profile Version 1.0, 2006) which addresses the main limitations of MIME and DIME and is the recommended approach to implementing Web service attachments.

WS-I SOAP with Attachment Reference Type

The WS-I organisation recently introduced an XML type for attachments (Attachments Profile Version 1.0, 2006). The WS-I "wsi:swaRef" reference type addresses the limitations associated with declaring MIME and DIME attachments within the concrete part of the WSDL interface (i.e., within the <wsdl:binding>). Declaring attachments within the concrete WSDL means that the attachments are not visible from the abstract part of the WSDL interface. In contrast to MIME and DIME, "wsi:swaRef" can be referenced from within the abstract WSDL. Furthermore, its location is not limited to message parts as it can be used to define an element or complexType in the schema(s) contained in the WSDL <types>. Listing 5 shows an example WSDL fragment and Listing 6 shows an example SOAP message. WS-I has defined only a single reference type so it automatically maps to the native objects of the service implementation. For example, for Java "wsi:swaRef" maps to the "DataHandler" class from the "java.activation" package.

Listing 5. XML Schema document using the 'wsi: swaRef' reference type for specifying attachments

```
  <element name="myAttachmentElem">
   <complexType>
  <sequence> <element name="octet" type="wsi:swaRef"/>
</sequence>
   </complexType>
  </element>
```

Listing 6. SOAP message with WS-I SOAP attachment reference type

```
<soapenv:Body>
  <sendDH xmlns="http://testproject">
    <myAttachmentElem>
      <octet> cid:1E019A6B976FD5AAD772F60A1
E510D7 </octet>
    </myAttachmentElem>
  </sendDH>
</soapenv:Body>
```

STRONGLY TYPED WEB SERVICES

A purely strongly typed WSDL interface defines a complete definition of an operation's input and output messages with XML Schema, with additional constraints on the actual permitted values. This means that the content of messages can be fully validated before invoking business logic, which offers important security and data integrity benefits. For example, even when considering the effects of a "man-in-the-middle" attack, the effects may be limited by restricting value changes (i.e., hacks) to expected or "nonharmful" parameter ranges. Although strong typing applies to both Document and RPC literal styles, strong typing is easier to implement in Document style services due to the limitations associated with RPC validation. The XML schema used to constrain the <wsdl:messages> can be either embedded directly into the WSDL document or imported using <xsd:import>. It is important to understand, that strongly typed services do not have to be solely strongly typed, as they may combine loose types where necessary. Strong typing is especially relevant for data-centric applications that require a tight control on message values (e.g., numerical ranges and string patterns). From our experiences related to the e-HTPX project (*http://e-htpx.ac.uk/*), the best approach involved mixing the different styles where appropriate. For mature Web services, where the required data is established and stable, the use of strong data typing is preferable. For immature Web services where the required data is often subject to negotiation and revision, loose typing proved useful.

Strongly Typed WSDL Example

Listing 7 shows an example of a strongly typed, Document-literal/wrapped WSDL file that describes a service developed for the e-HTPX project. The WSDL file imports a separately defined XML schema that is shown in Listing 8. The WSDL file defines the "executeBulkMR" service operation. The input and output messages for the operation reference single request and response elements that are globally defined in the imported schema (<executeBulkMR>, <executeBulkMRResponse>). The use of single, global elements for request and response messages enables each message to be validated according to the rules defined by the schema (Listing 7). As shown in Listing 7, XSD restrictions, patterns, and enumerations are all used where necessary to tightly constrain permitted values of important or sensitive parameters (e.g., the "sequence," "pdbIgnoreCodes" and "mrprogram" elements). In the following sections, these WSDL and schema files are used to demonstrate a number of different approaches to XML binding and validation.

Listing 7. Strongly typed WSDL file that imports a XML schema file with value constraints (BulkMRFinal.xsd - shown in Listing 8). The schema is imported within the <wsdl:types> element. The schema is used to constrain the input and output messages of the executeBulkMR Web service operation.

```
<?xml version="1.0" encoding="UTF-8"?>
<wsdl:definitions name="bulkMR"
  targetNamespace="http://e-htpx.ac.uk/bulkmr"xmlns:
import1="http://e-htpx.ac.uk/bulkMR"
  xmlns:soap="http://schemas.xmlsoap.org/wsdl/soap/
```

```
"xmlns:tns="http://e-htpx.ac.uk/bulkmr"
  xmlns:wsdl=http://schemas.xmlsoap.org/wsdl/
  xmlns:xsd="http://www.w3.org/2001/XMLSchema"
   xmlns:xsd1="http://e-htpx.ac.uk/bulkMR.xsd1">

  <!-- Types element used to import or directly declare the schema types -->
  <wsdl:types>
      <xsd:schema targetNamespace="http://e-htpx.ac.uk/bulkMR.xsd1"
      xmlns:SOAP-ENC="http://schemas.xmlsoap.org/soap/encoding/"
      xmlns:xsd="http://www.w3.org/2001/XMLSchema"
      xmlns:xsd1="http://e-htpx.ac.uk/bulkMR.xsd1">
        <xsd:import namespace=http://e-htpx.ac.uk/bulkMR schemaLocation="BulkMRFinal.xsd"/>
    </xsd:schema>
  </wsdl:types>

  <!-- Message elements describe the parameters and return values -->
  <wsdl:message name="Msg_executeRequest">
      <wsdl:part element="import1:executeBulkMR" name="parameters"/>
  </wsdl:message>
  <wsdl:message name="Msg_executeResponse">
   <wsdl:part element="import1:executeBulkMRResponse" name="result"/>
  </wsdl:message>

 <!-- portType element describes the abstract interface of a Web service -->
  <wsdl:portType name="bulkMR_PortType">
   <wsdl:operation name="executeBulkMR">
    <wsdl:input message="tns:Msg_executeRequest"/>
        <wsdl:output message="tns:Msg_executeResponse"/>
   </wsdl:operation>
  </wsdl:portType>

 <!-- binding and service elements not shown -->
 </wsdl:definitions>
```

Listing 8. XML Schema file (BulkMRFinal.xsd – shortened for clarity). The schema is imported into the WSDL file shown in Listing 7 and uses XSD restriction to tightly constrain permitted values (restrictions, patterns, enumerations). This tightly bound schema helps secure the message payload.

```
<?xml version="1.0" encoding="UTF-8"?>
<xs:schema ....targetNamespace="http://e-htpx.ac.uk/bulkMR" ....>

  <xs:complexType name="execute_BulkMR_Request">
   <xs:sequence>
    <xs:element name="email" type="xs:string"/>
    <xs:element name="jobid" type="xs:string"/>
    <xs:element name="sequence">
<xs:simpleType> <xs:restriction base="xs:string"> <xs:minLength value="1"/>
          <xs:pattern value="[A-Ia-iK-Nk-nP-Tp-tV-Zv-z\s\*]*"/>
      </xs:restriction> </xs:simpleType>
    </xs:element>
       <xs:element name="mrprogram" default="molrep" minOccurs="0">
     <xs:simpleType>
      <xs:restriction base="xs:string">
<xs:enumeration value="molrep"/> <xs:enumeration value="phaser"/>
      </xs:restriction>
     </xs:simpleType>
    </xs:element>
<xs:elementname="ignore"type="pdbIgnoreCodes"maxOccurs="1" minOccurs="0"/>
  ...........
 </xs:complexType>
 <xs:complexType name="pdbIgnoreCodes">
  <xs:sequence>
       <xs:element name="pdbCode" minOccurs="0" maxOccurs="unbounded">
    <xs:simpleType> <xs:restriction base="xs:string">
      <xs:pattern value=»[0-9][a-zA-Z0-9][a-zA-Z0-9][a-zA-Z0-9]»/>
     </xs:restriction> </xs:simpleType>
```

```
    </xs:element>
   </xs:sequence>
  </xs:complexType>
  <xs:complexType name="execute_BulkMR_Response">
   <xs:sequence>
  <xs:element name="stringArrayResponse" type="ArrayOf_
xsd_string"/>
   </xs:sequence>
  </xs:complexType>
  ..........
 <xs:element name="executeBulkMR" type="execute_Bulk-
MR_Request"/>
   <xs:element name="executeBulkMRResponse"
type="execute_BulkMR_Response"/>
 ..........
</xs:schema>
```

XML DATA BINDING AND VALIDATION: *HOW* AND *WHERE* DATA IS BOUND AND VALIDATED IN THE APPLICATION

Reliable binding and validation of XML is vital for the correct parsing of both the SOAP Body and SOAP Header. Indeed, the SOAP header, which is used to convey security-related information (e.g., SAML tokens), demands reliable binding and validation. Consequently, the chosen style of binding and validation is essential to all aspects of application security. The following section discusses the approaches and best practices of binding and validating the main security related specifications available today. In the context of Web services, XML that is said to be well-formed can be successfully bound, whereas malformed XML will fail binding (due to malformed elements, for example). Data validation checks the values for correctness and occurs after binding, but before business logic is invoked. Depending upon the service implementation style, data binding and validation can be:

- Performed by the SOAP engine, or,
- Separated from the SOAP engine and performed by the service implementation.

It is essential to realize the advantages and disadvantages of each style as each influence *how* and *where* binding and validation is performed—each style delegating responsibility to different parts of the application. Consequently, a clear delegation of binding and validation responsibility is crucial to ensure application security.

XML Binding/Validation Performed by the SOAP Engine

Data binding and validation can be performed by the internal binding-framework of the SOAP engine so that the Web service implementation is presented with an object representation of the message parameters. The SOAP engine is also responsible for reliably validating security constructs.

Advantages:

- *Simplicity*: The developer is not burdened with performing data binding and validation, and is presented with an object model representation of the Web service parameters that can be used directly.

Disadvantages:

- *Restricted choice of binding/validation framework*: For many SOAP engine implementations, you cannot use custom or preferred data binding and validation frameworks.
- *Semistandardized data bindings which are often not 100% schema compliant:* Some SOAP engine implementations may use semistandardized data binding frameworks to generate client and server classes for

manipulating the payload, but which are not 100% Schema compliant. This has very serious implications for application security, as partially validated data can enter the business logic. In our experience, this has often been a source of error and concern.

- *May need to manually unmarshal objects back into XML*: If the original XML is required (for storage in a database, for example), you may have to reconstruct the XML from the object representation of the payload.

Examples of XML Binding/Validation Performed by the SOAP Engine

Axis 1.4 (JAX-RPC 1.1 Implementation)

The Axis toolkit (*http://ws.apache.org/axis/*) is a popular implementation of the JAX-RPC 1.1 specification (Java APIs for XML Based RPC, 2002). The framework provides the WSDL2Java command line tool for building a Web service (or client) implementation from a WSDL file. This is known as the "WSDL first" or "contract driven" approach. After executing WSDL2Java on the tightly bound WSDL file shown in Listing 7, an implementation of the Web service is generated and is shown in Listing 9. The following important points must be emphasised:

- The Web service operation parameters and return types are "unwrapped" object model representations of the XML request and response messages. The request parameters correspond to the data contained within the <executeBulkMR> schema element. The same applies to the return types corresponding to the <executeBulkMRResponse>. It is also possible to receive and return single "document" objects that correspond to the global request and response elements.
- The Axis 1.4 binding and validation framework ***is not*** 100% XML schema compliant. Consequently, not all of the schema restrictions defined in Listing 8 are enforced, for example, the <xs:pattern> restrictions. Consequently, invalid <sequence> and <pdbCode> elements could pass validation and penetrate the business logic, which raises very serious security-related concerns. It must be noted however, that later versions of Axis (e.g., Axis2) binds and validates with a 100% XML schema compliance.

Listing 9. An Axis 1.4 generated Web service implementation class that relies on the SOAP engine for data binding/validation. The class has been generated from the WSDL file shown in Listing 7. The Axis binding and validation framework is not 100% XML schema compliant and so object parameters are not guaranteed to be valid according to the schema shown in listing 8 (e.g., the xsd:pattern restrictions). This can raise very serious application security concerns.

```
package uk.ac.e_htpx.bulkmr;
import uk.ac.e_htpx.bulkMR.*; // import auto-generated
helper classes and artefacts


public class BulkMR_PortTypeBindingImpl implements
BulkMR_PortType{

/** Web service operation */
public String[] executeBulkMR(String e-mail, String jobid,
String sequence,
    Execute_BulkMR_RequestMrprogram mrprogram,
Float evalue, String[]
ignore, String[] include) throws java.rmi.RemoteException
{

/** TODO implement business logic and return valid response
(ArrayOfXsdString)*/
 /** WARNING - parameters may not be valid if using a
binding framework
      that is not 100% XML schema compliant */
 }
}
```

JAX-WS

JAX-WS 2.0 (Java API for XML Based Web Services, 2006) is the next generation Web service API for Java and replaces JAX-RPC 1.1 (Java APIs for XML Based RPC, 2002). The framework was renamed to JAX-WS to help change the common misunderstanding that Web services are just another way of doing RPC. The most important feature of the JAX-WS framework is that the data binding and validation is delegated to the JAXB 2.0 (Java Architecture for XML Binding, 2006) framework, which supports all of the XML schema features (100% schema compliant). Consequently, the Web service message data is fully validated according to the rules defined in the schema(s). An example implementation is shown in Listing 10. The following important points must be emphasised:

- The Web service operation parameters and return types are "unwrapped" object model representations of the XML request and response messages. The request parameters correspond to the data contained within the <executeBulkMR> schema elements. The same applies to the return types corresponding to the data contained in the <executeBulkMRResponse>. It is also possible to receive and return single "document" objects that correspond to the global request and response elements.
- The XML schema restrictions are applied fully during validation. Consequently, the <xs:pattern> restrictions (i.e., regular expressions) are enforced when binding and validating the payload (only valid data will enter the business logic of the service, which imposes tighter control on securing the payload, SOAP body and header).

Listing 10. A JAX-WS generated Web service implementation that relies on the SOAP engine for data binding and validation via JAXB. The class has been generated from the WSDL file shown in Listing 7. The parameter values are guaranteed to be valid according to the schema shown in Listing 8 as JAXB is 100% Schema compliant). This helps impose tight control on securing the payload, SOAP body and header.

```
import javax.jws.WebService;
import uk.ac.e_htpx.bulkmr.* ; // import auto-generated
binding classes and artifacts

@WebService(serviceName="bulkMRService", portName
= "Port1",
endpointInterface = "uk.ac.e_htpx.bulkmr.BulkMRPort-
Type",
targetNamespace = «http://e-htpx.ac.uk/bulkmr»,
wsdlLocation = «WEB-INF/wsdl/BulkMRService2/bulk-
MRService.wsdl»)

public class BulkMRService2 implements uk.ac.e_htpx.
bulkmr.BulkMRPortType {
  @WebMethod
  public ArrayOfXsdString executeBulkMR(String e-mail,
String jobid, String sequence,
        String mrprogram, Float evalue, PdbIgnoreCodes
ignore) {

/** TODO implement business logic and return valid response
(ArrayOfXsdString)*/
  }
}
```

XML Binding/Validation Separated from the SOAP Engine

Data binding and validation can be separated from the SOAP engine and left to the sole responsibility of the service implementation. This approach requires a "message style" service endpoint implementation that is passed a raw, unbound XML payload. It is important to understand that in doing this, the service implementation has sole responsibility for fully binding and validating the payload before business logic is invoked (of both SOAP body and security constructs in the SOAP header). This can be performed using APIs and tools of choice. If implemented incorrectly, however, invalid or insecure data can pass to the business logic. Binding and validation can be performed using direct XML manipulation API's, such as DOM or SAX. However, it is more secure to use dedicated XML schema binding and validation frameworks such as JAXB 2.0 (Java Architecture for XML Binding, 2006) or XMLBeans (*http://xmlbeans.apache.org/*). Developers may still manipulate XML in the familiar format of objects (courtesy of the binding framework), but there is no dependency upon the SOAP engine. In doing this, the XML schema(s) that are imported within the <types> element of the WSDL file are manually compiled to produce an object-binding library (XMLBeans provides the "scomp" command line compiler and JAXB provides the "xjc" command line compiler). The compiled object library can be imported directly within the Web service implementation to bind and validate the unbound XML after service invocation. In doing this, it is easy to both parse and traverse the XML payload, and validate where necessary (e.g., "on-demand" validation of security constructs in the SOAP header. Please refer to the section titled "Binding and Validation of XML Security specifications").

Advantages:

- *Choice of preferred data binding/validation framework*: This could lever the preferred, or more powerful features of a chosen binding framework for securing the payload. For example, we have found the XML cursor functionality of the XMLBeans toolkit especially useful for isolating and parsing arbitrary XML that is defined in place of <xsd:any> and <xsd:anyType> elements.
- *Clear separation of roles*: The SOAP engine and the data binding/validation framework become clearly separated into "communication-specific" and "data-specific" roles. The clear delegation of responsibility helps ensure security across the whole application.
- *On-Demand XML Document Construction and Validation for "Out-of-Band" Processes:* A clear separation of roles allows construction of valid XML messages/documents when necessary (i.e., outside of the Web service class). The separation of the data binding from the SOAP engine is gaining popularity in the next generation of SOAP engines that are now beginning to implement "pluggable" data binding frameworks.

Disadvantages:

- *Manual Binding/Validation:* The developer is responsible for manually parsing, traversing and extracting data from the unbound XML payload that is received by the service.
- *Manually Construct Sensible Exceptions:* The developer is also responsible for throwing sensible exceptions with the occurrence of payload errors such as mal-formed XML and erroneous values.

Examples of XML Binding/Validation Separated from the SOAP Engine

Axis 1.4 (JAX-RPC 1.1 Implementation)

The Axis framework provides "Message" style service endpoint methods. Here, the endpoint implementations accesses the XML message directly, and does not perform data binding or validation. Listing 11 shows an implementation example that uses the XMLBeans toolkit to parse the SOAPEnvelope request. It would be equally valid to parse, bind, and validate SOAP body elements using SAX, DOM, or JAXB.

Listing 11. Axis Message style service implementation (used with the WSDL file shown in Listing 7). Data binding and validation is performed by the business logic rather than by the SOAP engine. Data binding and validation is performed using an XML schema compilation framework (e.g., XMLBeans).

```
package uk.ac.ehtpx.bulkMR.message;
import uk.ac.eHtpx.bulkMR.*;
import ....
public class bulkMRMessageService {
 /** Web service Method */
  public void executeBulkMR(SOAPEnvelope req, SOAP-
Envelope resp)
   throws SOAPException {
    // Get SOAPBodyElement ("executeBulkMR" - same
name as operation).
    SOAPBody reqBody = req.getBody();
    Iterator it = reqBody.getChildElements();
    SOAPBodyElement be; String content = null;
    while(it.hasNext())
         be = (SOAPBodyElement)it.next(); content =
be.toString();
 // PARSE – that is, check document for well-formed XML.
    ExecuteBulkMRDocument doc = null;
    try {
         doc = ExecuteBulkMRDocument.Factory.
parse(content);
    } catch(XmlException e){
      throw new javax.xml.soap.SOAPException
        ("Not well formed "+e.getMessage());
    }
 // VALIDATE – that is, check doc for correct values (accord-
ing to xsd restrictions)
    try {
      this.validateExecuteBulkMRDocument(doc);
    }catch(SOAPException ex){ throw ex; // rethrow }

    /** TODO implement business logic and build response
*/
      ExecuteBulkMRRequest reqdoc = doc.getExecuteB-
ulkMR();
    String sequence = reqdoc.getSequence(); // sequence
is validated !
     ...
  }
}
```

JAX-WS

The JAX-WS specification also provides message style Web service implementation endpoints that facilitate direct access to the XML payload by implementing the "Provider" interface and "javax.xml.ws.WebServiceProvider" annotation. Provider endpoints must declare the "@WebServiceProvider" annotation rather than the "@WebService" annotation, as shown in Listing 12. The "@ServiceMode" annotation may also be used to convey whether the endpoint requires access to the whole SOAP message (Service.Mode.MESSAGE) or just to the payload of a particular request (Service.Mode.PAYLOAD). It is important to understand that the XML binding and business logic of the Web service could be identical to that shown in Listing 11.

Listing 12. JAX-WS Message style service implementation (used with the WSDL file shown in Listing 7). Data binding and validation is performed by the business logic rather than by the SOAP engine (see business logic shown in Listing 11).

```
@ServiceMode(value=Service.Mode.PAYLOAD)
@WebServiceProvider(wsdlLocation="WEB-INF/wsdl/bulk-
MRService.wsdl",
portName="Port1", targetNamespace="http://e-htpx.
ac.uk/bulkmr",
```

```
serviceName="ehtpxProviderService")
public class bulkMRImpl implements Provider<Source> {

 /** Web service method – implements invoke of interface
javax.xml.ws.Provider */
  public Source invoke(Source source) {
   try {
     /** TODO implement same business logic here – see
previous code listing */
   } catch(Exception e) {
      throw new RuntimeException("Error in provider end-
point", e);
   }
  }
```

Binding and Validation of XML Security Specifications

The approaches to data binding and validation and the best practices discussed earlier for delegating *how* and *where* to perform binding/validation are equally applicable when working with security-related specifications. Indeed, these security specifications also define rule-sets and constraints in the form of accompanying XML Schema that should be fully bound and validated. Consequently, a correct binding and validation implementation and a good understanding of these schemas, including their design, structure, restrictions, and limitations are vital to incorporate effective security. A single specification alone may not fulfil all of the security requirements of an application. Consequently, familiarisation of the different specifications significantly complicates application development. The main security related standards are briefly outlined before presenting the approaches and best practices bind and validate these security specifications.

WS-Security Specifications

Security itself has three flavours; confidentiality, integrity, and authentication/authorization. Most of these core security concepts depend on technologies and various emerging standards that require effective XML binding and validation.

XML Signature: XML Signature (XML Signature Syntax and Processing, 2002) is a foundational technology for the WS-Security standard and is built on top of mature digital signature technologies. The purpose of a digital signature is to provide a mechanism for message integrity by encoding digital signatures into XML. XML Signature defines a strongly typed schema and associated processing rules recommended by W3C.

XML Encryption: XML Encryption (XML Encryption Syntax and Processing, 2002) is based on standard cryptographic technologies, particularly shared key encryption. The main purpose of XML Encryption is to provide a mechanism to encrypt selected portions of an XML document using standard algorithms.

SAML: SAML (Security Assertion Markup Language, 2004) allows trust assertions (e.g., "tokens") to be specified in XML. Assertions apply to an individual or an entity, which are attached to a message. SAML assertions take the form of authentication or authorization attributes. SAML defines a set of Web API's to be used to obtain these assertions from trust services and makes authorization and authentication decisions about individuals and entities.

WS-Security: WS-Security (Web Services Security, 2004) is used to define how XML Signature and XML Encryption should be used together in SOAP messages. WS-Security is a conceptual model that abstracts different security technologies into "claims" and "tokens." In summary, the packaging of security tokens into SOAP messages is the focus of WS-Security, which provides a mechanism to digitally sign all or part of SOAP message and pass the signature and encryption tokens in the SOAP header.

APPROACHES TO BINDING AND VALIDATING SECURITY SPECIFICATIONS

The following sections discuss the various approaches to implementing binding and validation the security specifications introduced in the previous section.

Manual Binding/Validation

One possibility is to construct, bind, and validate security constructs and secure SOAP messages manually by using low level DOM or SAX APIs. However, many Web service developers are not comfortable with raw XML and should avoid using these low level APIs as this increases the likelihood of introducing error. Indeed, this approach requires a thorough understanding of the specifications, including the structure, limitations, and restrictions of the security related schemas. Any change in specifications requires an extensive update of the application.

Use Dedicated Binding/Validation Frameworks

Java binding was discussed in detail in the previous sections, which introduced how to bind and validate XML using dedicated binding and validation toolkits (e.g., XML-Beans and JAX-B). These toolkits can also be used to construct, bind, and validate security constructs and secure SOAP messages. As shown previously, these binding toolkits parse the XML schema and create corresponding Java objects without compromising the schema constructs. XML Schema provides various features such as restriction, extension, and regular expressions. The translation of XML Schema into Java objects is complicated process and XML-Java binding toolkits use proprietary mechanisms to implement complete mappings. It is possible to generate 100% compliant XML schema mappings to implement security specifications. SOAP messages can be easily constructed through SAAJ (SOAP with Attachments API for Java) and security constructs can be added to the SOAP messages using the binding frameworks.

Adopt Pre-existing (Partial) Implementations

A number of existing research projects implement the security-related specifications of Web services. Often, these projects may have either partial or outdated implementations and are packaged as "black boxes" out of immediate control of the developer. These implementations may impose their own limitations:

1. Normally, different security implementations are packaged with large middleware stacks, for example, Globus Toolkit (*http://www.globus.org/toolkit/),* IBM Emerging Technologies Toolkit (ETTK) (*http://www.alphaworks.ibm.com/ettk*), and EGEE gLite (*http://glite.web.cern.ch/glite/*). It is usually required to understand the architecture of the entire middleware stack before making any effective use of selected components (e.g., security components).
2. For the most part, it is not possible to use different components of the middleware in isolation. These components are often too tightly integrated.
3. The middleware may only provide functionality that is crucial for the middleware resulting in partial implementations.
4. In some cases, toolkits extend the specifications in a nonstandard format to match their requirements. This negates the core purpose of Web services regarding interoperability and platform independence.

CODE FIRST OR WSDL FIRST

The complexity of XML schema and over-verbosity of WSDL is a major concern in practical development of Web services, especially for ensuring effective constraint of data and securing the message payload. As a result, two divergent practices for developing Web services and WSDL have emerged, the "code first" approach ("bottom up") and "WSDL first" approach ("top down" or "contract driven"). The code first approach involves auto-generation of the WSDL file from service implementation using tools that leverage reflection. In doing this, it could be stated, "*the WSDL describes the underlying implementation*." Alternatively, the WSDL first approach involves writing the original WSDL and XML Schema, and generating/writing the service implementation from the WSDL file. In this scenario, *"The underlying code implements the interface defined by a WSDL."* The advantages and disadvantages of each approach are summarized below.

Code First

Advantages

- Simplicity. Developers are hidden from the complexity of writing XML/WSDL.

Disadvantages

- WSDL generated from source code may introduce dependencies upon the implementation language. This is especially relevant when considering older, JAX-RPC implementations, which can lead to serious interoperability issues across different platforms (e.g., differences in how Java and .NET serialize value types in one language but are reference/nillable objects in the other).
- WSDL created from source code will always be less strongly typed than WSDL that is created from the original XML Schema. Indeed, many of the more powerful features of XML Schema are often lost when using automatic WSDL generators (e.g., xsd:patterns). As previously discussed, this has serious implications for imposing effective data constraints and for tightly constraining and securing message payloads, especially when considering the security related specifications.

WSDL First

Advantages

- Platform and language interoperability issues are prevented, as both the client and service are working from a common set of interoperable XML Schema.
- The data types available in programming languages are only subset of those available in XML Schema. Indeed, schema is more powerful and descriptive than the data types available in source code.

Disadvantages

- The developer requires a reasonable knowledge of XML Schema and WSDL.
- This approach is initially more time consuming.

In our experience, the WSDL first approach is the most suitable for developing robust, tightly constrained, and secured services, especially when integrating the security specification constructs previously outlined which usually mandates the WSDL first approach.

CONCLUSION

The WSDL interface style (RPC/Document, encoded/literal), dictates how SOAP messages are constructed, serialized, and to what extent SOAP messages can be constrained and secured during the validation process. Consequently, a good understanding and a correct choice of Web service style influences application security from the outset. Developments in the field of Web services, however, have largely focused on the RPC style services rather than on the Document style, which is more effective for the binding, validation, and constraint of SOAP messages and is recommended over RPC. The RPC/encoded style is not WS-I compliant and is deprecated. The RPC/literal style is WS-I compliant, but has validation limitations. As a result, the RPC style is increasingly being referred to as "CORBA with brackets" in the Web service community.

The strength of data typing, which is dependent on the chosen Web service style, dictates the extent to which SOAP message data can be constrained and secured. Loosely typed services encapsulate data within generic types and are easy and convenient to develop, which makes them suitable in a number of scenarios. However, loose typing can raise security concerns regarding propagating loosely bound or even unknown data to the business logic (e.g., erroneous/malicious/binary data). Loose typing also raises a set of limitations associated with ambiguous WSDL, which can lead to data integrity and security concerns between consumer and service. This is because additional manual negotiation is usually required to establish the format of encapsulated data. In contrast to loose typing, strongly typed services define all necessary information in the WSDL interface and provide parameter value constraints where necessary. Strong typing is easily implemented in the Document Web service style where the exchange of plain XML documents facilitates full validation of complex data before the business logic is invoked. This offers important security and data integrity benefits (e.g., the effects of "man-in-the-middle" may be limited by restricting parameter changes/hacks to expected or "nonharmful" ranges).

The chosen approach to binding and validation dictates *how* and *where* message binding and validation is performed (e.g., *how* – by manual XML manipulation APIs such as SAX/DOM or by dedicated frameworks such as JAXB/XMLBeans; for example, *where* - before the service implementation via the SOAP engine or "on-demand" within the service implementation). A clear understanding and effective implementation of binding and validation is therefore crucial for application security. This is especially relevant when processing security-related constructs in the SOAP header, which demands reliable processing of complex security related schema(s). For the most part, we recommend the use of dedicated binding and validation frameworks, which guarantee 100% XML schema compliance and are most appropriate for processing complex security schema. These frameworks also facilitate "on-demand" processing when required. If relying on the SOAP engine to perform binding and validation, it is vital for all application security to ensure the SOAP engine binding and validation framework is 100% XML schema compliant. We also recommend the "WSDL first" or "contract driven" approach to Web service design, as strong typing can be included as required.

REFERENCES

Attachments Profile Version 1.0. (2006). Retrieved June 11, 2007, from http://www.ws-i.org/Profiles/AttachmentsProfile-1.0.html

Basic Profile Version 1.0. (2004). Retrieved June 11, 2007, from http://www.ws-i.org/Profiles/BasicProfile-1.0-2004-04-16.html

Direct Internet Message Encapsulation (DIME). (2002). Retrieved June 11, 2007, from http://xml.coverpages.org/draft-nielsen-dime-01.txt

Extensible Markup Language (XML) 1.0 (Fourth Edition). (2006). Retrieved June 11, 2007, from http://www.w3.org/TR/xml/

Java APIs for XML Based RPC (JAX-RPC), (JSR 101). (2002). Retrieved June 11, 2007, from http://jcp.org/en/jsr/detail?id=101

Java API for XML Based Web Services (JAX-WS), (JSR 224). (2006). Retrieved June 11, 2007, from http://jcp.org/en/jsr/detail?id=224

Java Architecture for XML Binding (JAXB), (JSR 222). (2006). Retrieved June 11, 2007, from http://www.jcp.org/en/jsr/detail?id=222

Multipurpose Internet Mail Extensions (MIME) Part One, RFC 1521. (1996). Retrieved June 11, 2007, from http://www.ietf.org/rfc/rfc2045.txt

Security Assertion Markup Language (SAML). (2004). Retrieved June 11, 2007, from http://www.oasis-open.org/committees/download.php/6837/sstc-saml-tech-overview-1.1-cd.pdf

Simple Object Access Protocol (SOAP) 1.1. (2000). Retrieved June 11, 2007, from http://www.w3.org/TR/2000/NOTE-SOAP-20000508/

Universal Description, Discovery and Integration (UDDI), Version 3.0.2. (2004). Retrieved June 11, 2007, from http://uddi.org/pubs/uddi_v3.htm

XML Encryption Syntax and Processing. (2002). Retrieved June 11, 2007, from http://www.w3.org/TR/xmlenc-core/

XML Signature Syntax and Processing. (2002). Retrieved June 11, 2007, from http://www.w3.org/TR/xmldsig-core/

Web Services Description Language (WSDL) 1.1. (2001). Retrieved June 11, 2007, from http://www.w3.org/TR/2001/NOTE-wsdl-20010315

Web Services Security. (2004). Retrieved June 11, 2007, from http://docs.oasis-open.org/wss/2004/01/oasis-200401-wss-soap-message-security-1.0.pdf

Chapter XIV
Enhancing Web Service Discovery and Monitoring with Quality of Service Information

Christian Platzer
Vienna University of Technology, Austria

Florian Rosenberg
Vienna University of Technology, Austria

Schahram Dustdar
Vienna University of Technology, Austria

ABSTRACT

Web services provide a fundamental technology for developing service-oriented systems by leveraging platform-independent interface descriptions (WSDL) and a flexible message encoding (SOAP). Beside the functional description, quality of service (QoS) issues are currently not part of the Web service standards stack, although they provide valuable metadata of a Web service such as performance, dependability, security, or cost and payment. This additional information can be used to greatly enhance service discovery, selection, and composition. As a result of the latest research that is dedicated to this area, this chapter deals with the various ways of describing, bootstrapping, and evaluating QoS attributes. A strong focus is laid on client-side QoS assessment and the arising problems. Furthermore, a method to analyze Web service interactions by using our evaluation tool and extracting important QoS information without any knowledge about the service implementation will be presented and thoroughly explained.
Usually, taking performance measures for a specific Web service requires access to the service implementation or at least the server machine where it is hosted. This chapter will address a way to bootstrap the most important performance and dependability values form the client's perspective, and therefore overcoming these restrictions.

INTRODUCTION

QoS descriptions for Web services are gaining importance and are heavily investigated by different research groups. Their availability is a fundamental requirement to solve many problems researchers are currently encountering. These problems include dynamic composition, search and discovery of Web services, and performance-based selection of services.

Currently, the most severe drawback when dealing with Web services is a common lack of quality of service (QoS) attributes and their present values. These descriptions are necessary to appraise the value of a Web service in different respects. On the one hand, they can describe performance-related characteristics like availability, latency, and response time, and on the other hand, they are utilized to provide the necessary values for provider-specific settings like cost, security requirements, and similar values. With the current method to specify Web services by using WSDL descriptions, no technique to attach both, provider- and consumer-specific QoS values, exists. For the provider side it is simply because no common way to attach this valuable information to either a WSDL description or a service registry has yet been established.

The case is different for consumer-specific values, especially the performance-related aspects, because it simply does not make sense in most cases. A provider that guarantees a response time of 20 milliseconds for a Web service will run into serious trouble to fulfill this guarantee when a client operates on a slow modem connection, for instance. Furthermore, by appointing their own performance values, the providers would be forced to announce best-case values or even tempted to declare better values than they can possibly produce. Apart from the aspects mentioned above, QoS parameters related to performance are required by various researchers because they can be used to optimize workflows or enhance the results of search engines. For the time being, those very specific measurements must be assessed by the client invoking the service or a third party.

In this chapter, a framework is introduced which provides the possibility to assess QoS attributes for a given set of Web services. The approach is automated and is able to bootstrap and constantly monitor QoS parameters for existing services that are currently lacking such valuable descriptions. A tool, based on this approach, allows categorizing service repositories according to the most important characteristics, finally enabling QoS-driven development. Furthermore, existing standards are used to attach the bootstrapped values to a document description. Not all of these standards are applicable and can be used for the purpose of QoS propagation, while others have to be adopted to fit in the requirements discusses in the following chapter. First of all, we will discuss a proper QoS model which encompasses the most relevant nonfunctional properties of a Web service.

QoS MODEL

This section describes the QoS model and how it is used to express quality attributes of Web services. It is important to keep in mind that most of the presented attributes are dynamic and site-dependent. As a result, the produced values cannot be seen as global attributes, but as site-specific statistics with a strong local context. This is an intended behavior, because the parameters, influenced by the local conditions, increase the significance of the whole value. We assume two Web services, for example, named A and B, with the same implementation and the same hardware. The Web service consumer is located at a remote place where the routing of the actual IP packets is the only difference between the two services. Therefore, A may respond faster than B in this case, while B could be the faster service when queried from another place.

We begin with breaking down the QoS attributes into different categories and describing how they are evaluated in a real-world scenario.

Categorization

In general, QoS parameters are categorized into several groups, with each group containing related QoS attributes. Four main QoS groups, namely *Performance*, *Dependability*, *Security and Cost,* and *Payment* can be identified. As already mentioned in the introduction, automated bootstrapping and evaluation can only be applied to the first two groups. Nevertheless, the attachment strategies of the actual values are the same for all four groups.

Performance

Processing time: Given a service S and an operation o, the processing time $t_p(S,o)$ defines the time needed to actually carry out the operation for a specific request R. The processing of the operation o does not include any network communication time, and is therefore an atomic attribute with the smallest granularity. Its value is determined by the implementation of the service and the corresponding operation. To take Google as an example, t_p entitles the actual search time that is also displayed for search-requests sent by the Web interface.

Wrapping Time: The wrapping time $t_w(S,o)$ is a measure for the time that is needed to unwrap the XML structure of a received request or wrap a request and send it to the destination. The actual value is strongly influenced by the used Web service framework and even the operating system itself. In Wickramage and Weerawarana (2005), the authors even split this time into three subvalues where receiving, (re-)construction, and sending of a message are distinguished. For evaluation purposes, it does not matter if the delay is caused by the XML parser or maybe the socket implementation, because it is constant for the same request.

Execution Time: The execution time $t_e(S,o)$ simply is the sum of two wrapping times and the processing time:

$$t_e = t_p + 2 * t_w.$$

It represents the time that the provider needs to finish processing the request. It starts with unwrapping the XML structure, processing the result, and wrapping the answer into a SOAP envelope that can be sent back to the requester.

Latency: The time that the SOAP message needs to reach its destination service S is depicted as latency or network latency time $t_l(S)$. It is influenced by the type of the network connection the request is sent over. Furthermore, routing, network utilization, and request-size play a significant role for the latency.

Response Time: The response time of a service S is the time between sending a message M from a given client to S and the response R for message M returns back to the client. The response time is provider specific; therefore, it is not possible to specify a globally valid value for each client. The response time $t_r(S,o)$ is calculated by the following formula:

$$t_r(S,o) = t_e(S,o) + 2 * t_l(S).$$

Round Trip Time: The last time-related attribute is the round trip time $t_{rt}(S,o)$. It gives the overall time that is consumed from the moment a request is issued to the moment the answer is received and successfully processed. It comprises all values on both the requester and the consumer side. Considering the formula above, it can be calculated as:

$$t_{rt}(S,o) = [2 * t_w]_{Consumer} + t_l + [t_p + 2 * t_w]_{Provider} + t_l + [2 * t_w]_{Consumer}$$

Figure 1. Service invocation time frames

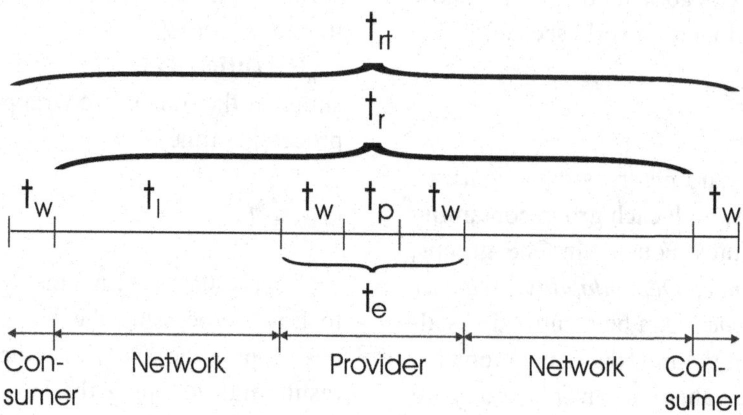

Figure 1 shows a graphical representation of all involved time frames within a service invocation.

Throughput: The number of Web service requests *R* for an operation *o* that can be processed by a service *S* within a given period of time *t* is referred to as throughput $t_p(S, o)$. It can be calculated by the following formula:

$$t_p(S,o) = \frac{\#R(S,o)}{t\ (in\ sec)}$$

This parameter depends mainly on the hardware power of the service provider and is measured by sending many requests in parallel for a given period of time (e.g., 1 minute) and counting how many requests return to the requester.

Scalability: A Web service that is scalable has the ability to cope with a great number of parallel requests without getting overloaded. A high scalability value states the probability for the requester of receiving the response in the evaluated response time $t_r(S,o)$:

$$sc(S) = \frac{t_r}{t_r(Throughput)}$$

The value $t_r(Throughput)$ is the response time which is evaluated during the throughput test.

Dependability

Availability: The probability that a service *S* is up and running. The availability can be calculated the following way:

$$av(S) = 1 - \frac{downtime}{uptime + downtime}$$

The downtime and uptime are measured in minutes.

Accuracy: The accuracy *ac(S)* of a service *S* is defined as the success rate produced by *S*. It can be calculated by evaluating all invocations starting from a given point in time and examining their results. The following formula expresses this relationship:

$$ac(S) = 1 - \frac{\#failed\ requests}{\#total\ request}$$

Robustness: The robustness *ro(S)* is the probability that a system can react properly to invalid, incomplete, or conflicting input messages. It can be measured by tracking all incorrect input messages and putting this value in relation with all valid responses from a given point in time:

$$ro(S) = \frac{\sum_{i=0}^{n} f(resp_i(req_i(S)))}{\#total\ requests}$$

In this formula, $resp_i(req_i(S))$ $resp_i(req_i(S))$ represents the ith response to the ith request to service S, where n is the number of total requests to S. The utility function f is calculated as:

$$f(r) = \begin{cases} 0, & !isValid(r) \\ 1, & isValid(r) \end{cases}$$

It is used to evaluate if the response was correct for a given input.

QOS MONITORING APPROACHES

Based on the above QoS model, there are several ways those measurements can be assessed in the real world. Each one has a certain level of advantages and disadvantages.

Provider-Side Instrumentation

The first and easiest way to bootstrap QoS parameters for Web Services is to directly instrument the service at the provider. It bears the enormous advantage of a known service implementation. The service provider has to choose if the dynamic attributes are calculated directly within the service code (invasive instrumentation) or by utilizing an artificial monitoring device (non-invasive instrumentation). Either case has two major drawbacks:

- All monitoring is done from the provider side, which means that network latency cannot be taken into account for a connecting client
- A service consumer has to trust the provider to publish correct values, which raises the same problems as mentioned in the introduction

The approach, visualized in Figure 2, allows a very accurate measurement of all provider-specific values, even those not measurable, like cost and security.

SOAP Intermediaries

By using an intermediary party, the traffic is not directly routed from client to server, but to an intermediate party that is responsible for maintaining QoS-related data. The big advantage with this approach lies in the trustworthiness of the received data. This third party is effectively a proxy who is able to handle incoming requests and forward them to the original destination. Although this approach solves the problem of

Figure 2. Provider-side instrumentation

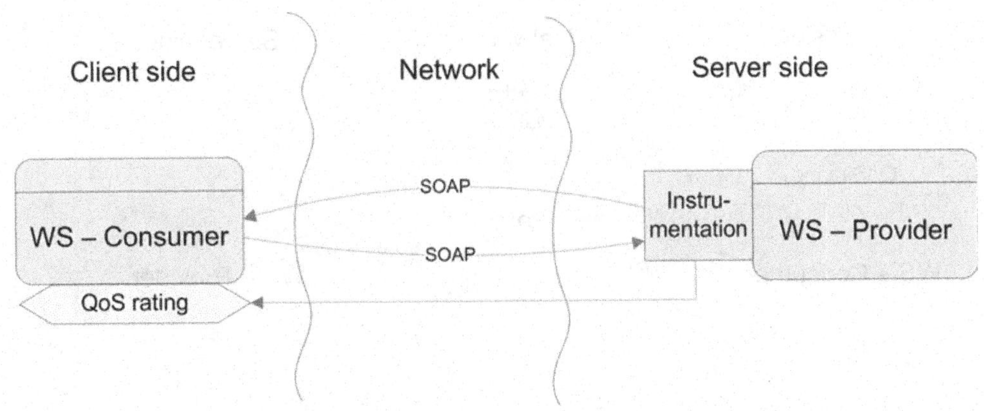

trustworthiness, and partially the latency issue, it still has an enormous drawback. Because of the proxy function, the third party will always be the bottleneck that limits scalability.

In Figure 3, a graphical representation of this approach is depicted. It is obvious that this method is unable to assess nonfunctional data like cost, because these values are explicitly created by the providing party.

Probing

Just like bots for search engines and Web crawlers, the possibility to implement probes to collect data about Web service endpoints must be considered. This method bears a lower runtime overhead compared to SOAP intermediaries, but still has the disadvantage of not being consumer-specific.

When invoking a service that is monitored by a probe as shown in Figure 4, the original message is not altered in any way and the QoS metadata is provided by the probing party which invokes the original services on a scheduled basis. As a result, providers might recognize when they are being probed and react different than to real clients and manipulate the performance measurement the probe produces.

Sniffing

The last method introduced here, makes use of a sniffer that captures all outgoing packets from the client side. This way, the real traffic can be monitored and used to produce the required QoS data. Other than all the methods presented above, the values produced here are really consumer-specific. The performance rating strongly depends on the used client and its location, which is the desired behavior.

Two major disadvantages come with this method:

- QoS parameters of unknown services are not available until they are invoked the first time.
- The capturing process can only measure the time from the moment the packet leaves until an answer is returned. This timeframe usually includes a subset of other timeframes, such as processing time, wrapping time, and so forth, that has to be distinguished.

The next section will focus on these two problems and how they can be solved.

Figure 3. Intermediary

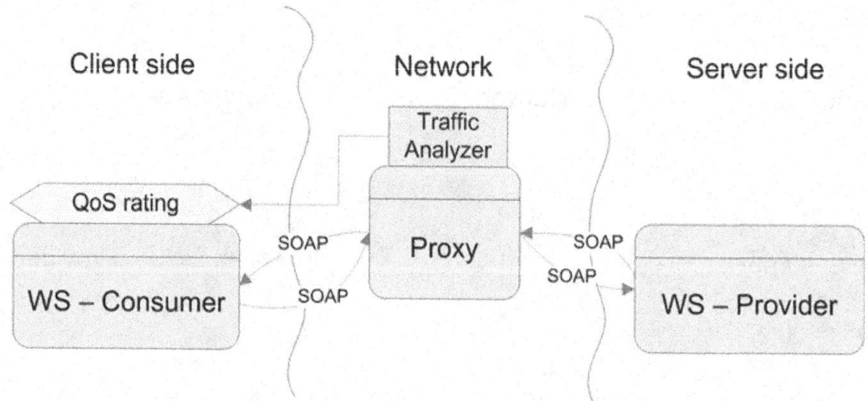

Figure 4. Probing

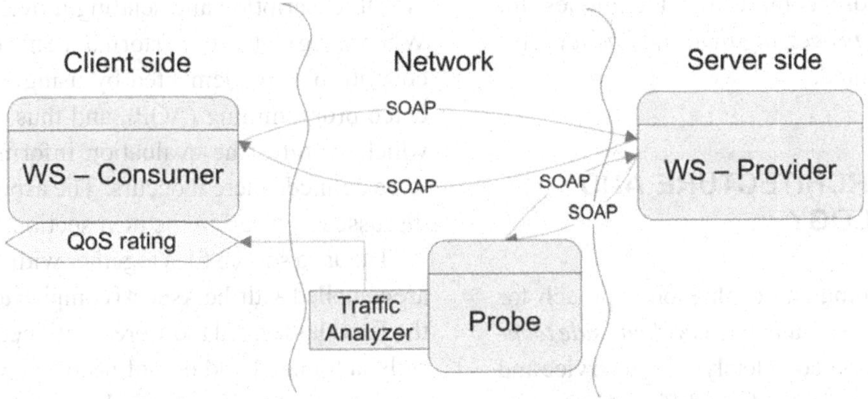

A BOOTSTRAPPING AND MONITORING APPROACH USING ASPECT-ORIENTED PROGRAMMING

A number of possibilities exist to design a QoS-based evaluation and monitoring approach for Web services, but all approaches share the previously mentioned premises concerning the knowledge and access about the Web service under evaluation.

Access to the Web service implementation: The approach seems to be the easiest one, because full access to the service implementation is available. This implies that performance measurements, such as latency or the service processing time of Web service requests, can be exactly determined by combining the evaluation software running on the client-side with information on the server side, for example, by implementing special handlers or loggers, as it is possible with the Apache Axis Web service environment (Apache Software Foundation, 2006). In practice, this approach is not feasible because the implementation is considered private property of the service provider and therefore not a public facility.

No access to the Web service implementation: This approach is a client-side technique, where only the WSDL file of the service de-

Figure 5. Sniffing

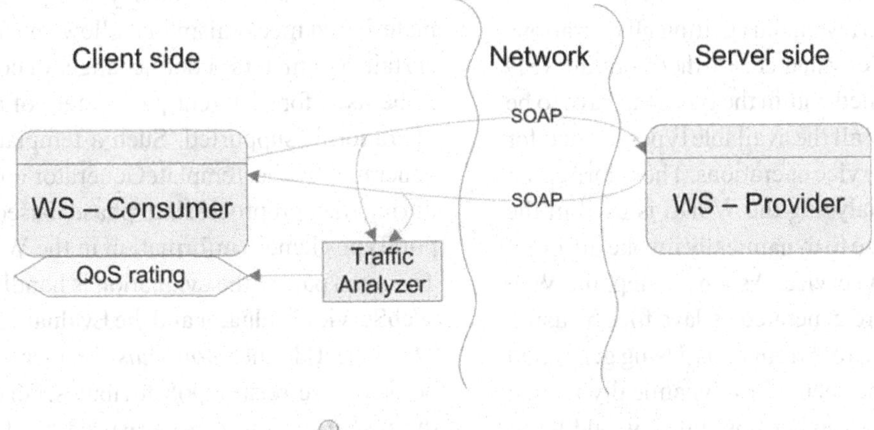

scription is available. Therefore, alternative and sometimes more complicated techniques for measuring the *processing time* and *latency* have to be implemented.

SYSTEM ARCHITECTURE AND METHODOLOGY

Our bootstrapping and evaluation approach for the different QoS parameters is a *client-side technique* which works completely as Web service and provider independent. Many different steps are necessary to successfully bootstrap and evaluate QoS attributes for arbitrary Web services. An overview of the main blocks of the system architecture and three different phases of the evaluation process are depicted in Figure 6.

The principal procedure is always the same for all approaches, but the various elements and their ways of interaction can, of course, differ. Basically, the following phases can be distinguished.

Preprocessing Phase

In this initial phase, the WSDL description is fetched as an input from a given URL or some local repository. Then, the WSDL file is parsed and analyzed to determine the SOAP binding name (Three different bindings are possible: SOAP, HTTP GET, and HTTP POST). From the binding name, the corresponding portType element can be retrieved, thus getting all operations which have to be evaluated. Furthermore, all XSD data types defined within the types tag have to be parsed to know all the available types needed for invoking the service operations. The information gathered by analyzing the WSDL is used in the evaluation phase to dynamically invoke different operations of a service. As a next step, the Web service stubs are generated as Java files by using the WSDL2Java tool from Axis. Using generated stubs is just one method to dynamically invoke a Web service. Another possibility would be to manually create a correct XML message for a WSDL description and sending it over a socket. When using stubs, the performance measurement code itself is implemented by using aspect-oriented programming (AOP), and thus, an aspect which captures the evaluation information has to be defined where it occurs. The aspect will be discussed in detail in the next section.

The Java source files together with the aspect are compiled with the AspectJ compiler to generate the Java classes. All the aforementioned steps are fully automated and do not need to be executed every time a specific service has to be evaluated. It has to be done only once, and then the generated code is stored in a local service repository and can be reused for further re-executions of the evaluation process itself.

Evaluation Phase

During the evaluation phase, the information from the WSDL analysis in the preprocessing phase is used to map the XSD complex types to Java classes created by the WSDL2Java tool. Furthermore, we heavily use Java Reflection, in this example encapsulated in the Reflector component, to dynamically instantiate these complex helper classes and Web service stubs. The WebServiceInvoker component tries to invoke a service operation just by "probing" arbitrary values for the input parameters for an operation. If this is not possible, for example, because an authentication key is required, a template-based mechanism that allows us to specify certain parameters or define ranges or collections to be used for different parameters of a service operation is supported. Such a template is also generated by the TemplateGenerator component during the preprocessing phase based on the portType element information in the WSDL file. The main part of the evaluation is handled by the WebServiceEvaluator and the EvaluationAspect. The aspect defines *pointcuts* for measuring the performance-related QoS attributes. For example, the response time t_r is measured by defining a

Figure 6. System architecture

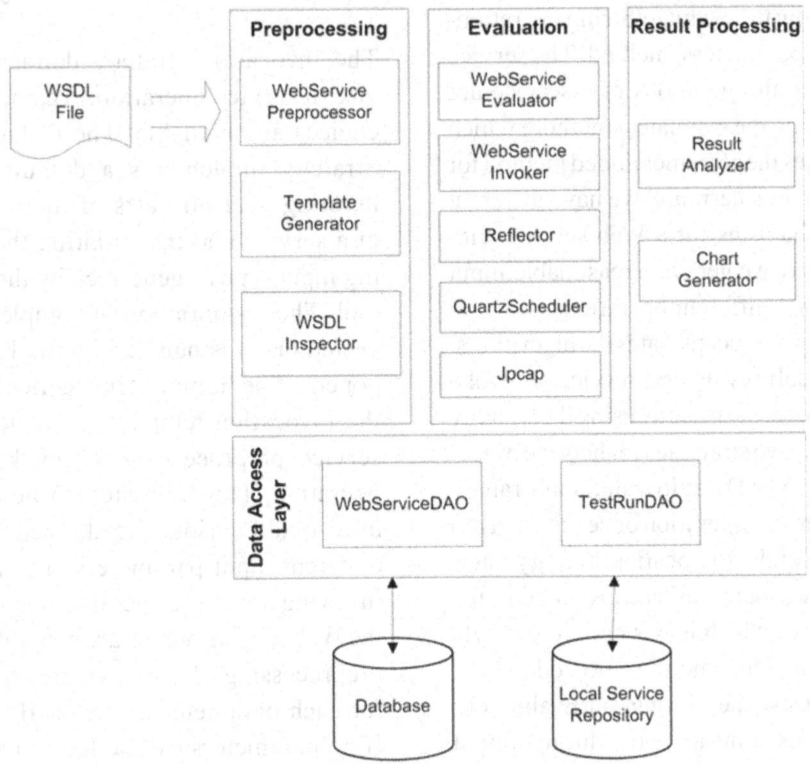

pointcut which timestamps before and after the invoke(..) method of the Axis Call class. The Call class handles the actual invocation to the Web service within the previously generated stub code. The response time itself is then calculated by subtracting the timestamp after the invoke(..) call from the timestamp before the call. Due to our client-side mechanism, the QoS parameter such as the latency t_l cannot be measured as comfortably as t_r. Therefore, we additionally use the packet capturing library Jpcap within the Evaluation-Aspect to measure the latency and the processing time on the server by using information from the captured TCP packets. We discuss details of the TCP analysis in the next sections.

Result Analysis Phase

In the final phase, the results generated from the WebServiceEvaluator and the EvaluationAspect are stored in a database. Afterward, the Result-Analyzer iterates over these collected results and generates the necessary statistics and QoS attributes. Moreover, these resulting QoS attributes can be attached directly to the evaluated service. It is relatively straightforward to do so, and therefore not explained in detail in this chapter.

ARCHITECTURAL APPROACH

In Figure 7, a subset of the architecture is depicted as an UML class diagram. The core class is the WebServiceEvaluator, which encapsulates all the evaluation specific parts. A WebService class encapsulates all information about a Web service (endpoint, reference to WSDL, location in repository, porttype, binding information, etc). An evaluation is either performed at the operation level or the service level. The operation level denotes that only one given operation of a service is evaluated by using the evaluate(String operationName, Object[] parameters) method. The service level means that all operations of a service are evaluated by using the evaluate() method, which implicitly invokes the aforementioned method for every operation. Furthermore, we have different invocation mechanisms for a Web service with respect to the way we generate reasonable input parameters for the different operations.

This architecture encapsulates the algorithms, and how we actually evaluate a service or invoke certain operations of a service by using the strategy pattern. We have two strategies for how we evaluate an operation. The DefaultEvaluationStrategy simply calls a service operation once with a given implementation of the IInvocationStrategy interface. The QoS attributes are encapsulated in the EvaluationAspect, which is woven into the byte code of our application and the stub code of the service. By contrast, the ThroughputEvaluationStrategy allows us to measure the throughput of a Web service by sending multiple requests in concurrent threads to the service, according to the formula given above in the QoS model.

Service Invocation Strategies

The invocation strategy defines how we invoke a service operation. Again, two different choices are available. The DefaultInvocationStrategy implements a default behavior by iterating over all parts of the input messages of a service and instantiating the corresponding input type as generated by the WSDL2Java tool. The instantiation of complex types (even nested ones) is handled by the Reflector component. The TemplateInvocationStrategy uses the invocation template generated during the service preprocessing to invoke the service operation. The template can be edited by the user to add various pre-defined values for the different input parameters. The algorithm for invoking a service operation uses the stubs for the Web service, which are generated during the preprocessing phase, and tries to find a value for each parameter in the XML template file. If no parameters can be found in the template or the template is not available, the Reflector tries to instantiate the required parameter type with a default value.

Figure 7. Architectural approach

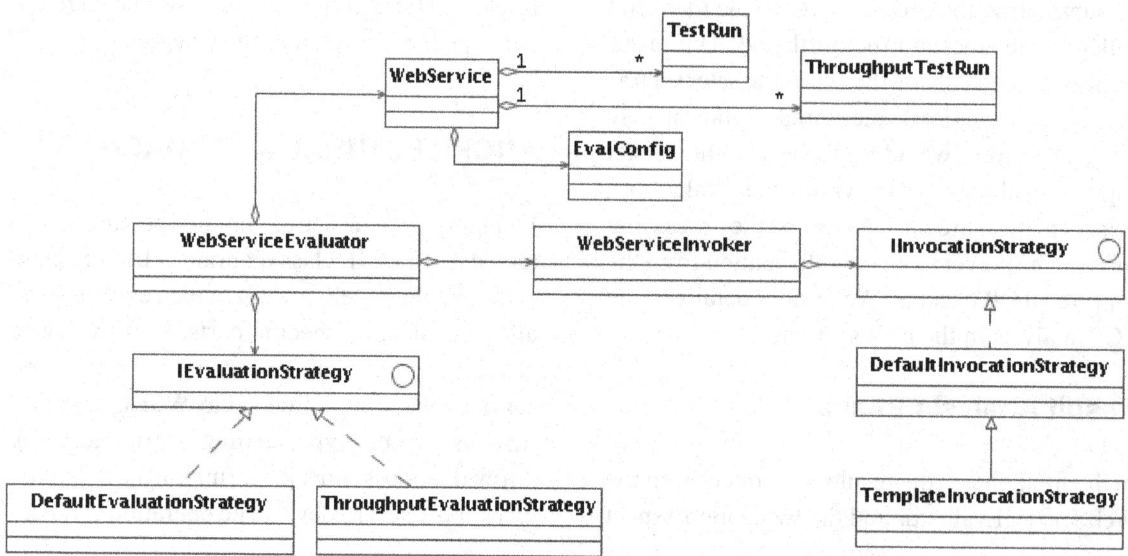

Listing 1. Invocation pointcut

```
pointcut wsInvoke(): target(org.apache.axis.client.Call)
         && ( call( Object invoke(..)) ||
            call( void invokeOneWay(..)));
```

The main advantage of this flexible architecture is the possibility of adding new evaluation and invocation mechanisms, or even selecting them at runtime without changing the structure of the system and the aspect.

Evaluating QoS Attributes Using AOP

This approach measures the performance related QoS values which is achieved by using aspect-oriented programming (AOP). It is an ideal technique for modeling cross-cutting concerns. The evaluation part is such a cross-cutting concern because it spans over each service that has to be invoked during the evaluation. The basic idea of the approach is described in Figure 8. During the preprocessing phase, the stubs for the service which should be evaluated by using the WSDL2Java tool have been created. For the Google Web service, as one example, the main stub class that is generated is called GoogleSearchBindingStub. Each stub method looks similar. First is the wrapping phase, where the input parameters are encoded in XML. Secondly, the actual invocation is carried out by using the invoke(..) method of the Call class from the Axis distribution. Finally, the response from the service is unwrapped and encoded as Java arguments and returned to the caller.

Therefore, the EvaluationAspect defines the pointcut in Listing 1 to measure the response time t_r.

Whenever a service operation is invoked by using the WebServiceEvaluator, the wsInvoke() pointcut defined for this join point is matched. Before the actual service invocation, the before advise is executed. This is where the actual evaluation has to be carried out. It mainly consists of a timestamp and the generation of an EvaluationResult, as well as starting the packet-sniffer to actually trace the TCP traffic caused by the following request.

After the wsInvoke() pointcut, the execution of the corresponding after advise is triggered, depending on whether the service invocation was successful or not. At this point, packet capturing can be stopped and the collected data can be extracted. The timestamps taken before and after the invocation can directly be used to calculate the response time. To distinguish between latency and execution time, we have to move one level deeper to the TCP level. The next section explains how the TCP reassembling is carried out.

TCP Reassembly and Evaluation Algorithm

The core element of the stub-based approach is the TCP sniffer and traffic analyzer. These elements finally make it possible to perform the service evaluation at the client side.

A service invocation, which is a TCP communication after all, actually consists of at least three submessages if the TCP level is observed. The first and the last are always handshake messages, with no payload attached. More precisely, the TCP handshake consists of two parts:

- The connection setup via a SYN packet, issued by the Web service client, and a following SYN/ACK packet by the Web service provider to confirm the established connection.
- The connection termination, again issued by the client to signal the end of the transmission via a FIN, plus an optional ACK flag

Figure 8. AOP schema

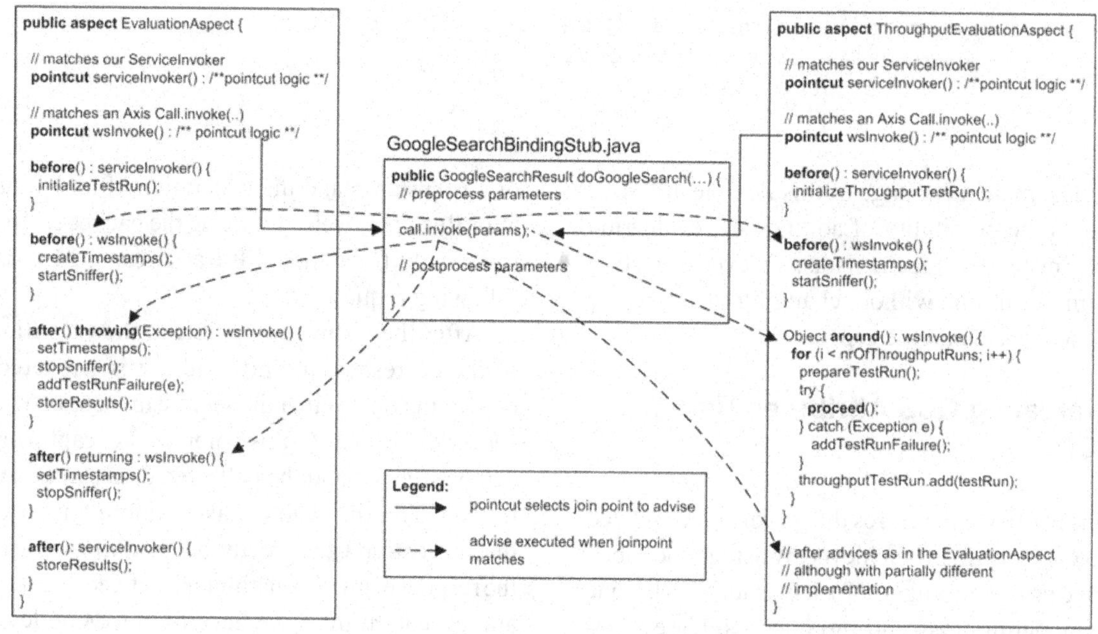

for previously received traffic, followed by the servers ACK and FIN, with ACK confirming the connection termination.

Each of those handshake messages only needs the time to overcome the network latency, plus some negligible time span the operating system uses to create an acknowledge packet and send it back. Therefore, we have at least two meaningful values for the network latency gathered from one single request. A complete trace visualized by the famous packet capturing tool Ethereal[1] is illustrated in Figure 9. The dashed lines highlight the handshake and connection termination message exchange.

Unfortunately, exploiting the traffic of the actual message transfer is not easily achieved because it is harder to predict how the traffic eventually looks. In a standard scenario, the client sends a single HTTP message with one POST and receives an acknowledgement packet that contains the SOAP encoded answer. Even in this very fundamental case, many variations are possible:

- The Web server may or may not return a result value for the request. Therefore, it is not clear a priori how large the payload of the server answer is.
- The original request or even the answer could be of a rather large size, exceeding the maximum TCP frame length, making either a multiframe transmission or a TCP frame length update necessary. The additional messages make it hard to isolate the packet where the Web Server executes the operation and therefore consumes the execution time we want to evaluate.
- The packet transmission may be disturbed at some point, forcing the sending partner to retransmit the lost packet. Again, the obsolete packets must not be used to calculate network latencies.

To overcome these obstacles, the following algorithm (see Listing 1) can be used to analyze the message flow seen in Listing 2.

What this sequence basically does is to put the packages in two hash tables, indexed by the

Listing 2. TCP message flow algorithm

```
TCPPacketList sourceList,destinationList;

foreach (TCPPacket p in TCPTrace) {
 if (p is outgoing) {
   if (p.sequenceNumber NOT IN sourceList) OR
     sourceList.getPacket(SequenceNumber) has no payload OR
     p has no payload)) {
            add p to sourceList with key p.SequenceNumber
   }
 } else if (p is incoming) {
  add p to destinationList with key p.AcknowledgeNumber;
 }
}
```

packet's sequence number for the client's packages, and acknowledge numbers for the server's packages. Packets from repeated transmissions or frame updates are omitted because they are mapped to the same position in the tables and will be overwritten. After all packets are received from a single request, the analyzing procedure iterates through the list of source packages and tries to find a packet in the destination list with a matching acknowledge number. Each match can then be used to calculate a latency and is added to the list of latencies for the whole request. The largest latency in this list is assumed to include the processing time and is not added to it. Finally, the arithmetic mean of all collected latencies is subtracted from the largest time to calculate the execution time without trailing latencies.

For massive amounts of requests at the same time, as it happens in a throughput test, for example, TCP packets sometimes interleave. We coped with this problem in two ways: Firstly, we use dynamic filter rules for the TCP sniffer. This way, the captured packets can be limited to a single endpoint IP and a port (which is 80 for HTTP in most cases). Secondly, we sort captured packets according to the outgoing port, which is determined by the operating systems' port allocation algorithm. This way, it is possible to distinguish between multiple requests to the same endpoint.

Figure 9. TCP handshake traffic

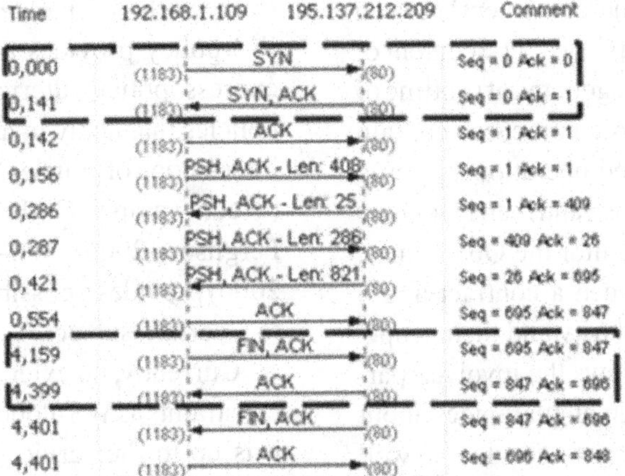

APPROACHES FOR QOS AND SLA SPECIFICATION

In the previous section, we presented an approach for how QoS attributes for Web services can be bootstrapped and constantly measured. A very important aspect for the service provider and requester is the question of how measured QoS attributes can be attached to various services and how these QoS attributes can be queried at runtime when selecting the services.

Currently, a few Web service-related standards and proposals exist which are trying to address the issues of how to specify and enforce a QoS from the provider perspective. These approaches share many communalities and differences; in a nutshell, they all can be classified into one of the following categories:

Policies

Policies represent a way to specify certain requirements on the service provider side to express constraints and regulations which have to be fulfilled to establish a successful interaction with the service. For example, a policy of a Web service can specify that messages can only be exchanged if WS-Reliable Messaging (OASIS, 2004) is used for the communication.

Contracts

A contract represents a formal agreement between two or more collaborating parties. The content of such an agreement can be negotiated at runtime or even fixed at design time. A contract can contain descriptions of the provided operations, pricing information, QoS guarantees, and metrics of how to measure and how to monitor the QoS values. The main difference between a contract and a policy is the level of granularity and their scope. The scope of a contract allows the involved parties to specify a whole range of guarantees about the nonfunctional attributes of a service, as well as penalties if certain guarantees are not met. Policies are used within contracts to specify or constrain different aspects.

Implicit

The QoS of a given service is specified implicitly by the service, for example, by hard-coding it directly into the application and allowing the service requester to retrieve the specified values. This approach is highly proprietary and is therefore not suitable for the use in interoperable service-oriented environments.

Despite the fact that a great number of Web services standards and standard proposals are published, no solution exists for specifying the QoS of Web services to allow service consumers to retrieve the accurate QoS attributes of a service in real-time. In the following paragraphs, some existing proposals are highlighted and we discuss possible integration methods of our proposed QoS monitoring solution presented above.

WS-POLICY

WS-policy (W3C, 2006) is a general purpose framework for the specification of policies for Web services. The specification aims at specifying nonfunctional characteristics of a service to provide a means to perform development time and runtime service discovery and selection. The framework is separated into two specifications: WS-policy provides a grammar that is used to express policy alternatives, merging multiple policies that apply to a common subject, and the intersection of policies to determine compatibility (Weerawarana, Curbera, Leymann, Storey, & Ferguson, 2006). WS-PolicyAttachment (W3C, 2006) provides a possibility for attaching policies to a certain subject.

Currently, no extension exists to specify QoS constraints as WS-Policy assertions, and therefore it is up to the service requestor to define their

Listing 3. WS-QoSPolicy schema

```
<!-- WS-QoSPolicy.xsd Version 0.5 -->
<xs:schema>
 <xs:element name="ExecutionTimeAssertion">
  <xs:complexType>
   <xs:attribute name="value" type="xs:integer" use="required"/>
   <xs:attribute name="unit" type="xs:string" use="required"/>
   <xs:attribute name="predicate" type="tns:PredicateType" use="required"/>
  </xs:complexType>
 </xs:element>
 <xs:element name="ThroughputAssertion">
  <xs:complexType>
   <xs:attribute name="value" type="xs:integer" use="required"/>
   <xs:attribute name="unit" type="xs:string" use="required"/>
   <xs:attribute name="predicate" type="tns:PredicateType" use="required"/>
  </xs:complexType>
 </xs:element>

 <!-- other assertion types -->
 <xs:simpleType name="PredicateType">
  <xs:restriction base="xs:string">
   <xs:enumeration value="Greater"/>
   <xs:enumeration value="Less"/>
   <xs:enumeration value="Equal"/>
   <xs:enumeration value="GreaterEqual"/>
   <xs:enumeration value="LessEqual"/>
  </xs:restriction>
 </xs:simpleType>
```

own QoS-Policy as extension to WS-Policy. A possible XSD Schema extension for representing QoS parameters and their metrics can be seen in Listing 3.

By using this schema, one can define different policy assertions which can be directly linked to Web service operations. A very simple policy example is presented in Listing 4, where an assertion for the execution time and the throughput are specified.

This policy can then be used by linking it with WS-PolicyAttachment directly to a Web service operation.

The experienced reader might have noticed that this WS-Policy approach represents some problems, especially when combining it with QoS values. Normally, QoS values are subject to constant changes, due to different load factors of the services or the network. Therefore, the service requestor has no chance to validate if the provider assertions are guaranteed, and if not, how to react to such violations. Therefore, higher level mechanisms are needed to specify a contract between multiple parties, which can be enforced by the involved parties. In the next section, we briefly discuss such approaches, generally referred to as service level agreements.

WS-AGREEMENT

Currently, WS-Agreement (Open Grid Forum, 2006) is a promising effort to develop a standard proposal within the Open Grid Forum for specifying service level agreements among a number of service providers. The current draft clearly points

Listing 4. WS-QoS policy example

```
<wsp:Policy xmlns:qosp="http://www.vitalab.tuwien.ac.at/ws/2007/01/qos/policy"
      xmlns:wsp="http://schemas.xmlsoap.org/ws/2004/09/policy" >
 <qosp:ExecutionTimeAssertion value="1000" unit="msec"
predicate="LessEqual" />
 <qosp:ThroughputAsseration value="25" unit="ops" predicate="GreaterEqual" />
</wsp:Policy>
```

out that the main objective of the WS-Agreement specification is to "define a language and a protocol for advertising the capabilities of service providers and creating agreements based on creational offers, and for monitoring agreement compliance at runtime." The structure of an agreement consists of a context, specifying the partner and the lifetime, and a set of terms. These terms are divided into the following parts:

- **Service terms:** These terms specify information about the service the agreement belongs to and where the guarantee terms apply.
- **Guarantee terms:** They specify the main service level objectives the involved parties agree on. These terms can then be used to monitor and enforce the defined guarantees by the agreement partners.

A full discussion of WS-Agreement is out of the scope of this chapter; nevertheless, it is obvious that an SLA-based mechanism offers several advantages compared to WS-Policy. Firstly, the negotiation of the guaranteed QoS values can be handled at runtime and if violated, the parties can specify a penalty if some assurances are not met.

Applied to our approach, one could use the WS-policy schema from Listing 2 and use these assertions to specify guarantee terms in terms of WS-agreement. The current draft does not specify how QoS values (expressed in terms of guarantee terms) are measured, thus making our QoS bootstrapping and measurement approach a possible candidate to use as a measurement party as part of an SLA-enabled middleware.

RELATED WORK

This section gives an overview of related work that already deals with QoS specific problems and various other aspects of performance for Web services.

Quality of service research encompasses different research domains such as the network, software engineering, and more recently service-oriented computing communities. A lot of research is dedicated to the area of QoS modeling and enriching Web services with QoS semantics. Most of this work leaves open the way how QoS parameters are bootstrapped or evaluated in the first place. Wickramage and Weerawarana (Wickramage & Weerawarana, 2005) define 15 distinguishable periods in time, a SOAP request goes through before completing a round trip. This value, which is also referred to as response time, can be split up into different components, where it is essential to bootstrap as much of them as possible.

Suzumura, Takase, and Tatsubori (2005) did some work on performance optimizations of Web services. Their approach is to minimize XML processing time (which we call wrapping time) by using differential de-serialization. The idea is to de-serialize only these parts which have not been processed in the past. In contrast to the approach presented here, this method tries to optimize the performance instead of measuring the different attributes.

A QoS model and a UDDI extension for associated QoS to a specific Web service is proposed in Ran (2003). The QoS model proposed here is very similar to the model presented in this paper; hence, the author does not specify how these values are actually assessed and monitored. It is assumed that the QoS attributes of a service are specified by the service provider in UDDI. In Tian, Gramm, Ritter, an Schiller (2004), another approach for integrating QoS with Web services is presented. The authors implemented a tool-suite for associating, querying, and monitoring QoS of a Web service. It is not specified how QoS attributes are actually measured and evaluated to associate them to certain Web services.

Song and Lee (2005) propose a simulation-based Web service performance analysis tool called sPAC which allows analyzing the performance of Web process (i.e., a composition) by using simulation code. Their approach is to call the Web service once under low load conditions and then transform these testing results into a simulation model. This paper also focuses on the performance aspects of Web services, whereas it does not deal with Web processes. Furthermore, no simulation code is needed, but the evaluation is performed on real Web services with the constraint that no access to the Web service implementation is available.

QoS attributes in Web service composition also raise a lot of interest due to the fact that they can be used by the compositor to dynamically choose a suitable service for the composition regarding the performance, price, or other attributes. A simple but illustrating example of such a composition is presented in Menasce (QoS issues in Web services, 2002). In Zeng , Benatallah, Dumas, Kalagnanam, and Sheng (2003) and Zeng , Benatallah, Ngu, and Dumas (2004), the authors propose a QoS model and a middleware approach for dynamic QoS-driven service composition. They investigate a global planning approach to determine optimal service execution plans for composite service based on QoS criteria, but it does not specify how QoS attributes for atomic services are measured and assessed. It is assumed that the atomic services already have QoS attributes attached.

CONCLUSION

In this chapter, we have introduced and discussed an approach for bootstrapping, evaluating, and monitoring performance-related QoS attributes for Web services which works independent from the Web service provider. Similar solutions can be implemented for all evaluation techniques.

Furthermore, this approach works completely service independent, allowing invocation of arbitrary services (at least semiautomatically). By using a combination of object-oriented and aspect-oriented programming techniques, a maximum level of flexibility can be achieved.

Nevertheless, there is a lot of additional research needed in this field. Future work will include the implementation and evaluation of all presented methods for QoS assessment, but for the time being, the client-side method proves to be the most feasible for real-world environments. Furthermore, an encapsulation of the current implementation as a Web service will allow easier integration with other applications, thus making it usable for other applications and research projects.

REFERENCES

Apache Software Foundation. (2006). Axis 1.4. Retrieved June 11, 2007, from http://ws.apache.org/axis/

Casati, F., & Shan, M.-C. (2001). Dynamic and adaptive composition. *Information Systems, 26*(3), 143-163.

Charles, P. (2004). *jpcap -- A network packet capture library.* Retrieved June 11, 2007, from http://jpcap.sourceforge.net/

Eclipse Foundation. (2006). Eclipse AspectJ. Retrieved June 11, 2007, from http://www.eclipse.org/aspectj

Fujii, K., & Suda, T. (2004). Dynamic service composition using santic information. In *Proceedings of the 2nd International Conference on Service-oriented Computing* (pp. 39-48). ACM Press.

Gamma, E., Helm, R., Johnson, R., & Vlissides, J. (1995). *Design patterns: Elements of reusable object-oriented software.* Addison-Wesley.

IBM, BEA Systems, Microsoft, SAP AG, Sonic Software, VeriSign. (2006). Web service policy framework specification. Retrieved June 11, 2007, from http://download.boulder.ibm.com/ibmdl/pub/software/dw/specs/ws-polfram/ws-policy-2006-03-01.pdf

Iwasa, K. (2004, November 15). Web service reliable m*essaging.* Retrieved June 11, 2007, from Web Service Reliable Messaging by OASIS: ttp://docs.oasis-open.org/wsrm/ws-reliability/v1.1

Laddad, R. (2003). *AspectJ in action: Practical aspect-oriented programming.* Manning Publications.

Liu, Y., Ngu, A.H., & Zeng, L.Z. (2004). QoS computation and policing in dynamic Web service selection. In *Proceedings of the 13th International World Wide Web Conference on Alternate Track Papers & Posters (WWW'04)* (pp. 66-73), New York. ACM Press.

Mani, A., & Nagarajan, A. (2002, January 1). Understanding quality of service for Web services. Retrieved June 11, 2007, from http://www-128.ibm.com/developerworks/library/ws-quality.html

Maximilien, E.M., & Singh, M.P. (2004). Toward autonomic Web services trust and selection. In *Proceedings of the 2nd International Conference on Service-oriented Computing (ICSOC'04)* (pp. 212-221), New York. ACM Press.

Menasce, D.A. (2002). QoS issues in Web services. *IEEE Internet Computing, 6*(6), 72-75.

Menasce, D.A. (2004). Composing Web services: A QoS view. *IEEE Internet Computing, 8*(6), 88-90.

OASIS. (2004). *Web services reliable messaging.*

Open Grid Forum. (2006, October 27). Web services agreement specification (WS-Agreement). Retrieved June 11, 2007, from http://www.ogf.org/Public_Comment_Docs/Documents/Oct-2006/WS-AgreementSpecificationDraftFinal_sp_tn_jpver_v2.pdf

Platzer, C., & Dustdar, S. (2005). A vector space search engine for Web services. In *Proceedings of the Third IEEE European Conference on Web Services (ECOWS'05).* Växjö, Sweden: IEEE Computer Society.

Ran, S. (2003). A model for Web services discovery with QoS. *SIGecom Exchanges, 4*(1), 1-10.

Rosenberg, F., Platzer, C., & Dustdar, S. (2006). Bootstrapping performance and dependability attributes of Web services. In *Proceedings of the IEEE International Conference on Web Services (ICWS'06)* (pp. 205-212). Chicago, IL, USA: IEEE Computer Society.

Schreiner, W., & Dustdar, S. (2005). A survey on Web services on Web services composition. *International Journal of Web and Grid Services, 1*(1), 1-30.

Song, H.G., & Lee, K. (2005). sPAC (Web Services Performance Analysis Center): Performance analysis and estimation tool of Web services. In *Proceedings of the 3rd International Conference on Business Process Management (BPM'05)* (pp. 109-119). Springer.

Suzumura, T., Takase, T., & Tatsubori, M. (2005). Optimizing Web services performance by differential deserialization. In *Proceedings of the IEEE International Conference on Web Services (ICWS'05)* (pp. 185-192).

Tai, S., Khalaf, R., & Mikalsen, T. (2004). Composition of coordinated Web services. In *Proceedings of the 5th ACM/IFIP/USENIX International Conference on Middleware* (pp. 294-310). Springer.

Tian, M., Gramm, A., Ritter, H., & Schiller, J. (2004). Efficient selection and monitoring of QoS-aware Web services with the WS-QoS framework. In *Proceedings of the International Conference on Web Intelligence (WI'04),* Beijing, China.

W3C. (2006). *Web Services Policy 1.2 - Attachment (WS-PolicyAttachment).*

W3C. (2006). *WS-Policy Framework Specification Version 1.2.*

Weerawarana, S., Curbera, F., Leymann, F., Storey, T., & Ferguson, D.F. (2006). *Web services platform architecture.* Pearson Education.

Wickramage, N., & Weerawarana, S. (2005). A benchmark for Web service frameworks. In *Proceedings of the IEEE International Conference on Service Computing (SCC'05),* Orlando, FL, USA.

Zeng, L., Benatallah, B., Dumas, M., Kalagnanam, J., & Sheng, Q.Z. (2003). Quality driven Web services composition. In *Proceedings of the 12th International Conference on World Wide Web (WWW'03)* (pp. 411-421).

Zeng, L., Benatallah, B., Ngu, A.H., & Dumas, M. (2004). Qos-aware middleware for Web service composition. *IEEE Transactions on Software Engineering, 30*(5), 311-327.

ENDNOTE

1 http://www.ethereal.com/

Compilation of References

Abadi, M., Burrows, M., Lampson, B., & Plotkin, G. (1993). A calculus for access control in distributed systems. *ACM Transactions on Programming Languages and Systems, 15*(4), 706-734.

Aggarwal, R., Verma, K., Miller, J., & Milnor, W. (2004). Constraint driven Web service composition in METEOR-S. In *Proceedings of the 2004 IEEE International Conference on Services Computing* (pp. 23-30). Shangai, China.

Akram, A. (2006). Web services resource framework resource sharing (Tutorial 9 and Tutorial 10). Retrieved June 11, 2007, from http://esc.dl.ac.uk/WOSE/tutorials/

Akram, A., Kewley, J., & Allan, R. (2006, October). Modelling WS-RF based enterprise applications. In *Proceedings of the Tenth IEEE International Enterprise Distributed Object Computing Conference* (EDOC 2006).

Aktas, M.S., Fox, G.C., & Pierce, M.E. (2005). Managing dynamic metadata as context. In *Proceedings of the Istanbul International Computational Science and Engineering Conference (ICCSE2005).* Retrieved June 11, 2007, from http://www.iccse.org/

Alexander, J. et al. (2004). *Web service transfer (WS – Transfer).* Retrieved June 11, 2007, from http://msdn.microsoft.com/library/en-us/dnglobspec/html/ws-transfer.pdf

Alexander, J. et al. (2004). *Web service enumeration (WS – Enumeration).* Retrieved June 11, 2007, from http://msdn.microsoft.com/library/en-us/dnglobspec/html/ws-enumeration.pdf

Alfieri, R., Cecchini, R., Ciaschini, V., Dell'Agnello, L., Frohner, A., Lorentey, K., & Spataro, F. (2005). From gridmap-file to VOMS: Managing authorization in a Grid environment. *Future Generation Computer Systems, 21*(4), 549-558.

Aloisio, G., Blasi, E., Cafaro, M., Fiore, S., Lezzi, D., & Mirto, M. (2003). *Web services for a biomedical imaging portal* (pp. 432-436).

Altintas, I., Jaeger, E., Lin, K., Ludaescher, B., & Memon, A. (2004). A Web service composition and deployment framework for scientific workflows. In *Proceedings of the 2004 IEEE International Conference on Web Services* (p. 814). San Diego, CA.

Anane, R., Chao, K-M., & Li, Y. (2005). *Hybrid composition of Web services and grid services* (pp. 426-431).

Ankolekar, A., Burstein, M., Hobbs, J.R., Lassila, O., Martin, D.L., McIlraith, S.A. et al. (2001). DAML-S: Semantic markup for Web services. In *Proceedings of the International Semantic Web Working Symposium (SWWS).* Standford University, CA.

ANSI (2004). Information technology: Role-based access control. ANSI INCITS 359-2004.

Apache Software Foundation. (2005). *AXIS Web services.* Retrieved June 3, 2007, from http://ws.apache.org/axis/

Apache Software Foundation. (2005). *Tomcat servlet container.* Retrieved June 3, 2007, from http://tomcat.apache.org/

Apache Software Foundation. (2006). Axis 1.4. Retrieved June 11, 2007, from http://ws.apache.org/axis/

Arkin, A. (2002). Business Process Modeling Language (BPML), Version 1.0. Retrieved June 3, 2007, from www.BPMI.org

Arora, A. et al. (2005). *Web service management (WS – Management).* Retrieved June 11, 2007, from https://wiseman.dev.java.net/specs/2005/06/management.pdf

Asokan, N. (1998). *Fairness in electronic commerce (Research Rep. No. RZ3027).* IBM Zurich Research Lab.

ASTM. (2006, September). ASTM E31.20 working draft 0.9k, privilege management infrastructure.

Atkinson, B., Della-Libera, G., Hada, S., Hondo, M., Hallam-Baker, P., (Ed.), Klein, C.K. et al. (2002). *Web services security (WS-Security) v1.0.* IBM, Microsoft, Verisign.

Attachments Profile Version 1.0. (2006). Retrieved June 11, 2007, from http://www.ws-i.org/Profiles/AttachmentsProfile-1.0.html

Avouris, N. M., & Gasser, L. (1992). *Distributed artificial intelligence: Theory and praxis.* Kluwer Academic Publishers.

Aydin, G. et al. (2005). SERVOGrid complexity computational environments (CCE) integrated performance analysis. In *Proceedings of the 6th IEEE/ACM International Workshop on Grid Computing.*

Bajaj, S. et al. (2006). *Web services policy framework (WS-Policy).* Retrieved June 11, 2007, from http://specs.xmlsoap.org/ws/2004/09/policy/ws-policy.pdf

Baker, M., Apon, A., Ferner, C., & Brown, J. (2005). Emerging grid standards. *Computer, 38*(4), 43-50.

Ballinger, K. et al. (2004). *The Web services metadata exchange specification.* Retrieved June 11, 2007, from http://specs.xmlsoap.org/ws/2004/09/mex/WS-MetadataExchange.pdf

Barkley, J., Beznosov, K., & Uppal, J. (1999). Supporting relationships in access control using role based access control. In Proceedings of the *Fourth ACM Role-based Access Control Workshop* (pp. 55-65), Fairfax, VA.

Basic Profile Version 1.0. (2004). Retrieved June 11, 2007, from http://www.ws-i.org/Profiles/BasicProfile-1.0-2004-04-16.html

BEA. (2005). *WebLogic 8.1 trading partner integration.* Retrieved June 3, 2007, from http://e-docs.bea.com/wli/docs81/pdf/tpintro.pdf

Bellwood, T., Clement, L., & Riegen, C. (2003). *UDDI Version 3.0.1: UDDI spec technical committee specification.* Retrieved June 11, 2007, from http://uddi.org/pubs/uddi-v3.0.1-20031014.htm

Beznosov, K. (2002). Object security attributes: Enabling application-specific access control in middleware. In *Proceedings of the 4th International Symposium on Distributed Objects & Applications (DOA)* (pp. 693-710). Irvine, CA: Springer-Verlag.

Beznosov, K. (2002). Overview of .NET Web services security. In *Proceedings of the OMG Distributed Object Computing Security Workshop,* Baltimore, MD.

Beznosov, K., Deng, Y., Blakley, B., Burt, C., & Barkley, J. (1999). A resource access decision service for CORBA-based distributed systems. In *Proceedings of the Annual Computer Security Applications Conference* (pp. 310-319). Phoenix, AZ: IEEE Computer Society.

Beznosov, K., Espinal, L., & Deng, Y. (2000). Performance considerations for CORBA-based application authorization service. In *Proceedings of the Fourth IASTED International Conference Software Engineering and Applications,* Las Vegas, NV.

Bhatti, R., Bertino, E., & Ghafoor, A. (2007). An integrated approach to federated identity and privilege management in open systems. *Communications of the ACM, 50*(2), 81-87.

Bhatti, R., Joshi, J. B. D., Bertino, E., & Ghafoor, A. (2004). XML-based specification for Web services. *IEEE Computer, 37*(4), 41-49.

Bhatti, R., Joshi, J.B.D., Bertino, E., & Ghafoor, A. (2005). X-GTRBAC: An XML-based policy specification framework and architecture for enterprise-wide access control. *ACM Transactions on Information and System Security (TISSEC), 8*(2), 187-227.

Bhatti, R., Sanz, D., Bertino, E., & Ghafoor A. (2006). A policy-based authorization system for Web services: Integrating X-GTRBAC and WS-policy (Tech. Rep. No. 2006-03). CERIAS. Retrieved June 4, 2007, from https://www.cerias.purdue.edu/tools_and_resources/bibtex_archive/archive/2006-03.pdf

Bilorusets, R. et al. (2004). *Web services reliable messaging protocol (WS-ReliableMessaging).* Retrieved June 11, 2007, from http://www-128.ibm.com/developerworks/library/specification/ws-rm/

Bilorusets, R. (2005). *Web services reliable messaging protocol (WS-ReliableMessaging)* (Specification). Retrieved June 3, 2007, from http://www-128.ibm.com/developerworks/library/specification/ws-rm/. BEA, IBM, Microsoft and TIBCO.

Birman, K. (2005). Can Web services scale up? *Computer, 38*(10), 107-110.

Blakley, B. (1999). *CORBA security: An introduction to safe computing with objects.* Reading, MA: Addison-Wesley.

Blue Titan Network. (2004, January 3). *Blue Titan Network Director.* Retrieved August 18, 2004, from http://www.bluetitan.com/products/btitan_network.htm

Bonner, A.J. (1999). Workflows, transactions, and datalog. In *Proceedings of the 18th ACM Symposium on Principles of Database Systems (PODS)* (pp. 294-305). Philadelphia.

Booth, D., Haas, H., McCabe, F. et al. (2004, February). Web services architecture, W3C Working Group Note 11. Retrieved June 11, 2007, from http://www.w3.org/TR/ws-arch/

Box, D. et al. (2004).*Web services addressing (WSAddressing).* Retrieved June 11, 2007, from http://www.w3.org/Submission/ws-addressing

Box, D. et al. (2004).*Web services eventing.* Microsoft, IBM, & BEA. Retrieved June 11, 2007, from http://ftpna2.bea.com/pub/downloads/WS-Eventing.pdf

Brickley, D., & Guha, R. V. (2004, January). *Rdf vocabulary description language 1.0: Rdf schema.* Technical Report, W3C Working Draft.

Bultan, T., Fu, X., Hull, R., & Su, J. (2003). Conversation specification: A new approach to design and analysis of e-service composition. In *Proceedings of 12th International World Wide Web Conference*, **Budapest, Hungary.**

Bunting, B. et al. (2003). *Web services context (WS-Context)* version 1.0. Retrieved June 11, 2007, from http://www.arjuna.com/ library/specs/ws_caf_1-0/WS-CTX.pdf

Business Application Software Developers Association (BASDA). (2005). *eBIS-XML Specifications ver. (3.05).* Retrieved from basda.net/twiki/pub/Core/DownloadTheSuite/eBIS-XML-3.05.zip

Carminati, B., Ferrari, E., & Hung, P.C. K. (2006). Security conscious Web service composition. In *Proceedings of the 2006 IEEE International Conference on Web Services* (pp. 489-496). Chicago.

Casati, F., & Shan, M.-C. (2001). Dynamic and adaptive composition. *Information Systems, 26*(3), 143-163.

Case, J., Fedor, M., Schoffstall, M., & Davin, J. (1990). *Simple network management protocol.* Network working group request for comments 1157. Retrieved June 11, 2007, from http://www.ietf.org/rfc/rfc1157.txt

CEN/ISSS e-invoicing Focus Group. (2003). *Report and recommendations of CEN/ISSS e-invoicing focus group on standards and developments on electronic invoicing.* Retrieved from www.cenorm.be/isss/Projects/e-invoicing

Chadwick, D.W., & Anthony, S. (2007, June). Using WebDAV for Improved Certificate Revocation and Publication. In *LCNS 4582, Public Key Infrastructure. Proceedings of 4th European PKI Workshop,* Palma de Mallorca, Spain. 265-279

Chadwick, D.W., & Otenko, A. (2003). The PERMIS X.509 Role-based privilege management infrastructure. *Future Generation Computer Systems, 19*(2), 277-289.

Chadwick, D.W., Otenko, S., & Nguyen, T.A. (2006, October 19-21). Adding support to XACML for dynamic delegation of authority in multiple domains. In *Proceedings of the 10th IFIP TC-6 TC-11 International Conference, CMS 2006,* Heraklion, Crete, Greece (pp. 67-86). Springer-Verlag.

Channa, N., Li, S., Shaikh, A.W., & Fu, X. (2005). Constraint satisfaction in dynamic Web service composition. In *Proceedings of the Sixteenth International Workshop on Database and Expert Systems Applications* (pp. 658-664). Copenhagen, Denmark.

Charfi, A., & Mezini, M. (2005). Using aspects for security engineering of Web service compositions. In *Proceedings of the 2005 IEEE International Conference on Web Services* (pp. 59-66). Växjö, Sweden.

Charles, P. (2004). *jpcap -- A network packet capture library.* Retrieved June 11, 2007, from http://jpcap.sourceforge.net/

Christensen, E. et al. (2001).*Web services description language (WSDL) 1.1.* Retrieved June 11, 2007, from http://www.w3.org/TR/wsdl

Christensen, E., Curbera, F., Meredith, G., & Weerawarana, S. (2001). *Web services description language (WSDL)* 1.1 (W3C Note). Retrieved June 3, 2007, from http://www.w3.org/TR/wsdl

Chun, S.A., Atluri, V., & Adam, N.R. (2004). Policy-based Web service composition. In *Proceedings of the 14th International Workshop on Research Issues on Data Engineering: Web Services for E-commerce and E-government Applications* (pp. 85-92). Boston.

Cline, K. et al. (2006). *Toward converging Web service standards for resources.* Events, and Management. Retrieved June 11, 2007, from http://msdn.microsoft.com/library/en-us/dnwebsrv/html/convergence.asp

Coffey, T., & Saidha, P. (1996). Nonrepudiation with mandatory proof of receipt. *ACM SIGCOMM Computer Communication Review, 26*(1), 6-17.

Connolly, D., Dean, M., van Harmelen, F., Hendler, J., Horrocks, I., McGuinness, D. L., et al. (2003, February). *Web ontology language (owl) reference version 1.0.* Technical Report, W3C Working Draft.

Cook, N., & Robinson, P. (2006). *NRExchange: XML schema and WSDL for Web service nonrepudiation protocols.* Retrieved June 3, 2007, from http://homepages.cs.ncl.ac.uk/nick.cook/ws-nrex/

Cook, N., Robinson, P., & Shrivastava, S.K. (2006). Design and implementation of Web services middleware to support fair nonrepudiable interactions. *International Journal of Cooperative Information Systems (IJCIS) Special Issue on Enterprise Distributed Computing, 15*(4), 565-597.

Czajkowski, K., Ferguson, D., Foster, I., Frey, J., Graham, S., Sedukhin, I. et al. (2004). *The WS-resource framework.* Retrieved June 11, 2007, from http://www.globus.org/wsrf/specs/ws-wsrf.pdf

Czajkowski, K., Ferguson, D., Foster, I. et al. (2004). From open grid services infrastructure to WS-resource framework: Refactoring & evolution.

Czajkowski, K., Ferguson, D., Foster, I., Frey, J., Graham, S., Maguire, T. et al. (2004, March). *From open grid services infrastructure to WS-resource framework: Refactoring & evolution* (White Paper No. Version 1.1). The Globus Alliance. Retrieved June 11, 2007, from http://www.globus.org/alliance/publications/papers.php#OGSI-to-WSRF

Czajkowski, K., Ferguson, D., Foster, I., Frey, J., Graham, S., Sedukhin, I. et al. (2004, March). *The WS-resource framework* (White Paper No. Version 1.0), The Globus Alliance.

Damianou, N., Dulay, N., et al. (2001). *The ponder policy specification language.* Policy 2001: Workshop on Policies for Distributed Systems and Networks. Springer-Verlag.

Dialani, V. (2002). *UDDI-M Version 1.0 API specification.* University of Southampton, UK.

Dierks, T., & Allen, C. (1999). The TLS Protocol Version 1.0, RFC 2246.

Direct Internet Message Encapsulation (DIME). (2002). Retrieved June 11, 2007, from http://xml.coverpages.org/draft-nielsen-dime-01.txt

Distributed Management Task Force, inc. (2005). *Common Information Model (CIM), Version 2.9.0.*

Eastlake, D., Reagle, J., Imamura, T., Dillaway, B., & Simon, E. (2002). *XML encryption syntax and processing (W3C Recommendation).* Retrieved June 3, 2007, from http://www.w3.org/TR/xmlenc-core/

Eastlake, D., Reagle, J., & Solo, D. (2002). *XML-signature syntax and processing (IETF RFC 3275 and W3C Recommendation).* Retrieved June 3, 2007, from http://www.w3.org/TR/xmldsig-core/. IETF/W3C

Eclipse Foundation. (2006). Eclipse AspectJ. Retrieved June 11, 2007, from http://www.eclipse.org/aspectj

e-mayor consortium D2.1. (2004). Deliverable D2.1: Municipal services–Analysis, requirements, and usage scenarios. *e-mayor project* (IST-2004-507217).

e-mayor consortium D3.1. (2004). Deliverable D3.1: e-mayor–System design. *e-mayor project* (IST-2004-507217).

e-mayor. (2004). Electronic and secure municipal administration for European citizens. E.C 6th Framework Programme, IST-2004-507217. Retrieved from www.emayor.org

Encommerce. (1999). *GetAccess design and administration guide.*

Enhydra. (2005). *Open source for eBusiness.* Retrieved from http://www.enhydra.org

ETSI. (2002). ETSI TS 101 903 V1.1.1 - XML Advanced Electronic Signatures (XAdES). (Technical Specification.)

Even, S., & Yacobi, Y. (1980). *Relations among public key signature systems* (Tech. Rep. No. CS175). Haifa, Israel: Technion Israel Institute of Technology.

Extensible Access Control Markup Language (XACML). (2005). Retrieved June 4, 2007, from http://www.oasis-open.org/committees/tc_home.php?wg_abbrev=xacml

Extensible Markup Language (XML) 1.0 (Fourth Edition). (2006). Retrieved June 11, 2007, from http://www.w3.org/TR/xml/

Ezhilchelvan, P.D., & Shrivastava, S.K. (2005). A family of trusted third party based fair-exchange protocols. *IEEE Transactions on Dependable and Secure Computing, 2*(4), 273-286.

Fensel, D. (2004) *Ontologies: Silver bullet for knowledge management and electronic commerce.* Springer-Verlag.

Fischer, M.J., Lynch, N.A., & Paterson, M.S. (1985). Impossibility of distributed consensus with one faulty process. *Journal of the ACM, 32*(2), 374-382.

Fitzgibbons, J.B., Fujimoto, R.M., Fellig, D., Kleban, S.D., & Scholand, A.J. (2004). *IDSim: An extensible framework for interoperable distributed simulation* (pp. 532-539).

Flamenco Network. (2004, January). *Flamenco Networks.* Retrieved August 18, 2004, from http://www.flamenconetworks.com/solutions/nsp.html

Foster, I. (2002). The physiology of the grid: An open grid services architecture for distributed systems integration. Retrieved June 11, 2007, from www.globus.org/alliance/publications/papers/ogsa.pdf

Foster, I., Czajkowski, K. et al. (2005). Modeling and managing State in distributed systems: The role of OGSI and WSRF. In *Paper presented at the Proceedings of the IEEE.*

Foster, I., Czajkowski, K., Ferguson, D.E., Frey, J., Graham, S., Maguire, T. et al. (2005). Modeling and managing state in distributed systems: The role of OGSI and WSRF. *Proceedings of the IEEE, 93*(3), 604-612.

Foster, I., Kesselman, C., Nick, J.M., & Tuecke, S. (2002). Grid services for distributed system integration. *Computer, 35*(6), 37-46.

Fox, G. (2004). Grids of grids of simple services. *Computing in Science & Engineering [see also IEEE Computational Science and Engineering], 06*(4), 84-87.

Fox, G., & Pallickara, S. (2005). Deploying the NaradaBrokering substrate in aiding efficient Web and grid service interactions. *Proceedings of the IEEE, 93*(3), 564-577.

Friedman-Hill, E. (2004, December). *Jess Manual, Version 7.0.* Distributed Systems Research, Sandia National Labs.

Fujii, K., & Suda, T. (2004). Dynamic service composition using santic information. In *Proceedings of the 2nd International Conference on Service-oriented Computing* (pp. 39-48). ACM Press.

Gadgil, H., Fox, G., Pallickara, S., & Pierce, M. (2006). *Managing grid messaging middleware challenges of large applications in distributed environments.* Paris, France.

Gamma, E., Helm, R., Johnson, R., & Vlissides, J. (1995). *Design patterns: Elements of reusable object-oriented software.* Addison-Wesley.

Gannon, D., Alameda, J., Chipara, O., Christie, M., Dukle, V., Fang, L. et al. (2005). Building grid portal applications from a Web service component architecture. *Proceedings of the IEEE, 93*(3), 551-563.

Genesereth, M. R., & Nilsson, N. (1986) *Logical foundation of artificial intelligence.* Morgan Kaufmann.

German Federal Ministry of Interior. (2003). *SAGA—Standards and Architectures for e-government Applications,* (version 2.0.)

Gibbs, K., & Goodman, B.D. (2003). *IBM Elias Torres.* Create Web services using Apache Axis and Castor. IBM Developer Works. Retrieved June 11, 2007, from http://www-106.ibm.com/developerworks/webservices/library/ws-castor/

Goland, Y., Whitehead, E., Faizi, A., Carter, S., & Jensen, D. (1999). HTTP extensions for distributed authoring – WEBDAV. RFC 2518.

Goth, G. (2002). Grid services architecture plan gaining momentum. *Internet Computing, IEEE, 6*(4), 11-12.

Gottschalk, K.D., Graham, S., Kreger, H., & Snell, J. (2002). Introduction to Web services architecture. *IBM Systems Journal, 41*(2), 170-177.

Grangard, A., Eisenberg, B., & Nickull, D. (2001). *ebXML technical architecture specification v1.0.4 (*OASIS Final Draft). Retrieved June 3, 2007, from http://www.ebxml.org/

Gravengaard, E., Goodale, G., Hanson, M., Roddy, B., & Walkowski, D. (2003). *Web services security: Nonrepudiation (Proposal Draft).* Retrieved June 3, 2007, from http://schemas.reactivity.com/2003/04/web-services-non-repudiation-05.pdf

Grid Resource Allocation Agreement Protocol (GRAAP) WG. (2005). *Web Services Agreement Specification (WS-Agreement)*, Version 2005/09, GWD-R (Proposed Recommendation).

Grimshaw, A. (2003). Grid services extend Web services [Electronic version]. *SOA Web Services Journal, 3*(8).

Gruber, T. R. (1993). *A translation approach to portable ontology specifications.* Knowledge Acquisition.

Gudgin, M. et al. (2003, June). *SOAP Version 1.2, Part 1: Messaging framework.* Retrieved June 11, 2007, from http://www.w3.org/TR/2003/REC-soap12-part1-20030624/

Gudgin, M., Hadley, M., & Rogers, T. (2006). *Web services addressing (WS-Addressing) (W3C Submission).* Retrieved June 3, 2007, from http://www.w3.org/TR/ws-addr-core/

Hallam-Baker, P., & Mysore, S. (2005). *XML key management specification (XKMS 2.0) (W3C Recommendation).* Retrieved June 3, 2007, from http://www.w3.org/TR/xkms2/

Hallam-Baker, P., Moses, T., Morgan, B., Adams, C., Knouse, C., Orchard, D. et al. (2001). *Security assertions markup language: Core assertion architecture.* OASIS.

Hartman, B., Flinn, D.J., Beznosov, K., & Kawamoto, S. (2003). *Mastering Web services security*. New York: John Wiley & Sons.

Hartman, B., Flinn, D., Beszosov, K., & Kawamoto, S. (2003). *Mastering Web services security.* Indianapolis, IN: Wiley Publishing.

Housley, R., Ford, W., Polk, T., & Solo, D. (1999). *Internet X.509 public key infrastructure: Certificate and CRL profile* (IETF RFC 2459). Internet Engineering Task Force.

HP. (2005). *Web service distributed management (WSDM).* Retrieved June 11, 2007, from http://devresource.hp.com/drc/specifications/wsdm/index.jsp

Hu, J., & Weaver, A.C. (2004). Dynamic, context-aware security infrastructure for distributed healthcare applications. In *Proceedings of the First Workshop on Pervasive Security, Privacy and Trust (PSPT).*

Hunter, R. (2004). E-government schema guidelines for XML. *Office of the eEnvoy*, (v3.1.) Retrieved from http://www.govtalk.gov.uk/documents/schema-guidelines-3_1.pdf

IBM, BEA, Microsoft, SAP, Sonic Software, & VeriSign. (2004, September). *Web Services Policy Framework (WS-Policy).*

IBM, Microsoft, & VeriSign. (2002, April 5). *Specification: Web Services Security (WS-Security)*, Version 1.0.

IBM, BEA Systems, Microsoft, Layer 7 Technologies, Oblix, VeriSign, Actional, Computer Associates, OpenNetwork Technologies, Ping Identity, Reactivity, RSA Security. (2005). Web services trust language (WS-Trust). Retrieved June 4, 2007, from ftp://www6.software.ibm.com/software/developer/library/ws-trust.pdf

IBM, Microsoft, RSA Security, VeriSign. (2005). Web services security policy language

IBM, BEA Systems, Microsoft, SAP AG, Sonic Software, VeriSign. (2006). Web service policy framework specification. Retrieved June 11, 2007, from http://download.boulder.ibm.com/ibmdl/pub/software/dw/specs/ws-polfram/ws-policy-2006-03-01.pdf

IBM Corporation. (2002). *Business Process Execution Language for Web Services (BPEL4WS)*, Version 1.0.

IBM DataPower. (2007). *WebSphere DataPower XML security gateway XS40.* Retrieved June 3, 2007, from http://www-306.ibm.com/software/integration/datapower/xs40/

IBM. (2003). Enterprise privacy authorization language (EPAL). Retrieved June 4, 2007, from http://www.zurich.ibm.com/security/enterprise-privacy/epal/Specification/index.html

IBM-MS WS-Security Roadmap. (2002, April 7). *Security in a Web services world: A proposed architecture and roadmap.* Retrieved August 18, 2004, from http://msdn.microsoft.com/library/en-us/dnwssecur/html/securitywhitepaper.asp

IDA BC. (2004). *IDA eProcurement XML schemas initiative—eOrdering and e-invoicing phases,* (v 2.0.) Retrieved from http://europa.eu.int/idabc/en/document/4721/5874

IHE. (2005). IHE IT infrastructure technical framework (vol. 1), Integration profiles. Retrieved June 4, 2007, from http://www.ihe.net/Technical_Framework/upload/ihe_iti_tf_2.0_vol1_FT_2005-08-15.pdf

IHE. (2005). IHE IT infrastructure technical framework (vol. 2), Transactions. Retrieved June 4, 2007, from http://www.ihe.net/Technical_Framework/upload/ihe_iti_tf_2.0_vol2_FT_2005-08-15.pdf

IHE. (2006). Integrated health care enterprise. Retrieved June 4, 2007, from http://www.ihe.net/

Imperial Collage. (2000). Ponder: A language for specifying security and management policies for distributed systems. Retrieved June 4, 2007, from http://www-dse.doc.ic.ac.uk/Research/policies/ponder/PonderSpec.pdf

Institute of Human and Machine Cognition. (2005). *IHMC ontology and policy management.* University of West Florida.

ITU-T. (1995). Security frameworks for open systems: Access control framework. ITU-T Rec X.812 | ISO/IEC 10181-3:1996.

ITU-T. (2005). The directory: Public-key and attribute certificate frameworks. ISO 9594-8 (2005) /ITU-T Rec. X.509.

Iwasa, K. (2004, November 15). Web service reliable m*essaging.* Retrieved June 11, 2007, from Web Service Reliable Messaging by OASIS: ttp://docs.oasis-open.org/wsrm/ws-reliability/v1.1

Java API for XML Based Web Services (JAX-WS), (JSR 224). (2006). Retrieved June 11, 2007, from http://jcp.org/en/jsr/detail?id=224

Java APIs for XML Based RPC (JAX-RPC), (JSR 101). (2002). Retrieved June 11, 2007, from http://jcp.org/en/jsr/detail?id=101

Java Architecture for XML Binding (JAXB), (JSR 222). (2006). Retrieved June 11, 2007, from http://www.jcp.org/en/jsr/detail?id=222

Jini Spec. (2003, September 12). *Jini technology specification.* Retrieved August 18, 2004, from http://wwws.sun.com/software/jini/jini_technology.html

Josang, A., & Sanderud, G. (2003). Security in mobile communications: Challenges and opportunities. In *Proceedings of the Australasian Information Security Workshop* (AISW2003) Conference on ACSW Frontiers (Vol. 21, pp.43-48).

Josefsson, S. (2003). *The Base16, Base32, and Base64 Data Encodings* (IETF RFC 3548): Internet Engineering Task Force.

Joseph, J., & Fellenstein, C. (2003). *Grid computing.* Upper Saddle River, NJ, USA: Prentice Hall.

Junginger, M.O. (2003). *High performance messaging system for peer-to-peer networks.* Kansas: University of Missouri.

Kagal, L., Finin, T., & Joshi, A. (2003). A policy based approach to security on the semantic Web. In *Proceedings of the 2nd International Semantic Web Conference,* Sanibel Island, FL.

Kagal, L., Paolucci, M., Srinivasan, N., Denker, G., Finin, T., & Sycara, K. (2004). Authorization and privacy for semantic Web services. In *Proceedings of the AAAI Spring Symposium, Workshop on Semantic Web Services,* Stanford University, Palo Alto, CA.

Kagal, L., Finin, T., & Johshi, A. (2003). *A policy language for pervasive computing environment.* Policy 2003: Workshop on Policies for Distributed Systems and Networks. Springer-Verlag.

Kaliontzoglou, A., Boutsi, P., Mavroudis, I., & Polemi, D. (2003). Secure e-invoicing service based on Web services. In *Proceedings of the 1st Hellenic Conference on Electronic Democracy*, Athens, Greece.

Kaliontzoglou, A., Sklavos, P., Karantjias, T., & Polemi, D. (2004). A secure e-government platform architecture for small to medium sized public organizations. *Electronic Commerce Research & Applications, 4*(2), 174-186.

Kaliontzoglou, A., Boutsi, P., & Polemi, D. (2005). E-invoke: Secure e-invoicing based on Web services. Electronic Commerce Research, Kluwer (accepted for publication).

Kaminsky, D. (2005). An introduction to policy for autonomic computing. Retrieved June 4, 2007, from http://www-128.ibm.com/developerworks/autonomic/library/ac-policy.html

Karantjias, A., Kaliontzoglou, A., Sklavos, P., & Polemi, D. (2004). Secure applications for the Chambers of Commerce: Functionality and technical assessment. In *Proceedings of EUROSEC 2004 15th Forum on Information Systems and Security,* Paris.

Karjoth, G. (2003). Access control with IBM Tivoli Access Manager. *ACM Transactions on Information and Systems Security, 6*(2), 232-257.

Kasera, S., Mizikovsky, S., Sundaram, G. (2003). On securely enabling intermediary-based services and performance enhancements for wireless mobile users. In *Proceedings of the 2003 ACM workshop on Wireless security* (pp. 61-68).

Kavvadias, G., Spanos, E., & Tambouris, E. (Eds.). (2002). Deliverable D2.3.1 GovML syntax and filters implementation. *E-gov project* (IST-2000-28471). Retrieved from http://www.e-gov-project.org/e-govsite/e-gov_D231.zip

Kent, A. (2003). Address and personal details schema. *Office of the eEnvoy*, (v1.3) Retrieved from http://www.govtalk.gov.uk/documents/APD-vl-3.zip

Keynote. (1999). The keynote trust-management system, Version 2, Matt Blaze, Joan Feigenbaum, John Ioannidis, and Angelos D. Keromytis. Request for comments (RFC) 2704, http://www1.cs.columbia.edu/~angelos/Papers/rfc2704.txt

Khalaf, R., Mukhi, N., & Weerawarana, S. (2003). *Service-oriented composition in BPEL4WS*. In Paper presented at the Budapest, Hungary. Retrieved June 11, 2007, from http://www2003.org/cdrom/papers/alternate/P768/choreo_html/p768-khalaf.htm

Koshutanski, H., & Massacci, F. (2003). An access control framework for business processes for Web services mechanisms. In *Proceedings of the ACM Workshop on XML Security*, Fairfax, VA.

Kosiur, D. (2001). *Understanding policy-based networking*. John Wiley & Sons.

Kremer, S., Markowitch, O., & Zhou, J. (2002). An intensive survey of fair nonrepudiation protocols. *Computer Communications, 25*(17), 1601-1621.

Krishnan, S., & Gannon, D. (2004). *XCAT3: A framework for CCA components as OGSA services* (pp. 90-97).

Laddad, R. (2003). *AspectJ in action: Practical aspect-oriented programming*. Manning Publications.

Laliwala, Z., Jain, P., & Chaudhary, S. (2006). Semantic based service-oriented grid architecture for business processes. In *Proceedings of the 2006 IEEE International Conference on Services Computing* (SCC 2006), SCC 2006 Industry Track.

Lampson, B., Abadi, M., Burrows, M., & Wobber, E. (1991). Authentication in distributed systems: Theory and practices. In *Proceedings of the ACM Symposium on Operating Systems Principles* (pp. 165-182), Asilomar Conference Center, Pacific Grove, CA.

Le Hégaret, P. (2004). *W3C document object model–DOM*. Retrieved from http://www.w3.org/DOM/

Leymann, F. (2001). *Web Services Flow Language (WSFL 1.0)*.

Li, J., & Yang, H. (2005). *Towards evolving Web sites into grid services environment* (pp. 95-102).

Liu, Y., Ngu, A.H., & Zeng, L.Z. (2004). QoS computation and policing in dynamic Web service selection. In *Proceedings of the 13th International World Wide Web Conference on Alternate Track Papers & Posters (WWW'04)* (pp. 66-73), New York. ACM Press.

Los Alamos National Laboratory (LANL). (2006). *The Interdependent Energy Infrastructure Simulation System (IEISS) Project*. Retrieved June 11, 2007, from http://www.lanl.gov/orgs/d/d4/interdepend

Ludascher, B., Altintas, I., & Gupta, A. (2003). Compiling abstract scientific workflows into Web service workflows. In *Proceedings of the 15th International Conference on Scientific and Statistical Database Management*, Cambridge, MA.

Maamar, Z., Mostefaoui, S.K., & Yahyaoui, H. (2005). Toward an agent-based and context-oriented approach for Web services composition. *IEEE Transactions on Knowledge and Data Engineering, 17*(5), 686-697.

Mani, A., & Nagarajan, A. (2002, January 1). Understanding quality of service for Web services. Retrieved June 11, 2007, from http://www-128.ibm.com/developerworks/library/ws-quality.html

Markowitch, O., Gollmann, D., & Kremer, S. (2002). On fairness in exchange protocols. In *Proceedings of the 5th International Conference on Information Security and Cryptology (ISISC 2002)*, Seoul, Korea.

Markowitch, O., & Roggeman, Y. (1999). Probabilistic Nonrepudiation without trusted third party. In *Proceedings of the 2nd Workshop on Security in Communication Networks*, Amalfi, Italy.

Martínez Pérez, G., García Clemente, F. J., & Gómez Skarmeta, A. F. (2005) *Policy-based management of*

Web and information systems security: An emerging technology. Hershey, PA: Idea Group.

Maximilien, E.M., & Singh, M.P. (2004). Toward autonomic Web services trust and selection. In *Proceedings of the 2nd International Conference on Service-oriented Computing (ICSOC'04)* (pp. 212-221), New York. ACM Press.

McIlraith, S., & Son, T.C. (2002). Adapting Golog for composition of semantic Web services. In *Proceedings of the 8th International Conference on Knowledge Representation and Reasoning*, Toulouse, France.

McRae, L., Nguyen, M., Cohen, A., & Vine, J. (2004). Signet functional requirements. Retrieved June 3, 2007, from http://middleware.internet2.edu/signet/docs/signet_func_specs.html

Meadows, B., & Seaburg, L. (2004). *Universal Business Language UBL 1.0. Official OASIS Standard.* Retrieved from http://docs.oasis-open.org/ubl/cd-UBL-1.0.zip

Medjahed, B., Bouguettaya, A., & Elmagarmid, A.K. (2003). Composing Web services on the semantic Web. *The VLDB Journal, 12*(4), 333-351.

Megginson, D. (2005). *Simple API for XML–SAX.* Retrieved from http://www.saxproject.org

Menasce, D.A. (2002). QoS issues in Web services. *IEEE Internet Computing, 6*(6), 72-75.

Menasce, D.A. (2004). Composing Web services: A QoS view. *IEEE Internet Computing, 8*(6), 88-90.

Meneklis, B., Kaliotzoglou, A., Polemi, D., & Douligeris, C. (2005). Applying the ISO RM-ODP standard in e-government. In *Proceedings of E-government: Towards Electronic Democracy: International Conference,* Bolzano, Italy (LNCS 3416, pp. 213). Springer-Verlag GmbH.

Microsoft. (2001). Securing XML Web services created using ASP.NET. *.NET framework developer's Guide.* Microsoft Press.

Microsoft. (2002). *Altering the SOAP message using SOAP extensions.* Microsoft.

Microsoft. (2002). *Building secure ASP.NET applications: Authentication, authorization, and secure communication.* Microsoft Press.

Milanovic, N., & Malek, M. (2004). Current solutions for Web service composition. *IEEE Internet Computing, 8*(6), 51-59.

Miles, S. et al. (2003). Personalized grid service discovery. In *Proceedings of the Nineteenth Annual UK Performance Engineering Workshop (UKPEW'03),* University of Warwick, Coventry, England.

Miles, S., Papay, J., Payne, T., Decker, K., & Moreau, L. (2004). Towards a protocol for the attachment of semantic descriptions to grid services. In *Proceedings of the Second European across Grids Conference,* Nicosia, Cyprus.

Milosevic, Z., Gibson, S., Linnington, P. F., Cole, J., & Kulkarni, S. (2004). On design and implementation of a contract monitoring facility. In *Proceedings of the 1st IEEE Workshop on Electronic Contracting,* San Diego, CA.

Minsky, N., & Ungureanu, V. (2000). Law-governed interaction: A coordination and control mechanism for heterogeneous mistributed systems. *ACM Transactions on Software Engineering and Methodology, 9*(3), 273-305.

Mobile Electronic Transactions. (2003). *MeT white paper on mobile ticketing.* Retrieved from http://www.mobiletransaction.org/

Modal Act. (2003). The State Agricultural Produce Marketing (Development & Regulation Act, 2003). Retrieved June 11, 2007, from http://agmarknet.nic.in/reforms.htm

Molina-Jimenez, C., Shrivastava, S.K., & Warne, J. (2005). A method for specifying contract mediated interactions. In *Proceedings of the 9th IEEE International EDOC Enterprise Computing Conference*, Enschede, Netherlands.

Multipurpose Internet Mail Extensions (MIME) Part One, RFC 1521. (1996). Retrieved June 11, 2007, from http://www.ietf.org/rfc/rfc2045.txt

Myers, M., Ankney, R., Malpani, A., Galperin, S., & Adams, C. (1999). X.509 Internet public key infrastructure: Online certificate status protocol – OCSP, RFC 2560.

Nadalin, A., Kaler, C., Hallam-Baker, P., & Monzillo, R. (2004). Web Services Security: SOAP Message Security 1.0 (OASIS Standard). Retrieved June 3, 2007, from *http://docs.oasis-open.org/wss/2004/01/oasis-200401-wss-soap-message-security-1.0.pdf*

Naseer, A., & Stergioulas, L.K. (2005). Resource discovery in computational grids: State-of-the-art and current challenges. In H. Czap, R. Unland, C. Branki, & H. Tianfield (Eds.), *Self-organization and autonomic informatics (I)* (2005th ed., pp. 237-245). Amsterdam, Netherlands: IOS Press.

Naseer, A., & Stergioulas, L.K. (2006). *Integrating grid and Web services: A critical assessment of methods and implications to resource discovery.* In Paper presented at the IWI-WWW 2006: 2nd Workshop on Innovations in Web Infrastructure, Edinburgh, Scotland, UK. Retrieved June 11, 2007, from http://www.wmin.ac.uk/~courtes/iwi2006/naseer.pdf

Naseer, A., & Stergioulas, L.K. (2006). Discovering HealthGrid services. In *Proceedings of the IEEE International Conference on Services Computing (SCC'06)* (pp. 301-306). Retrieved June 11, 2007, from http://dx.doi.org/10.1109/SCC.2006.44

Naseer, A., & Stergioulas, L.K. (2006). Resource discovery in grids and other distributed environments: States of the art. *Multiagent and Grid Systems - An International Journal, 2*(2), 163-182.

Nash, A., Duane, B., Brink, D., & Joseph, C. (2001). *PKI: Implementing & managing eSecurity.* Emeryville, CA: McGraw-Hill Osborn Media Publishing.

Nataraj Nagaratnam, Jason Philippe, Dayka John, Nadalin Anthony, Siebenlist Frank, Welch Von, et al. (2002, July). *OGSA security roadmap.* Retrieved August 18, 2004, from http://www.cs.virginia.edu/~humphrey/ogsa-sec-wg/OGSA-SecArch-v1-07192002.pdf

Nenadic, A., Zhang, N., & Barton, S. (2004). FIDES - A middleware e-commerce security solution. In *Proceedings of the 3rd European Conference on Information Warfare and Security (ECIW),* London.

Netegrity. (2000). *SiteMinder concepts guide.* Waltham, MA: Netegrity.

Nguyen, T.A., Chadwick, D.W., Nasser, B. (2007, September 3-7). Recognition of Authority in Virtual Organisations. Presented at *4th International Conference onTrust, Privacy & Security in Digital Business,* Regensburg, Germany.

Nolan, P. (2004). Understand WS-policy processing. Retrieved June 4, 2007, from http://www-128.ibm.com/developerworks/webservices/library/ws-policy.html

OASIS 2002, *Universal Description, Discovery and Integration UDDI v. 3.0,* UDDI Spec Technical Committee Specification.

OASIS. (2003). XACML profile for Web services. Retrieved June 4, 2007, from http://www.oasis-open.org/committees/download.php/3661/draft-xacml-wspl-04.pdf

OASIS. (2004, November). *Extensible Access Control Markup Language (XACML), Version 2.0.*

OASIS. (2004). *Web services reliability TC WS-Reliability.* Retrieved June 11, 2007, from http://www.oasis-open.org/committees/download.php/ 5155/WS-Reliability-2004-01-26.pdf

OASIS. (2004). *Web services reliable messaging.*

OASIS. (2004). WS-security 1.1 core specification. Retrieved June 4, 2007, from http://www.oasis-open.org/committees/download.php/16790/wss-v1.1-spec-os-SOAPMessageSecurity.pdf

OASIS. (2005). Assertions and protocol for the OASIS Security Assertion Markup Language (SAML) V2.0, OASIS Standard.

OASIS. (2005). Assertions and protocols for the OASIS security assertion markup language (SAML) V2.0. Retrieved June 4, 2007, from http://docs.oasis-open.org/xacml/2.0/access_control-xacml-2.0-saml-profile-spec-os.pdf

OASIS. (2005). Core and hierarchical role based access control (RBAC) profile of XACML v2.0. Retrieved June 4, 2007, from http://docs.oasis-open.org/xacml/2.0/access_control-xacml-2.0-rbac-profile1-spec-os.pdf

OASIS. (2005). eXtensible access control markup language (XACML) Version 2.0. Retrieved June 4, 2007, from http://docs.oasis-open.org/xacml/2.0/access_control-xacml-2.0-core-spec-os.pdf

OASIS. (2005). SAML 2.0 profile of XACML v2.0. Retrieved June 4, 2007, from http://docs.oasis-open.org/xacml/2.0/access_control-xacml-2.0-saml-profile-spec-os.pdf

OASIS. (2005). Web service security SAML token profile 1.1. Retrieved June 4, 2007, from http://www.oasis-open.org/specs/index.php#wssprofilesv1.0

OASIS. (2007). XACML v3.0 Administrative Policy Version 1.0, working draft 15. Retrieved June 3, 2007, from http://www.oasis-open.org/committees/tc_home.php?wg_abbrev=xacml

OASIS. *SAML 1.0 Specification.*

OASIS. *Web Services Business Process Execution Language (WSBPEL).*

OASIS-2. (2005). eXtensible Access Control Markup Language (XACML), Version 2.0. OASIS Standard.

Object Management Group. (2001). *CORBAservices: Common object services specification, Security Service Specification v1.7.* Object Management Group, document formal/01-03-08.

OGC. *The Open Geospatial Consortium.* Retrieved June 11, 2007, from http://www.opengis.org

OGSA Spec. (2003, April 5). *Open grid services infrastructure.* Retrieved August 18, 2004, from http://www.gridforum.org/ogsi-wg/drafts/draft-ggf-ogsi-gridservice-29_2003-04-05.pdf

Oh, S. et al. (2005). Optimized communication using the SOAP infoset for mobile multimedia collaboration applications. In *Proceedings of the International Symposium on Collaborative Technologies and Systems 2005.*

OMG (2001). *Security domain membership management service.* Final Submission, Object Management Group.

OMG. (2001). *Resource access decision facility.* Object Management Group.

Open Geospatial Consortium. (2006). *OpenGIS Web map service (WMS) Specification.* Retrieved June 11, 2007, from http://www.opengeospatial.org/standards/wms

Open Geospatial Consortium. (2006). *OpenGIS Web feature service (WFS) Specification.* Retrieved June 11, 2007, from http://www.opengeospatial.org/standards/wfs

Open Grid Forum. (2006, October 27). Web services agreement specification (WS-Agreement). Retrieved June 11, 2007, from http://www.ogf.org/Public_Comment_Docs/Documents/Oct-2006/WS-Agreement-SpecificationDraftFinal_sp_tn_jpver_v2.pdf

Orbital Library. Retrieved June 3, 2007, from http://www.functologic.com/orbital

OWL-based Web Service Ontology. Retrieved June 3, 2007, from http://www.daml.org/services/owl-s/

Pagnia, H., & Gärtner, F. (1999). On the impossibility of fair exchange without a trusted third party (Tech. Rep. No.TUD-BS-1999-02). Department of Computer Science, TU Darmstadt.

Pallickara, S. et al. (2005). On the costs for reliable messaging in Web/grid service environments. In *Proceedings of the 2005 IEEE International Conference on E-science and Grid Computing* (pp. 344-351), Melbourne, Australia.

Pallickara, S., & Fox, G. (2005). An analysis of notification related specifications for Web/grid applications. In Paper presented at the ITCC (2).

Papazoglou, M. P., & Georgakopoulos, D. (2003). Service-oriented computing. *Communications of ACM, 46*(10), 24-28.

Papazoglou, M.P. (2003). Web services and business transactions. *World Wide Web, 6*(1), 49-91.

Peng, J., & Law, K.H. (2004). *Reference NEESgrid data model* (Tech. Rep. White Paper Version 1.0, No. TR-2004-

40). Retrieved June 11, 2007, from http://eil.stanford.edu/publications/NEESgrid/TR_2004_40.pdf

Periorellis, P., Cook, N., Hiden, H.G., Conlin, A., Hamilton, M.D., Wu, J. et al. (2006). GOLD infrastructure for virtual organisations. In *Proceedings of the 5th UK E-science All Hands Meeting*, Nottingham, UK.

Perrin, T., Andivahis, D., Cruellas, J.C., Hirsch, F., Kasselman, P., Kuehne, A. et al. (2004). *Digital signature service core protocols, elements and bindings (OASIS Committee Working Draft)*. Retrieved June 3, 2007, from http://www.oasis-open.org/committees/dss

Plale, B., Gannon, D., Alameda, J., Wilhelmson, B., Hampton, S., Rossi, A. et al. (2005). Active management of scientific data. *Internet Computing, IEEE, 9*(1), 27-34.

Platzer, C., & Dustdar, S. (2005). A vector space search engine for Web services. In *Proceedings of the Third IEEE European Conference on Web Services (ECOWS'05)*. Växjö, Sweden: IEEE Computer Society.

Project Liberty Spec. (2003, January 15). *Project Liberty specification*. Retrieved August 18, 2004, from http://www.projectliberty.org/specs/archive/v1_1/liberty-architecture-overview-v1.1.pdf

Qin, C.L., Davenhall, A.C., Noddle, K.T., & Walton, N.A. (2003). Myspace: Personalized work space in astrogrid. In *Proceedings of the UK E-Science all Hands Meeting* (pp. 361-365), University of Southampton.

Quadrasis Firewall. (2004, January 2). *Quadrasis EASI SOAP content inspector*. Retrieved August 18, 2004, from http://www.quadrasis.com/solutions/products/easi_product_packages/easi_soap.htm

Ran, S. (2003). A model for Web services discovery with QoS. *SIGecom Exchanges, 4*(1), 1-10.

Ratnasingam, P. (2002). The importance of technology trust in Web services security. *Information Management & Computer Security, 10*(5), 255-260.

Reactivity Firewall. (2004, January 2). *Reactivity XML firewall*. Retrieved August 18, 2004, from http://www.reactivity.com/products/solution.html

Richard, F., Jenkins, J., & Frank, G. (2003). JTP: A system architecture and component library for hybrid reasoning. *In Proceedings of the Seventh World Multiconference on Systemics, Cybernetics, and Informatics*. Orlando, FL.

Rosenberg, F., Platzer, C., & Dustdar, S. (2006). Bootstrapping performance and dependability attributes of Web services. In *Proceedings of the IEEE International Conference on Web Services (ICWS'06)* (pp. 205-212). Chicago, IL, USA: IEEE Computer Society.

RosettaNet. (2005). *E-business standards for the global supply chain*. Retrieved June 3, 2007, from http://www.rosettanet.org/RosettaNet/

Rowell, M. (2002). OAGIS—A "Canonical" business language. *Open Applications Group, white paper*, (version 1.0.) Retrieved from www.openapplications.org/downloads/whitepapers/whitepaperdocs/20020429_OAGIS_A_Canonical_Business_Langugage-PDF.zip

Russell, S., & Norvig, P. (1995). *Artificial intelligence: A modern approach*. Prentice Hall.

SAML Interop. (2002, July 15). *SAML interoperability event*. Retrieved August 18, 2004, from http://xml.coverpages.org/ni2002-07-15-a.html

SAML Spec. (2003, September 2). *Security Assertions Markup Language (SAML)*. Retrieved August 18, 2004, from http://www.oasis-open.org/committees/download.php/2949/sstc-saml-1.1-cs-03-pdf-xsd.zip

Sandhu, R., Coyne, E.J., Feinstein, H.L., & Youman, C.E. (1996). Role-based access control models. *IEEE Computer, 29*(2), 38-47.

Sandhu, R., Coyne, E., Feinstein, H., & Youman, C. (1996). Role-based access control models. *IEEE Computer, 29*(2), 38-47.

SAPHIRE. (2006). Intelligent health care monitoring based on semantic interoperability platform. Retrieved June 4, 2007, from http://www.srdc.metu.edu.tr/Webpage/projects/saphire/

Schmit, B., & Dustdar, S. (2005). *Systematic design of Web service transactions*.

Schneier, B. (1996). *Applied cryptography.* John Wiley & Sons.

Schreiner, W., & Dustdar, S. (2005). A survey on Web services on Web services composition. *International Journal of Web and Grid Services, 1*(1), 1-30.

Security Assertion Markup Language (SAML). (2004). Retrieved June 11, 2007, from http://www.oasis-open.org/committees/download.php/6837/sstc-saml-tech-overview-1.1-cd.pdf

Security Assertions Markup Language (SAML). (2004). Retrieved June 4, 2007, from http://xml.coverpages.org/saml.html

Security in a Web services world: A proposed architecture and roadmap. (2002). Retrieved June 4, 2007, from http://www-128.ibm.com/developerworks/webservices/library/ specification/ws-secmap/

Semantic Web Services Initiative (SWSI). Retrieved June 3, 2007, from http://www.swsi.org/

Semantic Web Services Language (SWSL) Committee. Retrieved June 3, 2007, from http://www.daml.org/services/swsl/

ShaikhAli, A., Rana, O., Al-Ali, R., & Walker, D. (2003). UDDIe: An extended registry for Web services. In *Proceedings of the Service-oriented Computing: Models, Architectures, and Applications, SAINT-2003,* Orlando, FL, USA. IEEE Computer Society Press.

Shi, Y., Zhang, L., Liu, B., Liu, F., Lin, L., & Shi, B. (2005). A formal specification for Web services composition and verification. In *Proceedings of the Fifth International Conference on Computer and Information Technology* (pp. 252-256). Shanghai, China.

Simple Object Access Protocol (SOAP) 1.1. (2000). Retrieved June 11, 2007, from http://www.w3.org/TR/2000/NOTE-SOAP-20000508/

Sinnott, R.O., Stell, A.J., Chadwick, D.W., & Otenko, O. (2005). Experiences of applying advanced grid authorisation infrastructures. In *Proceedings of the European Grid Conference (EGC),* Amsterdam, Holland.

Sinnott, R.O., Watt, J., Jiang, J., Stell, A.J., & Ajayi, O. (2006). Single sign-on and authorization for dynamic virtual organizations. In *Proceedings of the 7th IFIP Conference on Virtual Enterprises, PRO-VE 2006,* Helsinki, Finland.

Sirer, E., & Wang, K. (2002). An access control language for Web services. In *Proceedings of the Seventh ACM Symposium on Access Control Models and Technologies,* Monterey, CA.

SOAP. (2000). Simple object access protocol (SOAP) 1.1. Retrieved June 11, 2007, from http://www.w3.org/TR/2000/NOTE-SOAP-20000508/

Song, H.G., & Lee, K. (2005). sPAC (Web Services Performance Analysis Center): Performance analysis and estimation tool of Web services. In *Proceedings of the 3rd International Conference on Business Process Management (BPM'05)* (pp. 109-119). Springer.

Sorathia, V., Laliwala, Z., & Chaudhary, S. (2005). Towards agricultural marketing reforms: Web services orchestration approach. In *Paper presented at the SCC '05: Proceedings of the 2005 IEEE International Conference on Services Computing,* Washington, DC, USA.

Sotomayor, B. *The Globus Toolkit 4 Programmer's Tutorial.* Retrieved June 11, 2007, from http://gdp.globus.org/gt4-tutorial/singlehtml/progtutorial_0.2.1.html

Spencer, B. (2004). *A Java deductive reasoning engine for the Web (jDREW), Version 1.1.*

Srinivasan, R. (1995). *Remote procedure call protocol specification version 2 (RPC) (RFC1831).* Retrieved from http://asg.web.cmu.edu/rfc/rfc1831.html

Stewart, C.A. (2004). Introduction. *Communications of the ACM, 47*(11), 30-33.

Strassner, J. (2003). *Policy-based network management: Solutions for the next generation.* Morgan Kaufmann.

Suzumura, T., Takase, T., & Tatsubori, M. (2005). Optimizing Web services performance by differential deserialization. In *Proceedings of the IEEE International Conference on Web Services (ICWS'05)* (pp. 185-192).

Tai, S., Khalaf, R., & Mikalsen, T. (2004). Composition of coordinated Web services. In *Proceedings of the 5th ACM/IFIP/USENIX International Conference on Middleware* (pp. 294-310). Springer.

Talia, D. (2002). The open grid services architecture: Where the grid meets the Web. *Internet Computing, IEEE, 6*(6), 67-71.

Thatte, S. (2001). *XLANG - Web services for business process design.* Microsoft Corporation.

The European Parliament. (2001, December 20). *Council Directive 2001/115/EC, amending Directive 77/388/EEC with view to simplifying, modernizing, and harmonizing the conditions laid down for invoicing in respect of value added tax.*

The Rule Markup Initiative. (2004, May). *SWRL: A Semantic Web rule Language combining OWL and RuleML, Version 0.6.*

The Rule Markup Initiative. (2004, August). *Schema specification of RuleML 0.87, Version 0.87.*

Tian, M., Gramm, A., Ritter, H., & Schiller, J. (2004). Efficient selection and monitoring of QoS-aware Web services with the WS-QoS framework. In *Proceedings of the International Conference on Web Intelligence (WI'04),* Beijing, China.

Tonti, G., Bradshaw, J. M., Jeffers, R., Montanari, R., Suri, N., & Uszok, A. (2003). Semantic Web languages for policy representation and reasoning: A comparison of KAoS, Rei, and Ponder. *The Semantic Web — ISWC 2003. Proceedings of the Second International Semantic Web Conference.* Springer-Verlag.

Tuecke, S., Welch, V., Engert, D., Pearlman, L., & Thompson, M. (2004). Internet X.509 Public Key Infrastructure (PKI) proxy certificate profile. RFC3820.

Tuecke, S., Czajkowski, K., Foster, I., Frey, J., Graham, S., Kesselman, C. et al. (2003). *Open grid services infrastructure (OGSI)* (No. Version 1.0), Global Grid Forum (GGF). Retrieved June 11, 2007, from http://www.globus.org/alliance/publications/papers.php#GSSpec

Twardoch, A. (2003). *Web services technologies: XML, SOAP and UDDI.* Retrieved June 11, 2007, from http://www.twardoch.com/webservices/

UDDI. (2004). Universal description, discovery and integration, UDDI Version 3.0.2. Retrieved June 11, 2007, from http://uddi.org/pubs/uddi_v3.htm

UK Office of the eEnvoy. (2004). *UK GovTalk portal.* Retrieved from www.govtalk.gov.uk

UMBC eBiquity. (2005). *Project Rei: A policy specification language.* University of Maryland, Baltimore County (UMBC).

Universal Description, Discovery and Integration (UDDI), Version 3.0.2. (2004). Retrieved June 11, 2007, from http://uddi.org/pubs/uddi_v3.htm

Uszok, A., Bradshaw, J., Jeffers, R., Suri, N., et al. (2003). *KAoS Policy and domain services: Toward a description-logic approach to policy representation, deconfliction, and enforcement.* Policy 2003: Workshop on Policies for Distributed Systems and Networks. Springer-Verlag.

van der Aalst, W.M.P., Dumas, M., & ter Hofstede, A.H.M. (2003). Web service composition languages: Old wine in new bottles? In *Proceedings of the 29th Euromicro Conference* (pp. 298-305). Belek, Turkey.

Van Engelen, R. (2003). Pushing the SOAP envelope with Web services for scientific computing. In *Proceedings of the International Conference on Web services (ICWS)* (pp. 346-352).

Van Engelen, R., Gupta, G., & Pant, S. (2003). Developing Web services for C and C++. *In IEEE Internet Computing* (pp. 53-61).

Verisign. (2004). *Verisign trust gateway: Simplifying application and Web services security (Verisign White Paper).* Retrieved June 3, 2007, from http://www.verisign.com/products-services/security-services/intelligence-and-control-services/application-security/index.html

Verma, K., Sivashanmugam, K., Sheth, A., Patil, A., Oundhakar, S., & Miller, J. (2003). METEOR–S WSDI: A scalable P2P infrastructure of registries for semantic publication and discovery of Web services. *Journal of Information Technology and Management.*

Verma, D. C. (2000). *Policy-based networking: Architecture and algorithms.* Pearson Education.

Vinoski, S. (2004). More Web services notifications. *Internet Computing, IEEE, 8*(3), 90-93.

Vinoski, S. (2004). WS-nonexistent standards. *Internet Computing, IEEE, 8*(6), 94-96.

Vordel Firewall. (2004, January 2). *Vordel XML security server.* Retrieved August 18, 2004, from http://www.vordel.com/products/xml_security_server.html

W3C. (1999, February). *Resource Description Framework (RDF), data model and syntax.* W3C Recommendation.

W3C. (2002). *SOAP Version 1.2 Part 1: Messaging Framework*, W3C.

W3C. (2002). *SOAP Version 1.2 Part 2: Adjuncts*, W3C.

W3C. (2002). *SOAP Version 1.2 Usage Scenarios*, W3C.

W3C. (2006). Web service policy 1.2-framework (WS-Policy). Retrieved June 4, 2007, from http://www.w3.org/Submission/WS-Policy/

W3C. (2006). *Web Services Policy 1.2 - Attachment (WS-PolicyAttachment).*

W3C. (2006). *WS-Policy Framework Specification Version 1.2.*

Wang, G. (2005). Generic fair nonrepudiation protocols with transparent off-line TTP. In *Proceedings of the 4th International Workshop for Applied PKI,* Singapore.

Wang, H., Huang, J.Z., Qu, Y., & Xie, J. (2004). Web services: Problems and future directions. *Journal of Web Semantics, 1*(3).

Warrier J., Besaw L., LaBarre L., & Handspicker, B. (1990). *The common management information services and protocols for the Internet. Network Working Group request for comments 1189.* Retrieved June 11, 2007, from http://www.ietf.org/rfc/rfc1189.txt

Watt, J., Sinnott, R.O., Jiang, J., Ajayi, O., & Koetsier, J. (2006). A Shibboleth-protected privilege management infrastructure for e-science education. In *Proceedings of the 6th International Symposium on Cluster Computing and the Grid, CCGrid2006*, Singapore.

Web Services Description Language (WSDL 1.1). (2001). Retrieved June 4, 2007, from http://www.w3.org/TR/2001/NOTE-wsdl-20010315

Web Services Description Language (WSDL) 1.1. (2001). Retrieved June 11, 2007, from http://www.w3.org/TR/2001/NOTE-wsdl-20010315

Web Services Policy Attachment (WS Attachment). (2006). Retrieved June 4, 2007, from http://www-128.ibm.com/developerworks/webservices/library/specification/ws-polatt/

Web Services Policy Framework (WS Policy). (2006). Retrieved June 4, 2007, from http://www-128.ibm.com/developerworks/webservices/library/specification/ws-polfram/

Web Services Security (WS Security). (2002). Retrieved June 4, 2007, from http://www-128.ibm.com/developerworks/webservices/library/specification/ws-secure/

Web Services Security. (2004). Retrieved June 11, 2007, from http://docs.oasis-open.org/wss/2004/01/oasis-200401-wss-soap-message-security-1.0.pdf

Web Services Trust Language (WS Trust). (2004). Retrieved June 4, 2007, from http://www-128.ibm.com/developerworks/library/specification/ws-trust/

Weerawarana, S., Curbera, F., Leymann, F., Storey, T., & Ferguson, D.F. (2006). *Web services platform architecture.* Pearson Education.

Welch, V., Ananthakrishnan, R., Siebenlist, F., Chadwick, D., Meder, S., & Pearlman, L. (2006). Use of SAML for OGSI Authorization, GFD.66. Retrieved June 3, 2007, from http://www.ggf.org/documents/GFD.66.pdf

Westbridge Firewall. (2004, January 2). *Westbridge XML message server.* Retrieved August 18, 2004 from http://www.westbridgetech.com/products.html

WFMC. (2007). Workflow Management Coalition (WfMC). Retrieved June 3, 2007, from http://www.wfmc.org

Wickramage, N., & Weerawarana, S. (2005). A benchmark for Web service frameworks. In *Proceedings of the IEEE International Conference on Service Computing (SCC'05)*, Orlando, FL, USA.

Wilkes, L. (2005). The Web services protocol stack. Retrieved June 11, 2007, from http://roadmap.cbdiforum.com/reports/protocols/index.php

Wooldridge, M. (2001). An introduction to multiagent systems. John Wiley & Sons.

World Wide Web Consortium (W3C). (2002). *Web Services Architecture Requirements.*

World Wide Web Consortium (W3C). (2002). *Web Services Description Language (WSDL) Version 2.0 Part 0: Primer*, W3C Candidate Recommendation, 27 March 2006.

World Wide Web Consortium (W3C). (2002). The *Platform for Privacy Preferences 1.1 (P3P1.1) Specification*, W3C Working Group Note, 13 November 2006.

World Wide Web Consortium (W3C). (2003). *SOAP Version 1.2 Part 0: Primer (Second Edition*, W3C Proposed Edited Recommendation, 19 December 2006.

World Wide Web Consortium (W3C). (2004). *OWL Web Ontology Language Overview*, W3C Recommendation, 10 February 2004.

World Wide Web Consortium (W3C). (2004). Web Services Choreography Description Language Version 1.0, W3C Candidate Recommendation, 9 November 2005.

World Wide Web Consortium [W3C]. (2002). *SOAP Version 1.2 Part 0: Primer*, W3C.

WS-Addressing. (2004). Web services addressing. W3C Member Submission 10 August 2004. Retrieved June 11, 2007, from http://www.w3.org/Submission/ws-addressing/

WS-BaseFaults. (2006). Web services base faults 1.2. Retrieved June 11, 2007, from http://docs.oasis-open.org/wsrf/wsrf-ws_base_faults-1.2-spec-os.pdf

WS-BaseNotification. (2006). Web services base notification 1.3. Retrieved June 11, 2007, from http://docs.oasis-open.org/wsn/wsn-ws_base_notification-1.3-spec-pr-03.pdf

WS-BrokeredNotification. (2006). Web services brokered notification 1.3. Retrieved June 11, 2007, from http://docs.oasis-open.org/wsn/wsn-ws_brokered_notification-1.3-spec-pr-03.pdf

WSDL. (2005). Web services description language (WSDL) 1.1. Retrieved June 11, 2007, from http://www.w3.org/TR/2001/NOTE-wsdl-20010315

WS-Eventing. (2006). Web services eventing (WS-Eventing). Retrieved June 11, 2007, from http://www.w3.org/Submission/WS-Eventing/

WS-Federation Spec. (2003, July 18). *WS-Federation specification.* Retrieved August 18, 2004, from http://www-106.ibm.com/developerworks/webservices/library/ws-fed/

WS-Notification. (2005). Web services notification. Retrieved June 11, 2007, from www.oasis-open.org/committees/wsn/

WS-Policy Spec. (2002, December 18). *WS-Policy Specification.* Retrieved August 18, 2004, from http://msdn.microsoft.com/library/default.asp?url=/library/en-us/dnglobspec/html/wspolicyspecindex.asp

WS-ResourceFramework. (2005). Web services resource framework. Retrieved June 11, 2007, from www.oasis-open.org/committees/wsrf/

WS-ResourceLifetime. (2006). Web services resource lifetime 1.2. Retrieved June 11, 2007, from http://docs.oasis-open.org/wsrf/wsrf-ws_resource_lifetime-1.2-spec-os.pdf

WS-ResourceProperties. (2006). Web services resource properties 1.2. Retrieved June 11, 2007, from http://docs.oasis-open.org/wsrf/wsrf-ws_resource_properties-1.2-spec-os.pdf

WS-SecurityPolicy. Retrieved June 4, 2007, from ftp://www6.software.ibm.com/software/developer/library/ws.secpol.pdf

WS-Security Spec. (2002, April 5). *Web services security (WS-Security).* Retrieved August 18, 2004, from http://msdn.microsoft.com/library/en-us/dnglobspec/html/ws-security.asp

WS-ServiceGroup. (2006). Web services service group 1.2. Retrieved June 11, 2007, from http://docs.oasis-open.org/wsrf/wsrf-ws_service_group-1.2-spec-os.pdf

WS-Topics. (2006). Web services topics 1.3. Retrieved June 11, 2007, from http://docs.oasis-open.org/wsn/wsn-ws_topics-1.3-spec-pr-02.pdf

Wu, F.F., Moslehi, K., & Bose, A. (2005). Power system control centers: Past, present, and future. *Proceedings of the IEEE, 93*(11), 1890-1908.

XACML Profile for Web Services (WSPL). (2003). Retrieved June 4, 2007, from http://www.oasis-open.org/committees/download.php/3661/draft-xacml-wspl-04.pdf

XACML Spec. (2003, February 18). *eXtensible Access Control Markup Language (XACML).* Retrieved August 18, 2004, from http://www.oasis-open.org/committees/download.php/2406/oasis-xacml-1.0.pdf

XACML-TC. (2003). *OASIS eXtensible access control markup language (XACML) version 1.0*, OASIS.

xCBL.org. (2003). *XML common business library version 4.00* (xCBL v4.00). Retrieved from www.xcbl.org/xcbl40/xcbl40.html

XKMS Spec. (2001, March). *XML Key Management Specification (XKMS).* Retrieved August 18, 2004, from http://www.w3.org/TR/xkms/

XML Encryption Syntax and Processing. (2002). Retrieved June 11, 2007, from http://www.w3.org/TR/xmlenc-core/

XML Signature Syntax and Processing. (2002). Retrieved June 11, 2007, from http://www.w3.org/TR/xmldsig-core/

XML-Encryption Spec. (2002, December 10). *XML Encryption Syntax and Processing.* Retrieved August 18, 2004, from http://www.w3.org/TR/xmlenc-core/

XML-Signature Spec. (2002, February 12). *XML-Signature Syntax and Processing.* Retrieved August 18, 2004, from http://www.w3.org/TR/xmldsig-core/

Xu, W., Chadwick, D., & Otenko, S.(2005). A PKI-based secure audit Web service. IASTED Communications, Network and Information Security CNIS, November 14 - November 16, Phoenix, AZ.

Yang, J., Papazoglou, M.P., Orriens, B., & van Heuvel, W.J. (2003). A rule based approach to the service composition life-cycle. In *Proceedings of the Fourth International Conference on Web Information Systems Engineering* (pp. 295-298). Rome, Italy.

Yang, X., Hayes, M., Usher, A., & Spivack, M. (2004). *Developing Web services in a computational grid environment* (pp. 600-603).

Yildiz, B., Pallickara, S., & Fox, G. (2006). Experiences with deploying services within the Axis container. In *Proceedings of the 2006 IEEE International Conference on Internet and Web Applications and Services,* French Caribbean.

Zang, T., Jie, W., Hung, T., Lei, Z., Turner, S.J., & Cai, W. (2004). *The design and implementation of an OGSA-based grid information service* (pp. 566-573).

Zeng, L., Benatallah, B., Dumas, M., Kalagnanam, J., & Sheng, Q.Z. (2003). Quality driven Web services composition. In *Proceedings of the 12th International Conference on World Wide Web (WWW'03)* (pp. 411-421).

Zeng, L., Benatallah, B., Ngu, A.H., & Dumas, M. (2004). Qos-aware middleware for Web service composition. *IEEE Transactions on Software Engineering, 30*(5), 311-327.

Zheng, W., Hu, M., Yang, G., Wu, Y., Chen, M., Ma, R. et al. (2004). *An efficient Web services based approach to computing grid* (pp. 382-385).

Zhou, J., & Gollmann, D. (1997). Evidence and nonrepudiation. *Journal of Network and Computer Applications, 20*(3), 267-281.

About the Contributors

Asif Akram studied chemical engineering at Punjab University, Lahore, Pakistan. He has since worked in the IT research field. He recently joined Imperial College, London, and the London E-science Centre to work on the EU-funded GridCC Project. He had also worked in the CCLRC, one of Europe's largest multidisciplinary research organizations on the Workflow Optimization for Scientific Applications (WOSE). His research interests are distributed programming, and particularly Web services. During his research career he has worked on various projects implementing Web services and orchestrating these Web services into complicated workflows. He has also contributed to various books, published numerous research papers, and written tutorials for IBM developerWorks. Before joining Imperial College and CCLRC, he taught at different universities.

Mehmet S. Aktas received an MSc from Syracuse University in computer science in 2001. He is a PhD candidate in the computer science department and graduate research assistant in the Community Grids Lab at Indiana University. His areas of research include distributed information systems for Grid and Web service-oriented architectures, geographical information systems, Web mining, and semantic Grid.

Rob Allan is head of the Grid Technology Group at CCLRC Daresbury Laboratory, with an interest in distributed service development and deployment and user interfaces for research, mainly in the natural sciences. Allan's background is as a researcher in theoretical atomic physics, doing large scale computational modeling. He has also developed numerical algorithms and parallel computing and Grid tools for the UK Collaborative Computational Projects and HEC communities, for example, through CCP2, CCP6, HPCI, and UKHEC initiatives. He has skills in FORTRAN, Perl, and C/C++. Rob has a practical knowledge of Grid and Web services middleware and helped to set up CCLRC's E-science Centre and the UK's Grid Support Centre, and has acted as PI or co-PI in numerous high-profile research council and JISC grants. He has written several technical evaluations, including the DTI-funded Globus evaluation report (December 2001) and the JISC Sakai Evaluation report (December 2004). Rob is currently acting as e-research representative on the Joint Framework Working Group (JISC UK and DEST Australia) and is chair of the Operations Board of the NW-GRID and chair of the Service Delivery Board of National Centre for E-social Science.

Elisa Bertino is a professor of CS and ECE at Purdue University, and research director of the Center for Information and Research in Information Assurance and Security. Her recent research focuses on privacy techniques for databases, digital identity management, policy systems, and security for Web service. She is a fellow of ACM and of IEEE. She received the IEEE Computer Society 2002 Technical Achievement Award and the IEEE Computer Society 2005 Kanai Award. She is an editor-in-chief of *VLDB Journal* and an editorial board member of *ACM TISSEC, IEEE TDSC*, and *IEEE Security & Privacy*.

Yildiz Beytullah is a PhD candidate in the Computer Science Department, and graduate research assistant in the Community Grids Lab at Indiana University. He received an MSc from Syracuse University in Computer Science in 2001. Most of his research work is connected with the study and development of message-oriented middleware, Semantic Web, Grid, and Web service architecture. His current research focuses on handler architecture for Web services.

Konstantin Beznosov is an assistant professor at the Department of Electrical and Computer Engineering, University of British Columbia, where he founded and directs the Laboratory for Education and Research in Secure Systems Engineering (*lersse.ece.ubc.ca*). His primary research interests are distributed systems security, usability and security, secure software engineering, and access control. Prior to UBC, Dr. Beznosov was a security architect with Quadrasis, Hitachi Computer Products (America), Inc., where he designed and developed products for security integration of enterprise applications, as well as consulted large telecommunication and banking companies on the architecture of security solutions for distributed enterprise applications. Dr. Beznosov did his PhD research on engineering access control for distributed enterprise applications at the Florida International University. He actively participated in standardization of security-related specifications (CORBA Security, RAD, SDMM) at the Object Management Group, and served as a co-chair of the OMG's Security SIG. Having published a number of research papers on security engineering in distributed systems, he is a co-author of *Enterprise Security with EJB and CORBA* and *Mastering Web Services Security*.

Rafae Bhatti is currently a post-doctoral researcher at IBM Almaden Research Center in San Jose, California. His research interests include information systems security, with emphases on design and administration of access management policies in distributed systems. His recent research focuses on the access management problems posed by the emerging federated paradigm of information sharing and collaboration. His work on XML-based access control framework for the role based access control (RBAC) model has recently been cited by the OASIS consortium in their official announcement of the RBAC standard. He is a member of the ACM, IEEE, and the IEEE Computer Society.

Barbara Carminati is an assistant professor of computer science at the University of Insubria at Varese, Italy. Carminati received an MS in computer sciences in 2000, and a PhD in computer science from the University of Milano, in 2004. Her main research interests include database and Web security, XML security, WS security, Web semantic security, secure information dissemination, and publishing. Dr. Carminati has served as program committee member of several international conferences and workshops (SACMAT, COOPIS, PST, MSW, etc.), and as reviewer for various international journals and conferences (IEEE TKDE, ACM TOIT, etc.). She is on the editorial board of the *Computer Standards & Interfaces* (Elsevier Press).

David Chadwick is a professor of information systems security at the University of Kent, and the leader of the Information Systems Security Research Group. He is a member of IEEE and ACM. He specialises in public key infrastructures, privilege management infrastructures, trust management, and Internet security research in general. Current research topics include: policy-based authorisation, the management of trust, the delegation of authority, and autonomic security. He actively participates in standardisation activities, is the UK BSI representative to X.509 standards meetings, and is the author of a number of Internet Drafts, RFCs, and Global Grid Forum documents. He has published widely, with over 80 publications in international journals, conferences, and workshops, including three books and 10 book chapters.

Sanjay Chaudhary is an associate professor at Dhirubhai Ambani Institute of Information and Communication Technology (DAIICT), Gandhinagar, India. His research areas are distributed computing, Grid computing, Semantic Web, and ICT applications in agriculture. He has authored a number of research papers in international conferences and workshops, including IEEE Wireless Communications and Networking Conference (WCNC), International Conference on Services Computing (SCC), Asia Pacific Software Engineering Conference (APSEC), COMmunication System software and MiddlewaRE (COMSWARE), International Conference on Advanced Computing & Communications (ADCOM), International Conference on Innovations in Information Technology, International Workshop on Innovative Internet Community Systems (I2CS), International Workshop on Distributed Event-Based Systems (DEBS), International Workshop on Semantic and Dynamic Web Processes (SDWP), and others. He has served on many program committees of international conferences and workshops, including Web Services track of International World Wide Web Conference Committee (IW3C2), International Conference on Business Process Management (BPM), International Workshop on Semantic and Dynamic Web Processes (SDWP), and others. He has authored three books and a number of book chapters. He holds a doctorate degree in computer science from Gujarat Vidyapeeth. Prior to joining DAIICT, he worked with Gujarat University, and he has also worked on various large-scale software development and consultancy projects for the corporate sector, the cooperative sector, and government organizations in India and the United States.

Nick Cook is a lecturer in computing science at Newcastle University. He has a BSc in mathematics from Manchester University, and an MSc and a PhD in computing science from Newcastle University. His research concerns middleware support for B2B e-commerce. He has worked on two major collaborative research projects, as a Ph.D. student for the TAPAS European project on complex service provisioning on the Internet, and as a research associate for the Gold UK e-science project on middleware support for virtual organisations.

Asuman Dogac is a full professor of the Department of Computer Engineering at the Middle East Technical University, and the founding director of the Software Research and Development Center. She is a graduate of the Department of Electrical Engineering, Middle East Technical University, and was a post-doc at the University of California, Los Angeles, in 1981. In 2004, Professor Dogac received the IBM (USA) Faculty Award. She is also the recipient of several local awards: the 1991 Mustafa Parlar Research Award, the 1994 Husamettin Tugac Research Award, the 1999 METU Achievement Award, the 2000 METU Tarik Somer Superior Achievement Award, the 2000 Mustafa Parlar Science Award, and the 2001 Tarik Somer Award.

Schahram Dustdar is a full professor of computer science with a focus on Internet technologies at the Distributed Systems Group, Information Systems Institute, Vienna University of Technology (TU Wien), where he is director of the Vita Lab. He is also honorary professor of information Ssystems at the Department of Computing Science at the University of Groningen (RuG), The Netherlands.

Elena Ferrari is a professor of computer science at the University of Insubria, Italy, since March 2001. She received an MS in computer science from the University of Milano (Italy) in 1992, and a PhD in computer science from the same university in 1998. Her main research interests are Web security, access control and privacy, and multimedia databases. On these topics, she has published more than 100 scientific publications in international journals and conference proceedings. Dr. Ferrari has served as program chair of the 4th ACM Symposium on Access Control Models and Technologies (SACMAT'04), software demonstration chair of the 9th International Conference on Extending Database Technology (EDBT'04), and co-chair of the First COMPSAC'02 Workshop on Web Security and Semantic Web. She has also served as program committee member of several international conferences and workshops. Professor Ferrari is in the editorial voard of the *VLDB Journal* and the *International Journal of Information Technology (IJIT).* She is a member of ACM and senior member of IEEE.

Geoffrey Fox received a PhD in theoretical physics from Cambridge University in 1967. He is a professor in the Department of Computer Science, School of Informatics and Physics at Indiana University. He is the director of the Community Grids Lab at Indiana University. He was also the director of the Northeast Parallel Architectures Center at Syracuse University from 1990-2000. He has led activities to develop prototype high performance Java and Fortran compilers and their runtime support. His research group has pioneered use of CORBA and Java for both collaboration and distributed computing. He helped set up the Java Grande forum to encourage use of Java in large-scale computations.

Arif Ghafoor is currently a professor in the School of Electrical and Computer Engineering at Purdue University, and is the director of the Distributed Multimedia Systems Laboratory. He is pursuing research in information security and multimedia systems. Dr. Ghafoor has served on the editorial boards of various journals and has co-edited a book entitled *Multimedia Document Systems in Perspectives* and has co-authored a book entitled *Semantic Models for Multimedia Database Searching and Browsing.* Dr. Ghafoor is a fellow of IEEE. He has received the IEEE Computer Society 2000 Technical Achievement Award for his research contributions in the area of multimedia systems.

Gadgil Harshawardhan holds a BE in computer engineering from Mumbai University, India, and an MS in computer science from Indiana University. He is interested in publish subscribe systems, Web services, and workflow technologies and management issues in large scale distributed systems. He currently works in the Distributed Systems Engineering Group at Amazon.com, Seattle. He is also pursuing his PhD in computer science from Indiana University, Bloomington.

Patrick C.K. Hung is currently collaborating with Boeing Phantom Works (Seattle, USA) and Bell Canada's Privacy Center of Excellence on security- and privacy-related research projects. Patrick has been serving as a panelist of the Small Business Innovation Research and Small Business Technology Transfer programs of the National Science Foundation (NSF) in the states. He is an executive committee member of the IEEE Computer Society's Technical Steering Committee for Services Computing, a steering committee member of IEEE EDOC "The Enterprise Computing Conference," and an associate editor/editorial board member/guest editor in several international journals, such as the *Journal of Web Services Research.*

Prateek Jain is student in Dhirubhai Ambani Institute of Information and Communication Technology. He is pursuing his PhD under the supervision of Dr. Sanjay Chaudhary. His research interests are Web services, workflow, and Grid services. He also worked on the IBM Eclipse Innovation Grant 2005 for a research project on "Framework for Processing and Visualisation of Critical Alerts for Risk perception and Efficient Decision-Making."

Zakir Laliwala is a PhD candidate in the Dhirubhai Ambani Institute of Information and Communication Technology (DA-IICT <*http://www.daiict.ac.in*>). He is currently working as a research assistant on the IBM Eclipse Innovation Grant 2005 project "Framework for processing and visualization of critical alerts for risk perception and efficient decision-making."

David Meredith is a software engineer for the UK National Grid Service and a member of the Grid Technology Group at CCLRC Daresbury Laboratory. Meredith's main research areas include distributed computing and enterprise systems, with special application to the physical sciences. Meredith's background is as a researcher in computational modeling of petroleum systems.

Tuncay Namli is working as a senior software engineer in Software R&D Center of Middle East Technical University (METU). He is a graduate of Department of Computer Engineering, METU. Namli is currently working on his MSc thesis in the graduate program of Computer Engineering Department of METU. In METU SRDC, he has worked on several IST projects, namely, EUMEDIS-311 DAEDALUS, IST-1-002104-STP SATINE and IST-1-002103-STP ARTEMIS.

Aisha Naseer (BSc, MSc) is a researcher at the Department of Information Systems and Computing at Brunel University, UK, where she is studying for a PhD in the area of HealthGrid development. She is a qualified computer engineer and has studied mathematics and statistical analysis in her first degree (1996) at the University of Punjab, and later received an MSc (2003) in computer science from the Hamdard University, Pakistan, specialising in software engineering and artificial intelligence. She worked as a lecturer in the Computer Science Department, Lahore College for Women University, Pakistan (2001-2003). Currently, she is also a lecturer at the Uxbridge College, London. In the last 5 years, she has taught various computer science courses at both the undergraduate and postgraduate level. She has published several papers in journals and international conferences. Her research interests include intelligent data management, health informatics, HealthGrid applications, Grid computing, and artificial intelligence.

Sangyoon Oh received an MS in computer science from Syracuse University and a PhD in computer science from Indiana University, USA (2006). He is currently a senior researcher of the SK telecom company, South Korea. Oh has worked in a variety of computer science fields focusing on mobile computing, Web service technology, Grid systems, and Semantic Web technology.

Shrideep Pallickara received his master's degree and PhD in computer engineering from Syracuse University (1998 and 2001, respectively). He is currently a researcher at the Community Grids Lab at Indiana University. His research interests are in the area of large-scale distributed systems with an emphasis on fault-tolerant and secure systems, Grid computing, and Web services. He also leads the NaradaBrokering project which facilitates the development of loosely-coupled distributed systems.

Sima Patel is a research associate/software engineer at the Community Grids Lab at Indiana University, Bloomington, Indiana. She got her master's degree in computer science from Illinois Institute of Technology in 2004. She is involved in the research and development of middleware software for Grids computing.

Marlon E. Pierce is the assistant director of the Community Grids Lab at Indiana University. He received a PhD in computational condensed matter physics from Florida State University in 1998. Subsequently, his research has concentrated on the application of Web services, Web portal gateways, messaging systems, and related technologies to scientific applications. He has worked on numerous Grid projects to support earthquake science, computational chemistry, and chemical informatics. He is also the project leader for the Open Grid Computing Environments Project, which provides a common software stack for science portals.

Christian Platzer is a PhD student at the Distributed Systems Group, Information Systems Institute, Technical University of Vienna. His research areas include Web service engineering, service-oriented architectures, and Web service technologies with an emphasis on service discovery and search engines for Web services.

Paul Robinson is a senior consultant engineer at Arjuna Technologies, where he leads transactional middleware consultancy and training. He has a BSc and a PhD in computing science from Newcastle University. While at the university, Robinson also contributed to the TAPAS European project and the Gold UK e-Science project.

Florian Rosenberg is research assistant and PhD student at the Distributed Systems Group, Information Systems Institute, Technical University of Vienna. His research areas include software engineering in general, service-oriented architectures, and Web service technologies with an emphasis on service composition and quality of service (QoS) aspects.

Daniel Sanz obtained the computer science engineering degree at Carlos III University in 2002. Then he started to work as assistant teacher at this university and as a PhD student in the CS Doctorate Program. His research topics are the application of RBAC to hypertexts, both at theoretical as well as practical/technological levels. He is also interested in the model-driven security paradigm, and is particularly concerned with the integration of access control concerns in hypermedia and Web development methods from a methodological point of view. Currently, he is developing his PhD thesis, titled "A role-based access control framework for hypermedia."

Santosh Shrivastava was appointed professor of computing science, Newcastle University in 1986, where he leads the Distributed Systems Research Group. He received his PhD in computing science from Cambridge in 1975. His research interests are in the areas of distributed systems, fault tolerance and application of transaction and workflow technologies to e-commerce, virtual organizations, and Grid-based systems. He has led and managed several European Union funded, multipartner research projects, beginning with BROADCAST (1992) to a project on complex service provisioning on the Internet, TAPAS, that started in 2002.

Lampros K. Stergioulas (BSc, MSc, PhD, MIEE, MIEEE, CEng, MIOP, CPhys, MCS) is a senior lecturer in the Department of Information Systems and Computing at Brunel University, UK, where he serves as director of the MSc programme in telemedicine and e-health systems. He is a qualified chartered engineer and has studied informatics and physics in his first degree (1991) at the University of Athens, and later received an MSc (1992) and PhD (1997) in electrical engineering from the University of Liverpool, UK, specialising in information engineering and communications. From 1996 to 1998 he worked as a research associate in the Cambridge University Engineering Department. He has held lectureship posts in the Manchester School of Engineering at Manchester University (1998-1999) and in the Communication Systems Department of Lancaster University (1999-2003). Over the past 10 years, he has taught a wide range of undergraduate and postgraduate courses in computer science and engineering. Dr. Stergioulas has published over 90 papers in journals and international conferences. He has supervised and examined several PhD dissertations in the areas of health information systems, information processing, grid computing, and computer science in general. He has held several National and European Grants in medical and health informatics, information processing, human-centred communications and computing, and intelligent systems. He has been a principal investigator in several UK and EU research projects. His research interests include intelligent data processing, biomedical informatics, health information systems, grid computing, human-centred computing, computing education, and intelligent information systems.

Damodar Yemme is a senior systems analyst at Wheaton Van Lines, Inc. He received his MS degree from the National Institute of Technology, Warangal, India, in 1997. He has worked for Fortune 500 companies as senior J2EE programmer. Most of his research work is connected with the portals and Web services architecture. His current research focuses on WS-reliable messaging and WS-reliability.

Index

B

C

D

E

L

M

N

O

P

Q

R

S

T